Speak Your Healing from the Homosexual Deception

Personal Testimony, Prayers of Faith, and Research

**A Biblical Account
of the
Walk of Purity
Through
an
Intimate Relationship with Jesus Christ**

BONNIE M. EGGLEHAND
via
REVELATION OF THE HOLY SPIRIT
2ND EDITION

WESTBOW·
PRESS
A DIVISION OF THOMAS NELSON
& ZONDERVAN

WestBow Press books may be ordered through booksellers or by contacting:

WestBow Press
A Division of Thomas Nelson & Zondervan
1663 Liberty Drive
Bloomington, IN 47403
www.westbowpress.com
1 (866) 928-1240

Because of the dynamic nature of the Internet, any web addresses or links contained in this book may have changed since publication and may no longer be valid.

The views expressed in this work are solely those of the author and do not necessarily reflect the views of the publisher, and the publisher hereby disclaims any responsibility for them.

Any people depicted in stock imagery provided by Thinkstock are models, and such images are being used for illustrative purposes only.

Certain stock imagery © Thinkstock.

ISBN: 978-1-4497-7444-8 (sc)
ISBN: 978-1-4497-7443-1 (e)

Library of Congress Control Number: 2012920885

Printed in the United States of America.

WestBow Press rev. date: 10/6/2014

Acknowledgements

I am grateful to the Holy Spirit Who guided me through the writing of this manuscript.

I am grateful to the Platt family who led me into my born again relationship with the Lord Jesus Christ.

I am grateful to the countless people who helped me to learn, to live, and to obey the Word of God. I give special thanks to: Dad, Mom, Uncle Walter, my brothers Carey and Louis, my sister Carol Rose, and my brother Thomas Daniel.

Rev. Ron and Joanne Highley and Dick Defiore of Life Ministries in New York City – for the dinners, the meetings, the personal ministry in counseling and for meeting my mother in the diner in New Jersey.

Rev. John and Penny Mac Arthur of Comforting Hearts Ministry in Avenel, New Jersey – for helping me with my ministry and including my writings in their newsletter.

Pastor and Mrs. Gibb Allen of Calvary Chapel in Santa Barbara, California.

Assistant Pastor and Mrs. Tim Anderson of Calvary Chapel in Santa Barbara, California- for their teaching of the Word of God and their guidance to help new Christians to stay accountable in their church home.

Pastors and friends of Vineyard Christian Ministries in Santa Barbara, California.

My friends Wendell Hyde, Joan Harkness, Monica Sherlock, Tommy and Becky Spadoro, Wayne Kingsbury and his daughter Heidi.

David and Barbara de Boer, Robert and Jean Wilson – partners in the Salvation Army Ministry.

The late Pastor Billy Joe Daugherty and present Senior Pastor Sharon Daugherty of Victory Chrisitan Center in Tulsa, Oklahoma, including Iru Daugherty and the entire Daugherty family.

Their ministry of pure love and acceptance assisted this baby Chrisitan to begin to walk in the truth of God's powerful Word. With countless impartations and prayers from many, I was blessed with a deposit of faith which kept me rooted and grounded in Christ through many trials on the front lines of ministry. Their TV production of Victory in Jesus helped me through a critical life crisis.

Pastor Bruce and Trudy Edwards.

Pastor Ron MacIntosh and John Fenn of Victory Bible Institute.

Pastor Marlene Burdock - for her counsel on the essential importance of speaking the Word of God when amidst the spiritual warfare.

Pastors Jerry and Lynn Popenhagen – for their anointed instruction at VBI.

Pastors Galen and Janet Nation – for their prayer ministry for the missionaries at Victory Christian Center

Pastor Jere Peterson, Director of Victory Fellowship of Ministries – for his anointed teachings and support.

Singles Pastors Ty and Debbie Barker – for their anointed worship and teaching of the Word and for their hands on ministry which brought me the peace and the joy of the Lord; Singles Pastor Dora Rodriquez – for her support and her anointed teachings of the Word of God with worship and praise.

Ron Tracy, Cliff Huntwork, Robert Taylor, Pastor J.O. Williams, and Floyd Jackson – for their friendship and support. Mrs. Carol Cate, Jayne L. Radcliffe, Mae Bennett, Theresa Wright, Bertha Fisher, Luther Robins – for their support and friendship, especially Carol, who was always standing by to support me especially through the final stages of these writings.

Care Pastors Harry and Nikki Latham of Celebrate Recovery at Victory Christian Center in Tulsa, Oklahoma – who welcomed me and supported me.

Melissa Slagle, Licensed Christian Counselor.

Katy Jones – for her partnership in ministry to the geriatrics at Maplewood Care Center.

Rebecca Robinson – my roommate during ORU attendance.

Pastors David and Diane Demola of Faith Fellowship World Outreach Center in Sayreville, New Jersey. His ministry of compassion and tough love led me to a deeper union with God, thus developing my true inner character. He inspired me to fight this battle God's way and to win against all odds.

Reverend Dr. Leo and Carole Natale of Faith Fellowship Counseling Department – Thank you, Leo, for your years of Christian support, counsel, prayers and your model of Jesus Christ to me. You helped me to see the forest from the trees when I needed a more godly perspective. You were always there for me with Chrisitan counsel with meekness, kindness, and with the wisdom of God.

Reverend Vinny and Nancy Longo of Victory in Jesus, who helped me to learn about my authority in Christ Jesus, how to take it, and how to win against all the wiles of the enemy in my life. Ms. Francine Zitz – Principal of Cornerstone Christian Academy – for her leadership and Christian modeling and friendship. Reverend David Sellers – prophet of God and orchestra conductor and music instructor of Faith Fellowship World Outreach Center. Dr. Carla (Hardy) Hammond - Christian Psychiatrist specializing in the healing of addictions – for her counsel, her friendship, hospitality, and her continued support for this ministry.

Pastor Dr. Thomas and Kim Keinath of Calvary Temple in Wayne, New Jersey - The anointing of the Holy Spirit which pours out of this man of God and his wife exemplifies a life of purity and prayer before God and man. Pastor Keinath is a great teacher of the Word of God and a humble teacher to his congregation of the essential necessity of prayer. Thank you for teaching me to pray and for allowing the New Dawn Ministry. Peter and I were enabled to help others and to grow closer in our walk with the Lord as well.

Pastor and Mrs. Rema Spencer of Calvary Temple – for supporting, overseeing, and counseling Peter and I through the New Dawn Ministry.

Mr. and Mrs. Ed and Dee Verhagen – for friendship, hospitality, support and especially the anointed personal counseling and the teaching of the Elijah House Prayer Ministry.

Dr. Adrianna Mueller – for your counseling and teachings.

Peter Psillas, leader of the New Dawn Ministry, for his loyalty and friendship and his partnership in this ministry. Danny Proudley, his mother Janet Proudley, Sister Marlene, and James Quaglietta for help with New Dawn Ministry. Rev. Bill Taylor of Exodus Ministries for his empathetic counsel and support.

Financial support of Paul Nagy, Carol Cate, and the Mr. and Mrs. Proudley.

Computer assistance from Ernie Dicks and Cliff Huntwork.

Hospitality from Nellie della Porta, Francine Zitz, Dr. Carla (Hardy) Hammond, Danuta Kurzig, and Kevin and Sharon Hedgecock.

Editors Bonnie Doebley and Minna Mikkonen.

Ted and Debbie Kosko – for their incredible support, hospitality as singles' ministers, and phone counselors at Calvary Temple of Wayne, New Jersey.

Ken and Joanne Kowalski and Ruthie –for their friendship and support of this ministry.

Pastor and Mrs. Jonathan Cahn of Beth Israel Messianic Fellowship in Garfield, New Jersey – for his words of wisdom and knowledge, his teachings about the Jewish culture and feasts, and his humble surrender to the Lord Jesus Christ.

Pastor Hamilton and Theresa Okotie of Miracle Lamb of God Church in Tulsa, Oklahoma –for the warm welcome to their church and for their prayers.

Pastor Mark and Janet Brazee of World Outreach Church in Tulsa, Oklahoma –The anointing of the Holy Spirit which fills his church as he preaches the uncompromising Word of God brought many healings, both physical and emotional. Pastors Jerry and Jill Spurell of World Outreach Church in Tulsa, Oklahoma, who welcomed me to the church.

Pastor Kenneth and Lynette Hagin of Rhema Bible Church in Broken Arrow, Oklahoma – Pastor Hagin's preaching and teaching of the ucompromising Word of God helped me to get back on track after ten years on the front lines in New Jersey. After laying hands on me with his wife at his side, I heard the audible voice of God. After just passing me in a crowd, I received a deep inner healing.

Rev. Craig Hagin, Rev. Bill Ray, Rev. Rick Fern, Rev. Tad Gingurich, Rev. Brent Bailey, and Rev. Richard King, worship leader of Rhema Bible Church.

President Dr. Mark and Mrs. Alison Rutland of Oral Roberts University in Tulsa, Oklahoma – President Rutland is gifted in eloquence and in deliverance. I was deeply inspired by his brilliant presentations at the ORU chapel services. I received a healing at one of his Ignite presentations in which he preached the power of preaching and speaking out the truth of the Word of God. This brought me a deep peace and also the loving presence of God. He convicted me of the necessity to seek help for self doubt and for any idols I had left in my life and I thank him for preaching the truth.

Special thanks to the library staff and students of ORU, especially Jane Malcolm, M.L.S., Annette Villines, M.L.S., Cheryl Holeman, M.A., Peggy Pixley, M.L.I.S., and students Tammie King, Sarah Cox, Davita, and Joseph.

Pastor Bob and Loretta Yandian of Grace Church in Broken Arrow, Oklahoma. Pastor Bob eloquently preaches a phenomenal and a practical application of the Word of God to everyday life. I thank God for his compassion to begin Restoration by Grace ministry . And for his son, Pastor Rob, who is now entering into the pastorate position under the leadership of his father.

Rev. Chuck and Betty MacConkey of Restoration by Grace Ministries - for their counsel, friendhship, and support.

Pastor David and Rosalie Roberson of The Prayer Center in Tulsa, Oklahoma – for his impartations, his teachings, and monthly newsletter and his openness to sharing Jesus from his heart.

Pastor Joel and Linda Budd and family of River Gate Church in Tulsa, Oklahoma – for their compassion to reach out to those who need Jesus, their anointing to lay hands upon the sick and see them recover, and for their teaching of the Word of God.

Thank you, Rita Bosico, for all your work on the website.

Thank you, Bo, for your special friendship and support.

Preface

The love of God is the strongest force of our supernatural experience. His love calls us from the depths of our innermost beings to speak to us, to correct us and direct us, so that we may encounter a union with Him that is the purest, most intimate relationship we could ever encounter in our short lifetime. He speaks to us and says,

"Fear not, for I have redeemed you. I have called you by your name. You are mine. Because you are precious in my eyes, because you are honored, and I love you." (Isaiah 43:1–4)

And for any force opposing this divine union, I say, with the authority of Christ Jesus Who dwells within me,

"I am convinced that neither death nor life, neither angels nor demons, neither the present nor the future, nor any powers, neither height nor depth, nor anything else in all creation, will be able to separate us from the love of God that is in Christ Jesus our Lord." (Romans 8:38 per.)

Receive His love, my friend,
It is His gift to you.
It is soft, not violent
It is gentle, not harsh
It is honest, truthful, and pure.
It is your Father's love,
Your Creator, the Creator of all the earth.
Watch Him reveal to you your "honest self"
As you drop every façade in your walk of purity before Him.

★★★★★★★★★★★

Platform

When we stop and sit before His presence, receiving His love, His forgiveness, and His acceptance, we enter the reality of Christ with us. As fear dissipates, faith only remains. The pristine silence of His presence reveals the holiness of each moment.

When we believe in the reality of the debt that Jesus paid for us at the cross of Calvary, we humbly receive Jesus' love for us in spite of our weaknesses. We thank Him for this free gift of love, forgiveness, and acceptance. All fear must go in the face of our faith in this provision. And we rest in His love.

We learn to trust and obey Him as He gently shows us how much He truly cares for us. When we surrender to Him, we accept our god given purpose to live for Him. To live for Him is to follow His commands to love others as we love ourselves. To live for Him is to surrender our flesh to Him daily, to repent daily, and to forgive ourselves and all who have sinned against us daily. Thus, we develop a heart of faith and we become more like Jesus.

The key to close the door on all deception is to forgive and release all judgment. The key to lock it is obedience to a holy God. He honors every step toward Him and we are pleasantly granted a natural connection between our mind and our heart. We feel life again as we settle into faith with a heart that readily surrenders to a holy God and a heart that readily repents and forgives. All the defilements, the inner pain, the lies, and the facades must go as we bow to a loving God. All fear must go in the face of a heart that has developed in faith.

When we settle the confusion of our deep inner pain and outward striving, we understand that the real enemy is Satan, the god of this world. He wars in the heavenlies using people and bloodlines to work against us. However, we offensively emerge with love and compassion for the very people who hurt us the most. We see their pain and their fear. We understand how the enemy used them against us. And we also see how we were influenced as well by the enemy's bite. All judgment must go in the face of this revelation. We are grateful for the revelation and we are stopped as our tears of truth break us free from the judgments. And we rest in the Lord's sovereign control over every man and woman. The earth is the Lord's and everything in it. (Psalm 24)

We rise up against the apathy and the hurt and speak with a heart of faith with submission, repentance, and forgiveness. We petition our Father God and take our delegated authority in Christ Jesus against all that is not of God. And we are changed by the words of our mouth. We speak in the name of Jesus. And we are changed by the words of our mouth. We speak the truth of the Word of God. And we are changed by the words of our mouth. With our words, we offensively fight every battle with love and compassion for the enemies who lash out in retaliation against us. Because they do not have the inner peace that only Jesus can give, their spirits are repelled by our spirits. And we pray for them. We fight the good fight of faith to stay firmly settled in "Christ in us". And we are changed by the words of our mouth.

Codependence dissipates in the face of our faith in a God who dwells within us and Who has not only forgiven our sins but has also forgotten them. The fear of man disintegrates as we draw our strength from Jesus Christ Who lives in us. For He is greater than any person, any spirit, any fear, any fantasy or phobia, any philosophy, any demonic foe, and any inner wounding or pain. Breakthrough comes with the catharsis of this emotional revelation. For then Jesus truly becomes Lord. He Who sets our divine anchor also loves us more than we love ourselves.

This is the walk of faith. Jesus is real and is for us. And with each step in His direction, our Father touches us with glimpses of our true identity, that whom we were created to be before we were even in our mother's womb. The lies of homosexuality dissipate because a life of purity in Christ Jesus decidedly removes the homosexual deception. Each step toward Him brings us closer to His image and we are changed. We emerge free to be exactly whom our Father God created us to be, with our spirits as that of an innocent child. Leaving all secrets with honesty and transparency before God and man, and forgiving ourselves, we emerge in our true identity with a heterosexual desire. And this desire for the opposite sex is as natural as apple pie. Leaving the judgments, the pretenses, the facades, the sins, and all idols, the stark truth remains. We find ourselves. We are found in Christ and Christ alone. Surrender to a holy God reveals the truth of who we are in Christ and Christ alone.

And the revelation of our purity in Him brings us back to the innocence we once had as children. We are no longer ashamed to view our bodies. We are no longer afraid to love. We are so grateful to experience ourselves as washed clean before a holy God. We are cleansed only because of the sacrifice that Jesus Christ paid for us, the ultimate sacrifice of His blood for us. And we emerge free as a butterfly to live life led by the Spirit of the living God, with a healthy will that has control of our flesh, our thoughts, and our emotions. The just shall live by faith. (Romans 1:17)

Table of Contents

Introduction

What the enemy (Satan) has intended for evil, God will turn around for good.

From the west, men will fear the name of the Lord, and from the rising of the sun, they will revere His glory. For He will come like a pent-up flood that the breath of the Lord drives along. "The Redeemer will come to Zion, to those in Jacob who repent of their sins," declares the Lord. (Isaiah 59:19, 20)

As I continue to heal from the deep emotional wounds of my past, I now stand with a godly perspective on them. After feeding on the Word of God, when the emotions begin to surface, as they often do, I have a choice to make. Will I cry tears of self- pity that will only serve to keep me in the memory of my past and give the victory to Satan? Or, will I choose to redirect my wounds toward the act of interceding for the multitudes that still stand in the valley of decision? I am referring to the thousands who still live in the darkness of this world, entrenched in the web of homosexuality without an intimate relationship with Jesus Christ. **All things work together for good to those who call upon the Lord and are called according to His purpose. (Romans 8:28)**

Truthfully, I had to take full responsibility for my own hurts because my reaction to the world's injustices caused me to cling to idols, whether human or material. These took me from the fullness of a submitted and an intimate born again relationship with Jesus Christ and the freedom and blessings that He had for me. In order to stand in the full revelation of His godly perspective, I had to face my own pain and humbly ask Him into my heart. I had to repent and leave all idols and sins. As I forgave and released judgment against myself and others, I closed the door to the enemy's entrance. My submission to the will of God and His Lordship and authority taught me obedience to leave sin, one day at a time. And, when my obedience was completed, I then not only closed the door, but also locked the door on Satan's authority and control in my life. **"Father, if you are willing, take this cup from me; yet not my will, but yours be done." (Luke 22:42)**

As I stepped into this yielded life in an intimate relationship with Jesus Christ, a life of faith with repentance and forgiveness, Jesus healed my wounded heart, and then reopened it to feel life again. As I deeply surrendered with a heart of repentance for my sins to His Lordship and His authority, He brought me the Holy Spirit and His presence and His power to enable me to do what I could not do in my own strength. He empowered me to forgive and to let go of blame and judgment by faith. He took away the brokenness and reconnected my mind with my emotions. He took away that painful feeling on the inside and brought me a comfort within my own skin.

The emotional hurt was very deep. Since I was a little girl, I knew that God was deeply with me. At the beginning of my healing, I did not know why I was hurting. Tears would flow frequently without reason at many altar calls. As I was approaching the altars with my faith to reach out to the grace of God, the Holy Spirit met me at the points of my wounding. The tears were a cleansing and a purging from the Holy Spirit, a holy washing if you will, of the poisons of my sins and idols which resulted from my ungodly reactions to the hurt, traumas, and abuses of childhood. Later in life the Lord revealed to me that there was a demonic intrusion to my soul and spirit that I was exposed to as a child due to the generational curse on the family bloodline.

Jesus' presence and His power replaced the hurts. The infilling of His presence in my heart restored peace and rest to my spirit and my soul. "Christ in us is the hope of our glory." (Colossians 1:27 per.) With my submission to Him, I came to trust in His majesty and His love. With trust, I became obedient to His Word. I came to know Him as a real and a personal God. With obedience, I came to receive my full rights of redemption, thus, freedom from the generational curse, and from Satan's authority and control in my life. This continued as a process of sanctification and holiness and, day by day, I came to know my true identity in Christ Jesus, as a godly woman, holy and pleasing to my Father.

"**Come to me, all you who are weary and burdened, and I will give you rest. Take my yoke upon you and learn from me, for I am gentle and humble in heart, and you will find rest for your souls. For my yoke is easy and my burden is light.**" (Matthew 11:28)

Healing is a Process of Sanctification

With the help of Holy Spirit filled counselors; I was able to identify some of the root issues for the habit patterns, the negative emotions and mindsets, and the sins and idols. I was able to repent of them and forgive and release others and myself, asking God to help me to change. There is an accountability and correction I received from Spirit filled counselors that I would never have gleaned on my own. My role as a "noble martyr" and as a "parental inverter" was essential to face in getting free from the codependent model that I practiced since childhood years.

In counseling and in the very presence of the Lord in prayer, I faced the deep hurt that I was not loved or wanted and Jesus gave me a revelation of His love for me. He also showed me in His Word that my problems were rooted in the spiritual realm. But greater is Jesus Christ within me than he that is in the world (1st John 4:4 per.), including any demonic force. And, I am redeemed from any and all curses by the blood bought sacrifice of Jesus Christ. (Galatians 3:13 per.) My false sense of responsibility, my self- condemnation and inferiority complex, my false belief that I had to make up for my sins through good works, my judgmental attitude, and my need to prove myself needed to be dealt with to correct and change the sin of perfectionism. My fear of man, inner vows regarding intimacy and control, and my difficulty with trust issues and with authority figures needed to be dealt with to correct and to change and to grow out of the tendencies toward homosexuality. I had to come to a place where I keenly discerned the Lord Jesus Christ within my very heart and my innermost being and that His love, acceptance, and forgiveness of me was all I needed for fulfillment. (1st Cor. 11:23-25)(John 14:15,16,17)

As I dealt with the pain in the very presence of the Holy Spirit, I made choices to obey His voice and His leadings. He convicted and empowered me by His Holy Spirit to turn from the fleshly and carnal ways of living and press into a life of holiness for God. With each step of faith to follow after His truth, I let go of sins by baby steps of faith, one step at a time. God showed Himself real to me as I trusted Him little by little in the small things first.

A lot of my healing was received as I pressed into the Christian lifestyle with all of my heart. I faced a lot of issues as the Holy Spirit brought memories to mind while in church services under the anointing of the Holy Spirit. As I wept, the Holy Spirit helped me to forgive. With prayer counselors and hands laid on me, I was loved back to life both in the pews, at many altar calls, and with special impartations from men and women of God. As I worshiped the Lord, I entered into His presence and I experienced life in the Spirit which led me away from fleshly ways and desires. I love to be in His presence. And worship took me there directly.

Holy men and women of God were essential to my growth as a Christian woman. I had a deep respect for many pastors, counselors, and ministers of God and I gladly placed myself under their authority because I knew and felt that they were under the divine authority of Jesus. I experienced divine impartations as they imparted the Word of God with the boldness of the Holy Spirit. I received miracles from God through many holy men and women of God.

As I read the Bible, I received direction and help from the Word of God. Certain scriptures would leap off the pages as if they were meant just for me that day. I gleaned from the Word of God both how to live for God and how to be more like Jesus Christ. I found His words of love, acceptance, and forgiveness there as well as chastisement and only because of His love for me. I learned from the lives of other men and women of the Bible how to deal with the challenges of life. I learned who I am in Christ from the Word of God and through the examples of men and women of faith.

I had to obey God in separating and severing ties with certain folks, and this was very difficult. I received counsel from my pastor and counselors and I did this with love and compassion, always retaining honor in my heart in my actions toward both Dad and Mom. "Honor your father and your mother, so that you may live long in the land the Lord your God is giving you." (Exodus 20:12) I have become an intercessor for them. I had to accept my mistakes and limitations, my part in the struggle, and let go of that which I had no control. Ultimately, I had to accept the tragedy of the situation of people suffering under the lack of knowledge and the consequences of that lack. I thank God for the seasons of time where I was given the opportunity to share my relationship with Jesus with them and to share the Word of God with them.

To this day, my offence against the tragedy is to pray with my heart of faith, (defined in next section), and petition my Father in the name of Jesus, to intercede for those who suffer without a personal relationship with Jesus Christ, to trust God for their salvation first, their divine protection, their divine healing of body, mind, and spirit, and to ask God to send laborers to them to share the truth of Jesus Christ.(Matthew 9:37,38) I cannot cast out demons against the will of any persons and/or where I have no legal authority, but I can bind, mute, and gag them from operating in their lives. (Luke 11:24-26; Matthew18:18) If I cannot be present physically, I pray and wait on the Holy Spirit for opportunities to minister to them in His perfect time.(See Appendix for prayers and further info about praying for other people)

Eventually, by turning inward and looking to Jesus to heal my brokenness, I was not only healed, but the Holy Spirit met me at the point of my greatest need. He showed me His reality in the many times He blessed me through His people and His children, at the most opportune times and at the most difficult places. He filled me with His presence, His strength, His power, and His purpose to continue to live for Him and with Him in faith and gratitude for His sacrifice for me.

This sanctification process began in 1981 and will continue until Jesus returns. I continue to listen to the leading of the Holy Spirit and have learned to live the life of faith with His presence in my life. In the process, I took the baby steps, one day at a time, toward Him. It started with a quiet trust and matured into a walking and a talking, trusting relationship with the living Lord. Meditating upon His Word, studying His Word, memorizing and speaking it in faith, I continue to use the Word of God in my everyday life. Living and speaking the Word of God transforms my soul (thoughts, will, emotions) and my life, even to my DNA. **For the Word of God is living and active. Sharper than any double-edged sword, it penetrates even to dividing soul and spirit, joints and marrow; it judges the thoughts and attitudes of the heart. Nothing in all creation is hidden from God's sight. Everything is uncovered and lay bare before the eyes of Him to whom we must give account."(Hebrews 4:12,13)** As I speak with a heart of faith, the power of God is released and I believe and receive the expected change, calling into existence that which I need as I speak to every mountain and every hindrance.

Pray With Your Heart in Proper Position of Faith – Surrender, Repentance, and Forgiveness

With a deep and honest surrender to the Lordship and authority of Jesus Christ, with daily repentance and turning from sin, with forgiveness and release of all judgment against myself and all who have sinned against me, I am properly positioned with a heart of faith. I then address all prayers and petitions to my Father God in the name of Jesus Christ, (John 16:23) (John 14:14), the name that is higher than any other name. (Phil. 2:9) And I, with a heart of faith, speak with my human spirit by the power of the Holy Spirit. (Acts 2:38) (Acts 1:8) (Mark 11:23-25) I, with a heart of faith, take Jesus' delegated authority, rebuking the enemy and declaring the Word of God in the name of Jesus, (Luke 10:19)(Mark 16:17)(Mark 11:23-25)(Hebrews 1:1-3), declaring those things that are not as though they are. (Romans 4:17) (Hebrews 11:1-3) I expect results.

I also confess the Word of God with faith and release the power of God into my life. Words spoken in faith release the power of God and move both the hand and the heart of the Father. (Hebrews 1:1-3) (Mark 11:22-25) And God changes me from the inside out as I speak the living Word of God with faith. (When we declare the Word of God, however, in taking Jesus' delegated authority against our flesh, our thoughts, our emotions, or any evil spirit, our words are spoken "in the name of Jesus." It then is a declaration spoken in Jesus' authority and not only a faith confession of the powerful Word of God.)

We initiate change to the spiritual environment with our words of faith. Our minds are being transformed as we read, meditate upon, and speak the living Word of God. Our hearts are convicted by its love and also by it limitations. Our faith is growing as the Lord speaks to us personally through His Word. And we expect the answers will come as we speak to the Father in faith against every mountain that rises up against us, in the name of Jesus Christ. The key to answered prayer is speaking God's will in faith, believing that God hears us, and expecting that He will answer us. (Mark 11:22-25) (All scriptures referenced)

"Have faith in God," Jesus answered. "I tell you the truth, if anyone says to this mountain, 'Go, throw yourself into the sea,' and does not doubt in his heart but believes that what he says will happen, it will be done for him. Therefore I tell you, whatever you ask in prayer, believe that you have received it and it will be yours. And when you stand praying, if you hold anything against anyone, forgive him, so that your Father in heaven may forgive you your sins." (Mark 11: 23-25)

Step One – Making Jesus Lord with a Humble and a Repentant Heart

Making Jesus our Lord and our loving authority is the first step to taking Jesus' delegated authority. We enter into a committed covenant relationship with Jesus Christ with a deep reverence for Him, asking for His forgiveness first for offending Him. He immediately receives us, forgiving us and cleansing us by our willful acts of faith and of repentance. With repentance, the Holy Spirit comes to empower us and to baptize us with divine assistance to help us to forgive ourselves and others, to say "no' to sin, to rise up out of the emotions of self condemnation and inferiority, to speak to every mountain that is against us, and to be witnesses for Jesus Christ here in the earth. We thus develop in our heart of faith in its proper position with submission to Jesus as Lord, with a heart to quickly repent when we need, and with forgiveness of ourselves and of others. We grow day by day into this heart position of faith and become more like Jesus Christ in our development. (1st John 1:9)(Acts 2:38)(Acts 1:8)(Matthew 28:18,19)(All scriptures referenced)

After we then enter into divine and intimate covenant relationship with Jesus Christ, we are privileged to enter into the new and divine bloodline of Jesus Christ. We then are honored to receive all His precious promises (2nd Peter 1:4) that we inherit as a result of the finished work of Jesus Christ. We are assured not only of eternal life, but also of divine healing of spirit, soul, and body, divine protection, divine prosperity, and wellbeing for ourselves and our families. (Psalm 103:1-5) (Romans 10:9,10) (Romans 10:13) (Psalm 91) (3rd John 2) (Luke 4:18) (Isaiah 53:3-5)(All scriptures referenced)

Step Two – Speak with Faith and with Compassion for those the Enemy is Using against Us

Our heart must be properly positioned in faith, surrendered to Jesus' Lordship and His authority, with a repentant and forgiving heart, in order to pray properly, safely, and effectively. Forgiveness includes releasing all judgment against ourselves and others. Faith believes that the words we speak are heard by our heavenly Father and that He will act upon our petitions to Him because He promises He will in His Word. Faith does not look at the circumstances. It speaks to them. Faith is not moved by feelings or senses. Faith simply believes that there is a God who is greater than the natural circumstances and greater than our feelings and our senses. (John 16:23)(Hebrews 11:1)(Romans 4:17) And the Lord is able to move every mountain out of our way. (Mark 11:23-25) **Now faith is being sure of what we hope for and certain of what we do not see. This is what the ancients were commended for. (Hebrews 11:1)**

With our hearts properly positioned in faith, then, we address all our prayers and petitions to the Father in Jesus' name. By our words of faith, we enforce Jesus' delegated authority to rebuke the enemy and declare the Word of God, in the name of Jesus Christ. By faith, we also confess the living Word of God over our lives. Our prayers of faith release the power of God. Our faith filled spoken words have power. Life and death are in the power of the tongue. (John 16:23)(Mark 11:23-25)(Hebrews 11:1)(Luke 10:19)(Hebrews 4:12)(Hebrews 1:3)(Proverbs 18:21)(All scriptures referenced)

A life of faith and self-control surrendered in a personal, intimate relationship with Jesus Christ replaces a life of flesh controlled by the emotions. Surrender, daily repentance, and prayers of forgiveness with release of judgment upon self and others lock the heart in its proper position of faith. Why? It takes faith and humility in Jesus Christ to surrender to an unseen God in a personal way. It takes faith and humility to ask Him to pardon our sins. It takes faith and love to forgive both ourselves and other people. Faith expresses itself by love. (Galatians 5:6) We forgive ourselves and others with the empowerment we receive from the Holy Spirit. Speaking in faith releases the power of God. We believe and expect without doubt for God to answer us. (Mark 11:23-25)(All scriptures referenced)

Jesus said, **"But you will receive power when the Holy Spirit comes on you; and you will be my witnesses in Jerusalem, and in all Judea and Samaria, and to the ends of the earth."(Acts 1:8)**

Peter replied, **"Repent and be baptized, every one of you, in the name of Jesus Christ for the forgiveness of your sins. And you will receive the gift of the Holy Spirit. The promise is for you and your children and for all who are far off – for all whom the Lord our God will call. (Acts 2:38)**

Step Three – Compassion

The Holy Spirit empowers us with compassion for the person(s) the enemy is using against us. The Holy Spirit gives us revelation knowledge that the enemy is not the person(s) but Satan is disguising himself and using the person merely as a physical vessel from which to tempt us and to distract us. This knowledge will keep the believer in faith with compassion for the person when praying against the enemy. Standing in faith is the victory.

Satan needs a physical body to work through. Satan worked through the snake in the garden. He works through people as well. Born again believers in relationship with the living God are His godly vessels in the earth. Our words and our deeds of faith successfully enforce Jesus' authority and dominion against the enemy, helping to set both ourselves and others' free. (Ephesians 6:12)(1st John 5:4)(Scriptures referenced) (See Appendix) **Therefore, whoever humbles himself like this child is the greatest in the kingdom of heaven. (Matthew 18:4) This is the victory that has overcome the world, even our faith. (1st John 5:4)**

The Issues of Abuse Start in the Spirit Realm

Whether injustices are premeditated or not are and never can be the issue. The issue is always whether we choose to forgive and we must! We must close out all of our abusers' accounts. Even to our deepest sorrow, as an act of our faith, and with obedience to God's Word, we must lock every door to the enemy's entrance. Thus, we enter into prayers of intercession for the very people whom Satan worked through to cause us deep hurt and inconvenience. Our enemy actually becomes the springboard to a higher level in God. And, as we grasp onto this revelation, and see the seeds of our love grow in those we pray for, we continue to grow in faith. It is a deeper love, an agape love, when we reach out to pray for those who need Jesus the most. **The only thing that counts is faith expressing itself through love. (Galatians 5:6 ref.)**

In life's battlefield, oppression begins in the spirit realm. Satan works in the spirit realm to oppress a person. He secretly and purposefully works to ignite unresolved emotions to react. It is as if a wall has been breached, and the wounded heart becomes an entry point from which the enemy can invade. We must resolve and settle these emotional wounds in order to close and lock all spiritual doors for Satan's entry.

Once the born again believer submits and turns to the Lord Jesus Christ in his or her woundedness, the Holy Spirit meets the person there, at the place of the wounds. When the brokenness is faced in the presence of a holy God, with or without a counselor present, the healing of the heart begins. There is a need for repentance for our ungodly reactions to the hurts, the traumas, and the pains we have experienced; for our sins, habits, co dependencies, idols, negative thoughts, negative emotions, and behavior patterns. We must face our inner pain to get to the truth.

The Holy Spirit is the divine counselor, and when we listen, He guides and directs us to the strategies and solutions. It may be to forgive someone. It may be to forgive oneself. It may be to pray daily. It may be to read the Word daily. It may be to get a job or volunteer somewhere. It may be to visit a friend or to give something away. It may be to keep a daily journal. Whatever is needed, He is the ultimate and the divine counselor.

The enemy will try to keep us locked into the spiral of the abuse, even if it is rooted in something that happened in childhood. It is so important to face these childhood issues so that we do not get stuck into a cycle of an abuse that happened thirty years ago. Jesus died two thousand years ago to free us from all suffering. The wounds of abuse make us vulnerable to the temptations, the invasions, and the accusations from the enemy. Once we enter into the temptation, we are in sin. And sin is the root cause of bondage. It separates us from God. To be strong in the Lord, we must annihilate the vulnerabilities to thus prevent successful attacks from the enemy.

I believe the healing for the person struggling with homosexual addiction will include both one to one Christian counseling and also divine counsel and cleansing from the Holy Spirit. This for me takes place when I am worshipping the Lord. He is faithful to cleanse me when I am in the very act of worship in that intimate place with Him. He meets me at that place and guides me in the way that I should go as I face the pain before Him Who knows me and loves me intimately.

When the surrendered believer identifies and faces the root issues of the pain in the presence of a holy God, repenting of his/her ungodly reactions to the pain, forgiving and releasing blame against self and others with obedience to leave sin, growth occurs. New godly behaviors will replace the ungodly behaviors and inner change will take place. It takes time, perseverance, and humbling oneself to God and others.

The anointing of God will come to bless the believer with His love and His presence. And the wounded heart emerges healed and honest identity is restored. With healing comes the reconnection of the mind to the emotions. Our confidence in Christ Jesus brings us to a sense of a life energized to do His will. Wholeness is restored and we are blessed with a new heart like that of a child, free and open to the leading of the love of God within our hearts. The walk of love is the greatest defense and offense for the believer to be victorious in his/her purpose and calling in life.

Now, with any enemy attack, the believer responds in faith and in the love of God and does not react to the attack. The person becomes now "alert" and "awakened" to the way the enemy is attempting to take control through the temptations. He/she has the ability to strategize and to respond the way Jesus would respond. The will is energized by the Holy Spirit to say "no" to sin and keep the enemy out! Love is our greatest weapon against the enemy. As we walk in love, we will not be moved by the distractions and lures of the enemy. (Galatians 5:6) (1st Cor. 13)(Scripture references)

The Holy Spirit will help us to strategize in order to rise above each trial. The baptism (fire) of the Holy Spirit works both within and upon the believer to help him/her to take control of his own responses to these temptations from both the demonic realm and also from one's own fleshly desires. And, as the believer yields to the Lord, the defiant willfulness of the "self" and "flesh" is transformed to a yielding to the Lord and a willingness to His will, and one's will is strengthened to make godly decisions, thus resisting the fleshly temptations. **When the enemy shall come in like a flood, the Spirit of the Lord will lift up a standard against him and put him to flight – for he will come like a rushing stream which the breath of the Lord drives. (Isaiah 59:19 –The Amplified Bible)**

If the brokenness remains unresolved, the door remains open and the person remains in a vulnerable position emotionally and is open prey for the enemy to continually invade the body, mind, and the spirit. This causes the person to continually react physically, emotionally, in negative thoughts, judgments, words, vows, and actions against oneself and/or others. Jesus will teach us through His Word and He will heal us as we are changed daily into His image. We are led by the Spirit of God to walk away from the flesh. In proper position of faith, with submission, repentance, and forgiveness, my heart spoke, "Thank you, Father God, through Christ Jesus, the Spirit of life set me free from the spirit of sin and death, in Jesus' name." (Romans 8:2 per.) "My body is a living temple for the Holy Spirit. I honor God with my body." (1st Cor. 6:19-20 per.)

It is important to see abuse for what it is. A person who causes pain or sins against oneself or another could have a demonic oppression or possession on him/her and/or is broken and wounded also. We all have inherited the rebellious nature from the fall of man, from Adam and Eve. We must close and lock the door to our own wounds so that we respond to all abuse as Jesus would, interceding with compassion for the abusers. And we must defiantly and obediently close and lock all our doors to our own rebellion.

Demonic influences from the spirit realm ignite the embers of the unresolved soul. This fire sends negative thoughts which then trigger painful memories and emotions, causing a person to act out against oneself or against another person. Self-condemnation or a sense of inferiority, for example, is abuse against one's own soul. Rejection from others will cause the unresolved soul to react and to want to lash back instead of responding in love and praying for the person. It also triggers the body to desire to sin against oneself or against another person, seeking a way of escape from the negative thoughts and painful emotions and memories.

The person may not even be aware of this process. He or she may just sense an intense physical energy like "electricity" from within his/her body or an intense energy pressing against him/her. This could be the Antichrist spirit or one of his cohorts, i.e. the spirit of lust. With issues that are still unresolved, we may not recognize the roots of this attack as coming from Satan and his demons. Satan's way of deceiving and luring people to sin is rooted and instigated from the spirit realm. And he works through people. Remember that Satan had to enter the body of a snake to present himself to Adam and Eve. People may or may not be aware of the domino effect this causes. The spirit realm works through the physical realm to cause havoc in the spirits, souls, and bodies of men and women.

The victory is found with the person first recognizing the enemy is Satan. And God is the ultimate judge of all men and women. The believer will look within his/her own heart and then identify and repent and turn from the flesh, the ungodly thoughts and/or emotions (desires), and submit to the Lordship and the authority of Jesus Christ. The Lord's presence indwells our body/soul/spirit and His love is shed abroad in our hearts. (Romans 12:1) (John 15:5) (Romans 5:5) The Holy Spirit meets us at our point of need and His presence and fruit, including the fruit of self-control, will eventually take over. He then helps us to no longer be controlled by our flesh and the negative thoughts and emotions as we mature in our spiritual walk with Him, focused upon His loving presence.(All scriptures referenced)

You, dear children, are from God and have overcome them, because the one who is in you is greater than the one who is in the world. (1ˢᵗ John 4:4)

Bondage

Millions of people are enslaved by some type of bondage. To be in bondage means to be enslaved or subjected to some force, compulsion, or influence; to be under the control or manipulation of something evil and destructive; to be led away from God's best and the path He has ordained for you to walk, keeping you from fulfilling all that He has called you to do. A person could be in bondage to wrong thoughts, a philosophy, an attitude, an emotion, feelings, or actions. If you are led by your flesh rather than by the Holy Spirit, here are some of the works of the flesh which will bring you into bondage: [1]

The acts of the sinful nature are obvious: sexual immorality, impurity and debauchery; idolatry and witchcraft; hatred, discord, jealousy, fits of rage, selfish ambition, dissensions, factions, and envy; drunkenness, orgies, and the like. I warn you, as I did before, that those who live like this will not inherit the kingdom of God. (Galatians 5:19–21)

Once the desire to be free of bondage exists, it's time to identify the root cause of those things that have held you in bondage. The root of worry and anxiety often appears to be insecurity as a result of things that happened while a person was growing up. The root cause behind the drive for materialism in many people appears to be the lack they experienced when they were growing up, the fear that if they don't stockpile and hoard, they won't have enough. Many people are caught in the trap of immorality, uncleanness, and pornography because of emptiness in their life. The root cause behind any kind of bondage could be emptiness, insecurity, a lack of acceptance, or something that happened in a person's childhood. However the real root cause for bondage of any type is sin. [2]

The late Pastor Billy Joe Daugherty speaks eloquently about the four keys essential to getting over the hurts, abuses, and traumas of the heart in his sermon, "Jesus Heals the Brokenhearted." Pastor Billy Joe says, "Jesus makes all things new." Pastor says, "There are four keys we need to get over past offenses. The blood of Jesus, which forgives you from your sins, is number one. You can repent and His blood wipes away your sins. For sins committed against you, the power from the Holy Spirit gives you the power to forgive and enables you to forgive others. The Word of God renews your mind. And with the name of Jesus, you declare in His name and take His delegated authority to stand against it (imaginations, thoughts, fears, memories, hurts, and traumas....). In prayer, we declare: 'I take authority over imaginations, thoughts, fears, memories, hurts. You cannot reign and rule in my life.' We have to release our faith. When you pray, confess, believe you receive it!" **[3]**

"Have faith in God." Jesus answered. "I tell you the truth, if anyone <u>says</u> to this mountain, 'Go, throw yourself into the sea' and does not doubt in his heart but <u>believes</u> that what he says will happen, it will be done for him. Therefore I tell you, whatever you <u>ask</u> for in prayer, believe that you have received it, and it will be yours. And when you stand praying, if you hold anything against anyone, <u>forgive</u> him, so that your Father in heaven may forgive you your sins." (Mark 11:23)

Fight the Good Fight of Faith – Put Your Spiritual Armor On

Your very inner being, "the honest self" is merely looking for love, acceptance, and forgiveness; legitimate needs which only a committed and intimate relationship with Jesus Christ can truly provide. But, if you are not born again, walking in faith and in the power and the leading of the Holy Spirit with Jesus Christ dwelling on the inside of you, when the homosexual demon comes knocking on the door of your heart, you will have no weapons with which to fight. The helmet of salvation, the breastplate of righteousness, the belt of truth, the sword of the Spirit, the shield of faith, the gospel of peace, and the Holy Spirit prayer language will mean absolutely nothing to you. You stand completely vulnerable to the attacks of the enemy without wearing your armor.

This is not merely an exercise or a metaphor. This is an actual dressing we place upon ourselves before leaving our place of residence. We place this armor on by faith and it is our covering against anything that tries to invade or attach to us during our everyday activities with other people. We live in a spiritual world. **Therefore put on the full armor of God, so that when the day of evil comes, you may be able to stand your ground, and after you have done everything, to stand. Stand firm then, with the belt of truth buckled around your waist, with the breastplate of righteousness in place, and with your feet fitted with the readiness that comes from the gospel of peace. In addition to all this, take up the shield of faith, with which you can extinguish all the flaming arrows of the evil one. Take the helmet of salvation and the sword of the Spirit, which is the Word of God. And pray in the Spirit on all occasions with all kinds of prayers and requests. With this in mind, be alert and always keep on praying for all the saints. (Ephesians 6:13-18)** As you stand with your armor on, take your authority as Jesus did in the desert when He was tempted of the devil, responding to his mocking accusations,**"It is written: Man does not live on bread alone, but on every word that comes from the mouth of God." (Matthew 4:4)**

Take Jesus' Delegated Authority

1st **Submit to God (James 4:7)**

2nd **Resist and Rebuke the Devil (James 4:7)**

3rd**Speak with Your Heart Properly Positioned in Faith**

(With surrender to Jesus as Lord, repentance for sins, and forgiveness with release of all judgments against self and others)

(Acts 2:38)(Matthew 6:12)(Luke 6:27,37)

4th **Enter into His Gates with Thanksgiving and Praise (Psalm 100:4)**

5th **Petition Your Father in the Name of Jesus Christ (John 16:23)**

6th **Rebuke the Enemy and Declare the Word of God in the Name of Jesus Christ (Luke 10:19) (Mark 16:17)(Hebrews 4:12)(All scriptures referenced)**

Scriptures for Jesus' Delegated Authority

Submit yourselves, then, to God. Resist the devil, and he will flee from you. Come near to God and he will come near to you. (James 4:7)

Enter His gates with thanksgiving and His courts with praise; (Psalm 100:4)

The following scriptures are the words of Jesus:

Do not judge, and you will not be judged. Do not condemn, and you will not be condemned. Forgive, and you will be forgiven. Give, and it will be given to you. (Luke 6: 37-38)

I tell you the truth, my Father will give you whatever you ask in my name. (John 16:23)

I have given you authority to trample on snakes and scorpions and to overcome all the power of the enemy; nothing will harm you. (Luke 10:19)

Forgive us our debts, as we also have forgiven our debtors. (Matthew 6:12)

Peter replied, "Repent and be baptized, every one of you, in the name of Jesus Christ for the forgiveness of your sins. And you will receive the gift of the Holy Spirit. (Acts 2:38)

Notice, he didn't say the devil would flee from God. Sometimes we have prayed for God to get the devil off of us. As born again believers in covenant relationship with Jesus Christ, we have been given Jesus' delegated authority. But we must first submit ourselves to God. Then resist the devil and he will flee from us. **[4]**

Jesus Christ was submitted to His Father. At the time of His baptism, He became filled with the Holy Spirit and was gifted with the power and anointing of the Holy Spirit. The authority of Jesus came from being born as a man. His power and anointing came from God. **[5]** Then, at age thirty, He was anointed with the Holy Ghost so that He could undo, loosen, and dissolve the works of the devil. He was the last Adam. Jesus had the authority of a man while God furnished the anointing and power. **[6]**

"Streams of Living Water Will Flow"

The Heart of Faith Speaks from the Human Spirit within the Man or Woman, (from your innermost being, not the voice box)

Jesus stood and said in a loud voice, "If anyone is thirsty, let him come to me, and drink. Whoever believes in me, as the Scripture has said, streams of living water will flow from within him." By this He meant the Spirit, whom those who believed in Him were later to receive. Up to that time the Spirit had not been given, since Jesus had not yet been glorified. (John 7:37-39). As born again believers, when we receive the Baptism of the Holy Spirit, we are also blessed with the power of the Holy Spirit from on high to do just as Jesus did and to undo the works of the devil. The Holy Spirit helps us to live above the emotions and to live by faith. We enter into the Father's presence with our hearts properly positioned in faith, with submission, repentance, and forgiveness, to present our petitions to the Father in the name of Jesus; to then take Jesus' delegated authority in the name of the Lord Jesus Christ. It is not how loud we speak.

The power of God is released by speaking with a heart properly positioned in faith, as we petition our Father in the name of Jesus. We operate from our human spirit, (where the Holy Spirit dwells), not from the voice box. We speak with a heart of faith from our human spirit. Thus, Jesus' delegated authority is taken by speaking with a heart properly positioned in faith from one's human spirit or innermost being (from the belly). Jesus' delegated authority is taken as we rebuke the enemy (with respect and not fear) off our own lives and in Jesus' name; we repent of, rebuke, and renounce our flesh, our negative thoughts, negative memories, negative emotions, all addictions, ungodly behavior patterns, and fears. We rebuke evil spirits off ourselves in the name of Jesus. And we also replace the negatives as we declare the Word of God against them in Jesus' name. I continued praying until the manifestation came and the enemy had no further control in each battle. And I grew more deeply submitted as I grew in faith. I grew more offensive in my love walk no matter what the circumstances said, and that made a decided difference. With respect to praying for others we cannot pray against their will and/or where we do not have legal authority, but we can bind, mute, and gag the enemy from operating against their lives. (Luke 11:24-26)(Matthew18:18)(See Appendix)

Taking Jesus' delegated authority victoriously commands a respect for the enemy but never a fear of him. It takes a compassion for the person the enemy uses against us with a delicate balance of knowing who we are in Christ. It commands that we stay rooted in Christ both in us and with us as we set healthy boundaries with other people. And it takes faith in the Lord Jesus Christ with a strong inner confidence that has fully received His love, His forgiveness, and His acceptance of us to get the job done and to move whatever the mountain may be in the way.

Whenever we are in enemy territory, we can be of no want or need there. We must not seek acceptance from those the enemy uses against us. We must know our total acceptance in the Christ Jesus. We must confidently and gratefully, but not boastfully, know who we are in Christ. See yourself in the person and your will stay humble on all counts. Know that we are neither better than nor inferior to any person. We are all God's children. We must walk in humility and in love and speak with faith from our spirits. **Do nothing out of selfish ambition or vain conceit, but in humility consider others better than yourselves. (Phil 2:3)**

In extending love to any person the enemy is using against us, we set healthy boundaries, firmly planted in our identity in Christ, and give with a pure motive of modeling the love of Christ, and of not expecting a return of any personal acceptance from them. We give love in small acts of kindness with the pure motive of winning them to Christ, thus saving their soul and perhaps extending their lives as well. We give seeds of kindness and let go and let God harvest them by showing the enemy Jesus' hand in it. We do not catch a fish in a day.

Always be led of the Holy Spirit in this area, and consider your safety the highest priority. Two is always better than one when in enemy territory. Sometimes it will be intercessory prayer without the need for your physical presence that will be the safest and the best alternative. The Holy Spirit will guide you. You may have to literally leave the premises. If so, seek support from both your church and from the police if necessary. Use the wisdom of God.

The focal point of our prayers should be God, not the devil. If the evil one is to be bound, it will take divine strength to do the job. Railing at the enemy is reckless and immature. It is also dangerous. We must never forget that we are dealing with a higher dimensional being whose capabilities greatly exceed our own. Spiritual swagger and clichés mean nothing to him. [7] This is why it is essential to prepare one's heart of faith before God and under His authority with submission, repentance, and forgiveness, before taking Jesus' delegated authority. (See Appendix)

God Gave Us Delegated Authority to Subdue and to Take Dominion over the Earth- Jesus Gave Delegated Authority to His Disciples – We as Born Again Believers are His Present Day Disciples

God created man in His own image, in the image of God He created him; male and female He created them. God blessed them and said to them, "Be fruitful and increase in number; fill the earth and subdue it." (Genesis 1:27,28)

It's important to notice that God did not say, "Just be humble and let circumstances of life bowl you over. Don't ever do anything about your circumstances." Just say, "What is to come will come'" and "Do nothing to change it." No! God said, Subdue it! In other words, if the earth or any living creature gets out of line, you put it back in line! That's quite different from some of our Sunday school ideas. God created man to be god over the earth. Man wasn't put here as a worm in the dust. God created the earth and gave it to him. It became man's to do with as he would, but God gave him some guidelines with the ability to carry them out. **[8] The highest heavens belong to the Lord, but the earth He has given to man. (Psalms 115:16)**

Prayers of Authority Must be Spoken by a Believer who is Under the Authority of Jesus Christ

We must be under the authority of God to properly and effectively exercise our delegated authority in Christ Jesus. In the gospel of Matthew, the centurion came to Jesus asking him for help for his servant who was paralyzed and who was suffering. He said to Jesus, **"Lord I do not deserve to have you come under my roof. But just say the word, and my servant will be healed. For I myself am a man under authority, with soldiers under me. I tell this one, 'Go' and he goes; and that one, 'Come,' and he comes. I say to my servant, 'Do this,' and he does it." (Matthew 8: 8, 9)**

Jesus was astonished with the faith of this man, who was a military man who understood authority because he was under authority. When you understand authority as the Bible sets it forth, you will rise to a new level of faith. You will rise to an understanding of God's Word that will set you free from the circumstances of life! **[9] Then Jesus said to the centurion, "Go! It will be done just as you believed it would." And his servant was healed at that very hour. (Matthew 8:13)**

The centurion believed that Jesus could and would heal his servant, even without traveling to his bedside. He believed that Jesus would send the Word to his servant's bedside and he would be healed, just like the soldiers who were under the centurion's authority obeyed his word. He understood and believed in authority.

We must be under Jesus' authority to truly forgive because forgiveness is an act of faith and it is a command of the Father to his children. We will never forgive if we listen to how we feel about the situation. Therefore, by faith in the finished work of Jesus Christ, I say a prayer of forgiveness with a release of all judgment against myself and against all who have sinned against me, even to the subconscious level of my heart (to things I may not even remember). I am now forgiving with a heart of faith under the Lord's authority. **So He said to me, "This is the word of the Lord to Zerubbabel: 'Not by might nor by power, but by my Spirit, says the Lord Almighty." (Zechariah 4:6)**

Jesus spoke to the Apostle Peter, **"And I tell you that you are Peter, and on this rock I will build my church, and the gates of Hades will not overcome it. I will give you the keys of the kingdom of heaven; whatever you bind on earth will be bound in heaven, and whatever you loose on earth will be loosed in heaven."(Matthew 16:18)**

In Proper Position of Faith, Address Father God in the Name of Jesus and Take Jesus' Delegated Authority

We take an active part in getting rid of the devil. As our submission to the Lord grows, our hearts are continually growing deeper in the proper position of faith with submission, repentance, and forgiveness. The first and most important key is submission to the Lordship and the authority of Jesus Christ. (James 4:7) (Romans 10:9,10) (Romans 10:13)We stand submitted to Jesus Christ as Savior and Lord and divine authority of our lives. (James 4:7) (Philippians 2:9) With repentance from sin and the works of the flesh, we are immediately forgiven and cleansed by the blood of Jesus. Repentance makes us right with God. It is a daily activity. (1st John 1:9) Our hearts must stand in forgiveness and release of all judgment against both ourselves and all who have sinned against us. Jesus is the Judge of all men and all women. (Matthew 6:12) (Mark 11:25,26)(Numbers 16:22) (Hebrews 10:30)(All scripture referenced)

Then, in this proper position of a heart of faith, we can effectively speak with our human spirit, by the power of the Holy Spirit, and take Jesus' delegated authority over the devil in our own lives. We address all prayers to the Father in the name of Jesus. (John 16:23) (John 14:14) This is the key to seeing our prayers answered. **[10]** Jesus spoke to the disciples, **"I tell you the truth, my Father will give you whatever you ask in my name. Until now you have not asked for anything in my name. Ask and you will receive, and your joy will be complete." (John 16:23,24)** Jesus spoke to Philip,**"You may ask me for anything in my name, and I will do it." (John 14:14)**

The negative thoughts immediately leave as I speak and replace them with the spoken Word of God. (You can only think one thought at a time.) All evil spirits and/or demons will flee the environment at the very discharge of words of rebuke spoken with a heart of faith and in the name of Jesus Christ (taking Jesus' delegated authority) and by speaking the living Word of God with a heart of faith and in the name of Jesus (taking Jesus' delegated authority). The presence of the Lord and the angels of God (Psalm 91:7) (Psalm 34:7) take over the environment as soon as I call upon His name, "Jesus." (All scriptures referenced) **Use your faith and change the circumstances! Subdue it! Take dominion over it! [11]**

I would literally get out of the bed and walk around the room speaking until the spirits left me. I would put on the praise tapes and then enter into praise and worship. If it is late at night and you are in an apartment, put on your earphones so you do not intrude upon your neighbors. Remember this is spiritual warfare. Respect and pray for your neighbors also. You cannot cast out any spirits where you do not have legal authority or against another person's will. But you can bind, gag, and mute any spirits that are oppressing folks to render them powerless. Casting them out against the will of the person(s) and/or where you do not have legal authority will bring in seven other spirits to live there. (Matthew 18:18)(Luke 11:24-26) In praying for neighbors, take no personal offence! If you perceive the disturbance is coming from them, immediately ask God to forgive them, bind and gag the demons in the name of Jesus, cover yourself with the blood of Jesus, and keep in your position of faith. Faith is your victory! (See Appendix)

Jesus also gave delegated authority to His disciples when He spoke to them in the gospel of Luke. Jesus had sent seventy two appointed people to go out "two by two" to spread His Word and heal the sick. **The seventy-two returned with joy and said, "Lord, even the demons submit to us in your name." He replied, "I saw Satan fall like lightning from heaven. I have given you authority to trample on snakes and scorpions and to overcome all the power of the enemy; nothing will harm you. However, do not rejoice that the spirits submit to you, but rejoice that your names are written in heaven."(Luke 10:17,18)** We are the spokesmen and spokeswomen for God here on the earth. We have been given delegated authority from God Who, since the beginning of time, gave Adam and Eve the privilege to subdue the earth. And Jesus Christ reaffirmed this by giving us His authority, "power over all the power of the enemy" (Luke 10:19) while He spoke to the disciples. Today, we act as His present day disciples. (All scriptures referenced)

Resist the Devil from the "Secret Place" of Faith

Because we are in covenant relationship with Jesus Christ, we are covered by the blood of Jesus Christ. (Hebrews 12:24) This is the "secret place". The enemy cannot touch us in this place. It is our godly defense! We are hidden in Christ with His divine protection in the "secret place" of the Most High God. (Psalm 91:1)

Forgiveness by Faith – with the Help of the Holy Spirit

The Holy Spirit empowers us to forgive and release all judgments we have held against both ourselves and other people. With forgiveness, we are motivated to obey by faith and leave anything that is unpleasing to God. (Matthew 6:12)(Galatians 5:6) The Holy Spirit empowers us also to obey and leave all sin and idols and lock the door against the devil's control and/or further entrance into our spirits, souls, and our bodies. (Acts 2:38) (Acts 1:8) (John 14:16,17) Thus, we submit to the Lord and resist the devil. (James 4:7,8) (All scriptures referenced)

Forgiveness closes the door to the enemy. And obedience locks the door to the enemy's entrance. Our strength to win and to progress in our identity in Christ is found in our acts of obedience which will eventually extinguish the impulses of the flesh. Spending time with Jesus keeps us locked into the "secret place" of faith. Guard this place of intimacy with all your heart! Here is where we are blessed with God's anointing, His holy presence.

My obedience to say "no" to the sin brings me His rest, because I know He is pleased with my choice, and I have a deeper assurance of His living presence both upon me and in me. I am able to hear His still small voice with a clear conscience. And because I know I have done the right thing, my inner confidence now grows with each act of obedience. Therefore, I expect a blessing is coming my way.

Jesus spoke to His disciples, **"But I tell you the truth: It is for your good that I am going away. Unless I go away, the Counselor will not come to you; but if I go, I will send Him to you….But when He, the Spirit of truth comes, He will guide you into all truth."(John 16:6,13)**

The Holy Spirit gives us divine assistance to resist the devil. If Paul didn't resist him (the devil), he wasn't going to flee. The messenger of Satan was not going to leave unless Paul resisted him. It was not God's responsibility. It was Paul's responsibility to exercise his God-given authority here on earth. Yet, it was God's anointing that Paul must rely upon for effective deliverance. [12]

Take Jesus' Delegated Authority against Self Condemnation in the Name of Jesus
Speak to Your Soul and to the Spirits of Self Condemnation and Inferiority

Prayer to Prepare Your Heart of Faith - "Jesus I humble myself to You. I believe You died for me and rose victoriously on the third day. I repent of all sin and ask You to come into my heart and to be the Lord, Savior, and loving authority of my life. Fill me with Your Holy Spirit. I commit to forgive and release all judgment against myself and all who have sinned against me. Thank You, Lord Jesus, for Your sacrifice of Your life for me. I now receive Your forgiveness, in Jesus' name."

Enter into the Father's Presence - "Father, I come into Your presence with thanksgiving and praise with my petitions in my heart and in the name of Jesus Christ my Lord and Savior." (Psalms 100:4) (John 16:23)

Take Jesus' Delegated Authority against Condemnation in the Name of Jesus - " Lord Jesus, you died two thousand years ago and paid the debt for all condemnation and inferiority on the cross for me by shedding Your own blood for me. (Hebrews 9:14)(Isaiah 53:3-5)(Luke 4:18,19)(Romans 8:1)(Roman 1:17) Thank you, Lord Jesus. (1st Thes 5:18) Now I speak to you, soul. Soul, there is now no condemnation to those who are in Christ Jesus. (Mark 11:23-25) I pray and believe this in the name of Jesus Christ, my Lord, my Savior, and my confidence. (Hebrews 11:1) (Romans 8:1) I receive the righteousness of God which is in Christ Jesus. The just shall live by faith and in dignity and integrity before God. (Romans 1:17) Thank You, Lord Jesus, for Your sacrifice for me, in Jesus' name. Amen." (1st Thes 5:18,19)(See Appendix)

"Spirit of condemnation and spirit of inferiority, get out of here, in the name of Jesus. (Luke 10:19) (Mark 16:17) Go wherever Jesus sends you to be held captive there by the angels of God. (Mark 5:8-13) You have no authority here. (Mark 16:17)(Luke 10:19)(Col. 2:10,15) There is now no condemnation to me because I have repented of all sins and I am in Christ Jesus, in Jesus' name. (Romans 8:1)(1st John 1:9) I declare that I have been delivered from all evil that is being used against me, in the name of Jesus Christ. (Colossians 1:13)(Matthew 6:13) I declare that my body is a living sacrifice, holy and pleasing to God – this is my spiritual act of worship, in Jesus' name. (Romans 12:1)(1st Cor 6:19,20) And I refuse to defile myself with any sin against my body or anyone else's body.(1st Cor.6:18) I commit to daily study of the Word of God and prayer with praise and worship to keep my vessel filled with God and to keep the enemy out. (Luke 11:24-26)(Romans 12:2)(James 5:16)(Psalm 33:1-3)(John 4:24) I will stay in an attitude of gratitude for this priceless gift of the Son of God, in Jesus' name, Amen."(1st Thes. 5:16-18)(All scriptures personalized) (See Appendix)

The blood of goats and bulls and the ashes of a heifer sprinkled on those who are ceremonially unclean sanctify them so that they are outwardly clean. How much more, then, will the blood of Christ, who through the eternal Spirit, offered Himself unblemished to God, cleanse our consciences from acts that lead to death, so that we may serve the living God. (Hebrews 9:13-14)

The Spoken Word of God is His Power

When we speak we know and believe that the faith-filled spoken Word of God has power. In the book of Hebrews, it says,**Who being the brightness of His glory, and the express image of His person, and upholding all things by the word of His power, when He had by himself purged our sins, sat down on the right hand of the Majesty on high. (Hebrews 1:1-3)**

"Upholding all things by the word of his power"…If He had said, "by the power of His Word," then you could say there is some power in His Word, but not all power. But He didn't say that. He upholds all things by the Word of His power. **The spoken Word of God is His power. It was His creative ability of words that released His faith. God's faith was transported by words. [13]** God created the world by His words, bringing into existence that which was not and it became that which He spoke. Look in the book of Genesis. "And He said," precedes His spoken words before He created the world and everything in it.

God created Adam in His image and in His likeness. Adam was meant to have dominion over the earth by releasing his faith in words just as God had done with His. God used words to bring forth all creation. He set it in motion by saying, Let there be… (Gen. 1:3) And there was! God's faith was transported by words. **[14] For we also have had the gospel preached to us, just as they did; but the message they heard** was of no value to them, because those who heard did not combine it with faith. Now we who have believed enter that rest. (Hebrews 4:2)

Receive the Grace of God and Receive the Holy Spirit

The main ingredient to successfully speaking in our delegated authority in Christ Jesus is humbly submitting with repentance, honoring Jesus Christ and His sacrifice and His authority, not a perfect soul. The Lord wants our hearts sold out to Him, committed to a life of purity, not perfection. We must accept that we are human. And resist self-condemnation at all costs. Receive the grace, the power, the loving kindness, and the unmerited favor of God. **For it is by grace you have been saved, through faith – and this not from yourselves, it is the gift of God – not by works, so that no one can boast. For we are God's workmanship, created in Christ Jesus to do good works, which God prepared in advance for us to do. (Ephesians 2:8 – 10)**

My sins of homosexuality, and habitual sins of perfectionism, with its obsessive compulsive components, kept me from the full surrender to God. I thought I had to do certain tasks before I would be free. This kept me in the law. And the law kept me from receiving all the Lord had for me, i.e., my confidence and right standing with Him. No! Jesus already freed us two thousand years ago. His gift of grace is the undeserved favor of God that we receive when we come into relationship with Him. Jesus loves and accepts us, in spite of ourselves, and our weaknesses. He meets us all in our place of repentance and brokenness with His grace (loving kindness, unmerited favor, and His power). Do not let the deception of self-condemnation keep you from receiving the grace of God. (Ephesians 2:8)(Romans 3:23) **There is no difference, for all have sinned and fall short of the glory of God, and are justified freely by His grace through the redemption that came by Christ Jesus. (Romans 3:23,24)** (Scriptures referenced)

The Lord loves us and wants to help us. But we must take the first steps toward believing His Word and receive His promises. The Word is clear that we must repent to receive the baptism and the gift of the Holy Spirit. (Acts 2:38) Jesus knew we would need the supernatural empowerment of the Holy Spirit to help us to receive the grace of God. As we yield our fleshly members, our spirits, and our souls to Christ Jesus, we begin to die to self. It is at this juncture that the Holy Spirit infills us and gives us the grace of God to live abundantly in Christ. (All scriptures referenced)

The good news is that God is for us. He knows we need Him and that is why He sent us the Holy Spirit. Just a turning of the heart to follow Him is what counts. He wants our hearts to turn toward Him. He honors a heart that reaches out to Him one day at a time. We are not perfect beings, only perfectly forgiven. We are in a process of becoming more like God, that of sanctification. When we turn in faith toward Him, He meets us at the point of our need.

Jesus came to free us from the law of sin and death. (Romans 8:2) We do not have the power to keep the law, to say "no" to sin, or to speak in our delegated authority in our own strength. He sent us the Holy Spirit to empower us to yield our flesh to him, to trust Him, and to enter into the life of grace with Him. Both His grace and the Holy Spirit are gifts from God to us. His grace cancels all obsessive compulsive tendencies. It is the rest of God that overrules the Antichrist spirits and all demonic spirits of addiction.

Live a Life Led by the Spirit of the Living God

Peter replied, "Repent and be baptized, every one of you, in the name of Jesus Christ for the forgiveness of your sins. And you will receive the gift of the Holy Spirit. The promise is for you and your children and for all who are far off – for all whom the Lord our God will call." (Acts 2:38)

So I say, live by the Spirit, and you will not gratify the desires of the sinful nature. For the sinful nature desires what is contrary to the Spirit and the Spirit what is contrary to the sinful nature. They are in conflict with each other, so that you do not do what you want. But if you are led by the Spirit, you are not under the law. (Galatians 5:13-14)

I remember the day I sent my last lover a letter of "goodbye." I knew that the Holy Spirit was there with me. As I said the words, "Thy will be done," I placed the letter in the mail. And the Holy Spirit gave me such a deep peace. I knew deep within me that I was doing the right thing. I knew my life was going to change. This one decision of faith would change a life controlled by fear and feelings to a life led by faith and by the Holy Spirit. And I would step into my divine purpose, as you, and touch other people for Jesus Christ. Fear would have no place in my life. I persistently refused fear until the full manifestation came, that of the grace and the rest of God. **Now we who have believed enter that rest... (Hebrews 4:3)**

The Fruits of the Holy Spirit

The Lord blesses us with the fruits of the Holy Spirit. **"For the fruit of the Spirit are love, joy, peace, patience, kindness, goodness, faithfulness, gentleness and self-control. Against such things there is no law. Those who belong to Jesus Christ have crucified the sinful nature with its passions and desires." (Galatians 5:22-24 refs.)**

The Holy Spirit gives us self-control over what our bodies sense and feel, what our minds think, and what our emotions feel. We still have the thoughts, feelings, emotions, and desires, but we mature with both the insight to recognize them and the power of mind to control them with our wills. As we become more like Jesus, we will become repulsed by anything that is ungodly. He makes us new, like children in His loving arms. **We demolish arguments and every pretension that sets itself up against the knowledge of God, and we take captive every thought to make it obedient to Christ. And we will be ready to punish every act of disobedience, once your obedience is complete. (2nd Cor. 10:5,6)**

Water Baptism and the Baptism of the Holy Spirit

With the water baptism of the Holy Spirit, we become new creatures in Christ Jesus, putting off the old man or woman, and we put on Christ. This is a baptism of repentance. **Therefore, if anyone is in Christ, he is a new creation, the old has gone, and the new has come! All this is from God, Who reconciled us to Himself through Christ and gives us the ministry of reconciliation. (2nd Corinthians 5:17)**

The Baptism of the Holy Spirit also is a gift from God and this gives us divine empowerment from the Holy Spirit to say "no" to the enemy's deceptions and to walk in the Holy Spirit's fire. "No" can be exemplified by simply walking away from evil as well as saying "no" with one's mouth. The Holy Spirit will direct us in this. With His divine empowerment to forgive and obey, we can then not only close the door, but also lock the door to Satan's control and entrance into our bodies, our souls, and even our spirits.

The Baptism of the Holy Spirit gives us the power to speak with our human spirit and to subdue all evil and all fleshly temptations, negative thoughts and emotions. We are also empowered to be a witness for Jesus Christ to other people. This is our primary commission from Christ Jesus. After Jesus died, He appeared to many,

On one occasion, while He was eating with them, He gave this command, "Do not leave Jerusalem, but wait for the gift my Father promised, which you have heard me speak about. For John baptized with water, but in a few days, you will be baptized with the Holy Spirit." (Acts 1:4)

He continued, **"It is not for you to know the times or dates the Father has set by His own authority, but you will receive power when the Holy Spirit comes on you; and you will be my witnesses in Jerusalem, and in all Judea and Samaria, and to the ends of the earth." (Acts 1:8)**

Jesus spoke to Satan in the desert, "It is written..." He spoke the Word of God in resistance to the enemy's mocking accusations. He did not speak "in Jesus' name." It was not necessary because He was Jesus! When we speak in Jesus' delegated authority, we speak, "in the name of Jesus" because it is in Jesus Christ Whose authority we are speaking.

After Jesus humbled himself to God and also to John the Baptist, he was baptized in the Holy Spirit at the Jordan River. He took authority and He rebuked evil spirits off of many people. All were healed and devils trembled and fled from the people at His spoken words of faith and authority. We also receive the baptism of the Holy Spirit by our humbling ourselves with a repentant or a contrite heart.

How God anointed Jesus of Nazareth with the Holy Spirit and power, and how He went around doing good and healing all who were under the power of the devil, because God was with Him. (Acts 10:38)

Jesus was victorious as He spoke to the devil in His proper heart position of faith, (submission, repentance, and forgiveness), under the divine authority and Lordship of His Father. Since He was God, there was no sin to repent of. He was sinless. He did, however, speak prayers of forgiveness to His Father at the cross, as He was still a man who suffered incredible physical, mental, and emotional, social, and spiritual torment and abuse for our sake. "Forgive them, Father, for they know not what they do." (Luke 23:34)

The prayer language is also one of the signs of the Holy Spirit baptism, which helps to build up our faith in this battle. (Jude 20) It is also included as the last piece of God's spiritual armor in Ephesians 6:18. **But you, dear friends, build yourselves up in your most holy faith and pray in the Holy Spirit. (Jude 20)**

Body, Mind/Soul, Spirit

Body, soul (mind, will and emotions), and spirit (the real you), must be united for a complete inner healing to take place. One must also have a personal relationship with Jesus Christ first in order to fight for one's own healing because without Him, we can do nothing. It is through His sacrifice that we receive all His promises, including the healing of our bodies, souls, and spirits. **"I am the vine; you are the branches. If a man remains in me and I in him, he will bear much fruit; apart from me you can do nothing." (John 15:5)**

The presence of the Lord becomes so real that one lives earnestly seeking His touch of love and His voice of "I love you, my child. I am with you and I will help you." Today, in praying for and desiring a mate, I pray for one who loves the Lord first, seeking a man of God, a friend, and a prayer partner first whom I can easily talk to and trust. **Flee the evil desires of youth, and pursue righteousness, faith, love, and peace, along with those who call on the Lord out of a pure heart. (2nd Timothy 2: 22)**

Body, soul, and spirit are the three parts of the human creation. As I grew stronger in spirit and soul in my walk with Jesus and my knowledge of the Word, my needs for fleshly pleasures not only decreased but I was eventually repulsed by the evils of this sin of homosexuality. I had to grow up and through the stages I had missed as a child. This came with facing issues in one to one counseling and with time spent in the presence of the Lord in praise, worship, and prayer. The spirit and soul of a person grow closer to Jesus to such an extent that the desires and the needs for bodily sensations are outgrown. We recognize love as a heart issue.

All three parts of my soul (heart) needed an overhaul. My mind needed the Word of God. Oh, I was very intelligent and held a few degrees, but without the Word of God, my soul would not have gone through the transformation it so desperately needed. Also, I would never have learned how to pray effectively or how to live victoriously by faith above the circumstances and the negative forces. My thoughts (mind) and emotions would never have reconnected. My emotions had been the ruling force of my existence. Little did I know that God had a plan to completely turn my emotions around to live by faith instead of by my feelings. And my will strengthened to do His will one day at a time as I moved out of willfullness into a new willingness to do God's will.

Root Issues

I was fortunate to have committed my life to Jesus Christ in 1981, which immediately regenerated my spirit. Studying the Word of God, my mind began to be changed. Leaving the homosexual lifestyle thirty years ago, I left all homosexual contacts and committed my body to the Holy Spirit and to celibacy. Deep down within me, I knew homosexuality was wrong. This decision allowed for my spirit and soul to be healed, and eventually I experienced full deliverance. However, I was missing one key ingredient.

I still worshipped the idol of perfectionism which kept me in a hiding place and from truly facing my deepest pains and emotions. In order to completely close the door on this harassing spirit of fear, I had to confess and repent of this stronghold, and get help. This was an idol I had developed since childhood to block out fears and unresolved painful emotions. The trauma and pain I felt was experienced while either observing or while being involved in the family fighting and arguments. And, the root of the chaos within the family relationships was from the Antichrist spirit, generational and ancestral spirits, and a family bloodline curse, in which demonic spirits were present to harass and to destroy our spirits. I was not aware of this fact until I studied the Word of God. The Word of God opened my eyes to my inherited rights against these wicked spirits. The Word of God clearly teaches that Jesus Christ has redeemed (freed) us from any and all curses.

I was vulnerable to not only my own hurts but also the hurts of other family members. I had an enmeshed relationship with my mother, whom I tried to please. And I tried for years to get my father to stop drinking alcohol. I could talk with him when he was drinking, but it was difficult to talk to him when he was sober. Also, when I was eight years old, while walking home from school, I was met by a man in a car who motioned to me to come closer to him. I innocently thought he wanted directions. When I drew near the car to help him, I noticed his pants were exposing his genitals. I ran in fear!

The enemy set me up in this experience to fear intimacy with a man, but God had another plan for me. Jesus Christ brought a deep healing within my soul through a growing respect I developed for holy men of God (pastors, ministers, and friends) in authority in many church memberships. I trusted and respected these men of God. Through one to one counseling with Dr. Leo Natale, I bonded with a man who truly understood me. In facing, forgiving, and releasing hurts and issues related to my earthly father, I believed and knew that when the season was right that I would enter into a godly marriage with God's best for me.

In the days and years ahead, Jesus would bring healing and faith would replace all my fears. My belief and honor of His sacrifice, with my commitment to live with Him and for Him would entitle me to receive the benefits of redemption into a new bloodline, that of Jesus Christ, my Savior and friend.

If some of the branches have been broken off, and you, though a wild olive shoot, have been grafted in among the others and now share in the nourishing sap from the olive root, do not boast over those branches. (Romans 11:17)

We are Made Whole in Every Aspect of Life!

Intellectually, I knew that Satan was at the root of all these injustices and that he was the master enemy, not any person. Once this became a revelation in my heart, I would be matured and enabled to forgive from my heart and to move on in freedom.

Mentally, I knew that I had to choose to forgive in order to protect my own mental health as well as the mental health of others. In forgiving, I would release my abusers from all blame and to the care and working of God in their lives. I would release myself from self-condemnation as well so that God could work in and through me as a yielded vessel to touch others' lives.

Ethically, I knew from the Word of God, that I was commanded to forgive and that I could not be completely forgiven for my sins or delivered from evil until I released both myself and my abusers.

Morally, I knew that I would have no power or authority in Christ Jesus to pray against the generational sins in my family and over my own life if I did not first repent of sin and surrender to Jesus as my Lord and authority. Forgiving those who had sinned against me was difficult and took the longest time, because the hurt and the judgments were deep within my broken heart. I was convicted by a pastor I highly respected that I was holding a grudge even though I thought I had already forgiven. I knew he was right because I was suffering with depression. I was visited by an angel who told me I had to forgive my mother. I was convicted also by the book of Numbers 16:22 when Moses and Aaron fell facedown and prayed for their enemies during Korah's rebellion. They knew the enemy was sinning against God and not against them. God is the judge, not us. And I was convicted by Ephesians 6:12, which clearly shows us that the enemy is Satan and not flesh and blood. The Lord revealed to me later that both my father and my mother were fighting against the same driving spirit of fear that was affecting my brothers, my sister, and me. Unfortunately, they did not have the essential knowledge on how to fight the good fight of faith. (Hosea 4:6) (1ˢᵗ Timothy 6:12) The Lord ordained times to minister to them in person, times set aside for intercessory prayer, and times and seasons for separation for my own healing to continue.

I asked God for a revelation and He gave it to me. And, in time, I was enabled by the Holy Spirit, to start to speak forgiveness with a heart of faith and to minister love to the people who hurt me. God honored my obedience to love by faith in the face of the deep hurts. He not only freed and delivered me, but He also healed many as I prayed for and released judgments I held against them. Releasing our right to hold any grudge or to avenge anyone was and is a crucial step to our healing, and to our purpose in life to help others as Jesus would. It would place my heart in the victorious position of utter surrender to Jesus Christ as my authority, my Lord, and my judge and the judge of all men and women. I believe that it is in this place of faith and obedience to walk in love by faith no matter how I felt that the Father God would then honor and answer the words that I spoke to Him. "The only thing that counts is faith expressing itself through love." (Galatians 5:6) It is a decision of will to speak words of love and kindness and thus our acts of faith contradict, cancel, and conquer the negative emotions. It is a win – win situation for all involved.

Emotionally, I knew that my life would not fulfill its divine purpose if I kept this hatred within me any longer. I could not hide from it any longer. I had to stop running from the pain. I had to face the pain to get to the truth of my identity in Christ Jesus.

Socially, I knew that I had a purpose. I had the revelation that no matter what sin I had committed, that I was neither superior nor inferior to any man or woman. (Phil 2:3) I was a valuable and integral part of the body of Christ. As I matured in my identity in Christ and was empowered by the Holy Spirit, I would go forward with my godly purpose. Our purpose is assigned to us by our Father before we were in our mother's womb. **"For I know the plans I have for you," declares the Lord, "plans to prosper you and not to harm you, plans to give you hope and a future..."(Jeremiah 29:11)**

Spiritually, the Lord Jesus gave me a revelation that I will never forget. He showed me in a vision that for every attack I endured against my personhood, my dignity, my mind, my will, and my emotions, He took it for me on the cross. For every tear I shed, He shed another drop of His blood for me. For every trauma, He received the nails into His very wrists for me. For every insult to my integrity, He was mocked, spit upon, and beaten for me. For every worry, nightmare, negative thought, hallucination, delusion, or illusion, He wore a crown of thorns for me. For every person I lost to heaven that I loved, He defeated death through His resurrection and holds them close to His heart in heaven. And I have the "blessed hope" to see them again.

As I laid my crowns before Him on this earth, I looked forward to the crowns I would receive in heaven. My purpose was and is to please my heavenly Father, not man or woman. I look forward to His words, "Well done, my good and faithful servant."

When I chose to forgive and release myself and my abusers, I died to my own pain in exchange for the truth of His love, acceptance, and forgiveness. As I obeyed the leading from the Holy Spirit, I then locked the door to Satan's control, and received the grace of God by faith. I began to live for Him and in His purpose, not mine; a life of faith and not fear.

It is a strange feeling when one can no longer blame one's hurt on any other person. We live in a fallen world. It is both a mature and an empathetic choice to press into our freedom in Christ when we choose to forgive. We must give up any right to avenge. Self-pity decomposes and a new bud of compassion begins to grow when we now fertilize our hearts with forgiveness. Judgment is reserved for the Lord only. And the reward is His glory and our true identity in Christ Jesus.

Satan works through people, especially families. He will strike at the point of our deepest needs. Our victory is found in living by the standard that our relationship with Jesus Christ is more important than our relationships with our immediate family members, our spouses, our children, our pastors, teachers, mentors, friends, our acquaintances, and even our pets. Our victory comes in obeying His still small voice in this process of healing. Our position of ultimate victory, even to the separation from loved ones, is in intercessory prayer for those who have not yet accepted Jesus Christ as Lord and Savior, for there is no distance in prayer. Sometimes it is essential to separate from loved ones to heal, whether temporarily or permanently. This decision must be made with the help and confirmation of godly Christian counselors. Jesus Christ must be our first love and the Lord and King of our lives.

In compassion and understanding for those still suffering, I remember how long it took for me to yield. I am patient and continue to pray for my loved ones. I know how stubborn I was and continue to be in certain areas. This gives me patience while on my knees, praying and believing God will help those who are suffering in the valley of decision. I remember.

Satan knows our buttons and will continually buffet us into the self-condemnation for our past sins. But, we must resist his lies and yield and receive the promise of the Lord's total forgiveness, acceptance, and love. When will His still small voice becomes sweeter and more real than the lies and condemning gestures of the world? What will it take for us to yield to His love? For some, our defiance will only be silenced with continual chastisements from the Lord because He loves us. I believe He allows the buffeting from the enemy until we totally surrender to Him. And, with that surrender, we will emerge as bold as lions and as gentle as doves, because, we know whom we have believed!(2nd Tim 1:12) Our total surrender to the Lord is our greatest act of resistance against the lies and temptations of the devil.

Will you dare to emerge out of this cocoon of hiding, hiding in the fear, the self-incrimination, the self-condemnation, the self-existence and fly free like a butterfly? I will! I must! Why? Because of Jesus and Jesus alone! Because of His sacrifice of His own life for me! I will follow Him and share this gospel of complete love, complete acceptance, and complete forgiveness with as many people as possible before His return. I will live, laugh, and I will love again! (Matthew 28:18-20 – The Great Commission) Yes, there is a hurting child who has suffered abuse and pain, but the Lord asks us to come to Him as His precious children. We must come to Him so He can heal us. **At that time the disciples came to Jesus and asked, "Who is the greatest in the kingdom of heaven?" He called a little child and had him stand among them. And He said, "I tell you the truth, unless you change and become like little children, you will never enter the kingdom of heaven. Therefore whoever humbles himself like this child is the greatest in the kingdom of heaven." (Matthew 18:1-3)**

To the Reader

During the days of Jesus' life on earth, He offered up prayers and petitions with loud cries and tears to the one who could save Him from death, and He was heard because of His reverent submission. Although He was a son, He learned obedience from what He suffered and once made perfect He became the source for eternal salvation for all who obey Him . . . (Hebrews 5:7-8)

Be patient with yourself. As you walk the walk of a life committed to an intimate relationship with Jesus Christ, you will also learn obedience as you suffer the consequences of both disobedience and disappointments. Do not be discouraged. There is suffering that is necessary in this life for the sake of the Gospel. **Then Jesus said to his disciples, "If anyone would come after me, he must deny himself and take up his cross and follow me. For whoever wants to save his life for me will lose it, but whoever loses his life for me will find it." (Matthew 16:24)**

You may ask God why He has chosen to test you in this particular area. First, remember that Jesus was tested to the point of death. We are only tested to the point of our identity. Personal identity is very precious to a person. In choosing homosexuality, I literally sold my true identity over to the devil himself. However, Jesus died for this and every other sin, sickness, and disease on the cross of Calvary. My responsibility was to humbly ask His forgiveness, receive it, and enter into an intimate relationship with Him.

One's sexuality is given as a gift from God reserved to be used as the tool to express the very depths of one's innermost being to one person in a marriage covenant. The shame of the abuse of that gift caused my "honest self" to go into hiding for years until I was fed up enough with the enemy's strategies to deceive and to keep me locked into that shame. I had to choose to be honest enough to seek counsel and to go through the proper steps for complete deliverance from this hideous lie.

I will repay you for the years the locusts have eaten . . . (Joel 2:25) Coming out of this deception requires a healing process. Be very patient with yourself as you go through each step. You are very special as is every child of God. There is a divine reason that God has allowed you to be tested in this area. A test of this nature calls you to a life committed to purity in Jesus Christ. As you obey His commands, you will be directed into an even deeper intimacy with Him through the leading of the Holy Spirit. **Blessed are the pure in heart, for they will see God. (Matthew 5:8)**

Much will be required of you and the road to healing is not easy. Homosexuality primarily manifests itself as a legitimate need that is met illegitimately. Unmet needs met illegitimately will cause even more pain. Why? We have to undo the damage caused by going through the improper channels first before we can even find healing in the proper ones. **Call to me and I will answer you and tell you great and unsearchable things that you do not know. (Jeremiah 33: 3)**

As you cry out to Jesus and trust in Him to bring you the miracle of deliverance, you will go through a painful process. There are layers of hurt and the ungodly reactions to these hurts in the form of behavior patterns that need to be faced, repented of, and turned from for change to come. I'm so glad that God's healing power is free. I would have spent millions of dollars paying for all the prayers I received from the saints that God had preordained to help me through this process.

It was a humbling process that, because of my own unconscious arrogance, was sometimes humiliating. If you are truly humble, you can never really be humiliated. I eventually grew up and matured as I stayed connected to my Lord, my Savior and my authority, Jesus Christ and His Word. **Trust in the Lord with all your heart and lean not on your own understanding; in all your ways acknowledge Him and He will make your paths straight. (Prov. 3:5,6)**

Be honest with God. The Holy Spirit will direct you to the ministry in which He wants you to be involved. He will show you who you should associate with, where you should work, and what you should say or not say. You'll know by your inner witness. You'll have peace when you listen and turmoil when you do not. We are all blessed by God with a measure of faith. Because of so much disappointment with people, God knew I would need Him and I thank Him for that faith. **Do not think of yourselves more highly than you ought, but rather think of yourself with sober judgment, in accordance with the measure of faith God has given you. (Romans 12:3b)**

For a brief moment I abandoned you, but with deep compassion I will bring you back. (Isaiah 54:7) God made us all special. He gave you a sensitive heart and will teach you to use it for His glory. As you grow closer to Him, your softness will be used to show love to the unlovely. It will not always be welcomed because many people hurt too much to let your light in. Always remember patience with the hurting. Jesus is our example. He continues to be patient with us. It takes time for hurting people to trust. Remember, God uses you in ways you may not even understand. Just keep your eyes on Him and He will continue to lift you up.

I am the Lord your God who brought you out of Egypt, out of the land of slavery. You shall have no other gods before me. (Exodus 20:3) You may have to sacrifice some of your most treasured friends and/or family members to continue to place God in the place of honor that only He deserves. Because you have a great capacity to love, you may have a weakness of loving people too much. When you accept yourself and emerge out of the self hate, the balance will come naturally. You will acknowledge the importance of maintaining healthy boundaries with people both for your own growth and for theirs. Your relationship with Jesus Christ will be your anchor to keep you focused and balanced in relationships with other people.

And God is a jealous God. Out of His love for you, He will deal with you until you are willing to put Him in His rightful place of honor, which is first place. Loving another person with agape love means that you want what is best for the other person. That may mean ending a relationship, especially if he or she is in your thoughts more than God. You will never get a complete deliverance from homosexuality until God truly becomes your first love. If and when you marry or if you are now married, God must continue to be your first love.

Break up your unplowed ground and do not sow among thorns. Circumcise yourselves to the Lord; circumcise your hearts. (Jeremiah 4:3) Homosexuality is an addiction. Freedom from homosexuality will require that you deal with the root cause(s). Otherwise, this addiction will manifest in other addictions. For most, the root can be traced back to the primary relationships between mother/daughter and father/son. Many of these relationships are influenced by generational sins rooted in demonic influences from the spirit realm.

Healing begins as we look within our own hearts. As children, we form ungodly reactions to the injustices, rejections, traumas, or abuses we have experienced. As a result of inner anger, hurt, and confusion, we have made inner vows, bitter root judgments, and expectancies. These areas of our hearts need to be recognized and repented of, choosing change. Healing starts with confession to God of our brokenness and sin. [15]

As I learned the Word of God and learned how to live it as a lifestyle, I matured in my Christian walk. I was able to face my mother and father in a mature manner. The Holy Spirit showed me that both mother and father loved me as much as they were humanly able.

I was traumatized by a demonic curse on my family bloodline; generational sins passed down through the generations with both familiar and ancestral spirits invading the atmosphere. The root force of Satan's Kingdom is called the "strongman." The Bible is very clear about this demonic force. It is the root spirit from which all other demons manifest. **This was the demon that affected me since childhood, entering my spirit, soul, and body without my knowledge, not Mom or Dad. Both were sincerely trying to love me and all their children and did the best that they could. I love them and am very grateful to them for all their efforts and sacrifices for me.**

The battle brought me to my knees in complete submission to the Lordship and the authority of Jesus Christ in a born again covenant relationship. I learned to live by faith and to rise above my flesh, the negative emotions and thoughts, and the painful memories that sought to bring me down. I learned to walk led by the Holy Spirit and to walk in the love and forgiveness of God, a walk of faith completely opposite to the walk of the fleshly emotions.

It was a total transformation and it began with my decision to leave homosexuality and enter into an intimate and a personal covenant relationship with the living God. I will never be the same. I will never go back to that sin. I have been divinely changed in the intimacy I have grown to cherish with my Lord and Savior Jesus Christ.

Through this walk led by the Holy Spirit, I was daily strengthened in my will. I gained a foothold over the strongman of my flesh, my thoughts, and my emotions through obedience. As I yielded in obedience to the Holy Spirit, I was strengthened to say "no" to the flesh. (John 16:13) (Acts 1:8) My willfulness to do what I wanted was changed to a willingness to yield to God's will. His will eventually became my will. Today I experience a life of freedom living led by the Holy Spirit, walking moment by moment in His presence. Only as I yield to the Lord and obey Him has He set me free.

The thief comes only to steal and kill and destroy: I have come that they might have life and have it to the full. (John 10:10) The thief, your enemy, is Satan himself, not people! Once you know your enemy, you can then start the forgiveness process. Yes, Satan works through people. Some people operate with a lack of knowledge of Satan's existence and hurt others because they ignorantly allow Satan to work through them. Some people, even knowledgeable believers, hurt others just because Satan deceives them. Some people cause injury to others because they are just blind to reality. People actually do not recognize the extent of the hurt they are causing. They are too hurt themselves to empathize with other peoples' pain. Hurting people hurt other people!

The strongman can be seen as an "alien intruder." **[16]** In Pastor David T. Demola's book, <u>Dominion Authority</u>, he makes this statement in reference to the Garden of Eden. There appears to be an alien intruder here, and we clearly see that he did not come after Adam and Eve were placed in the garden. This alien intruder was already here. Therefore, God placed Adam in the garden in order to take his rightful place and have dominion, which is the power, and right to govern and control. **[17]**

This strongman or alien intruder is Satan Himself. He comes to steal not only individuals, but families as well. Marilyn Hickey states, in her book, <u>Breaking Generational Curses</u>: **These things that harass and plague us are actually family or generational curses - problems that begin back with our ancestors and have been carried through our bloodline until today. [18]**

We have so much to be thankful for. Jesus came to set us free from anything that would hinder us from walking in love with Him on this earth. Don't let the word "curse" scare you. Jesus, through His death and resurrection, set us free from every curse, every generational sin, and every assignment of the devil. **Christ redeemed us from the curse of the law by becoming a curse for us, for it is written; "Cursed is everyone who is hung on a tree." He redeemed us in order that the blessing given to Abraham might come to the Gentiles through Christ Jesus, so that by faith we might receive the promise of the Spirit. (Galatians 3:13)**

After twenty-seven years of distance from family, I was blessed to experience reconciliation with both parents. The reconciliation had to begin with me. And my steps of obedience to reconcile with family led to complete deliverance from my own fears and childhood issues. Later on in my healing, I did have to separate to go further in the call that I had upon my life. The rubber met the road in life's trials and I learned to trust God. His peace overtook my worries as I cast my cares about my family unto the Lord and continued on with the life I was called to live. It was a supernatural transformation. God will always make a way against any and all odds. **If you believe, you will receive whatever you ask for in prayer. (Matthew 21:22)**

Here is proof of the promise of salvation from the Word of God: **They replied, "Believe in the Lord Jesus, and you will be saved - you and your household." (Acts 16:31)**

Pray and Believe for Yourself, Your Family, and Your Children Against the Generational Curse and All Demonic Assignments

Prepare Your Heart - "I surrender to You, Jesus, as my Lord, my Savior, and my loving authority. I repent of all my sins. I now, as an act of faith, forgive and release all judgment against both myself and against all who have sinned against me. I gratefully receive Your forgiveness and Your cleansing, Lord Jesus. I receive the righteousness (right standing) of God. Fill me with Your Holy Spirit." (1st John 1:9)(Acts 2:38) (Acts 1:8) (Romans 1:17) (All scriptures personalized)

Enter into Your Father's Presence –"Father God, I enter into Your gates with my petitions and with thanksgiving in my heart and with a heart of praise in the name of Jesus Christ my Lord, my Savior, and my authority. Thank You, Lord Jesus, for Your promises of eternal life, complete forgiveness of sins, divine health and healing of body, mind, and spirit, divine protection, provision of all necessities for living, and prosperity." (Psalm100:4) (John 16:23) (Isaiah 53:3–5) (1st John 1:9) (Luke 4:18) (Psalm 91:1-16) (John 3:16) (3rd John 2) (All scriptures personalized)

Prayer for Yourself "Jesus, I believe You are the Son of God and I believe in Your death, burial, and resurrection at Calvary.(Matthew 27:50,59)(Matthew 28:6) I believe and declare that I am redeemed and set free from the curse in Jesus' name. You became a curse for me. (Galatians 3:13) I declare that I am free from any generational curse and all demonic spirits and/or assignments by Your blood bought sacrifice, in Jesus' name. (Luke 10:19)(1st Peter 2:24) You became a curse for me. And by Your stripes (Your blood stained beatings), I declare myself whole and healed emotionally, mentally, physically, spiritually, financially, and socially in the name of Jesus. (Isaiah 53:5)(1st Peter 2:24)(Hebrews 9:14) (Luke 4:18,19)(See Appendix)

Prayer of Intercession for Self and Unsaved Blood Relatives; (i.e. father, mother, brother, sister, uncle, aunt, niece, nephew, cousins…)

I now stand in the gap as Moses did, for all of my family members. I ask You to forgive me of my sins and for the sins of my ancestors.(Lev. 26:45) (Matthew 6:12) I ask that You do not count my family members' sins against them. (Acts 7:60) For they operated with a lack of knowledge of the truth of the Word of God and are deceived by both the devil and by the traditions handed down through the generations.(1st Peter 1:18) (Hosea 4:6) Thank You, Jesus, that Your blood covers my blood relatives.(1st Peter 1:18,19)(1st Peter 2:24) (Hebrew 10:19-22)(Hebrews 9:14)(Lev. 26:45) Your Word says that You sent Your Son Jesus into the world so that none would perish but that all would have eternal life. You did not come to condemn the world but to save it. (John 3:16,17) I pray that the angels go before my relatives. (Psalm 91:11) The angel of the Lord encamps around those who fear Him, and He delivers them. (Psalm 34:7) I pray that no weapon formed against them will prosper.(Isaiah 54:14) I call forth laborers to them from the north, the south, the east, and the west to minister the truth of Your gospel to them.(Matthew 9:37,38) I ask You to touch them through media and internet. (Matthew 9:37,38) I believe that Your loving kindness will open their hearts to choose to humble themselves to You, to repent and turn from all sin, and to the commitment of a relationship with You, Jesus. (Romans 2:4)(Romans 10:9,10) (Romans 10:13)(John 3:16) (John 14:17) (John 15:5) I pray they are saved, redeemed, protected from all evil, freed from every fear, every deception, and every addiction. (Col. 1:13)(John 10:10)(Galations 3:13)(1st John 4:18)(John 10:10)(1st Peter 5:8) I pray that they will make the choice to make You Lord and to then take their own freedom from every demonic stronghold.(John 3:3)(Luke 10:19) I bind, mute, and gag every demonic spirit and/or demonic assignment that is oppressing them in Jesus' name. (Matthew 18:18)I render them powerless in Jesus' name.(Matthew 18:18) I declare and believe that these words will not return void but that they will accomplish all that they have been spoken in faith to perform in Jesus' name. (Isaiah 55:11) I ask, pray, believe, and receive all that I have spoken for them, in Jesus' name. I expect and hope for the answer to this prayer. (Mark 11:23-25)(Hebrews 11:1) As I continue to pray for them, I commit to daily study of the Word of God and to daily prayer with praise and worship to keep my vessel filled with God." (Luke 11:24-26)(Romans 12:2)(James 5:16)(Psalm 33:1-3) (John 4:24)(All scriptures personalized) (See Appendix) **Yet I am not ashamed, because I know whom I have believed, and am convinced that He is able to guard what I have entrusted to Him for that day. (2nd Tim. 1:12)**

One day, while riding on a train, the Lord gave me a vision of my entire family standing together in the heavenlies. They were all dressed up in their Sunday best with smiles on their faces. I believe the Lord graciously lifted the burden from me.

These are the words of Paul in prison in answer to the jailer who was about to take his own life. **The** jailer woke up, and when he saw the prison doors open, he drew his sword and was about to kill himself because he thought the prisoners had escaped. But Paul shouted, "Don't harm yourself! We are all here!" The jailer called for lights, rushed in and fell trembling before Paul and Silas. He then brought them out and asked, "Sirs, what must I do to be saved?" They replied, "Believe in the Lord Jesus, and you will be saved – you and your household." (Acts 16:27-31)

I believed and proclaimed the Words of 2nd Timothy: **Yet I am not ashamed, because I know whom I have believed, and am convinced that He is able to guard what I have entrusted to Him for that day. (2nd Timothy 1:12)**

A Parent's Prayer of Intercession for His/Her Unsaved Children
A parent has legal authority to pray in Jesus' delegated authority for his/her children

"Lord Jesus, I place the blood of Jesus Christ between my children and the sins of their father(s). (Exodus 20:5,6)(Lev. 26:45) I declare them saved, redeemed, protected from all harm, free from all addiction, and free from any demonic oppression/possession and/or assignments, in Jesus' name.(Galatians 3:13) (Luke 10:19)(Psalm 91:11)(Psalm 34:7)(Isaiah 53:3-5) I speak to every demon spirit oppressing and/or possessing (____name of child or children____). Go, in the name of Jesus Christ.(Luke 10:19)(Mark 16:17) Go wherever Jesus sends you to be held captive by the angels of God. (Mark 5:8-13) I commit to daily study of the Word of God and daily prayer with praise and worship as I stand in the gap for my children; to keep my vessel filled and to keep the enemy out. (Luke 11:24-26)(Romans 12:2)(John 4:24) I declare my children the "healed of the Lord." (Ephesians 6:20)(Mark 11:23-25) (Isaiah 61:1)(Luke 4:18) I pray that when they reach the age of knowing their calling they will make the decision to repent of their sins and to welcome and ask You, Lord Jesus, into their hearts with sorrow and renounciation for their sins, in Jesus' name. Amen." (1st John 1:9)(Rom. 10:9,10)(Rom. 2:4)(Acts 2:21)(John 3:3)(John 3:16)(John 15:5)(All scriptures personalized) (See Appendix)

He sent forth His word and healed them. He rescued them from the grave.(Psalm 107:20)
Pray With Expectation

When I prayed, I stood on the Word of God in Acts 16:27-31 and I believed that God was taking care of my family's every need. Against the negative pull to fear and worry, I willed to believe by faith that God was in control of my family. I conquered the worries and fears one day at a time. I do believe that the Word of God is true. By faith, I rose above the negative pull and believed that God loved and died for them two thousand years ago and that He would send laborers to them to minister Jesus to them. I prayed with expectation. Even when I did not feel the expectation, I spoke it by faith. "Lord, I expect a miracle!" Just as the prayers of one man, Moses, brought three million people across the Red Sea to deliverance from the control of Pharaoh's edicts, I determined that I, by an act of my will and by an act of my faith, would be the person to stand in the gap for my family members, as their intercessor.

So the prayers we pray are not, "If it be Thy will, Lord, please save my family or my x –lovers!" These are declarations of faith because we know and we believe that God died for every person's sins, sicknesses, and all diseases as well. Jesus said, **"Again, I tell you that if two of you on earth agree about anything you ask for, it will be done for you by my Father in heaven. For where two to three come together in my name, there am I with them." (Matthew 18:19, 20)** And Jesus spoke to the disciples, **"I tell you the truth, my Father will give you whatever you ask in my name." (John 16:23)**

I could not physically be there, but there is no distance in prayer and this became a higher call for them and for me as well as I released them to the care of the sovereign Lord. I always prayed for the time and opportunity when we would be joined together in this life. I knew by faith I would be joined with them in heaven and I took solace in that.

Know Your Enemy

Finally, be strong in the Lord and in His mighty power. Put on the full armor of God so that you can take your stand against the devil's schemes. For our struggle is not against flesh and blood, but against the rulers, against the authorities, against the powers of this dark world, and against the spiritual forces of evil in the heavenly realms. (Ephesians 6: 11,12) Coming out of homosexuality is a hellish battle. What are you fighting? A demon that is so grotesque that if you were to see it, you would probably be paralyzed, blinded, and muted by the very sight of it, that is, if you are not walking in the authority of Jesus Christ in your position of surrender and intimacy with Him. It is a demon that comes so suddenly and so subtly that you can easily be deceived by its blatant lies. Deception by its very nature deludes a person from the truth by making a lie appear to be true. The prophet Daniel tells us: **Some of the wise will stumble, so that they may be refined, purified and made spotless until the time of the end, for it will still come at the appointed time. (Daniel 11:35)**

My people are destroyed from lack of knowledge. (Hosea 4:6)

Many are Suffering

Multitudes, multitudes, in the valley of decision! For the day of the Lord is near in the valley of decision. (Joel 3:14)

There are thousands of people suffering in this so-called "alternative" lifestyle. As proud and self-righteous as these folk carry on to be, they are suffering. In their innermost being, they do not have peace. The mask of self-righteousness is only a cover-up for the deep pain and confusion imprisoned within their hearts. Some are Christian believers. Some are not. A large majority of them are suffering rejection both in the world's circles and in the church circles. They are afraid to speak out to the Christians because they do not want to experience any more rejection. They have established their own little havens to avoid rejection in the world's circles.

Homosexual communities in Los Angeles and New York City, for example, provide only an external environment of acceptance, peace, and safety. This can never serve as a substitute for the true inner peace and safety with complete acceptance found within our souls and spirits that we receive in a relationship with the living God. When we sincerely repent and leave this sin, turn away from it, and commit to a born again committed covenant and personal relationship with Jesus Christ, there we sit in peace at His table of complete and utter love, acceptance, and forgiveness. We are cleansed as white as snow from all sin. Jesus Christ has already provided a way out of this pain and a way out of this deception.

I once read in a poem that when snow covers the earth that it hides the world's scars and gives nature new birth. And then when a man comes to God in the Lord that forgiveness like snow covers him evermore. **[19]** A sense of rejection can never be resolved by running away. I had to face my own self-rejection as well as others' rejection in order to overcome it. Kate McVeigh states in her book, <u>Conquering Intimidation</u>: We actually reject ourselves because somebody else rejected us! **[20]**

Only through our submission to repent and leave the sins and, by faith, to welcome Jesus into our hearts, are we granted relationship with Jesus Christ. He then endows us with the "blessed assurance" that in whatever capacity we walk, live, work, or play, that we are completely forgiven and set free from this sin, walking in right standing before God. The power of Jesus Christ dwells on the inside of us. Nothing any man or woman has to think, say, or do to the contrary has the ability to change that. **For if God is for us, who can be against us? (Romans 8:31) The Lord is my strength and my sword. What can man do to me? (Psalms 27:1)**

God's Love for Us Allows Us to Rise Above All Abuse and All Fear

God's love for me became more and more real as I trusted in His love for me. I believe I was especially blessed to know He was present with me. Little by little, I took risks both in the world and in the Church, sharing my testimony with others. When Jesus walked the earth, He was rejected by men, but he didn't fear them or their opinions of Him. Because He was rejected even to His own death, He understands our deepest rejections today. And, as He shared His deepest self with His Father, He experienced a deep inner conviction. His Father's love for Him would enable Him to rise above the abuse. He knew there was a better place. His heart was heaven bound while He served His purpose here on earth. **He was despised and rejected by men, a man of sorrows, and familiar with suffering. Like one from whom men hide their faces He was despised, and we esteemed Him not. (Isaiah 53: 3)**

Be encouraged. Jesus knows exactly how you feel and His love for you is divine. He would say to you as he said to the prophet Isaiah: **Fear not, for I have redeemed you. I have called you by your name. You are mine. (Isaiah 43: 1b) Because you are precious and honored in my sight, and because I love you. (Isaiah 43:4)**

The Spirit World is Real

However, the spiritual state of the world still stands since the beginning of time. If we were to have three-dimensional spiritual eyeglasses provided for the purpose of seeing into the spiritual world, we would see Our Lord Jesus Christ high above all the other created spiritual beings, both angelic and demonic. The thief or Satan himself was created by God and was the first "alien intruder" [21] on the earth before Adam and Eve arrived. Satan has power but it is God Himself who created him. The greater power exists in the Creator, of course!

You must settle that your enemy never was and still is not your mother, your father, your brothers, your sisters, your spouse or children; not even your abusers, rapists, attackers, or anyone else "er's." Your enemy was and still continues to be Satan himself. Satan is the god of this world and he works through people. He receives much pleasure taking over and controlling your life. He desires to completely destroy both your life, your purpose in this life, and your will to live. **Be self-controlled and alert. Your enemy the devil prowls around like a roaring lion looking for someone to devour. Resist him, standing firm in the faith, because you know that your brothers throughout the world are undergoing the same sufferings. (1ˢᵗ Peter 5: 8-9)**

Deception, Conviction, Decision

Redeemed by Jesus, Not Tradition

We are a family of Roman Catholic and Italian descent. I was not the youngest but I was the quietest child in a family of five children. Everyone, except Dad, one brother, and myself, were outspoken. I had many weaknesses, but they seemed to be unnoticed by my family. They all seemed to be about their own business.

I believe God had given me the gift of helps since infancy. Having had the opportunity to view old family movies with Mom, I watched myself helping the younger children. I literally helped Mom to raise them. Even through high school, I was on the listener end of relationships, always trying to help solve all my friends' problems.

Since childhood, I always had a strong belief in God. When I was in need, I ran to talk to Jesus, usually by taking a walk on the beach. I knew Jesus loved me and I believed that He heard me when I talked to Him. However, I thought God was far from me, in the clouds somewhere. I didn't know He could come into my heart; and that He wanted an intimate and a personal relationship with me. (John 15:5) (John 14:17) (John 3:16)(Romans 10:9,10)(Romans 10:13)(All scriptures referenced)

These are the words of Jesus: **I am the vine; you are the branches. If a man remains in me and I in him, he will bear much fruit; apart from me you can do nothing. (John 15:5)**

You Enter Into a New Bloodline with a Divine Nature

When I became born again, accepting Jesus Christ into my heart, I made a lifelong personal commitment and I entered into a divine covenant relationship with the living God. (John 3:3) You can only get to Father God through His Son Jesus Christ. (John 14:6) When I committed to a relationship with Jesus Christ, I also entered into a new, a divine, and a completely separate bloodline from that of my family inheritance. (1st Peter 1:18,19) (Romans 8:15-17) I became adopted and grafted into the bloodline of Jesus Christ and I inherited all of His precious promises. (Romans 11:17,18)(2nd Peter 1:3,4) (Romans 8:15-17) I didn't realize that Jesus Christ would play an integral part in helping me to form my very identity as a godly woman.(All scriptures referenced)These are the words of Jesus to Nicodemus: **In reply, Jesus declared, "I tell you the truth; no one can see the kingdom of God unless he is born again. (John 3:3)** These are the words of Jesus in the gospel of John: **Jesus answered, "I am the way and the truth and the life. No one comes to the Father except through me. (John 14:6)**

For you know that it was not with perishable things such as silver or gold that you were redeemed from the empty way of life handed down to you from your forefathers, but with the precious blood of Christ, a lamb without blemish or defect. (1st Peter 1:18)

For you did not receive a spirit that makes you a slave again to fear, but you received the Spirit of sonship. And by Him we cry, "Abba, Father." The Spirit himself testifies with our spirit that we are God's children. Now, if we are children, then we are heirs - heirs of God and co-heirs with Christ, if indeed we share in His sufferings in order that we may also share in His glory. (Romans 8:15-17)

His divine power has given us everything we need for life and godliness through our knowledge of Him who called us by His own glory and goodness. Through these He has given us His very great and precious promises, so that through them you may participate in the divine nature and escape the corruption in the world caused by evil desires. (2nd Peter 1:3,4)

If some of the branches have been broken off, and you, through a wild olive shoot, have been grafted in among the others and now share in the nourishing sap from the olive root, do not boast over those branches. If you do, consider this; You do not support the the root, but the root supports you. (Romans 11:17,18)

Transgressions and Iniquities

I had faith but I did not know the Word of God which teaches about transgressions and iniquities. Holy prophets of God announce and vividly describe the coming of the Anointed Savior in the Old Testament seven hundred years before the actual arrival of Jesus Christ, the Messiah. **He was despised and rejected of men, a man of sorrows, and familiar with suffering. Like one from whom men hide their faces He was despised, and we esteemed Him not. Surely He took up our infirmities and carried our sorrows, yet we considered Him stricken by God, smitten by Him, and afflicted. But He was pierced for our transgressions, He was crushed for our iniquities; the punishment that brought us peace was upon Him, and by His wounds we are healed. (Isaiah 53:3-5)**

An iniquity implies a tendency or predisposition toward a certain sin. [22] A transgression is sin. It could be any sin; alcoholism, drug addiction, homosexuality, worry. I believe I have a tendency toward certain sins as drug and alcohol addiction, homosexuality, and a tendency toward fear and worry as a result of the fall of Adam and Eve and as a result of generational sins and ancestral spirits affecting my family bloodline. These iniquities became more pronounced after the death of my paternal grandfather. This event was a crisis point for my family in the early seventies. This crisis brought much strife and confusion to me and to many members of my family.

But, the good news is that Jesus was wounded for my transgressions (sins) and was bruised for my iniquities as well. Anyone who has surrendered to an intimate relationship with Jesus Christ and has become born again and has made a covenant commitment to Jesus Christ as the Lord, Savior, and authority of his/her life has the opportunity to be cleansed from all iniquity and from all sin. How?

By opening our hearts in humble submission to the Lordship of Jesus Christ and by asking His forgiveness for hurting Him, we repent. Repentance is a true sorrow for having offended God which includes a turning from the sin and a desire to change. The Lord Jesus lovingly forgives and cleanses us by His blood as soon as we come to Him with repentance in our hearts. And we are placed in the secret place of His divine protection, under His shed blood which was shed for all sin. (1st John 1:9) (Psalm 91:1) Repentance then brings us the Holy Spirit. The Holy Spirit then enables and empowers us to forgive and to release judgment toward both ourselves and others by faith. (Acts 2:38)(Acts 1:8) (Luke 24:49)(Luke 6:37)(All scriptures referenced) **The only thing that counts is faith expressing itself through love. (Galatians 5:6)**

The Prayer of Faith

First, we prepare our hearts to speak properly positioned in faith in submission to Jesus' Lordship and authority, in repentance for sins, and in forgiveness and release of judgment against ourselves and others. With a heart of faith, then, we first petition the Father in the name of Jesus. (John 16:23) "I honor You, Father God, with my substance and come to You with my petitions, in Jesus' name." With a heart of faith, we then take Jesus' delegated authority and rebuke the enemy in the name of Jesus in coming against the generational curse, any demonic spirits, and against all ungodly habits, emotions, and all negative thoughts and memories. (Luke 10:19) "Go, in the name of Jesus. You have no authority here." With our heart of faith, we also take Jesus' delegated authority, speaking the Word of God over ourselves in declaring what is not as though it is, (Romans 4:17) in the name of Jesus. (Phil. 2:9) "I am redeemed from the curse of the law, in Jesus name." (Galatians 3:13)

We always speak with a heart that is prepared in faith to release the power of God. Also, the spoken Word of God changes us from the inside out in speaking it, declaring it, and believing that God will change us as we confess His Word over our lives. "God has not given me the spirit of fear, but He has given me the spirit of power, and of love, and of self-discipline (sound mind)." (2nd Timothy 1:7) Our words spoken in faith release the power of God. (Hebrews 4:12) (Hebrews 1:1-3) (Hebrews11:1) It is that simple. Remember, God cannot and will not do anything without our taking the first step toward Him. He is a gentleman. (John 16:23)(All scriptures referenced)

Ask and it will be given to you; seek and you will find; knock and the door will be opened to you. For everyone who asks receives; he who seeks finds; and to him who knocks, the door

will be opened. (Matthew 7:7,8) His promises are true. The Word of God is settled and never changes. When I repent of sin and iniquity or tendency toward sin with true sorrow for having displeased the Lord, and ask Him to forgive me, He forgives. When I repent of sin and ask Him to help me break this ungodly tendency I have, He gives me strategy to act. I have to speak for Him to act! He is not looking for perfection, but He does want my heart to be honest before Him. **If we confess our sins, He is faithful and just and will forgive us our sins and purify us from all unrighteousness. (1ˢᵗ John 1:9)**

Jesus is our High Priest, and we can take our trespass offerings directly to Him. Once a trespass becomes a pattern of sin, however, it becomes an iniquity that is passed from generation to generation. Iniquities are only broken by confessing them, repenting for your forefather's participation and the part you have played in perpetuating them and applying the blood of Jesus. **[23]**

Breaking free from my own bondage requires that I repent of all sins and leave all idols. Repentance means that I am yielding to the Lord, cooperating with Him to change me and to form new behaviors and attitudes. I fought to leave self: self-pity, self-condemnation, and selfishness. I had to give out to others in whatever capacity I was able to give. This is not just a prayer to Father God in proper position of a heart of faith, with submission, repentance, and forgiveness. "Father God, I forgive them and I forgive myself and I am sorry for the hurt that I caused them, in Jesus' name," and now I am healed. Yes, I had to apologize to family members I had hurt.

The real work, however, came when I had to look within my own heart and see the dirt. The process of deliverance is about looking within my own heart and seeking to purify it. (Psalm 51:10,11) I had to repent, renounce, and rebuke, in Jesus' delegated authority and in Jesus' name, my part in the hurts and the abuses. I had to also crucify my flesh, my ungodly thoughts and behavior patterns, judgments, emotions, fantasies, and all impure motives. I had to take Jesus' delegated authority against all evil spirits oppressing me. I had to close the door on all sin and all idols.

This kept the enemy out and took away his power. I had to stubbornly refuse all sexual sin and its connections, and press into the walk of the Spirit of the living God. I had to also adamantly refuse to worry and lock the door on perfectionism. Obedience locks the door against Satan's control. It is the ultimate resistance against his ploys. Because it is an action of completed submission to God. (James 4:7,8)

Rebuke the Antichrist Spirits Over Yourself, in Jesus' Name

Prepare Your Heart – "I surrender to You, Jesus, as my Lord, my Savior, and my authority. I repent of all my sins. I now, as an act of faith, forgive and release all judgment against both myself and against all who have sinned against me. I gratefully receive Your forgiveness and Your cleansing, Lord Jesus. I receive the righteousness (right standing) of God. I ask You to fill me with Your Holy Spirit." (1ˢᵗ John 1:9) (Romans 1:17) (Acts 2:38)

Enter into Your Father's Presence – "Father God, I enter into Your gates with my petitions, with thanksgiving in my heart and with a heart of praise in the name of Jesus Christ my Lord, my Savior, and my authority." (Psalm100:4) (John 16:23)

Take Jesus' Delegated Authority against the Antichrist Spirit in Your Life, in Jesus' Name – "Lord Jesus, in Your delegated authority, and by faith, I now repent of, renounce, and rebuke all antichrist spirits, including any generational and ancestral spirits in Jesus'name.(Luke 10:19)(Mark 16:17) The blood of Jesus is against you.(1ˢᵗ Peter 1:18,19)(1ˢᵗ Peter 2:24)(Hebrews 9:14) I rebuke you and I renounce you, in the name of Jesus Christ.(Luke 10:19) I render you powerless in Jesus' name.(Phil 2:9,10)(Matthew 18:18)(Col. 2:10,15) Go wherever Jesus sends you to be held captive by the angels of God. (Mark 5:8-13) Jesus, I ask that You have mercy upon me for my sins and upon my ancestors' for their sins. (Lev. 26:45) (Acts 7:60) (John 15:7)(Matthew 7:7) I ask that You have mercy upon my parents and grandparents for their sins as well.(Acts 7:60) I forgive them.(Luke 6:28,37)(Matthew 6:12) Jesus, You dwell in me and greater are You within me than he (any person, place, thing, or any demonic spirit and/or assignment) that is in the world. (1ˢᵗ John 4:4) I repent of my part in this, Lord Jesus.(Acts 3:19) I believe that You, Lord Jesus, will honor this prayer because I am Your child and I expect that You will remove this mountain from me.(Mark 11:23-26)(Hebrews 11:1)Thank you that You have delegated me with Your authority here in the earth. (Luke 10:19)(Matthew 18:18)(Mark 16:17) Nothing shall be able to separate me from the love of God which is in Christ Jesus.(Romans 8:38) I commit to daily study of the Word of God and prayer with daily praise and worship to keep my vessel filled with God's Word. Amen." (Romans 12:2) (Luke 11:24-26)(John 4:24) (Psalm 33:1-3)(James 5:16) (All scriptures personalized)(See Appendix)

The Curse is Broken – The instant you repent of your sins, the curse is broken. But as long as you cop out, as long as you dump the blame on everybody else and what you think they've done to you, then the curse will not be broken in your life. [24]

Breaking the family curse first required repentance on my part. If I held even the slightest amount of bitterness toward any family member, I would lose both liberty and authority given me from Jesus Christ. Unforgiveness is sin. We are commanded to forgive. To this day I stand in prayer for my loved ones. Don't fall into Satan's traps to keep you bitter against them, no matter what the circumstances are!

If you are bitter against someone, you can't afford it! It's going to cost you your blessing. And it can cost your children's blessing too. You had better repent. You are wrong to be bitter, and you're going to live in depression and defeat until you do. **[25]**

My friend, please be wise to this trap! Do not take the bait of Satan! You will never feel like forgiving in your flesh. This must be done as an act of faith and obedience with the help of the Holy Spirit and a Spirit filled counselor(s) may be necessary to help you through. When you believe that you were never in this battle against people, but against rulers, authorities, and powers of this dark world and against spiritual forces of evil in the heavenly realms, (Ephesians 6:12 ref.) forgiveness and release of all judgment becomes possible with the divine help of the Holy Spirit. (Acts 1:8 ref.) With forgiveness comes your deliverance and freedom from this hellish spirit! There is no compromise here. You must forgive as an act of your will. Ask for help if you need.

As I closed the doors to all that was not of God, I stepped closer and deeper in my intimacy with the Lord, despite the persecution. I could stand and pray for those who hated, ridiculed, and rejected me because the Lord was with me. He enabled me to get through the tormenting spirits because my love for Him was greater than life itself and greater than any demonic entity. He knew and honored my heart to please Him and I knew and believed He would deliver me, no matter how difficult the test was. He was there with me all the time. He showed Himself real to me. My good works of having to be perfect was my open door and it had to close. When I obeyed the Lord, He baptized me with His power and presence and the demons fled! When they tried to torment again, I prayed for the people as if they were a brother or a sister. They had no power anymore because I had decidedly given my need for control over to my Lord and Savior. I closed the door to Satan's authority by closing the door on the "law" (the need to be perfect).

I know that I cannot give what I do not have. Only through the help of the Holy Spirit, I am strong against this enemy who uses every scheme possible to tempt me back into pride, envy, depression, jealousy, discouragement, hopelessness, lust, bitterness, self-pity, self-condemnation, and selfishness. His goal was and still continues to be to whip me of the freedom and power I have in Jesus Christ. He lost the battle two thousand years ago when Jesus showed His total acceptance, love, and forgiveness for me and triumphed over the devil and all his works. (Col. 2:15)

And having disarmed the powers and authorities, He made a public spectacle of them, triumphing over them by the cross. (Col. 2:15)

I would have given up had I leaned upon my feelings because I was bleeding from the wounds. It was the working of the Holy Spirit that helped to heal the wounds in my heart. As the bleeding subsided, scars began to form. These scars now form a base from which I experience incredible gratitude to the Lord for all He has done. I remember the events of childhood, but the pain no longer has a grip upon me. The memories remain as a legacy of deep gratitude to Jesus Christ for His sacrifice of His life for me on the cross.

The Story Begins

In 1973, I was twenty-three years old. I was in an emotionally vulnerable state when I left my home in New Jersey. I was headed toward California. I left with my father's blessing and my mother's hesitations about my move. After graduating with a bachelor's degree in music therapy, I was to practice as a music therapy intern on an adolescent drug rehabilitation unit at Camarillo State Hospital.

I met a woman there who was one of my coworkers. She acted as a drug counselor on the unit. As I stood and watched her counseling these drug-addicted youngsters, I stood in awe of her ability to capture their attention. She knew just how to touch them with her words and actions. I marveled at her ability to be in control. She was very tall and striking in appearance. I marveled at her demur of meekness. It was extremely attractive to me. I was especially drawn to her self-confidence, a character trait I did not have.

We became friends. We were living in the same dormitory connected to the hospital. As we became closer as friends, she asked me to become her housemate. I actually went up on a hill to pray about the decision. I sensed a small still voice say to me, "Follow your heart." I naively believed that this was God speaking to me. On the contrary, however, this was a deceptive lure and a blatant lie from Satan himself.

Lacking a committed relationship with Jesus Christ, completely ignorant and defenseless against Satan's schemes, and with a desperate and legitimate need to be loved and accepted, I was faced with the temptation to fall into the trap, the web of homosexuality. "How can love be a sin?" A demonic spirit whispered to me. "God is love, isn't He?" I rationalized and I further deliberated. "How can this good feeling be bad? This is my friend whom I care for and love. How can friendship be wrong?" Like Eve, I was also deceived.

Without realizing the deception I was falling for, I was setting myself up for an idyllic relationship that would take me away from reverencing God and would replace it with reverence for man or, should I say, for a woman.

Although they claimed to be wise, they became fools and exchanged the glory of the immortal God for images made to look like mortal man and birds and animals and reptiles. Therefore God gave them over in the sinful desires of their hearts to sexual impurity for the degrading of their bodies with one another. They exchanged the truth of God for a lie and worshiped and served created things rather than the Creator - who is forever praised. Amen. (Romans 1:21-25)

Body, Mind, and Spirit in a Process of Holiness before the Living God

We were created by the Almighty God with a spirit, a soul, and a body. The spirit is the "real you," the part of you that will live forever with Jesus Christ in heaven, if you are trusting in Jesus Christ as your Savior and Lord.

The soul of man is also comprised of three areas; his conscious mind, his preconscious mind, and his subconscious mind. <u>The heart of man is found in his soul area.</u> The word "heart" is literally translated from "lieb" or "nephesh" in Hebrew-Chaldean. The Greek counterpart is "psyche," which means soul. Both the original Hebrew and Greek describe the word "heart" as being the seat or center of man's intellect, emotions, and will. **[26]** The conscious mind is aware of what is going on. The preconscious mind is called the seat of your memory. But the subconscious mind is called the "heart of man." And the heart of man in the Bible is the center of man's intelligence, emotions, and will. **[27]**What does the Word of God say to us about the heart? **Above all else, guard your heart, for it is the wellspring of life. (Proverbs 4: 23) The heart is wicked above all, who can know it? (Jeremiah 17: 9)**

The heart connects the spirit to the body. The body is the very substance, the temple that houses the spirit and the heart. The goal of sanctification for the Christian believer is to cleanse the heart to a state of purification or holiness. Holiness with God renews the heart in such a way that bodily pleasures are delighted to come under the subjection of the spirit and heart/soul. Holiness is a state of gratitude to Him for every breath we take. Our Father God is the perfection of holiness, and has wiped our slate completely clean before Him because of the cross of His Son Jesus Christ. When we by faith reach out to receive the Lord Jesus Christ into our hearts, a divine merger occurs.

The spirit-man is perfect, and is created in the image and likeness of God, but the spirit and soul must be in agreement before the body can respond. [28] God's purpose for our lives is for us to be guided by our spirit, living spirit to Spirit with the living Lord. Satan tries to distract the heart/soul with negative thoughts and feelings, luring us to live by what our flesh desires. It is the heart or soul of man that determines the winning vote. As it becomes filled with the Word of God and becomes purified through the healing of the thoughts, emotions, and memories, the will begins to make godly decisions and not worldly ones.

Do not conform any longer to the pattern of this world, but be transformed by the renewing of your mind. Then you will be able to test and approve what God's will is - His good, pleasing, and perfect will. (Romans 12:2)

A Metaphor on Deception

In the animal kingdom, it is interesting to note that when the snake attacks its victim, its venom affects the nervous system first before attacking the respiratory system. After the initial bite, it takes only a few minutes before the victim is paralyzed. After paralysis occurs, the physical heart ceases beating and the victim dies.

Likewise, our enemy, the devil, attacks our soul realm, attacking the thoughts first. Venomous thoughts are targeted at our minds first. Once the thought enters, the poison is deposited. "How can love be a sin? God is love, isn't he?" No wonder the Lord warns us to guard our hearts! The venom then spreads as the victim progresses from the initial deceptive thoughts to intellectual deliberation and self-gratifying rationalizations. Satan has successfully deposited his initial deception or poison through the thought realm of our heart/soul.

The venom of the enemy then continues to spread its influence to the emotional realm of the heart/soul. A relationship develops between both parties in a same sexed relationship. The friendship becomes codependent in nature because it simply is not dependent upon God as its source.

Codependent relationships are addictive in nature. Because of the intense need to be needed, each party is desperately looking to the other to supply all his/her needs. The heart is operating under a false pretense, a fantasy assumption that all will be now satisfied through the other person. A simple friendship within several days or weeks will transform into a seduction.

The next deceptive thought is "I love this person." "I want this person." And, as the friendship grows, the person is not only convinced by the deception, but he or she is now convicted that there is nothing sinful or wrong with this homosexual encounter. Of course, this is another deception because only the Holy Spirit is able to truthfully convict. Friend, "I want" is rooted in pride, not conviction. Now the heart/soul becomes almost thoroughly saturated with the venom of Satan's deception.

However, for sin to conceive, the will must make a decision to enter into the act. Look at the scenario of Adam and Eve in the Garden of Eden. Listen to the tempter's words: **Now the serpent was more crafty than any of the wild animals the Lord God had made. He said to the woman, "Did God really say? 'You must not eat from any tree in the garden'?" (Genesis 3:1)** He also said, **"You will not surely die," the serpent said to the woman. "For God knows that when you eat of it your eyes will be opened and you will be like God, knowing good and evil." (Genesis 3:4)**

Notice the scripture states that the serpent was craftier than all the wild animals in the garden. The word "crafty" means "adept in the use of subtlety and cunning."[29] A crafty player will always attack the opponent at his/her weakest point. So far the enemy succeeded to deceive the thoughts and the emotions. Just as the viper deposits its venom in the victim's nervous system first, the devil starts to deceive us in our heart/soul realm first, and spiritual paralysis has begun.

However, for spiritual death to take place, the will must make a decision. In order for the will to now act on these thoughts and emotions, a moment of weakness is required. And, believe me, Satan knows our weaknesses. The more we dwell on a thought without replacing it and "taking it captive" to the obedience of Christ, the more access is allowed for the enemy to influence first and then to invade. His motive in the invasion is to distract us and to attack us unawares; to strip us of our power to control the very decisions of our own wills. When temptation knocks, we must think and act quickly, redirecting our thoughts and our emotions. We must take control of our own thoughts and not allow any foreign interference, other than the voice of the Holy Spirit.

For the weapons of our warfare are not carnal but mighty to the breaking down of strongholds. We demolish arguments and every pretension that sets itself up against the knowledge of God, and we take captive every thought to make it obedient to Christ. (2nd Cor.10:5)

The Story Continues

At the time, I was nowhere near taking my thoughts for this woman captive. I was not submitted to the Lord and was being controlled by my emotions. I was "captured by my feelings" for her. This rebellious attitude invited further demonic influence. She was my friend and I was very secure and happy to have a friend. Here I was face to face with this person whom I admired and respected as I watched her helping young adolescents. I really liked and trusted her. I wanted to learn from her and to be like her in many ways. I didn't know she was living the gay lifestyle but I found out one night when we were wrestling, playing in the dormitory room. In the excitement and the surprise of one moment, I acted on the sin and responded as she initiated a kiss.

At first, I was totally repulsed, wanting to resist. My entire being felt the unnaturalness of this act. The "real me," my spirit, knew deep down inside me that this was unnatural. However, my deep need to be loved, needed, and accepted, and to please this person, coupled by the awe and unconscious envy toward this person, further tempted my will to enter into the seduction.

Dr. Consiglio, a renowned speaker and counselor for strugglers of homosexuality, states that the envy for the person becomes eroticized. [30] My own lack of self-esteem or self-value, self- confidence, and self-image, my lack of personal autonomy and initiative to say "no," and my deep need to be loved, accepted, and needed and to please others were character flaws that kept me from resisting the gross repulsion that I initially felt. Unfortunately, my character weaknesses outweighed the repulsion. Lacking a personal relationship with Jesus, with no base of trust in a personal God, I was drawn to this woman for security. But, the Lord Jesus Christ would restore and rescue me from this gross deception.

Satan had his way and I was deceived. By an act of my own will, I submitted to the temptation. I take full responsibility for it was indeed my decision, no matter how deceived I was.

But….God still had a plan for my life and He would lead me into freedom from this addiction.

Summary

As you can see, the subtle deception of this crafty demon spirit starts out convincing the victim into "thinking that this friendship is not really a sin." As the friendship deepens, the demon spirit attacks the emotions and deceives the victims into "feeling good about the relationship." Finally, attacking the victim's weakest point of needing to be loved, accepted, and needed, and to please others, the deception reaches its climax. Once the demon succeeds at convincing the victim into a willingness to act on his/her feelings, Satan has won the victim over into his sinful realm and the victim will be under his control.

The act of the sin of homosexuality must be seen for what it is; a sin against God and against one's own body, soul, and spirit, against another person's body, soul, and spirit, and against both party's personal identity and integrity. Reverend Dr. Leo Natale so poignantly explains; initially, the soul is influenced by a deceptive spirit. After sin has conceived, the soul which is part of the spirit will be influenced by what the victim feels through the body. [31]

Once I conceived this sin, not only was my soul, (thoughts, emotions, and will) "paralyzed" by the deceptive demonic venom, but also I experienced a "death" in my spirit being. Sin brings separation from God. Unhealthy shame is a result of this sin. Thus, my spirit and soul were affected and would require repentance and healing. At this point, I allowed myself to be under the control of Satan.

For all have sinned and fallen short of the glory of God . . . (Romans 3:23)

Because of the shame of their sin, Adam and Eve had to cover their bodies which they loved before their sin. In the sin of homosexuality, not only was I shamed in my body but also in my personal identity. As a result, my "honest self" went into hiding as well. The "honest self" includes personality, dignity or self-respect, and personal integrity or character. The "honest self" also includes godly gender identity as a blessed woman of God.

The Consequences of Sin Bring Conviction

Because our sexuality is created by God as the tool for our deepest expression of love for one other person in the holy covenant of marriage, this sin does an extreme amount of damage to the soul. Only the supernatural healing power of Jesus Christ is able to restore and to deliver the soul. As a result of the sin of Adam and Eve, they were so shamed by their rebellion that they clothed themselves with fig leaves.

Their act of disobedience was willful and defied the commandment of God. Their sin, however, did not defy the very order of the natural creation of man. The sin of homosexuality, however, defies God's natural and original intended design for man and woman. **So God created man in His own image, in the image of God He created him; male and female He created them. God blessed them and said to them, Be fruitful and increase in number; fill the earth and subdue it. Rule over the fish of the sea and the birds of the air and over every living creature that moves on the ground. (Genesis 1: 27, 28) God saw all that he had made, and it was very good. (Genesis 1:31)**

God does not measure sin and I thank God that He does not. My sin of homosexuality was not only "a willful disobedience," but it was also an "unnatural act." Not only was I shamed in my body, but the "honest self," the woman God made me to be, my true identity, was repulsed and went into hiding.

Jesus in His infinite mercy forgave me immediately after I repented and turned from this sin. But I had to accept that it would take time and a painful process to heal. Why? The "honest self" in hiding is a traumatized child who needs to be healed of abuse, shame, hurt, rejection, loss, and tragedy. Also, there are demonic, ancestral, and familiar spirits throughout the family generational bloodlines that have influenced and oppressed the innocent and pure spirit of this child.

Dr. John Bradshaw defines this "honest" self as the "private self." [32] The private self goes into hiding and a false self or selves emerge out of protection and denial. The false self masquerades as a person who is happy and cheerful, when in reality, he or she is miserable. Underneath the shame, guilt, and false pride is a child who never faced his/her self. That "self" is a hurting child. The child is stuck in that place covering a deeper pain or the root pain. The root pain must be exposed, and dealt with.

Because the exposure of self to self lies at the heart of neurotic shame, escape from the self is necessary. The escape from the self is accomplished by creating a false self. The false self is always more or less than human. The false self may be a perfectionist or a slob, a family Hero or a family Scapegoat. As the false self is formed, the authentic self goes into hiding. Years later the layers of defense and pretense are so intense that one loses all awareness of whom one really is. [33] However, Jesus Christ redeemed us from all lies, including any "false selves." When we come honestly to Jesus and face those pains, all facades are shed, and we become the person(s) we were created to be by God. We become deeply aware of whom we are in Christ Jesus. It is an inner transformation that can only be found in our relationship with Jesus Christ.

The false self disguises that pain and hides in various addictions to work, alcohol, drugs, [34] or in ungodly relationships. The false self is under the delusion of false contentment. The disguise becomes fatiguing because it is an act. Meanwhile, the honest self or private self hides and prefers to be alone because it really is exhausting to keep pretending. When we repent and receive the cleansing of the blood of Jesus Christ, there is healing of the pain with no further need to hide in any addiction. All disguises and facades leave as we walk honestly before our God and other people. And the truth sets us free. (John 8:32 ref.)(1st John 1:9 ref.)

The shame tormenting the honest self keeps the person in hiding. And Satan is content to have the honest self isolated because he can bring discouragement and more torment in that place of solitude. Isolation is a very dangerous place. Until I decided to repent of my sin, turn my life over to Jesus, and humble myself to receive the Lord's forgiveness, acceptance, and love, staying connected to the body of Christ, I continued to live in the torment of the lies of shame and isolation. Even as a single person, my neighbors helped me to come out of the seclusion, even through the battles. The Lord will use the people who live next door to you to bring you to a higher level and come out of isolation. Stay connected to at least one other person. It will keep you connected to life!

I wondered if I had multiple personalities. No! This was another lie. Or if I had gone mad. No! I had to remind myself that the enemy wanted my life at all costs. And he'd try to torment me to the point of suicide if possible. The only way out of the torment of being under the control of a lying spirit is repentance from sin, receiving Jesus Christ into my heart as my Lord, Savior, and loving authority, letting go of false guilt and false burdens, letting other Christians in to help me to face and deal with the lies of the false self, and receiving forgiveness, love, and acceptance from a loving God and from other loving Christians.

The lying spirit must also be continually rebuked as it will continue to harass. The sin is only a symptom of a deep need that was not met during the early years and the ungodly reactions to the wrongs I had perceived were harming me. I personally experienced grief as a child who watched and grieved for the hurts and traumas of other family members. My ungodly reaction to the pain I experienced was a sense of responsibility for the hurt and the pain of others. This is a false sense of responsibility. I was playing God in this.

The spiritual atmosphere in the home had also allowed demonic forces to be in control due to a lack of knowledge of the leaders in the family. And these forces also grieved and affected my spirit and soul. My spirit (the real me) and soul (thoughts, emotions, and will), were wounded as well as a result of the grief. But, **"Blessed are the poor in spirit, for theirs is the kingdom of heaven." (Matthew 5:3)** God would restore the broken spirit as well. **"I will repay you for the years the locusts have eaten – the great locust and the young locust, the other locusts and the locust swarm!" (Joel 2:25)**

Leaving the Codependent Model

I had developed the "burden bearer's" heart since childhood. It was the mercy gift from God which became unbalanced in my desperate need to help those around me who were suffering. Compassion for others played out as codependence because I had not dealt with my own inner pain that I had experienced as a child. I had no healthy boundaries .

Codependence was and is an ungodly reaction to unfaced inner pain. I had to face my own false sense of responsibility for the pain of others, renounce the "burden bearer's role," and set healthy boundaries so that I could mature and deal with my own inner pain. Only Jesus can truly heal our inner pain with the power of His presence and of His anointing. He took our griefs and pains on the cross. When we come to Him with our painful and negative emotions, He then blesses us with His anointing, which breaks the power of the ungodly emotions over our lives. The Lord's presence and power take over. A divine exchange occurs when we come humbly to our God. We then are controlled by the Holy Spirit in a spirit of faith. Our emotions take second place to a walk of faith, living by what we believe and not by what we feel. And we are guarded against codependence by His "shield of faith." (Psalms 3:3) (Ephesians 6:16) (Scriptures referenced)

Experiencing much pain as a child, I had developed a need to help others and thus I flourished within the codependent relationships, hiding from the "honest self" in my perfectionism at work, my workaholic lifestyle as a nurse, and in my codependent relationships, always feeling comfortable in helping the one whom I perceived needed my help. I thrived on the "need to be needed." It became my identity and I hid in that place of codependence.

It began in the enmeshment with Mom and the helper role to Dad and plummeted into my career as a professional nurse, helping many. I was blessed with helping many and they helped me as well. Whatever we give always returns back to us. But the false sense of responsibility for others had to be dealt with. I had to let God be God and cast my cares about my family and other people upon the Lord to His care. I had to trust God. (Proverbs 3:5,6) As I stand in prayer, interceding for loved ones and friends, believing that God hears and answers my prayers, the burden is lifted.

I had to seek the face of Jesus and enter into conversation and prayer to ask for His help out of codependent structures in relationships and let God be God. I repented of playing God and of the burden bearer role that was out of balance. I had to develop in my own self-confidence and seek strong godly friends who would help me in life. I sought counsel in many seasons of my deliverance from strong men and women of God.

As I released the need to rescue others and started to work on myself in relating to Jesus in the divine exchange, the strong "burden bearer" structure started to come down. I learned to form healthy boundaries and help others without completely losing myself in the process of that exchange. "Christ in me" helped me to set the healthy boundaries. I was now separate from others and not enmeshed or easily influenced by others' personalities or their spirits. "Christ in me" helped me to form my own identity, thus, my confidence. I learned to say "no" to relationships that only took from me without giving in return. And I became strong in my own confidence and respect for myself as a giving person. Thus, the original mercy gift that I was blessed with by God blossomed as a flower within my own personality. I learned to have compassion for others without feeling a need to rescue them or to be their "Savior." Giving without a need to "save" or "change" others gives with the heart of Jesus, without any need for "payback".

Healthy relationships require confrontation. Because I was never a confrontational person, I did not feel worthy of healthy and strong relationships. I had to turn away from inferiority and press into my self-confidence. Bonding with others in activities brought me confidence, whether in school, in work, or in social activities. I had to dare to relate to strong people and learn from them. You can still be a sensitive person with strength and take the courage to confront. Confrontation takes honesty and love. Once you identify your weaknesses, you can overcome them and change with God's help. "Christ in you" gives you the strength to be yourself with all people. (However, always place your safety as a priority in all confrontations. Let the Holy Spirit guide you. It is best to have a witness with all difficult confrontations. Travel in two's is best.) **To them God has chosen to make known among the Gentiles, the glorious riches of this mystery, which is Christ in you, the hope of your glory. (Colossians 1:27)**

New Age Theology

Like the crafty serpent in the Garden, the world today has a tempter who is disguised with New Age Theology. This theology not only condones but also applauds homosexuality. This mind set does not even have the word "sin" in its vocabulary. The first commandment of the New Age Theology is "Love yourself as yourself." The second commandment is, "Do as you want to do, to please yourself." In other words, treat yourself as if you are a god or a goddess.

Therefore, instead of eating the fruit to become like God, as in Adam and Eve's scenario, New Age Theology does not even require a prerequisite to becoming like God. New Agers already treat themselves as if they are gods. Can you see that intimacy with your own gender would be construed as the epitome of self-love? New Agers applaud homosexuals with a standing ovation....**I have set before you life and death, blessings and curses. Now choose life, so that you and your children may live and that you may love the Lord your God, listen to His voice, and hold fast to Him. For the Lord is your life, and He will give you many years He swore to give to your fathers Abraham, Isaac, and Jacob. (Deuteronomy 30:19,20)**

God's Love Cuts through the Heart of Shame

Without knowing the supernatural touch of love that Jesus has for me, I was always searching for this fulfillment in people. Once I began to experience and live out a real intimate relationship with Jesus Christ as the number one love of my life, He showed me His reality and began to come in and heal my wounds.

The pleasures of the flesh are temporary. But the love of God is eternal. Desperation for love drove me to experience what I could see, taste, feel, hear, and touch, and Satan knew my weaknesses. The consequences of listening to Satan's deceptions took years of precious time away from me because healing takes time. However, the journey took me to a sweeter place with Jesus, a place of faith and a walk led by the Holy Spirit. I remember one evening I was sitting home on my couch in Tulsa. I was born again but still hiding behind this hideous lie. I could not forgive myself.

I thought I was happy in my nursing career. Deep within, I was hiding my "honest self" under the professional title of "nurse," living in the false identity of perfectionist to cover the neurotic shame of my past. I was deceiving myself. God blessed me anyway through all the people He brought into my life in this career. God blessed me in spite of myself! He is no respecter of persons; we are all His kids! I rested in His presence while caring for many people. Nursing was an awesome gift from God which kept me in the giving mode.

It was after I left the career, which was at the heart of the perfectionist mask, that I truly faced my honest self and was fully delivered. I thought I was "ok" in God's eyes because I was doing good works. Healing is never about how good we are or about the good work that we do. It is about how good God is. After living as a giver to so many, I had to learn to receive God's forgiveness, acceptance, and love into the deepest crevices of my own heart. Only then could I accept myself. When I began to receive from God, I began to experience the grace of God, His unmerited favor and loving-kindness, and His power working within me.

To be severed and alienated within oneself also creates a sense of unreality. One may have an all pervasive sense of never quite belonging, of being on the outside looking in. The condition of inner alienation and isolation is also pervaded by a low grade chronic depression. This has to do with the sadness of losing one's authentic self. Perhaps the deepest and most devastating aspect of neurotic shame is the rejection of the self by the self. [35] I determined to stay connected to the body of Christ and to get free from this condition.

Jesus comes to us and breaks through both the self-alienation and isolation. Reality sets in as He loves us back to life and into our true identity. We become more conscious of His presence and His love, and the fear of man loses its power over us as we rest under the loving control of the Holy Spirit. I received so much from the Lord in the very acts of worshiping and praising Him. **"The Lord your God is with you, He is mighty to save. He will delight in you, He will quiet you with His love, He will rejoice over you with singing." (Zephaniah 3:17)**

Repentance Allows Receiving Grace – We are Not Perfect – We are Only Perfectly Forgiven

I had to learn the hard way. In both sins of homosexuality and perfectionism, I sought personal affirmation through people. In both sins, I was acting out of the "wounded little girl" role. It was the "unaffirmed little girl" with very low self-confidence, who developed into an adult who did not even trust herself. Therefore, self-doubt developed. In the lifestyle, I always looked for the dominant partner who looked like "she had it altogether." In reality, we both were covering up wounds from childhood. In the perfectionism spiral, I was the "perfect little girl" doing good to cover up the pain and the wounds of childhood. I was still doing good also for Mom's approval or anyone who would pay me attention. Both these sins also exposed the "frightened little girl" afraid of being scolded or criticized. They exposed the "frazzled little girl" attempting to take control in an uncontrollable environment. They also exposed the "traumatized child" oppressed with demons from a bloodline curse from Satan himself. I was a young adult with low self esteem, low self confidence, and no relationship with Jesus Christ. And it was Jesus Christ Who would teach me, restore me, and develop me as a godly woman with purpose and identity in Him. I remained invisible until I got honest with myself and with one other person and began to deal with the root issues of perfectionism.

In perfectionism, I was trying, by works, to shake off this striving demonic spirit, the same spirit that controlled me in the homosexual lifestyle. Only by exposing the root pain and resolving it with the help of my Lord's healing power would I allow the power of God in to break these obsessive-compulsive cycles. Jesus already redeemed me from every curse, including self-doubt, because Jesus was and still is the Lord and

Savior of my life. In perfectionism, I had to double and triple check my own steps to end the self-doubt. Even after those steps, the tormenter came to me with the words, "Are you sure you did that right?" Remember Satan said to Eve, "Did God really say?" (Genesis 3:1) I had to stop the doubts and replace them with the Word of God and ask the Holy Spirit for a check in my spirit that the work was done. I had to step out of timidity and into a holy boldness. I resisted the doubts as I spoke in faith with submission, repentance, and forgiveness, "Nothing shall separate me from the love of God," in the very act of the checking rituals. (Romans 8:39)

As a young child, I had certain challenges. I had a stutter which cleared with speech therapy. I also had difficulty with reading comprehension and my listening skills were not up to par. My mother sent my brother and me to a special reading school. Then in my senior years, I took time away from television to strengthen my listening skills both in the natural and the supernatural realms. I listened for the Holy Spirit's confirmation and I then subdued the lies from Satan with an act of my will, by faith, and with the help of the Holy Spirit. When I had any difficulty, I sought a witness. My mistake was keeping perfectionism a secret, therefore allowing the control of the enemy in my life. Once we bring our secret sins to one person and confess them, then the pride cycle is broken. This step of honesty and humility will bring the Holy Spirit to you. This is essential to the healing process. No secrets allowed!

We are saved by grace through faith, not by any works that we do. (Ephesians 2:8) Perfectionism is a lie straight from the pit of hell. We are never perfect, only perfectly forgiven. It became a type of self-punishment. Jesus already took the punishment for my shame. Keeping focused on all these details also served as a mental block from all painful emotions and from enjoying life itself. Life became "robotic." This "wounded little girl" needed deep inner healing. And the Lord did restore. (Joel 2:25) The Lord spoke to me as I turned to Him for help out of this addiction. He said, "Free yourself." "Release yourself." "Let go." I needed to forgive myself and move on with life. **But He was pierced for our transgressions, He was crushed for our iniquities; the punishment that brought us peace was upon Him, and by His wounds we are healed. (Isaiah 53: 5)**

In idolizing my lesbian partners, Jesus came off the throne and I allowed the control of other persons into my life. Here my focus was on the creature (person), not on my Creator. The intimacy in these relationships covered my wounded heart's pain in the temporary pleasures of the flesh; and in the deeply emotional and codependent relationships. Severing and leaving the homosexual relationships served to free both myself and the partners to choose the healing power of the Lord Jesus Christ to free us and to discover our true identity in Christ Jesus.

With the sin of perfectionism as well as in the homosexual addiction, I needed to change my focus to Jesus and upon life itself. Not until I looked within to my faith, focused on the Lord within me, and listened to the leading of the Holy Spirit would the rest, the grace, and the peace of God come and replace the worry, the fear, and the obsessions. I stayed connected to the body of Christ and its activities. I changed from the "running" mode to the "receiving" mode, receiving love and forgiveness from the Lord and from His people. I got involved in making healthy Christian relationships; in my church fellowships, through prayer and support groups, attending regular services, attending Bible school, attending a Christian University, taking up work activities, attending Christian singles groups and outings, and in Bible study groups. I believed that I would change as I pressed into life and turned from all sin and idols.

Perfectionism was my hiding place for fears, traumas, and pains I had experienced as a child. It was a defense mechanism that deceived me to believe that if my outward environment was in order, that if all the details of my papers were in order, that I was ok. If I had control over the environment, then I deceived myself to believe that I also had control over my emotions. But they were only in hiding and would have to be faced sooner or later. Keeping busy cleaning the house as Mom's helper as a child, a high achiever earning degree after degree as an adult, and trying to be a perfect nurse, kept me plugged into the insidious spiral of perfectionism. And, the root of this sin was the spirit of fear or the Antichrist spirit, which was the driving spirit that attacked the family bloodline.

One of my biggest problems was not being able to grasp the concept of grace as a free gift from God.

Believing I had to "make up" for the sin of homosexuality by doing good works kept me from fully receiving from God. I lived under the false pretense that my good works kept me in His grace. Living by the law made me open game for the enemy to torment and control me. Spiritual arrogance developed out of this deception, blocking me from real gratitude for His sacrifice for me. I was too busy with my paperwork to stop and submit and just be thankful for His grace. The business of doing for God kept me from the fullness of His presence, especially with the pressure of having to be perfect. Yet, when I was with the people, I did have peace. Healing comes through healthy relationships!

God knows and understands our every trial and dilemma. He still loves us in spite of our stubbornness, but He will do everything He can to get our attention back to Him. He wants to get us His power, but we won't get it until we submit and obey. We have to stop and pay attention to the King of Kings and the Lord of Lords, our Creator and the lover of our souls. Our good works are needed to accomplish the Great Commission, but we must always remember that He can still do it without us, and that also, we can only successfully accomplish our assignments for God with Him in us and with us. **For it is by grace you have been saved, through faith - and this not from yourselves, it is the gift of God - not by works, so that no one can boast. (Ephesians 2:8)**

I had a large garbage bag full of garbage. Satan would have had me empty it and go through it again to "make sure" there was nothing important in it. I had already checked it. I ran to the garbage bin that I would not be able to reach back and retrieve, and threw it away, saying, "Jesus." The tormenting spirits of perfectionism would actually tempt me to recheck garbage! I would recheck laundry machines to "make sure" I did not leave anything. Some people have to check and recheck to make sure the door is locked or the lights are out. I didn't tell anyone about this because of shame and the enemy kept me in isolation until I revealed it in a recovery group. In a single opening of my heart, I broke the back of pride by humbling myself to a group of people in a support group. We have to turn the light of Jesus Christ on in the darkness so that it no longer holds us captive.

This is about a demon of fear that enters the soul of the broken person with self doubt and lack of self confidence. It is about a person who has not faced the root issues and inner pain, and, because of this, the mind and emotions become disconnected. The broken spirit and heart do not want to face the deep inner pain. It is easier to live in a mindless state of numbness than to think about the issues and to settle them in the presence of a holy God. Thus, the enemy takes advantage of the vulnerable mind and causes a mental fog as the mind blanks out. The enemy brings confusion and a spirit of fear to steal, to kill, and to destroy. But God! Jesus brings us a spirit of love, of power, and of self-discipline, (a sound mind). (2nd Timothy 1:7 ref.) He is the answer.

Perfectionism is rooted in worry and a false sense of responsibility. When there is worry, there is no trust. And, my friend, worry is sin; it steals your faith from you. The only way to break the cycle of this addiction is through steps of faith. Just as I had made a conscious decision to sin, I had to make a conscious decision to come out of the insidious spiral of worry. The Holy Spirit was convicting me at points where I literally got sick. I had to heed His commands and trust Him. This was a habit structure I had learned since childhood, being raised in a family where I could not control the tense and sometimes explosive surroundings. Out of my own need to find peace and a sense of my own control, I took control in keeping everything around me in perfect order. This was a survival mode which I developed to cope with life. It both covered and hid the "honest self."

In a counseling session, I was led to the cross and Jesus met this "little girl" there. Jesus spoke to me and said, "You are a good girl." This experience in the presence of a prayer minister set me free from the false guilt I had carried for years. I then released all judgment I had held against myself. **Therefore, since we have been justified through faith, we have peace with God through our Lord Jesus Christ, through whom we have gained access by faith into this grace in which we now stand. And we rejoice in the hope of the glory of God. (Romans 5:1-3)**

Prayer is Simply Speaking to God – Prayer to Repent, Rebuke. and to Renounce Perfectionism

Prepare Your Heart – "I surrender to You, Jesus, as my Lord, my Savior, and my authority. I repent of all my sins. I now, as an act of faith, forgive and release all judgment against both myself and against all who have sinned against me. I gratefully receive Your forgiveness and Your cleansing, Lord Jesus. I receive the righteousness (right standing) of God. I ask You to fill me with Your Holy Spirit." (1ˢᵗ John 1:9) (Acts 2:38)

Enter into Your Father's Presence – "Father God, I enter into Your gates with my petitions, with thanksgiving in my heart, and with a heart of praise in the name of Jesus Christ my Lord, my Savior, and my authority."(Psalm100:4) (John 16:23)

Renounce and Rebuke Perfectionism in the Name of Jesus Christ – "Jesus, I am so sorry for this sin of perfectionism. I renounce and rebuke it out of my life, in the name of Jesus Christ. (Luke 10:19)(Matthew 7:7) I repent of anything I have done to retain it in my life.(1ˢᵗ John 1:9) I ask You to come into my heart and apply the healing salve for the negative experiences that caused me pain and trauma. (Luke 4:18)(Isaiah 61:1) I ask you to help me to remove this mental block and help me to face the painful issues.(Matthew 7:7)(John 15:7) I repent of the need for control and surrender to Your loving and divine control in my life. (1ˢᵗ John 1:9) I receive Your loving presence. (Joshua 1:5) I surrender to Your perfect will. (Matthew 6:10) (1ˢᵗ Thes. 5:16–18) Please forgive me for hurting You. (Matthew 6:12) By faith, I receive your righteousness and renounce all false guilt, self-doubt, and inferiority, in Jesus' name. (Hebrews 11:1)(Romans 1:17)(Luke 10:19) I forgive and release myself to live an abundant life. (John 10:10) I have the mind of Christ and I ask you for a "check" in my spirit when I finish each project.(1ˢᵗ Cor. 2:16) Open my spiritual eyes and mind to listen for Your Holy Spirit. (Luke 24:31,45)(2ⁿᵈ Cor. 4:3,4) I commit to come out of isolation and self focusing and to become involved in activities with other people.(Psalms 133:1) I commit to do whatever it takes to leave this sin and to keep it out of my life.(Rom. 5:3,4)(Acts 1:8) I declare that I walk with a holy boldness and with confidence, with love, power, and a sound mind, in Jesus' name, the name that is above every name.(Hebrews 10:19)(Romans 1:17)(2ⁿᵈ Timothy 1:7)(Phil. 2:9) I believe for You to help me to get this ungodly habit out of my life once and for all.(Mark 11:23-26)(Matthew 7:7)(John 15:7) I believe that You will make a way for me.(Hebrews 11:1) I ask You to fill me with Your Holy Spirit, in Jesus' name. (Acts 1:8)(Acts 2:38) Without You, Lord, I can do nothing. (John 15:5) Spirits of inferiority, self doubt, and perfectionism, go, in the name of Jesus.(Luke 10:19)(Mark 16:17) The blood of Jesus Christ is against you. (1ˢᵗ Peter 1:18,19)(Hebrews 9:14) Go where Jesus sends you to be held captive by the angels of God. (Mark 5:8-13) I declare that through Jesus Christ, the law of the Spirit of life has set me free from the spirit of sin and death. (Romans 8:2) I commit to the daily study of the Word of God and prayer with praise and worship to keep my vessel filled with the Word of God and to keep the enemy out. Amen." (Luke 11:24-26)(Romans 12:2)(All scriptures personalized)(See Appendix)

Four Keys to Winning in Christ

Our prayers must be said using our faith! We must believe that when we pray, that our heavenly Father hears our prayers. In one of his many anointed sermons, "Jesus Heals the Broken Hearted," the late Pastor Billy Joe Daugherty said**,** "We are going to declare in the name of Jesus, using the Word of God, let the Holy Spirit work inside of us, and receive the power of His blood on the inside of our hearts." **[36]** Remember, when Jesus spoke the Word aloud, the people were healed. **"He sent forth His Word and healed them; He rescued them from the grave."(Psalm107:20)** Jesus spoke directly to the devil using the Word of God against all the temptations saying, **"It is written." (Matthew 4:4,7,10)**

Receiving the power of His blood on the inside of my heart means that I have received Jesus into my heart and His divine presence abides within my heart, and within my being. His divine abiding presence has the power to heal and purify my heart as I continue this walk of love in faith and obedience, teaching my heart daily to surrender, to repent, and to forgive and release all judgment by an act of my faith as I walk in the love of God. And His presence within me is greater than anything the devil uses against me. At times in my walk, His presence is an actual felt presence. He is still helping me to form my boundaries, and to restore what the enemy has taken from me. (Joel 2:25)(1st John 4:4) (All scriptures referenced) **For who has known the mind of the Lord that He may instruct him? But we have the mind of Christ. (1st Cor. 2:16)**

The Blood of Jesus is against You, Satan

Prepare your Heart of Faith – "Jesus, I submit myself to You. I believe You died for me; You were buried, and rose again for me at Calvary two thousand years ago. I honor Your sacrifice for me and I now repent of all my sins against You. I invite You into my heart, Jesus, and ask You to be the Lord and the Savior of my life. I accept Your loving authority. I receive complete forgiveness for my sins. Fill me with Your Holy Spirit. I forgive and release all judgment against myself and against all who have sinned against me. I receive the righteousness (right standing/confidence) of God. Thank You, Lord Jesus."

Enter into your Father's Presence – "Father God, I come to You, with praise and thanksgiving in my heart. I enter into Your presence and present my petitions to You, in Jesus' name." (Psalm 100:4) (John 16:23)

Take Jesus' Delegated Authority against the Enemy in Jesus' Name – "Satan, the Word of God and blood of Jesus Christ is against you. (Mark 11:23-25)(Matthew 4:4,7,10)(Hebrews 4:12)(Isaiah 53:3-5) (Hebrews 10:19-22) I declare this by faith as I place the blood of Jesus Christ around me in the name of Jesus Christ, the strong Son of God.(Heb. 11:1) (1st Peter 1:18,19)(Hebrews 9:14) By faith, the cross of Jesus Christ is now actively placed between me and any enemy weapons. (Colossians 2:15)(1st Peter 1:18,19)(Isaiah 53:3-5)(1st John 4:4) Get out, in the name of Jesus. (Luke 10:19)(Mark 16:17) Go where Jesus sends you to be held captive by the angels of God. (Mark 5:8-13) I am hidden in the secret place of the Most High God. (Psalm 91:1) I stand strong and in the rest of God, with no judgment against the people the enemy is using against me. (Hebrews 4:9-11)(Luke 6:37) I will take the offensive and will love them as an act of my faith and pray for them, and this will keep me in the love of God. (Romans 5:5)(1st Cor. 13)(Galatians 5:6) Satan, you have no authority over me.(Matthew 21:27)(Col. 2:10,15)(Phil 2:8) Jesus Christ is the head of all powers and authorities. (Col. 2:10,15) The angel of the Lord goes before me and the Lord delivers me because I stand in awe of Him. (Psalm 91:1,11)(Psalm 34:7) No weapon formed against me shall prosper. (Mark 11:23-25) (Isaiah 54:17) I am a friend of God.(Pro. 18:24) I am His child Whom He loves. (1st John 3:1) Nothing in all of creation shall be able to separate me from the love of God that is in Christ Jesus my Lord. (Romans 8:38) Greater is He Who is in me than He who is in the world. (1st John 4:4) I commit to daily study of the Word of God and prayer with praise and worship to keep my vessel filled with God. (Luke 11:24-26) In Jesus' name I pray and believe this, Amen." (Phil. 2:9)(Mark 11:23-25)(All scriptures personalized) (See Appendix)

And being found in appearance as a man, He humbled himself and became obedient to death even death on a cross! Therefore God exalted Him to the highest place and gave Him the name that is above every name, that at the name of Jesus every knee should bow, in heaven and on earth and under the earth, and every tongue confess that Jesus Christ is Lord, to the glory of God the Father. (Philippians 2:8)

And having disarmed the powers and authorities, He made a public spectacle of them, triumphing over them by the cross. (Colossians 2:15)

Declare and Receive Your Deliverance from Homosexuality

Prepare Your Heart of Faith – "Jesus I humble myself to You. I believe You died for me and rose victoriously on the third day. I repent of all sin and ask You to come into my heart and to be the Lord, Savior, and loving authority of my life. Fill me with Your Holy Spirit. I commit to forgive and release all judgment against myself and all who have sinned against me. Thank You, Lord Jesus, for Your sacrifice for me. I receive Your forgiveness."

Enter into your Father's Presence – "Father God, I come boldly to the throne of grace with my petitions.

I enter into Your presence with thanksgiving and praise in my heart. (Psalm 100:4) (John 16:23) I submit to Your spiritual guidance, Lord Jesus, and Your loving authority, in Jesus' name."

Take Jesus' Delegated Authority and Declare Your Healing from the Homosexual Addiction in Jesus' Name -

"Jesus, You are my Lord. I am truly sorry for hurting You, Lord Jesus. I rebuke, renounce, and make a decision now to turn from homosexuality, in Jesus' name.(2nd Tim. 2:22)(1st Cor. 6:18-20)(Acts 2:38) (Rom. 1:24-26)(2nd Cor. 6:17) I believe that as my relationship with You, Lord Jesus, grows, and as I mature and live by the Word of God, I will be saved and also changed into Your image. (Rom. 12:2)(Gen. 1:26) (Rom. 10:13) As my confidence in Your love and acceptance of me grows, (Isaiah 43:1-4) and as Your holy presence within and upon me is discerned,(1st Cor. 11:23-25) my need for codependence will come to a close.(Joshua 1:5) I release my wounded heart to You, Lord Jesus. (Isaih 53:3-5)And I come to You just as I am – a sinner who desires Your mercy and grace.(Luke 6:36)(Ephesians 2:8) I believe that as I come to You in all honesty, all my facades will drop, Lord Jesus.(Hebrews 5:8)(John 8:32) I belong to You, Jesus. (Isaiah 43:1-4)(1st John 3:1) As You become my number one love, with no idols in my life, I will be changed into Your nature and will be naturally and divinely healed of this unnatural tendency, thus becoming the godly and confident woman You made me to be before I was even born, in Jesus' name, Amen."(Exodus 20:3)(Jeremiah 29:11-14)(Isaiah 44:24)

"Jesus, thank You for forgiving me. I now forgive myself for this rebellion and forgive myself for the hurts I have incurred on both myself, on the people I was involved with, and also on my family. I have asked for my family's forgiveness as You, Lord Jesus, allowed a season of favor for this. (Ecc. 3:1) I am so grateful for that time I was able to share with my family.(1st Thes. 5:16-18) Lord Jesus, I commit to walk in daily forgiveness and to stay accountable to the body of Christ as well as to You in this walk of love.(Psalm 133:1)(Luke 6:28,37)(Mat.6:12)(Rom. 5:5)I stand in prayer for both my family members and for all past ungodly relationships that I have obediently severed as the Holy Spirit led me.(Rev. 18:4)(James 5:16) I act as their intercessor and trust You, Lord Jesus, to lead them to repentance so they may enjoy their benefits of eternal life, divine protection, divine provision, and divine healing, in Jesus' name. (Rom. 2:4)(Pro. 3:5,6)(2nd Cor. 4:3,4) I command all demon spirits that have come to me through these soul ties to leave me now, in Jesus' name. (Luke 10:19)(Mark 16:17) Go where Jesus sends you to be held captive by the angels of God. Amen." (Mark 5:8-13)(See Appendix) (Scriptures personalized)(See chapter on breaking ungodly soul ties, <u>Death Cannot Hold Me</u>)

"Thank You, Lord Jesus, for Your sacrifice for me. (1st Thes. 5:16-18) I now receive Your acceptance and Your precious and holy blood which covers and cleanses me from this sin. I thank You, Lord Jesus that Your precious blood has forgiven and cleansed me from this sin two thousand years ago.(Hebrews. 9:14)(1st Peter 1:18,19) I now receive the person of the Holy Spirit and His power within and upon me to comfort me, to empower me to forgive, to release all judgments, to continue to leave this sin and all idols, and to speak prayers and the Word of God against all enemy attacks and temptations of the flesh. (Acts 2:38)(Acts 1:8) I commit to obey You and to leave all ungodly soul ties and anything related to my activities in this lifestyle (Heb. 5:8)(1st Thes 5:21,22); any New Age and occult materials, any memorabilia or photos of persons I had relations with, gifts given to me as furniture or clothing connected with the lifestyle, records and cassette tapes, CDs, DVDs, books on mysticism, any Eastern philosophy of healing using auras and other New Age topics, magazines, journals, astrological charts, I Ching calendars, all Eastern religious articles, books, tarot cards, Ouija boards, crystals, ancestral or New Age statues (anything that exalts itself above You, Lord Jesus), incense, letters, any drug paraphernalia, and candles. (1st Cor. 10:14) I commit to flee even the mere appearance of evil. (2nd Cor. 6:17, 1st Thes. 5:22) Your Word says in 1st Thessalonians 5:21, 22, **Test everything. Hold on to the good. Avoid every kind of evil.** I believe that as I close and lock the door to all evil in my life, that the masks of pretense and all personality disguises and facades will be removed. I will emerge free as Your child and as a godly woman (man) with a pure heart.(2nd Tim. 2:22) (Matthew 5:8) I pray and believe this, in Jesus' name, Amen." (All scripture references personalized)

Ask the Lord if you have anything in your household that may have demonic spirits attached to them to be rid of. And follow His lead. Consider from where and from whom you have received them.

"Lord Jesus, by Your stripes (beatings),(Isaiah 53:5), and in Your precious name, I now, by faith, (Heb.11:1), take Your delegated authority and I declare that I am now healed of this homosexual addiction in Jesus' name.(Luke 10:19)(Matthew 6:13) I declare that homosexuality shall no longer rule and reign in my life, in the precious name of Jesus Christ.(Ephesian 6:20)(Phil. 2:9) I now receive the complete restoration of my true identity as a godly and anointed woman (man) of God. (Joel 2:25) I humbly and gratefully declare and receive my freedom and deliverance from this deception of Satan, in the name of Jesus Christ. (Mat. 6:13)(Phil. 2:9)(Galatians 3:13(John 10:10)(1st Peter 5:8)(Jer. 39:18) And I decidedly take back all that the enemy has stolen from me.(Joel 2:25) (Mark 16:18)(Psalm 39:13)(James 4:7) Thank You, Lord Jesus, for Your everlasting love, complete acceptance, and total forgiveness; (Isaiah 43:1-4)(1st John 1:9)(1st Cor. 6:19)(1st Thes.5:18) and for Your obedient sacrifice for me on the cross of Calvary.(Hebrews 5:8) You died for me. (Galatians 3:13)(1st Peter 1:18,19)(1st Peter 2:24) In Jesus' name, I pray and I believe, I receive, and I declare my deliverance from all fear, all evil deceptions, every curse, and every assignment of the devil. (Mark 11:23-25) Spirit of homosexuality, go,in Jesus' name. (Luke 10:19)(Mark 16:17) Go where Jesus sends you to be held captive by the angels of God. (Mark 5:8-13) Lord Jesus, I commit to daily study of Your Word and prayer, with praise and worship,(Psalm 33:1-3)(John 4:24), to keep my vessel filled with God and to keep the enemy out. In Jesus' name, Amen." (Luke 11:24-26) (Romans 12:2)(Pro. 4:20)(All scriptures personalized)) (See Appendix)

The words of Jesus to His disciples before His death, **"If you love me, you will obey what I command. And I will ask the Father and He will give you another Counselor to be with you forever – the Spirit of truth. The world cannot accept Him, because it neither sees Him nor knows Him. But you know Him, for He lives with you and will be in you. I will not leave you as orphans."(John 14:15-18)**

Respect the Enemy but Do Not Fear Him
And hope does not disappoint us, because God has poured out His love into our hearts by the Holy Spirit, Whom He has given us. (Romans 5:5)

We pray with a holy and convicted anger, (not a fleshly anger). The Word of God says to be angry but sin not. Prayer rises up from our human spirit, where the Holy Spirit lives, from the "living waters" that speak from our innermost beings, (John 7:37) with respect for the enemy, but never in fear. **Submit to God. Resist the devil and he will flee from you. Come near to God and He will come near to you. (James 4:7,8)**

We enter into a new and a holy lifestyle of daily repentance, walking led by the Holy Spirit, listening for His guidance, cherishing His comfort, and walking in the love of God, our greatest gift and spiritual weapon that we receive from God.(1st Cor. 13) (John 16:13) (Romans 10:9,10) (Romans 5:5)(All scriptures referenced)

Prayers
As the late Pastor Billy Joe Daugherty led the congregation of Victory Christian Center in prayer, he said, "Right now it may seem so far away. It looks impossible because there is so much pain. Let the walls of fear down, let down the walls and barriers. Lord, You're the healer of the brokenhearted. Lord, forgive me. The power of the Holy Spirit is coming to you. Whisper that name – say, 'Father, I forgive in the name of Jesus of Nazareth.' When you speak it out, the poison of bitterness, anger, and hurt comes out. Steven said, 'Do not lay this sin to their charge.' The Word of God is pouring into you and in the days ahead you are going to renew your mind. It may look like a dark deep river in your face. Take Joel 2:25- I will restore to you all the locust has stolen from you. You may ask yourself, 'What will I do when the thoughts come?' Say, "In the name of Jesus, I cast down all the pain, the imaginations, the negative thoughts, the fears, all brokenness incurred from traumas, and the remaining memories and hurts of my soul, in the precious name of Jesus Christ. You cannot rule or reign in my life anymore." [37]

Receive the Healing of Jesus – Declare Your Heart Whole and Clean

Prepare Your Heart of Faith - "Jesus I humble myself to You. I believe You died for me and rose victoriously on the third day. I repent of all sin and ask You to come into my heart and to be the Lord, Savior, and loving authority of my life. Fill me with Your Holy Spirit. I commit to forgive and release all judgment against myself and all who have sinned against me. Thank You, Lord Jesus, for Your sacrifice of Your life for me. I now receive Your forgiveness, in Jesus' name."

Enter into your Father's Presence - "Father God, I enter into Your presence with my petitions and with thanksgiving and praise in the name of Jesus Christ my Lord, my Savior, and my loving authority. (Psalm 100:4) I now apply the blood of Jesus to my spirit, my soul, and my body in Jesus' name. (Matthew 26:28) (1st Peter 1:18,19)(Heb. 9:14) I now put on the full armor of God. I take up the helmet of salvation (including my face shield⋆) and the sword of the Spirit which is the Word of God. I place the belt of truth buckled around my waist. I put the breastplate of righteousness on over my heart and fit my feet with the readiness that comes with the gospel of peace. I take up the shield of faith to extinguish all the flaming arrows of the evil one. And I build myself up in my faith as I pray the prayer language of the Holy Spirit. The prayer language builds my spirit up, and helps me when I do not know what to do. You calm my thoughts and my soul, O Lord. (Ephesians 6:13-18) (Jude 20) I pray this in Jesus' name, Amen." (Phil. 2:9)(All scriptures personalized)(⋆Face shield added by author)

Take Jesus' Delegated Authority, Declaring Your Heart Clean and Whole in the Name of Jesus Christ - "By Your stripes, (Your blood bearing beatings and Your suffering), Lord Jesus, I now declare that I am forgiven and free from all condemnation, shame, anxiety, inferiority, and fear, in Your name, O Lord Jesus. (Isaiah 53:3-5)(Luke 4:18)(Isaiah 61:1) (Romans 8:1) (2nd Tim.1:7)(Hebrews 12:1-3)(Galatians 3:13) (Colossians 1:13)(Rom. 1:16,17)(Heb.9:14) Spirits of condemnation, shame, anxiety,inferiority, and fear, go, now, in the name of Jesus. (Luke 10:19)(Mark 16:17) (2nd Tim. 1:7) Go wherever Jesus sends you to be held captive by the angels of God. (Mark 5:8-13) I declare my heart is cleansed of all woundings and all guilt. (1st John 1:9) (Ephesian 6:20)(Isaiah 53:3-5) I am clean and whole in the name of Jesus Christ. (Romans 8:1)(Hebrews 10:19-22)(Heb.9:14))(Phil.2:9)(Luke 4:18)(1st Peter 2:24) I commit to daily study of the Word of God and prayer with praise and worship to keep my vessel full. (Luke 11:24-26)(Romans 12:2)(Psalm 33:1-3)(John 4:24) (James 5:16)Thank You, Lord Jesus. I now enter into the rest of God. (Hebrews 4:9) In the precious name of Jesus Christ, the name that is above every other name. (Phil 2:9) Amen."(All scriptures personalized)(See Appendix) **There remains, then, a Sabbath rest for the people of God; for anyone who enters God's rest also rests from his own work, just as God did from His. (Hebrews 4:9)**

The Lord Will Harvest Our Words

When we speak with a heart of faith, with submission to the Lordship and the authority of Jesus Christ, with repentance for sin, and forgiveness and release of judgment towards ourselves and all who have sinned against us, we place our heart of faith in proper position to pray. We are convinced, convicted, and we believe that the prayers that we speak will remove any mountain that is in our way. Prayers are seeds planted that bring forth a new harvest. It is a heart of faith that speaks which moves the heart and the hand of God. (Hebrews 1:1-3) (Mark 11:23-25) (Genesis 1:3, 6, 9,14,20,24,26) (Matthew 4:4,7,10)

A divine interception takes place with our prayers spoken with a heart of faith that breaks the power of the negative thoughts and emotions that seek to distract us, the bodily sensations that seek to tempt us, and the fantasies and habit structures that seek to steal our peace. As we speak to the Lord, our words are seeds that we plant. As we continue to present our petitions and pray with a heart of faith to our loving Father in Jesus' name, (John 16:23), our heavenly Father hears us. And He will act to harvest the seeds of our faith-filled words. (Mark 11:23-25)(Matthew 17:20) (Malachi 3:10) Our part is to believe and receive His love and His answers to our prayers, and to continue to pray, believe, and expectantly wait in faith for the complete manifestation to come. (Mark 11:23-25)(All scriptures referenced) Jesus said...**Whoever welcomes me welcomes the One Who sent me. For he who is least among you all – he is the greatest."(Luke 9:47,48)** Jesus said these words,**"I tell you the truth, if you have faith as small as**

a mustard seed, you can say to this mountain, 'Move from here to there' and it will move. Nothing will be impossible for you." (Matthew 17:20)

You may not feel the transformation right away. Your life of living by what you feel, see, and sense will be changed by the anointed presence of the Lord and by a life of faith led by the Spirit of the living God. Press in and keep sharing with the Lord. Keep your heart in proper position of faith with submission, repentance, and forgiveness. So when you speak it will be by faith and not by flesh. It will be your true inner voice. Continue speaking the Word of God and prayers as you petition your Father in the name of Jesus Christ.

We receive His love, His acceptance, and His forgiveness by an act of our faith, no matter how we may feel about it or what the world may say. Faith is our victory! Continue to stay connected to the body of Christ and receive from God. Expect the miracles and the transformations to come to you as you continue to press into your faith by continuing to pray and believe, without doubting. The manifestation of your completed deliverance and your honest and true identity in Christ Jesus will come. Expect results!

Prayer against the Generational Curse
Enter into the New and Divine Bloodline Covenant with Jesus Christ – Believe God to Act
You have come to God, the Judge of all men, to the spirits of righteous men
made perfect, to Jesus the Mediator of a new covenant, and to the sprinkled
blood that speaks a better word than the blood of Abel. (Hebrews 12:24)

Prepare Your Heart of Faith – "Jesus, I believe You died for me on the cross of Calvary. I surrender to You. I believe in Your death, burial, and resurrection. (Luke 23:46,53)(Luke 24:6) I ask You now to forgive me of my sins. I am sorry for having offended You. I welcome You into my heart. I confess You as my Lord and my Savior. I declare myself born again in Jesus' name. (Romans 10:9,10) (Romans 10:13) (John 3:3) (Ephesian 6:20) I ask You to fill me with Your Holy Spirit. (Acts 2:38) (Acts 1:8)(John 14:16,17) I now commit to enter into an intimate and a personal covenant relationship with You, Lord Jesus. (Heb. 9:15) (John 15:5)(John 14:17)I now enter into Your divine bloodline, Lord Jesus. (Romans 11:17) I declare that I am now a recipient of all of Your precious promises in Jesus' name. (Hebrews 12:24) (Hebrews 13:20)(2nd Peter 1:4)(1st Peter 1:18,19) I come just as I am, surrendered to You as my Lord and Savior, and my loving authority. (Col. 2:10)(Col. 2:15) I acknowledge Your presence with me now and come boldly before the throne of grace. (Joshua 1:5)(Psalm 100:4)(Hebrews 13:5) (Romans 10,9,10)(Heb. 10:19) I humble myself to You, Lord Jesus. (2nd Chronicles 7:14) (Matthew 18:4) (Matthew 23:12) I forgive and release all judgment against myself and all who have sinned against me.(Luke 6:28,37)(Matthew 6:12) I ask that You do not count our sins against us. (Acts 7:60) I gratefully receive the cleansing and the washing of Your blood for my sins. (1st John 1:9)(1st Peter1:18,19)(Heb. 9:14) I thank You for the Holy Spirit, Who comforts and empowers me, and Who guides me into all truth. (Acts 1:8) (Acts 2:3)(John 14:15,16,17,18) (John 14:26) I pray and believe, in Jesus' name, Amen."(All scriptures personalized)

Enter into your Father's presence - "Father God, I submit my petitions to You as I enter into Your presence with thanksgiving and praise in my heart, in the precious name of Jesus Christ." (Psalm 100:4) (John 16:23) (Scriptures personalized)

Take Jesus' Delegated Authority against the Generational Curse in the Name of Jesus Christ – Declare Your New Bloodline in Jesus' Name - Thank God for Complete Restoration of Your Spirit, Soul/Heart, Body – Commit to Comfort Others – " I repent of, rebuke, and renounce the spirits of homosexuality, spirits of perfectionism, spirits of fear, envy, lust, lying, inferiority, and selfishness, including all New Age beliefs and mindsets in the name of Jesus Christ. (Luke 10:19)(Matthew 18:18)(1st John 1:9)(1st Thes. 5:21,22) In Jesus' name, I now declare that You have set me free!(Gal. 3:13) I ask You to reveal to me the roots of these sins so I can open myself to heal from my wounds." (Matthew 3:10) (Matthew 7:7)(John 15:7)

"Lord Jesus, I repent, rebuke, and renounce the generational curses and all demonic, familiar, and ancestral spirits and/or demonic assignments against me in Jesus' name.(Luke 10:19) (Galatians 3:13) (Phil 2:9) (Romans 2:4) (1st John 1:9) All demons, go in the name of Jesus. (Luke 10:19)(Mark 16:17) Go wherever Jesus sends you to be held captive by the angels of God. (Mark 5:8-13) I place the blood of Jesus between me and all curses, any ancestral, familiar, or demonic spirits, and/or all demonic assignments. No curses, ancestral, familiar, or demonic spirits, and/or demonic assignments can cross the divine bloodline or is higher than the name of Jesus Christ. (Romans 11:17,18)(Phil. 2:9,10)(Hebrews 9:14)(1ˢᵗ Peter 1:18,19) (Col. 2:10)(Col. 2:15) I am covered by the divine blood of Jesus Christ as a born again believing child of the living God.(1ˢᵗ Peter 1:18,19)(Heb. 9:14)(Hebrews 10:22,28)(1ˢᵗ Peter 2:24)(John 3:3) And the name of Jesus Christ is higher than any other name.(Phil. 2:9,10)(Col 2:10)(Col. 2:15) It is the blood of Jesus Christ that cleanses and heals me and that forgives me of all my sins the moment I repent. (1ˢᵗ John 1:9)(1ˢᵗ Peter 2:24) I commit to the daily study of Your Word and prayer with praise and worship, to keep my vessel filled with God and to prevent any further enemy entrance." (Luke 11:24-26)(Romans 12:2) (Psalms 33:1-3) (John 4:24)(James 5:16)(See Appendix)

"With my sincere commitment and surrender to a divine covenant relationship with You, Lord Jesus, as my Lord, my Savior, and my loving authority, I now declare that I am grafted into Your divine bloodline, in Jesus' name. (Romans 11:17,18) (John 15:5)(Heb. 9:14) (Hebrews 12:24) (1ˢᵗ Peter 1:18,19) By an act of my faith (Hebrews 11:1) and with thanksgiving in my heart, (1ˢᵗ Thes.5:18) I ask you to empower me with the courage to obey your commands and to turn from my sins of addiction.(1ˢᵗ Cor. 10:5)(John 15;5)(John 14:16-18)(Acts 1:8)(Acts 2:38) I know that obedience is key to breaking the curse.(2ⁿᵈ Cor 10:6)(Hebrews 5:8)(Jer. 42:6) I will no longer be moved by the sins that have passed down through the fourth generation, in Jesus' name.(1ˢᵗ Cor. 15:58) (Romans 11:17,18)(Exodus 20:5) (Lev. 26:45) I believe and declare in the precious name of Jesus Christ that I am redeemed from the curse of the law and from any generational curses, demonic, familiar, or ancestral spirits, and/or demonic assignments because You, Lord Jesus, became a curse for me. (Gal. 3:13) Thank You, Lord Jesus, that my sins are now completely covered and blotted out by Your blood sacrifice." (Hebrews 9:14,15) (Hebrews 4:12) (1ˢᵗ Cor.11:25) (Ephesians 1:7) (Hebrews 10:19-22)(1ˢᵗ Peter 1:18,19)(1ˢᵗ Thes. 5:18)

"I declare that the Holy Spirit abides in me and greater is He Who lives in me than he that is in the world in Jesus' name. (1ˢᵗ John 4:4) (John 15:5) (John 14:17) I declare that I who dwell in the secret place of the Most High God will rest in the shadow of the Almighty in Jesus' name. (Psalms 91:1) I declare that I am delivered from all evil, in Jesus' name. (Matthew 6:16) (Colossians 1:13) As an act of my will, I surrender my entire being to You; my body which is Your temple (Romans 12:1) (1ˢᵗ Cor. 6:20), my soul/heart, which are my thoughts, my emotions, and my will (Psalm 23:3), and my spirit, (the real me), (Matthew 26:41). As I submit to You, Lord Jesus, I also resist the devil and he will flee from me.(James 4:7,8) My greatest resistance to the enemy is my deep surrender and obedience to You, Lord Jesus.(James 4:7,8)(Hebrews 5:8) And I commit to comfort others with the same comfort that I have received from You, O Lord God."(2ⁿᵈ Cor. 1:3-4) (All scriptures personalized)

Christ redeemed us from the curse of the law by becoming a curse for us, for it is written; "Cursed is everyone who is hung on a tree." He redeemed us in order that the blessing given to Abraham might come to the Gentiles through Christ Jesus, so that by faith we might receive the promise of the Spirit (Holy Spirit). (Galatians 3:13,14)

Consecrate Yourself to the Lord
Bind the Devil from any Further Entrance to Your Body, Soul, and Spirit

Prepare Your Heart of Faith – "Jesus I humble myself to You. I believe You died for me and rose victoriously on the third day. I repent of all sin and ask You to come into my heart and to be the Lord, Savior, and loving authority of my life. Fill me with Your Holy Spirit. I commit to forgive and release all judgment against myself and all who have sinned against me. I receive Your forgiveness. Thank You, Lord Jesus, for Your sacrifice for me."

Enter into the Father's Presence – "Father, I humbly and boldly come to Your throne of grace with my petitions in the name of Jesus Christ my Lord, my Savior, and my loving authority. Thank You, Lord, for Your sacrifice for me." (Psalm 100:4) (John 16:23)

Consecrate Your Body to the Lord Jesus Christ in the Name of Jesus – "As an act of my faith and of my will, through the power of the blood of Jesus Christ on the inside of my heart, (1st Cor. 11:25) (Hebrews 9:14), and in the name of Jesus Christ, My Savior and Lord, (Phil. 2:9) Whose authority I am under, (Mark 2:10) (Romans 10:13) (Romans 10:9,10), I now consecrate and dedicate my body to You, Lord Jesus. (Romans 12:1) (1st Cor. 6:19) I now, by faith and of my own free will, repent of all my sins and ask the Holy Spirit to fill me with His presence and power. (Acts 2:38) (Acts 1:8)(1st John 1:9) I now, by an act of faith, of my own free will, and with the help of the Holy Spirit, release the poisons in my heart; the fears, the hurts, the inner pain, resentments, bitterness, inferiorities, fantasies and imaginations, traumatic and painful memories, and all grudges and judgments against myself and all who have sinned against me. (Matthew 6:12,14) (James 4:7) (Luke 6:28,37) Thank you, Holy Spirit, for empowering me to forgive and to let go of all judgments. (John 15:5) (John 14:15,16,26)(John 15:26) (John 16:13)(Acts 1:8) (Acts 2:38) (Luke 6:28,37) I am now, with a commitment to daily repentance and to the study of the Word of God and prayer with daily praise and worship, closing the door of my heart to any further entrance for the enemy to attack, attach, harass, or to invade. (1st John 1:9) (Romans 12:2)(Luke 11:24-26)(Psalm 33:1-3)(James 5:16)(John 4:24) I speak to the enemy of my soul to go now in the name of Jesus. (Mark 11:23-25) (Luke 10:19)(Phil. 2:9) Go where Jesus sends you to be held captive by the angels of God.(Matthew 18:18)(Mark 5:8-13) I ask and believe that You, Father God, will provide me with the power of the Holy Spirit, with strategies out of the temptations, and the strength of my will to resist all temptations of my flesh that try to separate me from Your presence, from the voice of the Holy Spirit, and from my personal intimacy with You, Lord Jesus. (1st Cor. 10:13) I believe Your Word that says that for every temptation, You are faithful and will provide a strategy and a way out. (John 15:26) (1st Cor. 10:13) In Jesus' name I pray and I believe, Amen."(See Appendix)

"Father God, I now take Jesus' delegated authority over my body, my soul, and my spirit, in the precious name of Jesus Christ. (Luke 10:19) I speak by the power of the Holy Spirit within me. (John 15:5)(John 14:17) I believe that my words of faith are seeds planted to release the power of the Holy Spirit to change and restore me into the image and likeness of God as I commit to a life of purity. (Genesis 1:26) (Matthew 5:8)(Gal. 6:9)(Pro. 18:21)(Mark 11:23-25)(Matthew 4:4,7,10) I now declare my entire being (body, mind, and spirit), saturated with Your presence and restored to complete wholeness, in Jesus' name. (Isaiah 53:3-5) (1st Peter 2:24) Thank You, Lord Jesus, for Your restoration power working within me. (Luke 4:18,19) (Joel 2:25) Thank You for Your grace, Your love, Your presence, and Your mercy.(Ephesians 2:8)(Isaiah 43:1-4)(Joshua 1:5)(Isaiah 61:1-3)(1st John 1:9)(Luke4:18) I pray and believe this in the name of Jesus Christ, my Savior and my Lord, in the name that is above every other name. Amen." (Phil. 2:9)(Hebrews 11:1) (Scriptures personalized)(See Appendix)

Therefore, I urge you, brothers, in view of God's mercy, to offer your bodies as living sacrifices, holy and pleasing to God – this is your spiritual act of worship. Do not conform any longer to the pattern of this world, but be transformed by the renewing of your mind. Then you will be able to test and approve what God's will is - His good, pleasing and perfect will. (Romans 12:1,2)

Jesus Suffered to Bring Us His Peace

The late Pastor Billy Joe Daugherty continues, "When Jesus stood up and read from the book of Isaiah in the synagogue in Nazareth, 'The spirit of the Lord is upon me…..Because He has sent me to heal the brokenhearted, to set at liberty those who are bruised, recovering of sight to the blind,' Jesus was claiming that what Isaiah had foretold He would now bring to pass. Jesus said, 'This day the scripture is fulfilled in your ears.' He was saying that He was the one that Isaiah foretold would come to heal the brokenhearted. What Isaiah was talking about that would one day come to pass, Jesus said, "It's here! It's now!"

Pastor Billy Joe Daugherty continues, "The curse of sin of Adam and Eve affected every area of man's existence. Jesus came to undo that curse and to announce good news. You don't have to live another day without peace, joy, the knowledge of God. You can live in the fullness of the blessing." Pastor Billy Joe

Daugherty continues, "Something hurts on the inside. Jesus will heal that brokenness. It is all paid for. He already took the suffering for our inner peace as well as for our sins." Isaiah 53:4,5 tells us, "The chastisement for our peace fell upon Him."**Surely He took up our infirmities and carried our sorrows, yet we considered Him stricken by God, smitten by Him, and afflicted. But He was pierced for our transgressions, He was crushed for our iniquities; the punishment that brought us peace was upon Him, and by His wounds we are healed. (Isaiah 53:4, 5)**

Pastor Billy Joe Daugherty continues with these words, "The chastisement for our peace fell upon Jesus. He took stripes, (beatings), for the healing of our bodies. He bore our griefs and carried our sorrows, was wounded for our transgressions (sins). All our iniquity (tendency toward sin), was placed upon Him. The spirit of God will raise you up. Receive the healing of Jesus." [38]

Inner Healing Awakens the Power and Presence of God in and Upon You

As I pray, speaking to Jesus, I feel the brokenness on the inside and the poison is then released. And I receive the love, acceptance, and forgiveness of God. I will continue to pray for healing is a lifelong process. For so long, I just wept and did not know why I was weeping. As the pain continued and areas of my life began to close, I got more honest with myself and others. The Lord then anointed me with His presence and the deep pain left. As doors closed and locked in my life, God got my attention to let the sins go, receive the healing, and fall more deeply in love with Jesus. As I closed the door to worry, my mind became clear to hear and to receive from the Lord. This will always be an area of challenge for me. As I closed the doors to lust and codependence, I received a divine peace within my body and I experienced Jesus as a real presence both within me and upon me.

During extremely difficult decisions, I had to press into fellowship with other believers because the isolation was causing a depression and physical illness to attach to me. Even when I felt unlovely, I continued attending church meetings and Bible studies with other believers, speaking the Word and worshiping Jesus in song. The battle is always very tough, but never impossible. Once I started to bow to Him and pray from my heart and leave the sins, He brought me His divine energy (His presence and anointing), to keep me going and to live for Him. Staying connected to the body of Christ is essential to the healing process. Accountability with other Christians and counselors still brings me inner strength amidst any battles.

However, there are times when it is just you and God, and it is in these times of personal prayer with Him, that He makes His presence and power very clear. Spend time with Him. It will bring you unforgettable times with Him that will bring clarity and confirmation to you that He is a real and a loving God. He will make His presence known. You will never feel alone because, even if there is no other human being present with you, you will be keenly aware of His presence.

Jesus spoke to Paul about His thorn, **"My grace is sufficient for you, for my power is made perfect in weakness." (2nd Corinthians 12:9)** His words, His thoughts and opinions, and His presence within me took over. And they became my direction, not the voices of the world around me. I knew that I knew that I knew that I was right with God and I was going forward in my calling. This has to be settled, my friend, or Satan will work overtime to distract your thoughts and your feelings. Stay focused on Jesus, no matter what you must do to stay disciplined, because it will cost you your healing and others' whom your life will touch as God uses you. The road gets narrower as you go along. Do not give up! Do whatever it takes to truly make Jesus the Lord of your life. **Dear friends, do not be surprised at the painful trial you are suffering, as though something strange were happening to you. But rejoice that you participate in the sufferings of Christ, so that you may be overjoyed when His glory is revealed. (1st Peter 4:12)**

I determined to receive my healing. I felt the brokenness as a real presence in my body, as if it were a force preventing me from life itself. But, praise God, this left me as I continued diligently in my commitment to live for Jesus and to follow Him daily in surrender, repentance, forgiveness, obedience, and thanksgiving. I began to receive from Him as I learned to rest in Him by acts of faith. I began asking Him to help me to change. A daily surrendering of my need for control as I released idols was eventually changed to a trusting in His presence and authority in my life.

For so long I was not even thinking, just existing. When you start to deal with the emotions, you will start to think clearly, and you will live and love again. I had trouble with listening and worked on this by turning off the TV for periods of time. I would listen to the radio instead and strengthen my listening skills.

The late Pastor Billy Joe Daugherty concludes in this awesome video with, "You can live in the fullness of the blessing. Jesus became poor so that we could become rich – rich in God's blessings in every area of our existence. He came to set at liberty those who are oppressed and bring restoration and release! You will live again. You will love again. You will even laugh again." **[39]**

Resist the Enemy

Submit yourselves, then, to God. Resist the devil, and he will flee from you. Come near to God, and He will come near to you. (James 4:7,8) When Jesus was continually beaten, He continually fell and got up again. It is the devil's plan to continually beat us up so that we will become so exhausted that we also will give up. Our greatest weapon against giving up is walking in love, refusing to get bitter, and keeping close to Jesus, His Word and prayer, praise and worship, and keeping connected to the body of Christ. Believe God that you have a divine destiny and a divine purpose and your life will touch many for Jesus Christ.

During my most trying seasons, I committed to the Lord that I would thank Him by blessing at least one person every day. I kept a record in a journal of people I would visit or talk to each day, sharing Jesus with them, or just being kind to them. This kept me walking in the love of God, no matter what the devil was up to. Acting as an evangelist even when I had no employment kept me locked into my real purpose on the earth. I kept busy doing His work and kept my spirits up in doing so, sharing the Word of God with homeless and indigent people I met along the way, always keeping my safety as the number one priority. Travel in two's and be led of the Holy Spirit when evangelizing. Even Jesus sent the disciples out in twos. This kept me accountable to the Christian lifestyle. To effectively touch people for Christ, we must be built up in prayer.

I kept ample tracts with the Word of God with prayers to receive the Lord in my car. And I knew that the Lord watched me. It kept me encouraged with a purpose and I refused to give up or give in. I was determined to get His word to others who needed it. I was determined to have my life count for others. There is always a way out of each test the Lord places in our path. We resist the plans of the devil for our lives and for the lives of others, through actively walking in love. But Jesus resisted to the point of shedding His blood for us! **No temptation has seized you except what is common to man. And God is faithful; He will not let you be tempted beyond what you can bear. But when you are tempted, He will also provide a way out so that you can stand up under it. (1ˢᵗ Cor. 10:13)**

Repentance as a Daily Activity

Repentance keeps us in an attitude of looking within ourselves to keep our hearts clean before the Lord. When I speak to Jesus, saying the words, "I am sorry," not only do I humble myself before Father God, but I break the power of selfishness and pride and from judging others. Submission to the Lord brings the victory because it keeps me in that "secret place," focused upon His presence, not on mine. Repentance brings us the Holy Spirit and His divine power blesses us.

Coming out of an enmeshed relationship with my mother placed the focus back on Jesus. She had always been the focus. Later, it was my friends and lovers who had my attention in codependent relationships or it was my patients whom I cared for. The Lord blessed me with a season of rest in my later years where I could concentrate on my relationship with Jesus Christ and fully heal. During this season, I had to actively seek out activities within the body of Christ to stay connected to life.

Jesus became my Lord, as I walked through life. The "things of earth became dim" as Jesus Christ and His presence with me became bright within my experience of life. At first, I felt it as a loss because I had no real self-image or identity. I always found identity in other people. Codependence upon people changed to dependence upon my Lord and Savior Jesus, and I found my confidence and my honest and true identity in Him. **In Him (Jesus) was life, and that life was the light of men. (John 1:4)**

Therefore, as Jesus becomes more real to us as living within us, and our identity becomes clear in Him, we become comfortable in our own skin. It is a revelation of His presence in us that takes the fear of man away. We are able to set healthy boundaries and to have healthy relationships. We are not anxiously looking for people to relieve us, but we are at peace, seeking to enjoy fellowship as we share the love of Jesus with others. We are able to truly give and love others with His love and kindness, without fear. And it all starts with repentance. For repentance places us in our rightful position with Our God, Our Maker, and Our divine authority. We can only repent when we are submitted and humbled under the mighty hand of the Lord. With submission, we stop in our own agenda and we then begin to receive from God; His love, His forgiveness, His acceptance. **Humble yourself in the sight of the Lord and He will lift you up . . . (James 4:10)**

Love Your Neighbor as You Love Yourself

I don't know what is more deceptive to the truth of a relationship with Jesus; worldly arrogance which says, "I'm right and the world is wrong." Or spiritual arrogance, which says, "I'm good because I'm doing the work of the Lord." Both attitudes are deceived to believe and to think that one is humble. In both attitudes I am walking in pride. Humility bows to our Lord and Maker. It was a giant step toward that humility in just saying to Him, "I am sorry."

Before I was saved, I acted as if I was so right when really deep down inside in the "real me," of my spirit, I knew I was wrong. After I was saved, I thought I was right because of good works. This was living by the Law and this actually kept me from receiving the very thing I needed the most, the grace and power of God working within me. The pride of "being right" or "being good" completely separated me from the true humility that God requires for me to receive His love and for His power to begin to work within and through me. We have to stop working for Him long enough to receive His presence and His power. Then when we work His plan, He is actively with us to empower us with His grace to perform it. We can easily deceive ourselves in "doing for God." I thought I was "so good" doing "so much" for Him. When, in actuality, everything I did He created me and equipped me to do. He must get all the glory!

It took much courage to learn humility after years and years of living as a survivor and doing everything without God. And this lesson continues. Why? Because the belief system of a survivor is one in which "Only the strong survive." A person can live in one's own strength for so long. It leads to "burn out." Only when I took steps toward surrendering to God and allowing myself to be transparent, honest, and humble myself to other people, no matter what they thought of me, did I find true freedom. I refused to let other people reject me. (Titus 2:15)

Love for self and others carries the greatest power against any demonic intention. The Lord will bless you with a godly wisdom that Satan is working through them, through their unresolved pain, to try to bring rejection or distraction to you. And they themselves need the love of God to get free. By faith, love them and you will always be on the winning side both for them and for yourself. In some battles, you will not even have a conversation with them, but you will pray for them in your hearts. (Galatians 5:6) However, use wisdom and be led of the Holy Spirit before you act in love for any enemy. Remember, your safety is always of the highest priority. Travel in twos is best.

You have to defiantly walk through the deceiving voices of shame and determine to connect with other Christian people, no matter what the situations are. Do not let others despise you and do not despise yourself. (Titus 2:15) If you feel rejection in a church circle, stay planted unless the Holy Spirit redirects you. Do not isolate yourself. The Lord commands that we love our neighbors as we love ourselves. We all are human beings; we are all sinners, saved only by the grace (loving kindness) of God. (Romans 3:23) **If my people, who are called by my name, will humble themselves and pray and seek my face and turn from their wicked ways, then will I hear from heaven and will forgive their sin and will heal their land. (2nd Chronicles 7:1)**

Jesus is My Psychiatrist – Warnings from God

You will know th truth and the truth shall set you free. (John 8:32)
The Lord tells us, "My thoughts are not your thoughts and
my ways are not your ways." (Isaiah 55:8)

The Holy Spirit is Our Divine Guide and Comforter

No matter how much I tried to rationalize that I was acting in truth having a relationship with this woman, the Holy Spirit continued to lead me into conviction against this lie. I tried to block out this inner witness even before I was born again, but the Holy Spirit was still standing at the door of my heart to "woo" me to the truth. I know there were people who were praying for me during this very critical time.

But it is like faith. Not a person could have changed my mind. The Holy Spirit can and did penetrate deeper than my heart. He touched my innermost being. He traveled to the deepest part of me, my spirit, revealing impressions, revelations, and visions. **Deep calleth to deep in the roar of your waterfalls: all your waves and breakers have swept over me. (Psalm 42:7)** No matter how much I tried to twist or turn it, I knew deep down inside myself that what I was doing was wrong. I really knew it!

The gospel of John tells us of the person of the Holy Spirit: **But when He, the Spirit of truth comes, He will guide you into all truth. He will not speak on His own; He will speak only what He hears, and He will tell you what is yet to come. (John 16:13)**

I defined my "honest self" as the true identity that goes into hiding as a result of the repulsion that is initially felt when entering into the homosexual act. I hid from my own soul (mind, emotions, and will). Mind and emotions disconnected, my will was weak, and I lived in a mental fog. The "honest self" is part of the soul. But my spirit, the "real substance of my creation," which lives forever with Christ because I am born again, never went into hiding. However, as soon as sin is conceived, both my soul and my spirit are separated from Jesus. Repentance brings the connection back. Nothing can ever be hidden from God.

The spirit, heart/soul, or body of a person can never hide from God. The spirit of man (woman) is the very life substance of a person that is housed in the body. When we by faith accept Jesus Christ as Lord and Savior into our hearts/souls, He literally takes up residence within our human spirit and our hearts/souls and He is also housed in our bodies. Jesus said, **Remain in me and I will remain in you. No branch can bear fruit by itself; it must remain in the vine. Neither can you bear fruit unless you remain in me. I am the vine; you are the branches. If a man remains in me and I in him he will bear much fruit; apart from me you can do nothing. (John 15:4,5)**

His love is poured into our hearts by the Holy Spirit. **And hope does not disappoint us, because God has poured out His love into our hearts by the Holy Spirit, whom He has given us. (Romans 5:5)** Only God Himself can touch the human spirit. This is the part of a person that comes alive when we bow to our Maker, the part that awakens when we worship God. This is the part that is strengthened when praying to the Father in Jesus' name. This is the part that only the breath of God could have created. This is the "real you."

In the gospel of John, Jesus expounds on the Holy Spirit Who is both with us and lives within our spirits and hearts/souls. And our bodies are the temples that house the Holy Spirit.

If you love me, you will obey what I command. And I will ask the Father, and He will give you another Counselor to be with you forever – the Spirit of truth. The world cannot accept Him, because it neither sees Him nor knows Him. But you know Him, for He lives with you and will be in you. (John 14:15-17)

Listen for the Voice of the Holy Spirit

After entering into homosexuality, I would now be ruled by my flesh. The Holy Spirit was very close by to both strengthen and teach me. I remember driving to a seminar in Los Angeles run by Desert Stream Ministries. While driving, I sensed a still, small voice saying to me, "I will help you." I felt so safe listening to the small still voice of the Holy Spirit. Learning to trust and obey His voice has brought me the most solace in my life. **Here I am! I stand at the door and knock. If anyone hears my voice and opens the door, I will come in and eat with him, and he with me. (Revelation 3:20)**

Choose to Believe God for a New Life! Call Sin Sin

It was my choice to enter into the sin of homosexuality. It would have to be my choice to repent and leave it. Yes, I was strongly influenced by a deceptive spirit straight from the pit of hell disguised as an inner voice saying, "Follow your heart." Yes, I had a legitimate need to be loved and accepted. Yes, there was a generational curse affecting the family bloodline on both my father and my mother's side that I was subjected to and oppressed by since I was in my mother's womb. Yes, I was subjected to lots of family feuds, both physical and verbal, which left scars on my heart. Yes, there were love needs that were not met as a child. Yes, I was fearful of intimacy with a man since a man exposed himself to me on the streets when I was a little girl and I was attacked by a man in my adult years.

Against these odds, and by faith, I chose to take responsibility for my choice to sin and to repent and seek the Lord, believing that He would deliver me out of this darkness. He would heal every traumatic memory and I would live and love again. He is a "Healing Jesus." I chose to believe that God would make a way even if I did not see it. I chose to believe the Lord Jesus Christ would help me to face any fears with faith, and that, when the right man of God showed up, I would know him. The Lord would direct me to him by the Spirit of God's direction in the proper season of my life. It will be possible, because with God all things are possible. **Jesus looked at them and said, "With man this is impossible, but not with God; all things are possible with God." (Mark 10:27)**

Here is where the rubber met the road. I had to decide to take responsibility for my own actions. It did not matter how victimized, weak, influenced, naive, bitter, angry, hurt, rejected, confused, envious, or needy I was. I had to come to both the recognition and the admission that I was wrong before God. I had to repent, no matter what, how, or why this all happened. I had to call sin "sin." I had to humble myself before God and ask His utter and complete forgiveness, making a conscious decision to change my life and to live for Him, His way.

For the wages of sin is death, but the gift of God is eternal life in Christ Jesus our Lord. (Romans 6:23) My sin separated me from my Creator. It was a death from my relationship with Jesus until I decided to turn from it. Jesus gives us the opportunity to confess and repent at every turn and He promises forgiveness and cleansing. He loves us but He hates our sins. So also we must hate our sins, repent and turn from them out of love for God, for ourselves, and for those whom our lives will touch.

In a counseling session in 2004, I was led by a counselor to go back to the bedroom scene with my first woman lover and to see my Father God watching me. The counselor led me to my Father's lap. As I sat on His lap, He hugged me and said, "I love you." It's the act of sin that He hates. This experience helped me to release my shame. **If we confess our sins, He is faithful and just and will forgive us our sins and purify us from all unrighteousness. (1st John 1:9)**

Defiance Sears the Conscience

It was in the seventies, out of stubbornness of flesh and a legitimate need to be needed and loved, I felt a sense of desperation. That desperate feeling I chose to meet through the flesh and through the codependence I plunged into with Monica, my first female relationship. I began living the homosexual lifestyle and I plunged deeper into the lifestyle with other lovers, both male and female. Promiscuity grossly retarded my growth and development as an adult.

But your iniquities have separated you from God; your sins have hidden His face from you,

so that He will not hear. For your hands are stained with blood, your fingers with guilt. Your lips have spoken lies, and your tongue mutters wicked things. (Isaiah 59:2, 3) The healing process is longer and harder as the conscience becomes seared by the continual defiance against the warnings of the Holy Spirit to stop sinning. In other words, the conscience is no longer moved by the convictions from the Holy Spirit. Despite many warnings from the Holy Spirit, I would not listen. As I continually defied the warnings, I became both mentally, emotionally, and physically sick.

The Spirit clearly says that in later times some will abandon the faith and follow deceiving spirits and things taught by demons. Such teachings come through hypocritical liars, whose consciences have been seared as with a hot iron. (1ˢᵗ Timothy 4:1, 2) In order to continue to live in the "normal" world, I now had a "secret." And in keeping my lifestyle a secret from family, coworkers, and friends, I was not at peace. I now was a liar. It was a "catch – 22." Even after telling my secret to my family and friends, I still was not at peace. Why? I was lying to myself by knowingly living this lie of homosexuality. As a result, my own body now cried out. In 1973, I was rushed to surgery with an ovarian cyst that burst in my womb.

When body, soul, and spirit are all in agreement with the Creator, there is a healthy state of being. However, when there is sin, especially habitual sin, there is a diseased state of being. My spirit and soul were separated from my heavenly Father because any sin separates us from God. My mind was tormented by the lie I was living and the unspoken lies I carried out as a result of the lifestyle I tried to hide. And there was more torment associated with the guilt I felt in my dishonesty with coworkers. I suffered in my need to both hide my sin from them and to impress them with my talents as a cover-up for the sin. With hypocrisy comes exhaustion and torment.

Why didn't I listen to the warnings? Why didn't I repent? I was blinded by this lust and the emotional connections to the women I was with. This hellish demon spirit of homosexuality had paralyzed my judgment and was controlling me. In not heeding these warnings, I became further deceived by the enemy.

About a year after my surgery, I left Monica. She later committed suicide by a drug overdose. Now I allowed Satan to deceive and control me with a spirit of condemnation. I blamed myself for her death. This was also a lie from Satan. It was a false sense of responsibility that the enemy deceived me with. At the time, I was not born again. I did not know Jesus personally and I did not know His Word. Had I known Jesus and the Word of God, I would have known that self-condemnation comes from Satan. I would have been able to speak and believe:**There is then no condemnation to those who are in Christ Jesus. (Romans 8:1)**

Since I was a little girl, I had believed in God. But I did not have a personal relationship with Him. I thought God was in the clouds somewhere. After Monica's suicide, I discovered I was also blaming God for this event. Years later, with the help of the Holy Spirit, the Word of God, and Spirit filled counselors, I was assisted to release both my anger toward God and this false sense of responsibility which plagued me for years to come.

The Lord's will for us is for abundant life. It is the enemy who seeks to steal from us and to destroy us. (John 10:10 ref) We are never responsible for the decisions of another human being. Our lives are all in the sovereign hands of Almighty God.

Sin's Insanity

In 1978, I literally drove my car from Santa Barbara, California to New York City to investigate the circumstances of Monica's death. I remember crying hysterically in the car while driving in the rain. When I arrived, I had an opportunity to speak to Monica's landlady, who lived in the apartment below. She told me that she heard Monica get down on her knees the night before she died. I believe that Monica called out to Jesus that night before overdosing.

I believe Monica lives in heaven today, standing at the feet of Jesus praying for us folks still living on earth. I know she was a believer because we attended an Easter Sunday service together on the beach one Sunday before she went home to the Lord. Even if she were not a believer, I am convinced that anyone can call out to the Lord Jesus, repent of sin and confess by faith that Jesus Christ is Lord at any moment before entering into eternity; I believe Monica is one soul of the "cloud of witnesses." **Therefore, since we are surrounded by such a cloud of witnesses, let us throw off everything that hinders and the sin that so easily entangles, and let us run with perseverance the race marked out for us. Let us fix our eyes on Jesus, the author and perfecter of our faith, Who for the joy set before him, endured the cross, scorning the shame, and sat down at the right hand of the throne of God. (Hebrews 12:1, 2)**

Not having any sense of Jesus in my heart, I was subconsciously angry with God. I felt responsible for Monica's demise and subconsciously felt guilty for the lifestyle I was living. The enemy literally had a party on me. I plunged further into a web of insanity. At this crisis point in my life, I felt so desperate for love because I actually felt unlovable. With so much vulnerability, and without a relationship with Jesus Christ, I was open prey for the enemy to come and to further deceive me to continue to sin.

For the next three years, I lived a promiscuous lifestyle, hopping from lover to lover, male and female, experimenting with drugs to block both the emotional pain of both her death and of my early childhood pain. Had I known the Word of God, I would have been rejoicing that she was at peace in her heavenly home with Jesus. I believe she called out to Jesus Christ and repented of her sins before taking her life. **When the perishable has been clothed with the imperishable, and the mortal with immortality, then the saying that is written will come true; "Death has been swallowed up in victory." "Where, O death, is your victory? Where, O death, is your sting?" The sting of death is sin, and the power of sin is the law. But thanks be to God! He gives us the victory through our Lord Jesus Christ. Therefore, my dear brothers (sisters), stand firm. Let nothing move you. Always give yourselves fully to the work of the Lord, because you know that your labor in the Lord is not in vain. (1ˢᵗ Corinthians 15:54–58)**

I was not only addicted to the pleasures of the flesh which blocked my deep inner pain and grief from childhood. I was also running wild with the driving spirit of fear that was oppressing and controlling me, also since childhood. And I was also tormented by the false guilt I had assumed for Monica's death. I suffered with poor judgment, confusion, a sense of inferiority and hopelessness, and a lack of self- confidence and self-respect. Here was yet another layer of the mental block, which hid my "honest self" even deeper within the crevices of my heart. What started as frivolity turned into insanity! I needed the Lord Jesus Christ and His healing presence and power.

Codependency versus Interdependence

A false sense of responsibility for her death plagued me. But God helped me to release this. He gave me a revelation of His sovereignty (authority) over every individual's life. We are never responsible for another person's decisions. I believe that this was one of the root reasons that my healing took so long. Codependency and a false sense of responsibility are mutually partnered.

When you are codependent with a person, neither partner is really separate. One becomes an idol to the other. Both parties are so enmeshed that when one partner makes a bad decision, the other assumes a false sense of responsibility for that decision.

The Lord expresses to us in His Word: **I will never leave you or forsake you. (Joshua 1:5)** The divine relationship which we are privileged to encounter in a born again intimate relationship with Jesus Christ is the only relationship which is purely interdependent; it is a divine partnership. Unless we accept Him into our hearts, we will always feel alone. With Him abiding within us, we may be alone, but we will never be lonely as we stand in reverent awe of Him.

There are ebbs and flows in this relationship, but once I made the commitment, I took it very seriously. This is a divine covenant relationship, as in a marriage. I may get off the track, but I will always return to Him. Because I know the truth of this relationship in my life and the peace it brings me, I have a divine taste of true freedom. And the peace that this relationship brings has become for me greater than life itself!

Although it was tragic that I experienced homosexuality and the death of my friend at such an early age, God used both experiences for my good. He had a divine plan in mind. **I know the plans I have for you, plans for good and not for evil, plans for a future and a hope. (Jeremiah 29:11)**

Reaching a Turning Point - Warnings from God

In l981, eight years after I entered the lifestyle, I reached a turning point in all this madness. After Monica's death, I would travel to my favorite spot on the shoreline at around sunset. There in sunny Santa Barbara, after asking God's forgiveness for my anger toward Him, I would go to the beach to talk to Him. I wanted to know why this happened. I wanted to know where Monica was. And I wanted to know what would happen to me after I died.

I decided, with the encouragement of one of my friends, to become a nurse. I guess I felt that if I couldn't help Monica when she needed me, perhaps I could help somebody else. The tragedy actually caught my attention and directed me to becoming "heavenly" minded. **And we know that in all things God works for the good of those who love Him, who have been called according to His purpose. (Romans 8:28)**

God continued to give me warnings to help me to come to my senses and turn to Him. I remember talking to my mother on the telephone. I was visiting a lesbian couple's home that night. This couple was dealing with the occult. One woman was engaging in tarot card reading. My speech was actually altered. It was far from spontaneous. It was as if the words I wanted to speak did not come out.

The Bible tells us that John the Baptist's father's speech was muted because of his unbelief. He did not believe the news of the angel Gabriel that his wife Elizabeth would bear a child. **The angel answered, "I am Gabriel. I stand in the presence of God, and I have been sent to speak to you and to tell you this good news. And now you will be silent and not able to speak until the day this happens because you did not believe my words, which will come true at the proper time."(Luke 1:19-20)**

While engaged in a relationship with an older woman, God gave me a severe warning that literally frightened me. This woman's eyes literally changed colors before my eyes. I knew in my spirit that this was a warning from God to get out of this relationship. She was a mother figure for me. She was a mother herself of four children. She helped to take care of me during nursing school. It was a difficult time to break this bond as she was stricken with bladder cancer. Satan will always make it hard to obey God and to turn to truth.

Again, the rubber met the road and a decision had to be made. I was attending nursing school in Santa Barbara. Because I was smoking marijuana while still relating to this woman, my judgment was poor. The school administrators placed me on probation. I was, however, allowed to graduate. Praise God! At this point, I made a conscious decision to leave the relationship. I will never forget the day I mailed the letter saying "goodbye." I said the words to the Lord, "Thy will be done" as I placed the letter in the mailbox. God honored my obedience.That was the year I began to consciously pray, even though I did not yet attend a church. I recall sitting in the cafeteria of St. Francis' Hospital in Santa Barbara during one of my clinical rotations. I was saying the Lord's Prayer while eating lunch. Now life began to change. **For a brief moment I abandoned you, but with deep compassion I will bring you back. (Isaiah 54:7)**

After the suicide of a second friend, Ronald, I was down on my knees, crying out to Father God, "Where is my spirit? I am nowhere near it." I opened the Bible to Romans 1:22-27 after Ronald's death. **Although they claimed to be wise, they became fools and exchanged the glory of the immortal God for images made to look like mortal man and birds and animals and reptiles. Therefore God gave them over in the sinful desires of their hearts to sexual impurity for the degrading of their bodies with one another. They exchanged the truth of God for a lie, and worshiped and served created things rather than the Creator – Who is forever praised. Amen. Because of this, God gave them over to shameful lusts. Even their women exchanged natural relations for unnatural ones. In the same way, the men also abandoned natural relations with women and were inflamed with lust for one another. Men committed indecent acts with other men, and received in themselves the due penalty for their perversion. (Romans 1:22-27)**

I called some church leaders to the house and we all prayed hoping that Ronald had committed his life

31

to Jesus Christ before he died. He was a heroin addict and he died of an overdose, just like Monica. After losing two friends through suicide, almost being kicked out of nursing school, losing my natural spontaneity and love for life, I was now ready to change. I was convinced that homosexuality was indeed sin. I now believed that the Bible was truly the Word of God, not just words of men, but men who were inspired by the Holy Spirit! **All Scripture is God-breathed and is useful for teaching, rebuking, correcting and training in righteousness, so that the man (woman) of God may be thoroughly equipped for every good work. (2nd Tim. 3:16)**

Whose Report Will You Believe? Secular Psychiatry vs. Spirit Led Counselors

I sought help from a psychiatrist. This did not prove fruitful because the doctor clearly was not Christian. I remember telling her my story. At the close of the session, she asked, "What do you want?" My reply actually surprised me. My Catholic upbringing set a good moral standard! "It is not what I want, Dr., but what God wants for me." I replied. And I left the office never to return again. The only counselors who helped me to get well were Spirit-filled Christians. **If you hold to my teaching, you are really my disciples. Then you will know the truth and the truth will set you free. (John 8:32)**

The Story Continues

After the suicides of both my friends Ronald and Monica, my attention was refocused upon the supernatural. Living in sunny Santa Barbara, surrounded by the vast deep blue ocean and the majestic mountains, I was faced with the astounding beauty of God's creation. I stood in awe of God. I believe that living in an environment that resembled an earthly paradise assisted me through much of my depression. The surrounding beauty alone helped to bring me out of myself, being constantly reminded of the Lord's majesty and presence in my life.

I was so grateful that God allowed me to stay planted there for ten years. The atmosphere certainly helped me during the infancy stages of my growth as a Christian believer. God used my sense of awe in that environment to prepare me for the real awareness and awe of His taking residence within me when I became born again. This began the restoration of my real identity, "the honest self," fully emerging out of its hiding place, with my identity in Jesus Christ. **Therefore, if anyone is in Christ, he is a new creation; the old has gone, the new has come! (2nd Corinthians 5:17)**

Heed the Warnings – Choose Life

Well, God now had caught my attention. At this time, the warnings of God weighed more heavily upon me than any of my needs, wants, or feelings for this or any other person. Finally, I proceeded to heed the warnings. I was afraid something worse might happen. And I know that prayers were answered for the many people who had been praying for me during those very dark years. It was time to choose life. **This day I call heaven and earth as witnesses against you that I have set before you life and death, blessings and curses. Now choose life, so that you and your children may live, and that you may love the Lord your God, listen to His voice, and hold fast to Him. For the Lord is your life, and He will give you many years in the land He swore to give to your fathers, Abraham, Isaac, and Jacob. (Deuteronomy 30:19, 20)**

Expect a Miracle

I remember writing a letter to my last girlfriend telling her that I loved her but that I was convinced that what we were doing was wrong in the eyes of God. I told her that I decided to "choose life." I never found out what happened to her with regards to her bladder cancer. However, I know that I was given explicit instructions from the Holy Spirit to leave this relationship. Every time I thought of her, I prayed for her salvation and for her healing. I never saw her again. The Word of God clearly says: **Return to the Lord your God, for He is gracious and compassionate, slow to anger and abounding in love, and he relents from sending calamity . . . (Joel 2:13)**

My cry for help to the Lord was answered. After many prayers, much study, and a decision to leave all homosexual relationships, I graduated from nursing school. And I believe the Lord allowed that because of my decision to obey Him. My first nursing job was a divine appointment. I took on a private duty job caring for a twenty-year-old girl, a born again Christian who was paralyzed from her neck down. Her family members were also born again Christians. I was ready to receive Jesus Christ as my Lord. God knew it and I believe He planned it. I'll never forget the button attached to her pillowcase, which said, "Expect a miracle!"

My first day of work, I knocked on the door. Her mother, Mrs. Platt said, "Come on in. You must be the nurse sent to take care of my daughter." "Yes," I said. I'll never forget the words she spoke to me before I entered the house. "You are a very nice girl, but there are a few keys you need to drop." I didn't understand all that she was trying to say. But soon I came to understand her words.

My job responsibilities not only consisted of nursing this beautiful child, but also Mrs. Platt insisted that I read the Bible to her child. As I read to her, she would smile so brightly that her countenance shone like that of an angel. I saw the glory of God in the radiance which shined upon this young child's face. God knew that I would be moved by this. **I sought the Lord, and He answered me; He delivered me from all my fears. Those who look to Him are radiant; their faces are never covered with shame. (Psalm 34:4,5)**

Well, the truth began to set me free. I would return home at night and read the Bible to myself in the privacy of my apartment. I was still not ready to actually attend a church with "normal" folk. Yet I continued working for the Platt's. There was love and acceptance there. And I continued to read the Word of God. It was so rich! I purchased a version I could easily understand and became immersed in it.

For the Word of God is living and active. Sharper than any double-edged sword, it penetrates even to the dividing of soul and spirit, joints and marrow; it judges the thoughts and attitudes of the heart. (Hebrews 4:12) I started attending both AA and al anon meetings. I felt secure in these rooms knowing I was not alone. I had friends there but there was no joy there. The Word of God was not spoken there. Whenever I read the Bible, however, the Word of God would minister to me deep within my spirit. I was tasting real truth.

You Must Be Born Again

A Pharisee named Nicodemus came to Jesus and asked, "Rabbi, we know you are a teacher who has come from God. For none could perform the great miraculous signs you are doing if God were not with him." In reply, Jesus declared, "I tell you the truth; no one can see the kingdom of God unless he is born again." "How can a man be born again when he is old?" Nicodemus asked. "Surely he cannot enter a second time into his mother's womb to be born!"

Jesus answered, "I tell you the truth. No one can enter the kingdom of God unless he is born of water and the Spirit. Flesh gives birth to flesh, but the Spirit gives birth to spirit. You should not be surprised at my saying, 'You must be born again.' The wind blows wherever it pleases. You hear its sound, but you cannot tell where it comes from or where it is going. So it is with everyone born of the Spirit." (John 3:1-8)

It was a sunny day in June of 1981 when I committed my life to Jesus Christ. I was led into the sinner's prayer by Mrs. Platt. I spoke the words, **"Heavenly Father, in Jesus' name, I repent of my sins and open my heart to let Jesus come inside of me. Jesus, You are my Lord and Savior. I believe that You died for my sins and that You were raised from the dead. Fill me with Your Holy Spirit. Thank You, Father for saving me; in Jesus' name. Amen."** [40]

The Word of God further confirms the born again commitment by saying: **If you confess with your mouth Jesus as Lord and believe in your heart that God raised Him from the dead, you will be saved." (Romans 10:9,10)** Being "saved" means that I am now assured of all the promises of God. I am now promised not only eternal life, but also well-being for myself and all my family members, divine provisions and protection necessary to live an abundant life, and divine health and well-being of body, mind, and spirit. **[41]**

The moment I spoke those words my life began to change. I became a new creature in Christ. All the old life had passed away. I was clean! My spirit was now united and alive with Jesus. I am so glad that Jesus gave me this free gift of abundant life on earth and eternal life through His grace. There is nothing I can do to receive this. I received it by faith. Salvation is a free gift from God because of Jesus and His ultimate sacrifice of His life for us on the cross. My faith in this provision reached out to receive the grace (unmerited favor and loving kindness) of God. **For it is through grace that you have been saved, through faith – and that not from yourselves, it is the gift of God – not by works, so that no one can boast. (Ephesians 2:8,9)**

This was only the beginning of a new life. Accepting Jesus as my Lord was the most important decision I have ever made. From that moment of commitment on, I entered into a divine and an intimate covenant relationship with Him. And He changed me, through His presence with me daily, through the still small voice of the Holy Spirit, through His Word, and through the love I received from my Lord and His people.

I knew the healing process of the soul was ahead and this would take time and pain. Healing is a painful process. It must be actively sought and worked through before the child of God can be used by God for His Kingdom in the fullest capacity. It would begin by reverencing God and getting to know Jesus through His Word. **Do not conform any longer to the pattern of this world, but be transformed by the renewing of your mind. Then you will be able to test and approve what God's will is – His good, pleasing, and perfect will. (Romans 12:2)**

From Defiance to Repentance to Reverence – Dr. John Bradshaw's Research – Receiving from God

I was immersed in the lifestyle for a period of eight years, from 1973-1981. Why did it take me eight years to come to a decision? Why did I not heed the many warnings the first time? Why did I have to go through so much pain before finally submitting to God and changing? The answer, I believe, lies behind an attitude of defiance. Oh yes, you can say I was driven by the spirit of fear and I was. It is the root spirit of all spirits in the demonic realm. But my healing process would have been accelerated had my attitude been one of reverence, repentance, forgiveness, obedience, and gratitude. **God opposes the proud but gives grace to the humble. (James 4:6)**

Face the Defiance and Receive the Righteousness of God

I accepted Jesus as my Lord. I stood in awe of Him and worshiped Him. But most of my healing took place in the intellectual realm before it even entered the heart realm. I believe there was a slowdown in my healing because of my heart's attitude. I went from one extreme to another; from worldly arrogance to a spiritual arrogance. Being so wounded, I was blinded by this arrogance. And this kept the wall up around my heart allowing people in "this far and no more."

Healing is a heart issue. We all have our own stories tracing the roots of our sins. Besides generational curses and generational and ancestral spirits from the demonic world that affect our spirits since childhood; besides iniquities (tendency toward sins) that we inherit from the fall of man; I believe sin is rooted in deep hurts, rejections, traumas, abuses and/or injustices committed against us. Our sins are the result of our deep need to annihilate the wounds caused by these human injustices. They are the ungodly reactions [42] to the injustices. Sin only temporarily numbs the pain but, sooner or later, the pain must be faced for the healing to transpire. There are no shortcuts.

Unresolved deep hurts cut off our ability to experience life victoriously and must be dealt with head on. The only way to truly deal with these hurts is to enter into the darkness of this pain accompanied by Light of the world, Jesus Christ Our Savior. Jesus is very acquainted with our grief because He lived and walked the earth as both God and as a man. Jesus experienced our every abuse and affliction. He understands our wounds. Jesus suffered the ultimate injustice in giving us His very life through crucifixion. And He also demonstrated complete victory over the devil and his tricks to keep us locked into the pain and hurts through His resurrection.

All sin is rooted in a spirit of rebellion, which is defiance against God. Defiance seeks to cover over the pain and not deal with it. Yet it is our unresolved hurt that opens the door for Satan to intrude and invade us with lies and more temptations. God is a gentleman. He did not make us puppets to be fully under His control. He created within us a free will to choose for ourselves a life reverently submitted to Him.

Sin is also a result of a willful and disobedient act that obeys Satan's voice, not the voice of God. Unless we submit to Jesus and repent of the sin, leave it, and then ask Him to help us to change, healing will never take place. To go forward in inner healing, it is essential that we receive the righteousness (right standing with God). This is part of our inheritance in Christ Jesus. Once we humble ourselves and repent, we are forgiven and cleansed of all unrighteousness. (1st John 1:9 ref.) **If we confess our sins, He is faithful and just and will forgive us our sins and purify us from all unrighteousness. (1st John 1:9) For in the gospel a righteousness from God is revealed, a righteousness that is by faith from first to last, just as it is written: "The righteous will live by faith." (Romans 1:16,17)**

It basically comes down to this. I decide to live either for God my Creator or for myself. There is only one way out of the torment of unresolved hurts and His name is Jesus Christ. No pleasure on earth can replace the bliss we experience when we are fully submitted to His will.

This is a choice each person must make. Billye Brim so explicitly describes one's will as the "choicer." With it a person makes the choices which determine eternal destiny. **[43] You were bought at a price; do not become slaves of men. Brothers (or sisters), each man (or woman), as responsible to God, should remain in the situation God called him (or her) to. (1ˢᵗ Cor. 7:23)**

Jesus paid the ultimate price for our freedom by sacrificing His life for us on the cross. We actually owe our lives to God not only because Father God created us, but also because He gave His Son Jesus to us. Jesus paid the ultimate price for all our sins and all our sicknesses, which includes any curse set in motions by the sin of Adam and Eve. Jesus paid the full price for sickness and disease by sacrificing His life for us. His divine blood paid for our freedom on this earth once and for all. All we need to do is receive it and enter into divine covenant relationship with Jesus Christ as an act of faith and as an act of our will.

Receiving righteousness or right standing in Christ Jesus is absolutely essential to continue walking in the love of Christ and to continue in victory over the snares of the devil's work through men and women. Why? Because this is our confidence in Christ, and Christ lives within us. Therefore, it is my self-confidence. Jesus' approval and my clear conscience with Him shuts off the need to please others. I can rest in Jesus' total acceptance, love, and forgiveness and respect myself and others as well. I am changed from the defensive victim position to an offensive place of confidence and rest within my own skin and with my peers. We are all sinners saved by the grace of God! **For the Lord will be your confidence and will keep your foot from being snared. (Proverbs 3:26) God made Him who had no sin to be sin for us, so that in Him we might become the righteousness of God. (2ⁿᵈ Corinthians 5:21)**

Will You Be Deceived By Envy? Strive to Be Content

But godliness with contentment is great gain. For we brought nothing into the world, and we can take nothing out of it. (1ˢᵗ Timothy 6:6) A sense of inferiority will cause a sense of unworthiness which will cause an envious attitude of wanting to be like someone else. This keeps us running after whatever we cannot have. As I got honest with myself and honest with Jesus, the need for more of God increased and I received the righteousness (right standing) of God by an act of my faith. My confidence in the Lord was restored as I matured in Christ.

For it is by grace you have been saved, through faith – and this not from yourselves, it is a gift from God – not by works, so that no one can boast. (Ephesians 2:8) As I obeyed the Lord and left sins, idols, and ungodly attitudes, my heart opened to receive His grace. This is God's loving kindness, His power, and His favor toward us. I then entered into His rest. Contentment begins with knowing Christ is with us and for us. Self respect and our own sense of integrity returns as we act according to His Word. This is an inside job, friend, that must be received and worked out between you and God. For me, self confidence naturally enfolded as my relationship grew with the Lord. As I grew in reverence to Him, I received more of Him and more of His grace.

No one is worthy of the grace or loving-kindness of God. It is a free gift which He extends to all His children. We do not receive it by any feelings we may have about ourselves. We receive it by faith and with gratitude to Him for the gift….**for all have sinned and fall short of the glory of God, and are justified freely by His grace through the redemption that came by Christ Jesus. (Romans 3:23)**

We must face and turn from our own envious attitudes toward others, choose to be happy for them, and seek contentment in Jesus Christ first. He will show us by revelation how valuable and special we are just the way we are. There is nothing that can compare to the liberty and contentment we experience when we receive the grace and rest of God into our lives, experiencing ourselves as forgiven, accepted, loved, and valuable to God! **He has made everything beautiful in its time. (Ecclesiastes 3:11)**

In the fall of Lucifer, the Bible clearly shows the pompous and arrogant position that Lucifer takes before he falls from his heavenly position. He was not content with his beauty and wanted to be like God. **How you have fallen from heaven, O morning star, son of the dawn! You have been cast down to the earth, you who once laid low the nations! You said in your heart, "I will ascend to heaven; I will raise my throne above the stars of God; I will sit enthroned on the mount of assembly,**

on the utmost heights of the sacred mountain. I will ascend above the tops of the clouds; I will make myself like the Most High." (Isaiah 14: 12- 14)

Lucifer is defined as the most beautiful being that God had created. He was called the archangel. The archangel was the angel who was the leader of all the other angels. Ezekiel, the prophet, describes Lucifer as: **You were the model of perfection, full of wisdom and perfect in beauty. (Ezekiel 28:12) You were blameless in your ways from the day you were created till wickedness was found in you. (Ezekiel 28:15)**

That wickedness or "gross injustice" [44] began with Lucifer's conscious and vulgar misuse of his own will. Lucifer's conscious decision to defy His Creator cost him the complete expulsion from the divine position he was so generously given. Defiance is a severe character flaw. When one walks defiantly for so long, it will take many falls to break its ugly head. It is like a wild animal that needs to be tamed because it is rooted in man's core, his flesh. The flesh is only concerned with wanting for itself. Be encouraged! God's love reaches for every lost sheep, even the most defiant. Jesus came for the sinners. He spent most of his time with sinners. Some of God's greatest men and women experienced great falls before becoming victorious leaders representing God's Kingdom.

What was in the heart of Lucifer? What caused him to choose to defy His Creator? I believe the rebellion was instigated by an intense jealousy on Lucifer's part. Instead of taking on the attitude of gratitude toward God because he was created in such a beautiful way and given a position of honor amongst his peers, he was envious and wanted more. The words "I want" are dangerously defiant against the divine will of God. Lucifer was burning with envy and this attitude caused him to defy God Himself. His envy would not be quenched until he became just like God. "I want" looks outside for fulfillment and finds an idol. "Not my will but thine" looks within, humbling oneself to God, and finds the truth. **If my people will humble themselves and pray, then they will hear from heaven. (2nd Chronicles 7:14)**

In Catholic school, envy was taught as a "near occasion of sin" and not as sin itself. But as I look at this "near occasion of sin" squarely, I can see how it got me into dangerous positions with both God and man. Envy says, "I don't accept myself for whom I am. I would rather be like someone else." Without consciously realizing it, I became motivated by envy in my initial rebellion against God. Because I did not feel good about myself, I suffered with a lack of self-esteem. Because I did not think well about myself, I suffered with a low self-image. When I saw another woman who had what I believe I did not have, my envy motivated me on a subconscious level, and I entered into the homosexual relationship. With Monica, for example, I wanted her confidence and her beauty. And this envy became eroticized. I sold my soul to the devil through an illicit homosexual relationship.

When we commit to a divine covenant relationship with Jesus Christ, He takes up residence within our spirits, souls, and bodies. This cannot even compare with all the physical beauty in the natural realm. Jesus Christ in us blesses us with right standing in Him, or righteousness, which is our confidence found in our right relationship with Him. Our physical eyesight is gradually changed to spiritual sight and we learn to see and perceive as Christ would, with our hearts, not just with the physical senses. His presence in our lives brings us the awareness of a supernatural world that is far greater than what we see and experience with our natural eyes.

We no longer need to compare ourselves to others because we learn a new-found contentment. We are content with Christ in and for us, in the Father God Who loves and watches over us, and in the Holy Spirit Who guides and empowers us. **I have learned the secret of being content in any and every situation, whether well fed or hungry, whether living in plenty or in want. I can do all things through Him Who gives me strength. (Phil 4:13,14)**

Had I recognized the enemy of my soul, I would have seen the trap and not fallen for it. I would have been alert to Satan's bait and taken steps to avoid the close encounters. For example, a recovering alcoholic will do well not to enter a bar. A recovering homosexual will also do well not to enter a gay bar. Passing by the bar will engage your mind to the temptation. Take another route home!

Be self-controlled and alert. Your enemy the devil prowls around like a roaring lion looking

for someone to devour. Resist him, standing firm in the faith, because you know that your brothers throughout the world are undergoing the same kind of sufferings. (1ˢᵗ Peter 5:8,9) Before I entered into covenant with Jesus, I had no real identity. So I chose a person whom I perceived as having a confident identity to help me to become a stronger, more confident person. Instead of seeking my confidence in God in my right standing with Him, I looked for it in my friend. Monica was actually an idol through whom I established my identity. She took God's place in my life. And I actually lost my real identity in the process. True identity is only found through an intimate and personal relationship with Jesus Christ. It is discovered within one's heart, not through any person, place, or thing. **The fear of man will prove to be a snare. (Proverbs 29:25)**

Worship and Praise Brings Healing – Let Your Spirit Take Hold of Your Soul

Our identity can only be truly found in a personal relationship with Jesus Christ. Self-esteem and self-image issues are heart issues that only Jesus can truly answer for us. Once I accepted the Lord Jesus Christ and decided to leave the gay lifestyle, I now started out on the journey of self-discovery, finding my true identity in Jesus Christ.

My self-esteem and self-image would be built up as I developed in my relationship with Jesus Christ. I found value in myself in studying His Word and I began to see myself as He saw me. Daily, as I repented of sin, the wall of shame started to come down. As I received His forgiveness, love, and total acceptance, and His right standing, my self-respect and self-confidence were restored. As I experienced His love for me, I began to love myself again. As I studied His Word and worshiped Him, I was courted and blessed by Him. As the Holy Spirit spoke to me in a small still voice, I was encouraged by His words of love to me and I grew in maturity as I heeded His directions. **Deep calls to deep in the roar of your waterfalls; all your waves and breakers have swept over me. By day the Lord directs His love, at night His song is with me – a prayer to the God of my life. (Psalm 42:7-8)**

I believe that the "honest self" of my soul began its rebirth the day I accepted Jesus Christ as my Lord and my Savior. As I grew in my relationship with Jesus, worshiping and praising Him, my human spirit, (the real me), grew in greater proportions. I was cleansed and purged in my soul, (my thoughts, emotions, and will), by the Holy Spirit and by the living of the Word of God. As my human spirit grew and my soul healed, I became repulsed by the sins of the flesh.

In becoming more aware of the Lord's presence, I did not want to displease Him with anymore sin. I also did not want to defile myself with sexual sin, negative thoughts, emotions, and fantasies, and separate from His loving presence. I believe that it was the "real self" of my spirit that fought to bring the "honest self" of my soul out of hiding, thus rebirthing it.

I loved to sing and worship the Lord and still do today. I had church in my car and would sing to the Lord to usher in His presence and to encourage myself in the Lord. There is a definite advantage to becoming "sold out" to Jesus! **Lift up your heads, O ye gates, be lifted up, you ancient doors that the King of glory may come in. Who is this King of glory? The Lord strong and mighty, the Lord mighty in battle. Lift up your heads, O you gates; that the King of glory may come in. (Psalms 24:7-9)**

Release the Sin of Judgment

When a memory sparks old emotions, I step back and ask the Lord for a godly perspective. I am still learning self-control in this area. When past memories attempt to cloud my reality when in the company of another woman, I stop and think, take control of my thoughts, speak to myself, and take the thoughts captive. The quicker I do this and not dwell on the fantasies, the better I get a grip on the reality of each situation. I may then choose to speak to the person in an attitude of faith through the love of God which dwells in my heart rather than to be ruled by any negative past memories which are only reflections of past feelings, and not a clear reflection of the present situation. I am a new creature in Christ Jesus. I do not know the old person. I remember her but I am gratefully not moved by her past actions. Jesus forgives me and so do I also forgive and release myself from any and all guilt and condemnation. I am in Christ Jesus and there is no condemnation to anyone who is in Christ Jesus. (Romans 8:1) (2nd Cor. 5:17) (Galatians 5:6) (2nd Cor. 10,4,5)

For this reason, make every effort to add to your faith, goodness; and to your goodness, knowledge; and to knowledge, self-control; and to self-control, perseverance; and to perseverance, godliness; and to godliness, brotherly kindness; and to brotherly kindness, love. For if you possess these qualities in increasing measure, they will keep you from being ineffective and unproductive in your knowledge of our Lord Jesus Christ. (2nd Peter 1:5-8) Remember, the enemy knows our buttons. Because it took so much for me to begin to love and accept myself after sinning in this area, the enemy continues to tempt me to bitterness if not against myself, against others who are accusing me or whom I perceive are accusing me. Sometimes my perceptions are correct. Sometimes they are not. Nonetheless, I choose to walk in faith through love! I refuse to be moved by others' opinions and/or judgments (Galatians 5:6) I am the righteousness of God. (Romans 1:17)

I really had to get to the point of accepting that I really didn't know for sure what other people thought. When you know you don't know, you are no longer distracted. Therefore, you can focus on the Lord instead of on man. Focus upon the Lord's presence in the very presence of others and you will become free from the fear of man. You are tuned into a different station altogether!

I also have learned that walking in love is the best offense and the best defense when treading upon the land of both friend and foe. I know that Satan works through people and it is never the people whom I come against. I ask the Lord for wisdom amidst every storm. Walking in love does not mean that I cast my every pearl upon swine, but that I walk as an ambassador for Christ and with the wisdom of God. I represent Him. Walking in love does not mean I put myself down to build someone else up. That is false humility. To truthfully walk in love, I must respect myself as well and either be honest with people, or, walk away and pray for them, using the wisdom of God. The Holy Spirit will be your guide. (1st Corinthians 13) Always be safe. Travel in two's.

When you were dead in your sins and in the uncircumcision of your sinful nature, God made you alive with Christ. He forgave us all our sins, having canceled the written code, with its regulations, that was against us and that stood opposed to us: he took it away, nailing it to the cross. And having disarmed the powers and authorities, he made a public spectacle of them, triumphing over them by the cross. (Colossians 2:13-15) One never has to fight Satan. He already was defeated at Calvary. Jesus resurrected, took the keys of sin and death from Satan and brought them to His Father in Heaven.

As I forgive and release myself and others from all judgment, Jesus forgives me. (Matthew 6:12)(Luke 6:27,28) This was the most difficult sin to release, the sin of judgment. I had deceived myself to believe that I carried no blame toward my enemies. Yet I was continually faced with having to forgive enemies. Yes, I prayed with my heart properly prepared in faith, with submission, repentance, and forgiveness, against the spirits that were oppressing the people, binding and gagging them in the name of Jesus, as I addressed my Father in the name of Jesus. (Matthew 18:18)(Luke 11:24-26) I could only bind and gag the enemy against them but could not cast out any demons with no legal authority and/or against the will of the people.(See Appendix)

I also had to pray directly for the people as well to be free from my sins of judgment. I had to see myself in them, with just as much need for forgiveness and healing as myself. When I got honest with God and with myself, I saw my own sins and afflictions. I was able to discern between the two. I gave up the lie that I was "better than my persecutors," and I prayed for God to forgive them and to save and deliver me as well. (Phil 2:3)(See Appendix)

Refuse to Be Bitter - Set Healthy Boundaries

I had to refuse to be bitter, no matter what the cost. It cost me jobs at times, but my peace with God was always the priority. I did leave jobs when the strife of mockery was overwhelming, when I felt taken advantage of to the point of abuse. I allowed much of the abuse because my confidence was not fully developed in Christ in a mature way. Many of my perceptions were incorrect because my confidence was not yet fully developed. Many perceptions were correct, but I remained hidden in the shame of the past and a people pleaser. Therefore I did not lovingly confront coworkers when the Holy Spirit led me to, when it would have been safe to honestly confront. However, I had to accept my limitations and do what I needed to do at the time. Everyone has their limits. **For the grace given me, I say to every one of you: Do not think of yourself more highly than you ought, but rather think of yourself with sober judgment, in accordance with the measure of faith God has given you. (Romans 12:3)**

As my relationship with Jesus becomes more secure, I became more successful at setting healthy boundaries. Jesus has taught me so much in this area. He has given me actual revelations of walking with His fire around me, and of walking clothed with real spiritual armor as that of Joan of Arc. I put my spiritual armor on when dressing. These revelations have helped me to set a precedent for the actual "shield" of God around me and the "rest" of God upon me, especially in the workplace. (Psalms 3:3) (Hebrews 4:9) I use my god-given imagination to help me until the full manifestation of "God with me" comes. I imagine the cross of Jesus between myself and others. I use this strategy to keep my focus upon the Lord and His presence deep within my innermost being, to see people as Jesus sees them, not as I may want or need them, and to set healthy boundaries.

I also have learned from godly coworkers. I have spent time with coworkers who exemplified the love of Christ and I have gleaned from their confidence and faith. I thank God for the many opportunities to work alongside so many certified nurse's aides who work diligently and humbly for the Lord serving others in need. Working with others is a good and a necessary thing.

Even if I am being mistreated, I am still commanded to love and not to judge. **Do not judge and you will not be judged. Do not condemn, and you will not be condemned. Forgive, and you will be forgiven. Give and it will be given to you. A good measure, pressed down, shaken together and running over, will be poured into your lap. For with the measure you use, it will be measured to you. (Luke 6:37–38)**

Defiance to Reverence – Connection of Mind, Will, and Emotions

There is a very good reason God did not want any idols before Him. With Him as first and foremost, we have the profound pleasure of experiencing His love, which is divine. His love for us is a truly satisfying affection. Living a life led by the Spirit of Christ Jesus is the greatest freedom we could ever experience in this life. We actually are afforded the awesome privilege of experiencing "a little bit of heaven" here on the earth.

The fear of the Lord is the beginning of wisdom. (Proverbs 10:10) Webster defines this fear of the Lord as a profound reverence and awe toward God. **[45]** Reverence demands that we see ourselves in the proper perspective to our Maker. The moment I say, "I am sorry," I place myself in a position of humility before God, a position of reverence in the sorrow that I express to Him and the awe that I experience in His loving presence.

Repentance is a daily exercise as we are still living in the flesh. We are all still sinners. **Godly sorrow brings repentance that leads to salvation and leaves no regret, but worldly sorrow brings death. (2nd Corinthians 7:10)** As the Lord spoke to Job, he said: **When I said, 'This far and no farther; here is where your proud waves halt'? Have you ever given orders to the morning, or shown the dawn its place, that it may take the earth by the edges and shake the wicked out of it? (Job 38:11,12)**

Repentance and acceptance of Jesus as my Lord and Savior were choices for life. Hope entered my heart and now I somehow knew that a supernatural helper was with me. I did not actually feel it but I knew He was with me. Faith told me. And a deep reverence for God kept me. I was no longer going through this fire alone. Accepting Jesus as Lord in 1981 was the initial step of revering and honoring God. It was a big step. God was pleased. He always honored my obedience. He has His ways of showing us His pleasure as well as His displeasure. **"Blessed are they whose transgressions are forgiven, whose sins are covered. Blessed is the man whose sin the Lord will never count against him." (Romans 4:6,7,8)**

The Holy Spirit continues to help me to turn from rebellion and pride to humility and a deep reverence for God. It is through His power working within me along with decided acts of my own will to yield to this power that I learned to listen for His voice. That is why Scripture says: **"God opposes the proud but gives grace to the humble." (James 4:6)**

Become a Prayer Warrior and Give Out of Your Need

The Holy Spirit has shown me that I am called as a prayer warrior. Intercessory prayer has served to annihilate self-pity. God has given me a burden for others' sufferings and that burden miraculously lifts off me when I pray for others from my heart. Working in both the teaching and in the nursing fields, self-pity has been transformed to a caring for others as I reach out to others. It helps so much to give to God in your career! (See Appendix)

This ultimately gave me a godly perspective of myself. I am merely one child of God out of millions of His children. Yet I am a valuable part of His creation. And I am His servant to be used to better His world. When I feel sorrow, I can either turn inward and feel sorry for myself staying in the flesh of this negative emotion. Or this feeling can be redirected outward upon the thousands of people in this world who, at this very moment, need prayer. Using sorrow as a springboard for intercessory prayer for others who suffer turns the tide from the flesh to the spirit – as I decide to make an impact upon those who need prayer.

Fears have been transformed to faith, one step at a time. Giving is a weapon that is irreplaceable. It is in giving that we bless others. We are, in turn, blessed in the very act of it. It is an act of love that no fear can invade, no anxiety can intercept, and no worry can interrupt. My world in the nursing profession provided me with people to love and to touch. It was a profession that served me as I served others. It is important to find your gift and seek the will of God in using that gift in serving others. And, in serving others, you will be blessed by the Lord. In whatever capacity you find yourself, you can and must make the choice to give. If you find yourself unemployed, you can volunteer. Stay involved as long as you have breath!

I placed a requirement upon myself. I told the Lord that I would reach out and bless one person every day. I made a point of sharing Jesus or just being kind with at least one person. I journaled my progress. As I reached out to others, the Lord was sure to bring folks to me who were less fortunate than I. And what started out as an exercise to free myself from self-pity transformed me into a compassionate human being. I had to choose to be joyful amidst the sorrow. It was a necessary attitude adjustment!

It Takes Humility to Receive Life

This is where defiance had to leave. Its ugly head kept me in shame until I fully accepted my Lord's total and complete acceptance, love, and forgiveness of me and all the mistakes I had made. This, my friend, has to be a revelation! Only the Holy Spirit can free us from the stigma and the facades we place upon ourselves in committing these sins of sexual immorality. Only through the precious blood that Jesus shed for us on the cross is the stigma, the guilt, and the shame of this and any other sin removed. We receive a clear conscience by reaching out to Him in great thanksgiving for the abundant life He has provided for us.

This cross must not be taken lightly, friend. This one event in human history is the only event that had the power to completely bring victory to the human condition. Jesus' blood paid for all sins, once and for all. It did away with the need for the laws of sacrificing of animals for the forgiveness of sins or for us making any sacrifices for Him. Jesus paid it once and for all.

I always knew this intellectually, but I never really believed it in my heart. So I would continually be affected by others' opinions. As I drove through the mountainous roads of Rockaway, New Jersey, to visit a beautiful child with Tay Sachs disease, the Holy Spirit spoke to me and He said, "I love you. You are accepted. You are so precious!" He also said, "You have nothing to worry about. I am living within you."

I have been crucified with Christ and I no longer live, but Christ lives in me. The life I live in the body, I live by faith in the Son of God, who loved me and gave himself for me. (Galatians 2:20)

Receive God's Sovereignty – Release the Need to Control Others

As I experienced my inability to control or to change my family, I experienced a deep surrender to God in prayer believing Him for their salvation. I had to trust God. There were times when I saw my family and was blessed. There were also times I needed to stay away. **Believe in the Lord Jesus, and you will be saved – you and your household. (Acts 16:31)**

We can try to manipulate or control people, but controlling them is impossible because we are fighting our will against their wills. Only God Himself can change people. But we do have influence by our attitudes, our words and prayers, and our actions towards others. For example, forgiving someone may be the open door to a person's accepting the reality of a risen Savior into his/her hearts, thus, the gift of salvation. Being kind to someone who has been unkind to you may be the only open door that person may have to learning about Jesus Christ.

We also always have the opportunity to pray for others, for there is no distance in prayer. I have felt burdens and the lifting of those burdens after prayers for people were answered. Sometimes the people are present. Sometimes not. In intercessory prayer, the Holy Spirit may give you a burden to pray for a particular person, and, after a season of prayer, the burden will lift and you will know, by the Spirit of God within you, that your prayer has been answered.(See Appendix)

However, we only have the ability to control our own thoughts. By accepting our limitations regarding others' choices, we take the correct steps toward living and toward changing our own lives. If you become entrapped in your imagination about others, God says we are to:

…demolish every argument and every pretension that sets itself up against the knowledge of God and we take captive every thought to make it obedient to Christ. (2nd Cor. 10:5)

I had to honestly face myself and come out of my fantasy world and take responsibility for my own thoughts and feelings, and my own life. I chose instead to listen for the voice of the Holy Spirit as He led me through each moment and through each decision. Yes, there was an enemy lurking, but I had to decide to close the door to allowing him any further entrance.

Receive God's Restoration

I learned to turn my stubborn streak to my advantage. I was going to get my healing no matter what! I remember how happy I was as a child. I was determined that, with the help of the Holy Spirit, Jesus would restore to me all that the enemy had stolen. This is God's promise to His children. **I will repay you for the years that the locusts have eaten. (Joel 2:25)**

I knew since I was a little girl that God would be using me to help others. He used me in spite of myself. Being a helper to many tragic situations in the nursing field, my wounds seemed insignificant compared to others. I was deeply humbled by the tragedy of others in the nursing profession.

No battles are won alone. If you look at the battles throughout history and in the Bible, armies were composed of hundreds and thousands of men and women with similar purposes under God. Once I hooked into a church family, I was well under way. I now had a team of healthy Christians as part of my family. I felt safe and accepted. I was growing. I also was accountable to them and this assisted me to live up to the demands of the Christian lifestyle. Even today I am accountable to a church family. Accountability is essential to staying on track!

There is power in unity! Iron sharpens iron. When you need a miracle, you must go through the miracle worker, Jesus. But remember, Jesus works through His people. **How good and pleasant it is when brothers (sisters) live together in unity! (Psalm 133:1)**

It's Humbling to Receive Your Completed Healing – Research from Dr. John Bradshaw
Healing is Not Just an Experience – It is a Decided Resolution and It is Taken by Faith
Therefore confess your sins to each other and pray for each other so that you may be healed.
(James 5:16) I have found that the most humble hearts are the hearts of children. God blessed me with ample opportunities to work with children. There is always room in the children's ministry for workers. There are crevices in my heart that will only be touched through the pure hearts of children. I let them in because I knew I could trust them. Children are pure and honest and they not only bring safety, but also much joy!

All attitudes are decisions of the will. Even to this day my will needs healing. Dr. John Bradshaw calls the will the executor of the personality. He believes that a person who has been severely wounded as a child forms what he calls emotional energy blocks that seriously affect one's ability to think and reason. He says that such people are contaminated in their judgment, perception, and ability to reason. Therefore, with our practical judgment shut down, the will is no longer reality grounded. And the emotionally shut down person then becomes filled with will, or "will-full." Willfulness is then characterized by attempts to control; it is playing God. He sees this as a result of the toxic shame. **[46]**

I experienced this willfulness as a feeble attempt to cover up for my secret sin of homosexuality, a form of a mental block. Even after leaving the lifestyle, I was enmeshed in so much shame that my only defense was to form a mental block. I became a workaholic and a perfectionist. These were my false selves which kept me from facing my shameful self. I blanked my mind from the shame of the sin, and the pain in my soul. This was just a temporary fix – a band aid hiding the real wounds. It didn't work. Hiding the shame behind the guise of "professional nurse" or any job was not the answer. The work became an obsessive and compulsive act, just another addiction. The root issues had to be faced and worked through in the presence of Holy Spirit-filled counselors who welcomed the Lord and prayer into the counseling sessions.

John Bradshaw found freedom from alcoholism. He found that the hurting child who is compulsive must return to the point of origin of the hurt and re-experience the hurt. These are old blocked feelings (unresolved grief) being acted out over and over again. He says that we either work them out by re-experiencing them or we continue to act them out in our compulsiveness. Also, we must leave home and become our own person in order to cure our compulsions. [47] I agree with Bradshaw's perspective in facing the pain to find the truth. However, I believe that the breakthrough comes not just with re-experiencing the pain. I would have been grieving from the pain throughout my entire life. Breakthrough comes with a decided resolution that we work through and settle within our own hearts. I also add that it was through the grace of God, with the help of the Holy Spirit, and with help from the people of faith who loved me back to life that I healed from the compulsivities. I believe we must confront the root of the pain and our ungodly reactions and sinful patterns that have resulted from that pain in the presence of godly counselors and in the presence of a holy God. We must break down the structures of judgment and expectancies, and of ungodly behavior patterns, thoughts, habits, and attitudes by taking them to the cross of Jesus Christ.

Recognition, repentance, confession, and prayers of forgiveness, restoration, and healing must take place. [48]

Therefore, my dear friends, as you have always obeyed – not only in my presence, but now much more in my absence – continue to work out you salvation with fear and trembling, for it is God who works in you to will and to act according to His good purpose. (Philippians 2:12,13)
Also, it was in counseling, in support groups, and in time spent with Jesus and His Word that my heart reopened and that Jesus came in and restored. And, as the wounds healed in a process of time spent with Jesus and His Word, the obsessive compulsive behavior lessened and the anointing of the Holy Spirit began to replace the driving spirit with the peace of God. The Holy Spirit convicted me of my ungodly sins, attitudes, and judgments, and also of the worldly distractions. Leaving worldly distractions, I set time aside

for the completed healing to manifest. I faced the pain, the idols, and the sins. It is then that I closed the doors to sin and idols, and settled issues within my own heart, in obedience to the leading of the Holy Spirit.

I repented of my ungodly behavior patterns of unbalanced burden bearing, parental inversion, noble martyr, and my false sense of responsibility. I then cast my cares upon the Lord, and redirected my concerns to intercessory prayer for my family and for the world.(See Appendix) I broke the mindsets and habits of childhood as I confronted myself with my sins, choosing obedience no matter how I felt. I listened to the Holy Spirit's leading.

The enemy tried to keep me from the victory. When the enemy brought me confusion, I spoke to the confusion with my heart of faith, with submission to the Lord, with repentance for my sins, and with forgiveness for myself and all who had sinned against me. "Father God, I cast all my burdens upon You for You are in control and know all things in Jesus' name. I will not worry." When fleshly temptations came, I spoke with my heart of faith, "Father God, I ask You to strengthen me against these temptations, in Jesus' name. I choose Your will and not mine, O Lord God." With issues that were difficult to accept, I spoke with my heart of faith, "Father God, I ask You to help me to accept what I cannot change, and to bring change to what I can change, in Jesus' name." When I was at a loss for words, I just said, "I love You, Lord." "I believe You are here."

The grace and rest of God came as I strengthened in my faith and in thanksgiving for the peace that He brought me because of my acts of obedience. My heart healed and reopened to life. I continued to develop my heart in its proper position of faith. And I grew daily in my faith. Being fully committed and submitted to a personal and intimate covenant relationship with Jesus Christ, I bowed my head to readily repent, forgive, and release all judgment against both myself and all who have sinned against me. A heart properly positioned in faith developed with time and practice and brought about the closing of the doors of my spirit, my soul, and my body against the temptations and the spiritual invasions to my spirit, my soul, and my body.

I came to the end of myself. I knew I had to obey because I reached a crisis point with the continual chastisements from the Lord. The pain of keeping the addiction becomes greater than the pain of leaving it. You come to a place where you no longer want to displease the Lord and you seek His approval, not the approval of man or of women. You no longer want to come under the chastisements and warnings from God, and the consequences of sin. You place your own standard against disobedience. And you win in Christ Jesus!

The weapons we fight with are not the weapons of the world. On the contrary, they have divine power to demolish strongholds. We demolish arguments and every pretension that sets itself up against the knowledge of God, and we take captive every thought to make it obedient to Christ. And we will be ready to punish every act of disobedience, once your obedience is complete. (2nd Cor. 10:4-6)

It is in the daily exercise of my heart of faith, with prayers and petitions to my Father for myself and for others in the name of Jesus Christ; it is in meditating upon the Word of God and in confessing and believing the Word of God over my life; and it is in taking my delegated authority in Christ Jesus with a heart of faith, rebuking the flesh, the ungodly thoughts and emotions, the fantasies, and any demonic spirits, declaring the Word of God in the name of Jesus Christ that the Lord continues to heal me from the inside out, blessing me with His grace (unmerited favor, loving kindness, and power). With a clear conscience, I gratefully enter into the priceless rest of God. (Ephesians 2:8) (Hebrews 4:9) **There remains, then, a Sabbath-rest for the people of God; for anyone who enters God's rest also rests from his own work, just as God did from His. (Hebrews 4:9)**

I chose to receive my healing from the obsessive and compulsive behavior patterns as I humbly chose to receive Jesus' forgiveness, His acceptance, His total love, and His righteousness. I sought accountability with other Christians to help me to change ungodly behavior patterns and habits learned since childhood. "Therefore confess your sins to each other and pray for each other so that you may be healed. The prayer of a righteous man (woman) is powerful and effective." (James 5:16)

I decidedly chose to live and to renounce inferiority and self-condemnation, and especially in the face of others who rejected me, knowing that Jesus loves me unconditionally, knowing that Jesus was condemned even to His death for me, knowing that my life is valuable to God, and that I was born with a purpose to be used by Him. I chose to receive His righteousness and renounced despair, because I know I needed to step into my divine destiny. I chose to accept that I would be persecuted but that God's love and divine protection would get me through every trial. Thus, I will live with the purpose that God has intended for me. **I will not die but live, and will proclaim what the Lord has done. The Lord has chastised me severely, but He has not given me over to death. Open for me the gates of righteousness; I will enter and give thanks to the Lord. This is the gate of the Lord through which the righteous may enter. I will give You thanks, for You answered me; You have become my salvation. (Psalms 118:17-21)**

I will bless others as I choose to receive the blessings from God for my life. And in choosing to obey Him and to walk away from this sin and all its contacts and agendas, I am no longer moved by the homosexual lure. I still seek His help with the perfectionist spiral. And fear is miraculously becoming transformed to a growing faith. I find the rest of God as His child with a pure heart totally in love with Him. The fear of man has lost its deceptive lure. I choose freedom and dare to be me.

When we stand transparent before our God, with all our pain and rebellion, then the miraculous occurs. The anointing of God, His grace and His loving kindness, blesses us with a new nature, as a pure child of God, changed, made whole and brand new, with the oil of gladness deep within our beings and the salve of thanksgiving forever within our hearts for what He has delivered to us. The pain of tragedy no longer controls our lives. We remember, but the pain of it is no longer there. On the contrary, and against all odds, we come out of it healed and ready to live victoriously. We will be used for the Kingdom to share what Jesus has done in us, to then share with and bless others with the healing power of Jesus Christ, and with the transforming power of the Word of God as we touch and speak to others.

Speak to the Pain in Jesus' Name – Declare Your Restoration in Jesus' Name

Prepare Your Heart - "Jesus, I humble myself to You. I believe You died for me and rose victoriously on the third day. I repent of all sin and ask You to come into my heart and to be the Lord, Savior, and loving authority of my life. Fill me with Your Holy Spirit. I commit to forgive and release all judgment against myself and all who have sinned against me. I receive Your forgiveness. Thank You, Lord Jesus, for Your sacrifice for me."

Enter into Your Father's Presence - "Father God, I come to You and enter into Your presence with thanksgiving in my heart with my petitions, in Jesus' name."(Psalm 100:4) (John 16:23)

Speak to the Pain and Walk into Your Divine Calling in the Name of Jesus Christ – "In the name of Jesus Christ, I speak to every hurt, every trauma, every rejection, and all the pain within my heart. (Mark 11:23-25) I declare that you no longer rule or reign in my spirit, my soul, or in my body in Jesus' name.(Luke 10:19) I declare that I have the mind of Christ in Jesus' name. (1st Cor 2:16)(Ephesians 6:20) I declare that my heart is now made whole in Jesus' name. (Luke 4:18)(Isaiah 53:3-5) I repent of, renounce, and rebuke my defiance and rebellion: all my sins, idols, ungodly habits, mindsets, thought and behavior patterns in Jesus' name. (1st John 1:9)(Luke 10:19)(Matthew 18:18) I replace all negative thoughts with the Word of God and praise and worship. (Pro.4:20-22)(Romans 12:2)(Psalm 33:1-3)(John 4:24) I now gratefully receive full cleansing and forgiveness for my acts of rebellion against You, Lord Jesus, through Your shed blood. (1st John 1:9)(1st Peter 1:18,19)(Hebrews 9:14)(Hebrews 10:19-22) I place all torment, condemnation, and pain at the foot of the cross. (Romans 8:1) (1st Peter 5:7)(Isaiah 53:3-5) I believe that You removed these torments from me at the cross! (Hebrews 11:1)(Isaiah 53:3-5)(Luke 4:18) Spirits of torment and condemnation, go, in the name of Jesus.(Luke 10:19) Go wherever Jesus sends you to be held captive by the angels of God. (Mark 5:8-13) Lord Jesus, You were buried and resurrected from the dead for me.(Luke 23:46)(Luke 24:7) (Luke 23:55) (Phil.3:10)(Matthew 28:6) It was finished at the cross! (Matthew 27:51)(Mark 15:38)(Luke 23:45) I commit to daily study of the Word of God and prayer with praise and worship to keep my vessel filled with God. (Luke 11:24-26)(Romans 12:2)(James 5:16)(Psalm 33:1-3)(John 4:24) Thank You, Holy Spirit. You guide me into all truth and are my Comforter. (John 16:13)You live in me and You are with me.(John 15:5)You are my Counselor.(John 14:15-17) (See Appendix)

"I will rise above my emotions to a life committed to walking in love by faith, especially for my enemies. (Luke 6:28,37)(Matthew 6:12)(Gal. 5:6)(Hebrews 11:1) I will step into the life of faith, knowing that the Lord's eyes are upon me to do His perfect will.(1ˢᵗ Thes. 5:18)(1ˢᵗ Chron. 16:9)(Romans 1:16,17) It is the Lord's good pleasure that I seek.(Luke 12:32) I know there is a reason I went through all this. (Ecc. 3:1) In compassion for those who do not yet know about the freedom we have in a relationship with Jesus Christ, (Luke 10:33), I will fulfill my divine calling and purpose in Christ Jesus. (John 8:32) (Matthew 28:18)(Mark 16:15)(Hosea 4:6) I will tell others of the freedom and authority we do have against any generational curse and/or demonic, ancestral, or familiar spirits and/or demonic assignments, and against any abuse, walking in daily repentance and forgiveness in a committed, submitted, intimate, and personal relationship with Jesus Christ.(Luke 10:19)(Galatians 3:13)(Hebrews 10:19-22)(1ˢᵗ Peter 1:18,19)(Romans 10:9,10)(Romans 10:13) (John 15:5)(John 14:16-18)(Joel 2:25)(James 4:7,8)(Matthew 28:18) I declare that I am the redeemed of the Lord, in Jesus' precious name.(Gal. 3:13) I declare that I am restored to wholeness and to the joy of the Lord, which is my strength, in Jesus' name.(Nehemiah 8:10) I am more than a conqueror in Christ Jesus. (Romans 8:37-39) Nothing shall be able to separate me from the love of God that is in Christ Jesus my Lord. (Romans 8:37-39) Nothing can breech the intimacy that I have with Him, in Jesus' name, Amen."(John 10:27)(1ˢᵗ John 4:4) All scriptures ref./per.)(See Appendix)

Continue to Pray for Restoration – Receive the Restoration of the Lord

We work at the healing of our hearts as we daily submit to Jesus as Lord and authority. We daily repent of sin and spend quality time with Jesus to deepen our surrender to Him. We speak forgiveness and release of all judgment upon ourselves and toward primary relationships as mother and father, husband or wife, sons and daughters, grandparents, step parents and the like, uncles and aunts, cousins, in-laws, sisters and brothers, nieces and nephews, children, friends and enemies, teachers, mentors, pastors, counselors, and all abusers. We expect and believe the Lord hears us when we pray. As we pray, the power and presence of God comes in to personally restore what has been broken. (Acts 2:8) (Matthew 6:12) (Luke 6:37) (Hebrews 4:9) (Hebrews 4:12) (Luke 4:18) (Isaiah 53:3-5) (Mark 11:22-26)

As we humble ourselves to the Lord, working through the difficult memories, Jesus will refresh our memories. He will bring good memories to us that we have blocked, of the good things we have experienced with the very people who have hurt us. He will bring us dreams and visions to restore what the enemy has stolen. He will restore a normal flow to our thoughts. He is a good God. (Joel 2:25) It is an abundant life that we live. (John 10:10) Even if you have been involved with drug or alcohol addiction, He provided your physical healing at the cross, including the brain and all its neurons. He heals all the cells in the body as we reach out by faith and speak our healing into existence.

It is the Holy Spirit within us Who empowers us to forgive and to release judgment from the heart and with an act of our will by faith. And it is the knowledge that Satan is working through other people that helps us to objectify the hurts. We rise above the hurts and forgive and release ourselves and others through acts of faith and with the help of the Holy Spirit. This is revelation knowledge from the Word of God. (Ephesians 6:12) To truly forgive, it takes a surrendered heart to step out and rise above the hurts to then receive the love, acceptance, and forgiveness of God, along with His righteousness (right relationship with God). (Acts 1:8) (Acts 2:38) (Ephesians 6:12)(Romans 1:16,17)

(All scriptures referenced)

Ironically, it was a deep love for my father, my mother, and my family, that went deeper than the hurt that brought me the victory of love by faith. I knew and believed that Satan was working through them and on the bloodline. And they suffered because of a lack of knowledge. I decided to release all the hurt, all the pain, and all the injustice and win not just for myself, but for them also, becoming both an intercessor for them after our separation and sharing the Word of God with them in the time that we did share together. (Galatians 5:6) And, in that release of judgment, I was able to glean from their strengths and apply them to my own life. It was a win-win situation. **For if you forgive men when they sin against you, your heavenly Father will also forgive you. (Matthew 6:14)**

(See Appendix)

Receive Your Freedom – Parental Respect and Thanksgiving for Their Sacrifices – Cutting Free

After the forgiveness process with my family, especially Mom and Dad, was completed, the "honest self" began to emerge from its cocoon. No one knew me better than Mom and Dad. Some of their words hurt, but I had to take an honest examination of them. Truth does hurt. With release of the hurt and judgment against others, I was able to look more honestly at my own weaknesses and sins against my Father. It was obedience to leave my own idols and sins to the best of my ability that completed the emergence of the "honest self." In spite of myself, the Lord still loved, forgave, and accepted me. The key was keeping my heart honest and repentant before Jesus.

Our liberty was purchased two thousand years ago because of Jesus' sacrifice for us. We work out our salvation in a day to day process until we see Him face to face. It is our heart He wants, not perfection. When we get a revelation of how much He loves us, it brings us to a deep thanksgiving for His grace and love, in spite of our humanity. Receive His love and grace today.

Remember, people change with time. Usually people mellow with age. Mom was a great help to me as I continued in this grueling process. She continued to love me unconditionally. She would cook for the family and shop with us kids to make sure we were ready for every school year. She sacrificed her life and cooked incredible five course meals for the family for the holidays. She was always there for us. And Dad as well always showed his love. He supported the entire family working very hard as a professional dentist. He taught me to be a dental assistant when I was sixteen. My sister, my cousin, and I were all his assistants. He provided all five children with new cars at graduation from high school, excellent education in private and Christian colleges for some of us, and great vacations to the summer resorts, with luxurious dining and wardrobes. His generosity was beyond words. He would stay home to work for us while we enjoyed our vacations, and would join us on the weekends in order to pay the high cost of the hotels and cottages on the seashore. Dad was the spiritual leader of the family and he drove the family to church services every Sunday. Both of my parents came out of the depression, yet they exemplified giving to their children to the max!

The deep healing comes when we truly appreciate the sacrifices our parents made for us and see clearly how the enemy perverted the love and brought addictive behaviors, and physical, emotional, and/or mental illnesses into our family bloodline. He creeps in so subtly and, if there is a lack of knowledge of a true intimate relationship with Jesus Christ with the benefits of that relationship, people suffer. (Hosea 4:6) My family members didn't know how to fight the good fight of faith. (1ˢᵗ Tim. 6:12) (Deuteronomy 5:9,10)

However, both Mom and Dad were uninformed that Jesus wanted to come into their hearts and have a personal and intimate relationship with them. They also were ignorant to the generational curse of Satan on the bloodline and to the power of speaking and living the Word of God with faith over their lives and their souls. They were uninformed of their delegated authority in Christ Jesus to take their rights as Christian believers, to take their liberty from the curse, and to be free from Satan's control upon their lives and their souls and upon their children's lives and souls.

You shall not bow down to them or worship them (idols in any form); for I, the Lord thy God, am a jealous God, punishing the children for the sin of the fathers to the third and fourth generation of those who hate me, but showing love to a thousand generations of those who love me and keep my commandments. (Deuteronomy 5:9,10) and (Exodus 20:5,6) I had the opportunity to receive healing because I was called away from the "traditions" of my parents. I obeyed the call. I came to know Jesus personally and I learned about His benefits of redemption. Our lives given to serve Jesus will touch many others for Christ. (2nd Peter 1:4)

I believe that God honored me with three beautiful years of reconciliation with Mom and I praise Him for that precious time in my life. It was very difficult and it was a time of growth. I remembered a lot that I had "stuffed." I thank God that some memories still have been kept from me.

After that season of reconciliation ended, I still had another hurdle. I had to let go of Mom and grow into the mature young woman I am. Elijah House speaks of this as the "cutting free" stage of deliverance. [49] It was the shedding of the little girl part of my personality. After completing this step, I emerged as a mature young woman.

It's Humbling to Receive – God's Gift of Grace – Stop and Receive His Anointing

For it is by grace you have been saved, through faith - and it is the gift of God - not by works, so that no one can boast. (Ephesians 2:8, 9) To receive any gift requires a humble and a grateful heart. It was so hard for me to receive the full healing. I guess I didn't feel worthy. No one is worthy, no, not one. We are all sinners saved by the grace of God. (Romans 3:10,23 ref.) This was very frustrating as I saw so many people being set free and accepting the "grace" and therefore, the "rest" of God. I continued to live by the law. His grace releases us from the doing mode. All of my efforts to take His grace by works were to no avail. I had to decidedly stop and receive from God. None of us are worthy of God's love and grace. This is a gift we must humbly accept by our faith in order to be free in life. **All of us have become like one who is unclean, and all our righteous acts are like filthy rags. (Isaiah 64:6)**

As I continued to go through the healing process, wonderful revelations occurred. The presence of the Lord fell upon me in a deeper way. This is the anointing of God, His very presence. Sometimes it can be felt. Visions can be very real. The anointing holds within it the power of God to "keep us steady" through all adversity. I actually saw a shadow of Christ standing in front of me at a church service. I did not see His face, but I saw His hair and one of His scarred hands. He walked into me and spoke, "I will now be your hands. I will be your eyes." What an awesome vision and revelation of the love and of the presence of Christ within me! This was revelation knowledge for me personally that He came to the earth as both man and as God. He knows our every trial and human affliction.

Jesus tells us that He will remain in us as we remain in Him. (John 15:4) The scripture also tells us that whoever acknowledges that Jesus is the Son of God that God lives in him, and he in God. And that he who lives in love lives in God and God in him, because God is love. And we know and we rely on the love God has for us. (1st John 4:15,16) **To them God has chosen to make known among the Gentiles the glorious riches of this mystery, which is Christ in you, the hope of glory. (Colossians 1:27)**

The adrenalin rush of always having to do something or go somewhere lifts as we fall deeper in love with Jesus. Rev. Benny Hinn states in his book, The Anointing:

My purpose in The Anointing is to further that beautiful, ongoing relationship and lead you into the reality of the power to serve the Lord Jesus in His particular calling on your life. The power is the anointing of the Holy Spirit as promised by Jesus after His resurrection: "Ye shall receive power, after that the Holy Ghost is come upon you; and ye shall be witnesses unto me." [50]

Isaiah further explains the anointing: **The Spirit of the Sovereign Lord is on me, because the Lord has anointed me to preach good news to the poor. He has sent me to bind up the brokenhearted, to proclaim freedom for the captives and release from darkness for the prisoners, to proclaim the year of the Lord's favor. (Isaiah 61:1-2a)**

The goal to bring spirit and soul into agreement is assisted by this anointing or the presence of God. The spirit-man is perfect, and is created in the image and likeness of God, but the spirit and soul must be in agreement before the body can respond. [51]

It's Humbling to Ask for Help – Receive Christian Counsel

I sought Christian counseling throughout the years. I was blessed with many counselors, support groups, and friends who mentored me. In 2004, when I went through counseling with Dee Verhagen, a Holy Spirit-filled woman of God, I made leaps in the victory.

Dee has been trained as a prayer minister through the Elijah House Ministry. It was in these sessions that I was escorted into the very presence of the Lord. I experienced His love, His acceptance, and His forgiveness. I honestly faced, admitted, and repented of my own ungodly reactions to the childhood traumas, my sinful behavior and habit patterns, and my negative mindsets, including any vows I had made as a child and as a teenager. Expression of feelings that I had "stuffed" for years also helped to set me free as Dee listened carefully and replied with godly answers. Roots of sin were finally uncovered and dealt with. Prayers of agreement, of repentance, and of forgiveness, and releasing judgment against me and others, were spoken. Having a Spirit filled counselor present brought accountability with loving confrontation. Dee was able to see and perceive things by the Holy Spirit that I could not see or perceive for myself. I thank God for her and for the many issues that were settled. What was imparted to me there at Calvary Temple, Wayne, New Jersey, I then was able to impart to others as I was granted a ministry position there. I thank God for the love of God that was shared to me through this anointed woman of God.

I strongly encourage wise counsel from Spirit-filled counselors when making decisions concerning family ties. Severance or separations, even temporary separations from family, are critical decisions and must be made with wisdom and with the guidance of Holy Spirit-filled counselors. The Lord may tell you to sever and it may also line up with one or more scriptures in the Word of God. But you need accountability and confirmation from Spirit filled counselor(s) to help you to rightly divide the Word of God in your particular situation.

Counseling will help you to stand firm in both making and keeping difficult decisions. It will provide you with accountability and support from those who care about you and your growth and maturity in Jesus Christ. You need counsel from those who are not emotionally involved in your situation, who will form a godly perspective on your particular circumstances, who have experience in pastoral care, and who will pray for direction from the Holy Spirit on your behalf.

Dee is a happily married woman who has three children. There was a clear boundary already drawn in the sand in this godly exchange which literally changed my life and my thinking. I was comfortable with Dee from the very onset of our relationship for two reasons. She walked in the love and the wisdom of God and she really cared for me as a person. She respected me even after I shared my testimony with her. When I related to her, I sensed no judgment, only love and respect. She actually saw God's hand upon my life and, in sharing this with me, I was deeply encouraged. She helped me to set up a ministry for the struggling homosexual with my friend Peter Psillas. We had her and her husband's support. I also had the support of the head pastor, Pastor Dr. Thomas Keinath, and his wife, Kim Keinath, and all the supporting pastors there. Pastor Rema Spencer headed up the support groups and followed us closely. We reported to him on a regular basis both privately and in group meetings.

I believe the Lord honored my heart to heal from this insidious lie from Satan. I was granted a leadership position to help others, twenty years after I had left the lifestyle and made Jesus Lord of my life. This was in 2001. I continued to heal as I gave into the ministry. I believe the Lord granted me this position also out of my obedience to leave the ungodly soul ties many years before this. This step was the most difficult step, but it was imperative to my healing. (See Chapter on breaking ungodly soulties, <u>Death Cannot Hold Me</u>)

Receive Self-Respect and Integrity

In counseling, I was able to come out of deep introspection and actually talk to another human being who listened to me, comforted me, and also helped me confront the root issues. What a relief after years of isolation with this problem! I faced the lies that deceived me for years.

My focus started to return to the place of rest in Jesus. He told me how much He loved me. He told me that I was His special child. And He, not man, restored my identity. As I faced the deep pain behind my addictions, repenting of ungodly reactions, idols, sinful behavior patterns, and negative mindsets, the "honest self" began to emerge out of hiding. As I humbled myself in counseling sessions, I began to receive from God.

But you, O Israel, my servant, Jacob, whom I have chosen, you descendants of Abraham my friend, I took you from the ends of the earth; from its farthest corners I called you. I said, 'You are my servant'; I have chosen you and have not rejected you. So do not fear, for I am with you; do not be dismayed, for I am your God. I will strengthen you and help you; I will uphold you with my righteous right hand. (Isaiah 41:8-10)

These are the words of Jesus,**"Come to me, all you who are weary and burdened, and I will give you rest. Take my yoke upon you and learn from me, for I am gentle and humble in heart, and you will find rest for your souls. For my yoke is easy and my burden is light." (Matthew 11:28-30)**

Self-respect and integrity are very important. They are the lifelines of a person's self-confidence. The key to human dignity comes simply from honesty with self, with others, and with God and obedience to lock the door on sin, leave it and all its temptations and attachments. We cannot hide anything from God. One's true dignity I believe is formed when we submit to our accountability to the living God and refuse to behave in any way that is displeasing to God; in words, thoughts, and actions, especially when there is no one but God watching us...

We must see ourselves as imperfect people who are forgiven by our Maker. Our identity comes from Christ and Christ alone. We must receive His approval. It is our confidence. We do not need the approval from others. Spending time with Jesus in prayer brings us the righteousness of God because He blesses us when we draw near to Him in our right relationship with Him. (James 4:8)(Matthew 23:12) Because of His great love for us, we are saved by His grace and forgiven by His mercy. His love for us is divine.

Humble Yourself
Humble thyself in the sight of the Lord. And He will lift you up. (James 4:10)

I was led into such a conscious communion with My Father that I overcame the fear of man and the need to please. I stepped out of the mindless state of existence into a place of comfort in my own skin because I knew He was with me. True humility is a precious thing. When we are truly bowing before God with reverence and thanksgiving, fear and all its cohorts as worry, anxiety, panic, and terror have to take their rightful places and bow to the Father. The fear of man must leave because we know who we are in Christ; blessed, forgiven, and completely loved and accepted.

No one could have told me that I was wrong when I was immersed in this sinful lifestyle. The deception of "being in love" coupled with a desperation to be loved and, later, the shame and self-hatred I lived with because of the sexual sin, blinded me from the true liberty in Christ Jesus. All was a cover up for the "honest self" who was hiding deep within a broken heart.

But God came and spoke to me through His Word, through apostles, pastors, teachers, counselors, godly leaders, friends and family, and through the children! He spoke also through revelation knowledge, through visions and dreams, through miraculous impartations, and through fellowship with other believers. The Holy Spirit spoke to my innermost being in a still small voice. And I know there were people praying for me. Faith replaced my fears and anxieties one day at a time and my loneliness and despair was replaced with the awesome and sometimes even with the felt presence of the Holy Spirit within and upon me.

Receive God's Forgiveness, Acceptance, and Love – From Rebellion to Reverence

In coming out of the sin of homosexuality, as in any other sin, we are commanded to revere God. As my vertical relationship grew with Jesus, my horizontal relationships within the body of Christ also grew with healthier boundaries. I was able to blend in with others, feeling the safety and being a part of a community of Christian believers. I received my sins as forgiven and stopped measuring my sins against others because I now esteemed the love and the mercy I was receiving from God more highly than the acceptance from people.

I believed from the Word of God that God does not measure sin. God never discriminates about any sin. He merely forgives us of all of our sins when we confess and repent. **If we confess our sins, He is faithful and just and will forgive us our sins and purify us from all unrighteousness. (1ˢᵗ John 1:9)**

In receiving God's love, I began to love myself again. Repenting of my critical attitude toward others, God helped me to respect others. As I grew to respect myself, I esteemed others as well. I taught myself to see the strengths in others instead of the weaknesses. I learned from others yet I maintained my own self-respect amidst the lessons learned. I began to obey God's voice and speak only life. I was more careful with my words, no matter how I felt.

Do nothing out of selfish ambition or vain conceit, but in humility consider others better than you. Each of you should look not only to your own interests, but also to the interests of others. (Philippians 2:3,40)

Who's Running This Show Anyhow? The Roots of Addiction

When I was a child, I talked like a child; I thought like a child, I reasoned like a child. When I became a man (woman), I put childish ways behind me. (1st Corinthians 13: 11)

As children, we are under the care of our parents. Isn't it interesting that before the words "Mommy" and "Daddy" are spoken, the word "No" takes the lead for many toddlers? The child's need for control is demonstrated even at this early stage. Some psychologists label these children as "strong-willed children."

What is the root of this need for control? Some experts say it is genetically rooted while others argue that it is a behavioral or a learned response. What does God say? **He who spares the rod hates his son, but he who loves him is careful to discipline him. (Proverbs 13:24)**

Because the child has not been appropriately disciplined, he or she acts out of impulse. An impulse is an uncontrolled urge that is either spoken or acted out. It is the motion or effect produced by a sudden action or applied force. **[52]** It comes directly from the child's flesh. It is through the use of clear directives and the setting of limitations from a caring parent that these impulses are brought under control.

Proper parenting sets up the foundation for the child's later years. As the child grows to maturity, early disciplinary procedures will first influence adolescent decisions and later, adult decisions. A disciplined child will grow up with self-discipline as an adult. A child who was raised without proper discipline will have difficulty with impulse control in later years.

Moses shared with the Israelite people these words of the Lord on Mt. Horeb:

I am the Lord your God, who brought you out of Egypt and out of slavery. You shall have no other Gods before me. (Deuteronomy 3:7)

Daniel Webster defines the word "addict" as meaning "to devote or surrender (oneself) to something habitually or obsessively." **[53]** To "obsess" means to "be excessively preoccupied by the mind."**[54]** One who struggles with addictions is a person devoted excessively with a mental preoccupation to some person, place, or thing. Because the devotion is excessive, it is repeated over and over again.

This is the insanity of addiction. There is never any peace of mind if there is a constant preoccupation with a thought. Preoccupation of thought ultimately leads to a compulsive action or a "compulsion." A "compulsion" is "an irresistible urge to do something irrational." **[55]** "Compelling" by its very nature is "forceful." **[56]**

There is a cycle to every addiction. The thought is followed by the act. A resultant feeling of remorse instigates another thought which starts the cycle over again. Remorse is directly related to shame. The roots of this must be identified and faced.

There is no victory over any addiction until the addict accepts his/her sin as sin, coming out of denial, and gives his/her control over to Jesus Christ as Lord and authority. I am very grateful to the Lord Jesus Christ for His sacrifice that allows for an actual personal relationship with Him. This relationship gives me His love and presence living on the inside of my heart. I am equipped with the Word of God, my greatest weapon against the fleshly habits, the negative thoughts and emotions, and the painful memories. I am grateful for my relationship with Jesus. He lives within my heart to help me to attack any problem. The Holy Spirit leads me through every obsessive and compulsive thought with strategies and diectives with His still small voice.

God has poured out His love into our hearts by the Holy Spirit, whom He has given us. (Romans 5:5) We must learn to tune into the Holy Spirit, to His voice within our innermost beings, speaking and directing our steps. We must have conversation with Him. He will give us divine strategy and even the wisdom of God through whatever the difficulty is. No fiery dart of the enemy can break through the breastplate of righteousness (Romans 10:17) that I wear because I am in right standing with Jesus. No thought pattern can break through this personal and intimate relationship that I have with the living God. (Romans 10:9,10) No obsessive thinking the enemy tries to bring to me is able to penetrate Jesus' love, acceptance, and forgiveness working on the inside of my heart or the small still voice of the Holy Spirit. (Romans 5:5)

Speaking and Meditating Upon the Word of God Breaks the Obsessive Thoughts

Therefore, in this proper position of a heart of faith, surrendered to the Lordship of Jesus Christ, with repentance and forgiveness in my heart, I confess the Word of God. Now I take the offensive and I meditate on and speak the powerful and the living Word of God in the face of the fleshly temptations, the negative thoughts and emotions, habits, memories, and any negative distractions of the enemy. My Lord's presence is deeper than the distractions. His Word is a double edged sword against the evil one. I stand in the most powerful position, the place of faith, with my heart developing each day in deeper surrender to Jesus Christ, my Lord, my Savior, and my loving Authority. (Phil 2:9) (Romans 10:9,10) (Romans 10:13) (Acts 2:38) (Acts 1:8) (John 15:5) (John 15:26) (John 14:14-18) (Luke 10:19) (Luke 6:37-38) (Luke 11:10) (Mark 11:22-26) (Matthew 6:12) (1st John 1:9) (Hebrews 4:12) (Hebrews 11:1) (Revelation 12:11)(1st John 4:15,16)(Hebrews 9:14) (1st Peter 1:18,19) (1st John 5:4) (All scripture references)

One More

This is the blatant lie of all addiction. It can be expressed in three words, "Just one more." This is referring to the cycle of addiction that will continue to deceive our minds until we say "no" to it. It is the lie of one more. 'If I just take care of this one thing, if I just take one more look, one more bite, one more program or video, one more encounter with this person, one more hit, one more cigarette, and then I will stop; one more, one more….. And the cycle will never end until we take responsibility to end it. Jesus and our life and purpose in Him must become more important than whatever our "one more" is. We must be so exhausted from the corrections from the Lord. With His corrections, the pain of leaving the addiction is no longer greater than staying in it. We must say, "No more." And do whatever it takes to call it quits.

With perfectionism still an addiction in my life, I was not successfully fighting the good fight of faith. I was getting discouraged and distracted by depression, and there were demons I believe that were visiting me in the middle of the night. When I asked God to stop them, He told me to humble myself to Him and repent of sin and to get rid of all the papers, reports, and all impure motives. All illegal open doors had to close and lock. No cheating is allowed. We can hide nothing from Jesus! Perfectionism is a form of pride and a cover up for the deep hurt. **It is written: "I believed; therefore I have spoken." With the same spirit of faith we also believe and therefore speak, because we know that the one who raised the Lord Jesus from the dead will also raise us with Jesus and present us with you in His presence. (2nd Corinthians 4:13)**

We Have to Choose to Take Jesus' Delegated Authority
and Take Back Control over Our Lives

Addiction has its very roots in poor impulse control. There are various viewpoints as to the origins of these impulses. Some say the cause of addiction is generational, implying that some people are genetically prone to addiction. Some say addiction is caused by poor behavioral control, implying improper parental discipline. Needless to say, whatever the roots, there cannot be any blame here.

As born again believers, we are empowered by the Holy Spirit to take control over all addiction, which includes any generational or demonic spirits. And we have been given free will to choose obedience and self-control, no matter how our parents disciplined us. Self control is also a fruit of the Holy Spirit, Who helps us to say "no" to whatever the addiction is because we have heard from Him and His word settles the matter. By acts of faith and of will, we take back control of our lives. (Galatians 5:22,23) And we have the privilege and the benefit delegated to us by Jesus Christ to take His authority here in the earth over all that is not of God. (Luke 10:19) (Mark 16:15) (Mark 11:23-25)

I believe that when we take one step in God's direction to obey and to control the flesh, the Holy Spirit then steps in and further empowers us with an inner strength to continue in that obedience. Because we have obeyed Him, He is pleased with us. His Word tells us to repent and then we will be baptized and receive the gift of the Holy Spirit (Acts 2:38) Repentance is not just saying, "I am sorry." There is action in faith that we choose as we obey God and turn from addiction, sin, and its temptations. We turn from sin and decidedly change and do something else. Then our repentance is complete and thus honored by the Lord. As we do the heart work and forgive and release judgment against both self and others, we enter into a place of peace with God. Then, with a clear conscience, we are further empowered to rise above the addictions and to obey God and to stop and redirect the energy. Jesus then graciously rewards us with His grace. And we enter into the divine rest of God.

His love and assistance is the victory! Let Him know you believe in Him. Ask Him to help you.

If you do away with the yoke of oppression, with the pointing finger and malicious talk, and if you spend yourselves in behalf of the hungry and satisfy the needs of the oppressed, then your light will rise in the darkness, and your night will become like the noonday. (Isaiah 58:9,10)

The Word of God, however, clearly teaches us: **We do not wrestle against flesh and blood but with principalities and powers in high places. (Ephesians 6:12)** When I was enmeshed in the snares of addiction, it was as if there was a force beyond me that was in control of me, trying to force me to continue in the insanity of it. We allow demonic spirits to have power over us when we are living in the flesh. By flesh I do not just refer to sexual sin. It could be any number of carnal presentations to our flesh; selfishness, greed, pornography, lust, envy, pride, grief, gluttony, vanity, greed, and indulging in any pleasure without the correct balance.

Our spiritual and emotional wounds keep us vulnerable to sin, and sin opens the door for the enemy's entrance to our bodies, souls, and spirits. Dealing with the root issues of childhood was the starting point to locking the doors on both my vulnerability and on my sins. Why was I still living in the flesh? I had to practice self-control to discipline and control fleshly impulses, and to strengthen my will against the attacks of the enemy. As I continued to live in the carnal world with the worries of work, I was still hiding from the root pain and traumas of childhood with the sin of perfectionism. Going over the details compulsively was a mental masturbation. It actually was a replaying of the tapes of the hurts, fears, pains, and traumas from childhood.

I had to ask the Holy Spirit to help me to take control of my will by saying "no" to the temptations. Even though I had left the homosexual lifestyle, I was still living carnally with perfectionism. One addiction will beget another until the roots are removed and new seeds are planted in fertile soil.

I thank God for the power of the Holy Spirit to both convict and to intervene in the disciplining of my will. These wounds would take time to heal. I had to humble myself and ask for the help of the Holy Spirit to strengthen my will. As I yielded to the Holy Spirit, my willfulness transformed to a willingness to follow the Lord's lead. My will then was strengthened. When I called upon the Holy Spirit, He showed up. The power of the Holy Spirit is a divine force of the Person of the Holy Spirit which ignites my will to resist these urges and to subdue the enemy's temptations.

Breaking addiction requires two actions, an act of faith and an act of the will. I believe addiction is stopped by bringing the preoccupations of the mind to the cross of Jesus Christ, in a decided and willful act of surrender to God. I had to believe and obey the voice of the Holy Spirit when He told me to leave the homosexual lovers. I had to believe and obey Him when He said the work was finished and not to worry. With obedience, my inner life with Jesus became bigger than my fleshly and carnal life. The Lord actually brought clarity to my mind and I received a "check" in my spirit that the work was completed.

And it also takes an act of the will to "subdue" it. I remember saying, "Thy will be done" when I placed the farewell letter in the mail to the last female lover. Webster defines "subdue" as "to bring under control especially by an exertion of the will."[57] I will never forget receiving the words of Pastor Dr. Thomas Keinath while at the altar of Calvary Temple in Wayne, New Jersey. He said, "Subdue it with an act of your will." [58] I was convicted. We must take an active part in our healing. God will meet us as we obey Him.

I will give them an undivided heart and put a new spirit in them; I will remove from them

their heart of stone and give them a heart of flesh. Then they will follow my decrees and be careful to keep my laws. They will be my people and I will be their God. (Ezekiel 11:19–20)

Addiction is Fantasy

All addiction is a distraction from reality and it is sin. The addict is always caught in some lying fantasy that not only separates him/her from God, but also blocks the "honest self" from hearing His voice. The addict lives in a fantasy world and, in it, the false self is stealing life away from the honest self.

All addiction is based on lies that block the heart from experiencing the love, communication, and relationship with both God and man. The addiction to sexual pleasure keeps the person distracted in the sense realm of "It feels good." The addictions to food, alcohol, or drugs also keep the person distracted in the same lie. The addiction to self distracts the person to his/her own reflection, rather than looking to God and others for friendships. The addiction to perfection keeps the person distracted to the details of the job or of the environment. Performance orientation locks the person into doing for others' acceptance. The addiction to gambling keeps the person focused on winning money, which keeps the mind distracted to owning things. The addiction to alcohol distracts the person from reality itself. The addiction to cleaning distracts the mind to a false sense of responsibility for all the germs, a mental delusion of sorts. The cleaning addict believes that by continual cleaning, she or he will protect oneself or others from disease. There must be a balance in this as cleanliness is important in disease prevention. Whatever the distraction is, this becomes the idol because it is the focus instead of an intimate relationship with Jesus Christ.

When I plunged into praise and worship, into the study of the Word of God, and bonding with other Christians, new ways of living were being established. I plunged into my relationship with Jesus as my Lord and as my friend. Thus, the fantasy world of addiction was replaced with the reality of a living God Who walked and talked with me. Mental fantasies were replaced with the still small voice of the Holy Spirit.

All addiction is motivated and controlled by a spirit of fear. The Word of God clearly tells us, **For God hath not given us the spirit of fear; but of power, and of love, and of a sound mind. (2nd Timothy 1:7)** All addicts operate from the physical realm of what is felt, seen, heard, or desired. The antidote is living in the spiritual reality of what is felt and seen by faith, what is heard with the spiritual ears, eyes, and heart, and what is the simply the desire to please God. When we live the spiritual life, the real presence of God with us and in us becomes a walking and a talking reality. Only when we begin to walk by faith will the truth be made available and freedom from bondage experienced. **The righteous will live by faith. (Romans 1:17)**

In the co-dependent addictive relationship, both parties are distracted from the truth of God because their focus of attention is on one another and not on God. This addiction says, "If I can get my needs met through this person, I do not need God. I can therefore control my own state of well-being through this relationship." In this, there is an actual release of control over my own life in allowing another person to take the place of God. **One can only find out how to become an individual person when free of dependency on another. [59]**

It's a catch-22. The addict needs love yet runs from it because of past rejection, pain, abuse, trauma, or hurts. He or she finds a substitute love in the addiction. For example, the alcoholic actually has a fantasy relationship with the alcohol. In order to fight the lies of addiction that the devil oppresses the hurting person with, that person must find Jesus. Jesus is greater than any fantasy. An intimate and divine covenant relationship with Jesus Christ is the only lasting way out of the insanity of any addiction. Jesus fills the void.

Every addiction runs its course from unreality to the truth of the pain within. The rubber meets the road in all of life's addictions because we live in a real world and we are real people. Addictions can mentally block the pain inside for so long. Sooner or later, and better off sooner, the pain must be faced squarely and dealt with in order to conquer the addiction.

I made a lot of money as a nurse and I helped many, but it became a place of pride as I was independent and making money. The busyness of the job kept me from facing my own needs for healing. I stayed in the place of control because of the addiction to the details; and stayed in the place of independence, not really needing a human soul mate or desiring a life-long relationship. I was too busy for this. I had no time to face my own pain squarely and to deal with my own issues. I was proud to be a nurse and I was too busy helping other people to stop and even realize that I needed to help myself; I had to face my own heart issues. Always having people to take care of kept me in a zone of the "fast lane." Jesus wants us completely dependent upon Him, not codependent on any job, any person, or any amount of money. He must take first place, no matter how good the work is we are doing for Him. There can be no idols before Him. Even your ministry cannot take God's place. He can do it all without us. He must be first. **"'Do not make idols or set up an image or a sacred stone for yourselves, and do not place a carved stone in your land to bow down before it. I am the Lord your God.'" (Leviticus 26:1)**

The word of the Lord came to the King of Tyre,**"'In the pride of your heart you say, "I am god; I sit on the throne of a god in the heart of the seas. But you are a man (woman) and not a god, though you think you are as wise as a god. Are you wiser than Daniel? Is no secret hidden from you?" By your wisdom and understanding you have gained wealth for yourself and amassed gold and silver in your treasuries. By your great skill in trading you have increased you wealth, and because of your wealth your heart has grown proud. '" (Ezekiel 28:2-5)**

Addiction takes our focus away from God to a person, a place, or a thing. Our addictions take the place of God and become our idols. Idolatry is the sin of addiction. Remember, you are the deciding factor in this battlefield. Idols are controllable. You have the ability to decide how much money you will make according to how many hours you are willing to work. You have the ability to decide how many hours a day you will spend cleaning your house or office. And you can decide with your own will whether you will continue to drink, to gamble, to watch pornographic web-sites or movies, or to stay in an ungodly relationship.

God is in Control – Conquer the Fear of Death

Addiction is primarily a problem that is centered on the issue of control. Its core motivational force is the fear of death. A person sold out to Jesus Christ conquers the fear of death and already lives in the presence of God. A believer stands firm in faith knowing that he/she will live eternally with Jesus Christ. A believer chooses to live a life of faith submitted in an intimate relationship with Jesus Christ. The power of the Holy Spirit is abiding within and upon the believer who lives peacefully under the divine love from Father God, because God is love. (1st John 4:15,16)

Or the person chooses to be in control of one's own life and defies the very presence of and the awesome reverence for God. Defiance refuses the opportunity for a walking/talking relationship with Jesus Christ. Defiance turns from the loving control, empowerment, and guidance from the Holy Spirit. And defiance turns its back on Father God and His eternal love. Defiance is deadly. It is an open invitation to the oppression and the control of evil spirits. The primary demonic spirit is the spirit of fear. The heart of the addictive soul says out of need and desperation, "I want" and not "Thy will be done." I want is rooted in selfishness and pride and thrives on obsessive thinking that leads to compulsive acting out. I remember the Lord telling me, "Obsess on my Word!"

No one can victoriously defeat addiction alone. This is spiritual warfare that must be tackled with the divine aid of Our Lord and Savior, Jesus Christ. Whatever the addiction is, it is a stronghold that distracts us from our intimate and personal relationship with Jesus Christ. It is an idol, which takes the place of the living God. I remember walking at Big Sur in California, on a mountaintop overlooking the Pacific Ocean. I asked the Lord, "Do you really love me?" I will never forget His reply. In His gentle voice, He said, "As much as you love children and even more than that do I love you." A revelation of God's love for you will transform you. **Call out to me and I will answer you and tell you great and unsearchable things you do not know. (Jeremiah 33:3)**

Truth vs. Fact

There exists a lot of controversy regarding the roots of addiction from scientific experts today. But what does God say about it? He clearly says that we do not wrestle against flesh and blood but against powers and principalities. (Ephesians 6:12) Also, Satan comes to steal, to kill, and to destroy but Jesus came so that we might have abundant life! (John 10:10) Satan enters through our flesh, our thoughts in negative thinking, through our senses, through our emotions, through our imagination, through fantasies, dreams, and even through delusions. Delusions can lead to hallucinations. These are the counterfeits to the Holy Spirit's revelations, visions, and dreams. Our surrender to Jesus Christ is our greatest defense against the counterfeits from the devil. And Jesus has blessed us with an alert spirit and mind that is wise to anything with which the devil uses to distract. We must be alert and quickly take the negative emotions and thoughts captive to the obedience of Christ. (2nd Cor. 10:4,5)(All scriptures referenced)

Leave the Demons of Babylon – Dr. Consiglio's Research

Angelic and Demonic Visitations

I remember one day while cleaning my bathroom, God allowed me to see into the spiritual realm. I actually saw an ugly being that looked like a large insect hovering over me, laughing at me as I struggled with the fear of germs. I felt like I was swept into the fierce winds of a tornado. It was the driving spirit of fear that was oppressing me. I wanted to stop but I just couldn't without help. However, God showed me in this vision that there was indeed a force other than myself that was tormenting me. Satan wanted me to believe that I had no power or control against it. But I knew and I believed that I had delegated authority in Christ Jesus to petition my Father with my heart of faith (submission, repentance, and forgiveness), and to rebuke this demon spirit and speak the Word of God all in the name of Jesus. (Luke 10:19) (Psalm 91)

First, I took some deep breaths and tried to calm down. I knew that the Lord was with me, even though I was in the frenzy of cleaning. Then I acknowledged my Father's presence and the presence of the angels around me. I bowed my head to the Father God and made my heart stop to acknowledge Him first to break the power of the frenzied emotions. Now ready to petition my Father, I prepared my heart to speak in faith and in the name of Jesus with submission, repentance, and forgiveness. Then I took Jesus' delegated authority and both spoke the Word of God and rebuked the demon spirit in the name of Jesus.

I first spoke to my Father, "Father, I submit to and acknowledge Your presence. I prepare my heart of faith now." I then spoke to Jesus. "Jesus, I humble myself to You. You are my Lord. I love you, Jesus. I am sorry for my sins, Lord, and I rebuke and renounce them in Your precious name, O Lord. I forgive myself and all who have sinned against me." Then I entered into the throneroom boldly to petition my Father in the name of Jesus. (Psalm 100:4)(Hebrews 10:19-22) I took Jesus delegated authority and spoke the Word of God in the name of Jesus.(Luke 10:19)(Mark 11:23-25) "You, O Lord, have not given me the spirit of fear, but of love, and of power, and of a sound mind in Jesus' name." (2nd Tim. 1:7) I went a step further in Jesus' delegated authority and I rebuked the evil spirit in the name of Jesus. "In the name of Jesus Christ, spirit of fear, get out. (Luke 10:19) Go wherever Jesus sends you to be held captive by the angels of God. (Mark 5:8-13) I will study and meditate upon the Word of God daily with prayer, praise, and worship to keep my vessel filled with God." (Luke 11:24-26) As I spoke in faith and in the name of Jesus, the control that the spirit of fear had which was driving me stopped. And with a decision of my will, I took control and stopped myself, obeyed the Lord, and stopped cleaning.(See Appendix)

After praying in the bathroom, I phoned a couple of friends from my Bible study group. By phone, we entered boldly with our hearts of faith, coming into the Father's presence to petition Him in the name of Jesus and to take Jesus' delegated authority against the demon spirit and to declare the Word of God in Jesus' name. Then they came to my apartment and prayed over it, anointing the doorways with oil. They agreed with me in prayer (Matthew 18:19,20) and we took Jesus' delegated authority (Luke 10:19) and cast out the tormenting spirits (Psalm 107:20)(Mark 16:17) and spoke the Word of God in the name of Jesus. (Mark 11:23-25)(Romans 12:2)(Matthew 4:4,7,10)(Phil. 2:9)(See paragraph above) We sent them to the depths of the earth to be held captive by the angels of God there. (Mark 5:8-13)(Matthew 18:18) And I recommitted to my relationship with Jesus and to spending time daily in the Word of God and prayer with praise and worship.(Matthew 18:18)(Luke 10:19) (Luke 11:24-26)(Psalm 33:1-3)(John 4:24)(James 5:16) (See Appendix)

Jesus will fight for us when our hearts are surrendered to His Lordship. His power will work through our weaknesses. (2nd Cor. 12:9) Sometimes we need the help of others to bring us to the other side of our weaknesses. The goal of the enemy is to get us into fear so that evil spirits can continue to harass us and keep us in the victim's position. A Christian witness or two helps to keep the presence of God against these pests. The following scripture are the actual words of Jesus, **"Again, I tell you that if two of you on**

earth agree about anything you ask for, it will be done for you by my Father in heaven. For where two or three come together in my name, there am I with them." (Matthew 18:19, 20)

I believed that the Lord and His angels were present with me even while in the grips of this evil, addictive, and obsessive, compulsive spirit. **In all their distress he too was distressed, and the angel of his presence saved them. (Isaiah 63:9) For the eyes of the Lord range throughout the earth to strengthen those whose hearts are fully committed to Him. (2ⁿᵈ Chronicles 16:9)** Truthfully, while in the snare of the evil spirit, the emotions are in a frenzy. There is a strong pull to stay in the frenzy of that fear. There is a <u>strong delusion</u> to believe that there is something present that has power over me. However, at the same time, there is a deeper and a stronger pull within my spirit that knows, believes, and senses the presence of God, even while in the grips of the emotions and of the frenzy. I know this is a spirit that is not of God. And I know and believe that God is there with me, dwelling on the inside of me, and that He is greater and more powerful than any spirit! (1ˢᵗ John 4:4)

The Holy Spirit within me steps in and helps me to rise up and speak and take control of the environment and of the evil spirit. This act of my will brings me above the delusion (false belief) and deeper than the frenzy of the emotions. I first acknowledge my Father's greater presence and immediately recommit my heart to Jesus Christ as Lord and loving authority with my heart bowed before my Father God. The act of bowing my head is my first act of resistance against the control of the spirit of fear. Something transpires with this action of humility that will bring change to the negative mindset and to the heightened emotions. <u>It is this physical act that breaks the frenzy and the panic</u>. Now I experience God's tangible presence. It is more than a knowing through the intellectual realm. I know His presence in my spirit and in my heart.

In first submitting my heart to Father God, the Holy Spirit honors my act of submission. In recommitting my heart to Jesus as Lord, the Holy Spirit brings His presence and power because I am repenting in the act of recommitting. My words of repentance are accompanied by words to forgive and release judgments. This then brings my heart into a place of faith. Faith can now resist and replace the fear. I now can speak as I am properly positioned with a heart of faith (with submission, repentance, and forgiveness). By the power of the Holy Spirit, and through the finished work of Jesus Christ, I can then enter into my Father's presence, petitioning Him, and taking Jesus' delegated authority all in His name, against this demonic spirit. In my proper position of heart, then, I can speak, "Now devil, get out, in Jesus' name! (Luke 10:19) Go wherever Jesus sends you to be held captive by the angels of God." (Mark 5:8-13)

As soon as I speak in faith, the power of that emotion (could be panic, fear, doubt, anger, lust, apathy, or any negative emotion) is broken, and the driving spirit leaves. Thus, I usher in the presence of the Lord. I am restored back into the peace and the presence of God and under the loving control of the Holy Spirit.

As I continue to speak with my heart of faith, I take further delegated authority speaking the Word of God in Jesus' name. (Luke 10:19)(Luke 11:24-26) And I usher the light of God's presence into the room as I enter into my Father's presence with further petitions, (Psalm 100:4)(Heb.10:19) in the name of Jesus.

"Father God, I come into Your presence with thanksgiving and praise with my petitions in the name of Jesus."(Psalm 100:4)(John 16:23) I then speak to Jesus. "Thank you Jesus, that You have not given me the spirit of fear, but of love, and of power, and of a sound mind. (2ⁿᵈ Tim. 1:7) Nothing shall be able to separate me from the love of God which is in Christ Jesus my Lord. (Romans 8:38,39) Thank you, Jesus, that I have the mind of Christ. (1ˢᵗ Cor. 2:16) In righteousness I am established. I am far from oppression. I do not fear. I am far from terror. It will not come near me. (Isaiah 54:14) No weapon formed against me shall be able to prosper. (Isaiah 54:17) My body is a temple for the Holy Spirit. I will not defile it. It is set aside for the use of my Lord. (Romans 12:1; 1ˢᵗ Cor. 6:19,20) I thank You, Lord, that all things work together for good in my life because I love You, Jesus, and I am called according to Your purpose. (Romans 8:28) (All scriptures personalized) In Jesus' name I pray this and believe, Amen."

I am the vine; you are the branches. If a man remains in me and I in him, he will bear much fruit; apart from me you can do nothing. If you remain in me, and my words remain in you, ask whatever you wish, and it will be given you. (John 15: 5,7)

If I feel that there is an evil spirit coming to me from a person who is not under my legal authority, I guard my heart and place my focus on the Lord. I prepare my heart of faith with submission, repentance, and forgiveness. I enter into my Father's presence and petition my Father in the name of Jesus in intercession for the person. I cover myself with the blood of Jesus and place a divine boundary around my spirit, soul, and body. I take Jesus' delegated authority as I then bind and gag the spirit and speak the Word of God in Jesus' name. (See Appendix)

With my heart of faith, with submission, repentance, and forgiveness, I pray:

"Father God, I come to You with my petitions in the name of Jesus. I cover myself and this person with Your precious blood.(1ˢᵗ Peter 1:18,19)(Hebrews 9:14) Lord Jesus, I pray that (this person) is the healed of the Lord, in Jesus' name.(Isaiah 53:3-5) I pray that You bless (this person) with Your Holy Spirit. (Acts 1:8)(Acts 2:38) I cover (this person) with the angels of God to guard over and to protect him/her.(Psalm 91:11)(Psalm 34:7) In Your name, Lord Jesus, I now bind and gag the devil from oppressing (this person). (Matthew 18:18) I ask that you open his/her spiritual eyes and heart to repent of his/her sins and to commit to a relationship with You, Lord Jesus; so he/she will be able to pray using his/her own authority in You, Lord Jesus. (2ⁿᵈ Cor.: 4:3,4)(Romans 10:9,10)(Luke 10:19)(Luke 24:31,45)(Romans 2:4)(Matthew 7:7) I pray that he/she is delivered from all evil.(Colossians 1:13)(Matthew 6:13) I pray you send laborers to him/her to convict him/her of the truth of the gospel of Jesus Christ.(Matthew 9:37,38) I pray and believe this, in Jesus' name. Amen." (Phil. 2:9)(Hebrews 11:1)(All scriptures personalized)(See Appendix)

Awakened

It takes a willingness to listen to the promptings of the Holy Spirit. It requires that we act quickly in faith as we objectify our emotions. With the power of the Holy Spirit within us, it is a divine privilege to enter into the throneroom of God and to take ourselves out of fear, lust, anger, apathy, or panic. We speak with a heart of faith, with submission, repentance, and forgiveness, to any evil spirit petitioning the Father in Jesus' delegated authority and in His name.

You have the deposit of the power of the Holy Spirit and your deep faith in the Lord Jesus Christ in you to do this. His power is within you and His Word is hidden deep in your heart to fight this good fight of faith. When you first accepted Jesus Christ into your heart as the Lord and Savior of your life, the Holy Spirit was already with you. You cannot accept the Lord Jesus Christ except by the Holy Spirit. Baptism in water and in the Holy Spirit brings the power of the Holy Spirit to us in a greater way. The Apostle Paul tells the Corinthian church; **No one can say, "Jesus is Lord," except by the Holy Spirit. (1ˢᵗ Cor. 12:3b)**

The enemy works double time in the night and early morning hours. He loves to work in darkness. We must prepare our hearts in faith before sleep. With my heart in a submitted and a reverent position to Jesus Christ and His Lordship and authority in my life, I repent of sin before I sleep. And I also, by faith, and with the empowerment of the Holy Spirit, forgive and release myself and all who have sinned against me. Then my heart is properly prepared to speak in faith if I am distracted in the middle of the night.

One night, while in my bed, I was awakened in the middle of the night. Jesus gave me a vision of two angels, one on either side of me and a demonic being standing right in front of me. I spoke directly to the demonic spirit being that I sensed coming toward me. Before sleep, I had submitted to Jesus as my Lord and loving authority with repentance for sin and with forgiveness prayers for myself and all who had sinned against me.

By the power of the Holy Spirit within me, I did rise up and speak to this demon spirit with my human spirit and with my heart in proper position of faith (with submission, repentance, and forgiveness). In this case, there was no opportunity for a formal entrance into my Father's presence. However, by faith, I was already there with my Father because I was submitted to Jesus as my Lord. We can only get to the Father through His Son. (John 14:6) I had prepared my heart of faith before sleep. Therefore, I was ready to speak and petition my Father with my heart of faith.

I rose up and spoke. I took Jesus' delegated authority as I both rebuked the spirit and as I also released my spiritual sword of faith, the Word of God, in the name of Jesus. And, as I spoke, I had a revelation of the two angels standing on either side of me to protect me. I rose up in confidence and spoke directly to the demon spirit and spoke the Word of God, "You cannot harm me because my Lord Jesus Christ is protecting me with His angels who are with me now. The angel of the Lord encamps around those who fear Him (the Lord), and He (the Lord) delivers them. (Psalm 34:7) Leave, now, in the name of Jesus Christ!"

My words of faith in this instance, were spoken executing Jesus' delegated authority, as an act of my faith with my heart, in the power of the Holy Spirit, and not in my own strength, in my intellect, in fear, in anger, or in any fleshly emotion. I confidently spoke with a deep conviction and I believed that I would have what I said. My words spoken in faith carried the power of God. The evil spirit left me as I spoke to it in the name of Jesus Christ. It never has returned since that incident. (Mark 11:23-25) **Then He showed me Joshua the high priest standing before the angel of the Lord, and Satan standing at his right side to accuse him. The Lord said to Satan, "The Lord rebuke you, Satan! The Lord who has chosen Jerusalem, rebuke you! (Zechariah 3:1,2) In all their distress he too was distressed, and the angel of his presence saved them. (Isaiah 63:9)**

It does not matter how I felt! But I fought the fight of faith and was determined that I would have victory in Christ Jesus over this evil spirit! I just did it in faith! I knew and believed deep down inside that Jesus loved me and that He would honor my faith and my spoken words of faith. I spoke these words believing God to answer my prayers. And the Lord showed me how absolutely awesome and powerful He truly is as the evil demon spirit left me as I spoke and believed.

I actually experienced the peace of God to enter and the demons to flee as I spoke!

Jesus disarmed the powers and principalities and gave us His delegated authority over them:

When you were dead in your sins, and in the uncircumcision of your sinful nature, God made you alive with Christ. He forgave us all our sins, having cancelled the written code, with its regulations, that was against us and that stood opposed to us; he took it away, nailing it to the cross. And having disarmed the powers and authorities, he made a public spectacle of them triumphing over them by the cross. (Colossians 2:13-15)

But, recall, my friend, Satan could not touch Jesus because He had no sin in Him. Freedom in Christ requires that we say "no" to sin. As we press into obedience to the still small voice and the promptings of the Holy Spirit to say "no" to sin, His presence and power deepens within and upon us. We know how real He is as He blesses us with each step of obedience. Strive for a sinless life.

During the days of Jesus' life on earth, He offered up prayers and petitions with loud cries and tears to the one who could save Him from death, and He was heard because of His reverent submission. Although He was a son, He learned obedience from what He suffered and, once made perfect, He became the source of eternal salvation for all who obey Him and was designated by God to be high priest in the order of Melchizedek. (Hebrews 5:7-10)

Seek Pastoral and/or Physician's Care
Medications Can Help Some People Who Have a Chemical Imbalance in the Brain

If there is any torment in your life, if you are having delusions, hallucinations, or any problems staying connected to life, please see a Christian physician, psychiatrist, and/or Spirit filled counselor you can trust. Seek a Christian physician and/or a Christian Psychiatrist to help you determine if medications will be helpful for you. I encourage you, if you are being harassed by evil spirits, to seek pastoral care from deliverance ministers and from experienced men and women within the body of Christ. Ask them to pray with you and for you and to help you win the victory for yourself that Jesus already won for you. I exhort you to go to a deliverance minister that is recommended by your pastor and/or a Spirit filled counselor. And go with a friend. There may be something in your life that you are not even aware of that can be easily remedied with the help of ministers who will pray with you and for you. It could be generational spirits that are harassing you. These trustworthy ministers are trained with a godly and objective perspective that we do not have. And they can also refer us to other helpful resources.

The Lord ordained physicians and also medications to help us through every physical, emotional, and mental challenge that we have. It could be a part of a chemical imbalance in the brain and/or demonic activity (familiar spirits), taking advantage of your vulnerability and/or your gifting. You may need healing for past traumas you have experienced. Or it can be an area of unforgiveness and/or disobedience that keeps the flesh shouting out. There may be many areas that need assistance. Use both the medical system and God's system to fight against the devil's attacks upon your life. Refuse to be tormented at all costs. Medications were helpful to me through stressful periods in my life.

I was being beat up by the devil. Why? I gave the devil my delegated authority. If we do not use it, the devil will take everything he can to steal, kill, and destroy us. (John 10:10 ref.) He will take everything he can get, even our will to live. I thought I was resisting by meditating the Word of God in my mind. Our prayers and petitions to the Father must be the audible and the spoken word, spoken with a heart of faith (with submission, repentance, and forgiveness), and in the name of Jesus! Remember, the angels hearken to His Word. (Psalm 103:20 ref.) Remember, people were healed by Jesus' spoken words. Remember, God created the world by His spoken words. (Genesis 1:3,6,9,14,20)(Acts 10:38)(Scripture references)

After many trials with demonic attacks, I saw a Christian physician. I was being affected in every area of my life, unable to keep down jobs, difficulty in every apartment with neighbors, and, in social situations, after interaction with others; I would become sick or very anxious. Sometimes my body would shake or become unusually exited for no apparent reason, as if there were demon spirits present. This is very possible coming out of this lifestyle. There are familiar sexual spirits that will attempt to harass the body of a person, to tempt the person to sin. We must close and lock all doors to prevent them from any entrance. We must repent of sin and crucify the flesh. We must humble ourselves under the love and authority of our Savior and Lord Jesus Christ. And we must release ourselves from self condemnation and the judgment of others, receive the grace of God, and walk free from the devil's torment! Jesus already paid for our sins on Calvary.

I experienced celestial visions of angels and of demons. Yes, I believe that my spirit is receptive and sensitive to the spirit realm. Perhaps this is a gift, but, with torment present, I needed help. I had to open my mind to the possibility that I may need medication to balance my brain chemicals in order to live a normal life. I was convinced that it was all coming from external spiritual entities and that there was an evil assignment against me. Perhaps so, and I continued in prayers of authority against all curses and /or demonic assignments and continued to believe that the Lord would take me through this.

After visiting with family, I literally felt like I was in a fog. I would speak things that I know I would not normally speak in my natural personality. Sometimes I heard what sounded like animals growling in my ears and sounds in my head. Sometimes there was itching or just feelings on my skin which I believe were demon spirits. I would be awakened by a shaking in my legs and the atmosphere would be very dark, tense, or very hot. I slept more than necessary and suffered with depression. I would be awakened with sexual excitement many times. I believed these were demonic attacks and not a physical malady. The Lord Jesus Christ has delivered me from this "affliction." During stressful times, it tries to return. However, prayer, physical exercise, and medication continue to help me. I take my medication, "in Jesus' name." I continue in the sanctification process to keep all ungodly doors closed and locked and to strengthen my spirit.

Sometimes I would come from visiting family and literally feel like a different person. I was attacked with fear, anxiety, lust, lethargy, confusion, depression, suicidal thoughts, panic, and nightmares. Many times I was visited by demons, usually at stressful times in my life. I still had idols in my life and a vulnerable spirit so I was open prey for the oppression from demonic entities. Always look within your own heart to see if there is an open door for the enemy to enter before placing blame on the outside. I believe the Lord literally sent me angels to stop the demonic activity. I have resisted with great success many a demonic spirit petitioning my Father with my heart of faith (submission, repentance, and forgiveness), and taking my delegated authority all in the name of Jesus Christ.

When I experienced sounds in my brain, I believed that I might have a chemical imbalance as well. I was advised by many physicians for some time. Many meds I tried had side effects. For so long, I was convinced that I did not need medication. I guess I was in denial. I finally went to a Christian physician whom I trusted and whom treated me with respect and compassion. After one of the medical team prayed in the authority of Jesus Christ to break any evil assignment against me, I accepted the physician's counsel to try a medication to balance the chemicals in my brain. Perhaps these sounds also were rooted in demonic attacks, perhaps I was hallucinating. I do not know. However, after many years of dealing with this, I chose to do whatever was necessary to come out of this torment, even if I needed to take medication, whether temporarily or permanently.

In a week's time, after taking the medication, I noticed a change. I was not so sensitive to the environmental cues and I felt like I was more connected and much more comfortable in my own skin. I was more firmly connected with my own thoughts and I was not so easily distracted by outside sounds or spirits. The sounds in my head almost completely stopped. It seemed as if my boundaries were more naturally in place and I was able to have normal conversations with others, without fear. The "hypervigilence" I had experienced stopped. It was as if I had experienced a disassociation from my own self, and now I was back within my own skin. It was a miraculous breakthrough for me. The medication helped me tremendously and I am grateful that we have medications to help us when there is a chemical imbalance.

God uses all avenues of healing. However, I continue in the good fight of faith as well because any kind of torment a person is subjected to is rooted in the satanic realm. Jesus is still our divine Healer Who took on all our infirmities on the cross of Calvary. I believe that He will restore me completely as I continue to petition my Father and to pray with my heart of faith, believing God in Jesus' name for the total healing of my brain. I believe that I am redeemed from all the enemy's schemes as I continue to fight taking my delegated authority in Christ Jesus against all of his wiles. With my heart of faith developing in Him, with submission, repentance, and forgiveness; believing, speaking, and expecting my completed healing in Jesus' name, I am free.

Now, I thank God that I am more fully equipped to fight the good fight of faith with balance being restored in my brain. I thank God that I accepted this treatment. I will continue in Christian counseling as well. My prayer life stays active as well. There is no stigma attached to seeking a balance in our mental health when we know and believe that we have the mind of Christ, no matter what the world says. Remember, the brain is a part of the physical body. The mind is a part of our soul. Do not worry about the world's definitions. It is God who justifies! (Romans 8:33) The Word of God is what defines us, not the world. (Hebrews 4:12)

Some people need the medications temporarily, some permanently. I believe God for the full manifestation of healing of brain chemicals to come. Until that time, I will continue with the medication speaking my healing, "in Jesus' name," when I take it. Today, medication continues to help me. We are all made differently, and there are medications that have helped countless people with brain and/or chemical challenges. Medications along with Christian support and counseling have prevented much suffering for many people.

Support groups are invaluable sources of assistance. I have benefited tremendously in many support groups within the body of Christ. I have met many people who have been helped through the use of medications. I continue in this fight by committing to a physical exercise program and to a good nutritional diet to keep my entire body healthy, including my brain, physically fit. And I will keep connected with people whether I am employed or unemployed. Always seek your physician's counsel regarding a proper physical exercise program and/or a good nutritional diet if you have any health conditions, medical issues, are pregnant or lactating, or are taking any medications.

I believe that there are some people who are extremely vulnerable to the spiritual world and that Satan takes advantage of their vulnerabilities and giftings, if you will. However, we have a God Who restores and brings us into balance through our relationship with Him, through a life of prayer, with repentance and forgiveness, closing and locking all doors against the enemy entrance. For some folks, as in my case, in the latter years of my ministry, balance also was restored through the use of medications as well.

Jesus wants us connected to other believers to help us with our weaker areas and to be accountable to others. **"How good and pleasant it is when brothers (and sisters) live together in unity." (Psalm 133:1)** The Bible tells us that the enemy is out to steal, to kill, and to destroy, and we must, whether taking medications or not, continue to fight this good fight of faith. (John 10:10) (1st Timothy 6:12) Victory is won by taking advantage of every resource that is available to us.

Today I believe that the demon spirits were taking advantage of me. However, I do believe I have an imbalance of brain chemicals. I may be diagnosed by the secular medical world with depression with tendencies toward OCD (obsessive compulsive disorder). But, with obedience to the Lord, with ongoing healing of my heart issues, with the working and washing of the Word of God, with daily prayer and praise and worship to the Lord, and, with the use of a medication to balance the brain chemicals, I am able to live a balanced life. I give the Lord all the glory and I am thankful to be released from torment. Deliverance comes and there is no shame in taking a medication to bring the brain into balance.

Were these demonic spirits or hallucinations? Probably both in my case. I only know that Jesus died for all physical, emotional, and mental torment two thousand years ago. And I have the victory over it through the precious sacrificial blood of my Savior and Lord Jesus Christ. And I will use every avenue available, even medication, to relieve mental torment. No person should live in a state of torment! My thinking is much clearer now. I have a deeper peace with the Lord. I am much more aware of the Lord's presence and my boundaries are more naturally set. I am able to carry on normal conversations with people, but I still must be more of a listener than a talker. And I am grateful to God and to the physicians who honestly challenged me as I stubbornly resisted their recommendations. I will never be the same.

But you have come to Mount Zion, to the heavenly Jerusalem, the city of the living God. You have come to thousands upon thousands of angels in joyful assembly, to the church of the firstborn, whose names are written in heaven. (Hebrews 12:22,23)

Cover Every Base – Pray for Complete Mental and Emotional Health

In 2012, I started on a medication to balance the chemicals in my brain. And I believe that the combination of the medication with a life pressing into purity sold out to Jesus Christ continue to work together toward my total healing. I will continue under an excellent Christian physician's care to praise God for the healing. I will continue to pray and believe God for completed healing of my body (including my brain), my mind, my emotions, my will, and my spirit. (Isaiah 53:3-5)

Prepare Your Heart - "Jesus I humble myself to You. I believe You died for me and rose victoriously on the third day. I repent of all sin and ask You to come into my heart and to be the Lord, Savior, and loving authority of my life. Fill me with Your Holy Spirit. I commit to forgive and release all judgment against myself and all who have sinned against me. Thank You, Lord Jesus, for Your sacrifice for me."

Enter into Your Father's Presence - "Father God, I come to You, in the precious name of Jesus Christ, my Lord, my Savior, and my loving authority. I enter into Your gates with thanksgiving and praise in my heart. (Psalm 100:4) I make my petitions known to You now, in the name of Jesus Christ." (John 16:23)

Take Jesus' Delegated Authority and Declare the Word of God over Your Brain (lay your hands on your head) in Jesus' Name - "Brain, I now speak to you. (Ephesians 6:20) I rebuke any mental illnesses and/or chemical imbalances, in the name of Jesus Christ. (Luke 10:19)(Mark 11:23-25) Line up with the Word of God. (Pro. 4:20) (Hebrews 4:12) I command the spirit of mental illness to go, in the name of Jesus Christ. (Matthew 18:18) (Luke 10:19) Go wherever Jesus sends you to be held captive by the angels of God. (Mark 5:8-13) I am of sound mind in Christ Jesus. (2nd Timothy 1:7) I cover my mind, my thoughts, my brain, my eyes, my ears, and all chemicals in my brain with the blood of Jesus Christ.(Hebrews 9:14)(1st Peter 1:18,19)(1stPeter 2:24) I now command every neuron and neural connection to rise up and live in Jesus' name. (Psalm 118:17)(Luke 10:19) Nervous system, line up with the Word of God. (Heb. 4:12)(Luke 10:19) (Ephesian 6:20)(Mark 11:23-25) Jesus, Your blood covers my sins and diseases once and for all. (Hebrews 10:19-22)(Hebrews 9:14) I believe that through Your name, O Lord, (Phil. 2:9), and through Your finished work on the cross, (Hebrews 9), I am healed in all these areas. (Luke 4:18)(Isaiah 53:3-5)(Mark 11:23-25) Jesus, Your name is higher than any chemical imbalance or disorder. (Phil 2:9) I declare my brain and all chemical in my brain to be completely balanced and covered by Your blood, in Your name, O Lord Jesus. (Hebrews 9:14) (1st Peter 1:18,19)(Ephesian 6:20) Thank you, Jesus, for healing me. (1st Thes.5:18) I declare that I am free from any symptoms of depression, confusion, anxiety, epilepsy, sleeplessness, panic, delusions, hallucinations, or emotional disorders, in Jesus' name. (Luke 10:19)(Ephesians 6:20) I rebuke obsessive compulsive disorders, any memory problems, or any dementia, in Jesus' name. (Luke 10:19)(Matthew 18:18) My mind will not be passive, but active in the Word of God. (Heb. 4:12)(Rom. 12:2) I declare that I have the mind of Christ in Jesus' name. (1st Cor. 2:16) I am redeemed from the curse of the law in Jesus' name. (Gal. 3:13) I believe that the Word of God, which I meditate upon and speak in faith, will change me and heal me even to my DNA. (Heb. 4:12)(Rom. 12:2)(Mark 11:23-25) I declare that my brain is now healed because of the death, burial, resurrection, and the ascension of Jesus Christ, in Jesus' name. (Luke 24:7) (Luke 23:46)(Luke 23:55)(Luke 10:19)(Isaiah 53:3-5) I commit to daily study of the Word of God and prayer with praise and worship of my Creator. Amen (Luke 11:24-26)(Romans 12:2)(Psalm 33:1-3)(John 4:24)(James 5:16)(All scriptures referenced and personalized)(See Appendix)

Note: Even today, I stand believing God for my total healing in these areas. I pray over my eyes when my sight seems to be affected and I have been healed on all counts! I continue to speak to these mountains and believe God for the completed healing. (Mark 11:22-26) And I exercise to keep the oxygen flowing to my brain and spinal column. Consult your physician regarding a safe exercise program that will help you if you have any health issues, medical problems, are pregnant or lactating, or are taking any medications.

But when they believed Phillip as he preached the good news of the kingdom of God and the name of Jesus Christ, they were baptized, both men and women. Simon himself believed and was baptized. And he followed Phillip everywhere and was astonished by the great signs and miracles he saw. (Acts 8:12,13) Remember, Jesus gave different directions to people for different healings. I encourage you to listen to the Holy Spirit and he will guide you and direct you. One time when my eyesight was weak, He told me to visit a friend who had Parkinson's disease. I obeyed, and after the short conversation with him, my eyes were completely healed. Another time I visited this man at the Holy Spirit's direction. He gave me a hug during the visit and I went home and slept like a baby that night. When we take care of God's business, He takes care of ours!

These are the words of Jesus, **"Go into all the world and preach the good news to all creation. Whoever believes and is baptized will be saved, but whoever does not believe will be condemned. And these signs will accompany those who believe; In my name they will drive out demons; they will speak in new tongues; they will pick up snakes with their hands; and when they drink deadly poison, it will not hurt them at all; they will place their hands on sick people, and they will get well."(Mark 16:15-18)**

Resistance Requires Honesty With God

I stress the importance of speaking with your spirit and with your heart properly positioned in faith, with submission, repentance, and with forgiveness. Because I was still not properly submitted under the authority and the Lordship of Jesus Christ with a repentant and forgiving heart, I made many mistakes deceiving myself to believe that I was in proper position of heart taking Jesus' delegated authority over demon spirits. Without true surrender to the Lordship and the authority of Jesus Christ, without full repentance for all hidden sin, and without a forgiving heart, I was resisting in my own flesh. I was trying in my own strength to rebuke evil spirits from my spirit, soul, and body. Therefore, that driving spirit of fear was still controlling and pushing me. I had to let go and let God take control by His Spirit. (Zechariah 4:6 ref.) **'Not by might nor by power, but by my Spirit,' says the Lord Almighty. (Zechariah 4:6)**(See Appendix)

Repentance and forgiveness with submission before prayers of authority places our hearts in right relationship with the Lord. We may still have addictions we are working to remove from our lives, but God knows we are working with a humble and an honest heart before Him. It is pride that steps out in the flesh and slanders the devil. Our hearts must be right with God. Humility and honesty before Him keeps us safe under His wings and keeps us speaking out in faith and not in the flesh. We cannot hide anything from God.

I had hidden sin with the perfectionism; papers that needed to be discarded after turning them into authorities. These represented worries that took me from the full surrender to God. Because of my need for control and because I did want anyone to know I had a secret and a problem, I was in rebellion and pride. Not asking for help, and having a false sense of responsibility to every detail, my heart was closed because my mind was on the details and not on God. It kept me in a proud and an isolated place! It kept me from my greatest source of ammunition, my faith.

Not believing I was in sin, I was hiding sin from God and from myself. I was lying to myself. I did not consider this rebellion against God, but it was, just as was homosexuality. I was open prey for Satan's attack. I had to call sin sin with no compromise. The first step to getting free from addiction is to accept that we have a problem and to then come out of the denial of the deception. Homosexuality is sin. Perfectionism is sin.

When the archangel Michael spoke to the devil, he said, "The Lord rebuke you." We still use the name of Jesus to exercise our authority because we are still speaking under the authority of Jesus Christ. The demonic beings, which are fallen angels of the spiritual world, do not have greater power than the power of Jesus Christ Who resides on the inside of the born again believer, but they are of a higher order than us human beings. Remember, God also is their original Creator.

But even the archangel Michael, when he was disputing with the devil about the body of Moses, did not dare to bring a slanderous accusation against him, but said, "The Lord rebuke you!" Yet these men speak abusively against whatever they do not understand; and what things they do understand by instinct, like unreasoning animals – these are the very things that destroy them. (Jude 1:9, 10)

Temptations will continue because Satan is still the god of this world. We must turn our hearts sincerely toward the Lord Jesus Christ in surrender and ask for His help. When we turn our hearts to Him, with all our brokenness in our complete need for Him, His power comes to us with this decision to submit to His will and not ours; a decision to submit to His control and not ours.

Jesus waits for our hearts to turn to Him. He is waiting with love for us to respond to Him as Lord and to come to Him as Savior and as friend. He has already provided the payment for our addictions two thousand years ago. But we must reach out to Him to receive it. He is a gentleman. He will not force His love and grace upon us. Friend, this is no game. The spiritual realm is real and Satan has a certain amount of power, but his power can only be brought under by the divine power of Jesus Christ working on the inside of our hearts. This is spiritual warfare and it can only be won spiritually by the words we speak with our hearts properly positioned in faith with submission, repentance, and forgiveness.

As long as we have hidden sin in our lives, we will not be able to successfully resist the devil. Hidden sin keeps the walls of pride up as it keeps the sin hidden from God and from others. As soon as we get honest with God and man, the defensive spiritual walls come down and God can work His power in us and through us. An honest heart sincerely surrendered and submitted to the Lord, not a perfectly sinless person, is the essential step we need to take before we can successfully resist the devil and take proper delegated authority. This heart stands victorious in faith because this heart has a clear conscience before God. This heart has honestly submitted to God before resisting any enemy. (James 4:7,8)

Jesus already conquered the devil at Calvary. But we can only step into our delegated authority in Christ Jesus when we are properly submitted under His authority. To fully make him Lord, we must take an honest assessment of ourselves and repent of all idols, all fears, and all addictions, bring all hidden sin to the light, and ask for His help. There is no reason to hide anything from God. He knows everything anyway. Then, with our hearts humbled and honest with Him with repentance and forgiveness, we will rise up with our hearts properly positioned in faith and successfully take this privilege of His delegated authority. It is not our authority. It is His and He gives us the privilege of using it for victory in our lives.

The words of Jesus in the gospel of Luke describe Jesus' delegated authority given to us,

I have given you authority to trample on snakes and scorpions and to overcome all the power of the enemy; nothing will harm you. (Luke 10:19)

Respect All Spirit Beings but Do Not Fear Them – Speak with Holy Emotions
Be sure that in all prayers of authority that you have legal authority to pray for the people.
(See Appendix)

Prepare your heart in proper position of faith to speak submitted only under the authority and Lordship of Jesus Christ with repentance and forgiveness in your heart. Petition the Father in the name of Jesus. And take Jesus' delegated authority, in Jesus' name, with a holy anger, not from your fleshly emotions of fear or anger. There is a "holy anger" that speaks firmly with faith and not in the flesh. This holy emotion does not react to the persons or to the circumstances. It does not take Satan's bait. It is firmly anchored to the rock of Jesus Christ. And the holy emotion of anger can still love amidst the hate that is coming toward it. Any hatred we feel is from a demonic spirit. A holy anger is fully submitted to the Lordship of Jesus Christ. A holy anger places faith higher and deeper than the emotions and exercises self control. It is not seeking man or woman's approval. It speaks firmly with conviction and truth, and with love. It boldly speaks God's Word. Holy anger is not ashamed of the gospel of Jesus Christ. It speaks in faith and discounts the fleshly emotions. (2nd Tim. 1:12)(Rom. 1:16)(Mark 11:23-25)

Do not fight in your emotions against evil spirits, no matter how frustrated or angry you may become in your flesh. The enemy does have some power, and we must respect that, but "greater is He that is within us than he that is in the world." (1st John 4:4) Stay in reverent submission and in faith, focused in on Jesus Christ as your Lord. Yield to His loving position of authority over you as you stand before him with a humble, honest, and a repentant heart. (Col 2:10) It is for your safety and for your protection. It is His power that wins over your enemies both in the natural world and in the spiritual realm.(Col. 2:15)

You must take the first step to stop and acknowledge the greater power of God within and with you while in spiritual warfare. Demonic spirits, fears, panic, apathy, anxiety, anger, unbalanced grief, obsessions, compulsions, and all addictions will bow in the presence of the Lord Jesus Christ when you enter into the Father's presence with a heart of faith properly positioned in submission, repentance, and forgiveness. Ask the Father in the name of Jesus Christ to work on your behalf. When you take Jesus' delegated authority, rebuking the enemy and declaring the word of God all in the name of Jesus Christ, He will move on your behalf. **Therefore God exalted him to the highest place and gave Him the name that is above every name, that at the name of Jesus every knee should bow, in heaven and on earth and under the earth, and every tongue confess that Jesus Christ is Lord, to the glory of God the Father. (Phil. 2:9,11)**

You are Valuable – Choose Life

The eyes of the Lord are upon all His children. Jesus already won this battle for us through His resurrection when He traveled to the bowels of hell. He took the keys of sin and death away from Satan and brought them back to the right hand of His Father in heaven. (Colossians 2:13-15) He still sits at the right hand of the Father, making intercession for us. (Colossians 3:1) He took away the law of sin and death and gave us His grace, His unmerited favor, His loving kindness, and His power. We receive it by faith alone, not by any works or good behavior. It is a free gift! (Ephesians 2:8) Jesus made a public spectacle of all the evil rulers, and He disarmed all the evil powers! In this victory, He gave us the benefit of enforcing this disarmament by taking His delegated authority over them here in the earth and in hell as well. (Luke 10:19)(Col. 2:15)(All scriptures referenced)

When you were dead in your sins, and in the uncircumcision of your sinful nature, God made you alive with Christ. He forgave us all our sins, having canceled the written code, with its regulations, that was against us and that stood opposed to us; He took it away, nailing it to the cross. And having disarmed the powers and authorities, He made a public spectacle of them triumphing over them by the cross. (Colossians 2:13-15)

And praise God in the midst of all battles, because to get to the victory, there will be difficult battles. Praise Him in the midst of all battles! You already have the victory through your covenant relationship with Jesus Christ.

If you are fearful in any given situation, call a Christian witness to come and pray with you. Don't isolate yourself for any reason. It can lead you to death! **[60]** We do not fear death, because the one who conquered death lives within us and has given us abundant life here on earth as well as eternal life in heaven. Death for a believer is just a step into another realm of life, in which we will all be alive with Christ in a face to face relationship. We have the "blessed hope" to be reunited with our loved ones there as well. **Where, O death, is your victory? Where, O death, is your sting? The sting of death is sin, and the power of sin is the law. But thanks be to God! He gives us the victory through our Lord Jesus Christ. (1st Cor. 15: 55, 56)**

I love the words of Paul in Philippians who was persecuted countless times and who chose to stay and be a servant of the Lord: **For to me to live is Christ, and to die is gain. If I am to go on living in the body, this will mean fruitful labor for me. Yet what shall I choose? I do not know! I am torn between the two: I desire to depart and be with Christ which is better by far; but it is more necessary for you that I remain in the body. Convinced of this, I know that I will remain, and I will continue with all of you for your progress and joy in the faith, so that through my being with you again your joy in Christ Jesus will overflow on account of me. (Philippians 1:21-26)**

The Apostle Paul knew his value on earth and withstood much persecution to stay and spread the gospel of grace to a world that was caught up into the law. Our lives are in the hands of God. To take our own life is to go against God's plan for our lives. Like Paul, our lives are valuable also. Do not let Satan steal another minute of life away from you. Share your life with other people. This is our call.

Nothing shall be able to separate me from the love of God which is in Christ Jesus my Lord. (Romans 8: 38-39)

From Pain to Truth

The path to freedom is through the pain to the truth. [61] The only way to conquer addiction victoriously is through the intervention of the Holy Spirit. **I have seen his ways, but I will heal him; I will guide him and restore comfort to him. (Isaiah 57:18)**

I had to face the pain of my past. I had to come home and face myself in the company of my family. I had to face, forgive and release the childhood hurt that was hidden inside for so many years. Then, in honest submission to God and Spirit filled counselors, I would identify my sins and my ungodly reactions to the deep hurts and pains and traumas of my earlier years. I would be assisted to bring them into the light through expression with Christian counselors present to assist me in the restoration process. This included not only identification of the root issues, but also confession, repentance, renunciations, forgiveness, with wise counsel and Spirit led prayers to strategize new behaviors to replace the addictive cycles. Until dealt with, the ungodly reactions remain as unexpressed emotions that hide in the subconscious heart and ensnare us into repetitive addictive and obsessive compulsive activities.

The unexpressed emotions contain unrepented sin and ungodly reactions to pain. Because of them the child draws the wrong conclusions about him/herself, the opposite sex, God, and life in general. When the child joins in with these emotions, Satan is able to take up residence in them and has access to the child's mind. As the mind separates from the emotions they are sealed off by demonic power. A blockage is put in place making the emotions seem "unreachable." When these emotions are stirred, the rational mind is put on hold, blanks out, locks up, or fogs over. The unexpressed emotions become strongholds from which Satan motivates the child to sin. [62]

There is no easy recipe by which one can face the unexpressed emotions and, while doing so, reunite the mind with the emotions and thus strengthen the mind and will. Because the stored emotions are very painful, the mind has separated from them. **[63]** LIFE Ministries of New York City uses the modality of "journaling" to facilitate the healing process. I still journal today. It has been very helpful. As I faced the pain and settled issues within my heart and mind, I began to relax and think more clearly.

It was a combination of expressing and facing the painful emotions both in my private time with the

Lord and in Christian counseling, and with the day to day living the Christian lifestyle that brought me inner change. It was my intimacy with Jesus Christ that kept me spiritually aware of His presence in my life. I continued to confess the Word of God over my life. Daily my heart grew in proper position of faith in submission to Jesus as Lord and authority, with repentance (His blood cleansing me from all sin and blessing me with the Holy Spirit), and with forgiveness with release of blame (closing the door to the enemy's control). In proper position of a heart in faith, I continued to then petition my Father in the name of Jesus, and to then take Jesus' delegated authority in the name of Jesus Christ, rebuking my flesh, the ungodly thoughts and memories, emotions, fantasies, and evil spirits, and speaking the Word of God.

And, the leadings of the Holy Spirit brought me daily encouragement and guidance as I listened with my spiritual ears. The Holy Spirit empowered me to forgive, to rise up and speak to the mountains, and to stop myself in the midst of the obsessive compulsive rituals. I drew a line in the sand. I knew this wa a lying spirit. His presence with me brought me out of every trial. I knew He was there with me. I knew it by faith, faith that was deeper than any fear or any darkness that was presenting itself. **With the same spirit of faith, we also believe and therefore speak, because we know that the one who raised the Lord Jesus from the dead will also raise us with Jesus and present us with you in His presence. (2ⁿᵈ Cor. 4:13,14)**

I had many tears of sadness, but Jesus shed tears of His own blood for us. I spent much time healing from the inner wounds, but Jesus was both physically and emotionally wounded for us. I lived with persecution, but Jesus received the ultimate persecution for us. I experienced much rejection, but Jesus experienced the ultimate rejection of crucifixion on a cross for us. And I became an evangelist for Jesus Christ in the process of my own deliverance because I wanted to share what Jesus did for me with other people. And in the very act of my giving to others, Jesus' death and resurrection provided me freedom from the generational curse and from all fear, shame, inferiority, and guilt. I humbly stepped out to receive His divine provisions. And I entered gratefully into His rest and His love. The words of Jesus are as follows, **But when you give to the needy, do not let your left hand know what your right hand is doing, so that your giving may be in secret. Then your Father, Who sees what is done in secret, will reward you. (Matthew 6:3,4)**

Thank You Lord

I was determined to find the full deliverance and to walk humbly before my God. For He alone has taken me out of this terrible enslavement. I thank Him for the courage He gave me to face and rid myself of this hellish demon and of my painful emotions. The Word of God has been my recipe book. It commands us to forgive others and ourselves. Those commands must be obeyed. It also commands us to love our neighbor as well as ourselves. Love is our most powerful weapon against the enemy. The Lord gives us His strength to fight with faith.

I thank Jesus for His sacrifice on the cross for me. It cancelled the law that I lived by for most of my life and brought me the grace and loving kindness, the power and the favor of God and His rest. I thank Him for leading me every step of the way and for all the real Christians who helped me and loved me through the process. Mostly, I thank Him for the Holy Spirit whose presence and loving voice has always been there with me. **You have made known to me the path of life; You will fill me with joy in Your presence, with eternal pleasures at your right hand. (Psalm 16:11)**

The Story Continues

Here I was in sunny Santa Barbara, the year is 1981, and I had just made a commitment to Jesus Christ as my Lord and Savior. The moment I spoke the words of the sinner's prayer, "I am sorry," I chose life. I also took the first step in kicking the hellish, vicious, and defiant homosexual spirit off of me. The angels in heaven triumphed over my decision and wrote my name down in the book of life.

To "commit" by its very definition means "to connect or to entrust." **[64]** My spirit immediately was connected and made alive with Jesus Christ. Sin had produced an invisible wall which had severed me from a relationship with Jesus. Until repentance, sin does separate spirit <u>and</u> soul from that divine relationship.

The arms of God are forever reaching out to us. Jesus literally threw me a supernatural rope from heaven and I grabbed onto it for dear life. My Savior began to pull me out of the quicksand that I had been immersed in for the last eight years of my life. **He who overcomes will, like them, be dressed in white. I will never blot out his name from the book of life, but will acknowledge his name before my Father and his angels. (Rev. 3:5)**

Repentance and Trust

Repentance is also the first step in the maturing process. Why? Because the hurting child within actually experiences a conscious awareness of his or her "condition" which is "out of control." **Dr. Consiglio states that the homosexual begins to experience breakthrough when he or she begins to objectify his/her emotions. [65]** Repentance opens one up to allowing the supernatural power of Jesus Christ to come into the blocked mind and the hurting heart and the healing begins. It takes a trust in the Lord to repent. **Trust in the Lord with your whole heart and lean not on your own understanding. In all things acknowledge Him and He will direct your steps. (Psalms 3:5)**

Trust, I said to myself, is going to be difficult. After all I had encountered, it was difficult to trust anyone. Everyone I had related to including me had so many problems. I believe that out of the disappointments I experienced coupled with the suicides of my two friends; I came to the decision to accept Jesus as Lord out of complete desperation.

Yet, since I was a little girl, deep within me, I had an indelible faith that God was watching me. This faith rose up within me in spite of all the pressure I felt from the enemy and I took the step to turn from homosexuality. By faith and with my heart turned toward God, I boldly resisted the enemy's pressure and decided to turn my life back over to the care of a loving God. I knew I was doing the right thing.

Commitment to Jesus Christ

This one decision of will to commit my life to Jesus Christ was the best decision of my life. I thank God for the Platt family who led me to Jesus. I know God had this divine appointment planned even before the very foundation of the earth. Even though I was in the dredges of despair, God had His holy hand upon me.

When I repented and committed my life to Jesus that summer day, hope entered my heart and now I somehow knew that a supernatural helper was with me. I started on the journey of learning to trust God. Trust is foundational to the psychological growth and maturity of all persons. **[66]** In the years to come, I would learn to trust God to heal my heart from the inside out.

As my relationship with Jesus grew, I would dare to forgive others with the help of the Holy Spirit, and eventually, to forgive myself. The process of my healing actually began in the intellectual realm. The Word of God transformed my thinking first. And as my focus was redirected upon God and I made healthy relationships within the body of Christ, my heart started to open and to feel again.

Leaving Homosexuality

I had to leave all homosexual contacts in obedience to the Lord. I had much inner healing work to do and I could not be distracted with any more idols. Emotional dependence upon any lovers or friends in the lifestyle had to be severed. I had to separate from them. They were idols. My emotional codependence upon them took both me and them away from total dependence upon Jesus. My sins committed with them separated me and them from the presence of the Lord Jesus Christ. Also, my security in these friendships served to keep both me and them from identifying and facing the flesh, the negative thoughts and emotions, judgments, habit structures, behavior patterns, and vows made as a result of childhood traumas. **Only through intimacy with Jesus Christ and facing the pain of the past are truth, freedom, peace, and identity in Christ and our true purpose in life discovered!** When I left these relationships, the painful emotions surfaced. Even though I was severely tempted to go back to the comfort zone of my friends, I pressed into the deeper truth, pressing into God, knowing deep within myself that I had to heal in my own heart and do the right thing, both for myself and for my friends.

I knew that God was with me and that He would use me to bless others with my testimony in the future. He would bless me for doing His will. I just knew and believed this deep within my soul and my spirit. I had to leave all dependencies and sins in faith and only in faith. My emotions would try to pull me back into the dependencies! I knew it would be best both for me and for my friends also in the long run! I committed to pray for them as I went forward in my healing process. I asked the Holy Spirit to assist me to rise above the emotions and dependencies as I forged ahead building my faith. I did not leave the area at first, but, as I moved ahead in my walk with the Lord, the Holy Spirit led me out of the land. I obeyed and left the land. It was for the best. Father always knows best. **Therefore come out from them and be separate, says the Lord. Touch no unclean thing and I will receive you. I will be a Father to you, and you will be my sons and daughters, says the Lord Almighty. (2nd Corinthians 6:17,18)**

The flesh must be crucified! Only through a decision to totally surrender to God will He step in and help us to crucify the flesh. When I gave my body away to a partner, I gave up my spirit, soul, and my body. I sold my spirit, soul, and my body to the devil, and I was ruled by my flesh and its pleasures. I was controlled by my emotions with whatever felt good, whatever would numb the inner pain. When I chose to leave homosexuality and commit my spirit, soul, and my body back to Jesus Christ, I regained not only my spirit, soul, and my body back, but also my "honest self" was restored back to me. This is a priceless jewel! No amount of money in this world can buy our "honest selves" back. Only through the blood of Jesus Christ are we bought back from the curse of sin and from the lies of the devil! **You are not your own. You were bought at a price. Therefore honor God with your body. (1st Cor. 6: 20)**

Friend, there is no amount of acceptance from any person in this world that could bring you the true peace of mind that honesty with oneself and with God brings: a clear conscience with complete self acceptance because you know that your Creator God has accepted you. There is an emptiness inside every human being that only the love of God can truly fill to bring inner contentment. And it lasts. It is not just a fleeting momentary pleasure. It is a deep lasting peace within that determines our very dignity and value as human beings. It is only through our steps to humbly receive the divine love, complete acceptance, and total forgiveness of Jesus Christ that we discover this treasure. We must reach out and receive it. It is a free gift for us.

Do we deserve it? No. Did we earn it? No. And, to let us know how much He really cares for us, He blesses us with His presence and with a clear conscience. He takes up residence within our hearts as we humbly receive His gifts of grace. And we gratefully rest in His Lordship as He forgives and He forgets our sins and embraces us with His outstretched arms.

Satan is a mastermind of deception, and he works against your flesh, your thoughts, your emotions, and your will. But he cannot touch your faith or the presence of God in your life, which is deeper than your will, your flesh, and any thought or emotion. If you believe the Word of God is true, then you have an active strategy against the enemy's lies. As you obey the Word of God, you will heal and change. Obedience is the strongest and the greatest step we can take toward surrender to the Lord.

As difficult as it is for us to face the truth at times, the Word of God will convict us of the truth. Friend, let no one deceive you, the Word of God is completely true and it was written by men and women of faith who were inspired by the Holy Spirit. (2nd Timothy 3:16 ref.) It is God's Word! **All Scripture is God-breathed and is useful for teaching, rebuking, correcting and training in righteousness, so that the man (woman) of God may be thoroughly equipped for every good work. (2nd Timothy 3:16,17)**

It is the Word of God that convinced and convicted me to the truth about the sin of homosexuality after the suicide of one of my friends. I was given the Word of God and taken to the book of Romans by some ladies at my church who came to pray and encourage me at my home after he took his life.

For although they knew God, they neither glorified Him as God nor gave thanks to Him, but their thinking became futile and their foolish hearts were darkened. Although they claimed to be wise, they became fools and exchanged the glory of the immortal God for images made to look like mortal man and birds and reptiles. Therefore God gave them over in the sinful

desires of their hearts to sexual impurity for the degrading of their bodies with one another. **They exchanged the truth of God for a lie, and worshiped and served created things rather than the Creator – who is forever praised. Amen. Because of this, God gave them over to shameful lusts. Even their women exchanged natural relations for unnatural ones. In the same way the men also abandoned natural relations with women and were inflamed with lust for one another. Men committed indecent acts with other men, and received in themselves the due penalty for their perversion. (Romans 1: 21-27)**

I knew when I read this that homosexuality was wrong. I needed proof from the Word of God and I also needed an explanation of the problem. I knew I was in sin through my spirit because I was not at peace with myself, but the Word of God confirmed it for me. My feelings for the woman I was relating to were very strong and the Word of God confirmed to me that I was actually worshiping her. She had become the center of my life. She was more important to me than any other person, any other activity, and certainly more important than God. Even if I was still worshiping God, she was still in my thoughts more than God. I could not lie to myself about this another day. She was an idol in my life and she took the place of God.

It became so clear to me that I not only was wrong but that homosexuality is sin and is also a perversion against God's natural and original intentions. I was convinced after seeing it written in the Word of God that God's natural and original intention for sexuality has always been reserved for the deep and holy intimacy to be shared between a man and a woman in the marriage covenant. **The Lord God said, "It is not good for the man (woman) to be alone. I will make a helper suitable for him (her)." (Genesis 1:18)**

Only Jesus can touch and heal our wounds. Not even a man could heal me. Healing is a supernatural impartation from the Lord because the wounds are in our spirits and in our souls (mind, will, and emotions). Healing is a work of the Holy Spirit. The negative emotions eventually leave us as the power of the Holy Spirit comes in and fills us with "living water." He gently heals the wounded emotions. (John 7:37-38 ref.) His peace replaces the griefs and we receive the fruit of the Holy Spirit, including the fruit of self-control. (Ephesians 5:22)(Colossians 3:15) With the help of the Holy Spirit and with acts of faith and of our will, we are then able to take control of the emotions and not let them control us.

Only the love of Jesus Christ can heal and fill the void in our souls with His awesome love, acceptance, and forgiveness, and His presence living and abiding within us to empower us with His grace. When we humble ourselves to Him, He meets us at our point of brokenness and faith. As we repent and turn from sin, He forgives and cleanses us. As we forgive ourselves and others, He also forgives us. He forgave us two thousand years ago at Calvary. But it is through our faith in Him to humble ourselves, to repent, and to forgive that we reach out to receive what He has already bought for us at the cross. And with our decided daily acts of repentance and forgiveness, the heart heals as it obeys the Lord, learning true submission to a holy God. It purifies. It reopens to feel again, to trust again, and to love again. And we emerge free to live an abundant life with our hearts healed and whole like that of a child. (John 10:10 ref.) (Ephesians 2:8 ref.)

The Holy Spirit can also convict your heart that you are sinning against God. I encourage you to ask God to reveal the truth to you. (Matthew 7:7) He will always answer our prayers. I not only got physically ill and needed female surgery, but I knew deep within my spirit that I was wrong. My disobedience and rebellion to live this homosexual lifestyle opened the door for Satan to bring disease to my ovaries. Later I needed a complete hysterectomy. It is never God's will to bring disease or to punish. However, sin and rebellion open the door for Satan to enter. God is a good God and wants us to come to Him with a humble and a repentant heart. Therefore, when the spirit and the soul are not in agreement, the body can be affected.

I also could not be honest with my coworkers and that was proof enough that I was not living with a clear conscience. My spontaneity for living was waning. I was living a double life. However, honesty with myself and with God would pull me out of the quicksand of sin. **Do not think of yourself more highly than you ought, but rather think of yourself with sober judgment, in accordance with the measure of faith God has given you. (Romans 12:3)** These are the words of Jesus to the church in Laodicea, **Those whom I love I rebuke and discipline. So be earnest, and repent. Here I am!**

I stand at the door and knock. If anyone hears my voice and opens the door, I will come in and eat with him, and he with me. (Revelation 3:20)

Your Vision is Your Baby!

Once you know your vision, you will be better motivated to die to selfish needs because you will realize that your one life will affect perhaps thousands more lives. Each decision you make will either help or hinder God's divine plan. Tough decisions build character!

There were many times in the process that I was tempted to go the wrong way. And I made mistakes along the way. There were many times, because of a self-hatred, that I cared more for others than for myself. Until I determined to break that spirit of self-condemnation over me, I made a lot of decisions to help others before even helping myself.

But as my desire to be used by God grew, I began to feel an inner satisfaction for the sacrifices I made to help others. I knew that Jesus was pleased with me and that was all I needed. **Give and it will be given to you. A good measure, pressed down, shaken together and running over, will be poured into your lap. For with the same measure you use, it will be measured to you. (Luke 6:38)** Despite all odds, God made me a winner. Because in helping others, I received much more back. Look at the pregnant mother who gives nine months of her life carrying the infant, sacrificing her life for the good of her own child. The rewards of childbirth are immeasurable after the physical pain of giving birth. Your vision is your baby. There is a divine delivery process after giving birth to the "honest self." And, as you bless others, God will give you spiritual children. Your healing will be used to share with other people who are suffering in this deception.

Mothering is Nurturing Others

Throughout my life, I was blessed to have been part of the "helping profession." It always helps me more to help others. It takes me out of "self" and teaches me "a lighter side to life." Helping others has and still is gratifying and keeps my perspective balanced. This is why I loved nursing. I was able to help others who were in need and keep healthy boundaries in the process. I loved working with children because they were so completely accepting. Their love is so pure.

I have not given birth physically to any children, but the Lord has given me many spiritual children: **"Sing, O barren woman, you who never bore a child; burst into song, shout for joy, you who were never in labor; because more are the children of the desolate woman than of her who has a husband," says the Lord. "Enlarge the place of your tent, stretch your tent curtains wide, do not hold back; lengthen your cords, strengthen your stakes, for you will spread out to the right and to the left; your descendants will dispossess nations and settle in their desolate cities." "Do not be afraid; you will not suffer shame. Do not fear disgrace; you will not be humiliated. You will forget the shame of your youth and remember no more the reproach of your widowhood.**

For your maker is your husband - the Lord Almighty is His name - the Holy One of Israel is your Redeemer; He is called the God of all the earth. The Lord will call you back as if you were a wife deserted and distressed in spirit - a wife who married young, only to be rejected," says your God. "For a brief moment I abandoned you, but with deep compassion I will bring you back. In a surge of anger I hid my face from you for a moment, but with everlasting kindness I will have compassion on you," says the Lord your Redeemer. (Isaiah 54:1-8)

Frank

In the early 1980's, I met a young man whom I was drawn to on the streets of Santa Barbara. His countenance was shining and I saw "truth" in his bright eyes. He was attending a small Word church, which just happened to be down the street from my apartment. It was the Open Bible Church.

He invited me to join him there. I really liked the church. I met with the Pastor who encouraged me.

After sharing my testimony with him, he said that I was not possessed because I was born again. I was only oppressed. The devil cannot live in a vessel that houses Jesus Christ, but he can surely try to barge into the doors. This is why it is so important to get sin out of our lives and to lock the doors.

Leave It!

This time was so precious for me and I was very vulnerable. I was actually cutting sin out of my life and being transformed into the image of Christ. I had to stay away from all my homosexual contacts. As cold as that sounds, if I spent any time with gay friends at this time, it would only serve to give Satan a chance to lure me back into the lifestyle. But I knew that God was not only saying, but He was commanding me: **Flee from Babylon! Run for your lives! Do not be destroyed because of her sins . . . (Jeremiah 51:6)**

This was the hardest thing to do. But, with the help of the Holy Spirit, I did it. Today I can honestly say I am delivered from the homosexual addiction. I want to touch lives for Jesus now as He has touched mine. Friend, during my infancy years of turning away from this sin, I wouldn't have been able to touch any lesbian or gay person for Christ because I was still not strong enough.

I had to obey God on this one. I had to sever all ties to all gay friends and/or lovers. The enemy tried to steer me back just as if Lucifer in the Garden of Eden were saying to me, "Aren't they your friends whom you love? Don't you want to save them too? Or are you only out for yourself? What kind of Christian are you anyway?"

Remember, he challenged Eve in saying, **"Did God really say?"** and **"You will not surely die." (Genesis 3:1,4)**The enemy will try everything to keep us from taking steps toward the Kingdom of God. I was in the infancy stage of Christianity. I had to help myself first before helping anyone else.I had to realize my own weakened state!

Perhaps, in the future, I would be used of God to help other homosexuals, but only in God's time. There could be <u>no compromise</u> on this command. There must be a clear separation and severance from all immoral relationships for inner healing to take place. The devil will use whatever he can to keep us locked into sin. If there is a soul tie to a person, it must be broken by physical separation and through prayer. See chapter, <u>Death Cannot Hold Me</u>, for prayers to break ungodly soul ties. The Word is clear about fleeing even the sight of temptation.

Do not put out the Spirit fire; do not treat prophesies with contempt. Test everything. Hold on to the good. Avoid every kind of evil. (1ˢᵗ Thessalonians 5:22)

Lucifer is a deceiving liar. We can, out of our own needs and desperation, deceive ourselves as well. We must be alert and smarter than the devil. This decision to leave all gay friends and lovers was pivotal not only to my healing but to theirs as well. Had I rationalized and lied to myself about it, I would never have found total freedom from this sin. Had I stayed in the emotional dependencies of these relationships, I would never have left the homosexual lie. It was like a deep nudging of the truth within my soul. I would never have faced my own emotional issues and healed. The Holy Spirit convicted me to leave. My friends were the salve for my wounds, subconscious as most of them were, but I had to choose to face the pain of those wounds to get to the truth of my identity in Christ Jesus.

I had to be honest with myself also. Tough love is not easy, especially when we believe that we are helping another by staying in a relationship. Do not take the bait of Satan and listen to his lies! The longer you stay, the harder it is to leave! Staying friends in these codependencies gives the enemy access into both your life and soul and into your friends' lives and their souls. You may need to move to another area if you are closely associated with a gay community. Follow the Holy Spirit's guidance step by step.

Jesus must be Lord for the healing to both begin and to be completed. Satan will try every trick in the book to keep you connected in your codependencies. You must be under the godly control of the Lord Jesus Christ, and this will replace the control you may feel with your partner. Even if you do not feel controlled in the gay relationship, you must leave it because it is sin and sin separates you from your intimate relationship with Jesus Christ.

We must bow to obey God and trust that He has control over every individual's life. He is sovereign over their lives. Only God can convict others! We do not have that power. Because of my own brokenness, I held people so tightly and it was so hard to let go. But I knew I had to release them and let God's love replace my need for them both for my good and for theirs as well. I had to move on.

Farewell

Praying for your friends will serve as part of your healing. It did mine. Interceding for them in prayer will help to connect your mind with your emotions and will bring peace within your own heart.

Deep down, I knew I was doing the right thing, even if I did not feel it. I knew by an inner conviction of faith and by a deep peace that I experienced. When you do the right thing, the Lord will bring you His peace. We must obey God and not men. (Acts 5:29) You will have a deep inner peace, no matter how difficult the decision is. You will discern the presence of the Lord in your heart. (1st Cor. 11:23-30) **And the peace of God, which transcends all understanding, will guard your hearts and your minds in Christ Jesus. (Philippians 4:7)**

I will never forget the day I mailed the farewell letter to my last female lover. I had such peace when I said to Jesus aloud, "Thy will be done," as I mailed it. This step of obedience confirmed my deep, personal, and committed relationship with Jesus Christ. I knew He was with me as I stepped out in obedience. I knew He was pleased.

Despite my confusion, I knew I had to break the tie. At that time, there was more of a dependency and a sense of indebtedness I attached to the lover I left. I had to redirect that dependency to Jesus. The only debt we owe people is to love them. Leaving all homosexual relationships was the highest expression of love both for God in obedience to Him and for myself and for the women I released to His love and His care. **Let no debt remain outstanding, except the continuing debt to love one another, for he who loves his fellowman has fulfilled the law. The commandments, "Do not commit adultery," "Do not murder," "Do not steal," "Do not covet," and whatever other commandment there may be, are summed up in this one rule: "Love your neighbor as yourself." Love does no harm to its neighbor. Therefore love is the fulfillment of the law. (Romans 13:8-10)**

I sought confirmation through accountability with my Christian friends within the body of Christ. I asked the Lord for divine courage to go through with the decision. Staying friends would only present the temptation to sin again. It would also serve to continue to cover the root issues that had to be faced and dealt with in order to get free of the homosexual attractions. I had to face my own inner pain and allow my partners to face theirs also. I had to get out of their way as well. Breaking addictions requires accountability with other caring Christians and compassion for others without compromising the Word of God. **It seemed good to the Holy Spirit and to us not to burden you with anything beyond the following requirements: You are to abstain from food sacrificed to idols, from blood, from the meat of strangled animals and from sexual immorality. You will do well to avoid these things. Farewell. (Acts 15:28, 29)**

The Lord Will Promote You

I remember praying for my friend as thoughts and feelings for her entered my mind. She had helped me through nursing school and I was a part of her family; she was divorced with a few children. I felt indebted to her for all she had done for me. She was an older woman. She was very "motherly." Friend, this was a tough call, but I had to do the right thing.

I knew I had to leave this relationship to go forward with my divine purpose in life. As difficult as the decision was, the Lord helped me to release her as I prayed for her. Believe me, you will never receive complete deliverance unless you say "farewell" to all your gay friends in the lifestyle and all illegal partners and lovers. It is a tough love that loves without compromising the Word of God. It is a tough love that refuses to have any sin or idols before God. It is a tough and a courageous love that goes against the flow of the crowd and takes steps of faith to do the right thing for all involved. And for the few I left, there were countless others who reaped the benefits of those obedient steps taken later in life. There is always a sacrifice involved in living for the Lord.

Unfortunately, my friend developed cancer at that time. This was the enemy's tactic to keep me plugged into the relationship. It was a set up to lure me into disobeying the voice of God. Whenever you make a decision to obey God's will, the enemy will do everything he can to stop you from making the right decision.

I had to trust that God would take care of her. I had to accept that her healing was not my responsibility. Only the Lord can heal. I obeyed God and severed the tie. I prayed for her healing. I never saw her or her family again. However, the Lord lifted the false guilt and burdens from me supernaturally. I entered into praise and worship of the Lord. I made new friends within the body of Christ. I received Christian counsel for accountability and to keep my obedience complete. The Ephesians desired that Paul stay in Ephesus: **But when they asked him to spend more time with them, he declined. But as he left, he promised, "I will come back if it is God's will." Then he set sail from Ephesus. When he landed at Caesarea, he went up and greeted the church and then went down to Antioch. (Acts 18:20, 21)**

Making New Friends within the Body of Christ

As a newly reborn Christian, I became a member of Calvary Chapel in Santa Barbara, California. I was surrounded by people who loved God and who would help me to live a new life in Christ. I had a place of both safety and accountability, a new family. And the Lord blessed me with every step of obedience as I made decisive steps toward bonding with the body of believers. With each step in the right direction, the Lord showed Himself true. I knew He was with me. Something good happened every time I obeyed Him. My faith was growing. I knew there was a supernatural helper with me.

I was loved and accepted there. Even if I did not have the capacity to reach out to them, they did reach out to me. I was in such great need for healthy friendships. Being welcomed and actively supported in a home church made a decided difference for me to continue making the lifestyle change and sticking with it. I had to be connected with people who were stronger than me to grow out of the sludge I was in. I volunteered in the children's ministry and the music ministry and loved it! I made friends in Bible study groups in peoples' homes and in singles' ministry activities. The body of Christ loved me back into abundant life and showed me the love of God.

Ron and Joanne Highley of L.I.F.E. Ministries in New York City write candidly about the importance of being free from the dependency in the homosexual relationship and are adamant about the necessity of separation of the partners when they state in reference to a former lesbian couple:

It may seem to some that homosexual lovers are friends, but we must remember the deceptive quality of this attachment. Though these women are not lovers any longer, there is great benefit in separation, because then the emotions can come to the surface and be processed. One can only find out how to become an individual person when free of dependency on another. During this separation, the person can ask God to reveal and break up any old resentment or other blockages to loving Him and to help us deal with the feelings that were covered by the idolatry. We can then go to God with our needs and learn the boundaries of true friendship and love. It is a precious time not to be missed, and we believe that everyone who has had homosexual desires and/or activity should have a period of separation for repentance, cleansing and making peace with God. [67]

Consecrate Your Body to the Lord

Dealing with Masturbation and Fornication
How good and pleasant it is for the brethren to dwell together in unity! (Psalm 133:1)
The Prayer of Agreement

I sought the counsel of Spirit filled Christians at Vineyard Christian Church in Santa Barbara, California. I remember going to an altar call and confessing to a young man, an altar minister, that I had left the lifestyle but that I was having trouble with masturbation. He said, "I have the same problem." I was so relieved! I was in a delusional state, imagining that the partner I had left was still with me.

Prepare Your Heart of Faith - At the altar, then, this young man and I properly positioned our hearts in faith, as we repented of the sin of masturbation and as we resurrendered to Jesus Christ as our Lord, our Savior, and our loving authority. (Romans 10:9,10)(John 14:6)(John 3:3)(Romans 10:13)(John 14:6) We then committed to forgive and release judgments against both ourselves and others. (Matthew 6:12)(Luke 6:27,37)(Scriptures referenced)

Now, with a release of judgments, with a reception of the Lord's acceptance, forgiveness, and love, we both were ready to speak with our hearts of faith. There is power in the prayer of agreement. **Therefore confess your sins to each other and pray for each other so that you may be healed. The prayer of a righteous man (or woman) is powerful and effective. (James 5:16)**

These are the words of Jesus to His disciples,**"I tell you the truth, my Father will give you whatever you ask in my name. Until now you have not asked for anything in my name. Ask and you will receive, and your joy will be complete." (John 16:23, 24) But if we walk in the light, as He is in the light, we have fellowship with one another, and the blood of Jesus, His Son, purifies us from all sin. (1ˢᵗ John 1:7) If we confess our sins, He is faithful and just and will forgive us our sins and purify us from all unrighteousness. (1ˢᵗ John 1:9)**

Enter into Your Father's Presence - "Father God, we enter into Your gates with thanksgiving in our hearts and offer to You our petitions, in Jesus' name." (Psalm 100:4) (John 16:23)

Take Jesus' Delegated Authority Against the Spirit of Lust and Self-Condemnation in the Name of Jesus — Repent from Dead Works — Ask the Lord for Divine Strategy - We then took Jesus delegated authority against the spirits of lust and self-condemnation. We repented, we rebuked, and cast them out, and we renounced these spirits off ourselves in Jesus' name. (Luke 10:19)(Matthew 18:18)(Psalm 107:20)(Psalm 103:4) We sent them to the depths of the earth to be held captive by the angels of God. (Mark 5:8-13) We committed to a life led by the Holy Spirit.(Acts 1:8)(Acts 2:38) We declared ourselves free from the spirit of lust and self-condemnation in the name of Jesus. (Romans 8:1)(1ˢᵗ Cor. 6:20)(Ephesian 6:20) We committed to a personal relationship with Jesus Christ. (John 3:3)(Romans 10:9,10) We committed to daily time spent studying the Word of God and prayer with praise and worship of our Creator God to keep the enemy out. (Luke 11:24-26)(Romans 12:2)(John 3:3)(Psalm 33:1-3)(John 4:24) We repented for sinning against our own bodies, spirits, and souls; in masturbation, and in fornication, (sex outside of marriage); and against other peoples' bodies, spirits, and souls (in fornication).(1ˢᵗ John 1:9) (1ˢᵗ Cor. 6:18-20)(1ˢᵗ Thes. 5:22) And we thanked Jesus for His divine provision of mercy through the finished work of His shed, divine, and holy blood on the cross of Calvary. (1ˢᵗ Thes. 5:18)(Hebrews 9 & 10)(Luke 23:46)(Luke 24:46,50) (See Appendix)

As we repented, we humbly received complete forgiveness and healing from the Lord with the washing and the cleansing of our bodies, spirits, and souls because of the sacrificial blood of Jesus Christ. (1ˢᵗ John 1:9)(Heb. 9:14)(Hebrews 10:19-22)(1ˢᵗ Peter 2:24) We thanked Jesus for His blood sacrifice which cleanses our consciences from such acts that lead to death so that we may serve the living God. (Hebrews 9:14) We placed a Holy Spirit seal upon our petitions as we released judgment against both ourselves and against the others we had been involved with.(Acts 1:8)(Acts 2:38) We committed to sever and leave all ungodly soul ties. (Proverbs 4:27) (1ˢᵗ Thes. 5:22)(Rev. 18:4) We prayed for those we were involved with, releasing judgment and blame, and prayed that they would be convicted of their purpose and calling in Christ Jesus. (Ephesians 1:18)(Romans 2:4)(Luke 24:31,45)(Luke 6:28,37)(Matthew 28:18-20)(Mark 16:15,16) We prayed that laborers be sent to them and that they would come to repent of their sins and enjoy the benefits of salvation through repentance. We petitioned that they surrender their lives to Jesus Christ. (Matthew 9:37,38)(Romans 10:9,10)(Romans 2:4)(See Appendix)

We then thanked the Lord for His blood sacrifice that took these sins for us on the cross. (1ˢᵗ Thes.5:18) We committed to taking our ungodly desires, thoughts, fantasies, and emotions captive to the obedience of Christ. (2ⁿᵈ Corinthians 10:4) We committed to daily study of the Word of God and prayer to lock the door to further enemy entrance. (Luke 11:24-26)(Rom. 12:2) We then asked the Lord for supernatural strategy to continue to resist the fleshly temptations. (1ˢᵗ Corinthians 10:13)(James 4:7,8) We committed to a life of purity in Christ. (Matthew 5:8)(All scriptures referenced)(See Appendix)

No temptation has seized you except what is common to man (woman). And God is faithful; He will not let you be tempted beyond what you can bear. But when you are tempted, He will also provide a way out so that you can stand up under it. (1ˢᵗ Corinthian 10:13)

Declare and Recommit Your Bodies, Spirits, and Souls
Back to the Lord in the Name of Jesus

With our hearts still positioned with faith in the holy presence of our Father God, we continued to take Jesus' delegated authority in Christ as we spoke the Word of God and recommitted our bodies, spirits, and souls back to the Lord also in Jesus' name. We declared Jesus' delegated authority over our bodies, spirits, and souls, declaring them holy and clean, as white as snow, and covered by the blood of Jesus in the name of Jesus Christ. We committed to live a life of purity and to wait until marriage before engaging in intimacy. In faith and as prayer partners, the altar minister of Vineyard and I then became accountable to each other to continue in our obedience and our pledge of purity before Christ Jesus. **Blessed are the pure in heart, for they will see God. (Matthew 5:8)**

And, by faith, we received the righteousness (right standing) of God. (1ˢᵗ John 1:9) (Romans 1:16,17) We accepted His justification, "just as if we had never sinned." (Romans 3:23-25)(All scriptures referenced) **For all have sinned and fall short of the glory of God and are justified freely by His grace through the redemption that came by Christ Jesus. God presented Him as a sacrifice of atonement, through faith in His blood. (Romans 3:23-25)**

Consequently, just as the result of one trespass was condemnation for all men (women), so also the result of one act of righteousness was justification that brings life for all men (women). For just as through the disobedience of the one man the many were made sinners, so also through the obedience of the one man the many will be made righteous. (Romans 5:18,19)

Act to Break Habits – Invite the Lord into Your Bedroom

I did have to sleep for many months with my hands above my head and that helped. And I asked God to help me break the fantasy I still retained of my last partner being with me. (John 16:23,24) I was in a delusional state when I masturbated, imagining that my previous partner was there with me. I had to cast down this imagination and stop and pray for her to come to Jesus with a repentant heart. (2ⁿᵈ Cor. 10:4-6) (Ephesians 1:18)(2ⁿᵈ Cor. 4:3,4) (Romans 2:4) And transfer to my godly imagination of God with me. (Deut. 31:6) (All scriptures referenced)(See Appendix)

...God's kindness leads you toward repentance...(Romans 2:4)

I then acknowledged the presence of the Lord there with me. (Joshua 1:5) I invited the Lord into my bedroom and felt His loving authority with me. I prepared my heart of faith with submission, repentance, and forgiveness. I then entered into my Father's presence with my petitions in the name of Jesus. The real battle must be initiated by our words. We must rise up as we take Jesus' delegated authority against the demonic spirits in Jesus' name (Luke 10:19) and against our own flesh (using self-control as a choice we make with our will). We must speak the Word of God in faith with our human spirit led by the Holy Spirit. It is our privilege and our responsibility to put the lights back on. I refused to be moved by this spirit of lust. I determined to rise above this relentless foe. After many trials, it left for a season only to return but I continued to resist and refuse to give Satan victory in my life.

I did aerobic exercises until I received the peace of God and the presence of the Lord back into my body. A warm bath or a professional massage does wonders to bring the body into a relaxed state. You do what you need to do to get the darkness out. Eat a sandwich. Go to a recovery group or a church meeting. Call a friend. Pray in the Holy Spirit. Ask the Holy Spirit for direction. Become involved in a volunteer group at your church. Consult your physician regarding a physical exercise program if you have any medical conditions, health issues, are pregnant or lactating, or are taking any medications.

Continue to enter boldly into the Lord's presence to petition your Father and take your delegated authority with a heart of faith. And, as a born again believer, rebuke spirits that are oppressing you in the name of Jesus. (Luke 10:19) Send them to the depths of the earth to be held captive by the angels of God. (Mark 5:8-13) Continue to speak the Word of God over your life and over any negative circumstances. (Mark 11:23-26) Commit to a life of daily prayer, praise, worship, and to the daily study of the Word of God to keep your vessel filled with God. (Luke 11:24-26) (See Appendix)

I had accountability with my friend from the church and that motivated me to continue fighting with faith against the unclean spirits and against my own flesh. (James 5:16) This was essential to my victory over this sin. Once I called the sin "sin" and I repented with another Christian, the power of both the delusion and of the sin was broken. Once I repented and welcomed the Lord into my bedroom, I was consciously aware of His loving presence there with me. I had to be stubborn to get to the other side of this sin. It is a fight but it is possible.

**Therefore confess your sins to each other and pray for each
other so that you may be healed. (James 5:16)**

I am God's child and His holy hand touches me. After confessing and repenting of the sin of masturbation, another layer of fog representing the guilt and the shame lifted off my mind. Masturbation was pure lust which kept me isolated from normal social interactions, from the truth of my "honest self," and from my complete deliverance from homosexuality. It kept me hooked into an ungodly lying fantasy relationship. My choice to continue in this activity kept me from quality relationships. I always felt so paranoid the next day after engaging in masturbation. I couldn't look people in the eyes. I felt not only guilty, but ashamed. I felt unclean. I had to receive the Lord's forgiveness as soon as I repented. Masturbation had to go! I sought the love, acceptance, and forgiveness of Jesus until this habit was completely extinguished from my life.

With each trial, I directed my imagination to the truth of the divine touch of the Lord Jesus Christ upon my life and upon my body. I believe that imagination has been given to us by God to see, feel, hear from, and also to touch and be touched by God Himself. **For we do not have a high priest who is unable to sympathize with our weaknesses, but we have one who has been tempted in every way, just as we are - yet was without sin. Let us approach the throne of grace with confidence, so that we may receive mercy and find grace to help us in our time of need. (Hebrews 4:15,16)**

I did have to be selective with whom I chose to spend time with. Codependence to a person you are intimate with, especially with any New Age involvement, is a strong ungodly soul tie, but with Jesus, anything is possible. I literally turned the light of Jesus Christ on in my bedroom and the Holy Spirit helped me to extinguish this habit. The Lord was pleased with my repentance and my honesty before Him, my obedience to sever the tie, and my prayer of agreement and accountability with this young man whom I met at the altar.(James 5:16)

I continued in intercession for the person whom I was codependently and obsessively attached to until the burden lifted. Repentance and intercessory prayer for my x- partners turned the tide to the Lord's favor and broke me of the delusional fantasies. I believe my prayers of intercession were heard and honored by my Lord. And my need for codependence to people broke as I leaned upon the Lord, step by step. He then anchored me to Him with a keen discernment of His divine presence with me. His presence within and upon me became my very identity and there was no further need for codependence. The Lord always meets us at the point of our need. His strength is made perfect in our very weaknesses. (2nd Cor. 12:9)(See Appendix)

Today, I am still harassed by this spirit of lust, but I have strategies that I use against it. Whenever I fall into this sin, I immediately repent, receive the Lord's forgiveness, and enter into right relationship with Him again. We are not perfect, only perfectly forgiven. The tendency toward this sin will be extinguished with healing of the heart, with persistent prayer, with persistent obedience to leave ungodly soul ties, with physical exercise, and with the forming of healthy relationships. The ultimate remedy for this sin is a love relationship with Jesus Christ, a commitment of daily study of the Word of God and prayer and worship, with a defiant "no" to the flesh lest the enemy get any foothold upon our walk of purity. (Luke 11:24-26) Even in marriage, Jesus Christ must be our first love. (Rev. 2:4)(See Appendix)(See chapter Death Cannot Hold Me on breaking soul ties)

Also the power of lust to control us is extinguished when we come to receive the rest and the grace of God, and His complete acceptance of us. We deeply discern His presence, His love, and His power within us. This helps us to continue to bring the flesh under our control as we come to a gratitude for these provisions in our lives. (1st Thes 5:18)(1st Cor. 11:23)(John 14:17) We fall deeply in love with Jesus. Wisdom tells us that our decisions for purity will not only bring our healing but will touch others' lives as well. Thus, we do not want to bring our Lord any further displeasure. Finally, we annihilate these spirits of lust out of our lives as we mature in a deep gratitude for His shed blood which covers these sins the moment we repent. His mercy also cleanses our consciences and our bodies with pure water. (Hebrews 10:19-22)(Hebrews 9:14)

The body does come into a restful state, no longer taunted by the unclean spirits, fleshly thoughts and memories, fantasies, imaginations, and emotions which ignite our flesh to sin. We come to a place of deep surrender and repentance, with a true forgiveness and release for ourselves and for all who have sinned against us. God has also given us the holy covenant of marriage to enjoy real intimacy embracing one other person, heart to heart.

'I saw the Lord always before me. Because He is at my right hand, I will not be shaken.' (Acts 2:25)

Prayer to Honor God with Our Bodies

Prepare Your Heart – "Jesus, I submit my heart to You as my Lord and Savior, and my loving authority. (Psalm 100:4) (Romans 10:9,10) (John 16:23) Lord Jesus, I am heartily sorry and I renounce every sin I have committed against both my body, my soul, and my spirit, and against any other persons' bodies, souls, and spirits, in my thoughts and/or in my actions. I humbly receive Your forgiveness from all these sins. I now willfully release all the shame and the guilt attached to them. Thank You, Lord Jesus. Now I forgive and release all judgments and all blame against both myself and all who have sinned against me. I commit to turn away from these behaviors and to change. Fill me, O Lord, with Your Holy Spirit. (Acts 2:38) (Matthew 6:12)(Luke 6:37) Thank you, Lord Jesus. Amen." (Romans 1:16,17)(All scriptures personalized)

Enter into Your Father's Presence – "Father God, I enter into Your gates with thanksgiving in my heart and offer to You my petitions, in Jesus' name." (Psalm 100:4) (John 16:23)(Scriptures personalized)

Rebuke the Spirit of Lust; Commit to Leave Sexual Sin and All Its Connections –

"I confess and accept masturbation as both sin against You and against my own body, soul, and spirit. It has separated me from You.(Rom. 3:23) It is an idolatrous fantasy addiction, Lord Jesus. (Gal. 5:20) I rebuke the spirit of masturbation in Jesus' name. (Luke 10:19)(Matthew 18:18) Go, in the name of Jesus. (Luke 10:19) Go wherever Jesus sends you to be held captive by the angels of God. (Mark 5:8-13) I repent and renounce my sins of masturbation. (1st Cor. 6:18)(1st John 1:9) I also confess and accept homosexuality, (any sexual activity with a member of the same sex), as sin against You, against my own body, soul, and spirit, and against my partner(s)' body(s), soul(s), and spirit(s). (Romans 1:22-23)(2ndTim. 2:22)(1st Cor. 6:10,18) (Ephesians 5:3) I realize, Lord Jesus, that all sexual sin is the ultimate act of selfishness and a lack of self-control. (1st Thes. 4:3,4) (Matthew 15:19) I rebuke the spirit of homosexuality in Jesus' name. (Luke

10:19)(Matthew 18:18) Go, in the name of Jesus. (Luke 10:19)) Go wherever Jesus sends you to be held captive by the angels of God.(Mark 5:8-13) I also repent and renounce my sins of homosexuality.(1st John 1:9) I confess and accept fornication, (any sexual activity with any other person, (male or female), before marriage, as sin against You, against my own body, soul, and spirit, and also against another person's body, soul, and spirit. (1st Thes. 5:22)(2nd Tim. 2:22) I rebuke the spirit of fornication in Jesus' name. (Luke 10:19) (Matthew 18:18) Go, in the name of Jesus. (Luke 10:19) Go wherever Jesus sends you to be held captive by the angels of God. (Mark 5:8-13) I repent and renounce all my sins of fornication. (Leviticus 18)(1st Cor.6:18) (1st Cor. 6:13) (Galatians 5:19) (Colossians 3:5) Thank You, Lord Jesus, for Your mercy to forgive me of these sins. Thank You for Your love for me that loves me but that hates all sin.(Isaiah 43:1-4) I commit to the study of Your Word and prayer with praise and worship to keep my vessel full of God and to keep all lustful spirits from oppressing me. (Luke 11:24-26)(Rom. 12:2) (James 5:16)(Psalm 33:1-3)(John 4:24) I also commit to pray for all I have had relationships with. (All scriptures personalized) (See Appendix)

"I now repent of _(identify your sin(s) to the Lord)_. (1st John 1:9) I believe the Word of God is true, (Heb. 4:12), and, in my heart of faith, (Heb. 11:1) I now ask You and believe that I will be empowered by the Holy Spirit to help me to stop sinning in this (these) way(s). (Acts 1:8) (Acts 2:38) Your Word is clear that I must flee all sexual immorality. (1st Cor. 6:18)(1st Thes. 5:22)(Rev. 18:4)(1st Cor. 6:17) I commit to separate and sever myself from all ungodly soul ties that I have made with anyone I have been sexually active with in immoral ways, writing them and telling them that the relationship is over. (1st Thes. 5:22) (Rev. 18:4) I also commit to separate and sever myself from all ungodly soul ties that I have developed in my imagination through images via magazines and/or the internet and/or social networks. (2nd Cor. 10:4,5)(1st Cor. 5:9-11) I will also sever all friendships I have formed that are ungodly and all soul ties with connections to the New Age and/or occult, including all memorabilia associated with these mindsets. (1st Cor. 6:18) (1st Thes. 5:22)(Rev. 18:4) I will do this in obedience to Your Word and Your will. (Matthew 6:10)I commit to continue to grow in you, Lord Jesus. I do not want to be separated from You any longer, Lord Jesus. I will go forward with the call and the purpose that You have designed for me in this life. (Matthew 28:18-20)(Mark 16:15-18) In Jesus' name, Amen."(Ephesians 1:18)(All scriptures personalized) (See Chapter Death Cannot Hold Me for breaking of soul ties)

"Lord Jesus, I am aware that there are issues and wounds in my heart that I must face and deal with in order to have a divine and completed peace in my body. (Col. 3:15) And I also confess that my immoral sexual behavior is a way of escape from the ungodly thoughts and emotions that must be faced in the presence of a holy God.(1st John 1:9)(Rom. 3:23)(Heb. 9:14)(Heb. 10:19-22) I know and believe that I must repent, forgive, and release all judgment against both myself and all who have sinned against me for that peace to manifest. (1st John 1:9)(Luke 6:28,37)(Matthew 6:12) I stand on the Word of Epheisian 6:12, knowing that I do not fight against flesh and blood but against principalities, powers, and rulers in heavenly places and against spiritual forces of evil that are working havoc through people. (Ephesians 6:12) I release all false guilt to You, Lord.(Rom. 8:1)(Hebrews 9:14) I let go of the past. And I do now receive Your forgiveness, Your unconditional love, and Your righteousness to enter into Your peace.(Isaiah 26:3) Jesus, I receive Your forgiveness and love.(Isaiah 43:1-4)(Rom. 1:17)(1st John 1:9) I now declare that I am in right standing with You, in Your name, O Lord. Thank You, Jesus."

"Only You, Lord Jesus, can bring me the peace of God that surpasses all understanding. (Isaiah 26:3) (Col. 3:15) It is an inner peace that is supernatural because it is the very discernment of You, Lord Jesus, and Your deep and unconditional love within me that fills me, that identifies me, and that brings me the peace that only You can bring. (Col. 3:15)(1st Cor. 11:23)(Jer. 29:11-14) Only You, Lord Jesus, can fill the void and emptiness in my heart. I commit to work through this pain and to get to the other side of sexual sin, to be the person You have called me to be, and to bless other people for the kingdom of God.(Mark 16:15-18)(Matthew 28:18-20) Help me, O Lord, to change. (Matthew 7:7)(Pro. 51:10) In Jesus' name I pray and believe."(All scriptures personalized)

"Whenever I am tempted in these ways, Lord Jesus, I will picture You, Lord Jesus, on the cross of Calvary, dying for me. (Rom. 3:25) You died for me, Lord! (Luke 23:46) I will never be the same. Lord,

I now ask for an accountability person to help me to keep this commitment.(Psalm 133:1) I commit to a strong Bible believing church body, to support groups, and to ministry work. I commit to humble myself and to come out of isolation.(Matthew 23:12)(Psalm 147:6) I declare that I will become active in Your work in the earth, in Jesus' name. (Matthew 28:18) I believe and trust that, at the right time and in the right season, Lord, you will bring the right person (marriage partner) to me. (Ephesians 5:22-33) I open my heart to that possibility. (Acts 16:14) I believe that I will know by the Spirit of God who that right person is. (John 16:13) Until then, Lord Jesus, I will continue to walk in purity before You as best as I can. (Matthew 5:8) And I will make a difference in other peoples' lives, in Jesus name. Amen" (All scriptures personalized)

"Lord Jesus, I now recommit my body back to You. My body is a temple and a dwelling place for the Holy Spirit. (1st Cor 6:19) The Holy Spirit lives within my body. (John 14:20) I have received the Holy Spirit. (Acts 2:38) (Acts 1:8) I also have received my body from You, Father God. (Genesis 1:26) You are my Creator. My body is a living sacrifice, set aside as holy and pleasing to You, Lord Jesus. This is my spiritual act of worship and thanksgiving to You. (Romans 12:1) Thank you for giving me a body, healthy, whole, and able to be used for Your kingdom. I am not my own. I have been bought with a price, the price You paid for me at Calvary. (1st Cor. 6:19,20) I will honor You, Lord Jesus, with my body. (1st Cor. 6:20) You sacrificed Your body giving Your life for me at Calvary's cross. I belong to You and am accountable to You on this earth. I do not want to bring You any further disgrace or displeasure. I now, as an act of my will, give my body back to You, Lord Jesus, to be used for your service here in the earth in Jesus' name. (Matthew 28:18) Thank You for Your sacrifice for me. (Luke 23:47)(Heb. 9:14)(Heb. 10:19-22)(1st Peter 1:18,19)(1st Peter 2:24) In you name, Lord Jesus, Amen."(All scriptures personalized)

"I thank You for the blood of Jesus that also cleanses and washes my soul clean from this sin. I now declare that I am as white as snow in the name of Jesus. (Rom. 3:25)(1st Peter 1:18,19)(Heb. 9:14) (1st John 1:7,9) I thank You for the Holy Spirit Who is in me and Who empowers me to forgive myself for this. (John 14:17,20) I now, as an act of my will, accepting the power of the Holy Spirit within me, and as an act of my faith in the finished work of Jesus Christ, forgive and release myself from the guilt and the shame of all sexual sins I have committed against You, O Lord Jesus. (Rom. 3:25) (Acts 1:8) (Romans 8:1)Thank you, Jesus. I also forgive and release all judgment against any person who has ever sinned against my body, whether against my will or with my consent, whether through physical acts or through spiritual rape. (Name the person(s) to the Lord). (Luke 6:28,37) (Matthew 6:12) I pray that You would convict their hearts to come to repentance, reconciliation, and a personal relationship with You, Lord Jesus. (James 5:16) (Romans 2:4)(2nd Cor.4:3,4) I thank You, Lord Jesus, that You have forgiven and have also forgotten my sins as far as the east is from the west.(1st John 1:9)(Hebrews 10:17) I pray and believe this, in the name of Jesus Christ."(Psalm 103:12)(All scriptures personalized)(See Appendix)

"Lord Jesus, I now declare that my spirit, soul, and my body are washed clean, as if I had never sinned in Jesus' name. (Heb. 10:17)(Rom. 3:24)(Rom. 5:1) I am cleansed by the blood of the spotless Lamb of God, holy and pure in Your sight. (1st John 1:9)(Hebrews 9:14) (Hebrews 10:19-22)(Romans 1:16,17) I declare in Jesus' name that I am justified and made righteous, not by anything that I have done.(Ephesians 2:8) I declare this in my faith in the sacrificial act of Jesus Christ for me,(Luke 23:46), and in the name of the strong Son of God. (Phil. 2:9)(Romans 5:1) (Romans 1:17) I am now covered by the precious blood of Jesus Christ. (1st Peter 1:18,19) (Hebrews 10:19-22) I rebuke and renounce the spirit of lust in Jesus' name. (Luke 10:19)(Mark 16:17) Go, in the name of Jesus. (Luke 10:19) I render you powerless to attach to my body, my soul/heart, my spirit, or to my life. (Rom. 12:1) Go wherever Jesus sends you to the depths of the earth so that the angels of God will hold you captive. (Mark 5:8-13) I commit to daily study of the Word of God with prayer and praise to keep my vessel filled with God and to keep the enemy out."(Luke 11:24-26)(Romans 12:2)(James 5:16)(Psalm 33:1-3)(John 4:24)(All scriptures personalized)(See Appendix)

"I now stand with a clear conscience before You, Lord, in surrender to You that would never have taken place without these trials. (Heb. 9:14)(Heb. 10:19-22) Therefore, I give thanks to You even in the trials.(1st Thes. 5:18) I now declare that I have peace in my body, in Jesus' name.(Col. 3:15) I declare that this is settled deep within my heart in Jesus' name. (Pro. 4:23)(Gal. 5:23) And I thank You, Lord Jesus, for Your mercy upon me.(1st John 1:9) I know You do not measure sin.(Heb. 10:17) I also know there will always be trials from people the enemy uses who seek to humiliate and bring insults to me only because of their own lack of knowledge and their unrepented sins against You.(1st Peter 5:8) I pray for them. (Luke 6:28) But deeper still is my anchor of faith in Your finished work at Calvary and my conviction of Your love for me which far outweighs the judgments of others. (Isaiah 43:4)(Luke 6:37) You see me just as if I had never sinned.(Rom 5:1)(Rom. 3:24)(Hebrews 10:17) I will carry the "living remembrance" of Your sacrifice within my heart with great thanksgiving. (1st Cor. 11:23) And my confidence in You, living in me, Lord Jesus, will grow to reign greater than anything coming against me from the world. (John 15:4) (John 14:17,20) As I continue to pray for those whom the enemy uses against me, I will keep my heart pure before You. (Matthew 5:8) I will live by faith which is higher and deeper than any emotion, feeling, thought, or opinion. (Hebrews 11:1)(2nd Cor. 4:18)(Rom. 1:17) Because love is the greatest weapon against anything the enemy brings. (1st Cor. 13) And faith expresses itself through love. (Gal. 5:6) Thank You for Your love, Lord Jesus. In Jesus' name, Amen." (Romans 8:28)(Jer. 29:11)(Isaiah 43:1-4)(All scriptures personalized)(See Apppendix)

I am Forgiven and My Sins are Forgotten - For as high as the heavens are above the earth, so great is His love for those who fear Him; as far as the east is from the west, so far has He removed our transgressions from us. As a father has compassion on His children, so the Lord has compassion on those who fear Him; (Psalm 103:11-13)

I am Justified in Christ Jesus - Therefore, since we have been justified (just as if we have never sinned) through faith, we have peace with God through our Lord Jesus Christ, through whom we have gained access by faith into this grace in which we now stand. And we rejoice in the hope of the glory of God. (Romans 5:1)

I am the Righteousness of God in Christ Jesus - For in the gospel righteousness from God (right standing with God) is revealed, a righteousness that is by faith from first to last, just as it is written: "The righteous will live by faith." (Romans 1:17)

Flee sexual immorality. All other sins a man (woman) commits are outside his (her) body, but he (she) who sins sexually sins against his (her) own body. Do you not know that your body is a temple of the Holy Spirit, Who is in you, Whom you have received from God? You are not your own; you were bought at a price. Therefore honor God with your body. (1st Cor. 6:18-20)

He (she) who unites himself (herself) with the Lord is one with Him in spirit. (1st Cor. 6:17)

Jesus comforts His disciples. He answers Thomas who asks Jesus where He is going after His discourse on leaving the disciples to go to heaven and also on His second return. **Jesus answered, "I am the way and the truth and the life. No one comes to the Father except through me. If you really knew me, you would know my Father as well. From now on, you do know Him and have seen Him." (John 14:6)**

Prayers to Silence Shame

Enter into the Holy Place with Your Heart Prepared with Faith - "I stand with a heart of faith that has accepted and surrendered to Jesus Christ as my Lord, Savior, and authority, with repentance for my sins, and with forgiveness and release of all judgment against myself and others. I enter into the gates of my Father with thanksgiving in my heart and petition Him in the name of Jesus Christ, my Lord."(John 16:23)(Psalm 100:4)(Scriptures referenced)

Prayer to Silence Shame Using the Spoken Word of God - "I am cleansed, purified, and covered with the precious blood of Jesus Christ by my repentance and by my commitment to a covenant relationship with Jesus Christ. (Heb. 9:15)(1st John 1:9)(1st Peter 1:18,19)(Romans 10:9,10)(John 14:17,20) I am safe under

His divine blood covering in this secret place of fellowship with Him.(1ˢᵗ Peter 1:18,19) (Psalm 91:1) With repentance, the Holy Spirit comes to empower and to baptize me. (Acts 1:8)(Acts 2:38) The anointing of the Holy Spirit breaks the yoke of shame. (Galatians 5:1)(Matthew 11:28) I am dressed in the armor of God. (Ephesians 6:14-18) Faith with perfect love shuts the door on all fear."(1ˢᵗ John 4:18)(Hebrews 11:1) (Galatians 5:6)(All scriptures personalized)

Take Jesus' Delegated Authority to Silence the Spirit of Shame in Jesus' Name – Jesus Already Died for This – You Don't Need to Take it upon Yourself! Take Back Your Confidence in Christ Jesus –

"I speak to you, spirit of shame, and, with the delegated authority of my Lord and Savior, Jesus Christ, I put you on notice and tell you to leave me now, in the name of Jesus Christ of Nazareth. (Luke 10:19) (Mark 11:22-25) You have no authority here and you must leave, in the mighty name of Jesus Christ. (Matthew 16:16-18) Go wherever Jesus sends you to be held captive by the angels of God. (Mark 5:8-13) I repent of taking shame on and entertaining it.(1ˢᵗ John 1:9) This is not God's will for my life. (1ˢᵗ Thes. 5:18) (Matthew 6:10) Lord Jesus, I commit to daily study of the Word of God, prayer, and praise to keep my vessel filled with thoughts of You, Lord, and to keep the enemy of shame out permanently."(Luke 11:24-26)(Psalm 33:1-3)(John 4:24)(James 5:16)(Rom. 12:2)(See Appendix)

"Lord Jesus, I now receive complete and divine love, acceptance, and forgiveness from my Father God. (Isaiah 43:1-4)(1ˢᵗ John 1:9) I declare that I will stop sinning and annihilate shame from my life, in Jesus' name. (Romans 1:16,17) (1ˢᵗ Cor. 15:34) I am the righteousness of God in Christ Jesus. (Romans 3:21,22) (Romans 1:17) There is nothing I can do to earn this right standing with You. I receive it as an act of my faith." (Hebrews 11:1)(Ephesians 2:8)(Rom. 3:23)

"Thank You, Lord Jesus, for taking this torment of shame from me on the cross of Calvary two thousand years ago. (Isaiah 53:4,5)(1ˢᵗ Thes. 5:8-13) Thank You, Jesus, for Your sacrifice for me on the cross in which You despised the shame for me. (Hebrews 12:2) You are now seated at the right hand of the Father, speaking prayers of intercession (prayers on my behalf) for me. (Romans 8:34) I am not ashamed, because I know whom I have believed, and am convinced that You, Lord Jesus, are able to guard all that I have entrusted to You." (2ⁿᵈ Timothy 1:12) (Romans 1:17)

"I now receive full forgiveness for all my sinful acts, negative thoughts, sinful fantasies, and negative emotions. (Acts 2:38)(1ˢᵗ John 1:9) I rebuke and renounce every negative mindset from each traumatic experience I have endured in the name of Jesus.(Luke 10:19)(2ⁿᵈ Cor. 10:4,5) I stand with forgiveness toward all intruders.(Luke 6:28,37) I release all judgments against them and rebuke any demons or self judgements that have come to me because of my judgments of others, in Jesus name. (Luke 6:37)(Luke 10:19) I commit to the daily study of the Word of God with prayer and praise to keep my vessel filled with God." (Luke 11:24-26)(Psalm 33:1-3)(See Appendix)

"I now ask You, Lord Jesus, to come into my heart and to heal every wound in my heart and restore it to wholeness. (Matthew 7:7)(Rom. 10:9,10)(Luke 4:18)I open myself to love again.(Acts 16:14) I declare that my mind and my emotions are reconnected and restored to wholeness and purity in Jesus' name. (Joel 2:25)(Matthew 5:8)(1ˢᵗ Cor. 2:16)Thank You, Lord Jesus, that I can stand with my head lifted up, (Psalm 24:9,10), in confidence and with a deep thanksgiving for Your sacrifice for me. (1ˢᵗ Thes. 5:18) Thank You, Lord Jesus, for providing complete freedom from shame for me.(1ˢᵗ Cor. 15:34)(Heb. 12:2) In Jesus' name I pray and believe this to be true. Amen." (All scriptures personalized)

Continue This Prayer as You Declare Your Confidence and Right standing in Christ Jesus Speaking the Word of God

"I declare that I now walk in the confidence of God in Jesus' name. (Romans 3:21,22)(Ephesians 6:20) Lord Jesus, I declare that shame is now removed through Your name and through Your shed blood. (Roman 1:16,17)(Mark 11:23-25)(Heb. 9:14)(Heb. 10:19-22) I now receive the blessings and benefits of my divine inheritance from You, O Lord Jesus. (Colossians 1:12) (1ˢᵗ Peter 1:18,19) (Galatians 3:13) You despised the shame for me on the cross of Calvary. (Hebrews 12:2) It is done by the power of Your blood, O Lord. (1ˢᵗ Peter 1:18,19) You have forgiven and purified me from all confessed sin. (1ˢᵗ John 1:7,9) You have sprinkled my heart to cleanse me from a guilty conscience. (Hebrews 10:22) You have washed my body with pure water. (Hebrews 10:22) Lord Jesus, it is You in Whom I have believed and committed my life and my heart. (2nd Timothy 1:12) I declare that I am in right standing with my Father God in Your name, Lord Jesus. (John 3:3, Romans 10:9,10, John 3:16, Romans 10:13, Romans 1:16,17) I am forgiven. I am released from all guilt.(Romans 8:1) I now receive complete cleansing by the Your blood into my heart and my body. (Hebrews 10:19-22) There is now no condemnation to those who are in Christ Jesus, my Lord. (Romans 8:1) I declare that I stand fully accepted into the family of God, in Jesus' name, Amen. Thank You, Lord Jesus." (Isaiah 43:1-4)(All scriptures referenced/personalized)

Let us fix our eyes upon Jesus, the author and the perfecter of our faith, who for the joy set before Him endured the cross, scorning its shame, and sat down at the right hand of the throne of God. (Hebrews 12:2) I continue to enter boldly into the throneroom of God, petitioning my Father in Jesus' name, (John 16:23), and speaking with my heart of faith, with submission, repentance, and with forgiveness; until the full manifestation of freedom from shame is revealed in my innermost being. (Hebrews 10:19-22)(Heb.11:1) I will submit first to God and resist all enemy distractions and delusions. (James 4:7,8)(1st Peter 5:8,9)(Acts 2:25) I shall not be moved by shame or any self-condemnation. (1st Cor. 15:58)(Romans 8:1) I will commit to keep my heart humble and repentant toward the Lord.(Matthew 18:4) No one can take my faith in a forgiving God away from me. (Acts 2:38)(Psalm 147:6)(Heb. 11:1) The Lord is my rock and my fortress. (Psalm 62:2) He accepts me despite my weaknesses and loves and accepts a humble and a contrite heart whose desire is to please Him. (2nd Cor. 12:9) He is not looking for perfection, but He is looking for an honest heart of faith that is pressing into holiness (a desire to become more like God), one day at a time. (2nd Cor. 12:9)(Psalm 51:10,16,17) Because I see the Lord always before me, I shall not be moved by shame.(1st Cor. 15:58) (Acts 2:25)(Psalm 16:8) I will obey the Lord's command and love myself. (Leviticus 19:18)(All scriptures referenced/personalized) **You do not delight in sacrifice, or I would bring it: You do not take pleasure in burnt offerings. The sacrifices of God are a broken spirit; a broken and contrite (humble) heart, O God You will not despise. (Psalm 51:16,17)**

Goodbye Shame and Self - Doubt

The obsessive compulsive behavior was triggered somewhere in the first six years of life. Something happened which set off the shame spiral. It was all rooted in lies from the demonic realm, from generational and familiar spirits, not Mom or Dad. It was the "little girl" in me somehow feeling falsely responsible for things I didn't cause. Shame says, "I am a mistake." and "It's my fault." From these feeling of shame and self-doubt, an unaffirmed little girl developed. **Therefore, there is now no condemnation for those who are in Christ Jesus, because through Christ Jesus the law of the Spirit of life set me free from the law of sin and death. (Romans 8:1 per.)**

As my heart healed from the wounds, I settled it in my heart that I did my best and I did the right thing with all persons I loved and was connected with. As I obediently left all idols, sins, ungodly soul ties, and all activities and connections with New Age theology, I emerged out of living by the Law of perfectionism. I received Christian help with all of this in different seasons of my growth process. Eventually, I began to hear the voice of God in my spirit. I began to listen to myself when I spoke. And the check in my spirit was clear.

My mind was no longer blocked by the worries of perfectionism. However, I did leave the nursing profession as this catered to the problem. If worry came back to distract me, I would and still confess the Word of God with my heart of faith, with submission, repentance, and forgiveness, "I cast all my cares upon You, Lord Jesus." (1st Peter 5:7 per.) If I started to worry about something and the Lord told me not to worry, I had to obey Him. Good judgment returned to me as I learned to trust God and myself. In time, I knew what things were important to take care of and what things were insignificant. **My confidence returned with both my obedience to leave sin and when I received forgiveness from the Lord. I believed I was totally loved, and the Lord, not man or woman, affirmed me. And His grace came upon me to bring me into the "rest of God." (Hebrews 4:3 per.)**

I then arose victorious over self-doubt in most situations. However, because I have habits of checking things since childhood, I still will recheck things today. A double check is sufficient, however, and the torment of continual checking has been annihilated from my life, praise God! **Therefore, my dear friends, as you have always obeyed – not only in my presence, but now much more in my absence - continue to work out your salvation with fear and trembling, for it is God who works in you to will and to act according to His good purpose. (Philippians 2:12,13)**

In perfectionism, self doubt was transformed to self confidence, as I listened to myself, to the voice of the Holy Spirit, and to others. I opened my spiritual ears to receive the check in my spirit from the impression I received from the Holy Spirit. In homosexuality, shame was transformed to honesty, godly character, and integrity, as I entered into divine relationship with Jesus Christ, receiving and accepting His forgiveness, His acceptance, and His love for me. I now walk in His righteousness, or His right standing.

When I decided to take God seriously and receive His grace, believing that He loved, accepted, and forgave me, I received His blessings and my confidence grew in Him. This busy "little girl" had to stop and receive from God. I grew into this confidence knowing that He lived inside of me and that He was working His love both to me and also through me.

Self doubt has been replaced by a confidence that the Lord affirms me and my spiritual ears are now opened to listen to His still small voice. I am no longer frantic and panicky. I have the peace of God and a check in my spirit from the Holy Spirit when I have completed a task. If I have any glitches, I seek a witness. And my need for codependence has been replaced by the precious and divine relationship I have with Jesus Christ, my Lord and with healthy relationships with Christian men and women. **So do not throw away your confidence; it will be richly rewarded. You need to persevere so that when you have done the will of God, you will receive what He has promised. (Hebrews 10:35, 36)**

Prayer to Silence the Spirit of Lust – Molestation?

If you were sexually molested as a child or at any time, or involved in sexual sin, that spirit of lust will try to badger you, but Jesus within you is greater than any spirit in the world. (1st John 4:4) When you have intimacy with Jesus Christ, your surrender in your love relationship with Him will overpower any spirit that tries to invade and/or harass you. Jesus Christ living in you is greater than any spirit in the world. **Lift up your heads, O you gates; be lifted up, you ancient doors, that the King of glory may come in. Who is this King of glory? The Lord strong and mighty, the Lord mighty in battle. (Psalm 24:7,8)**

I encourage you to follow the Holy Spirit in His lead regarding where you should work, where you should worship, whom you should befriend, and on all your endeavors. Always follow His lead. Strive to spend time with Christians who are stronger than you as you will glean and grow from their influence upon you. Ask the Holy Spirit to lead you to the church that will best serve you to grow more deeply in love with Jesus.

When you repent of your sins and stand firm in your walk of surrender to God in and with you, the anointing of God is present and the blood of Jesus covers you from all condemnation and all spiritual invasions. When you stand firm in forgiveness, releasing all judgment against any and all molester(s) or bullies, and against yourself, the door of your heart is closed to any demonic entrance, i.e. the spirit of lust. However, it is with honesty before God and with obedience to leave the sins of fornication and all the ungodly soul ties, including all memorabilia connected with them, (leaving all New Age connections as well), that you will finally lock the door to the spirit of lust's successful entrance, control, and authority in your life. He will still badger you, but you will have the strength of will to resist because of <u>your refusal to give him entrance</u>, with your submission to the Lord, and with the empowerment of the Holy Spirit. A commitment to live a life of purity in Christ Jesus is essential to silence lust and to crucify the flesh.

The devil has no legal access unless you give it to him. You have the privilege of drawing a divine bloodline, that of Jesus Christ in and with you, because you have inherited redemption (freedom from Satan's authority) from the blood bought sacrifice of Jesus Christ. Take the offensive against the spirit of lust and against your own flesh.

The spirit of lust knows my name. It has been relentless in trying to badger me. Unforgiveness can ignite the body to desire fleshly pleasures in order to quiet the unrest rooted in the bitterness, the deep pain, or the ungodly reactions and negative thoughts, fantasies, and emotions as self-condemnation, self-pity, apathy, and selfishness. Forgiveness for yourself as well as for others brings the rest of God even to the physical body and includes a release of judgment and also a release of our right to avenge ourselves and others. The Lord is the judge. (Hebrews 10:30,31)

Faith Requires Action

Perseverance must finish its work so that you may be mature and complete, not lacking anything. If any of you lacks wisdom, he should ask God, who gives generously to all without finding fault, and it will be given to him. (James 1:4) We do not inactivate the enemy by simply ignoring him and neutralizing our walk. We decidedly ambush the spirit of lust and crucify our flesh by committing to a life of purity in Christ Jesus. For me, it took a "Daniel fast" to break the hold of the spirit of lust upon me. This fast also strengthened my will to defiantly say "no" to this spirit of lust and/or to just say "no" to my own flesh. Remember to seek your physician before any fast if you have any medical conditions or health issues, are pregnant or lactating, or are taking any medications. (Please refer to Daniel 10 for further understanding of the Daniel fast).

Also we must "clean house" of anything that may have soulish or demonic attachments to any sexual partners, soul ties, and any New Age mindsets. Read further information and prayers on breaking all ungodly soul ties in the chapter, <u>Death Cannot Hold Me</u>. There may be articles or pictures related to an old lover(s) in your dwelling place that need to be burned and gotten rid of. Spirits and demons can attach to materials of any kind; furniture, clothing, dishes, pictures, letters, or any memorabilia related to past soul ties. These must be discarded and burned and taken away from your dwelling! Any idols or memories of the relationships must be gotten rid of as well, like videos, phone numbers, addresses, clothing, gifts, jewelry, tickets to shows, et cetera. Ask the Lord if He wants you to relocate. Sometimes this is helpful in cutting off ungodly soul ties.

God is Faithful

I had to ask myself, "Where did I go and with whom did I spend time?" This was clearly the spirit of lust. You don't have to visit a gay bar to pick up the spirit of lust. It is everywhere as we live in a carnal world. Next, I had to ask myself, "How did I pick this up? Was I walking surrendered to Jesus Christ? Did I pray early in the morning to prepare myself against enemy attacks? Was I walking with the anointing of the Holy Spirit, the very presence of God upon me? Did I have the Word of God in my mind? Was I walking in the confidence of Christ in me or was I passively walking through the day? Was I alert? Did I have my spiritual armor on? Or was I naked to the attacks of Satan? Who was I choosing to be in fellowship with? Was I properly setting boundaries with other people? Was I walking in my flesh or being led by the Holy Spirit.

We live in a carnal world. Satan is the god of this world. _ñí_The spirit of lust knows my name. I lived the homosexual lifestyle for eight years. But I know who he is too. I can smell him a mile away. He may not come in anymore. When you are right with God, the power of the Holy Spirit within and upon you is greater than any created demon. (1st John 4:4) There can be no compromise when it comes to the spirit of lust. It is relentless. You must dedicate and consecrate your body as a temple for the Lord to dwell in. You must guard your heart and soul with what you allow into it. Do whatever it takes to keep your temple clean. Consecrate and dedicate your eyes and ears also to what you allow to come into your temple. Watch what you say. Speak what is pleasing to God. Discipline your tongue! Keep good company! **Therefore, I urge you, brothers, in view of God's mercy, to offer your bodies as living sacrifices, holy and pleasing to God – this is your spiritual act of worship. Do not conform any longer to the pattern of this world, but be transformed by the renewing of your mind. Then you will be able to test and approve what God's will is – His good, pleasing, and perfect will. (Romans 12:1,2)**

Prayer before Sleep – Bind the Spirit of Lust in the Name of Jesus

Before sleep, I surrender my heart to Jesus Christ as my Lord and authority, with reading the Bible and journaling, with repentance for sins, (the blood of Jesus cleanses me of my sins and the Holy Spirit empowers me to resist the devil, to forgive, and to speak), and forgiveness prayers for myself and others, with a release of all judgment. I thank the Lord Jesus Christ for His sacrifice.

Sometimes it is just a bowing of the head first to get me into the right attitude and out of the daily activity mode. I therefore have prepared my heart of faith in proper position to speak if the spirit of lust attempts to intrude upon me in the middle of the night. If and when the intrusion comes, I first enter into the Father's presence to petition Him and to take Jesus' delegated authority, binding the devil and speaking the Word of God all in the name of Jesus Christ over myself.

Prayer against the Spirit of Lust

Prepare Your Heart – "Jesus, I believe You died for my sins on Calvary two thousand years ago and You were raised from the dead, conquering all sin, sickness, and spiritual death for me. I now submit and recommit to You as my Lord and Savior, and as my loving authority. I am sorry for my sins. I ask You to come into my heart and to live within me as my Lord and my Savior for the rest of my life. I forgive and release all judgment against myself for my sins and against all who have sinned against me as well, Lord Jesus. I receive Your forgiveness, Your love, and Your complete acceptance of me."

Enter into the Father's Presence – "Father God, I come to You with these petitions, in the name of Jesus Christ, Who is my Lord, my Savior, and my authority." (Psalm 100:4) (John 16:23)

Bind the Spirit of Lust and Speak the Word of God in the Name of Jesus Christ – "In the name of Jesus Christ, I renounce the devil. (James 4:7,8) Spirit of lust, you are now put on notice. (Luke 10:19) I declare that the blood of Jesus is against you, in Jesus' name.(Heb. 9:14)(Heb. 10:19-22)(1st Peter 1:18,19) You have no authority here. (Col. 2:10,15) I take Jesus' delegated authority against you now.(Luke 10:19) You must leave my body, my soul (my intellect, emotions, and my will), and my spirit, in Jesus' name. (Mark 11:23-25) I declare the peace of God that surpasses all understanding both rules and reigns in my body, my soul, and my spirit in Jesus' name.(Col. 3:15)(Isaiah 26:3) Spirits of lust, go, in the name of Jesus. (Luke 10:19) Go wherever Jesus sends you to be held captive by the angels of God. (Mark 5:8-13) I speak to all past and present traumas and wounding, painful memories, lying imaginations, and immoral fantasies.(Mark 11:23-25) You will no longer rule or reign in my life, in Jesus' name.(2nd Cor. 10:4,5) I will meditate, confess, speak, and study the Word of God daily.(Mark 11:23-25)(Luke 11:24-26) My mind will be transformed by the Word of God. (1st Cor. 2:16)(Pro. 4:20-22) My vessel will be continually filled with God's Word and prayer.(Rom. 12:2) By acts of my faith and with complete surrender to Jesus Christ as my Lord, with the help of the Holy Spirit, and with decisive acts of my will against you, I stand in resistance against you, spirit of lust.(Heb.11:1)((Rom. 1:16,17)((1st Cor. 6:19)(1st Cor. 15:58)(James 4:7,8)(Gal. 5:23)(Acts 1:8) I am controlled by the Holy Spirit and it is the Word of God only that shall define my thoughts. (John 15:5) (John 14:17,20)(Pro. 4:20-22)(Acts 1:8)(Acts 2:38)(John 16:13)(Luke 11:24-26)The spoken Word of God is a living sword against you."(Heb. 4:12)(Ephesians 6:17) (See Appendix)

"Jesus, You are the Lord and the authority of my life.(Col. 2:10,15)(Rom. 10:9,10) I declare that from this day forward, my body is a living temple of the Holy Spirit set apart for holiness to You, Lord Jesus, in the mighty name of Jesus Christ.(1st Cor. 6:19,20) I am committed to an intimate personal relationship with You, Jesus. (John 14:17,20)(John 15:5)(1st Cor. 11:25)I declare that I refuse to compromise my walk with You, Lord Jesus, in Your precious and holy name.(James 4:7,8)(1st Cor. 15:58)(Acts 2:25) Thank you, Lord Jesus, for giving me Your Holy Spirit to empower me to defiantly resist this spirit of lust and to say "no" to my flesh.(Gal. 5:23)(James 4:7,8)(Acts 1:8)(Pro. 6:25) Thank You, Lord, for the fruit of the spirit, self-control.(Gal. 5:23) I pray and believe that You, O Lord, will honor my prayer as I honor You with my body, in Jesus' name, Amen. (1st Cor. 6:20)" (All scriptures personalized)(See Appendix)

Because the Sovereign Lord helps me, I will not be disgraced. Therefore have I set my face like flint, and I know I will not be put to shame. (Isaiah 50:7)

Today I cherish the private time I spend with the Lord and welcome His touch of love upon my life; my spirit, my soul, and my body. The need for touch from another human being has been divinely transformed to the divine touch I have received from the presence of and from the still small voice of the Holy Spirit in my life. I know that not only His eyes but also His touch is always upon me. And I am ready to reach out and shake the hands of other people in greeting them as well.

I look forward to a godly relationship with a man who loves the Lord with all his heart, a man whom I will be able to trust because of his complete dependence upon God. Lust will have no place in this relationship because God will be at the center of it. And the power of the Holy Spirit that is within both of us will be used to supernaturally touch and bless one another.

People were bringing little children to Jesus to have Him touch them, but the disciples rebuked them. When Jesus saw this, He was indignant. He said to them, "Let the little children come to me, and do not hinder them, for the kingdom of God belongs to such as these. I tell you the truth; anyone who will not receive the kingdom of God like a little child will never enter it." And he took the children in his arms, put his hands on them and blessed them. (Mark 10:13–16)

The Holy Spirit Will Empower You /Baptism in Water/ Baptism of the Holy Spirit and Power

I began to experience some real inner confidence in these years and some real joy. After meeting a man named Wayne, I joined the Calvary Chapel congregation in Santa Barbara, California. Wayne was my landlord and I really liked him. He wasn't the greatest looking guy I had ever met, but I really liked him. He was bluntly honest, very funny, and that was very attractive to me. He led me to Calvary Chapel and we started getting to know each other. He was a widower and had a young daughter. They became my friends. Wayne encouraged me to be baptized in water at the swimming pool at the YMCA in 1986.

John the Baptist addresses the Pharisees and the Sadducees, teaching about water baptism and of the promises of the baptism of the Holy Spirit that is to come. **I baptize you with water for repentance. But after me will come one who is more powerful than I, whose sandals I am not fit to carry. He will baptize you with the Holy Spirit and with fire. His winnowing fork is in His hand, and He will clear His threshing floor, gathering wheat into the barn and turning up the chaff with unquenchable fire. (Matthew 3:11)**

I was water baptized in Calvary Chapel's swimming pool. I will never forget Pastor Tim, speaking over me while I was submerged in the water. He spoke publically over me proclaiming that I was now a "new creature in Christ". (2nd Cor. 5:17) Water baptism is an outward expression of the believer's heartfelt repentance and the confession of Jesus Christ as Lord....**having been buried with Him in baptism and raised with Him through your faith in the power of God, who raised Him from the dead. (Colossians 2:12)**

If you look at the events in the Bible, Jesus Christ was first water baptized in the River Jordan by John the Baptist. After His baptism, He was tempted by the devil in the wilderness. He won over in all three temptations; the lust of the eyes, the lust of the flesh, and the pride of life through His words of faith and the spoken Word of God, spoken in answer to the devil's temptations. Then He started His three year ministry on earth, preaching, teaching, and performing miracles. **Or don't you know that all of us who were baptized into Christ Jesus were baptized into His death? We were therefore buried with Him through baptism into death in order that, just as Christ was raised from the dead through the glory of the Father, we too may live a new life. If we have been united with Him like this in His death, we will certainly also be united with Him in His resurrection. (Romans 6:3–5)**

In water baptism, we declare that we are now new creatures in Christ Jesus. Our sins are washed clean because of His sacrifice and because of our repentance and faith in His sacrifice. We commit to live in that faith and to live with a deep thanksgiving for His sacrifice for us. **Therefore, if anyone is in Christ, he is a new creation; the old has gone, the new has come! (2nd Corinthians 5:17)**

My friend Wayne did not attend the water baptism, but it was for the best. He always told me not to talk to him but to talk to Jesus about my problems. I felt rejected when he said this, but these were wise and loving words! He taught me a lot about putting God first. He also made me laugh! **And this water symbolizes baptism that now saves you also – not the removal of dirt from the body, but the pledge of a good conscience toward God. It saves you by the resurrection of Jesus Christ, Who has gone into heaven, and is at God's right hand – with angels, authorities and powers in submission to Him. (1ˢᵗ Peter 3: 21, 22)**

The baptism of the Holy Spirit, however, is a very special gift from God. It is a gift which endows the believer with power from on high. This baptism endows us with a supernatural covering and with a divine empowerment within us that helps us to do what we cannot do in the natural. I believe that there are deeper levels of greater empowerment that we receive from the Holy Spirit. As I have yielded more to the Holy Spirit, I have experienced deeper levels of His power working in and through me. The Holy Spirit is our helper and will assist us to remove all that is unnecessary from our lives. Perhaps this explains why this baptism is like a "fire." The fire of the Holy Spirit burns the chaff. Webster describes "chaff" as the seed coverings and other debris separating from the seed in the threshing grain. It is also defined as something comparatively worthless. **[68]**

Jesus prepared His disciples for the coming of the Holy Spirit's power. He confirmed John the Baptist's promise of the Holy Spirit baptism in the following: **On one occasion, while He was eating with them, He gave them this command; "Do not leave Jerusalem, but wait for the gift my Father promised, which you have heard me speak about. For John baptized with water, but in a few days you will be baptized with the Holy Spirit." (Acts 1:4)**

He said to them, "It is not for you to know the times or dates the Father has set by His own authority. But you will receive power when the Holy Spirit comes on you; and you will be my witnesses in Jerusalem, and in all Judea and Samaria, and to the ends of the earth." (Acts 1:7, 8)

The Holy Spirit actually arrived on the day of Pentecost, which is explained in Acts 2:4: **When the day of Pentecost came, they were all together in one place. Suddenly, a sound like the blowing of a violent wind came from heaven and filled the whole house where they were sitting. They saw what seemed to be tongues of fire that separated and came to rest on each of them. All of them were filled with the Holy Spirit and began to speak in other tongues, as the Holy Spirit enabled them. (Acts 2:4)**

The late Pastor Billy Joe Daugherty spoke about the Holy Spirit prayer language saying, "Praying the Holy Spirit is the seventh piece of armor. When you pray in the Holy Spirit, your spirit man is strengthened and it'll sustain the physical man. Like a hydroelectric engine, when you let the rivers of the Holy Spirit run, it generates God's divine power in you." **[69] And pray in the Spirit on all occasions with all kinds of prayers and requests. With this in mind, be alert and always keep on praying for all the saints. (Ephesians 6:18)**

He who speaks in a tongue edifies himself... (1ˢᵗ Cor. 14:4)

It was the summer of 1986 when I received the prayer language. Praying in the Holy Spirit has really helped to heal my mind because it helps me to "get a grip." It erases the ungodly thoughts and fantasies as I redirect my focus upon God. Remember, you can only think of one thought at a time. So when I pray in the Spirit, it immediately hooks me into the communication I have with the Lord. It turns off the negative thinking and the mindless chatter. It is a great defense against the enemy's mental lures. It sets me from the defensive to the offensive mode because I become deeply and reverently aware of the presence of the Lord within me to guide me into all truth. And, as I listen to His leadings, He guides me into truth. (John 16:13)

For God did not give us a spirit of timidity, but a spirit of power, of love and of self-discipline. (2nd Timothy 1:7) The prayer language helps me through times of crises. When I don't know what to do or I don't know what to say, I pray in the Holy Spirit. I am then strengthened on the inside and the Holy Spirit will give me directives on what to do in each situation. It also will quiet my emotions and get me back into the Spirit. **And you, dear friends, build yourselves up in your most holy faith and**

pray in the Holy Spirit. Keep yourselves in God's love as you wait for the mercy of our Lord Jesus Christ to bring you to eternal life. (Jude 20, 21)

Since, then, you have been raised with Christ, set your hearts on things above, where Christ is seated at the right hand of God. Set your minds on things above, not on earthly things. For you died, and your life is now hidden with Christ in God. When Christ, who is your life appears, then you also will appear with Him in glory. (Colossians 3:1-4)

Positive Effects of Male Friends

I did not have many socialization skills. Since the sin of homosexuality, I did not easily blend in with "normal" folk. Even though I had stepped by faith into the promise of eternal life through a born again relationship with Jesus Christ, I was still a hurting person. I had not yet received or experienced the full forgiveness from the Lord. I still liked to smoke cigarettes, even more than having a good conversation with a group of people. But, as I became more honest with God and worked through my issues, I entered into socialization more readily. And I enjoyed the companionship of many friends.

I believe my boyfriend Wayne sensed this and saw my hurt. He was actually trying to help me. I felt completely safe with him. He, his daughter, and I did a lot of fun things together; flying kites on the beach, having meals together and such. His friends became my friends and we all attended Calvary Chapel. I felt like I belonged. I was accepted. These were cherished years. That was the year I was called home to ask for Mom and Dad's forgiveness and, of course, I got it. My parents were always happy to hear from me. And they loved me. That was also the year I got down to business with God. Because I felt a lot of disappointment still within me, I asked God to forgive me for being angry with Him. I figured I must have been angry with Him if I still wanted to isolate myself from people. Anger turned inward turns to depression. This conversation with Jesus brought breakthrough.

I remember Wayne asking me to go on a fishing trip with him and the "gang." I turned him down because I could not imagine myself going that long without smoking a cigarette alone. I had to have "my space." It was "that space" I needed that kept me from honestly sharing my life with others. It had to go. It was rooted in fear that was already changing to faith as I enjoyed the fellowship of Wayne, his family, and church associates. Jesus, through His people, transformed my life.

Wayne was the joker of the party. He asked me to go to Las Vegas and marry him once. I don't know if he was serious. But, as it turned out, he fell in love with another gal and is happily married today. I am happy for him. I never laughed so much with a man.

I got involved in the children's ministry at Calvary Chapel and I really loved working with the children. It was always such a joy to be with God's salt of the earth. I learned to work with others and I grew, one day at a time. I loved to get off work and go to service to worship the Lord. I gained so much strength in that. I was honored when I was accepted as a part of the worship team. I accompanied them on the piano. What an honor to play before the congregation! I enjoyed feeling accepted and part of my church family.

I met an older man who was holding Bible studies at his home. He has gone home to Jesus now. He was a father image to me and he helped me to look to Jesus in all things. I went through a course on Missions that he helped to sponsor. I loved and respected him so much that I thought I was "in love" with him. He was much older than I. I felt so comfortable and safe with him. He became a lifelong friend.

Because my confidence in my identity in Christ was still growing, I guess I was looking for that "older and wiser" man to take care of me. He was a gifted man of God and I thank God for his influence upon my life. He probably knew my feelings for him but, thank God, he continued to love me as God would. He did not take advantage of my vulnerability. This man's godly influence upon me literally changed my life. He was an unforgettable and precious gift from God. I know I will see him again in heaven.

I got involved with the Salvation Army in a ministry with three other Christians. One of them was very fond of me and wanted to marry but, again, I was not ready. He truly loved the Lord and loved the Word of God. He ministered to others with a real caring heart. And he was gentle and meek. But I was fearful of any commitments. He would have been a great husband for me. The presence of God was so strong in and upon him, but I was still very fearful of commitment. The anointing upon him was bringing me healing and I was responding to that healing with tears of purging. Unfortunately, I was not ready for this gift from God. **Iron sharpens iron, so one man sharpens another. (Proverbs 27:17)**

It has always been easier for me to give than to receive. Yet there was a grieving child inside that had to trust myself in forming healthy relationships. I needed to learn to receive from God and from other people. Yet, my freedom from my own pain continued to be lived out by giving comfort to others in the nursing profession. I was a classic codependent and I reaped so much love from my patients and the children whom I helped. But God wanted me totally free to experience life at its fullest by receiving love and comfort from Him first and, later, from an intimate relationship with a spouse. He was preparing me to receive love from a man as I first learned to receive His everlasting love.

A Deep Call

I remember that there were many times, while driving down the streets of Santa Barbara, I had the impression that the Holy Spirit was telling me, "Go Home!" Although I had obeyed God to this point, this was one directive I resisted for years. I did not want to face the pain. I was not ready or willing.

God knew this. Even though I was living in the Christian world in sunny California, I was still a workaholic. I was still trying to make it up to God. I couldn't receive the full grace and forgiveness for this because I was still running with the shame of the past, with this driving and condemning spirit pushing me. Pride kept me doing for God, leaving no room to humbly receive from God. I was so busy doing that I couldn't stop long enough to yield to Him and receive His full forgiveness, acceptance, and love. These were habit patterns developed since childhood. I needed more growth in God to prepare me to go home to face the root of all this pain. And God knew just what I needed.

It was a deep call to move from Santa Barbara, California and go to Tulsa, Oklahoma. I didn't know it, but God would prepare me to return to my family in New Jersey by sending me first to the "Bible belt." It was a call from God that went deeper than my intellect. This call went straight to my innermost being. In 1990, I literally experienced a tugging at my heart that was beyond anything I could rationally explain. I knew that if I did not heed the Lord's call, I would never know what great and precious things God had in store for me there. I knew it was something wonderful but I didn't know what. It was like a child crying out for help in a distant land. And I was the only one who heard the cry. I had to respond to this call!

In 1990, I attended a missions meeting in Urbana, Illinois and there the call was confirmed. I met Dean Wessman of Oral Roberts University of Tulsa, Oklahoma. She offered me a five-year scholarship for my B.S.N. and Masters in nursing. Of all the people I met there representing groups from all over the world, Dean Wessman and the ORU group was the only one that left a deposit in my heart. I knew it was God. I knew I had to visit Tulsa and see what God wanted for me. My visit confirmed that I was called of God to go there and study.

In Tulsa, I would be well trained. I received a deposit of faith that stayed with me throughout the following ten years of my home visit to New Jersey. It was that faith deposit that sustained me through the trials I faced in New Jersey. It was that faith deposit which brought me the ultimate victory over the curse of sin, sickness, and spiritual death, victory over all evil spirits and evil assignments, and victory over the generational curse over my family bloodline.

Tulsa to Heal

Therefore, I urge you, brothers, in view of God's mercy, to offer your bodies as living sacrifices, holy and pleasing to God – this is your spiritual act of worship. Do not be conformed any longer to the pattern of this world, but be transformed by the renewing of your mind. Then you will be able to test and approve what God's will is – His good, pleasing and perfect will. (Romans 12:1,2)

I was now born again. I had been water baptized. And I knew by a deep conviction of the Holy Spirit that God had called me to Tulsa to heal. I was a baby Christian and the Lord was now, in His infinite love, going to raise me as His child. He sent me to one of the most spiritually fertile places in the country in which to grow me up. I call it a "Christian womb." Tulsa is a Christian training camp in which many believers are being raised up to study and live the Word of God, to hear the voice of God, and to live by faith. Many are called and launched off to other lands to continue to spread the Gospel as evangelists, missionaries, apostles, pastors, teachers, and in whatever capacity the Lord has called them. **My people are destroyed for lack of knowledge. (Hosea 4:6)**

Power in the Spoken Word of God

The Lord knew what I would have to face when I would finally arrive home to my roots. He saw the beginning from the end. He knew I was born again as His child and I had some knowledge of the Word. He saw my torment with the obsessive compulsive behaviors and knew that I needed more of Him and more of His Word to find complete victory in Jesus.

However, I was still a baby Christian. He wanted to solidify my knowledge of His Word. He would begin the inner healing in this "safe womb" first before launching me home to my roots. As my heart softened, the Word of God began to penetrate deeper. In Tulsa, I would learn that I was literally in a spiritual battle. I would learn that there is power in the spoken Word of God. There is power in walking in the love of God. And that I would press in to receive His love.

In Tulsa, God would literally change my positional identity from a girl with a victim mentality to a godly woman of character, confidence, and dignity in Christ Jesus. I had to grow and mature. Tulsa is a place of restoration. I was away from any distractions from my past in California and I was not anywhere near my family. This was a holy season of six years of separation, sanctification, and preparation. It literally changed my entire life. This season left an imprint of faith and courage within me which I literally carried with me through the years that followed.

God Is Watching

For the eyes of the Lord range throughout the earth to strengthen those whose hearts are fully committed to Him. (2ⁿᵈ Chronicles 16: 9) The Lord knew my heart. He was well acquainted with all I had been through and knew just what I needed. He knew I needed to learn His Word to not only live abundantly, but to fight the fight of faith that was ahead of me in the land where I was raised. And I needed to be away from the environment and the memories of the people with whom I was involved in California. Father God always knows best.

The Lord is My Rear Guard

Driving to Tulsa for a college weekend, I asked the Holy Spirit to let me know in a sure way if He really wanted me to move to Oklahoma. It was in April of 1991. As I entered the city, I saw the larger than life size sculpture of a man's praying hands standing in front of Oral Roberts University. I was in the right place and it was the right time. It was time to get serious with God. Many people had come to seek God's will that weekend.

Reverend Ron McIntosh was preaching that Saturday night at the Mabee Center. He was preaching about sacrifice and about taking up our crosses to follow Jesus. I went forward for the altar call and the power of the Holy Spirit fell upon me. It was during this call that Isaiah 58 became alive to me:

Is not this the kind of fasting I have chosen; to loose the chains of injustice and untie the cords of the yoke, to set the oppressed free and break every yoke? Is it not to share your food with the hungry and to provide the poor wanderer with shelter -- when you see the naked, to clothe him, and not to turn away from you own flesh and blood? Then your light will break forth like the dawn and your healing will quickly appear; then your righteousness will go before you, and the glory of the Lord will be your rear guard. Then you will call and the Lord will answer, you will cry for help, and He will say: Here am I. If you do away with the yoke of oppression, with the pointing finger and malicious talk, and you spend yourselves in behalf of the hungry and satisfy the needs of the oppressed, then your light will rise in the darkness, and your night will become like the noonday. (Isaiah 58: 6-10)

At the altar, I experienced the Holy Spirit as a "real presence." It was as if He were standing on the same platform with me. I literally felt His presence directly behind me. It was an awesome experience! From that day forward I had a greater awareness of the presence of the Holy Spirit.

For every bad memory, God has given me either a heavenly vision or a revelation to show His love for me. As I have grown in the Lord, memories of the past surface but without the pain attached to them anymore. Facing a lot of the pain and the guilt with godly counselors has brought Jesus into the memories with a realistic perspective upon them. What a tremendous blessing from God to be able to look back, and instead of seeing myself as a worthless sinner, I see myself as a forgiven, an accepted, and a loved vessel for His Kingdom. **Wisdom is supreme; therefore get wisdom. Though it cost you all you have, get understanding. Esteem her, and she will exalt you; embrace her, and she will honor you. (Proverbs 4:7,8)**

I know that bitterness toward people will change the power of Christ to work through me. I have decided to repent immediately whenever anger sets in. My anger is not against people but against the devil himself who works through them. Because I am human and still vulnerable to others' opinions, many times I forget this. Satan works through people and his lies to us can keep us from the truth. I ask God to keep me alert to Satan's tricks and to create a clean heart within me. As godly knowledge is learned, my application of this knowledge will bring wisdom.

This is why I have to get alone with God and pray, repent of any bitterness, and ask Him for divine wisdom and strategy against any persons who are causing me distress. Physical exercise is a tremendous tool for releasing anger. Think of anger as energy. Satan would have us lash out at someone. The wisdom of God would have us redirect it and offer it up as a sacrifice of praise and worship to Him. Go for a brisk walk. Run. Swim. Take a bike ride.

In your anger do not sin. Do not let the sun go down while you are still angry. (Ephesians 4:26)

It was also at this altar call that the Holy Spirit confirmed to me that I was to move to Tulsa. Some ministers teach this as your "knower." This is the inner part of you or your human spirit to which the Holy Spirit beckons or speaks to you; your gut, so to speak. **But when He, the spirit of truth comes, He will guide you into all truth. (John 16:13)**

As the healing process took place, my focus changed. My perspective switched from the creature to my Creator. And I learned to listen to this small still voice of the Holy Spirit. **Then you will know the truth and the truth will set you free. (John 8:32)**

The Lord is My Healer

Sow for yourselves righteousness, reap the fruit of unfailing love, and break up your unplowed ground; for it is time to seek the Lord. (Hosea 10:12)

Little did I know the fullness of the plan that God had prepared for me. I thought the Lord's plan was to further my education in the nursing profession at Oral Roberts University. In hindsight, however, I understand that His plan was much greater than I had ever imagined.

Tulsa is literally a "Christian womb" that this baby Christian had the honor of growing up in for a period of six years. My mind became renewed with the Word of God through a committed membership at Victory Christian Center and Grace Fellowship. I also had the privilege of attending Victory Bible Institute under the divine guidance of the late Pastor Billy Joe Daugherty and Sr. Pastor Sharon Dougherty. I attended Grace Fellowship under the authority of Pastor Bob and Loretta Yandian. And I had the honor of studying at Oral Roberts University.

I would have spent a million dollars paying for all the prayers and the hundreds of altar calls I attended if God's help were not free. I received so much of the Father's love to heal the years of my youth through the body of Christ. Many tears were shed as I was purged, cleansed, and started on the road to complete restoration in this Christian boot camp. I felt totally safe and free to step forward for prayer because the ministers showed a "genuine love and concern" for me. God's love showed through them like beaming lights. God was going to bless me so that I would become a blessing. I was truly comforted by many in Tulsa.

Praise be to God and Father of our Lord Jesus Christ, the Father of compassion and the God of all comfort, who comforts us in all our troubles, so that we can comfort those in any trouble with the comfort we ourselves have received from God. (2nd Corinthians 1:3)

My plan was to help God by training to become a missionary to the children in Africa after receiving my masters in nursing at ORU. However, God had a greater plan for me. He was going to "feed this spiritually starving child" in the "land of the living." **I am still confident of this; I will see the goodness of the Lord in the land of the living. (Psalm 27:13)**

During this time, I was provided with two special Christian counselors to assist me through the healing process. One gave me very realistic counsel about my situation. We dealt with family issues and issues centering on anxiety and fear. The other counselor dealt more in the spiritual realm, praying for me with the help of two other prayer warriors.

The first counselor focused on both solidifying my relationship with Jesus Christ and giving me real answers to real problems. I remember in one session, she gave me a small stone to carry around that would serve as a reminder to me that I was standing on the "Rock" of Jesus Christ. Whenever I was tempted to anxiety, I would hold onto that rock and speak the Word of God, confessing in faith aloud, "I am standing on the rock of Jesus Christ. No weapon formed against me will prosper." (Isaiah 54:17)

The second counselor was a prayer minister. Her assistants were prayer warriors. After I would be led by the primary therapist to share my issues verbally, they would literally lay hands upon me and pray. It was in this therapeutic modality that the Lord helped me deal with my feelings toward my mother even as far back as the womb and breast-feeding time. There were fears that were faced at this time. I know there were layers lifted from me in broken areas of my heart. I am so grateful to the Lord for this provision. **Before I formed you in the womb I knew you, before you were born I set you apart; (Jeremiah 1:5)**

Fellowship with other believers built my self-esteem. Many of the men and women I associated with in both church and in nursing school had absolutely nothing to do with the homosexual lifestyle. I was a part of their team. The enthusiasm they exhibited toward their relationship with Jesus Christ was inspiring and contagious.

I began to feel good about myself. We followed a dress code at Oral Roberts University which further built my self-image. We wore dresses and skirts to both classes and to services. Pants were only allowed in designated areas. I thought well of myself because I looked feminine and I dressed well.

God divinely blessed me with a born again believing and a joyful roommate for three of the years I spent there. What a tremendous blessing Rebecca was to me! She loved me with the love of Jesus. She shared her heart, her friends, and her family with me. She always showered me with kindness in both her words and her actions. She always set healthy boundaries and walked in love. This was a "clean" Christian friendship through which the Lord divinely blessed me. I am so grateful to the Lord for Rebecca.

I became friends with many Christian believers at nursing school. I bonded easily with my classmates because they were so open to share with me. We all shared a common goal of reaching the lost for Jesus Christ as we trained to become Christian nurses. Who said that going back to school at age forty-one is impossible? I was encouraged by the students for the three years of my nursing training at Oral Roberts University-Anna Vaughn College of Nursing. The joy of the Lord was contagious as we all shared a common purpose and worked diligently to reach our goals together. We were a team of believing Christians. I was no longer in isolation. **How good it is for the brethren to dwell in unity. (Psalms 133:1)**

The master' program closed. So I did not pursue that as planned. God had another plan. I completed the B.S.N. in Nursing and then I enrolled in Victory Bible Institute as the Holy Spirit led me. Under the teachings of many anointed men and women of God, I learned the Word of God. Classes were taught in Old Testament, New Testament, Authority of the Believer, Gifts of the Holy Spirit, Praise and Worship, Divine Healing, and Prayer. We also spent precious time in praise, worship, and prayer before each teaching time. This baby Christian was learning to walk!

These were years of decision and discipline. A dear friend of mine once told me. When you come forward and do what is right in the natural, then God will honor that and do for you what you could not do in the supernatural. **Call upon me in the day of trouble; I will deliver you, and you will honor me. (Psalms 50:15)**

I encourage you that whenever opportunity knocks, you must reach out and take it. Your healing will require a life of discipline and a determination to change patterns. There will always be a deep resistance to change. But obedience to do whatever the Holy Spirit directs is critical to progress!

My focus of attention now shifted from my past lovers to my love relationship with Jesus Christ Himself. My love would be turned toward Jesus and I learned to put God first, no matter what the cost. Bible College was an eternal investment. It not only changed my life, but it would serve to change others' lives as I later would share the Word of God and Jesus as an evangelist both on the streets and in ministries within the body of Christ. **For the Word of God is living and active. Sharper than any double edged sword, it penetrates even to dividing of soul and spirit, joints and marrow; it judges the thoughts and attitudes of the heart. (Hebrews 4:12-13)**

Not only was my mind awakened by the Word of God, but I was learning how to live it. It was a revelation to me to learn that I had been given delegated authority by Jesus Christ over every enemy of my soul. This was powerful information! I would learn how to enforce it.

I was determined to make the Word of God an active part of my everyday thinking and living. I trained myself to walk through my day meditating on the Word of God. I would literally speak scriptures over myself while walking through my nursing jobs. Being in the nursing profession, I had the opportunity to petition my Father in the name of Jesus with my heart positioned in faith (submission, repentance, and forgiveness). I had many opportunities to take Jesus' delegated authority to rebuke diseases as I laid my hands upon the sick, speaking healing scriptures over many people in the name of Jesus. When employed by Christian organizations that cared for the elderly, I had more people open to the laying on of hands to pray. Always ask folks if they would like prayer before the laying on of hands and prayer.

Submit yourselves, then, to God. Resist the devil, and he will flee from you. (James 4:7)

Set Your Heart in Faith and Submit to the Lord to Win against the Spirit of Fear

Addiction is rooted in fear. It is the spirit of fear that must be faced and taken authority over with the help of the greater One Who lives within us. In the very act of the compulsion, I stopped and acknowledged the presence of the Lord there with me.

Prepare Your Heart - "Lord Jesus, I believe that You died and resurrected from the dead on the third day. I surrender to You, Lord. Jesus. I am sorry for having offended You. I ask You to come into my heart and be the Lord of my life. Lord Jesus, I forgive myself and all who have sinned against me. I release all judgment and blame against myself and against any other persons who have sinned against me. Lord Jesus, I forgive and release myself from the guilt and the shame of my sins. I now receive Your forgiveness, Your grace, Your love, and Your Holy Spirit."

Now my heart is properly positioned to speak with faith, to petition my Father, and to effectively take Jesus' delegated authority, in the name of Jesus Christ. With my heart attitude of submission, repentance, and forgiveness, and in the very act of the compulsion, therefore, I now petition my Father and take Jesus' delegated authority against fear in Jesus' name. I intercept and annihilate the spirit of fear as I speak with an act of my faith and with a decided act of my will.

My love and submission to God draws me to repentance. Repentance is most important because it both covers and cleanses our sins with the blood of Jesus and also brings us the Holy Spirit with His supernatural empowerment. We are assisted by the Holy Spirit to forgive by an act of our faith and of our will, thus rising above our emotions. With a pure heart before Him, then, the Holy Spirit empowers us to do what we could not do in our own strength against the fear and the compulsions. (1st John 1:9)(Acts 2:38)(Acts 1:8)(All scripture referenced)

Enter into Your Father's Presence - "Father God, I come into Your presence with thanksgiving and praise in my heart. (Psalm 100:4) I petition You in the name of Jesus Christ my Lord and my Savior."(John 16:23)

Take Jesus' Delegated Authority against the Spirit of Fear and Compulsion in Jesus' Name

"Spirits of fear and compulsion, I speak to you now.(Mark 11:23-25) I rebuke and cast you out, in the name of Jesus Christ. (Luke 10:19) I speak by power of the blood of Jesus Christ, Who lives in my heart. (Heb. 10:19-22)(Heb.9:14)((1st Peter 1:18,19) Go where Jesus sends you to be held captive by the angels of God. (Mark 5:8-13) You have no authority here. (Col. 2:10,15)(Matthew 4:4,7,10) For God has not given me the spirit of fear, but of love and of power and of a sound mind." (2nd Timothy 1:7) In Jesus' name, I pray and believe."(All scriptures personalized)(See Appendix)

"I walk by love and not fear. Perfect love casts out all fear. (1st John 4:18) (1st Corinthians 13) God is love and He dwells within me. (John 14:17,20)(John 15:5) Greater is He Who is in me than he who is in the world. (1st John 4:4) (1st John 4:16-18) I am more than a conqueror in Christ Jesus my Lord. (Romans 8:37) Nothing shall be able to separate me from the love of God that is in Christ Jesus my Lord."(Romans 8:38)(All scriptures personalized)

"Thank you, Lord Jesus, I am now covered by the Your precious blood because I have repented and renounced my sins. (1st John 1:9) I have submitted to Jesus Christ as my Lord and my Savior. (Rom. 10:13) (Rom. 10:9,10)(John 3:3) I have accepted His authority in my life. (1st Peter 1: 18,19)(Col. 2:10:15) (1st Tim. 2:11) I am in covenant relationship with Jesus Christ, covered by the shed blood of Jesus Christ. (1st Cor. 11:25)(Romans 10:9,10) (John 3:3) (1st Peter 1:18,19) This places me in the "secret place" of the Lord's divine protection and the devil has no power over me in this place. (Psalm 91:1)(James 4:7,8) I am under the loving control of the Lord. (Matthew 21:27)(Isaiah 43:1-4) Forgiving and releasing all blame against myself and all who have sinned against me closes the door on the enemy and places me into the rest of God. (Heb. 4:11)(Luke 6:28,37) I have received His divine love, His total acceptance, and His complete forgiveness.(Isaiah 43:1-4)(1st John 1:9) I now, with an act of my will and by my faith, turn from this compulsion and lock the door of my soul to any further enemy intrusions. (Heb. 11:1)(Rom. 10:17)(James 4:7,8) I will commit to daily study of the Word of God with prayer, praise, and worship to keep the enemy from reentrance. (Luke 11:24-26)(Romans 12:2)(Psalm 33:1-3)(James 5:16)(John 4:24) I pray this in Jesus' name, Amen. Thank you, Lord" (All scriptures personalized) (See Appendix)

As soon as I speak aloud, I become aware of a change. Fear lifts as soon as faith speaks! And, with the spoken Word of God, the devils flee at the very mention of the name of Jesus. The spiritual atmosphere has changed and the Lord brings the ministering angels along with His presence and ushers in His peace, His love, and His power. I then enter into thanksgiving for the Lord has answered my prayers. I am free from all fear and I will live by faith, living not by what I see, hear, feel, sense, or think in my rational mind, but by faith, knowing that the things that I pray for will be taken care of by the Lord Jesus Christ, who lives in me, who watches over me, and who loves, accepts, and forgives me of all sins the very moment I repent. I am grateful for the privilege to take and enforce Jesus' delegated authority here in the earth!

The spoken word carries power. **The tongue has the power of life and death, and those who love it will eat its fruit. (Proverbs 18:21)**

97

For who has known the mind of the Lord that he may instruct him? But we have the mind of Christ. (1ˢᵗ Corinthians 2:16)

Come to Jesus in the Midst of the Compulsion

Any compulsion is only a symptom of the unhealed wounds in the heart. The wounds keep us running because the mind and emotions are not connected. We are either running physically or mentally in our actions or thoughts to escape the pain in our hearts. We need to settle it. The Lord has already won the battle against addiction and has provided us His peace, but He is a gentleman and He will not invade our wills. We need to come to Him in our brokenness. Repentance brings us to the humble place of seeking Him with all our heart to help us out of the confusion. There are areas we need to retrain ourselves in as our thought processes become clearer. During times of confusion, I had to tell myself to think and to then come out of the panic states. This was a breakthrough!

We come out of the broken place and receive this incredible gift of grace, God's unmerited favor, His power, and loving-kindness in our lives. Sometimes He gives us this gift without us even knowing from whence it came. As we obey Him, He endues us with more of His power. This gift endues us with His power against any addiction. It is a supernatural strength given to us from the Holy Spirit. It empowers us to do what we cannot do in our own strength, and assists us to divinely overthrow the devil and all of his lies. And the Holy Spirit assists us to live a life of faith and to face the pain. He empowers us to settle the unsettled issues with submission to Him, with repentance, turning from our part in the abuse, and from our sins and idols.

The spirit of fear will continue to harass and try to control us. I needed help to face the childhood issues, to settle the issues of my heart, and to get back into the peace of God. With the deep pain faced and with a heart that has forgiven self and others, the mind and emotions connect and our hearts reopen to feel life again.

In dealing with the deep hurts of childhood, we learn how to forgive ourselves and others with the help of the Holy Spirit and with Spirit filled counselors. We learn from other brothers and sisters within the body of Christ what true submission and honor to the Lord is about, and what true repentance is. We grow up and out of the childhood wounds. Then change comes as we emerge into our "honest self," of our true identity in Christ.

With any compulsion, we are rising up out of the evil of generational curses and the bondages of ungodly reactions to deep pains of childhood. Jesus redeemed us from any and all curses by His death, burial, and resurrection. We must claim this and receive it for ourselves. We must believe that the Lord will take us through. With honest submission to the Lordship of Jesus Christ and His authority in our lives, the Lord meets us at the point of our needs and enters into our hearts. With a true repentance for our sins, the blood of Jesus immediately cleanses us from sin, washing us clean. We are then made righteous in Him. No more secrets. And with repentance, the Holy Spirit baptizes us with His power to rise above the abuse. We begin to walk in the love, peace, and joy of the Lord as we are changed and become intercessors, interceding for the sins of others, including our loved ones.(See Appendix)

God changed my attitude toward my enemies because I understood their pain and the difficulty of rising up out of it. I could then pray for them, both understanding and knowing the torment of their self-condemnation and guilt. Their chastisements of me taught me compassion as I pondered the depths of their torment which was once my own. **And if the Spirit of Him Who raised Jesus from the dead is living in you, He who raised Christ from the dead will also give life to your mortal bodies through His Spirit, Who lives in you. (Romans 8:11)(See Appendix)**

Jesus lives in us to awaken and stop the enemy's driving spirits to keep us under his control. The spoken Word of God transforms our thinking from fear to faith. **My son (daughter), pay attention to what I say: listen closely to my words. Do not let them out of your sight, keep them within your heart; for they are life to those who find them and health to a man's whole body. (Proverbs 4:20)**

The Lord is My Redeemer

The root problem of "shame" has to be faced. Shame says, "I am a mistake." Guilt says, "I made a mistake." Until fully healed from homosexuality, I stayed away from all gay bars, gay contacts, and New Age literature. Anything I had in my household was destroyed, including pictures that held memories, letters, and gifts of any kind, in order to break all the ungodly soul ties. I also released the persons to the care of God. (See Chapter-Death Cannot Hold Me with prayers on breaking ungodly soul ties).

Until I am completely healed in the area of perfectionism, I do have to stay away from management positions as this will cater to the compulsion. I have the peace of God in doing this. I have to acknowledge my weak areas and concentrate on my strengths. The more I tried to be perfect, the more imperfection I would find. There was no end to the viscous spiral until I did the inner healing work. Doing the healing work strengthens you in your will, mind, and your emotions to counterattack the devil's lies and lures. When your body and soul are in agreement the enemy has no place; he is under your feet. You live by faith.

Everyone has an area of challenge. It may be pornography or addiction to other things such as food, alcohol, money, or sex. Mine was homosexuality and then perfectionism. When I was in the homosexual struggle, the tormenting spirit whispered, "You will find love and complete acceptance and happiness in this relationship." Because I had no personal relationship with Jesus Christ and no intimacy with Him living on the inside of my heart and loving me unconditionally and personally, I looked to natural realm for my spiritual needs to be met. Because of my deep need to be needed, because of lack of self-confidence, low self esteem, lack of autonomy to say "no" and to set healthy boundaries, because of envy that became eroticized, and seeking to relieve this deep hurt inside that only Jesus Christ could heal, I fell into the trap, the lie of the homosexuality.

There is also a deep deception here in the emotional realm that lured me into this lie. This lying spirit whispered, "All your emotional needs will be met here. This person will love you and understand you in a way no one else can." Not true. There is no one on earth who knows, loves and understands our emotions and how we feel more than Jesus Christ. He knows every hair on our head and every thought we think and emotion we feel. And Jesus is not only God, but also He came to earth as a man. He is acquainted with everything we have been tempted with, all our griefs, our sorrows, our traumas, torments, disappointments, and our sins. Homosexuality is a lie and a distraction from the peace of God like all addictions.

Speak to Your Mountains

Through all the agony, I had written my prayer need down on paper. I believed God for complete mental health. I was standing on Mark 11:23-25. I had spoken, believed, and prayed for my miracle and I was expecting that God would give it to me in His perfect timing. He healed my broken heart and delivered me from homosexuality. I believed that He could and He would heal me from the entire addiction spiral. And He will do the same for you! For by His stripes, we are healed! (Isaiah 53:5)

My attitude, no matter how harassing the devil was during the temptations, had to be of persistent faith. I was convinced that my miracle would manifest as I stood on the Word. I tried to obey whatever the Lord told me to do. And I knew He knew my heart. I was praying and believing God to be freed from fear. As I was prepared further in Tulsa, God would eventually free me from this monster. I would get to the root issues of the hurt and trauma in New Jersey when I arrived home.

Of course, I was helped to keep this momentum of faith because I had the support of so many believers surrounding me both in Church and at Bible College. I also lived in a Christian community. The city of Tulsa is filled with Christian believers. God was helping me, through the Word, the teachings, and the models of Christ whom I sat under daily, to rebuild my inner character.

I believe that these were the days in which the Lord was taking my self-condemnation and shame and showing me, through His presence, through His holy scriptures, and through the body of Christ, that I was loved and truly forgiven for this sin; that He loved me and that it was the sin only that He hated. This was the key ingredient. Revelation is essential to receive!

I remember the late Pastor Billy Joe Daugherty sharing the story of Pastor David Wilkerson and his dealings with the gangster, Nicky Cruz, on the streets of New York City. Pastor Dave demonstrated the love of God when he said in answer to a hateful remark toward him, "You can cut me in a million pieces, but I <u>still</u> will say that I love you." That story gave me another revelation of how much God really loves me. **Fear not, for I have redeemed you. I have called you by name, you are mine . . . Because you are precious in my eyes, because you are honored, and I love you. (Isaiah 43:1–4)**

Bible College was a place of refuge and a total break from the torments of temptation. Without the Word of God firmly planted, and without a relationship with Jesus growing, I would not have had the adequate preparation for the trial that would follow in New Jersey. **For nothing is impossible with God. (Luke 1:37)**

Habit Patterns

Patterns are formed since childhood. I believe my obsessive compulsive pattern was not only a result of fear of failure and a need for acceptance but it started when I was a child out of a need to "take some form of control" in an uncontrollable environment. I remember many behaviors I had since childhood that would mimic an obsessive compulsive pattern. I was meticulously clean. I would count the cracks in the sidewalk while walking home from school as a child. Desiring order in a disorderly environment is a normal need. It is when it gets knocked out of balance that it begins to harm us.

There were also generational sins which affected me since childhood. These allowed for demonic oppression to affect me as a child. I believe that the spirit of fear is cousins with the spirit of condemnation. My spirit and soul were invaded by demonic influences that were active within the spiritual environment of the family. My family was completely ignorant to the power of faith filled words spoken to the Father in the name of Jesus Christ. They were not taught the power of the spoken Word of God. (Hebrews 1:1–3) (Hebrews 4:12) Or of the delegated authority we have been given by Jesus Christ as born again believers over every demonic attack of the devil against our spirits, souls, and our bodies. (Luke 10:19) Therefore, we all suffered in a spiritually dark environment.(Hosea 4:6) They are all believers, but without the knowledge of the benefits and blessings of their inheritance when entering into a divine covenant relationship with Jesus Christ, there is no working knowledge of how to fight the good fight of faith and how to receive His precious promises. (1st Timothy 6:12)(2nd Peter 1:4)

My people are destroyed from lack of knowledge. (Hosea 4:6)

I Believe Therefore I Speak God's Word

It is frustrating when you do not have any answers for the problems. Yet I was blessed to have been led to the truth and a way out of the evil. I was determined to stay with Jesus and His Word. Friend, there may not always be a counselor available. But we always have our Lord and Savior, Jesus Christ, living on the inside of our hearts and the Word of God within our souls.

It is God's living Word and it works by speaking it with a heart of faith to remove any mountains that are in our way. We speak and believe that what we say will come to pass as we stand with proper positioning of our hearts of faith, surrendered to Jesus' Lordship and authority, in repentance of all sins, and in forgiveness and release of judgment toward ourselves and others. To speak with His power, we must be submitted under His authority. You cannot execute delegated authority if you are not under proper godly authority. He is looking at our hearts sold out in honesty and humility toward Him, not perfectly sinless people. **The grass withers and the flowers fall, but the Word of our God stands forever. (Isaiah 40:8)**

Friend, there is power in the spoken Word of God. Mark 11: 23 commands us to speak the Word from our hearts of faith. Prepare your heart with submission to Jesus as Lord and authority, with repentance for all sin, and with forgiveness for self and others. Believe that what you say is heard, and has the power of the living God behind it. The Word of God is Spirit and it is truth!

When guilt comes knocking at the door of my heart, I speak to it:

There is then no condemnation to me because I am in Christ Jesus. (Romans 8:1)

I speak to the shame:

My body is a temple of the Holy Spirit. It is a living temple for the Holy Spirit. I will honor God with my body. (1ˢᵗ Corinthians 6:19) (Romans 12:1)

I am the righteousness of God in Christ Jesus. (Roman 1:16,17)

I speak to confusion saying:

I am of sound mind in Christ Jesus. (2nd Tim. 1:7) I have the mind of Christ. (1st Cor. 2:16)

I speak to fear, inferiority, and to any intrusive spirits:

Greater is He Who is in me than he that is in the world. (1ˢᵗ John 4:4)

I speak to the low self- confidence and say:

I am more than a conqueror in Christ Jesus. (Romans 8:37)

I speak to timidity and say:

God has not given me the spirit of fear, but of love and power and of a sound mind. (2ⁿᵈ Timothy 1:7)

I speak to unbalanced grief:

The joy of the Lord is my strength. (Nehemiah 8:10) My grief will be turned to joy. (John 16:20)

I speak to any distractions from the enemy:

Nothing shall be able to separate me from the love of God that is in Christ Jesus my Lord. (Romans 8:37-39)

I speak to self-doubt:

I can do all things through Christ Jesus Who strengthens me. (Phil. 4:13)

I speak to depression:

To them God has chosen to make known among the Gentiles the glorious riches of this mystery, which is Christ in me, the hope of glory . . . (Colossians 1:27)

I speak to anxiety and worry:

The peace of God which surpasses all understanding shall rule and reign in my heart. (Colossians 3:15)

I speak against all curses and assignments from the devil:

Jesus Christ has redeemed me from the curse of the law by becoming a curse for me so that the blessing of Abraham may come to me and so that I may receive the promise of the Holy Spirit through faith. (Galatians 3:13)

I have been rescued from the dominion of darkness and brought into the kingdom of God's dear Son, the Son He loves, in whom I have redemption, the forgiveness of all my sins. (Colossians 1:13)

I speak to apathy and despair because I have been born with a divine purpose:

The Lord has called me by name. I am called with a purpose to spread the gospel to a dying world. He has commissioned me to go into all of the world and to make disciples of all nations baptizing them in the name of the Father and of the Son and of the Holy Spirit. (Isaiah 43:1) (Matthew 28:19 - The Great Commission) (All scriptures personalized)

Speaking the Word is not just a positive thinking exercise. It is more than that. When the Word of God is spoken to the Father with a heart of faith, with submission, repentance, and forgiveness, it carries power with it because it is His Word and not a human being's opinion. Moreover, the fullness of the power of the spoken Word of God lies in the faith with which we speak. Even though I was still wounded, the Word of God began to heal my wounds as I studied it, meditated upon it, and, finally, began to speak it with faith. Speaking it brought His presence to me and I knew that I was not alone, but in the presence of a holy God. The Word of God taught me who I was as a child of God.

The Lord is All – Merciful

I ask the Lord to teach me to love again in the midst of so much wounding. And He always answers, "I love you with an everlasting love." (Jeremiah 31:3) Or, in a still small voice, Jesus says, "I will help you." "I love you. You are my child and I am with you. Do not fear. Only believe."

I write to you, dear children, because your sins have been forgiven on account of His name. I write to you, fathers, because you have known Him who is from the beginning. I write to you, young men, because you are strong, and the Word of God lives in you, and you have overcome the evil one. (1ˢᵗ John 2:12, 14) I knew that God had forgiven me. However, when I heard the scripture about His incredible mercy that actually cancels out all sins and blocks them from His memory, I felt a deep peace. **I will remember their sin no more. (Jeremiah 31:34)**

Sexual sin carries bondage of shame from which it is very difficult to get free. Only the supernatural workings of a loving God could completely free me from this bondage. A revelation that the Lord gave me of Jesus hanging on the cross helped me to release any residual shame to Him. I then opened my heart to receive the righteousness (right standing) of God. Receiving this from the Lord did not happen overnight. It was a process. A counselor shared with me that the answer to my bondage was to see Jesus on the cross dying for me and for all my shame every time I was tempted to sin.

Jesus, who for the joy that was set before Him, despised the shame . . . (Hebrews 12:2)

It was so hard for me to receive the forgiveness from God. The same spirits of fear and rebellion from the homosexual sin were still oppressing me with the perfectionist spiral. Same spirit; different sin. It had to go. Basically, the Lord Jesus was reaching out to me saying to me: "I died for this sin. Take the gift of forgiveness. Take my grace."

Just as Paul flicked the snake off his hand in the book of Acts, Jesus was showing me during these years how to flick this shame and guilt off also.

But Paul shook the snake off into the fire, and suffered no ill effects. (Acts 28:5)

God always shows up with a correction to Satan's every deception.

When the enemy comes in like a flood, the Lord raises up a standard. (Isaiah 59:19)

The Lord is a Strong Tower

The name of the Lord is a strong tower; the righteous run to it and are safe. (Proverbs 18:10) I not only had the protection of the Lord, but I was surrounded by men and women whom I could trust. My pastors were all human representatives of Jesus Christ Himself. They were divinely guided by the Holy Spirit and filled with the love of God. The late Pastor Billy Joe Dougherty was candid about the essential value of spending time with Jesus on a daily basis. This is where I came to discern the power of God working on the inside of me. As I set myself inward toward prayer, the presence of the Holy Spirit actually placed a deposit of this holy presence within me and upon me.

When I found Victory Christian Center in Tulsa, Oklahoma, I literally found a safe haven. I was home. I knew that this was where I would grow up in Christ. I felt totally safe and loved there by genuinely caring people who were there to help. Their compassion for others was awesome to me. And I wanted to be like them. I remembered experiencing this love for others when I was a little girl and I wanted that feeling back. These folks walked the walk and talked the talk. It was like a dream come true.

The late Pastor Billy Joe Daugherty and Pastor Sharon Daugherty were such a special and anointed team. In every service, Pastor Sharon would sing anointed worship and praise songs and then Pastor Billy Joe would preach the message. He preached in the spirit of meekness and love with a healing anointing that was very special. I literally learned how to relax under this precious, peaceful, and powerful anointing of God. I felt so clean under this anointing. Now, as Pastor Billy Joe Daugherty has gone home to the Lord, Pastor Sharon preaches with a powerful anointing with the support of her beautiful family. **Blessed are the pure in heart, for they will see God. (Matthew 5: 8)**

I love the songs that Pastor Sharon has written and published on tape. One of my favorite pastimes was singing along with her on tape while driving through the city of Tulsa. My car has been my praise and worship center for years. I knew that there was much healing that Jesus ordained while I was praising Him. **I will enter His gates with thanksgiving in my heart . . . I will enter His gates with praise. For the Lord is good and His love endures forever. (Psalms 100: 4, 5)**

In Tulsa, I truly learned a new lifestyle of prayer and praise necessary to succeed in this world today. I was surrounded by courageous men and women of God with vision to spread the Word of God to a dying world. God had supplied me with role models who lived disciplined lives devoted to this purpose. I learned to live a life of self-discipline devoted to time spent with the Lord and daily prayer. I learned to speak the Word of God both through meditation and speaking it aloud on a daily basis. I learned that the greatest knowledge one can retain in this life is the Word of God. As the Word entered my mind, the soft voice of the Holy Spirit came alive in my innermost being. Peace would become my umpire. I began to feel again as I spoke my petitions to my Father, and I believed that God would answer my prayers spoken from my heart of faith in the precious name of Jesus Christ.

I was involved in several Bible study home groups in which I not only studied the Word of God at Sunday services, but I also studied on a weekly basis with small groups of Christians. I not only was learning the Word but I was now also accountable to other Christians. Some of them became my friends. I learned how to pray in prayer groups. And some of these folks I still am in contact with today. Accountability helped me out of isolation. As I connected, I felt like I belonged.

And the children! My time in the children's ministry was, as always, a healing time. My friend, I could never have given children as much as they gave to me. Their joy literally crushes my sorrow. Their purity devours any of my own impurities. Their innocence crowds out any suspicion I could have in my heart. And their love truly is awesome because they are children, the salt of God's great earth. Time spent with the children is always precious and healing indeed! It is a breath of fresh air to be in the company of God's children. I believe children are God's secret agents!

The Lord Has Commissioned Us
Many are suffering in the valley of decision . . . (Joel 3:14)

The magnitude of those who have not been as fortunate as I to receive Jesus as Lord and His precious promises of love, acceptance, and forgiveness dawned upon me. I knew the time was coming soon that I would be called to leave Tulsa and to return home to complete the healing process. I knew that I would be used to help multitudes who are still suffering.

I had been given nuggets of truth here in Tulsa. I had accepted Jesus into my heart to live and to serve Him. I learned to use the Word of God as a powerful tool for living. I now had a choice to make. Was I going to continue to live for myself and let the enemy win in his temptation to keep me in the shame and guilt of the past mistakes I had made? Or was I going to go and share the Word of God with other people who perhaps did not have the same opportunities as I?

I believe God was calling me and I believe He calls every believer to go and preach His Word. This is the Great Commission. This is God's heartbeat. He wants to use us to share His love and His good news (the gospel) with a dying world. Will we answer the call or not? It doesn't matter where we have been. I could have said that I am not healed yet. And I would have waited an entire lifetime because I will never be completely or perfectly healed on this earth. Only by faith and by receiving the finished work of Jesus Christ am I perfectly healed. It can only be received by an act of my faith. And it must be received for us to be free and to also free others. God wants to use us just where we are. As a matter of fact, He needs weak vessels so that He can be strong through us. Look at the great men and women of the Bible. He used the greatest sinners as the greatest leaders. Why? Because of their humility and repentance before God, they were honored and used mightily for God's glory.

Then Jesus came to them and said, "All authority in heaven and on earth has been given to me. Therefore go and make disciples of all nations, baptizing them in the name of the Father,

and of the Son and of the Holy Spirit, and teaching them to obey everything I have commanded you. And surely I am with you always, to the very end of the age." (Matthew 28:18)

The Lord is My Shepherd

Throughout these six years in Tulsa, Oklahoma, I was in spiritual warfare and this is only because I was growing closer to the Lord. Satan never likes defeat. When he saw this child of God drawing closer and becoming more knowledgeable in the Word of God, he did all he could to destroy my relationship with Jesus Christ. It is and continues to be a good fight of faith. (1st Tim. 6:12 ref.) **And no wonder, for Satan himself masquerades as an angel of light. It is not surprising, then, if his servants masquerade as servants of righteousness. (1st Cor. 11: 14)**

In Bible College, I grew closer to Jesus. I learned to meditate upon Word of God. I grew in my confidence as I learned it, lived it, and discovered who I am in Christ Jesus. Because I had the support of so many Christian soldiers, I was able to grow in Christ. And the Holy Spirit filled me to overflowing before I left for my home in New Jersey.

I knew that it was time to move on. I knew the Holy Spirit's voice. And He was beckoning me to return home. I really did not want to leave Tulsa. I was so comfortable there. But I had to obey God and leave my comfort zone to go deeper in Christ.

God was calling me home and I was ready to obey. This would be a fight not only for my own deliverance from fear, but also for the salvation of my entire family. God would now show me that as I followed Him, one step at a time, He would help me to walk the walk of faith and be completely restored. I would now go home to face my past and the root issues of my sins accompanied by my Savior and Lord, Jesus Christ, armed with the Word of God, as I walked led by the Holy Spirit. **When you pass through the waters, I will be with you; and when you pass through the rivers, they will not sweep over you. When you walk through the fire, you will not be burned; the flames will not set you ablaze. (Isaiah 43:2)**

This was a season of decision and determination. I made the decision to leave because I knew it was the voice of the Holy Spirit. I was determined that with God on my side, nothing and no one could stop me from what God had planned. As Pastor Demola says, "When God tells you to do something, you better do it." **[70]**

Go Home to Be at Home – Soul Ties

It was July of 1997. I was now ready to return home to my roots. I knew that God wanted me to have the key to the door that would unlock the root problem. I had to face the root problem before I could lock it out of my life forever.

I remember walking at Victory Campground one day to spend quality time with Jesus. I was sitting on the edge of a crystal blue lake. It was the end of the summer season and I saw on the horizon the rich green pine trees standing. They were not standing tall and erect, but rather leaning toward the eastern sky.

It was on this day that the Lord spoke to me about my "roots." Just as the pines were not standing straight up with their greatest strength, I was not at the height of my strength in God. Just as the roots of the leaning pines were not firmly planted in the earth, I also would not be firmly planted in my Christian walk had I not returned home to my family, to confront the root issues of the deep hurt that wounded me as a child. I had to uncover the pain and look at my ungodly reactions to it squarely. It was time to return home to New Jersey where Mom lived and many other relatives, including my sister and my three brothers. Dad had gone home to be with the Lord in 1992.

I now had three years of study with a Christian family at Oral Roberts University and had completed my studies at Victory Bible Institute. I had received much prayer and counsel from gifted ministers at Victory Christian Center, Grace Fellowship, Oral Roberts University, and also from professional Christian counselors in the Tulsa area. I had made many friends and had bonded closely with a few. I loved my pastors and friends at Victory Christian Center. I had a great job working at St. Simeon's Episcopal Home nursing the elderly. The Holy Spirit had prepared me well.

But the comfort there was transformed to a sense of restlessness as the Holy Spirit continued to prompt me to leave the area. I did not know God's entire plan. We never do when He calls us to something. But I knew from this revelation and other confirmations from the Holy Spirit that I needed to start packing. And so I obeyed.

Coming home for me was not only a step of obedience but it was also a step of desperation; it was the voice of a hurting little girl who was saying, "I will do all that is necessary to be free again." I was still dealing with the bondage of perfectionism on the job and was not free of this obsessive compulsive behavior. I had to get to the root. I was sick of the torment of it!

I remembered what a happy little girl I was, always laughing and quick to help people. I loved people. This step of faith to return home after twenty-four years of living independently was also the adult woman taking a stand saying, "I am a new creature in Christ. (2nd Corinthians 5:17) I am going to take a step of faith. I am going to find the happy little girl again and in stepping on the head of Satan himself, *I will* find the beautiful woman inside that God made me to be."

I had all the ammunition I needed. I was born again. I had developed an intimate relationship with Jesus Christ. I had learned the Word of God and had developed a very good attitude. I had lived a lifestyle of worshiping God without any distractions from family issues and/or past lesbian or other illicit relationships. I had grown strong in faith in Jesus Christ. I knew He was with me. It was God's timing for this step of faith. I was relying on Him for this step of obedience to blossom. I knew He had a divine plan in mind for my total deliverance.

Perspective is Everything

My dear friend Ron drove me home. We arrived at Glen Ridge, New Jersey on a hot summer evening in July of 1997. Mom and I were so happy to see each other. The enemy had his plans to keep us from this wonderful reconciliation, but I was strong in God. I remember I would sing and worship the Lord in the bathroom to keep my spirits up while living home with Mom in the beautiful mansion my dad had provided for us. I would be sure to read the Bible every morning. I was committed to spending time with Jesus daily.

It was a precious three years of reconciliation and friendship which the "little girl" within me so desperately needed and wanted. Mom was so very helpful to my healing. You know people change with time. My father's "home going" in 1992 had been difficult for everyone, especially for Mom. My heart went out to her and I was there for her as much as possible. I laughed more in those three years than I have in my entire life.

My mother's mother died when she was seven. She was raised by her two older sisters. I talked with Mom about her life in great detail. She put her husband and her children before anything else in her life. She professes a belief in God. After 911 in New York City, we joined hands together in prayer at the kitchen table and said the sinner's prayer, receiving Jesus into our hearts as Lord and Savior.

Losing her mother early in life was extremely challenging for her. I believe as she immersed herself in her own family, some of her own pain was eased. Mom was and still is very loving and caring toward all her children. Italian moms are the very best. She cooked great meals for us! She gave me great advice on many different subjects. She was and still is the life of the party and a great story teller.

Mom and Dad's generation went through much suffering. Because they endured a war and the depression, they learned to depend upon each other. The necessity of blending together and helping each family member was exemplified as a comradery that is rare in circles today. The unselfishness they modeled was Christ like. They sacrificed everything for their children. It was as if their children were their "jewels."

However, there is a deception connected with this attitude of giving <u>all</u> for your children. Many parents actually idolize their children in attending to them so much. Without realizing it, parents' subconscious fears and inner hurts may cause them to hold their children too closely. I didn't have children, but I held onto my patients' medical reports and felt a similar attachment. I understand that need to "hover".

This is a possessive love which is rooted in the spirit of fear and in a codependent attachment to the children. This love can stunt the child's personal growth through the developmental stages to maturity. This attachment is never developed to intentionally cause harm to the child. It is a trap of unbalance that is naively entered. Agape love, however, is rooted in a desire to give to the child by allowing for his/her personal growth. Agape love actually releases another to what is best for him/her. The greatest challenge of parenthood is in balancing trust in the Lord with the proper parenting of the child. **Train a child in the way he (she) should go, and when he (she) is old he (she) will not turn from it. (Proverbs 22: 6)**

Without the center of one's love experience rooted in a love relationship with Jesus Christ, all other relationships become unbalanced rather than enhanced. It is only through personal intimacy with Jesus Christ in our divine and vertical relationship with Him that a person develops the strength of confidence in his or her own identity in Christ. We are grounded in Jesus Christ first. He is our anchor. It then naturally follows that healthy boundaries are formed with loved ones and friends in our horizontal relationships.

As I mature in my relationship with Jesus Christ, I am learning to love others unconditionally with the agape love which loves without wanting anything in return, and without judgment upon others. It is a love which finds the wisdom of God to assist another to grow in his or her own relationship with Jesus Christ. The greatest act of love we can give someone is to share Jesus with them.

Honor Your Father and Mother
"Honor your father and mother" - which is the first commandment with a promise -"that it may go well with you and that you may enjoy long life on the earth."(Ephesians 6:2)

I believe that the culture of each generation greatly affects attitudes. My parents came from a culture of survivors. Because they went through a lot of suffering, they learned to work hard and to rely upon each other to survive the war and its resulting financial burdens.

Their motto was and still is, "God helps those who help themselves." Today, we help ourselves by our faith and submission to God. As we yield, we help ourselves and then God helps us. Submission to His authority and Lordship ensures us of our inheritance. We receive His grace to help us through every tribulation. We become heirs to His blessings of eternal life, divine protection, divine health, and divine prosperity. Submission is the ultimate act of humility that reaches out in faith to God for the grace we desperately need. We are not only forgiven for sins, but we also receive healing from all diseases and torments because of His sacrifice. (Psalm 103:1-3) (Isaiah 53:3-5)

Even though this motto is biblical, many families in this generation became deceived in a sense of pride in all they did to help themselves and each other. As a result, my generation also became deceived in pride for all that was given freely to us in material goods. Our parents accomplished much and through a great deal of hard work and comradery. Their comradery was shown in the acts of humility and honor that they exemplified as they reached out toward one another in the love of God.

However, because of this, they relied heavily upon their own strength to reach the goals they set. However, in the Christian ethic, we believe to reach out in faith to receive the benefits of the Lord. We also receive divine strength from the Holy Spirit to help us to do what we cannot do in our own strength.

Personality Clash – Developmental Milestones Underdeveloped

So I ask myself, "What went wrong?" When I examine my relationship to Mom, I am first led by the Holy Spirit to examine the different temperaments between us. She has a sanguine personality and is very extroverted, whereas I have a choleric personality and am more introverted. I believe that because of our very different personality types, we were set up for an imbalance. While growing up, because Mom has a very strong personality, and I was not yet developed in my own, I was extremely dependent upon her. Normal developmental stages were stunted because my relationship to Mom was one of enmeshment as a child and of codependence in my teen years and my early twenties.

Of course, Mom was just being a "good mom" when we would go shopping and she would give me her opinion of what dresses looked best on me. It usually turned out that I would "just agree" with her opinions. My compliant attitude toward Mom's dominance stunted some normal developmental stages.

Mom and I had an enmeshed and codependent relationship. Because of this, personal autonomy or self-government was not developed within me as a child. This explains why I still have trouble establishing personal boundaries as an adult. Without autonomy, there is not a clear difference between "me" and "you."

Growth in the area of initiative was also underdeveloped. Without this, there is little inner confidence for proper decision making. This developmental stage is crucial to maturity. And trust in God and parents is foundational to properly develop a sense of initiative. Trust is also the root stage of development from which all others are built.

Mom was merely acting in her "element" when she would converse with all my friends when they came to visit me. I felt "left out" of many conversations. I really didn't develop my own self-image and self-confidence until I went away to college. Without her realizing it, Mom's love for me manifested itself in a controlling manner because she was holding me very tightly. Did she consciously hold me too tightly or leave me out of conversations? Of course not!

All I really wanted was for Mom to tell me she loved me and to hug me. I would do everything around the house to gain her approval and affirmation. I became her helper. I helped with the house chores as well as raising my younger brothers and sister. I became a "doer," not a receiver. Out of my desperate need for acceptance, I did all I could do to "earn" her approval. Here is where performance orientation, or perfectionism, started.

In the years that followed, I continued in that "helper" role as a nurse and as music therapist and music teacher. I believe that God did bless me with the gift of helps. The key to the proper use of this gift is to do one's best and leave the rest to the Lord. As I heal from perfectionism, the striving in my own doing for God is being divinely transformed into a momentum of doing with the Lord, "in His strength." Actually, I am a lot like Mom. She is a "doer" also, always doing something for someone else. She would be cooking, cleaning, taking care of the children, or pleasing her husband. It was and still is very difficult for her to receive. Even today, it is difficult to buy her a gift because she is not pleased that I spend money. She prefers that I spend it on myself or save it.

Being survivors of the depression, Mom and many from this generation still save money scrupulously. Her generation includes the "penny-saved, penny-earned" survivors. I commend them in their unselfishness on the one hand. On the other hand, in always giving and not being able to receive, they unfortunately kept themselves in the masculine model or the initiator's mode. The feminine model is the more receptive mode.

I couldn't settle. I couldn't rest. I believe this is attributed to the lack of the proper development of the receptive mode. In becoming a "doer" to please Mom, I set myself up to stay hooked into the masculine mode. Why did I continue in the "doing" role? This was a pattern I developed since childhood and, in time, it became an unhealthy mindset. Doing to please not only was seeking approval from the outside, but it also served to block out the hurt I felt on the inside.

Until I accepted Mom for who she is and reached out to Jesus for the love, acceptance, and the total forgiveness that I needed, I would not go further in my maturity or in my healing. Until I developed in my own identity in Christ, I would continue in this enmeshed and codependent model with Mom and in other relationships. It was a relationship without boundaries. And it was ungodly because Jesus was not the Lord of my life. Mom was. The relationship needed mending and boundaries needed to be set.

I Want to Be Free

I did have lots of boyfriends at college but my personal integrity was not confidently established. Relationships were immature because of this. Gender identity in those days was based upon my looks and how I dressed. I was physically attractive. I was very attracted to the "guys." I liked to get dressed up and go to dances and proms. I wore makeup and had a great wardrobe that Mom and Dad so generously provided for me for college.

I had a fear of commitment. Every time one of my boyfriends would propose, I would say "no." I was playing. I was not fully mature as a woman. I was not ready, nor was I desirous of a really committed relationship. Because of the enmeshment with Mom, I did not want to be controlled by anyone. I obviously needed her affirmation on one hand. Yet, on the other hand, I was resentful of her dominance. I wanted her love but hated her control.

I must have subconsciously made a vow never to be controlled by anyone. This vow had to be confronted, repented of, and dealt with in Christian counseling before I would be open to a committed relationship in a marriage covenant. Today, as I grow into maturity, I am no longer running from controlling personalities. I no longer fear their control because I am controlled by the Holy Spirit. He is my anchor. I am learning, however, to set healthy boundaries and limits and to relate appropriately to these personalities. Yet I do not get too close to them. I have developed the courage to say "no" and to set proper boundaries. I follow the leading of the Holy Spirit. As I gain a comfort with my own value, I am not afraid to "be me".

Homosexual behavior has been found to be motivated not only by legitimate needs for love, acceptance, and identity, but also by ungodly responses to hurt, rejection, and abuse. [71]

Ungodly Soul Ties Must Be Severed by the Child who is Redeemed from the Curse

I thought I broke away from the enmeshment with Mom when I physically left the area and was filled with the Holy Spirit in 1991. Yet I have to admit that there still was that "little girl" inside who wanted "Mommy to love her the way she desired to be loved." And there were communication patterns that had been formed since childhood that had to change. This demonstrates how deep these ties are. I had been physically away from Mom for twenty-four years!

I actually had an ungodly soul-tie to Mom. Because of a generational curse on the bloodline and the codependence in the relationship, there was an evil spirit working between us, and I had to separate and spend time away from contact with Mom. After I was restored to wholeness and was walking in the freedom of the Lord, then measures to reunite in a different type of relationship would hopefully be possible.

I encourage the reader to be led of the Holy Spirit and also to be assisted with the help of Spirit filled

Christian counselors in working through difficult issues in primary relationships. The decisions and issues regarding family ties must be worked through with or without the family members present. If separations, whether temporary or permanent, are necessary between family members, there must be godly Christian counsel for accountability and mature decisions regarding the perfect will of God to be made. There must be this accountability in order to rightly divide the Word of God.

If you are being led to attempt to establish new patterns and standards for the relationship, a third party is suggested. Old ways of communication are so easily reignited since we are dealing with childhood patterns. If trying to change patterns and reconcile in a controlling type relationship, the controlling party needs to recognize the new freedom you are walking in with the Lord or restoration of the relationship is not possible. **[72]** In an ungodly soul-tie one individual pulls another away from his/her commitment to God's laws of morality and obedience. We think of such pulls as evil soul-ties, wherein the one who becomes linked with another person finds himself to be evilly corrupted by the association. **[73]**

All human soul-ties must be counterbalanced by a love for Jesus. **[74]** We must live a life totally and desperately devoted, dependent upon, and belonging to Jesus Christ. Even in a godly marriage, Jesus must be on the throne of both partners' lives. **Anyone who loves his father or mother more than me is not worthy of me; anyone who loves his son or daughter more than me is not worthy of me; and anyone who does not take up his cross and follow me is not worthy of me. Whoever finds his life will lose it, and whoever loses his life for my sake will find it. (Matthew 10:37-38)**

Loss of focus on Jesus can come so quickly and so subtly when there are ungodly soul ties to parents, lovers, or even friends. Breaking the ungodly soul-tie to Mom does not mean I do not love my mother. On the contrary, it confirms a deeper love for her. Without breaking the ungodly soul tie, I not only forfeit the promises of God upon my life, but also I would never have been used of God in a godly relationship to Mom. My obedience to breaking that tie opens the door for both of our inherited blessings in Christ Jesus and my ability in Christ to bless Mom in the future. It also helps Mom to release me to the care of the Lord and it gives her the opportunity to focus on Jesus Christ as her Lord. Maturing in the pure walk of sanctification in Christ requires that I break all ungodly relationships.

If you fully obey the Lord your God and carefully follow all his commands I give you today, the Lord your God will set you high above all the nations on earth. All these blessings will come upon you and accompany you if you obey the Lord your God: (Deuteronomy 28:1-2)

If you read the many blessings listed in Deuteronomy 28, you will be motivated to obey the Lord with all your heart and mind and soul. I am so encouraged by His promise of protection against the enemy: **The Lord will grant that the enemies who rise up against you will be defeated before you. They will come at you from one direction but flee from you in seven. (Deuteronomy 28:7)**

A soul-tie is a cleaving together, a relationship whereby two souls are joined or knitted together, and, in a sense, become as one. The word "tie" is defined by Webster as meaning "to attach, bind, fasten; a bond of kinship or affection, as to unite in marriage: but it also carries another connotation: "to restrain from independence or freedom of action or choice: constrain by, or as if by authority, influence, agreement or obligation." The individual being so controlled feels obliged, and as if his independence must be sacrificed due to the influence or authority of the other party, who is controlling. **[75]**

God's intention was for man and woman to bond and form godly soul-ties. Godly soul ties are a part of God's original design. Remember that God had a walking, talking relationship with His son, Adam, in the beginning of creation. **[76]**

In the homosexual soul tie, there is an ungodly soul tie both in the fornication of the relationship and in the emotional attachment of the relationship. The physical tie is to be set aside for the marriage bed. The emotional attachment, whether the controlling element exists or not, must be surrendered to the Lordship of Jesus Christ. Each partner becomes codependent upon the other. Even if both partners attest to a love and commitment to Jesus Christ, codependence is an idol which takes each partner away from complete loyalty and allegiance to Jesus Christ. The codependence masks the real issues which must be faced for the homosexual to be freed from the bondage of such an erroneous and unnatural affection. (Romans 1:26-27)

In human reproduction, the mother-to-be is vitally linked to her unborn child via the connection which exists through the umbilical cord. The child draws sustenance, nourishment and life through that vital union with the earthly source of his natural life. This is a vertical umbilical relationship which provides us life... and it tends to be involuntary on the child's part. **[77]**

Initially, the child is totally dependent upon the mother for life, blood, oxygen, nourishment. On the subtler, less obvious side, she passes on to the child the DNA which will direct the child's growth, determining physical attributes, and many other factors which will affect the personality. Oftentimes the mother also passes down curses or spirits, such as alcoholism, drug addiction, or fears. All information passes to the developing child through the umbilical cord and is carried by the blood. **[78]**

All of this physical inheritance changes when we are born again and thus grafted into the bloodline of Jesus Christ. We are healed and freed through the blood of Jesus Christ of any curses, fears, iniquities, addictions, spirits, and any diseases when we reach out in faith and take our deliverance. We take it through our speaking with a heart of faith; with submission, repentance, and forgiveness. We take it as we present our petitions to our Father God in the name of Jesus. We take it through our delegated authority in Jesus Christ, rebuking the enemy and speaking the Word of God, with faith to receive our complete deliverance in the name of Jesus Christ. (Romans 11:17)(Galatians 5:6)(Mark 11:23-25)(Galatians 3:13)(Isaiah 53:3-5)(1st Peter 1:18,19)(All scriptures referenced)

Satan is the Enemy of the Bloodline, not Dad or Mom

Remember, any spirits or curses that are passed down through the bloodline originate from the father of lies, Satan, and not from Mom's blood or Dad's seed. (John 10:10) Furthermore, when a child of God becomes born again, he or she enters into a divine covenant relationship with Jesus Christ. (John 15:4,5) (Romans 10:9,10) Any curses, demonic assignments, or generational sins are broken over his/her life because of the redemption (freedom) promised through the precious shed blood of Jesus Christ.(Galatians 3:13)(1st Peter 1:18,19) It is our choice to then reach out and to take this freedom from God through our spoken words of faith. (Mark 11:23-25) **To be "redeemed" is to be bought back or to be freed from what distresses or harms. It means to free from captivity by payment of a ransom. Jesus' obedience to die for you and I is the payment that restores us to sanity in a relationship with Him. As we enter into covenant with Him, we are grafted into the bloodline of Jesus Christ. That frees us from any and all curses that Satan attempts to deceive us to believe about ourselves. [79]**

We, as born again believers, enter into a divine covenant relationship with Jesus Christ.(John 15:4,5) (Romans 10:9,10) We are grafted into a new and a divine bloodline with the Lord Jesus Christ. (Romans 11:17) We are free from any hindrances inherited spiritually, mentally, emotionally, or even physically to our DNA. The Word of God changes us even to our DNA. (Hebrews 4:12) We are now covered by the blood of Jesus Christ for complete healing in every area of our lives. (1st Peter 1:18,19) We now inherit the blessings and promises of God. (2nd Peter 1:4) As we receive the grace of God, we will increase in our capacity to be changed and to become more like God. (Ephesian 2:8) As we obey Him, He heals and restores us. (Luke 4:18)(Isaiah61:1) **If some of the branches have been broken off, and you, though a wild olive shoot, have been grafted in among the others and now share in the nourishing sap from the olive root, do not boast over those branches. If you do, consider this: You do not support the root, but the root supports you. (Romans 11:17) For you know that it was not with perishable things such as silver or gold that you were redeemed (made free) from the empty way of life handed down to you from your forefathers, but with the precious blood of Christ, a lamb without blemish or defect. (1st Peter 1: 18-19)**

For you have been born again, not of perishable seed, but of imperishable, through the living and enduring Word of God. (1st Peter 1:23) Christ redeemed us from the curse of the law by becoming a curse for us, for it is written: "Cursed is everyone who is hung on a tree." He

redeemed us in order that the blessing given to Abraham might come to the Gentiles through Christ Jesus, so that by faith we might receive the promise of the Spirit. (Galatians 3:13)

Releasing Family as an Idol

We release even our family to the care of God, repenting to the Lord for any idols and/or ungodly soul ties we have formed with them. **You shall not make for yourself an idol in the form of anything in heaven above or on the earth beneath or in the waters below. You shall not bow down to them or worship them; for I, the Lord your God, am a jealous God, punishing the children for the sin of the fathers to the third and fourth generation of those who hate me, but showing love to a thousand generations of those who love me and keep my commandments. (Exodus 20:4-6)**

The late Pastor Billy Joe Daugherty, in his book, Breaking the Chains of Bondage, states,

When you declare the name of Jesus as you are humbly submitted to the Lord, every bondage, imagination, and stronghold must leave you. Jesus' name has been given to you with the power of attorney. If a business person goes out of the city and wants business to go on as usual, he can confer upon another person in writing the power of attorney. The person will be named and the responsibilities, duties, and privileges he is to exercise will be spelled out so business can go on as usual.

This is exactly what Jesus did before He left earth. He assigned His work to those who believe in Him (Mark 16:15-18). He gave His name to those who believe in Him to carry on the Father's business as usual. It's time to accept you power of attorney in the name of Jesus Christ of Nazareth and declare your freedom! This is your day of liberation! And once you are free, you can set others free!

Breaking the Chains of Bondage Confession

Speak this confession aloud, believe it in your heart, and begin to act as if it is already true in your life: "By an act of my will, I cast down imaginations, arguments, and everything that exalts itself against the knowledge of God and bring them into captivity to the obedience of Christ. In other words, I capture my thoughts and attitudes and bring them under the control and the Lordship of Jesus Christ in Jesus' name, Amen." (2nd Cor. 10:4.) I exercise the weapons of warfare to pull down strongholds of bondage in my life. These are:

1. The blood of Jesus.
2. The Word of God.
3. The name of Jesus.

Jesus' blood has set me free from Satan's authority and it cleanses me from all sin. Speaking God's Word with accuracy keeps me free of bondage and helps me to mature in Christ. Using the name of Jesus gives me power of attorney to declare my freedom over the devil and to keep him under my feet!

(References: 2nd Cor. 10:5, Ephesians 1:7, 1st Peter 1:18, 19, 1st John 1:7) **[80]**

It is interesting to note that even Jesus' physical presence did not necessarily change circumstances – generally people were not delivered or healed until He spoke. **[81]**

Look with Your Spiritual Eyes

The great difference now is that I try not to look for my affirmation from Mom or anyone else, but first and foremost in the unconditional love and acceptance I receive from Jesus Christ. And it is through my errors that Jesus continues to teach me more and more about His love for me. I've made a lot of mistakes. Jesus continues to love and teach me in spite of them.

Did Mom consciously reject me? Of course not! She really didn't reject me at all in her eyes. But I perceived it that way. I sensed her inner turmoil as rejection against me until I realized that she was also tormented by oppressive spirits. Did she consciously try to dominate me? Of course not! Perspective is everything, my friend. It's a catch-22. Mom was playing out her own scenario. She had a mother whom she never knew. The loss of her mother hit her deeply as a seven-year-old child. She and thousands of other mothers live through their children to help them forget the pain of their past hurts. We are all human!

Likewise, I believe Mom was effectively blocking her own pain by redirecting it and giving all to her family. She not only did her best but she also did a remarkable job! Because of her own pain, she was driven to dominate her children and live through them. She held on so tightly because of emotional hurts from her childhood and her need to block them out.

She also shared with me that, because her mother had died at an early age that her overprotection was a result of wanting to give her children what she did not have. I'll never forget her words, "I wanted to give you what I did not have." Had I not obeyed the Lord and come home, I would never have heard her side of it. What a precious woman!

When you take a hard look at any criticism of someone else, it usually is a mirror reflection of your own behaviors. I did the same thing in my nursing profession. I held on too tightly to my patients. I became a perfectionist to block out my emotional hurts which had to be faced for healing to transpire. Instead of holding too closely to children as my mom did, I held onto my patients' case histories. This preoccupation also kept anyone from coming into my life. So I also became a controller. I just had a different outlet!

It is the law of sowing and reaping. We reap (receive back) what we sow (give). Likewise, I did not want to be controlled by anyone. Therefore, I became a controller myself because of my judgment and lack of forgiveness toward those whom I allowed to control me. If I do not take responsibility for my ungodly reactions to that control, I will stay in the quicksand of the victim's mud. I must not only forgive those whom I have allowed to control me, but I must rise up with confidence and set my boundaries, no longer allowing myself to be a "doormat," and dare to blend in and form relationships with other people.

The Earth is the Lord's

The little girl who then feared the control of another then found a place of "self-defense" and a hiding place in assuming the very same posture as the one who had controlled her. Out of a sense of self survival then, I assumed the need to "take control" and this became the very bondage which only Jesus could remove.

"Possession" is defined as the act of having or taking into control. **[82] The earth is the Lord's and everything in it. (Psalm 24:1)** The "strongman" or "unclean spirit" took total advantage of my vulnerabilities. In the homosexual lifestyle, I entered into ungodly covenants with women, looking for the affirmation I perceived that I did not receive from Mom. Satan took advantage of me because of my promiscuity and the unclean spirit, the spirit of lust, took control of me. Later, after renouncing the homosexual covenants, I was still afraid of being controlled. In defense, I assumed controlling positions in my work.

The unclean spirit is a designated leader of the spirit world. He is a ruler who has authority to command cadres of demons who are subservient to him. This is the strongman that Jesus refers to, and he is the one we must dethrone, in the name of the Greater One, Jesus Christ, in order to set a person free. His actions reveal his authorized position and power when he attempts to reenter a person's life again and again even after he or she comes to Jesus. **[83]**

Just As I Am

I am glad I did not marry in those early years. I truly was not ready or mature enough in Christ. I was not yet born again. Only through a personal and intimate relationship with Jesus Christ, living the Word of God, and through healthy relationships within the body of Christ would I be brought into my full identity in Christ as a blessed woman of God. And it would only be through healthy Christian relationships that I would be prepared for marriage. I had to first learn to trust and submit to the Holy Spirit before I would ever be ready to submit to a man in a marriage relationship.

Trust in the Lord and do good; dwell in the land and enjoy safe pasture. Delight yourself in the Lord and He will give you the desires of your heart. (Psalm 37: 3, 4)

Because of this lack of maturity, I actually needed more emotionally than I received from the attention my boyfriends were able to give. Had I reached out to Jesus, my inner needs for love and affirmation would have been divinely grounded. I would have then been able to reach out and give love with the love of Jesus within me. But I related to women instead and learned the hard way. These women were also victims of this hellish spirit of homosexuality. **I am the vine; you are the branches. If a man (woman) remains in me and I in him (her), he (she) will bear much fruit; apart from me you can do nothing. (John 15: 5)**

Gender Identity – Dr. Elizabeth Moberly's Research

So God created man in His own image, in the image of God He created him; male and female He created them. (Genesis 1:27-28) God created us with a gender orientation from the moment we were conceived in our mother's womb. We were created with the distinct physical orientation to either the male or the female gender. Our gender orientation is a result of God's "original and intended will" for us at the exact moment of creation.

The Word of God Changes Us to the Core of Our Being – the Marrow of Our Bones

The Word of God actually penetrates our bodies even to the very marrow of our bones. (Hebrews 4:12) Our blood cells which contain our DNA are manufactured in the marrow of our bones. Think about it! The Word of God penetrates to the marrow of our bones. As we commit to speak with faith and to live our lives by the Word of God, we not only begin to think as Jesus thinks, but the Lord physically transforms us even to the very marrow of our bones, where our DNA is made. Our DNA is our genetic material. Therefore, God changes us through His Word even to our DNA.

Therefore, anything we have inherited through our family bloodline can be changed through the spoken Word of God, and received by faith, as we enter into humble submission in the covenant relationship we have with Jesus Christ. We change as we are grafted into His divine bloodline. (Romans 11:17) The words we speak in faith are seeds from which growth and development in Christ transpire.

There is no statistical evidence to prove that our sexuality is from genetic origins. However, even if there were a homosexual gene, this would be no excuse for the homosexual addiction, because the Word of God still has the power to change us even to the very core of our DNA. The necessary changes, however, take place in the spirit, and the soul, (the emotions, the mind, the will), and through our words spoken in faith, not from our genetic material. I attest that true gender identity is both uncovered and discovered by each person from within his/her spirit and soul.

For the Word of God is living and active. Sharper than any double-edged sword, it penetrates even to dividing soul and spirit, joints and marrow; it judges the thoughts and attitudes of the heart. (Hebrews 4:12) For as he thinketh in his heart, so is he. (Proverbs 23:7) (King James Version)

As we think and live as Christ directs us in His Word, our very nature even to the cellular level is changed into the image we were created to be even before the very foundations of the earth! [84]

For those God foreknew He also predestined to be conformed to the likeness of His Son, that He might be the firstborn among many brothers. (Romans 8:29) There is no gender attached to our spirits and souls; whether thoughts, emotions, or will. We are all changed to be like Jesus as we enter into the born again intimate and personal covenant relationship with Jesus Christ. We all think, feel, and have a will, both men and women alike.

How Do We Experience Gender Identity?

I believe true gender identity is experienced as an inner conviction in our human spirits and souls in relation to our divine covenant relationship with our Father God, with Jesus Christ, and with the Holy Spirit. We sometimes also experience this inner conviction as revelation knowledge as we are guided into all truth by the Holy Spirit. Gender identity naturally emerges as we study, meditate upon, and speak the Word of God And we experience true gender identity as an inner perception as we bond to and relate in healthy relationships with both men and women. Relationships with other men and women are essential to the healthy formation of our true identity in Christ. **(Hebrews 4:12)**

Gender Identity - Inner Conviction as We Receive from the Father, Son, and the Holy Spirit

True gender identity is not something which is formed as a result of one's outward appearance. It forms when a person comes into full agreement with God, whether a person is born male or female. As I surrender to Jesus as Lord and loving authority in my life, I am experiencing an inner conviction in my spirit and soul of my own femininity through both the learning and the living out of His Word. I am walking in a personal relationship with Jesus and my identity is further revealed as I learn what He says about me in His Word. In my human spirit/soul to Holy Spirit interactions, I am listening with my spiritual ears to the Holy Spirit's leadings. His still, small voice beckons to me to both comfort me and to direct my steps. He reveals pieces of this puzzle as I listen for His lead. And the love that Father God has for me also reveals more pieces of the gender puzzle in both spirit and soul.

A man, I believe, will experience the same inner conviction of his masculinity in his human spirit and soul also in his divine covenant relationship with his Father God, Jesus Christ, and the Holy Spirit, and in the study of God's Holy Word. I say this because there is no gender in our spirits or in our souls. But our gender identity is revealed to us through our connection to our God.

Both male and female are created with a human spirit and a human soul. The human spirits of both the male and the female enter into that submitted posture to Jesus Christ in the intimacy with Jesus first, walking and talking with Him daily. Here the soul matures as the mind is transformed by the washing of the Word, the emotions are kept under by faith, and the will is strengthened through the submitted relationship with the Lord. As we grow more in love with Jesus, He then is able to grow us into the men or the women He originally designed for us to be, thus "honest self."

We get to our Father God through our relationship with Jesus Christ, in a day by day relationship led by the Holy Spirit. **Jesus said, "I am the way and the truth and the life. No one comes to the Father except through me." (John 14:6)** Jesus also sent us the person of the Holy Spirit to guide us into all truth. The human spirit and the human soul open up to receive the Holy Spirit with His comfort and guidance. Jesus also promises the Holy Spirit to the disciples, **"If you love me, you will obey what I command. And I will ask the Father and He will give you another Counselor to be with you forever – the Spirit of truth. The world cannot accept Him, because it neither sees Him nor knows Him. But you know Him, for He lives with you and will be in you. I will not leave you as orphans; I will come to you. (John 14: 15–18)** As a child seeks guidance and direction from the parent, so we as male or female seek guidance from our Lord, human spirit and human soul to Holy Spirit. It is through the guidance of the Holy Spirit and through the revelations discovered through our walk with Jesus Christ and His Word that the love of the Father is revealed to us. Our true identity in Christ is found as we humbly and gratefully receive His completed love, acceptance, and forgiveness through the Father, Son, and the Holy Spirit.

Deep calls to deep in the roar of your waterfalls; all your waves and breakers have swept over me. By day the Lord directs His love, at night His song is with me – a prayer to the God of my life. (Psalm 42:7)

Gender Identity – Inner Perception through the Reflection of Others

There is also an experiential and conscious awareness of our true gender in the real world as we connect with other people. We acknowledge ourselves as male or female as a result of an inner perception as we bond and relate to both sexes. Bonding to the same sex reflects our own similarities. Bonding to the opposite sex reflects our differences as well as our similarities. Therefore, gender identity develops as we inwardly perceive ourselves through the reflections of those we relate with.

Therefore, I attest that gender identity is both an inner conviction found as we receive from the Lord and His Word and an inner perception found through our bonding with other people. It is not an outward exemplification. **Your beauty should not come from outward adornment, such as braided hair and the wearing of gold jewelry and fine clothes. Instead, it should be that of your inner self, the unfading beauty of a gentle and quiet spirit, which is of great worth in God's sight. (1st Peter 3:3)**

Identity in Christ and Through Others

Therefore, we experience our gender identity first as an inner conviction in our relationship with the Lord Jesus Christ and His Word, which serves to define us in our identity in Christ. Through the leading of the Holy Spirit, our godly identity is revealed to us through the revealed presence of God in us, with us, and working through us. As we come into agreement with the Word of God and as we take steps to obey daily, the honest self emerges. Our gender as male or female is discovered primarily through Jesus Christ our Lord and our relationship with Him. (Galatians 5:6) (Romans 1:16,17) (Hebrews 11:1) (All scriptures referenced) The Father shows both spirit and soul His love. Jesus teaches us who we are, both spirit and soul, through His Word. And the Holy Spirit dwells in our human spirits and souls to bring us clear convictions, revelations, impressions, and perceptions.

This divine relationship breaks down all facades. We "see ourselves" not in our visual reflected mirror image but through our inner perceptions as we relate with other people. With Christ living within us, we see now with the eyes of our heart, with Christ abiding in us. The reflections we receive from others are clear because there are no blinders to block the true image. We are graced only because of what Jesus has done within our hearts to experience clear reflections from both the male and the female genders. We see and then perceive with the eyes of our human spirit and with our human soul, (emotions, mind, and will), not just with the eyes of our flesh, looking outward.

Therefore we are always confident and know that as long as we are at home in the body we are away from the Lord. We live by faith, not by sight. (2nd Corinthians 5:6,7)

Free in God's Natural and Original Intention of Creation and Free in Our Natural Attractions and Intended Desires

Jesus makes us brand new, with a new nature, as children with complete trust in Him. A walk of purity before our God brings us to this place of our natural creation. And the unnatural attraction for the same sex is no longer even a part of our identity or our nature. We are now changed into His created image, the natural and the original intention God created for us before we were even in the womb. We put on the new creation in Christ Jesus. (2nd Cor. 5:17) He has done a new thing, and our natural attractions and intended desires we were created with are also restored back to us. The Lord restores back to us that which He created for us before we were even in our mother's womb, a man for a woman and a woman for a man. (Jeremiah 1:5)(Isaiah 44:24) (Isaiah 43:1) He is a God of restoration. (Joel 2:25)

But for Adam no suitable helper was found. So the Lord God caused the man to fall into a deep sleep; and while he was sleeping, he took one of the man's ribs and closed up the place with flesh. Then the Lord God made a woman from the rib he had taken out of the man, and He brought her to the man. The man said, "This is now bone of my bones and flesh of my flesh; she shall be called woman, for she was taken out of man. For this reason a man will leave his father and mother and be united to his wife, and they will become one flesh. The man and his wife were both naked, and they felt no shame. (Genesis 2:23-25)

The Bible is clear that God's purpose in creating both male and female is twofold. He did not want man to be alone and He created the woman from man as a "helpmate." God also intended for man and woman to reproduce and populate the earth. (Genesis 1:27,28)

God Has Assigned Roles for the Male and the Female

Both genders have been blessed with many similar attributes, gifts, and talents. But God has intended "roles" for the male as the "initiator" and the female as the "helper" to the male. He commands submission of the female towards the male and love of the male for the female in the marriage bond.**The Lord God said, "It is not good for the man to be alone. I will make a helper suitable for him. (Genesis 2:18)**

Wives, submit to your husbands as to the Lord. For the husband is the head of the wife as Christ is the head of the church, His body, of which He is the Savior. Now as the church

submits to Christ, so also wives should submit to their husbands in everything. Husbands, love your wives, just as Christ loved the church and gave Himself up for her to make her holy, cleansing her by the washing with water through the Word, and to present her to Himself as a radiant church, without stain or wrinkle or any other blemish, but holy and blameless. In this same way, husbands ought to love their wives as their own bodies. He who loves his wife loves himself. After all, no one ever hated his own body, but he feeds and cares for it, just as Christ does the church – for we are members of His body. For this reason a man will leave his father and mother and be united to his wife, and the two will become one flesh. This is a profound mystery – but I am talking about Christ and the church. However, each one of you also must love his wife as he loves himself, and the wife must respect her husband. (Ephesians 5:22-33)

When we are united with Jesus, we stand naked before the Lord without shame. With God in a marriage, both believing partners stand together before God, unashamed. There is no shame when God is present.

Healed, Unashamed, Blessed
Heterosexuality is as Natural as Apple Pie
We are Called by God

The Lord called Jeremiah when he was a young boy as a prophet and as a priest. **The word of the Lord came to me, saying, Before I formed you in the womb I knew you, before you were born I set you apart; I appointed you as a prophet to the nations." (Jeremiah 1:5)**

And we unashamedly enter into the rest of God, with a clear conscience. (Hebrews 4:9) Jesus heals us and frees us from the lies of the past; the abuses, the fears, the painful memories and hurts, the rejections and traumas, the fantasies and imaginations, and all demonic oppression and/or possession. Jesus heals us from the painful memories and they have lost both their pain and their power to condemn or to control us. And because of His love, acceptance, forgiveness, and His grace, (unmerited favor and loving kindness), we take courage to emerge free to be what He created us to be.

Because of Jesus' ultimate sacrifice of His life for us on the cross of Calvary, through the shedding of His pure and divine blood, we inherit not only eternal life, but we also inherit healing and deliverance from all addictions, freedom from all condemnation, freedom from all demonic curses and perversions, and freedom from all fear! (Romans 8:1) (Galatians 3:13) (2nd Tim. 1:7) Receive the restoration from the Lord! (Matthew 7:8) This is His gift to you.

We are made whole in our sexual orientation by the stripes (wounding) of Jesus Christ. **Surely He took up our infirmities and carried our sorrows, yet we considered Him stricken by God, smitten by Him, and afflicted. But He was pierced for our transgressions, He was crushed for our iniquities (tendencies toward sin); the punishment that brought us peace was upon Him, and by His wounds we are healed (changed). We all, like sheep, have gone astray, each of us has turned to his own way; and the Lord has laid on Him (Jesus) the iniquity of us all. (Isaiah 53:4-6)**

The man/woman emerges healed, whole, and changed to his/her God-created natural and original intentions of creation with its natural attractions and its intended desires, with a changed and a pure heart as that of a precious child. The Lord gives inner conviction to the believer, Holy Spirit to human spirit and Holy Spirit to human soul. And other people provide us with reflections for our inner perceptions that we receive with both our spirits and our souls/hearts. The words of Jesus,

He called a little child and had him stand among them. And he said: "I tell you the truth, unless you change and become like little children, you will never enter the kingdom of heaven. Therefore, whoever humbles himself like this child is the greatest in the kingdom of heaven. (Matthew 18:1-4)

And we, no matter what age or how long this process has taken, have found the key ingredient to our honest identity in Christ Jesus, which is humility before a holy God. Now with a humbled heart of a child, with a clear conscience before Him, in right standing before Him, we emerge free into the natural and the original intention of our creation. Thus, our heterosexual identity created by God becomes as "natural" as apple pie. When we are rightly related to God, we are naturally aware of our God- given and our true sexual orientation toward the opposite sex. **He has made everything beautiful in its time. (Ecclesiastes 3:11)**

The Word of God, His people, prayer, and my commitment and surrender to an intimate and personal friendship and relationship with Jesus Christ, my Lord and Savior, all brought me out with His mighty hand. And He will do it for you as well. Remember, we are all sinners and we are all welcome to receive the incredible gift of the Father's love, Jesus and His healing power, and the Holy Spirit's guidance and comfort. Receive His love! Receive your healing! **Then Moses said to the people, "Commemorate this day, the day you came out of Egypt, out of the land of slavery, because the Lord brought you out of it with a mighty hand. (Exodus 13:3)**

Therefore, my dear friends, as you have always obeyed – not only in my presence, but now much more in my absence – continue to work out your salvation with fear and trembling, for it is God Who works in you to will and to act according to His good pleasure. (Phil. 2:12,13)

The truth of God's Word actually changes scientific facts. The truth is that man and woman are made in the image and the likeness of God. (Genesis 1:26) **Then God said, "Let us make man (woman) in our image, in our likeness, and let them rule over the fish of the sea and the birds of the air, over the livestock, over all the earth, and over all the creatures that move along the ground." (Genesis 1:26)**

The woman was created by God from the man. And she will be reunited in marriage to become one again with man. [85] This is God's plan. If the power of God can cause miraculous healings of people in the days of Jesus and today, it can also restore a person who has been led astray in his or her sexuality. I am convinced of this because I sought the Lord through all the confusion and the pain and He changed me from the inside out. He proved Himself faithful and true to me. And I came to myself – my "honest" self. And this is where my true gender identity was birthed.

Jesus said, **But seek first His kingdom and His righteousness, and all these things will be given to you as well. Therefore do not worry about tomorrow, for tomorrow will worry about itself. Each day has enough trouble of its own. (Matthew 6:33-34)**

Call to me and I will answer you and tell you great and unsearchable things you do not know. (Jeremiah 33:3)

Lastly, I must admit that I never had inner peace while engaging in this lifestyle. I did, however, experience a peace that could not be taken from me through each step of obedience to follow what I knew the Lord was telling me to do. **My son (daughter), do not despise the Lord's discipline and do not resent His rebuke. Because the Lord disciplines those He loves, as a father the son He delights in. (Proverbs 3:11-12)**

Gender Confusion

God's original intention for each individual is furthered influenced through the model behaviors of both parents. Because we live in a fallen world as a result of the sin of Adam and Eve, many of God's intentions for our lives have intentionally been thwarted by Satan's devises. As a result of Satan's deceptions, fear and rebellion lead to oppression; oppression leads to sin; homosexual or bisexual sin leads to gender confusion.

We feel most comfortable with the "familiar." For example, since childhood, we have established behavior patterns of relating to our parents who may have had abusive patterns because of their own unresolved inner pain. This is why we feel more comfortable with the temperaments and the personalities which most resemble our parents. We feel "at home" with the familiar.

However, these may or may not be God's best choice for us as helpmates. If there have been abusive patterns learned in these early parental relationships, the issues need to be dealt with first before entering into a marriage covenant with another person who resembles a parent. Remember, we take all the unsettled issues of childhood into adulthood. Premarital counseling is essential and can be very helpful before marriage.

If our parental models do not line up with the Word of God, we always have the divine and the human example of the love of Jesus Christ to help us through gender confusion. The Holy Spirit also speaks words of love to us. If we did not experience loving parents as children and/or our parent(s) were absent or possessive, receiving our Father God's love and following His Word are the keys to healing our wounds from childhood. The Lord may have also blessed us through another family member as an aunt, an uncle, or even a grandparent who may have positively influenced our choices for a godly spouse.

Through a lifestyle of Christianity, I experienced the depths of a loving God and His love for me changed my identity first. My readiness for mature bonding in relationships proceeded only from that divine relationship. This is foundational to forming other healthy relationships.

After coming out of this lifestyle, I believed that Jesus Christ would change me. I believed that as I followed Him, my honest and true identity would eventually be revealed. And, as I continue to go through the inner healing process, He continues to change me from the inside out. I grow closer to Him each day finding my honest and true identity in Christ Jesus.

Blessed are those whose strength is in you, who have set their hearts on pilgrimage. As they pass through the Valley of Baca (weeping), they make it a place of springs; the autumn rains also cover it with pools. They go from strength to strength, till each appears before God in Zion. (Psalm 84:5-7)

As a child, I lived through my mother. As a dating adolescent, I was just playing "dress up" and thought that my appearance defined my femininity. I always felt "gender-less" when I was practicing the homosexual lifestyle. I sold my true identity to the devil in this lifestyle.

After renouncing the lifestyle, it took much healing before I would begin to assume a confidence about my core identity in Christ. The more I surrendered to His will and went through the painful process of healing, the "honest self" emerged out of its hiding place of protection. There was a stepping out, a courage that I took to walk by faith and begin to let God work in me. With this came a comfort to "be me" without facades needed. Somehow the Lord stepped in and allowed for the transformation.

As I continue to submit to Jesus in daily repentance, believing and obeying His Word, forgiving and releasing blame against both myself and all who have sinned against me, the original intention of God for me as a woman of God becomes more of a reality. Coworkers say to me today, "You are so beautiful. Did you forget to get married?" I just say, "It wasn't always this way. I just thank God for what He has done in my life." And I look forward to the day I will marry a godly man, God's best choice for me.

The Feminine Gender - Finding the Rest of God

Leanne Payne describes the gender drive in a woman as the drive to respond to and receive the male. [86] Fear blocks us from the receptive mode. The need to be in control and always "doing" is a symptom of that fear. **He who dwells in the shelter of the Most High will rest in the shadow of the Almighty. (Psalm 91:1)**

It is impossible to experience fear and rest at the same time. A woman must respond to and receive Jesus Christ within her heart first as her divine soul mate before her true identity as a woman is experienced. A man must do the same for his masculine identity to be revealed. It is in that secret place that I am learning to trust and love God first. It is in that place that I am discovering my true identity in Christ Jesus my Lord.

I have spent many years learning to worship the Lord in song. I have grown to love Christian worship songs. I have found much strength in worshiping Jesus. And the Lord continues to do much healing as I continue to worship Him. I have literally become His bride. He has shown me year after year what it truly means to trust Him. Songs of worship have literally replaced negative thoughts, emotions, and painful memories that were deeply embedded in my soul.

As a bridegroom rejoices over his bride, so will your God rejoice over you. (Isaiah 62:5)

I find rest in that place of love. Today, I am *listening* more to what the Holy Spirit is saying instead of doing all the talking. I have grown to cherish the quiet times with Him. As I listen for Him, I become more receptive. Instead of the masculine role of initiating, my true feminine gender continues to form. My spiritual ears are opening to hear from Him. It is so precious to hear His voice! He will gently and lovingly tell me He loves me. He will tell me to rest and not to worry when I am anxious. He will tell me I did a good job. He says all the right things. His still small voice is the actual proof that we are not alone on this earth.

Even though I have not yet responded to an earthly man as a husband, I believe God continues to teach me my womanly role through His love for me. In response to my Creator as my first love, I began to learn my true identity as a beautiful woman of God, fit to be His bride. **For the wedding of the Lamb has come, and His bride has made herself ready. Fine linen, bright and clean, was given her to wear. (Revelation 19:7, 8)**

My Mother, My Self

I knew that the root issue of the sin of homosexuality would be discovered in my relationship with my mother. Daniel Webster defines the word "identify" as originating from the Latin word "idem," which means "the same." To "identify" with another, Webster further stipulates, is "to conceive as united." [87]

Therefore, in order for the female gender identity to be influenced from mother to daughter and the male gender from father to son, there must be a positive bonding first. No person wants to form an identity with or a feeling of "sameness" with a person to whom one is not bonded. Working through troubling issues in these primary relationships is mandatory. Troubling issues must be settled either directly with the person(s) or indirectly in therapy. Restoration is always possible with the Lord, whether the person is present or not. Forming godly relationships with Christian men and women can also serve to work through many issues. **As Jesus was saying these things, a woman in the crowd called out, "Blessed is the mother who gave you birth and nursed you." (Luke 11:27)**

Normal same sexed bonding is foundational to the healing of gender confusion. In some cases, the Lord provides us with "substitute" mothers and fathers where that gender identity can be experienced. The Lord appointed many older women nurses as "mother figures" for me in the nursing profession. In the church, I befriended older godly women who extended love to me like a mother would love a daughter. I also had female counselors within the body of Christ who were excellent role models. The Lord restores through relationships. (Joel 2:25)

Stunted Developmental Stages – Dr. Elizabeth Moberly's Research

While in training at Restoration by Grace Ministries under Reverend Chuck and Betty McConkey, I was introduced to Dr. Elizabeth Moberly's research. She works as a research psychologist in Cambridge, England, specializing in psychoanalytic developmental psychology.

Dr. Moberly has an answer for the root issue of homosexuality. Just as Dr. Consiglio states that an unmet emotional need becomes eroticized because of envy, Dr. Moberly makes a comparable statement. She candidly states that there are normal psychological needs between the mother/daughter and father/son relationship that are not met. [88] As a result of this, there is a deep hurt and pain that is experienced. [89] Jesus will come to restore all our pain and hurts. (Isaiah 53:3-5)

Legitimate Need for Love Met Illegitimately

Exodus International, an international ministry to the homosexual struggler, defines homosexuality as a sin committed as a result of a "legitimate need that is met illegitimately." What is this unmet need? Is it a psychological or emotional need or both? I believe it is rooted in the need for an "affirming love" that is not experienced to its fullest potential. As a result, both psychological and emotional deficits are experienced.

Of course, everyone has their own set of circumstances and perceives the love they received or did not receive from their primary care givers in various ways. These areas must be explored and dealt with in therapy. We must turn the light of Jesus Christ on in the emotional and psychological realms of our hurting hearts. We must forgive the hurts to turn off the darkness and repent of our ungodly reactions to them. And we must forgive ourselves.

And now these three remain; faith, hope and love. But the greatest of these is love. (1st

Corinthians 13:13) The unmet love need can be experienced as an emotional void because of either an absent and/or a domineering parent(s). As a result, the relationships between mother and daughter and/or father and son are either detached or enmeshed. Both types are unbalanced. **Detachment from or enmeshment with the Holy Spirit is impossible. He is a gentleman and will neither leave us nor intrude upon us.**

As a result of parental imbalances, normal childhood developmental milestones may also have been stunted. For example, in the early years, there must be a learned sense of trust, autonomy, and initiative for the normal maturing process to occur. Without trust, there is mistrust. Without autonomy, there is shame. And without initiative, there is guilt.

Without Trust, There is Mistrust

Trust, my friend, is faith. Faith believes in something we do not see, hear, smell, taste, feel, or sense. Trust is putting faith in God, in ourselves, or in another human being. It begins with our trust in God. Because of so many disappointments with people, relearning to trust others had to begin with my trust in God.

Trust is the cornerstone upon which all other developmental milestones are built. My trust even in myself in certain areas was poorly developed. I had to cry out to God for trust to be developed within me; first through Him, and then through men and women of God who helped me to heal. I was very insecure and had a sense of inferiority and self-doubt throughout most of my life. The Lord restored me in ways I do not even understand. **Trust in the Lord with all your heart and lean not on your own understanding; in all your ways acknowledge Him, and He will make your paths straight. (Proverbs 3: 4, 5)**

As I learned to trust God and fear the Lord, standing in awe of Him, I learned the necessity of relinquishing all idols: **But those who trust in idols, who say to images, 'You are our gods,' will be turned back in utter shame. (Isaiah 42:17)**

Without Autonomy, There is Shame

In my situation, the love was acted, not spoken. Actions actually speak louder than words. This does not mean that Dad and Mom didn't love me. Of course they did. I don't know of any father or mother who truly does not love their children. My perception, however, was that I was not loved as much as the other children. However, when I returned home to New Jersey after six years of studying the Word of God and living the Christian lifestyle in Tulsa, the Lord brought healing to my relationship with Mom. At that season of time, Mom's love for me was clearly felt and cherished. There are seasons for healing, friend, and people change. So be patient in the process.

As a child through my young adult years, my relationship to Mom was enmeshed. I responded to her strong overprotection by allowing her to make decisions for me. Mom was my resting place, not God. Therefore, due to poor development of autonomy, I had difficulty saying "no" to others and wanted to please others more than myself. Patterns of development were set in place early in life. As a result, there was a weakened development of personal autonomy or "self-government." **[90]**

An autonomous person can make decisions quickly. Without my own sense of control, I was set up to allow the control of others in my later years. Immaturity in this area is exemplified by passive behavior. In not saying "no" to the lesbians I was surrounded by, I set myself up for the shame spiral until I allowed Jesus to take it away from me by His marvelous mercy and love.

I had to work through basic communication skills in therapy. I had to learn to be assertive with controlling people. I not only forgave Mom, but also released her and realized my love for her. Then I discovered my leadership abilities. I discovered I had a lot of the same strengths of personality as my mother. As I matured and surrendered my need to be in control, I allowed the Lord to take control and to guide my steps. The effect that the controlling personalities had upon me actually changed. I was no longer intimidated by them because I rose up out of the victim mentality with Jesus as my anchor.

Even after leaving homosexuality, I allowed myself to be controlled by a condemning spirit which was broken by the power of the Holy Spirit and a decision of my will to no longer tolerate its torment. As I looked into the face of Jesus, with all my shame and guilt, He still smiled lovingly at me. As I learned reverence and submission to the Lord, I became more aware of my identity in Jesus Christ living on the inside of me.

I am not ashamed of the gospel because it is the power of God for the salvation of everyone who believes: first for the Jew, then for the Gentile. (Romans 1:16)

No Boundaries/Feeling Invisible/ Self Esteem and Self Image

There are no boundaries in these codependent relationships. As a child and a teenager, I was so attached to Mom that I literally did not see myself. I really felt invisible and Mom was my identity. My identity was also falsely based upon my outward appearance and my achievements in school. This produced a false sense of self-image and self-esteem.

Self-esteem identifies how I feel about myself. Self-image identifies how I think about myself. Both are properly developed from within the soul, not through another person, through achievements, or through outward appearances. Feeling invisible, being enmeshed with Mom, being a high achiever, and focused on my physical appearance all confirmed the void within me that only Jesus could fill.

I may have felt good about my physical appearance and my achievements in the academics, and I may have felt secure in the mother/daughter codependence, but these were all false external securities. Without a personal relationship with Jesus Christ, I was empty on the inside. Without a sure confidence of Jesus Christ living and working on the inside of me, I had little or no self-image or self-esteem and, thus, thought and felt poorly about myself. A keen moment by moment discernment of the presence of the Lord with and in me changed me. My confidence was restored because I determined to receive His gift of righteousness (right standing with Christ). (Romans 1:16) I received it by faith. (Hebrews 11:1)(Romans 1:17) **In righteousness you will be established: Tyranny will be far from you; you will have nothing to fear. Terror will be far removed; it will not come near you. (Isaiah 54:14)**

Friend, a total reliance and trust upon the Lord does not make one invisible. With Jesus Christ taking residence within me, my identity is seen, felt, and experienced through His presence within me, working in me, and working through me. All our defensive walls will eventually be brought down in this divine and intimate covenant relationship. We become as transparent as the truth of His love, His presence, and His Word becomes alive on the inside of us. And our true identity becomes a reality. Only through Jesus Christ is our self image formed.

From one man He made every nation of men that they should inhabit the whole earth; and He determined the times set for them and the exact places where they should live. God did this so that men would seek Him and perhaps reach out for Him and find Him, though He is not far from each one of us. 'For in Him we live and move and have our being.'(Acts 17:26–28)

Without Initiative, There is Guilt

Here I am! I stand at the door and knock. If anyone hears my voice and opens the door, I will come in and eat with him, and he with me. (Revelation 3:20)

Psychology books will explain that when one has a normal development of the sense of autonomy, one feels confident to "initiate" decisions. Webster defines "initiative" as "acting independently of outside influence or control." **[91]** As a result of the enmeshment with Mom, I did not develop a strong sense of social initiative in my teen or early twenties. It was when I went away to college that my social identity was formed. My identity in Christ came alive in Tulsa, as I worked on my relationship with Jesus and studied His Word and healed from the inside out. From this divine relationship, Christ in me, I developed a social identity. I stepped forward and made acquaintances and friendships setting healthy boundaries.

The Holy Spirit Restores Any Missing Milestones

Today, as a Christian woman, I listen to the prompting of the Holy Spirit as the divine director of my steps. I am living in more confidence, stepping out in faith and in obedience to the leading from the Holy Spirit. He speaks to me in my innermost being. I learn godly autonomy (initiative) in my responses to His directives.

My decisions are made more confidently because He helps me to make the best ones, bringing Him glory as I follow His lead. Saying "no" to the flesh and all carnal relationships is a part of that autonomy. I refuse to make the same mistakes in my adult life that I made in my twenties.

As I listen to His directives, I am confident to step out and initiate godly decisions and actions. With each baby step of faith, He rewards me with His peace and lets me know how real He is. It is and continues to be an awesome journey with the Holy Spirit. Being under the divine control of the Holy Spirit has blessed me in every way imaginable through both good and difficult times in my life. **But when the Spirit of truth comes, He will guide you into all truth. (John 16:13)**

As a child, I gave my control away to "people I needed to please." As a mature "Christian" woman, I now have a divine helper who controls me with His love, and, in that control, assists me to make wise decisions.The boldness of those decisions comes as a result of His strong directives. There is always a deep inner peace that follows obedience, no matter how difficult it may feel in the natural. And the peace I am given makes it all worthwhile, both for myself and for the people my life will touch through those decisions. **The mind of sinful man is death, but the mind controlled by the Spirit is life and peace. (Romans 8:6,7)**

A Psychological Viewpoint – Dr. Moberly's Research

Dr. Moberly continues to explain that as a result of these unmet needs, there remains a deep hurt. And there are mixed emotions of conscious love and unconscious hatred, hostility, and ambivalence because of the hurt. As a result of this hurt, there is "defensive detachment" which the person forms toward the parent of the same sex.

The defensive detachment vis-à-vis members of the same sex originated when the child experienced the parent of the same sex as hurtful. The hurt was such that the child repressed its normal need for attachment to that parent (even if at a conscious level there might appear to be little difficulty in the relationship). The defensive detachment marks an inability to trust the needed love-source, a 'decision' not to receive love from that love-source any longer. The 'decision' is, however, beyond conscious and voluntary control. It is a pre-adult decision, and in some cases may even date from the earliest years. It cannot be reversed merely by a conscious effort of will power, but requires healing. **[92]**

Homosexuality is an attempt to make up for the missing needs that were unmet in the primary relationships. The female homosexual is seeking her feminine identity through her female partner. The male homosexual is seeking his male identity through the male partner. Dr. Moberly goes on to say that the sense of hurt becomes unresolved into adult life, which leaves a repressed yearning or a love need. She comments that the hurt can be resolved in adult life and that normal attachment to the same sexed parent was blocked by the hurt. She further states that the hurt must be resolved. **[93]**

Poor Choices made from a Hurting Child's Heart

When I look back at the female partners in whom I was involved, most of them were more dominant and possibly more masculine in that dominance than I. As my mother was always the more dominant figure, I see now that I was comfortable with what was "most familiar" in these relationships. Receiving what I thought was love from female lovers to make up for what I felt I didn't receive as a child was a blatant deception. As my relationship with Mom was enmeshed, so also my lesbian relationships were codependent. I envied the confidence of the more dominant women and that envy became eroticized. **They exchanged the truth of God for a lie, and worshiped and served created things rather than the Creator – Who is forever praised. Amen. (Romans 1:25)**

I was involved in transference reactions from my relationship to Mom to the females I encountered. Webster's dictionary defines transference as a redirection of desires and feelings and especially those unconsciously retained from childhood toward a new object. **[94] For where you have envy and selfish ambition, there you find disorder and every evil practice. (James 5: 16)**

In continuing to be a people pleaser, I actually had no real identity. I just molded to whatever I thought the people wanted me to be. Why? I needed that "affirming love" from people. As I continued to feel both invisible and gender "less," relating to women only proved to reinforce my low self-esteem, poor self-image, and underdeveloped sense of trust, autonomy, and initiative. This did not remedy my low self-esteem and self-image. On the contrary, I plunged further into the darkness of not feeling good about myself and not thinking well of myself.

Only a relationship with Jesus Christ could repair the damage that was already done. Jesus would love me back to life through the gentle voice of the Holy Spirit, His Word to me as I studied the Bible, and through loving Christians. We must allow others to care for us and learn our true identity in Christ. We cannot heal without relationships! We must love ourselves enough to set healthy boundaries.

New Creature in Christ

Therefore if anyone is in Christ, he is a new creation; the old has gone and the new has come! (2nd Corinthians 5:17) Becoming born again now meant that I received unconditional love from my heavenly Father. My purpose on earth is to please Him and Him alone. As I gained revelation knowledge of His loving presence in my life, I began to see myself in a fresh and a new way.

Healing Comes Through Healthy Same Sexed Relationships

Foundational to healing is the forming of godly relationships with women. I did have many normal same-sexed relationships throughout my Christian walk. These were healthy friendships, which I believe prepared me for the transfer to desiring fellowship with the opposite sex.

The Holy Spirit spoke to me and encouraged me to make friends with men. I had many male friends. I was in the early stages of healing but I did have some good friendships. I still had walls up. The men who respected me and who had morals I still remember today. I thank God for them. But I still had not healed and still felt gender "less." I was always in a hurry to "do something" or to "go somewhere" to accomplish something. I was not ready for commitment. Yet I knew that once I entered into the "rest of God" that He would take care of both the "gender part" of my development and my willingness for a committed relationship.

Dr. Moberly expounds further to say that no amount of opposite sex contact can resolve the problem. She states that the only way to meet this need is for healthy same-sexed relationships to form. She gives the example of the healthy same-sexed therapist as a possible answer. The therapist would provide love, identification, and dependency and assist the healing homosexual to resolve the same sex hurt of the past. She also gives the example of Christian-based relationships within the body of Christ to provide god given channels for healing. **[95]**

Healthy Christian women friends assisted me in affirming and resolving my feminine identity. And this affirmation continues even today! Encouraging love from Christian women enhance God's healing power within me. The restoration continues as I continue to be fulfilled by the clean love I received from Christian women. God works through His people. When you find a woman of God who moves in the love of God, you have found a jewel!

Cast Down Negative Memories, in Jesus' Name

Throughout my Christian walk, I have been faced with women who remind me of Monica, my first homosexual relationship. These were not homosexual women. Until my spiritual eyesight was fully developed, the memory was ignited only by their physical appearance. These used to be challenging situations, especially while on the job. I would handle it by talking to the women about Jesus and the freedom I had found in my intimate relationship with Jesus. I used it as an opportunity to evangelize and share my testimony with wisdom. Conversation broke the deception of the delusion.

However, today, as I stand in a more mature place of healing, I am now able to have normal conversations with women. Not only has the presence of God defined my identity from the inside, but the lure from the physical realm does not distract or capture me as it used to. My focus is inward, listening for His voice, talking to Jesus in prayer, worshiping Him in songs in my heart, and in my prayers to the Father. As you mature in Christ, you begin to see with the eyes of your heart and with your spirit, and not just looking outwardly with physical eyesight from your flesh. You see as Jesus would see. It is spiritual eyesight.

You can speak to people who are taking advantage of you firmly with discretion and still maintain the love of Christ in your heart. Or you can just be silent. Setting boundaries and exhorting does not cancel love. Love confronts! Let the Holy Spirit be your guide. However, always regard your safety as the highest priority in all situations of confrontation. Two is always better than one. (Matthew 18:19 ref.) These are the words of Jesus,**"Again, I tell you that if two of you on earth agree about anything you ask for, it will be done for you by my Father in heaven. For where two or three come together in my name, there am I with them." (Matthew 18:19)**

The memory of Monica, my first homosexual relationship, is still present, but the pain and the and the shame of it are completely forgotten. I have broken the soul-ties to every woman with whom I was illegitimately involved. This is mandatory to our healing from homosexuality. Soul-ties are broken in prayer, committing our spirit, soul, and body back to the Lord Jesus Christ and severing all physical, spiritual, mental, and emotional ties, and all memorabilia we have in connection with these relationships. (See chapter entitled, <u>Death Cannot Hold Me,</u> for prayers to break soul-ties and more information on breaking soul ties).

However, if and when I find myself uncomfortable emotionally while in any woman's presence, I ask the Holy Spirit for direction. Sometimes He tells me to just smile and walk away. Sometimes He will direct me to speak to them and thus break the delusive spell of the fantasy. The Holy Spirit may direct me to share my testimony with them and to evangelize to them on how to be saved. Conversation breaks the ice of the fantasy and brings me into the reality of the encounter. Godly perspective brings both strategy and reality into the situation. The bottom line is that this is a person who needs to know Jesus both intimately and personally!

It is normal to experience difficulty in this area. Always take it to Jesus first and commit to break the soul tie to the woman (women) or man (men). I encourage you to break all ungodly soul ties if not yet broken with the help of a Christian Spirit filled counselor. You may need professional help to pray this through with prayers of agreement. You will also need to destroy any remnants of gifts, pictures, furniture, clothing, letters and memorabilia of any kind that would serve to keep the memories and attachments alive. All contact with the person or persons must come to an end!

After going through this, ask the Holy Spirit to give you a spiritual heart for this person, not a heart of flesh that wants or needs anything more from him or her. Pray for the person when the thoughts come to your heart about them. (See Appendix) And the Holy Spirit will let you know when you are delivered and when you are free to go into ministry to assist others who are trying to get free from homosexuality.

If you are involved in any gay/lesbian support groups to get free from homosexuality, spend a time of preparation with Jesus first, in submission to His Lordship and His authority. Praise Him and thank Him for what He has done in your life so far. Put your armor on. (Ephesians 6:14-18) Cover yourself with the blood of Jesus. (1st John 1:7, 9) (1st Peter 1:18,19) Prepare your heart, repenting of all sins before you attend. (Acts 2:38) Set your heart in forgiveness and release toward both yourself and all who have sinned against you with both your attitude and prayers before you enter the group. (Matthew 6:12) (Luke 6:37) Call upon the angels to encamp around you. (Psalm 34:7) (Psalm 91:11)(All scriptures referenced)

The enemy works in the spirit realm and you must stay aware of this to stay connected to the Holy Spirit and keep your focus on Jesus even in the meetings. Even if it is a support group, be aware that there is always a spiritual environment for every situation. Set healthy boundaries with all people you are in contact with. Keep the Word of God close to your heart that you can confess it over yourself and quickly replace all imaginations with the Word of God. Pray in the Holy Spirit. After the meetings, ask the Lord to refresh your soul and spirit and to remove anything that may have attached to you in the spirit realm that is not from God. <u>And</u> thank Jesus for His divine protection.

Satan Works through the Imagination – Forming Healthy Relationships with Women

There are many women I speak to today who are out of the active homosexual lifestyle and are even leaders in the ministry. They share with me that they are still attracted to women. Friend, I have been caught in the same deception. When faced with a certain type of woman, I am still challenged, but I am conscious that it is the memory that is being ignited, not my desires. Challenge yourself to become friends with someone who has never been challenged in this area, a godly Christian woman who reminds you of someone you broke soul ties with. And, with the progression of a healthy relationship, the lure of this memory will lose its power. The Holy Spirit will guide you into the right season.

This is where you must step back and take an objective and a godly perspective on your own emotions. Satan works through the imagination. He places thoughts, ungodly fantasies, and memories in our minds that we need to replace with the spoken Word of God and with pure images. Remember the scripture reference 2nd Cor.10:5, which teaches us to demolish arguments and every pretention that sets itself up against the knowledge of God and to take captive every thought to make it obedient to Christ. And do it quickly, replacing the thought or the image with the Word of God and another memory. The more healed you become of the past issues and life goes on into other areas, even the memories lose their power to distract your focus from the new reality the Lord places in your life. His anointing takes you into a completely different realm.

These are not always our own thoughts but Satan brings his demons to our ears to place the thoughts there. He knows our buttons! We must be alert to his schemes if we are going to progress through the lies. He reminds us of the past encounters only to try to stop our inner healing progress and to prevent the formation of godly relationships with other women. He will try to pervert anything that God has done and devalue your worth as a woman or as a man of God. He will also work through godly women (and godly men) within the body of Christ to keep you inactive within the body of Christ through deceptive lies and imaginations. Press through the lies and be determined to become active within the body of Christ. Cast down these imaginations to the obedience of Christ. (2nd Corinthians 10:4,5 ref.) Know who you are in Christ.

Friend, stay connected to the body of Christ. Remember, there is a healthy bonding to other women that comes from God and that is necessary for life and for your deliverance. And it will come out of godly relationships only. You must bond with women who do not deal with the same issues and who are confident and free in Christ. You will learn and grow from and with them. You will have accountability with them. God gave us the attraction to women as a godly attraction, loving each woman with the love of Jesus. Sharing with other women is essential to our growth and maturity. Press on through! Attend a woman's support group at your church.

As we become closer in our walk with Jesus, He becomes our inner reality; our very identity found in this intimate relationship; His presence, His power, His still small voice guiding us moment by moment. And we are able to discern the lies from the devil. As we connect with our family within the body of Christ, our sins and the past memories attached to them lose their power over us. We begin to live in the present and the past loses its power to distract and to control our thoughts.

Being honest with godly women and developing friendships with them has served to connect me with new and healthier bonding with women. I have bonded with many women in Bible studies, for example, and with godly women leaders. Volunteering in children's ministries, under the direction of godly women and also godly men, has connected me more closely to my Christian role and identity as a woman of God. Counseling and mentoring relationships with women of God, married and single, have helped me also.

I worked with many young married wives in helping them to nurse their critically ill children, and that position in the helping mode was a powerfully healing place for me. My relationships with my sister, my aunts, and cousins have been powerful places of healthy bonding to other women. In the latter years, the Lord graced me with special time with my mother for healthy bonding and reconciliation. The Lord will provide what you need in every area of your life.

I had to ask God to help me to respect these women, and to hold them in the highest regard, and I had to resist any temptation to envy them, especially if they were married or had children. This has always been humbling but God gave me the grace. I came to the point of accepting that I now was married to Jesus and that I had spiritual children. When I accepted my call and position as a woman of God, I did not have to compare myself with other women. I knew I had to go forward in my development. I thank God for all the godly women in my life. **...I have learned to be content whatever the circumstances. I know what it is to be in need, and I know what it is to have plenty. I have learned the secret of being content in any and every situation, whether well fed or hungry, whether living in plenty or want. I can do everything through Him who gives me strength. (Philippians 4:11-13)**

One woman, Carol, a mother, a grandmother, a missionary, and a teacher of many children, turned out to be one of my dearest friends and greatest supporters through the final stages of writing this book. She is blessed with a strong anointing of the Lord upon her life. God always knows what we need.

I was blessed to have many Christian friends and leaders in the body of Christ to lead and guide me through the reconciliation process with Mom. With guidance from the Holy Spirit, I was enabled to resolve the normal attachment with Mom as an adult woman for a precious season of my life. God literally restored that relationship in that special season. God granted me wisdom to fully love Mom just the way she is and we actually developed a good friendship of mutual support for each other for a cherished season in my life. It was a precious time of about three and one half years!

There is a time for everything, and a season for every activity under heaven: a time to be born and a time to die, a time to plant and a time to uproot, a time to kill and a time to heal, a time to tear down and a time to build, a time to weep and a time to laugh, a time to mourn and a time to dance, a time to scatter stones and a time to gather them, a time to embrace and a time to refrain. (Ecclesiastes 3:1-5)

Because my self-worth was measured by how I looked as a child and as a teen, I always kept involved with the Hollywood scene, shopping for the latest fashions. When I dedicated my eyes to the Lord, I stopped the over indulgences of cosmetics and the bright colors on my face and nails. I want to look nice, but not unnatural. Then I feel better about myself. Red nail polish has become mauve or pink and lipstick colors have toned down also. I represent Jesus as His ambassador, and that is how I want to present myself. My clothing has become more conservative as well, covering body parts that are reserved for intimacy. I have become attractive to the godly man as I continue walking out my healing as a godly woman. **Since you are precious and honored in My sight, and because I love you. I will give men in exchange for you, and people in exchange for your life. Do not be afraid, for I am with you; (Isaiah 43:4,5)**

Dealing With Immorality, Idols, the Occult, and New Age Deceptions

Say "No" to All Occult Activity – Nothing Hidden from God
Leave Independence for Complete Dependence upon God

You shall not make for yourself an idol in the form of anything in heaven above or on the earth beneath or in the waters below. You shall not bow down to them or worship them: for I, the Lord your God am a jealous God. (Exodus 20:4,5)

Truthfully, I still had the perfectionism addiction while going through the emotional healing. It was the last addiction to go. I had severed and left all lesbian relationships and repented and renounced any other addictions, including cigarettes and drugs, as well as all occult/New Age activities, while going through the healing process. I renounced, repented, and turned from all involvement in astrology, transcendental meditation, I Ching, and spiritualism. All drug involvement stopped, and any books or readings in the area of mysticism or anything like this was rid of and stopped, as in literature on healing and auras, which is an Eastern philosophy of healing. I, of course, severed and stopped all association with women who led me into goddess dances and rituals, who spoke in tongues but not from the Holy Spirit, and who were involved in the psychic realm; i.e. clairvoyance, healing through touch therapy, and any other involvement. As we leave all that is not of God, it is always the last layer that is the most difficult to part with. It is our security blanket that keeps us from the fullness of the presence and the workings of God in our lives. **The arrogance of man (woman) will be brought low and the pride of men humbled; the Lord alone will be exalted in that day, and the idols will totally disappear. (Isaiah 2:17,18)**

No one could have ever told me I was proud in those days, because I was doing good works as a nurse. However, my pure motives of helping others eventually brought me to a high place where I did not need anyone. I was completely independent of the need for deep interpersonal relationships. I lived contented with acquaintances with many people. If God did not take the nursing profession from me, I would never have been humbled to see my need for quality relationships. I would have stayed hidden in the "high place of independence." I would never have recognized my deep discernment of "Jesus in me" or my need for quality interpersonal relationships. I needed to "stop" long enough to discern the Lord's presence within and upon me and to fully heal as I yielded and opened my heart to Him. And I needed quality relationships with other people.

My faith in the Lord also grew as I learned to live with what I needed, instead of living frivolously. I went on social security disability because I entered into a vulnerable season of healing in which it was difficult to hold down any job. The Lord brought me to a humble place. And the Lord met my every need while I went on social security and learned to enter into His rest. It was God's gift to me. I became rich in Jesus and found the "jewel of His presence" in my heart, as it opened up like a butterfly, opening its wings to fly free of the world's standards or of any amount of money.

And my God will meet all your needs according to His glorious riches in Christ Jesus. (Philippians 4:19)

Sexual Immorality Defiles the Spirit, Soul, and the Body
The Holy Spirit Touches and Heals Us with Rivers of His "Living Water"

Our reverence for God will deepen as we yield to Him in greater degrees in our lives. As we become so filled with the Lord's presence, led by the Holy Spirit, the road narrows. People and places we used to enjoy are no longer enjoyable. The things of the world are not only unsatisfactory, but they become distasteful. We long for more of the Lord and His presence in our new reality of living in the truth. With our decided allegiance to Jesus Christ, we are blessed by the Holy Spirit who leads us and blesses us with His "living water." And His "living water" heals every part of our being as we yield to Him; body, mind, and spirit, and as we allow ourselves to be touched by His divine power. (2nd Cor. 2:5-11)(Matthew 7:14)(John 8:32) (John 7:37)(All scriptures referenced)

On the last and greatest day of the Feast, Jesus stood and said in a loud voice, "If anyone is thirsty, let him (her) come to me and drink. Whoever believes in me, as the Scripture has said, streams of living water will flow from within him (her)." (John 7:37-38)

Boundaries are Crossed Illegally – We Will Reoccupy Our Own Spirits, Bodies, and Souls

It is hard enough to leave a relationship in which there is codependency. But, when there is also intimacy involved, you are not only addicted to the physical pleasures you have received in your body through the illegal crossing of physical boundaries. But there are also mental, emotional, and spiritual boundaries that have been crossed through the illegal joining. This makes you more susceptible to continue listening to the lies of the enemy to stay connected because you are hooked into the pleasures of both the intimacy and also the mental and the strong emotional support you are receiving, whether negative or not. The codependency wounds the human spirit as well because it steals from your relationship with the Lord. It also steals from your very identity. Sin separates both soul and spirit from the Lord. It opens the door of the soul and welcomes satanic influences. Codependency is sin because it places a person above God. It is an idol.

It is the flesh that lures you to stay connected intimately because of its pleasure and the pull is strong because of the deep mental and emotional bonding in the friendship. It is this mental and emotional component of the codependency that covers over the root issues of our hearts' pain. These issues must surface and be faced in the presence of a holy God in order to restore and recover the "honest self" and come out of the homosexual deception. There must be repentance and a leaving of all the ungodly relationships for the divine healing to transpire.

Being separated from the Spirit of God brings further darkness. In boundary crossing, especially in intimacy, there is also a spiritual joining or connection. There are spirits and principalities influencing your spirit from the other person's spirit and influencing their spirit from your spirit as well. It is these demonic spirits that will also drive you to stay in the relationship. These demonic spirits attempt to deceive you further into believing that you are not sinning. These are lying and relentlessly driving spirits and they are unclean spirits. The spirit of lust, for example, is a highly energetic spirit and will entice you to stay centered on your fleshly desires.

The enemy wants to steal even the slightest amount of headway we make in the Kingdom of God. Be alert. You may not be dealing with an evil spirit possessing you. A born again believer cannot be possessed. However, there are spiritual beings that oppress us from the outside, even as born again believers. You may think you are merely leaving a fleshly soul tie, a human and emotional codependency, and a person with whom you have developed a friendship.

But, friend, there are spiritual forces that influence and oppress us in any ungodly and/or sexual relationships that are not under covenant with God (marriage). Yes, greater is He (Jesus Christ) that is within us than he that is in the world. (1st John 4:4 ref.) But, when we willingly enter into illicit intimacy joining with another person, outside of the holy covenant of marriage, we break covenant with Jesus Christ and demonic spirits are given legal access to influence, to oppress, and to harass our bodies, our souls, which includes our minds, wills, and emotions, as well as our spirits. Sin opens the door for Satan to oppress and to invade. Intimacy with another person is not only a joining of bodies, but it is also an exchange and a joining of souls and spirits as well. Immorality and idolatry makes one unclean or defiles. Homosexuality is a form of idolatry. It is also immoral behavior. We are open prey for defilement (violation from Satan) on both counts. (Mark 7:15)(Matthew 15:16-20)(Ezekiel 20:7)(Scripture references)

And I said to them, "Each of you, get rid of the vile images you have set your eyes on, and do not defile yourselves with the idols of Egypt. I am the Lord your God." (Ezekiel 20:7)

Jesus said, **"What comes out of a man (woman) is what makes him (her) 'unclean.' For from within, out of men's (women's) hearts, come evil thoughts, sexual immorality, theft, murder,**

adultery, greed, malice, deceit, lewdness, envy, slander, arrogance and folly. All these evils come from inside and make a man (woman) 'unclean.' (Mark 7:20)

You may wonder why you do not talk, think, or feel the same way you did before the relationship started. There has been not only a temporary bodily joining, but a spiritual and soulish joining as well. And it will take a decisive severance of the ungodly soul ties with prayers of submission, repentance, forgiveness, and recommitment to Jesus Christ as Lord in your life to restore you back into His peace with your healthy boundaries in Christ Jesus.

We must petition the Father first in the name of Jesus with a heart of faith (submission, repentance, and forgiveness). We will also speak in our delegated authority prayers with a heart of faith in the name of Jesus to rebuke the unclean spirit and anything not of God that has transferred to us; to get us back into a proper spiritual alignment with the Spirit of the living God. We will also speak the Word of God in the name of Jesus with a heart of faith in Jesus' delegated authority over ourselves to refesh ourselves in body, in mind, and in spirit with the help of prayer counselors. We also must commit to severing all ungodly soul ties and to speaking the Word of God over our own bodies, our souls, and our spirits. (See chapter <u>Death Cannot Hold Me</u>)

The Lord Jesus Christ will bring restoration to us as we obey and honor His Word and our intimacy with Him. Consider a fast to restore yourself to purity in Christ Jesus. Consult your physician if you have any health issues, medical problems, are pregnant or lactating, or are taking any medications. Follow the Holy Spirit's lead.

However, let me stress the power of taking Jesus' delegated authority by the believer. To resist all enemy harassments, the believer must fight for oneself. The enemy seeks to harass when we are not within our church fellowship. Let us face the fact that the church is a teaching springboard from which we learn to walk and then to stand in our own confidence and strength in the Lord. We must pray over ourselves with our hearts positioned in faith (submission, repentance, and forgiveness), in the privacy of our own homes as we petition our Father God and take Jesus' delegated authority against all the wiles of the devil in Jesus' name.

We must speak the Word of God over ourselves continually until it becomes a part of our normal thought pattern. His Word will become stronger than your thoughts for the ungodly soul tie as you pray for that person or persons whenever they come to mind. The Holy Spirit will give you peace within as you continue to walk in obedience. Prayer places you in submission to the Holy Spirit. Surrender to the Lord is the key ingredient to bring change during this transition period. You may feel the anointing (the tangible presence of God) as you change from fear to faith. These are the words of Jesus Christ,

When an evil spirit comes out of a man, it goes through arid places seeking rest and does not find it. Then it says, 'I will return to the house I left.' When it arrives, it finds the house unoccupied, swept clean and put in order. Then it goes and takes with it seven other spirits more wicked than itself, and they go in and live there. And the final condition of that man is worse than the first. (Luke 11:24-26)

We must reoccupy our own spirits, our souls (thoughts, emotions, and wills), and our bodies as we develop our hearts of faith with resubmission to Jesus as Lord, repentance from sin, and with forgiveness and a release of all judgments. We must commit to keeping our temples filled with the Word of God. We must harvest healthy Christian relationships, spend intimate and personal prayer time with Jesus Christ, engage in activities within the body of Christ, including praise and worship, and be accountable to Spirit filled counselors, especially when initially leaving the addictions and the co- dependencies.

Fornication is defined as human sexual intercourse other than between a man and his wife. [96] All sin is a result of disobedience. There are consequences for our disobedience. Disobedience opens the door for demonic influences to invade and to oppress. (Mark 7:20)(Matthew 15:16-20)(Ezekiel 20:7) Just as parents pass on spiritual influences to their children, so also we are influenced by the spirit, soul, and body of any other individual(s) with whom we have had immoral sexual relationships. And we, in turn, touch and influence their spirit, soul, and body. Being in any sin, we invite invasion and oppression from the satanic realm because sin separates us from the Lord Jesus Christ. The spirit of lust attacks with sexual demons which have power to gain a significant stronghold in each individual spirit, soul, and body. True, greater is Jesus Christ in us than any other influence in the world, but our disobedience to the Lord weakens our resistance against the worldly influences. (All scriptures referenced)

But among you there must not be even a hint of sexual immorality, or of any kind of impurity, or of greed, because these are improper for God's holy people. Nor should there be obscenity, foolish talk or coarse joking, which are out of place, but rather thanksgiving. For of this you can be sure: No immoral, impure or greedy person - such a man is an idolater - has any inheritance in the kingdom of Christ and of God. Let no one deceive you with empty words, for because of such things God's wrath comes on those who are disobedient. Therefore do not be partners with them. (Ephesians 5:3-7)

The bottom line to defilement (uncleanness) of the soul is disobedience. This is clearly spelled out in Deuteronomy 28:

However, if you do not obey the Lord your God and do not carefully follow all His commands and decrees I am giving you today, all these curses will come upon you and overtake you: You will be cursed in the city and cursed in the country. Your basket and your kneading trough will be cursed. The fruit of your womb will be cursed, and the crops of your land, and the calves of your herds and the lambs of your flocks. You will be cursed when you come in and cursed when you go out. The Lord will send on you curses, confusion and rebuke in everything you put your hand to, until you are destroyed and come to sudden ruin because of the evil you have done in forsaking Him. The Lord will plague you with diseases until He has destroyed you from the land you are entering to possess. (Deuteronomy 28:15-21)

The Lord will cause you to be defeated before your enemies. You will come at them from one direction but flee from them in seven, and you will become a thing of horror to all the kingdoms on earth. (Deuteronomy 28:25)

The Lord will afflict you with madness, blindness, and confusion of mind. (Deuteronomy 28:28)

Once for all Jesus did away with exterior fears of defilement and consequent rituals to cleanse. No Christian need fear defilement from outside by things. But He retained warnings of inner defilement; "Out of the heart come evil thoughts, murders, adulteries, fornications, thefts, false witness, and slanders. These are the things which defile the man." Not what touches us from outside but <u>what we feel inside and do outside, immorally or idolatrously</u>, is what defiles. **[97]** (Mark 7:15)(Matthew 15:16-20)(Ezekiel 20:7) (Scriptures referenced)

This in itself supports the importance of severance of the ties. Once lovers with someone and believing one can still be friends is playing with Satan's deception. Homosexuality is <u>idolatry as well as immorality</u>. As long as any remnant remains of the soul tie, Satan will continue to distract the person with the temptation to reenter into the relationship and to then sin again.

Breaking Ungodly Soul Ties and Renouncing All Idolatries, including New Age/ Occult Activities - The Healing Will Proceed With Obedience – Reoccupy So that Satan Might Not Outwit Us (2nd Corinthians 2:5-11)

Jesus will honor your obedience to break the ungodly soul ties. He will heal and restore you back to your honest identity. I had a deep peace when I obeyed him in this arena. I knew I was doing the right thing for myself and for those with whom I was involved. Every time I thought of them, I prayed for them. (See Appendix) That helped me to stay focused on my commitment to the Lord. He is the restorer! (See prayers on breaking soul ties in chapter, <u>Death Cannot Hold Me</u>.) **The Lord is my shepherd, I shall not be in want. He makes me lie down in green pastures, He leads me beside quiet waters, He restores my soul. (Psalm 23:1-3)**

You may see these as very tough decisions, and they are for you now, but they are essential for your healing, for your partner's healing, and also for your divine purpose, salvation, divine protection, and divine prosperity. The Lord wants to bring you His salvation in every area of your life. The Word of God is very clear that homosexuality is sin. And we know that sin separates us from God.

For me what started in frivolity turned into insanity because I became involved with women who were involved with other idolatries as the occult and New Age activities. I had to repent and turn from the women and all the activities and practices. I burned all articles and books related to New Age, astrology, occult, mysticism, spiritualism, I Ching, transcendental meditation, drug involvement, the study of auras in the healing arts, witchcraft, the worship rituals of women, and anything that placed me in control instead of God.

Even though I had renounced and repented of all this, the enemy still had entrance to my spirit, soul, and my body, because I was still ensnared in the idol and the worries of perfectionism which kept me abnormally fixated on the paperwork and not on God. This idol gave the spirit of lust legal access to harass me continuously until I repented and turned from this sin. As soon as I repented and asked for the Lord's help and spoke the Word of God to cast every burden on Him, my Lord honored my heart of faith, humility, and repentance. The Lord spoke to me and said, "Do not worry about anything." He then covered me with His blood and His anointing. There were times in my battle against worry that I actually felt the presence of God. And He actually gave me strategies to work toward the victory.

I may not have had complete victory over the sin, but my heart of faith was right with the Lord. The spirit of lust still tried, but I was strong in the strength of the Lord to resist. Whenever I fell, I quickly repented. And I emerged grateful for His forgiveness. The witchcraft spirits that sought to invade my skin could no longer hurt me. I used to feel an itching or a "biting" as if something was crawling on my skin. With an honest turning to God with my sins of worry, the fullness of the grace of God came to me. "Jesus. I cast all my cares upon You. Help me to trust You. I will not worry about anything." And I claimed my freedom.

It is very difficult to get free from Satan's agendas against us, but not impossible. What I am saying is that you must decide to leave whatever is hindering your walk with the Lord, whatever sin has tried to ensnare you, as soon as possible, and the sooner the better! Like any other addiction, the further you involve yourself, the more difficult it is to leave it.

I personally have received special impartations and have been freed from demonic spirits oppressing me and possibly possessing me from the prayers and the laying on of hands from anointed men and women of God. These were special impartations I received and will continually give thanks to God for. God works through His surrendered and anointed people! But my completed freedom came from my obedience to the Lord to rid myself of all idols and sin to the best of my ability on a daily basis. And this continues to this day.

Me and God – I Have a Secret

When in the homosexual lifestyle, I lived a double life. I was one person at work and another at home. I did not want anyone to know at work that I was living with a woman and that she was my lover. Only a select few knew and they were also gay. The sense of acceptance I received from the "click" of gay friends kept me from facing the truth. I so wanted to belong. And the dishonesty with others at work kept me in a secret hiding place of isolation. This is a dangerous place! Friend, there is no more fulfilling place to be in life than to belong to Jesus Christ, totally accepted and loved, forgiven, and free to be a part of the family of God. It is also fulfilling to be connected with His people who live by faith in the Lord Jesus Christ. It is invaluable to know that we have eternal life with Christ Jesus.

Dishonesty took from me a clear conscience and my natural spontaneity for life I had enjoyed before I entered into this sin. I was living in guilt and shame, even though I had feelings for Monica. Deep down, I knew I was wrong. The marijuana smoking helped to blank out my mind to the reality of my guilt and I lived in denial. Besides that, my brain and my self esteem were altered negatively from the drugs.

At that time, I did not have Jesus in my heart. I believed in God but I needed to come to Jesus and leave the ungodly soul tie with Monica. I had to run to Jesus, welcome Him into my heart, and repent and ask Him to help me to change. I was lost and, deep down, I knew that I was wrong. I lived secretly in shame until I reached out to Jesus and told Him that I was not only sorry for my sin, but that I also believed in Him and His power to help me to change.

When in perfectionism, I was also in a hiding place of control where no one was allowed into my life until I finished the work. And the work was never done. It continued from job to job until the Lord took the jobs away from me. Self pity which masked itself in spiritual pride and criticism for others was broken when I took the courage to actually repent and be honest enough with myself and with at least one other person whom I trusted. Even then, only God fully knows and understands the full of it. I humbled myself to ask God to forgive me of my own sins of judgment, pride, self-pity, envy, fear, lust, selfishness, and worry, which are the sins that manifest with the addictions of homosexuality and perfectionism.

All of this manifested as a form of witchcraft as I was playing God in thinking that I could handle this myself. I had the "me and God" syndrome. I would get out of this hole with God's help. I didn't want anyone to know I had a problem with homosexuality and with obsessive compulsive behavior. Had I emerged out of hiding and sought help sooner, I would have been healed sooner. Pride and "wanting my own space," which is selfishness, kept me in the cycle of sin and self abuse. It was me and God. I kept people at a distance. When the rubber meets the road, when I came to the end of myself, I came out of the cave. I knew I needed help. I knew I needed to share my life with someone.

Sin separates us from God and gives Satan access to our souls. I asked Jesus to help me. And He did. It was difficult to seek help from people as I did not want anyone to know about any of these weaknesses. I received much cleansing and purging from biweekly church services as the Word of God was deposited into my soul and spirit, with praise and worship being top priority to becoming close to the Lord. I involved myself with children and music ministry activities, Bible studies, and singles activities. And the Lord brought me the right people as I got involved. I was changed and blessed with divine impartations and prayers from the saints of God at countless altar calls. I stayed close to Jesus, His Word, His people, and worshiped the Lord, until I was humbled to reach out for one to one counseling. I sought counsel in many church memberships throughout the years. And Jesus and His people changed me as I was loved back to life by them. I continued to devote myself to the Christian life.

Jesus provided ways out of the temptations as I sought Him in prayer for strategies against the enemy's temptations to stay hooked into the lifestyle. Before active counseling, I stayed active in full time jobs and in church memberships and ministries. This helped me to stay away from the temptations to stay in the lifestyle. I knew I had to commit to this and I knew it would be hard but I knew I would change as I stuck to my commitment to stay with the truth of my relationship with Jesus and with healthy Christian people. They had something I did not have and I saw it in their eyes. I saw light in their eyes. They had the truth!

Leave by Faith

If you are being harassed from the spirit realm, always check your own heart first to close and lock any open doors allowing the enemy to interfere with your spirit, soul, or your body. Remember, Satan had no entrance to Jesus's soul or to His spirit because He had no sin in Him. He chose crucifixion.

We must be wise and fly higher than the enemy because Satan will intrude at every corner to keep us locked into deception. He wants to keep us in the darkness of the homosexual relationship and will use the closeness we "feel" in the "friendship" as the very tool to keep us deceived. I never "felt" like leaving. But I "knew" by faith, deep within my spirit and my heart that I had to leave. When I did, the peace of God came. And I learned a new way of living, that of living by faith led by the Holy Spirit and not by my feelings led by my flesh.

By a force deeper than emotions, by faith, you know you must leave the physical relationship to get right with God. You may also be hooked in and addicted mentally and emotionally in the relationship, deceived by the human acceptance of one person and the false sense of security you receive from the relationship, or from the "click" that is involved.

Jesus spoke these words, "Because you have so little faith. I tell you the truth, if you have

133

faith as small as a mustard seed, you can say to this mountain, 'Move from here to there' and it will move. Nothing will be impossible for you."(Matthew 17:20)

Spirit-Filled Counselors

I encourage you to seek Spirit filled counselors to receive prayers of agreement to not only repent and turn from the ungodly relationships, but also to fully break and sever the ungodly soul ties. You will also need prayers of agreement to rebuke any demonic attachments, possessions, or oppression you may have received as a result of the illegal joining of spirits, souls, and bodies. You will need prayer counselors to help you remove all "remnants" and "keepsakes" of the relationships and to speak the Word of God over you. Severance is difficult enough and you will need an accountability partner with an objective viewpoint to help you to break away and to stay accountable to your commitment. You will need prayer counselors to help you to begin to face and settle the negative thoughts and emotions that surface when you do sever the ties.

At this time, accountability with another believer who is not in the lifestyle is essential to stay grounded in your decisions. Seek an anointed prayer partner to help to keep you accountable and pray the prayer of agreement for your obedience to leave the relationship. Ask your prayer partner to pray and rebuke any demonic defilement(s) which has had entrance to your spirit, soul, or body. The prayer partner will usher you into the presence of the Father with your petitions in the name of Jesus. He/she will then take Jesus' delegated authority rebuking all unclean spirits and speaking the Word of God in the name of Jesus over you with a heart of faith that is submitted to Jesus Christ as Lord and authority, with repentance for sins and forgiveness and release of all judgment. This will be a model for you to continue to pray for yourself in the privacy of your own home. Submit your heart to walk in the love of God with forgiveness toward all persons you have been involved with, including forgiving yourself.

The sooner you identify and face the painful emotional issues, the closer you are to your healing and your deliverance in Christ Jesus. Ask God for the Christian counselor who will best be able to help you to face these issues and get to truth, Jesus' way. I found the greatest help from people who were not even involved with homosexual sin. These were anointed men and women in the body of Christ who were filled with the Spirit of God and His love and they knew His Word. They were much stronger than I and walked in love and compassion for all human turmoil. Truthfully, the secular counselors did not help me at all. They will ask you what you want. Jesus said, "Father, if You are willing, take this cup from me; yet not my will, but Yours be done." (Luke 22:42)

You will need to start replacing homosexual relationships with the development of your intimate relationship with Jesus Christ, healthy Christian relationships within the body of Christ, and filling your mind daily with the Word of God and prayer with worship, praise, and thanksgiving. You must also be accountable to a church body with a pastor and a church leadership that you honor and respect. Be led of the Holy Spirit regarding your church home. Dr. Moberly further states, **Homosexuality is the kind of problem that needs to be solved through relationships. [98]**

Oral Roberts always used to say that God's time is "now." I refuse to be deceived by living in the past. As I obey the Holy Spirit in this process, leaning upon Him for the strength I need, He keeps me in the present and always provides strategies and opens new doors for me as I heal. I am still healing today and I will be drawing closer to Him until He returns. **Not that I have already obtained all this, or have already been made perfect but I press on to take hold of that for which Christ Jesus took hold of me. Brothers, I do not consider myself yet to have taken hold of it. But one thing I do: Forgetting what is behind and straining toward what is ahead. I press on toward the goal to win the prize for which God has called me heavenward in Christ Jesus. (Philippians 3:12-14)**

Jesus Must Be Our First Love – Idols Bring Defilement

There continues to be seasons in the reconciliation with Mom. Why? As the inner healing process continues, the "little girl" part is being transformed into a beautiful mature young woman. Behavioral patterns of relating to Mom have to change because the relationship is changing.

While living with Mom, I made a big mistake. I lost my total focus upon the Lord. I had unconsciously set up two idols; Mom and the attachment to the details of work. Both idols prevented my sanctification in Jesus Christ and left the door of my soul open for the enemy to both attack and attach to my mind and try to enter my body.

As a born again Christian, there can be no possession or entrance of the demonic inside the spirit, soul, or the body. The enemy can hover, but cannot enter because Jesus Christ is dwelling on the inside. It may feel like there are demons inside, but it is not possible for the born again Spirit-filled Christian to be possessed. It is oppression and not possession! Jesus Christ dwells on the inside of the born again believer.

If and when the oppression is very strong, I will go to fasting and prayer to get back to the place of peace with God. Please seek your physician before fasting if you have any medical or health conditions, are pregnant or lactating, or are taking any medications. Fasting is a great tool to use if you need to hear from God. I will hear from God during the fast. He will reveal anything in my life that requires change. As I read the Word, He speaks to me through it.

During the "golden years" with Mom, this "hurting little girl" now had "Mommy's attention and love," and my focus changed. As my focus of attention was redirected from the Lord to Mom, I was becoming depressed. Not only did Mom become an idol but my compassion for her became a detriment to my own spiritual joy. I believe that I was being affected by her grief over the loss of my father and by demonic spirits. Godly compassion turned to sympathy and I took on her burdens. Without the full healing of my own heart, the oppression I experienced was intense. And, I admit, Mom became an idol and this took me from Jesus as my first love. Thus, with this idol, as any idol, defilement followed, especially with demonic attachments on the generational bloodline. The enemy had access to my body, my soul, and my spirit.

Burden bearing is a form of intercession in which we bear another's hurts just as Jesus bore ours. **[99]** However, this gift can become unbalanced. To the extent the child in us has not trusted God with our own wounds, we will not trust God with the wounds of others, and so will try to become their savior. **[100]**

Cast all your anxiety on Him because He cares for you. (1st Peter 5:7)

It is most difficult to keep one's center in Christ when it comes to family. Our patterns of communication and behaviors in bonding are so strong that we easily become pulled into Satan's schemes. It is wise to visit family with the accountability of another Christian, a spouse if married, even a counselor, especially if family members are not living for the Lord. This territory can be food in the enemy's playground if we do not exercise wisdom. **Then Jesus went around teaching from village to village. Calling the twelve to Him, He sent them out two by two and gave them authority over evil spirits. (Mark 6:7)**

Leave and Cleave – Tough Decisions – The Road Narrows

The idol of perfectionism was still a part of my everyday lifestyle. My concerns about the details on the job kept me from the rest of God and His grace. I was living by the law! Perfectionism, which was an abnormal fixation, and an idol, kept me from feeling from my heart and kept me from the true rest of God.

We are never good enough. The Lord wants us to enter His presence just as we are! All I needed to do is repent and get rid of the idols and enter into His presence. It is in that place of intimacy with Him that I would be changed, not in any of the work or in the codependent relationships. Change is an inside job. Of course my addictions also kept me from quality relationships with others, including Mom.

I had to be real with her, not perfect. The "good little girl" persona I played out with Mom had to go. The Word tells us to speak the truth in love. By playing this role with Mom, I also gave the enemy access because no facade is real. The Holy Spirit can only work through real and honest people.

I was so blind to the facade. I had to have it pointed out to me by a counselor. We can be so blinded by our own facades because we have lived in these patterns of communication and these pretenses for so many years. Friend, we need feedback from others to get a more real perspective on our communication patterns.

I am in a season now of learning whom I am at the deepest level of my identity. I have refrained from contact with Mom. This was done with love and respect. With the help of my church, with a firm "no" against any addictions, leaving all that is not of God and consecrating my life and lifestyle to Jesus, I am truly blossoming into the "honest self." I hope and believe that God will bring Mom and I back together in the future. Sometimes the Lord takes us away from the comfort zones which to a lot of us are the very place of our wounds. We cannot fully heal from a wound if we keep opening it. I bless Mom every day as I heal. I intercede for her in prayer.(See Appendix)

I am daily praying for and releasing Mom, trusting in God's protection over her life. I speak to the Lord, "Lord, I trust you." And, with this, I am changing and coming out of the need to bear everyone's burdens, out of my need for control, and I am beginning to enjoy life with healthy boundaries. **He who gets wisdom loves his own soul; he who cherishes understanding prospers. (Proverbs 19:8)**

There are some situations where relationships must be severed completely. However, these decisions must be made with the confirmation of two or more Holy Spirit-filled counselors and/or pastors and with the Holy Spirit's guidance. Jesus spoke to Peter in the gospel of Matthew: **"And everyone who has left houses or brothers or sisters or father or mother or children or fields for my sake will receive a hundred times as much and will inherit eternal life." (Matthew 19:29)**

I separated from Mom after counsel by my Pastor and three Spirit filled counselors, got started healing from the perfectionism spiral, and got back into the presence of the Lord. My relationship with Mom was an ungodly one because there were demonic spirits on my family's bloodline that oppressed me in my connections with her, and because she also became an idol in the power I allowed her to have in my life. Idols defile. And I must admit she was the center of my life. It was a love that was true but it was an unbalanced love because the emotional component and the codependency caught me unawares. I lost my center in Christ and the enemy took advantage of both my innocence and my ignorance. Being a noble martyr, I did not see that I was in sin in trying to help her. Taking on her burdens, I did not see the danger and the imbalance of the position I placed myself in, placing her welfare in my hands and losing my trust and focus on the Lord. The homosexual relationships I had were reflections of this one. My emotions blinded me and yet I learned the importance of setting healthy boundaries in every relationship to keep God first on all counts. Thank God her heart was compassionate toward me and we parted with love.

Therefore come out from them and be separate, says the Lord. Touch no unclean thing, and I will be a Father to you, and you will be my sons and daughters, says the Lord Almighty. (2ⁿᵈ Corinthians 6:17-18) Only Jesus can convict a person to Himself. There is no distance in prayer. I had to heal without any distractions from family. I was distracted enough now. The enemy thought he could get me to lose my joy and my deep faith in God, but he was and still is wrong. He tried to get me back to the depression I experienced as a child, but I said "no." **Therefore, my dear brothers, stand firm. Let nothing move you. Always give yourselves fully to the work of the Lord, because you know that your labor in the Lord is not in vain. (1ˢᵗ Corinthians 15:58)**

I experienced demonic oppression and defilement in this codependent relationship. I would later learn to confront with love and take back my identity as a Christian woman who set healthy boundaries, especially with people who had strong personalities. I had to repent of and leave the noble martyr role and the codependent burden bearing role so that I could mature in my own womanhood and my identity in Christ.

This was part of the generational bloodline curse. Even though I had entered into a new bloodline, that of Jesus Christ, and I am no longer a part of that traditional bloodline with all its spiritual influences and generational sins and curses, I still was not grounded enough in Christ or in my own healing process to minister to Mom on a daily basis. The Lord ordained a set time for us. I had to heal and deal with my own sins and wounds of my own heart. I had to leave and grow apart from her. I do value the time we spent because I received love from her that I needed as a child and that contributed to my deliverance. I was able to share my relationship with Jesus Christ and the Word of God with her as well. I led her to the Lord as well. I became an intercessor for her and the entire family, learning to trust in God's protection and care for them all. (See Appendix)

Jesus said, **"Haven't you read," He replied, "that at the beginning the Creator 'made them male and female,' and said, 'For this reason a man (woman) will leave his (her) father and**

mother and be united to his wife (her husband), and the two will become one flesh'? So they are no longer two, but one. Therefore, what God has joined together, let man (woman) not separate."(Matthew 19:4-6)

Dealing with the Antichrist Spirit/Angelic Visitations and Occult- An Undeserved Curse Cannot Come

This is not about blame. It is about identifying the root causes for our sins and the ungodly reactions to the deep pain within. It is about repenting and turning from all that is not of God. Many people turn to the occult as a means of finding "control" and "power" over demonic control, but it is in itself a demonic tool. Occult means "hidden" and nothing can be hidden from God for His power to successfully manifest in our lives. Hidden sin opens us up for enemy attacks and torment. Get it out of your life. Get help if you need. It is not worth the torment the enemy will bring to you.

In my case, I was dealing with the antichrist spirit that was coming against me and it was affecting my spiritual, mental, and emotional health. I will never fully understand the complete roots from whence it came. I believe there were multiple origins. I believe the primary root was from the spiritual realm, from the antichrist spirit, who operated through the generational curse on my family bloodline. There is a history of addiction on my father's side and emotional/mental disease on my mother's side. I believe because there was sin in all our lives, we allowed for the legal entrance of the antichrist spirit to harass and to attach and to defile us. I believe some suffered more from the demonic attacks due to vulnerable personality types and due to a lack of knowledge of their blood bought rights in Jesus Christ.

By faith we are blessed to reach out to receive our freedom from Satan's authority over both our bloodlines and over our lives through Jesus Christ's redemption. He paid for all sins, generational curses, demonic assignments, addictions, and all physical, emotional, mental, and social diseases at the cross. He also conquered death and all evil spirits through His sacrifice and His resurrection. And He delegated us with His authority in our covenant relationship with Him over all evil, over all curses and evil spirits, over death, over all diseases, and over all addictions. (Isaiah 53:3-5)(Luke 4:18)(Isaiah 61:1)(Col. 2:15)

Our repentance for sin is our way back into right relationship with Him. Our born again committed relationship with Him brings us eternal life and all of the promises of God. (2nd Peter 1:4) We must reach out in faith to receive what has already been purchased for us. By faith, we speak our healing and our complete deliverance into existence.

There are consequences for sin and all idols in our lives. I was knowledgeable of my delegated authority in Christ to pray against the antichrist spirit, but I was not strong enough in Christ to take it until I got to a place of decided honesty before God. I had to leave the ungodly relationships and make Jesus fully Lord of my body, my mind, and my spirit. I had to break free from the attachments to family and allow Jesus to heal my wounds of spirit, soul, and body. I knew I could not give what I did not have. I keep the hope alive within me that someday I will marry a godly man, and, with a human covering along with the Holy Spirit's covering, perhaps I will reconnect with family. If the Lord does not allow it, I know I will see them in heaven. In the meantime, I pray for their freedom and believe God they already are saved. Today, I live and obey the last word of the Lord to me, "Do not open that door." Unless the Holy Spirit redirects me, I have no contact at all. I continue as their intercessor.

I myself had renounced and broken all ungodly soul ties from the homosexual lifestyle, but I went through a deliverance minister to pray with me and to sever and break the ties again. In that healing, I found that even though I had severed the ties, I was still in rebellion and not in complete submission to the Lord. I had to then "clean house," ridding myself of all perfectionistic reports or papers that would keep me in that "control" mode. I had to get under Jesus' complete authority as Lord and Savior. I had to seek God's perfect will and close and lock all doors for the enemy to invade. I had to get on my knees in my prayer closet and seek the Lord with all my heart! I began a daily discipline of prayer in the morning upon rising and started attending a single's Bible study ministry weekly. Daily prayer changed my life!

It is so important to leave all that is keeping us from a clear conscience with God, from a completed submission to Him. We must sever all ungodly soul ties and activities not of God; repent daily of all dealings with any sinful activity. I forgave and released all judgment, placing no blame on anyone, even upon myself. God is the judge of each person. Look within your own heart and you will be changed by the Lord. Friend, without that accountability partner in the deliverance prayer meeting, I would never have seen my own rebellion or have been corrected of it. **Like a fluttering sparrow or a darting swallow, an undeserved curse does not come to rest. (Proverbs 26:2)**

If you have truly made Jesus Christ Lord of your life, "an undeserved curse does not come to rest."(Proverbs 26:2) When you enter into the born again covenant relationship with Jesus Christ, you are able to be restored and protected from any curse. No one can successfully put a curse on a blood bought child of the living God. In that divine covenant and personal/intimate relationship, we are delivered out of our family's traditional bloodline and all its iniquities (tendencies toward sin and disease) and are brought into the Kingdom and the bloodline of Jesus Christ. We were already set free or redeemed from any bloodline or generational curses by the blood bought sacrifice of Jesus Christ at Calvary two thousand years ago. It has already been paid for. We receive it by faith and by our obedience to His commands. (Deuteronomy 28)(Galatians 3:13) Obedience is the key to receiving what Jesus already purchased for us. (All scriptures referenced)

Declare Your Redemption (Freedom) in Jesus' Name –
Enter into the Divine and New Bloodline

Prepare Your Heart – "I believe in Your death, burial, and resurrection, Jesus. I surrender and commit my heart to You, Jesus, as my Lord, my Savior, and my authority. I heartily repent of all sin. I forgive and release all judgment against myself and all who have sinned against me. Fill me with Your Holy Spirit. I receive the full payment You made for me, the forgiveness of my sins, in Jesus' name. Thank You, Jesus."

Enter into the Father's Presence – "Father God, I come to You with thanksgiving and with my petitions, in the name of Jesus Christ, my Lord and my Savior."(Psalm 100:4) (John 16:23)(Scriptures personalized)

Declare Your Redemption in Jesus' Name

"Thank You, Lord Jesus. I declare that I am redeemed from the hand of the enemy, no longer bound, in Jesus' name. (Galatians 3:13) I declare that my DNA is lined up with the Word of God, in Jesus' name. (Hebrews 4:12)(Rom. 12:2) I now enter into the divine bloodline of Jesus Christ. (Romans 11:17)(John 15:1-5) I am made in Your image and likeness. (Genesis 1:26) Thank You, Lord Jesus, for You are changing me from glory to glory. (Psalm 24)(1ˢᵗ Cor. 15:51) I declare that I am redeemed and set free from all curses and/or demonic spirits and/or demonic assignments, in Jesus' name. (Galatians 3:13)(Mark 11:23-25) Demons of those curses and assignments, go, in Jesus' name.(Luke 10:19)(Phil. 2:9) Go where Jesus sends you to be held captive by the warring angels of God. (Mark 5:8-13) I declare that I am set free from all evil and brought into Your marvelous light and life, in Jesus' name, Amen."(Colossians 1:13)(See Appendix)

"As a result of my repentance, (1ˢᵗ John 1:9), I now receive the gift of the Holy Spirit with thanksgiving and praise to You. (Acts 2:38)(Psalm 113:1-3) I commit to You, Jesus, as my Lord and I commit to the daily study of Your Word with daily prayer, praise, and worship of You.(Luke 11:24-26)(Romans 12:2) (Romans 10:9,10)(Rom.10:13) (John 3:3) (Proverbs 4:20)(Psalm 95:6)(John 4:24)(Psalm 33:1-3) Thank You, for Your Word is true, Lord Jesus, and it is changing me to my honest identity in You. (2ⁿᵈ Tim. 3:16) (Hebrews 4:12) (Proverbs 4:20)(1ˢᵗ Cor. 15:51) I declare and believe that You are changing me from glory to glory, in the name of Jesus Christ. (1ˢᵗ Cor. 15:51) Thank You for Your sacrifice for me at Calvary. Amen."(1ˢᵗ Thes. 5:18-20)"(All scriptures personalized)(See Appendix)

Be imitators of God, therefore, as dearly loved children and live a life of love, just as Christ loved us and gave Himself up for us as a fragrant offering and sacrifice to God. But among you there must not be even a hint of sexual immorality, or of any kind of impurity, or of greed, because these are improper for God's holy people. Nor should there be obscenity, foolish talk, or coarse joking, which are out of place, but rather thanksgiving. For of this you can be sure; No immoral, impure or greedy person – such a man (woman) is an idolater – has any

inheritance in the kingdom of Christ and of God. Let no one deceive you with empty words for because of such things God's wrath comes on those who are disobedient. Therefore do not be partners with them.

For you were once darkness, but now you are light in the Lord. Live as children of light (for the fruit of the light consists in all goodness, righteousness and truth) and find out what pleases the Lord. Have nothing to do with the fruitless deeds of darkness, but rather expose them. For it is shameful even to mention what the disobedient do in secret. But everything exposed by the light becomes visible for it is the light that makes everything visible. This is why it is said: Wake up, O sleeper, rise from the dead, and Christ will shine on you. (Ephesians 5:1-14)

Angelic Visitations – Love is Confrontive

Recently, in December of 2010, I believe an angel of the Lord visited me. I walked into my apartment and I saw a bright light and, in my spirit, I heard a small still voice, "Your prayers have come up as a memorial." These are the word the angel declared to Cornelius, a Roman centurion. (Acts 10:4) I had been praying for my family now for almost four years, for their salvation, deliverance, and protection. **Suddenly an angel of the Lord appeared and a light shone in the cell. He struck Peter on the side and woke him up. "Quick, get up!" he said, and the chains fell off Peter's wrists. (Acts 12:6,7)**

I was convicted that I should contact Mom. I reconnected with Mom and was informed of my baby brother's suicide. He was a believer, but did not know how to fight the fight of faith. The knowledge of our benefits as believers is essential to our lives on this earth. I believe he was tormented by this antichrist spirit whom he could have rebuked in faith had he known his delegated authority in Christ Jesus and had he accepted Jesus as his Lord and Savior. He had two divorces, two beautiful children, and lost many friends in the 9-11 episodes in New York City. This was a window of time that the Lord miraculously opened for me to speak to Mom and to have compassion on her for the loss of my brother. God allowed me to speak to her with love and compassion.

My mistake in that conversation was that I should have had a Christian witness with me to pray with me before the call. A witness would have agreed with me and cover the conversation with the blood of Jesus. I should also have sought godly counsel even before making the call. Had I done so, I would have had a witness with the call. Unfortunately, I was attacked by demonic spirits after two conversations without a witness. I am grateful, however, for it was a precious connection of love.

I had a short season of grief which is to be expected for the earthly loss of my brother. My church family comforted me as I shared with them. However, I believe my brother went home to Jesus, so in that I rejoice. I had been standing in the gap for him for years! So many suffer without a relationship with Jesus Christ. We are God's ambassadors in the earth to spread His gospel and truth to a dying world. (Mark 16:15-18) **They replied, "Believe in the Lord Jesus, and you will be saved – you and your household." (Acts 16:31)** We do not grieve like the world does because death of the body brings to the believer eternal life with the Lord. **Godly sorrow brings repentance that leads to salvation and leaves no regret, but worldly sorrow brings death. (2ⁿᵈ Corinthians 7:10)**

The Lord showed me that there was danger lurking with further contact. In my spirit, after hanging up the phone with Mom, I felt a band swirling around my head and it almost took my peace and my very sanity. But I quickly and properly positioned my heart of faith, addressing Father God first, in the name of Jesus and submitting to Jesus as Lord and authority (with repentance and forgiveness). "Father God, I come humbly to You with my petitions, in the name of Jesus Christ, my Lord and Savior, with repentance for my sins, and with forgiveness in my heart." I then resisted with my heart of faith. I spoke in Jesus' delegated authority against the demonic spirit in the name of Jesus, "I rebuke you, Satan, in Jesus' name." Then, I took further delegated authority as I declared the Word of God in Jesus' name, with my heart of faith, believing I would have what I said, "No weapon formed against me shall prosper, in Jesus' name."(Isaiah 54:17 ref.) The Lord has ways of warning us when danger is lurking.

Unfortunately, I was not far enough along in my own healing process of surrender and sanctification to continue the relationship face to face. Thus, I continued in intercessory prayer for my mother and my family and continued on in my own inner healing process. I committed to daily time in the Word of God and prayer to keep my vessel filled with God. (Luke 11:24-26)(Romans 12:2)(Proverbs 4:20)(See Appendix) As I spoke, I believed that I would have what I said. (Mark 11:23-25) And the evil spirits left as the presence of the Lord remained with me with multitudes of the heavenly hosts (angels) also present with me. (Joshua 1:5 ref.) (Psalm 91:11 ref.) I believe the Lord broke the power of the enemy off of me and off of many enemies. It is a win-win situation when you stand in faith with your words of faith.

I reclosed the door for further communication and the Lord directed me to minister to Mom by mail for a short period of time, educating her about generational curses and the power the enemy has to intrude into our lives and souls if doors are left open, allowing him to operate. I also gave her the prayer of salvation to recommit to Jesus as Lord. I am so grateful for the opportunity to speak the truth of the Word of God to her.

And He (Jesus) said to them, Go into all the world and preach the good news to all creation. Whoever believes and is baptized will be saved, but whoever does not believe will be condemned. And these signs will accompany those who believe; in my name they will drive out demons; they will speak in new tongues; they will pick up snakes with their hands; and when they drink deadly poison, it will not hurt them at all; they will place their hands on sick people, and they will get well. (Mark 16:15-18)

I boldly and discreetly spoke to Mom by mail and directed her to "clean her house" as I myself had to also "clean my house" of all papers that had to do with my perfectionistic sin and any other secret sin in my life. I would later seek a witness to assist me to completely rid myself of all papers related to the perfectionistic fixation as these would resurface throughout the years. This was my weakest area and I needed to get help with it. Sometimes perfectionism is a result of covering up a sin that we do not own up to or an escape from reality. It also is a childhood ritual of making everything perfect in an imperfect environment. It can also be the child who tries to receive affirmation from the parent in pleasing them with the "perfect work."

I continued as my family's intercessor, (mother, sister, brothers, nieces, nephews, aunts, uncles, cousins), praying for laborers to be sent to them to lead them to repentance and to a commitment to Jesus Christ as Lord. (Romans 2:4) (Matthew 9:37,38) I prayed for the family members to be comforted by the Holy Spirit,(Isaiah 57:18), and to be quickened to the truth of the Word of God and of Jesus Christ in their lives. (Luke 24:31,45) I prayed the Word of God over all the letters I sent home, that the Lord would bless them with His presence. I started a Daniel fast for them as well, taking no meat but only fruits and vegetables. (Before any type of fasting, if you have any medical conditions or health related issues, are pregnant or lactating, or are taking any medications, please consult your physician.)(See Appendix)

I had found tarot cards in Mom's kitchen which she claimed she never used. She said she did not even believe in Satan. People suffer for their lack of knowledge. (Hosea 4:6) In the letter I asked Mom to get rid of the tarot cards, teaching her that even if she were not using them, they were bait for Satan to enter the house.

When I was in the homosexual lifestyle, I could have told you what your astrological sign was as I studied astrology. I repented and renounced all my dealings with the occult and New Age activities with a Spirit filled counselor present. And I burned and rid myself of all literature and memorabilia related to the activities, including books, tapes, CDs, DVDs, and all other objects and remnants. I committed to the Lord and one other person (a Christian counselor) to stop the practice of all related activities.

I also had to reexamine my heart for any impure motives in my life which would cause me or someone else to stumble. I had to examine my motives for my relationships. Were they proper and pure? Did I act in love for the other person's greatest good or for mine? I had to look myself squarely and honestly. The Holy Spirit showed me areas in which I was a taker and not a giver in relationships. I had to repent and turn around my motives.

The secret things belong to the Lord Our God, but the things revealed belong to us and to our children forever, that we may follow all the words of this law. (Deuteronomy 29:29) I told my mother I visited a spiritualist church in Santa Barbara after my girlfriend Monica died in 1978 to see where she was. This is necromancy! Years later, I would hear voices in my mother's house as well. I told my Mom about the chasm that divides all spirits that have left earth and that there is no rite of passage for the spirits of the dead to visit the earth. If any spirits of the deceased loved one presented, these would be demonic spirits representing or charading as the spirits of the dead. (See Luke 16:19-31) **He reveals deep and hidden things; He knows what lies in darkness, and light dwells with Him. (Daniel 2:22)**

In my family holiday dinners and weddings, they would pray and invite departed spirits to the dinner tables when they said grace – they were operating with a complete lack of knowledge and inviting demons into the room with this prayer. I would follow their prayers at the dinner tables, and I would speak directly to Jesus in my prayer publically showing them that my relationship to Jesus Christ, the King of Kings, was indeed personal and believe God that this would minister to them the reality of my covenant and intimate relationship with Jesus. I hoped that my example would inspire them of their rights to this divine relationship with Jesus Christ.

I, too, before accepting Jesus as Lord and learning the Word of God, was also operating with a complete lack of knowledge in my activities with astrology and the spiritualist church, as well as my involvement with the study of yoga, meditation, astrology, and literature about mysticism, Eastern healing techniques and auras, and the I Ching. These activities and also my past drug involvement opened the door for Satan's entrance to my spirit, soul (mind, will, emotions), and my body. The Lord used my deliverance to help to educate my family.

So there was no blame or judgment in my confrontational letter. I felt a deep sense of remorse that they did not have the truth and it inspired me to a deeper trust and belief in the Word of God that both my prayers and letters to them would make a difference. I only presented the truth of God in love, educating them to the Word of God, and believing God to remove the mountain of their lack of knowledge and to open their spiritual ears to the truth. (Luke 24:31,45)(See Appendix) **My people are destroyed from lack of knowledge. (Hosea 4:6)**

The acts of sinful nature are obvious: sexual immorality, impurity and debauchery; idolatry and witchcraft; hatred, discord, jealousy, fits of rage, selfish ambition, dissensions, factions, and envy; drunkenness, orgies, and the like. I warn you, as I did before, that those who live like this will not inherit the kingdom of God. (Galatians 5:16-21)

I made lots of money when I was a nurse and spent it frivolously. We know that the love of money is the root of all evil. Mom told me that she was being taken to court by another relative who was fighting over a will of an aunt. I told Mom that the love of money is the root of all evil. (1st Timothy 6:10) I encouraged her to use this as an opportunity to forgive my niece who was taking her to court. **For the love of money is a root of all kinds of evil. Some people, eager for money, have wandered from the faith and pierced themselves with many griefs. (1st Timothy 6:10)**

I left and did what the Holy Spirit directed me to do without judgment, and in love, hoping to perhaps save someone else's life and/or soul. I did the best I could while I was there. I asked God to help me to accept the tragic consequences of my brother's suicide. The Lord answered my prayer and He blessed me with a deep inner conviction and a deep faith about the reality of heaven. I have an inner peace knowing that my brother is indeed with Jesus in heaven and that I will see him again.

And I continued praying for them. I believe that the Lord brought me out of the family to then bring me back in to share the truth of the Word of God with them. I believe the Lord allowed communication with Mom on the telephone in December of 2010 to grant me a window of time to encourage her after my brother's suicide. I believe He also allowed me to minister the Word of God to Mom and other family members for various seasons by mail. These connections also allowed for closure with love for me with Mom and for her with me, which we both needed for "peace of mind;" a "letting go" so to speak. I believe the Lord allowed this short window of time of reconnection because of my obedience to sever the tie as He and several counselors and my pastor had directed. And I healed as I interceded for them for seven years while I was in Tulsa and still continue today, believing God for their salvation and their deliverance from the generational curse.(See Appendix)

The Lord instructed me to ask them for nothing at all, not even any inheritance money. There was to be no dependence upon them in any way. My dependence had to be totally on the Lord. I relied upon the Lord and He provided for my every need here in Tulsa. (Phil. 4:19) These were tough decisions, but for the highest good of us all. I believed for their salvation and especially for their eternal life and healing. No amount of money could ever buy that. Jesus paid it all on the cross. The truth of Jesus Christ as my Lord and the living out of His Word in my life won out over any other want, need, or earthly desire I may have had. Or still have today. All things work together for His good. (Romans 8:28)

I am not the judge of anyone's sins, but I do have a responsibility to flee even the appearance of evil and to follow the Lord in all my ways. The Lord gave me the strategy to leave with love and to continue to stand on Mark 11:23, praying for myself and for my family's salvation and deliverance from the generational curse. After sending Mom prayers and letters of condolence for my brother's loss, I had a deep peace within that she was free and had peace. The glory of God was upon me in a very clear presence. The Holy Spirit lifted the burden from me and told me to leave and wait as I continued to pray for my family. I had received godly counsel years previously to leave the land and the family ties. I learned to trust the Lord for their salvation and for the full manifestation of their freedom and deliverance from the generational curse.(See Appendix)(Please seek godly counsel before any physical severances from primary loved ones.)

Having to leave family is the hardest decision of my life, but I had to finally accept that God has a plan for me to share His truth with others who may be in a similar circumstance as I. Friend, I was attacked by harassing spirits wherever I went, but when I obeyed the voice of God, left the land, severed the family tie, and made a firm commitment to follow the Lord, a line was drawn in the sand. As I turned from my sin of homosexuality first, leaving all ungodly soul ties and all occult and New Age activities, leaving all drug involvement, and then the addiction and idol of perfectionism, honoring Jesus with complete truth and thanksgiving, and truly making Him Lord, the peace of God came to me. The harassment from the enemy did not stop, but I had the greater resistance of faith against it because of my deeper submission to the Lord.

Knowing I am also a sinner saved only by the grace of God and that judgment belongs to the Lord allows me to forgive the abuse and to take no offense to the abusers. With each step of obedience, my surrender to the Lord deepened and I became stronger in my resistance against the enemy's tactics to lure me back into sin. With a clear conscience due to a discipline of daily repentance, I stood strong and continue to stand strong against the enemy with the help of the Holy Spirit dwelling on the inside of me. With each step of obedience, I saw myself as separate from others. I could set healthy boundaries in social situations and enjoy other people. Christ in me awakened me to the reality of a person who was and who is now alive in Christ Jesus. **Jesus looked at them and said, "With man this is impossible, but not with God; all things are possible with God." (Mark 10:27)**

I was strengthened by the Lord to fight the fight of faith as I "gave up this need to be in control" and surrendered to seek His perfect will for my life. God has to have the final say. Let God be God! We must leave our life in order to find it! Friend, I came to the end of my "self" and I knew I needed to share my life with someone and walk in love with someone in a marital bond. And, until that manifested in my life, Jesus would continue to be the husband and the Lord of my life and I would bond and stay accountable with other Christians within the body of Christ. No matter what, I would make my life count for Jesus. **Then Jesus said to His disciples, "If anyone would come after me, he must deny himself and take up his cross and follow me. For whoever wants to save his life will lose it, but whoever loses his life for me will find it. What good will it be for a man if he gains the whole world, yet forfeits his soul? Or what can a man give in exchange for his soul? For the Son of Man is going to come in His Father's glory with His angels, and then He will reward each person according to what He has done. (Matthew 16:24-27)**

In the Bible, in the story of David's life, there was sin, but he confessed and repented of his sin. There were, however, consequences for his sin. His son, born from David's adulterous relationship with Bathsheba, died. The Apostle Paul lived with a thorn in his flesh. Paul experienced much persecution. Despite the consequences of both men, they were unstoppable! They both spread the Word of God to a dying world and continued in God's call upon their lives. King David encouraged himself in the Lord as he wrote and sang the (songs) psalms. He was also a great King of Israel, a man after God's heart. Paul wrote one third of the Bible and carried the gospel throughout many lands, despite the suffering and the persecution he endured.

Deceased Loved Ones are With Jesus – They are Part of the Great Cloud of Witnesses

Therefore, since we are surrounded by such a great cloud of witnesses, let us throw off everything that hinders and the sin that so easily entangles, and let us run with perseverance the race marked out for us. Let us fix our eyes on Jesus, the author and perfector of our faith, who for the joy set before him endured the cross, scorning its shame, and sat down at the right hand of the throne of God. (Hebews 12:1-2)

Mom once shared with me that it was very hard for her to go to my deceased aunt's house because she said she felt her presence there. The Lord had me humbly share with her, "Mom, perhaps the presence you are feeling is the presence of God." And she thanked me for sharing this. Friend, we must use discretion with correction. Discretion commands respect. **My people are destroyed from lack of knowledge. (Hosea 4:6) Brothers, if someone is caught in a sin, you who are spiritual should restore him gently. But watch yourself or you also may be tempted. (Galatians 6:1)**

The Word of God is very clear about deceased loved ones. There is a great chasm that divides us from the deceased souls. Before Jesus' resurrection, departed souls were known to go to Abraham's bosom. In Luke, there is an account of two departed souls. Lazarus was a poor beggar who was covered with sores and ate from the rich man's table.

The time came when the beggar died and the angels carried him to Abraham's side. The rich man also died and was buried. In hell, where he was in torment, he looked up and saw Abraham far away, with Lazarus by his side. So he called to him, 'Father Abraham, have pity on me and send Lazarus to dip the tip of his finger in water and cool my tongue, because I am in agony in this fire.' But Abraham replied, 'Son, remember that in your lifetime you received your good things, while Lazarus received bad things, but now he is comforted here and you are in agony. And besides all this, between us and you a great chasm has been fixed, so that those who want to go from here to you cannot, nor can anyone cross over from there to us.' (Luke 16:22-26)

Many people are filled with grief at the loss of their loved ones and their grief takes them to a place of deception if they do not know the truth of the Word of God. Many folk actually call back loved ones because of their mourning. Demon spirits disguised as the deceased loved one will actually come to deceive the mourner that they are in fact the loved one who has returned to the earth. The Word of God is very clear. There is no rite of passage for departed souls and/or spirits to return to the earth. Divination is a sin against God. If you read further on in Luke, the rich man also asks Abraham to send Lazarus to earth to warn his five brothers about the torment of hell. Abraham forbids this, saying,

'They have Moses and the Prophets; let them listen to them.'

'No, father Abraham,' he said, 'but if someone from the dead goes to them, they will repent.'

He said to him, 'If they do not listen to Moses and the Prophets, they will not be convinced even if someone rises from the dead.' (Luke 16:29-31)

We must always be on guard lest we fall, judging others, especially people who are not knowledgeable of the Word of God. Remember, Jesus spent His time with sinners and came for the sick. For so many years, I was spiritually proud and thought I was so good. So many deceptions! I had to almost lose my family before realizing that I was still judging. I was blind to many of my judgments because I thought I was so "noble." I thought I was their Savior, not Jesus. If anyone confronted me with this, I'd probably deny it. The Lord had to take me away from my family so I could take a real honest look at my own broken heart and my own behavior.

I did write Mom a letter educating her about Satan's deception used against mourners who are grieving the loss of loved ones. I wrote with discretion and with love giving her truth and the Word of God. I began the letter with an acknowledgment that I myself have been deceived in this area in my life as well. These are the words of Jesus in the gospel of Matthew: **Therefore, if you are offering your gift at the altar and there remember that your brother has something against you, leave your gift there in front of the altar. First go and be reconciled to your brother; then come and offer your gift. (Matthew 5:23, 24)**

When I was a practicing homosexual, I attended a "Spiritualist" Church after Monica's home going (my first gay relationship) to see if I could recontact her. So I also was deceived in this area. At that time, I had no knowledge of the Word of God. I continued in this deception until I was convicted by the Word of God. (Luke 16:22-31)(Hebrews 12:1,2) (Scripture references) I then left this church's services, and the sin of necromancy, as I repented.

Now, whenever a person who has gone home to the Lord enters my heart, I go immediately to my Lord Jesus and ask Him to thank the person I am thinking about or to tell them I love and miss them. I may miss their presence in my life but I do not grieve for them as they are face to face with Jesus Christ and are interceding (praying) for me. I do not dwell on the part of me that misses them as this is Satan's lure to keep me in his "death camp." I do not speak to any departed souls. Conversely, I celebrate their lives in the realm of the spirit, face to face with Jesus Christ. And I celebrate my hope to later be joined with them in heaven.

Put God First and He Will Make a Way

Jesus spoke these words to his twelve disciples before sending them out,

Do not suppose that I have come to bring peace to the earth. I did not come to bring peace, but a sword. For I have come to turn a man against his father, a daughter against her mother, a daughter-in-law against her mother-in-law – a man's enemies will be the members of his own household. Anyone who loves his father or mother more than me is not worthy of me; anyone who loves his son or daughter more than me is not worthy of me; and anyone who does not take his cross and follow me is not worthy of me. Whoever finds his life will lose it, and whoever loses his life for my sake will find it. (Matthew 10:34-39)

It was all so miraculous. I knew my enemy was Satan and just prayed for my family. And God honored my obedience to put Him first, to obey His voice, and to physically leave the land of my family with love. I had godly counsel and the conviction from the Holy Spirit on this decision. (Please seek godly counsel if you are also considering severance of family ties). I became my family's intercessor. Two years after leaving New Jersey, and living in an apartment in Tulsa, Oklahoma, I believe I had a visitation from an angel. I sensed the presence of a divine and angelic being who said to my spirit, as I was crying out to the Lord, "You must forgive your mother!" I thought I had forgiven her, but not fully. I continued in prayer for her daily. (See Appendix)

Two years after this angelic visitation, after about four years of prayer for my family, the Lord opened up for me another window in time. It was December of 2010, and it brought me a confirmation that I had completed the forgiveness of Mom. In one expression of compassion to her, my heart was opened! I spoke my love by faith saying, "You are a marvelous person." I then saw that the enemy of my family and of myself was truly Satan and not Mom, Dad, or anyone else. I released all judgment and all blame and I was free! Even if the words out of her mouth were not positive, I was then no longer controlled by them. I perceived them as coming from the oppressive spirit of fear that was controlling and also tormenting her. I spoke to that voice that sounded so frantic and condemning, "I cannot be what you want me to be." And I prayed for her deliverance from the oppressive spirit that was upon her.

I am free from any condemnation of the enemy working through any person. My words of compassion and confrontational love toward Mom broke through the condemning voices. Love is our greatest weapon! I am grateful to the Lord for the wisdom of God. He truly made a way for me in the midst of an extremely difficult situation. He made a way where I did not see it, even in the most difficult places. Ask and believe God for an opportunity to resolve and settle whatever your situation is. If your loved ones are home with the Lord, it doesn't matter. You can still forgive and release any abuser, living on the earth or in heaven, from your heart, between you and the Lord.

And, friend, remember that your decision not to place blame on any person(s), knowing that your enemy is Satan and his influence upon that person(s) and/or on the bloodline, could mean someone else's salvation and/or their life! Ask God for a revelation of this! It will change your perspective! It will change your life!

Releasing the Old Behavior Patterns and Embracing the New

Going through the Elijah House prayer ministry teachings at my church in counseling sessions with Dee really helped me. These sessions brought me insight and brought me to my knees and to a deeper place with Jesus. "Cutting free" of old patterns of relationships and traditions is difficult, but not impossible.

Childhood memories were being brought to mind and, in the safety of my church, with a female counselor. I was able to face them in the presence of a holy God. The Lord gave me revelation knowledge about further issues. I was able to "settle" these issues as I prayed prayers of repentance and forgiveness and prayed for the people who had caused me pain and/or rejection. In one to one counseling sessions, I was confronted with my noble martyr and parental inverter behavior patterns, my false sense of responsibility, and my unbalanced burden bearing role. Working through these issues was essential to the healing process and entering into the rest of God. These behavior patterns were areas of weakness that contributed to my abuse. (See chapter Mom and Me)(See Appendix)

It was difficult to separate from Mom each season I was directed to, but I learned to trust God for her salvation and her healing as well. Whenever she would come to mind, I would pray for her, and the physical separation served to bring both Mom and me closer to Jesus. There is no distance in prayer. I grew and matured in the separations. I learned who I am in Jesus Christ, without the codependence upon Mom. As with the codependent behaviors in the lifestyle, I also grew and matured as I left each one, prayed for them, and turned to Jesus for complete dependence upon Him.(See Appendix) **For wisdom will enter your heart, and knowledge will be pleasant to your soul. Discretion will protect you, understanding will guard you. (Proverbs 2:10–11)**

I Love You, Dad – Familiar Spirits

Forgive Your Father

I remember when I was attending Calvary Chapel in Santa Barbara, I went to the Pastor about a problem I had with my relationship with my Dad. I felt uncomfortable with Dad but did not know why. He led me to a female counselor and she led me in a prayer. I remember her saying, "You do the natural and then God will take over the supernatural." She led me in these words, "Daddy, I forgive you." Even though I wasn't sure what the primary reason was for my discomfort, it didn't matter. God honored my desire to remove the wall that I had built. This was my mountain that would be removed with my act of forgiveness, believing without doubt that I would have what I said. (Mark 11:23-26) The counselor prayed after I spoke the words. She told me that I had done all that I could do in the natural and that God would now take over the supernatural to reconcile the relationship. **Again, I tell you that if two of you on earth agree about anything you ask for, it will be done for you by my Father in heaven. For where two or three come together in my name, there am I with them. (Matthew 18:18)**

The following Christmas when Daddy picked me up from the airport for a family visit, there was a real peace between us. I felt totally comfortable with him. After speaking and standing on the Word in the prayer of agreement with another sister in the Lord, God had answered my prayer. **And I will do whatever you ask in my name, so that the Son may bring glory to the Father. (John 14:13)**

We are accountable to God to forgive and to release all those who have sinned against us. As we forgive others, we also release them to the care of God. He is then able to work on both our behalf and on theirs. **Forgive us our debts as we also have forgiven our debtors. (Matthew 6:12)** And, remember, Mark 11:25 ends with, **And when you stand praying, if you hold anything against anyone, forgive him, so that Your Father in heaven may forgive you your sins. (Mark 11:25)**

I actually felt a release in my spirit as I let go of anger and hurt. I felt lighter. I allowed myself to give up more of my control as I surrendered more to Jesus. Surrender is a daily decision and healing is a lifelong adventure. As I went through this process, I actually had more control because I was walking in the divine flow of the Holy Spirit. It was the Holy Spirit walking in me now and I was walking in His confidence because I chose to surrender the flesh, the self, and all of "my wants." In this surrender, my prayer is, "Lord Jesus, please send me Your will for me. Send me what I need."

When the addict reaches out for help, he also kicks the devil out of his/her life. Seeking to get out of the heinous pattern of playing God, the "honest self" is now telling the "proud self" to leave once and for all. The "proud self" fights back and says, "I don't need anyone. I can lick this myself."

My friend, resist the "proud self." The beautiful result of releasing the "pride" is the entrance of the divine power and presence of the Holy Spirit into your life and into your soul. This is your life and your very soul you are fighting for. Seek accountability. Seek wise Christian counsel. Seek your God. For: **With God, all things are possible. (Mark 10:27)**

My Discomfort with My Dad Faced - A Deep Healing

At Calvary Temple in Wayne, New Jersey, they have church prayer meetings. During one such meeting, while being led in prayer by Pastor Thomas Keinath, I went before the Lord. I had attended church that night in a difficult place emotionally. I walked into the chapel with overwhelming feelings, being attacked with childhood memories of being with my earthly father and memories of feeling uncomfortable with him, but not knowing why.

It is not my usual stance to come to church in such disarray, yet I knew I had to go there. I was in such a state that I did not want to be alone. I was seeking a touch from God. Any embarrassment for how I felt and looked had to be overlooked. I am just thankful that I listened to the Holy Spirit and went to the service.

I am thankful that I had developed such a deep trust for my pastor and the leaders there. I went through a breakthrough at the altar I never would have experienced had I hidden in pride and not attended.

The prayer meeting began with Pastor Keinath's lead, and we were all in agreement, submitted to the Lordship and under the authority of Jesus Christ. My heart of faith was submitted to Jesus as Lord and authority and was properly positioned with that submission, with repentance, and with forgiveness. My heart of faith was ready as we all were ushered into the Father's presence to present our petitions in the name of Jesus. I was ready to speak in faith to also take Jesus' delegated authority in the name of Jesus. At that time, I was coleading a ministry for the homosexual struggler and had a heart of compassion for many who had spiritual oppression upon them.

As Pastor Keinath prayed for the unsaved, we all agreed in prayer at the altar. He continued praying for the missionaries, the children, and many different needs as we agreed with him in prayer. When, however, he started to pray warfare prayers, my spirit was quickened. He prayed against spirits and principalities of different sorts. When he, however, prayed against the spirit of "perversion," I rose up out of my emotions of self-pity and desperation. A holy boldness of compassion rose up within my innermost being which crushed through the darkness as soon as I started to speak prayers and intercede for the folks I knew who were struggling with this oppressive spirit.(See Appendix)

I do not have legal authority to cast out spirits from folks who were not asking for prayers to cast them out, whether saved or unsaved. This would be praying against their wills. But I could pray to bind, mute, and gag them from operating against their lives and their souls.(Matthew 18:18) Casting out any spirit against a person's will can allow for seven more spirits to go in and live there. (Luke 11:24-26) An unsaved person who asks for such prayers must commit to Jesus Christ as Lord first before anyone can successfully cast out any demons. And, all born again believers who ask for such prayers must commit to fill their vessels with the study and meditation of the Word of God, with daily repentance and prayer, speaking the Word of God, and with ongoing praise and worship. This will keep their vessesl filled with God and will prevent further demonic invasions.(See Appendix)

When an evil spirit comes out of a man/woman, it goes through arid places seeking rest and does not find it. Then it says, 'I will return to the house I left.' When it arrives, it finds the house swept clean and put in order. Then it goes and takes seven other spirits more wicked than itself, and they go in and live there. And the final condition of that man is worse than the first. (Luke 11:24-26)

At the prayer meeting, I interceded for those I knew were battling against the spirit of perversion. I prayed with a heart of faith, (with submission, repentance, and forgiveness), as I entered into the throneroom of my Father to petition Him in the name of Jesus Christ: "I bind, mute, and gag the demons of perversion from operating in _____(names were kept anonymous to protect privacy)_____'s lives; bodies, spirits, and souls, in Jesus' name. (Matthew 18:18) I pray, Lord Jesus, that you open their hearts to repentance (Rom. 2:4) and to a personal relationship with You so that they will be able to use their own delegated authority in Christ Jesus against the spirits oppressing them." (Rom 10:9,10)(Luke 10:19)(See Appendix)

Prayer of Faith Against the Spirit of Perversion

Prepare Your Heart of Faith - "Jesus I humble myself to You. I believe You died for me and rose victoriously on the third day. I repent of all sin and ask You to come into my heart and to be the Lord, Savior, and loving authority of my life. I receive Your forgiveness. Fill me with Your Holy Spirit. I commit to forgive and release all judgment against myself and all who have sinned against me.

Thank You, Lord Jesus, for Your sacrifice for me."

Enter into Your Father's Presence - "Father God, I come boldly to the throne of grace with my petitions. I enter in with thanksgiving and praise in my heart. (Psalm 100:4) (John 16:23) I submit to Your spiritual guidance and Your loving authority, in Jesus' name, Amen." (James 4:7,8)(All scriptures personalized)

Take Jesus' Delegated Authority over the Spirit of Perversion in Your Own Life in Jesus' Name

"I rebuke you, spirit of perversion, in the name of Jesus Christ. (Luke 10:19)(Matthew 18:18) Go wherever Jesus tells you to go to be held captive there by the angels of God. (Mark 5:8-13)You cannot have my dignity.(Rom. 1:16,17) I am God's creation. (Gen. 1:26) I am honored and precious in the sight of the Lord. (Isaiah 43:1-4) His love is upon me. (Isaiah 43:4) I commit to daily study of the Word of God and prayer with praise and worship of my Creator.(Luke 11:24-26)(Psalm 33:1-3)(John 4:24)(Rom. 12:2)(James 5:16) I commit to a membership and fellowship at a Bible believing church. (Psalm 133:1) Thank You, Lord Jesus." (All scriptures personalized)(See Appendix)

Words of Life Bring Life

Praying with such conviction and in the spirit of faith, my emotions were strong, but I was not in the flesh. I was in control of my emotions through my submission and my deep faith in Jesus Christ. A heart properly positioned in faith is deeper than any emotion and will help us to stay in control of our fleshly emotions by the power of the Holy Spirit working within and upon us. It is a holy boldness that cherishes and keenly discerns the presence of the Lord within us that rises up in faith. And it is that keen discernment of the presence of the Lord within us, with an attitude of thanksgiving for His love, acceptance, and forgiveness, that puts us in active gear to speak in faith.

The corporate anointing under the leadership and the anointing of Pastor Dr. Tom Keinath of Calvary Temple, of Wayne, New Jersey, helped to keep me in the proper position of faith, under both the Lord's authority and under the leadership of Pastor Keinath. It served as a covering in this corporate prayer setting. There is a holy anger, not a fleshly anger that rises up and speaks from the human spirit, by the power of the Holy Spirit. In these holy emotions, then, we can still stand firm in our proper heart position of faith in Jesus Christ as Lord. We have submission to His authority and His Lordship, with repentance for our sins, and with love and forgiveness and release in our hearts for ourselves and even for our enemies. When we pray for our enemies, there is a divine transformation that takes place and our anger, our hurt, even our deep hurt turns to compassion for them. Depression is annihilated. There is power when we pray in agreement with other anointed prayer warriors. **How good and pleasant it is when brothers (sisters) live together in unity! (Psalms 133:1)**(See Appendix**)**

This is why the Lord has given us the seedtime and harvest principal. What we sow (give) on earth we will reap (receive). When we speak, our words carry the power of life or death. They are seeds and will produce after their own kind. Words of life will bring us life as the Lord harvests our words. Whatever measure we give will be measured back to us. (Luke 6:38)(Gal.6:7)

Being in ministry, praying for men who are trying to get free from homosexuality, God implanted within my heart a compassion for those men and women who are suffering in this area. My compassion for them acted as a seed in my own life to free me from any unforgiveness, any fears, and any discomfort toward my dad, my mom, or anyone who had abused me in the past. **The Lord is gracious and compassionate, slow to anger and rich in love. The Lord is good to all; He has compassion on all He has made. (Psalm 145:8)**(See Appendix)

Do not be deceived: God cannot be mocked. A man reaps what he sows. The one who sows to please his sinful nature, from that nature will reap destruction; the one who sows to please the Spirit, from the Spirit will reap eternal life. Let us not become weary in doing good, for at the proper time we will reap a harvest if we do not give up. Therefore, as we have opportunity, let us do good to all people, especially to the family of believers. (Galatians 6:7-10)

Inner Peace After Prayers of Faith

After praying this prayer, I felt a beautiful peace settle over me. My thoughts went toward Dad, and the Holy Spirit showed me that he, as well, was oppressed by an addictive and a perverted spirit. He also had a mute spirit that was oppressing and attaching to him. I had been told through revelation knowledge of a prayer counselor that he was sexually molested by his father. I never asked my dad about this. His closest friend, however, another dentist, was living the gay lifestyle.

Dad's addiction to alcohol allowed for legal entrance of demonic spirits to oppress his spirit and his soul. And I believe that there were spirits oppressing him through the bloodline curse passed down through many generations. He always denied that he had an addiction, because he knew when he could and could not drink. He knew when to stop. He was only comfortable to speak freely in conversation with others when he had a few drinks. He was a firm believer in Jesus Christ, but he did not know how to fight the good fight of faith. He did not know his delegated authority in Jesus Christ to take his freedom from these spirits. Therefore, he suffered from his lack of knowledge. (Hosea 4:6)

This is why I had a discomfort with him as a child and in my teen and adult years. But we had a close connection. I asked the Holy Spirit to take this discomfort I had with Dad away from me. Before he went home to the Lord, I was able to help him at the end of his life as he suffered with a terminal disease. Praise God, as I helped my Mom to nurse him, not only did I feel comfortable with him, but I kissed him and shared the Word of God with him. I led him through the sinner's prayer. I know he is with Jesus today face to face praying for all of us in the heavenlies. (Hebrews 12:1) Mom and I prayed the Lord's Prayer over him before he went home to the Lord. Daddy said his favorite verse in the Bible was the famous Psalm 23, verse 1, "The Lord is my Shepherd, I shall not want." (Psalm 23:1) It was a cherished time. **For if you forgive men when they sin against you, your heavenly Father will also forgive you. But if you do not forgive men their sins, your Father will not forgive your sins. (Matthew 16:14)**

My Uncle Walter became my second father after my father's home going. The Lord always brought me who I needed at every difficult season. And, the Lord blessed me with a precious little baby girl to nurse after my Dad's home going. I know and I believe that I will see him again in heaven.

Even though the natural reconciliation took place between Dad and I, Jesus knew that I had to face and deal with the childhood memories. I had to see the discomfort as rooted in a demonic oppression that was attached to Dad, not in my father himself. Only then could I forgive him from my heart. I loved him very much and I know he now lives face to face with Jesus praying for me in the heavenlies. He is one of the saints in the great cloud of witnesses. **Therefore, since we are surrounded by such a great cloud of witnesses, let us throw off everything that hinders and the sin that so easily entangles, and let us run with perseverance the race marked out for us. (Hebrews 12:1)**

I have countless wonderful memories of him as I was his pride and joy and his helper in his dental office as a teenager. I was his friend. He was the spiritual leader of the family. He made sure we all got to church every Sunday morning. He was a firm believer in Jesus Christ. He committed to rise early every Sunday morning and cook breakfast for the entire family after church services. He was a giver and sacrificed his life for his family. He gave to the poor, volunteering weekly at a Public Health clinic, and was very generous to all his children.

Remember, there are weaknesses and strengths in all people. Imperative to our healing is to face both sides and be willing to get to the truth of our ungodly thoughts and emotions as we look honestly within our own hearts. In facing the truth, the pain is discovered, and must be dealt with in order to move on in our lives. The very idea of marriage would be out of the question unless I dealt with the male side of things.

There were phallic insinuations throughout the years of that relationship which I thought had to do with the alcohol that affected Dad. He was a professional dentist. I knew his smell and always felt so comfortable in the dental chair as he took care of my dental needs. I would give him massages as a child and he would always ask for a kiss after, on the lips. Even though I have no recollection of any incest or penetration, boundaries were still crossed and I was not comfortable. Dad was familiar with techniques of hypnotism as a dentist. Hypnotism is not of God. He used this technique to reduce pain in his practice. I used to think he knew my thoughts. I know now that there were demonic familiar spirits oppressing him that were also oppressing me as a child and, later, in my teenage years.

For every gift of the Holy Spirit, the devil will come and try to mimic and pervert it. My father was a Georgetown graduate and a genius as well. I believe he could have operated in the office of the prophet, had he developed it. I believe both his alcohol ingestion coupled by his lack of knowledge of the power of the spoken Word of God prevented this. However, his life was a living testament to his wife and his children of the importance of living in love for one another. He walked in meekness and humility before God and was a model of a life of sacrifice. When we attended Church services together, he would pray aloud with me during the services.

I am a lot like him. The Lord instructed me never to take alcohol. My obedience to this command I believe has brought me deliverance from all evil.

Sexual Molestation? Forget It and Go On – Turn the Light on in the Darkness

You see, it is in the sly wiles of the devil that can keep us unaware of what really was rooted in our childhood traumas. These are the hardest ones to uncover because there is actually no memory and/or evidence of physical fornication with my father. Yet there was a discomfort. It could have been a mere discomfort with the perverted spirit that was attached to him and that affected my spirit. I don't know. Friend, be alert to your discomforts! They will be the keys to unlocking many stuffed feelings that must be faced, forgiven, and brought to the cross. Some memories the Holy Spirit will reveal. Some He will not.

In the privacy of my alone time with the Lord, I prayed and forgave Dad, in case there was any sexual molestation that I had no memory of. My knowledge of the Word of God brought me the revelation that had this occurred, it was rooted in the demonic oppression attached to my father. And I freed myself from any judgment against any man even in my subconscious heart, with this step of obedience to love, to release, and to forgive whatever transpired with my father. **The light shines in the darkness, but the darkness has not understood it. (John 1:5)(See Appendix)**

What it comes down to is this. The details of any forgotten memories are not important. I just trust God that perhaps there are some memories that He is purposely keeping from me, and, if so, I still know that Dad loved me very much and with a godly love. Whatever transpired in my childhood is now over. I refuse to let Satan continue to badger me with deception of the past memories and/or with fear of future intimacy. I will go forward in forgiveness and trust that God will work out the details in a marriage. As long as I take God's best choice for me, it will be a godly man and the Lord will be there with us to work through the areas of intimacy and any other areas that need work. I know that marriage will be a great step of faith, because with God all things are possible.

As I have developed Christian relationships within the body of Christ, and my spiritual walk with the Lord has matured me with spiritual eyes, the fear of man is leaving as I now look to the heart of the man and not to a body or to the physical appearance as priority. I am so thankful to God for blessing me with many male pastors, teachers, ministers, counselors, and friends whom I have grown to respect. They have truly grown me up in Christ through their godly influence upon my life. **Though one may be overpowered, two can defend themselves. A cord of three strands is not quickly broken. (Ecclesiastes 4:12)**

He Makes All Things Beautiful – a Fearful Childhood Memory is Dealt With

In the meantime, the enemy will use your discomforts against you, so be alert. Do not take the chidings or mocking or gestures from others with their sexual innuendos personally. I dealt with sexual innuendos from people I knew, coworkers, and strangers all of my life. I was very perturbed by it until I decided that God made all things beautiful in His creation. As a nurse, I had no fear of taking care of men. The male penis is made by God just like any other organ and it is all flesh and skin. It is a part of the body that is beautiful and clean. **God saw all that He had made, and it was very good. (Genesis 1:31)**

When I was eight years old, while walking down a street, I was stopped by a man in his car who motioned to me to come to his car window. I innocently went to the window and his genitals were exposed. I ran in fear. That incident brought me a fear of a man's body and stayed with me until I brought the memory to my Father God with my heart properly positioned in faith, with submission, repentance, and forgiveness. I petitioned Him to remove the fear from me in the name of Jesus Christ. I then took Jesus' delegated authority over the memory. I placed the memory at the cross of Jesus Christ and declared that it will no longer rule or reign in my life, in the name of Jesus Christ. And I declared the Word of God in Jesus' name, "Every person's body is a temple of the Holy Spirit, made in the image and the likeness of God in Jesus' name." (1ˢᵗ Cor. 6:19) (Genesis 1:26)

I believe that Jesus will help me to deal with any residual discomfort I may have in a godly marriage. The memory will always be there, but as I have had many godly relationships with men throughout the years, the fear connected to this memory is no longer present. The Lord Jesus Christ restores us to see both men and women with spiritual eyes in a heart to heart relationship first before any physical relationship starts.

Because I carry no shame of my past sins, I walk now as a child of God and do not take shame from others. I realize that any shame that another person tries to place upon me is coming from the master of lies who is using the person against me. I refuse to take it in. Sometimes I will speak to the person in love, give them a scripture, or just pray silently for them and smile. Sometimes the Holy Spirit will tell me to just walk away and not make any comment. Sometimes I discreetly repeat back to them what they have given me. **Always regard your safety as first priority when dealing with bullies. Two is better than one. Listen to the leading of the Holy Spirit.**

When your station is tuned to the Master of the universe, you will not be offended. It is a whole different realm! It becomes a different channel altogether! This is very important! You will not be thinking or perceiving from the victim's position but from your position in Christ as you develop your intimate relationship with Jesus Christ as the most important relationship in your life. When you have conquered shame in your life, it will have no power to distract you. We are seated with Him in heavenly places! **But because of His great love for us, God, Who is rich in mercy, made us alive with Christ even when we were dead in transgressions – it is by grace you have been saved. And God raised us up with Christ and seated us with Him in the heavenly realms in Christ Jesus, in order that in the coming ages He might show the incomparable riches of His grace, expressed in His kindness to us in Christ Jesus. (Ephesians 2:4-7)**

Settle the Lies of Abuse and Rape

Perhaps your situation is different. There are many needs that may have been unmet, which left you with a feeling of not being "affirmed" by the parent of the same or of the opposite gender. Perhaps you have unresolved issues with one or both of your parents. Perhaps you have had a bad experience in the past with abuse of some kind. Nevertheless, the deep hurt in our hearts is rooted in a "lie" from Satan that we were not loved or accepted or that we were not worthy to be loved. If you experienced a sexual assault or a violent crime, the enemy will badger you with lies bringing the negative thoughts or the humiliating feelings back to you through other events and/or through other people. **"No weapon forged against you will prevail, and you will refute every tongue that accuses you. This is the heritage of the servants of the Lord, and this is their vindication from me," declares the Lord. (Isaiah 54:17)**

Remember, the enemy always uses experiences of abuse to bring us self-condemning thoughts, self-doubt, self-defeating thoughts, shameful emotions and even anger to deceive us and to hold us in the victim's position. We must be wise to his devises. Be still amidst the accuser's accusations. Stand on God's Word. Be persistent to pray for all that comes against you. **"Be still and know that I am God; I will be exalted among the nations, I will be exalted in the earth." (Psalm 46:10)**

Remember, all spiritual oppression is rooted in lies and deceptions from the spiritual realm. Satan is the enemy and he works through people, especially hurting people. Hurting people hurt other people. Jesus Christ died for all our abuse as well as our trauma, pain, and grief. He loves us all and wants us free from all lies and all painful memories in order to fully receive His love. His love fills the void that only He can fill. He first heals our brokenness, and then He fills us with His love to then give out and love others with His compassion. Once we are healed of abuse, we can be used for others who have been through the same hurts and abuses, because we have the understanding and the wisdom of God to reach out and to touch them.

Unless we settle that this sense of unworthiness or of not being loved is a lie from Satan himself, we will never attempt to resolve and rise above the hurt, the injustices, and/or the abuses we have experienced. And we will continue to blame the abusers for the hurt and the abuse. This is the ploy of the enemy to keep us in the wounded position, thus keeping us in the bondage of sin, (unforgiveness is sin), and from our true identity, liberty, and purpose in Christ Jesus. Remember, all deception is rooted in a lie from Satan himself. Even if we were in a controlling relationship with one or both parents, this does not equate with the assumption that we were not loved! We are all human and no one is perfect! We are all sinners. Even if we were abused, God still holds us responsible for our ungodly reactions to any and all abuses. Remember, Jesus was abused to the point of death. He forgave and also released His abusers. And He commands that we do the same.

In 1986, I was attacked in the middle of the night by a man. I screamed, as he jumped on top of me, "Please do not rape me, I was raped as a child!" Friend, I have no recollection of ever being raped as a child, but these are the words that came out of my mouth. I believe the Lord divinely gave me those words because, after speaking them, we made eye contact for about one second, and then he immediately left me. I thank God for His guardian angels that provided divine protection for me that night. A very kind policeman came to my apartment and stayed with me in a diner for several hours, just talking to me and being an open ear for me as he gathered all the data he needed for the police report. He was great! He bought me a meal and actually made me laugh!

The day after the episode, after being examined at a hospital for evidence, and after the police investigations, I visited my Pastor and he stood in prayer and in agreement with me. I wept with him present, and, with the divine help of the Holy Spirit, forgave the perpetrator. We prayed also for the man that he would come to know and accept Jesus Christ as his Lord and Savior.(Rom. 2:4) I refused to give Satan the upper hand in my heart and in my life. I refused to give in to any bitterness or rage about this shocking experience. I am not excusing the injustice, but we are commanded to forgive and we can, with God's help. I did forgive with the help of the Holy Spirit and with the help of my Pastor.(See Appendix)

The knowledge that all abuse originates from the oppression and sometimes the possession that Satan and his demons have on the abusers is divine revelation. This will help you to not only forgive, but to also pray for your abuser(s).You can ask the Lord to open their hearts to the truth of the Lord and of His gospel and to bring them to repentance. You can bind and gag the enemy from operating in their lives. (Luke 24:31,45))(Rom. 2:4)(Matthew 18:18)(See Appendix)

As a matter of fact, most rapists have been raped themselves. Rape is not a sexual act, but a violent act against the offenders' unsettled issues of childhood. And it carries with it a defiantly controlling spirit. (John 10:10) These criminals are often victims of satanic influences and/or of satanic control. Don't take Satan's bait to hate; forgive and be free! When you let go of your unforgiveness, you will be free from their abuse once and for all. Draw close to God amidst all memories of any abuses. Release the pain to Jesus for He is there with You and He is in you. When you release the pain, He will cleanse you of the bitterness and give you an agape love and compassion for the offender(s).(See Appendix)

Had I not forgiven and prayed for him, I would still be the victim giving him, or Satan's hold on him, power in my life. I certainly would have no hope left to love and care for any man holding onto any rage against this man. I would not step out to face my fear of intimacy had I not released my fears attached to the assault. My heart would never have completely healed and opened to trust men or to have feelings for any godly man again had I held onto the rage or the fear. I am so glad I did release him and pray for him, because I can tell you that since that time, I have made many men friends within the body of Christ. When I am in the company of a godly man, I have no fear. Those memories are there if I purpose to bring them to mind. But the shock of the experience with all its rage and fear has lost its lure to distract me. The memories carry absolutely no pain. The presence of God with me is greater than any memory. I knew this was part of Satan's plan to keep me in bondage and to keep me from my destiny and purpose as a godly woman. And he will do all he can to steal your purpose, your destiny, and the love of God from your heart as well!

I am so grateful to God for godly men in the body of Christ who have contributed significantly to my Christian growth They also have truly shown me the love of God through their leadership, through special impartations, and through their clean and godly love. I have bonded to many godly men as friends and have been influenced by many godly counselors, pastors, and teachers who have blessed me abundantly! I believe that with the right man, God's best choice, the Lord will make a way out of any fear of intimacy. I will probably laugh myself through the honeymoon. Because it will be a walk with a "God man," a man sold out to Jesus Christ. I will respect him and be connected with him in a heart to heart trust and friendship first, with healthy boundaries. Jesus will be in this relationship to strengthen our relationship and each of us in our individual callings. There is no fear big enough that can stand in the face of the perfect and pure love of God with us and in us. **Though one may be overpowered, two can defend themselves. A cord of three strands is not quickly broken. (Ecclesiastes 4:12)** The Holy Spirit will guide us in and through every new relationship. Don't let Satan steal the love of God that dwells on the inside of your heart, no matter what happens in your life. This is your jewel!

When I went to a Rape Crisis counselor, I was told that I said the best thing I could say telling my attacker that I was raped as a child because the man was most likely an incest victim himself. Rape is a violent crime, not a sexual one. Very often the rapist has been raped himself as a child and his crime is an act to avenge the abuse he suffered in his past. That spirit of fear could also have been following him down through the generations on his family bloodline.If he has not accepted Jesus Christ as his Lord and entered into the divine bloodline of Jesus Christ, He would have had no knowledge of his delegated authority in Christ against any generational curse and against all fear. When I told him I was raped as a child, he very possibly was moved in his heart by it because he himself may have also been raped as a child or involved in an incestuous encounter(s).

I did scream when I first encountered him. I believe that my shouting, the words I spoke, and the eye contact with the abuser all broke through the darkness of whatever evil spirit was present, bringing the very presence of the Lord and His angels to the scene. Remember the battle of Jericho was won by shouts. I was a born again believer at the time and one of the benefits to that relationship with Jesus Christ is divine protection from the Lord. He commands His angels charge over us. (Psalm 91:11) I also believe the very presence of angels in the room not only protected me but also moved the man out supernaturally. He fled through the same window that he entered. I then called a friend and the police.

The seventh time around, when the priests sounded the trumpet blast, Joshua commanded the people, "Shout! For the Lord has given you the city! (Joshua 6:16) When the trumpet sounded, the people shouted, and at the sound of the trumpet, when the people gave a loud shout, the wall collapsed; so every man charged straight in, and they took the city. (Joshua 6:20)

I have heard of stories of folks who led abusers to the Lord who had initially intended harm to them. The intended victims used wisdom and shared their testimony and/or the gospel of Jesus Christ with them, winning them to the Lord. Always be led by the Holy Spirit if you are ever faced with these situations. Your safety is the most important thing. I always carry a cell phone with me when I travel alone so I can dial 911 in case of any emergency. Some people learn self defense and some carry defensive weapons with them. Self protection is essential in the days we live in. Travel with a witness(es). Travel in two's.

Once you know that the root of all abuse comes from Satan, you will then be able to settle it. Your mom and dad did their best with who they were, what knowledge they had, and the generation from which they were raised. Remember, hurting people hurt people, and that Satan works through people. You must resolve to say "no" to all rage, fear, bitterness and self-pity, no matter what you have been through! And trust in God to make a way for you out of the past and into a new and a wonderful life, into healthy and godly relationships. **Get rid of all bitterness, rage and anger, brawling and slander, along with every form of malice. Be kind and compassionate to one another, forgiving each other, just as in Christ God forgave you. (Ephesians 4:32)**

Prayer to Receive Your Freedom to Live and Receive from Others

Prepare Your Heart of Faith – "Father, I submit my life to You. I believe that You died and rose again the third day. (Luke 24:6,45) I ask You now to come into my heart and to be the Lord, Savior, and loving authority in my life. I repent of all sin. I forgive myself and all who have sinned against me. I release all judgment against myself and all who have sinned against me. I accept Your forgiveness, Your love, and Your complete acceptance. I ask You to fill me with Your Holy Spirit."

Enter into Your Father's Presence – "Father God, I petition You as I come into Your presence with thanksgiving in my heart and in the name of Jesus Christ, my Lord, my Savior, and my loving authority." (John 16:23) (Psalm 100:4)

Take Jesus' Delegated Authority and Declare Your Freedom by His Shed Blood in Jesus' Name

"I am redeemed (freed) by the blood of the Lamb, in Jesus' name.(Galatians 3:13) No weapon formed against me shall be able to prosper in my life. (Isaiah 54:17) I am free to live as a servant of the most High God. (Galatians 3:13)(Matthew 9:35) Thank You, for the knowledge of Your Word which has taught me the truth about spiritual warfare. (Hebrews 4:12)(Pro. 4:20) All abuse originates in the spirit realm, from evil principalities, powers, and rulers. (Ephesians 6:12) This knowledge has given me the wisdom to forgive and release judgments against all abusers with empowerment from the Holy Spirit. (Luke 6:28,37)(Pro. 1:7)(Pro. 2:1-5)(Acts 2:38)(Acts 1:8) Thank You for bringing godly men and women into my life so that I could rebuild my trust in them.(Psalm 133:1) Thank You for restoring relationships that needed mending. (Joel 2:25)(Matthew 5:24)(2nd Cor. 5:18) And thank You, Lord Jesus, for Your sacrifice for me. (1st Thes. 5:18-20) I open my heart to receive from a man." (Acts 16:14)(Proverbs 10:8) (All scriptures personalized)

Idols Invite the Demonic and Familiar Spirits

Idols set me up for the enemy to attack my body and mind. We live in a spiritual world. And, until Jesus comes back, there will always be challenges from the enemy. There were and still are today "familiar spirits" that operate in the spiritual realm that attempt to actually inhabit our physical bodies. They have a devious goal of stopping the working of God for full victory in our lives. These spirits are very acquainted with us. They know us intimately from childhood. Until we fully grow away from family and succeed in our own Christian lifestyle, we will have difficulty taking authority here. The unclean spirit is restless because it must inhabit a physical body. **[101] Now the serpent was more crafty than any of the wild animals the Lord God had made (Gen. 3:1)**

The serpent was more subtle than any beast of the field which the Lord God had made. (Gen.3:1 ref.) God created the earth and put man on it. Satan came on the scene in the form of a serpent. He had to enter a body so he could be manifested on earth. He had to come through some form of creation to reach Adam, so he used the body of a serpent. Satan can't come directly to your spirit; he has to approach your body — and you can shut him off with your will! **[102]**

The word, familiar, is defined as that "of a household, domestic; having to do with a family." In other words, a familiar spirit is one that is familiar with you and your family tree. It has followed your family line from generation to generation, and is intimately aware of and familiar with those hereditary weaknesses that run in your bloodline. It is equally aware of just how and when to plague you or your loved ones with the iniquities of the past. **[103]**

When you become born again, the curse of iniquity is broken in you and your future generations. The evil spirits that were accustomed to influencing and controlling you no longer have authority over you because they were evicted from their place of residence. For example, as a Christian, I took authority over mental and emotional breakdowns in my life, my children's lives, and in my family tree. Although my father and grandfather both had nervous breakdowns, as a born-again believer, I inherited a new bloodline, the bloodline of Jesus Christ, who has redeemed me from the curse of family iniquities. [104] (See Appendix)

Familiar spirits are pests. It takes faith, spiritual discernment, and a holy boldness to rise up out of the victim's mentality and to speak to them. The Holy Spirit within you and upon you will help you. Always prepare your heart in faith, surrendering to Jesus as Lord and authority, with repentance and forgiveness first. As you enter into the Father's presence with your petitions spoken with a heart of faith in the name of Jesus, you then take Jesus' delegated authority and rebuke the enemy and speak the Word of God to them in the name of Jesus.

With all our past wounding and ongoing healing process, we are vulnerable to the enemy attacks. It is best to stay away from dark territory until strong enough and healed enough. Follow the leadings of the Holy Spirit. The enemy will want you to place blame on your loved ones and will try to keep you bitter against them to steal your healing. Refuse bitterness at all costs. If you are wise, you will pray and seek the heart of God. It is dangerous to enter Satan's territory if the season is not ordained by God. Only go where the Lord leads you.

Your First Line of Defense – Get Sin Out of Your Life

Your main objective should be to get the sin out of your life. Repentance is the key! This will place you in a surrendered position of His power, the power of the Holy Spirit working within, upon, and through you. (Acts 1:8) (Acts 2:38) Obedience to leave sin locks the door to the enemy's entrance. "To obey is better than sacrifice." (1st Samuel 15:22)(All scriptures referenced) **"Does the Lord delight in burnt offerings and sacrifices as much as in obeying the voice of the Lord? To obey is better than sacrifice, and to heed is better than the fat of rams." (1st Samuel 15:22)**

The wages of sin is death. (Romans 3:23) Jesus came to bring us life. (John 10:10) And do whatever it takes to accomplish this goal. Do not let the enemy condemn you for past sins. Once you have repented and left them, it is done, over, forgiven! You are free and forgiven. Receive the Lord's love! Keep your spiritual ears open for the leading of the Holy Spirit. (Luke 24:31,45)

There was no way Satan could get a hold on Jesus. There was no sin in Him. Satan could not lay any kind of claim to Him. The blood of God flowed in His veins. Jesus was a union of the Word of God and human flesh. **[105]** He was closely connected to His Father. Jesus gave us the perfect example of how to defeat the devil. After Jesus was baptized by the Apostle John, He was empowered by the Holy Spirit. He spoke the Word of God directly to Satan when He was tempted in the wilderness. He spoke the Word of God as Satan attempted to use it against Him. "It is written," He spoke three times against the lust of the flesh, the lust of the eyes, and the pride of life.(Matthew 4:4, Luke 4:4) He called into existence those things He could not see, feel, hear, or sense by His words. (Romans 4:1) After this wilderness victory, He embarked on His healing ministry and "rebuked" the evil spirits off of all the people He touched, and He healed <u>all</u> their infirmities with His words.(Matthew 9:35)(Matthew 4:23))(Acts 10:38) **When evening came, many who were demon-possessed were brought to Him and He drove out the spirits with a word and healed all the sick. This was to fulfill what was spoken through the prophet Isaiah: "He took up our infirmities and carried our diseases." (Matthew 8:16)**

Prayer to Bind the Devil

Prepare Your Heart - "Father, I submit my life to You. I believe that You died and rose again on the third day. I ask You now to come into my heart and to be the Lord, Savior, and loving authority in my life. I repent of all sin. I forgive myself and all who have sinned against me. I release all judgment against myself and all who have sinned against me. I accept Your forgiveness, Your love, and Your complete acceptance. I ask You to fill me with Your Holy Spirit."

Enter into the Father's Presence - "Father God, I enter into Your presence with thanksgiving and praise in my heart and in the name of Jesus Christ. I submit my petitions to You, Father." (Psalm 100:4) (John 16:23)

Take Jesus' Delegated Authority and Cast Out and Rebuke the Devil from Your Body, Soul, and Spirit in Jesus' Name

"Now devil, I rebuke you, in Jesus' holy name. (Luke 10:19)The blood of Jesus Christ is against you. (Heb. 9:14) You cannot cross the bloodline of Jesus Christ. (Rom. 11:17)(1st Peter 1:18,19) You have no authority here. (Col. 2:10,15)(Matthew 21:27) Go, in the name of Jesus. (Luke 10:19)(Matthew 18:18) Go wherever Jesus sends you to be held captive by the warring angels of God. (Mark 5:8-13) The angel of the Lord encamps around me.(Psalm 34:7) Because I reverence the Lord my God, He protects and delivers me. (Psalm 34:7)(Psalm 91)(Psalm 103:1-5) I commit to daily study of the Word of God and prayer with praise and worship to keep my vessel filled with God. (Luke 11:24-26)(Romans 12:2)(Proverbs 4:20)(James 5:16) (Psalm 33:1-3) I pray and believe this in Jesus' name. Amen." (All scriptures personalized)(See Appendix)

This will keep the enemy out for awhile. However, he will not stop pestering you. He will find another time and place to pester you. With each trial, you will submit to Jesus Christ in a deeper and a more transparent and honest place of surrender and repentance. (Rom. 2:4) You will begin to see and discern the Lord with your spiritual eyes and with your heart of faith. (Luke 24:31,45)(Hebrews 11:1)(Rom. 10:17) And you will forgive and release judgments in deeper crevices of your heart.(Luke 6:28,37) Keep speaking the Word and believing that God will make a way and answer your prayers. (Mark 11:23-25)(See Appendix) **He is our Father in the sight of God, in whom he (Abraham) believed – the god who gives life to the dead and calls things that are not as though they were. (Romans 4:17)**

Come Out of the Victim Mentality

David said about Him: I saw the Lord always before me. Because He is at my right hand, I will not be shaken. Therefore my heart is glad and my tongue rejoices; my body also will live in hope. (Acts 2:22,23;25,26) As I pressed into healing and became obedient to get the habit structures out of my life leaving all idols and all the Holy Spirit led me to leave, I came to a stopping place and to the rest of God. I continue to daily submit to the Lord with a desire to please Him. And I stand with my heart of faith in submission, repentance, and forgiveness and with a will to say "no" to the temptations by the power of the Holy Spirit within and upon me. Amidst the devil's temptations, I petition my Father with thanksgiving, in the name of Jesus, and with a heart of faith. I take Jesus' delegated authority and rebuke the devil and speak the Word of God in the name of Jesus with my heart of faith. "No more, devil, in Jesus' name. I am healed by the stripes of Jesus Christ." (James 4:7,8) (Luke 10:19) (Isaiah 53:3-5)(All scripture references)

Now with the Holy Spirit within me, I have a greater victory over the darkness. He honors my obedience. He is working in divine partnership with me. It is because of His victory on the cross that allows for every victory I receive and walk out in my life. My faith in Jesus Christ grows stronger through every battle.

Peter replied, "Repent and be baptized, every one of you, in the name of Jesus Christ for the forgiveness of your sins. And you will receive the gift of the Holy Spirit. (Acts 2:38)

The Apostle Paul said, "There is no power but of God; the powers that be are ordained of God." (Rom. 13:1) The reason the evil ones have no power is because Jesus stripped them. They no longer have any authority in the earth, unless you give them your authority. **[106]**

And there is suffering in this life for Christ as well just because we are Christians sold out to Jesus Christ. The Apostle Peter speaks of this. **Dear friends, do not be surprised at the painful trial you are suffering, as though something strange were happening to you. But rejoice that you participate in the sufferings of Christ, so that you may be overjoyed when His glory is revealed. (1ˢᵗ Peter 4:12)** In all you do, keep your focus on the crucifixion and also on the resurrection of Jesus Christ, who gave us His very life!

Jesus Took the Keys from Satan – We Have Delegated Authority Over the Devil

But Jesus, the Son of God, arose – born again of the Spirit of God. He walked over to Satan and stripped from him the keys of death, hell, and the grave, and tore the gates off their hinges! Then He crossed the gulf to the place of the righteous dead and preached to them, saying, "There's no need for you to stay here. Your resurrection has come!" He led captivity captive. Paul said in Colossians 2:15, **"And having spoiled principalities and powers, he made a show of them openly, triumphing over them in it." The Word "spoiled" literally means "stripped off or unclothed." Satan doesn't have a thing to wear. His authority is gone. [107]**

The enemy of lust, fear, and demonic activity continued to tempt me but after I left the territory, got back into the reading, meditating upon, and the speaking the Word, praise and worship, I began to heal. I came to the end of myself and sought other believers to share my life with.

I sought the Lord and He sent me out of the geographical area of New Jersey completely for restoration and healing. In 2007, I traveled back to Tulsa, Oklahoma at the leading of the Holy Spirit. I became strong in faith as I released my idols to Jesus and made Him Lord and authority in a deeper commitment. The Holy Spirit was and continues to be my helper and this makes all the difference. I can fight the good fight of faith now with the Word of God more effectively because I am pressing into a life submitted to Jesus Christ as my Lord and Savior and realize that if the devil is in my life, it is I who have allowed it.

Paul had a thorn in the flesh. Every time the messenger of Satan stirred up trouble, Paul would go to another place and the anointing of God would come upon him. Remember what Paul said, "I will glory in my weakness, in the fact that I can't control the situation that the power of Christ may rest upon me." But when the anointing of God came on him, he destroyed the work of the devil. I imagine the devil wanted to know why the buffeting had not stopped Paul. It was because Paul was operating in the power of the Spirit, not his own strength. **[108]**

To keep me from becoming conceited because of these surpassingly great revelations, there was given me a thorn in my flesh, a messenger of Satan, to torment me. Three times I pleaded with the Lord to take it away from me. But He said to me. "My grace is sufficient for you, for my power is made perfect in weakness." Therefore, I will boast all the more gladly about my weaknesses, so that Christ's power may rest on me. That is why, for Christ's sake, I delight in weaknesses, in insults, in hardships, in persecutions, in difficulties. For when I am weak, then I am strong. (2nd Corinthians 12:7–10)

Spiritual warfare is real and it is ongoing for the dedicated Christian. I continue to walk with Him at my side, within me, and watching over me, living and believing that He will protect me against the wiles of the enemy. Follow the leading of the Holy Spirit in every decision you make on a daily basis.

Godly Relationships With Godly Men – Set a New Mindset

The Lord has given me so many wonderful opportunities to find comfort, enjoyment, and trust with men in both friendships and in the counseling relationships I have developed, especially with Dr. Leo Natale. He poured his loving counsel and the wisdom of God into me, praying for me, encouraging me, and inspiring me to continue in my call. For several years, I had the opportunity to be under his godly counsel. He prayed for me and counseled me with a sincere and a godly love. I have been under the godly authority of many other anointed men of God; pastors, family members including uncles, professors, teachers, cousins, and many friends

Nothing is impossible with God. We can do all things through Christ Who strengthens us. (Phil. 4:13) I still speak to the mountain of fear of intimacy with a man. I believed that God will remove all fear when the Lord's best for me arrives. Love will conquer all fear. (1st John 4:18) I open my heart to the possibility of change. When my healing reached a certain maturity, the Lord prepared me to believe for it. **There is no fear in love. But perfect love drives out fear, because fear has to do with punishment. The one who fears is not made perfect in love. (1st John 4:18)**

The Grace of God

Chastisement is God's Love Reaching Out to Give Us His Grace

God is a good God and the devil is a bad devil. It is a catch-22. God is sovereign over all things, even over the devil and his ploys. Remember, He spoke to the devil about Job and told him not to take his life. The Lord gave Job back twice as much as he lost because, through all his persecution, Job chose to continue to trust God. **The Lord blessed the latter part of Job's life more than the first. After this, Job lived a hundred and forty years; he saw his children and their children to the fourth generation. And so he died and full of years. (Job 42:12, 16)**

In the healing process, there is persecution from the enemy and we grant the enemy access to our souls because we are vulnerable. This is why it is so important to seek counsel and face those hidden things which keep us in the rebellion and the bondage of our negative emotions, thus causing sin in our lives and giving access to the demonic. The Lord will allow the chastisement to get us to our knees with our attention upon Him and to swallow our pride and seek assistance from other believers. **My son (daughter), do not despise the Lord's discipline and do not resent His rebuke, because the Lord disciplines those He loves, as a father the son he delights in. (Proverbs 3:11-12)**

He wants us to repent and come completely to Him so that we will receive His cleansing and His power to fight the good fight of faith against the enemy's lures and condemning lies. Without Jesus and the power of the Holy Spirit, we cannot successfully resist the enemy. We must be totally sold out to Jesus, with no secrets! And Our Father God can handle whatever it is.

There is Someone Else at the End of Your Obedience

Your Word says, **"Come, let us return to the Lord. He has torn us to pieces but He will heal us; He has injured us but He will bind up our wounds. After two days He will revive us; on the third day He will restore us that we may live in His presence. Let us acknowledge the Lord; let us press on to acknowledge Him. As surely as the sun rises, He will appear; He will come to us like the winter rains, like the spring rains that water the earth." (Hosea 6:1-3)**

I had to refuse to be bitter against anyone. Even the slightest amount of bitterness would be bait for Satan to use against me. The strategy is found in the Word of God, for we know by Ephesians 6:12 that Satan is at the root of all abuse, not people. Satan will try anything He can to keep you in the shame, hurt, anger, or bitterness against yourself or against anyone else.

The Word of God is a living word; it is God's word to us. It carries with it the power of God. (Proverbs 18:21) When we speak the Word of God, it is a seed planted that will be watered by the Lord. What we plant with our words, we will receive a harvest in return. (Galatians 6:7) The harvest we receive is the transformation of our minds, our emotions, and also of our wills as we step forward to make godly decisions. We step out of the fleshly life and begin walking into the life of faith. We are changed by the Word of God and are led by the Holy Spirit. As we not only speak but also live the Word of God, our hearts are healed and reconnected to our thoughts; mental and emotional clarity results; and the Lord gracefully reopens our hearts to feel again and to live the abundant life. We are changed from a life of survival to a life of abundance. (John 10:10)(All scripture referenced) **The tongue has the power of life and death, and those who love it will eat its fruit. (Proverbs 18:21)**

We must seek to keep our hearts pure as a child's heart before the Lord. And have the expectancy of being used of God in helping others to get free in their call as Christian soldiers. There is always someone else at the other side of our obedience. This is what motivates us to continue going forward in Christ. **People were bringing little children to Jesus to have Him touch them, but the disciples rebuked them. When Jesus saw this, he was indignant. He said to them, "Let the little children come to me,**

and do not hinder them, for the kingdom of God belongs to such as these. I tell you the truth, anyone who will not receive the kingdom of God like a little child will never enter it." And he took the little children in his arms, put his hands on them and blessed them." (Mark 10:15, 16) Blessed are the pure in heart, for they will see God. (Matthew 5:8)

Blessed is the man (woman) whom God corrects; so do not despise the discipline of the Almighty. (Job 5:17) Doors were closing in my life. When I got to the point of, "Jesus, You are the only one who can help me to change," my life made a "360" degree turn. Instead of looking to the idol to run from the issues that needed to be faced, I looked to Jesus, my Lord, to help me to release the idols to Him. Just as I had placed the "Goodbye" letter in the mail to my last lover, saying, "Jesus, Thy will be done," I also placed my hands upon the paperwork which represented the law of sin and death, speaking the Word of God to Jesus with my heart of faith, "Jesus, I cast all my cares upon You, Lord, because I know You care for me."(Psalm 55:22)(1st Peter 5:7) "Jesus, You redeemed me from the curse of the law, by becoming a curse for me. Jesus, You died for this torment. I will not pick it up again."(Galatians 3:13)

And I expressed my gratitude to the Lord for His sacrifice for me. "Thank You, Jesus, for You took this torment from me at the cross two thousand years ago. I am now taking back Your peace as my blood bought inheritance. I will bless You every day of my life, in Your name, Lord Jesus, I pray, Amen." (All scriptures personalized) **Every day I will praise You and extol Your name forever and ever. (Psalm 145:2)**

God's Grace is His Kindness Toward Us

Even if I did not yet throw them away, I took a step in faith by submitting and acknowledging the Lordship of Jesus Christ by bringing the work to the Lord and praying over it. It would take a step of faith to fully receive the gift of God's grace. And be finished with this habit once and for all. His grace is His loving kindness and His unmerited favor toward us in spite of ourselves. God will honor even our baby steps to take the sin to Him and to another person for help with our willingness to admit that we are wrong.

Grace is God's willingness to use His power and His ability on our behalf, even though we don't deserve it. The Lord spoke to Paul when he asked Him to take away the thorn in his flesh, "My grace is sufficient for you." In other words, God's grace was sufficient to deliver him, but Paul must act on God's Word and resist the devil. The Lord was saying, "Paul, My willingness to use My power and My ability on your behalf is sufficient for you. And I am willing to back you up with My ability, but you must first exercise your authority by resisting the devil." **[109]**

The depth of our surrender with repentance and honesty to Jesus and sometimes with one other person determines the strength of our resistance against the enemy. With our surrender and with a repentant heart comes an honesty of self to self and to God and, with that honesty, brokenness before Him. He meets us there at that place of brokenness. And He blesses us with His power, the power of the Holy Spirit.

Prayer to Ask For Help from the Lord Jesus Christ – Receive the Grace of God

Prepare Your Heart –"I believe in Your death, burial, and resurrection, Jesus. I surrender and commit my heart to You as my Lord and my loving authority. I heartily repent of all my sins. I am sorry to bring You displeasure. I forgive and release all judgment against myself and all who have sinned against me. Fill me with Your Holy Spirit. I humbly receive the full payment You provided for me, the forgiveness of my sins, and Your acceptance and love for me with thanksgiving in my heart. Thank You, Lord, in Jesus' name, Amen."

Enter into Your Father's Presence – "Father God, I come to You with thanksgiving and with my petitions, in the name of Jesus Christ, my Lord and my Savior." (Psalm 100:4) (John 16:23)

Ask the Lord to Help You to Completely Surrender

"Lord Jesus, I ask You to help me to surrender totally to You as my Lord and my Savior. (Romans 10:9,10)(Matthew 18:19,20) You know I have fears and I am sorry for my sins against You. (1st John 1:9)

Help me to live by faith and to turn from my sins, Jesus. (Heb. 13:6)(Isaiah 41:10) Create in me a pure heart and renew a steadfast spirit within me, O Lord. (Psalm 51:10) I receive Your forgiveness and Your cleansing and thank You, Lord Jesus, for Your sacrifice for me. (1st Thes 5:18-20)(Heb. 9:14)(Heb. 10:19-22) Lord, I ask that You do not cast me away from Your presence or take Your Holy Spirit from me. (Psalm 51:11) I commit to study Your Word and to prayer with praise and worship daily. (Luke 11:24-26)(Romans 12:2) (Proverbs 4:20)(James 5:16)(Psalm 33:1-3) I believe and expect that Your help is on the way. (Heb. 11:1) (Rom. 10:17)(Isaiah 41:10) I receive Your grace,Your power, and loving kindness, (Ephesians 2:8,9), in Jesus' name, Amen." (All scriptures personalized)(See Appendix)

Restore to me the joy of Your salvation and grant me a willing spirit, to sustain me. (Psalm 51:12)

Seek the Lord's Best for Your Church Family – Touch Not the Anointed of God

There is no replacement for the power and grace that the Lord Jesus Christ refreshes us with when we spend time alone with Him in daily morning prayer. I learned how to pray by attending prayer groups. When we truly know His presence within and upon us, we will hear His voice and follow Him, whether alone or in the company of other people. We stop looking outward for our security even within the church meetings. It is in this place of prayer that He meets with us. He shows Himself faithful and true to us in our place of intimacy with Him, in worship and praise.

I had to leave some churches because I became too connected spiritually and/or emotionally to the pastor. I did not guard my heart as I was being ministered to. These attachments will form from our naivety and our vulnerability. We must be mindful to form healthy boundaries. It is best to seek one to one counsel from pastoral care and not to depend on the pastor for ministerial care. A female should minister to a female and a male to a male. If the pastor has an altar call, which many do, and you feel led to go, keep your focus on the Lord, for it is Jesus who brings healing through the man of God.

Keep healthy boundaries within the congregation and during church services. With the laying on of hands, I feel much safer to go to an altar call if both the man of God and his wife are present. Remember, the pastor is there as the shepherd of the entire flock. We cannot in any way touch the anointed of God or cause God's anointed to stumble. The enemy can delude us so easily in this area and we must be aware in every interaction with the leaders of our church. We need to develop the attitude of protection for our pastor and his wife, praying for them as the leaders of the church. If we are unable to keep this attitude, this probably is not God's choice for your church home.

Even a godly minister or a pastor cannot take the place of God. This can become a trap for the enemy to use against the single woman or single man of God. I had to seek the face of God and repent. I had to make mature decisions and take responsibility for my actions. What is best for all involved? Because so many of us are bleeding on the inside, we may not even be completely aware of how we are influencing others or how deep our attachments are to those in leadership. The Holy Spirit will convict us if our motives are wrong. We must follow His lead and He will always bless obedience.

We must act in respect for all authorities, keeping healthy boundaries, and be mindful of our behavior with our pastors, especially if they are married. In a church service, you may not even have a conversation with your pastor, but it could be a glance, a look, or a gesture that might take his attention from the Lord. Dress modestly. Keep alert to yourself and keep yourself focused on the Lord.

Seek God's best for your church family and membership and follow the leading of the Holy Spirit. The Lord always makes a way when we seek to please Him and keep all our actions, behaviors, and motives pure. Use this as your guide. Would I do this (whatever the activity) if Jesus were present? Well, friend, He is. He is present and He wants to be your first love in every arena.

Face the Deception

When I was involved in the sin of homosexuality, I did not think I was in lust, envy, vanity, or fear. I thought I was in love. The enemy deceived me at first. But the Holy Spirit eventually convicted me. And I also knew deep within me that I was wrong. I knew that it was an unnatural act from the moment I entered into the intimacy. The Word of God proved to me that I was in sin from Romans,

Therefore, God gave them over in the sinful desires of their hearts to sexual impurity for the degrading of their bodies with one another. They exchanged the truth of God for a lie and worshiped and served created things rather than the Creator – who is forever praised. Amen. Because of this, God gave them over to shameful lusts. Even their women exchanged natural relations for unnatural ones. In the same way the men also abandoned natural relations with women and were inflamed with lust for one another. Men committed indecent acts with other men, and received in themselves the due penalty for their perversion. (Romans 1:24-27)

We will never be perfectly healed in this life. But we are perfectly forgiven by the grace and loving kindness of God, because of the sacrifice of Jesus Christ on the cross of Calvary for us. One of my greatest breakthroughs to my healing was in receiving this sacrifice Jesus made for me into my life. Sometimes we get complacent in our oppressive state. I had to rise up out of it. I had to stay connected to the body of Christ and attend church meetings and Bible studies. Being single, I sought the fellowship of other believers and this kept me connected in the momentum of life and away from the addictive influences.

The Word tells us that if we are truly repentant for our sins, that God forgives us. To repent is to be sorry for and to leave the sin. We must strive to leave all sin and all idols to operate in the fullest power of God. His power is made strong in our weakness. (2nd Cor. 12:9) Our surrender to Him must be from the heart, even if it is broken. Because it is He Who will heal our hearts. It is He Who will empower us. Our love for God and others will be our greatest weapon against the enemy's ploys to keep us in depression and/ or bitterness. It will motivate us to operate with the compassion of God for those whom the enemy uses against us. **There is no fear in love. But perfect love drives out fear. (1st John 4:18)**

Since Satan is the god of this world, he will continue to harass and steal from us. We must be fully sold out to Jesus to win the battle. Jesus knows our hearts. **Or again, how can anyone enter a strong man's house and carry off his possessions unless he first ties up the strong man? (Matthew 12:29)** When you open the door to the demonic, Satan will stretch it as wide as he can. He will shove every dirty thing he can at you. You will feel like he has actually come within your being, but, if you are born again, he can only hover over and try to oppress. He cannot possess you. Keep yourself pure in every way. **[110]** Do not let the enemy distract you from your focus on Jesus Christ and His awesome presence in your life.

Pray in the Holy Spirit and sing to the Lord. Submit to God and the enemy will flee. (James 4:7,8) **For if I pray in a tongue, my spirit prays, but my mind is unfruitful. So what shall I do? I will pray with my spirit, but I will also pray with my mind; I will sing with my spirit, but I will also sing with my mind. (1st Cor. 14:14-15)**

Pray over Your Dwelling

Bless your apartment or house before you ever move in, anointing the doorposts with oil and pray over every doorpost and room. Remember, at the Passover time, the people were directed to take a spotless lamb and roast and eat it, and to take some of the blood and place it on the sides and tops of the doorframes of their houses. Today, we can, by faith, and in prayer, apply the blood of Jesus Christ, our Spotless Lamb of God (John 1:36) over our doorposts. His precious shed blood is our divine protection.

Prepare Your Heart - "Jesus, I humble myself to You. I believe You died for me and rose victoriously on the third day. (1st Peter 1:3) I repent of all sin and ask You to come into my heart and to be the Lord, Savior, and loving authority of my life. Fill me with Your Holy Spirit. I commit to forgive and release all judgment against myself and all who have sinned against me. I receive Your love and Your complete forgiveness, O Lord. Thank You, Lord Jesus, for Your sacrifice for me."

Enter into Your Father's Presence - "Father God, I enter into Your presence with thanksgiving and with my petitions in the name of Jesus Christ, my Lord, my Savior, and my loving authority." (John 16:23) (Psalm 100:4)

Declare Your Dwelling Place Holy in Jesus' Name (as you pray and anoint the doorposts with oil)

"I believe and I declare that my house (apartment) is holy and set apart for the Lord to dwell in, in Jesus' name. (Luke 10:19)(Ephesian 6:20) I stand on Exodus 12:12,13 and Psalm 91:1. I cover all doorposts with oil representing the precious blood of Jesus Christ. (Exodus 12:12,13)(1ˢᵗ Peter 1:18,19)(1ˢᵗ Peter 2:24) (Rom 3:25) I declare that the blood of Jesus Christ, the spotless Lamb of God, is my divine covering against any demonic spirits and/or assignments in Jesus' name.(Heb. 9:14)(Heb. 10:19-22) I declare that I am now divinely protected in the secret place of the Most High God in Jesus' name. (Psalm 91:1) I now declare that no plague will come near my dwelling, (Exodus 12:12,13)(Psalm 91:10), in Jesus' name, Amen."(All scripture personalized)

The Israelites prayed over their dwellings in obedience to Moses' and Aaron's instructions which they had received from the Lord. This would protect the Israelites from the plague which struck Pharaoh's firstborn child and other firstborn children and animals of Egypt. The Lord comforted the Israelites and told them that He would pass over them and the blood they applied to their doorposts would be the sign of their obedience. It was also a pledge of the mercy and grace of God to the Israelites who placed themselves under the sign of the blood.

The Lord said to Moses and Aaron, **"On that same night I will pass through Egypt and strike down every firstborn – both men and animals – and I will bring judgment on all the gods of Egypt. I am the Lord. The blood will be a sign for you on the houses where you are: and when I see the blood, I will pass over you. No destructive plague will touch you when I strike Egypt. (Exodus 12:12,13)** This Old Testament story is a type and a shadow of the coming spotless Lamb, the Savior Jesus Christ, Who, through the sacrifice of His blood at Calvary, would take away our sins. His blood acts as a supernatural covering and protection for all His committed children. There is no need to fear the darkness of the night nor any plague that attempts to come near your dwelling tent. The blood of Jesus Christ is against the enemy! (Psalm 91) (Hebrews 9:12) A person's spirit and soul can be influenced by fear. Persistent fears cause spiritual paralysis. No one is able to do great feats with a heart filled with fear. The spirit of fear is a chain that binds the soul. **[111] For God has not given us a spirit of fear, but of power and of love and of a sound mind. (2ˢᵗ Timothy 1:7)**

The Holy Spirit Brings Healing Through Times of Cleansing and Purging

Some of the pain I experienced was necessary for my healing process. The "grieving child" needed to weep tears of forgiveness after years of unexpressed emotions. When the Holy Spirit cleanses you after a purging of forgiveness, you feel peace, not depression, lethargy, or despair. **Let the peace of Christ rule in your hearts, since as members of one body you were called to peace. And be thankful. (Colossians 3:15)**

I went through many hours of purging and cleansing at many altar calls and in the privacy of my own home. I believe that my healing process would have been shortened had I sought help sooner. With a godly counselor, you feel and release the pain, with an objective person there to guide you and help you to identify the root issues. I suffered needlessly because of pride. I didn't want anyone to know.

Be advised! Healing comes through relationships and with accountability with wise Spirit filled counselors, not in isolation. Facing the pain with an accountability partner brings resolution to many issues. There are many Christian ministries available today with support groups. One to one counseling is also available through some of these ministries.

The human spirit and the soul, (mind, emotions, and will), must also be strengthened with the Word of God. Jesus will bring healing to the broken spirit and wounded soul.The believer will then open to change with the healing. Mind and emotions will reunite and clear thinking will be renewed. Walls will come down and the stony heart will be transformed to one that feels and lives an abundant life. This new creature in Christ will be realized in a process of daily repentance and in time spent in the Word of God. Daily surrender to the Lord with growing faith brings the believer into the reception of the Lord's precious love and grace.

We are healed as we face the deep hurts with its accompanying negative thoughts and emotions. We are healed as we face and bring change to the ungodly behavior patterns as codependence, parental inversion, noble martyr role, unbalanced burden bearing, perfectionism, and a false sense of responsibility. We are healed as we enter into repentance for our part in the abuse and forgiveness and releasing of all judgments against both ourselves and others. We are healed as we enter into offensive intercessory prayer for those who have hurt us. (See Appendix) True gender identity also emerges as we study, meditate upon, and speak the Word of God. We become conscious of who we are in Christ. And we are healed with repentance of inner vows we may have made with a decided willingness to open our hearts to change. Time spent with Jesus, in the Word of God, in praise and worship, with early morning prayer, and in fellowship with other believers, brings us into the surrendered life of walking by faith and grace led by the Holy Spirit.

Give to Others Out of Your Need

Jesus said, **"Give, and it will be given to you. A good measure, pressed down, shaken together and running over, will be poured into your lap. For with the same measure you use, it will be measured to you." (Luke 6:38)** I found people who were less fortunate than I. I visited friends in nursing homes. I conquered the fear of man as I handed out tracks to homeless folks on the streets and shared in a church ministry at a nursing home. I encouraged them out of my own need for fellowship. And I was blessed in the giving. You have to be active in the warfare; you have to choose to come out of the apathy of depression and live in the grace and loving kindness of God. Decide to live by faith and not by what you feel.

I believe I am challenged with anxiety and with panic attacks, but when I acknowledge the presence of the Lord, entering into His presence, I take control, speaking with my mouth and believing with my heart. My audible words of faith break through the darkness and extinguish the fear.

I actually felt the presence of evil leave me after speaking. Also, I had to seriously leave all idols, all ungodly soul ties, all ungodly connections with the soul ties, and all sins to truly get the victory. Sins and idols give the enemy legal access to our souls. Since addiction is a tough sin to completely extinguish, I believe that the Lord honored my heart of repentance and my faith for His healing. I stayed connected to the body of Christ. I sought the Lord, Christian counselors, friends, and support groups as I went through the process of inner healing until I was fully delivered of each addiction and fully free from the enemy's control. As I came out of the proud place, my will strengthened to obey His will, and inner change came.

As I left the idols, one step at a time, the Holy Spirit brought me more of His grace and power to resist in a greater submission to Him. As we leave the idols, we no longer resist in our own strength, but in the divine strength of the Lord. There can be no compromise when fighting the good fight of faith in spiritual warfare. The enemy knows every button and vulnerability we have. And He will not have any mercy on us. He is a relentless enemy. We have to be tougher and smarter than the devil by decidedly crucifying all flesh! The Lord then honors our obedience and brings us His anointing and His power to resist.

The Love of Money is the Root of All Evil – a Lust for Things

There was a time during my healing process that I could not work, but God provided me with social security disability and every need I had was cared for by His provision. During that time I repented of greed and the love of money. As a nurse I made lots of money and spent it quickly because I always had it. I grew to respect people and have compassion on the poor because I also became indigent. I learned a simpler and a more peaceful life. **And my God will meet all your needs according to His glorious riches in Christ Jesus. (Phil. 4:19)**

There is no amount of money that can buy the inner peace, grace, and the love that God has shown to me through my time with Him, though His people, and through life itself! I found life when money and material things ceased to be my focus. Today I live on what I need, not on what I want, giving my tithes and offerings to the Lord. I continue to give to a child through World Vision. I appreciate that the Lord always provides for me as I continue to give to Him and into His Kingdom. I am not a slave to the world's system as I have now entered God's system and He provides every one of my needs. And I thank Him for

the deep peace I have within because my heart is right before God and fear is far from me. **For the love of money is the root of all kinds of evil. Some people, eager for money, have wandered from the faith and pierced themselves with many griefs. (1ˢᵗ Timothy 6:10)**
The earth is the Lord's, and everything in it, the world, and all who live in it; for He founded it upon the seas and established it upon the waters. (Psalm 24:1,2)

You Have Victory Over Generational Spirits:

In speaking about generational spirits, Marilyn Hickey says this, "This spirit will try to reenter a future generation. It will stalk your child or grandchild like a rapist stalks his victim. It will watch for the perfect timing – the right age or circumstance – to attack. If you used to smoke, drink, or take drugs, then it will watch for a certain age to tempt your child with the same thing." **[112]**

The good news is you don't have to put up with Satan's tactics! You can stop him in his tracks and let him know that your family tree is off limits because God's covenant or generational blessings have been promised to you and your family, and it extends to a thousand generations. **[113]**(See Appendix)

The Lord did not set his affection on you and choose you because you were more numerous than other peoples, for you were the fewest of all peoples. But it was because the Lord loved you and kept the oath He swore to your forefathers that He brought you out with a mighty hand and redeemed you from the land of slavery, from the power of Pharaoh King of Egypt. Know therefore that the Lord your God is God; He is the faithful God, keeping His covenant of love to a thousand generations of those who love Him and keep his commands. (Deuteronomy 7:9)

Defilement

Don't you see that whatever enters the mouth goes into the stomach and then out of the body? But the things that come out of the mouth come from the heart, and these make a man 'unclean.' For out of the heart come evil thoughts, murder, adultery, sexual immorality, theft, false testimony, slander. These are what make a man (woman) 'unclean.' But eating with unwashed hands does not make him 'unclean.' (Matthew 15:17-20)

And I said to them, "Each of you, get rid of the vile images you have set your eyes on, and do not defile yourselves with the idols of Egypt. I am the lord your God." (Ezekiel 20:7)

'This is what the Sovereign Lord says: Will you defile yourselves the way your fathers did and lust after their vile images? When you offer your gifts – the sacrifice of your sons in the fire – you continue to defile yourselves with all your idols to this day.' (Ezekiel 20:30,31)

Our sins and idols open us up to demonic distractions, harassments, and delusions from the spirit realm. The bottom line about defilement is that "Greater is the Lord Jesus Christ within us than he that is in the world."(1ˢᵗ John 4:4) Remember Jesus had no sin in Him and He had complete victory over the devil by His obedience and by the words of His mouth as He spoke the Word of God to the devil. Amidst all persecution, He kept a humble and a meek (strength under control) spirit. Defilement is usually about our own open doors. Look within your own heart first. See what door remains open to allow defilement to come from the spirit realm.

As we receive the Father's love, our submission to the Lord Jesus Christ strengthens us against what is in the spirits of other people. He is our shield, His blood covers us, and the power of the Holy Spirit is both upon us and in us. (Psalms 3:3) (1ˢᵗ Peter 1:18,19)(Acts 1:8) We must take hold of our righteousness in Christ Jesus. (Rom 1:17)(Heb. 11:1) This is our confidence. We are the righteousness of God in Christ no matter what issues, sins, or addictions we are working through. He knows our heart and wants us to know His love. Certainly, obedience to close off open doors will strengthen our resistance against that which is in the world. But God does not ask for perfection; He wants our hearts right with Him.

It is Satan who will try to bring us condemnation. Refuse to take it. There is no condemnation to those who are in Christ Jesus. (Rom. 8:1) Be on guard, however, that when we are at our weakest points, which include vulnerable and disobedient points, the enemy will use condemnation to attempt to bring us defilement through other people. Stay alert. Jesus is looking for a heart that is honest (contrite) before Him. Always prepare yourself with prayer before going into the world, with submission, repentance, and forgiveness. And place your spiritual armour on. Cover yourself with the blood of Jesus Christ. Keep your focus on the Lord.

Therefore, when we become aware that what is in the spirits of others can defile us, we need to counterbalance that with simple faith. We do not need to fear, only to pray away whatever we sense invading our heart and mind through our spirit's involvement with others. "Greater is He who is in you than he who is in the world." (1 John 4:4) Above all, Christians must not retreat from the world. We must learn not to celebrate the strength of the flesh. [114]

As John and Paula Sandford traveled in their ministry to the wounded hearted, they grew in their maturity against the demonic in cleansing prayers over themselves after they had been ministering in dark areas. They started to "pray up a storm and chase demons" and it left them "puffed up with ourselves and our soldierly power and quite distracted us from the King of Kings." [115] We need to fight in the power of the Holy Spirit, speaking with our human spirit. The baptism of the Holy Spirit empowered the apostles to spread the gospel to many people. (Matthew 28:18-20) We cannot effectively take our delegated authority in Christ Jesus against the demonic in our flesh. We invite retaliatory spirits if we pray without faith and in our fleshly emotions because we are not under God's authority. We also invite more spirits to enter a person's temple and our own temples as well if we pray without having legal authority to pray in Christ' delegated authority. (Luke 11:24-26)(Matthew 18:18)(See Appendix)

John Sandford shares, 'We learned there is a better way to accomplish the same cleansing. We might, along the way, still say a short, "Clear the air, Lord," but that is relatively unimportant. We have learned that when we know He has already won the victory, we carry that power with us. He transmits it and it flows through us. Now we ignore the devils and start praising Jesus. Pretty soon they can't tolerate that and depart, leaving Jesus with all the glory and them with none at all because nobody paid them any attention.' [116] Knowing you are righteous, (in right standing with God), no matter what sins you have committed or what addictions you are trying to get free of, you will be able to stand and carry the power of God wherever you go. He will empower those who are humble and repentant toward Him.

These, then, are the things you should teach. Encourage and rebuke with all authority. Do not let anyone despise you. (Titus 2:15)

God has given us a wonderful weapon to use, the blood of Jesus. This is our weapon, our shield, our hiding place. In Revelation 12:11 we are told that, "They overcame Him by the blood of the Lamb, and by the word of their testimony."[117] Jesus urges us to keep our minds filled with the concept of God's control over everything, which means that a disciple must maintain an attitude of perfect trust and an eagerness to ask and to seek. Not even the smallest detail of life happens unless God's will is behind it. [118]The Lord still uses us, even in spite of ourselves.

Post note:
Spend time with Jesus in prayer and He will anoint you for service. He will bless you with His presence. After the September eleventh terrorist attack, I wrote a letter to all my family members, telling them how much I loved them. I told them that I wanted to see them in heaven and told them that in order to get to heaven, they needed to commit their hearts and lives to Jesus Christ, repent of all their sins, and believe and submit to Jesus Christ as their Lord and Savior. Many of us held hands in a restaurant that year and said the sinner's prayer together.

It may be difficult to reach some people through a conversation. A letter can be a great tool. I always take advantage of the Christmas season to minister to unsaved relatives and friends via Christmas cards and worship CDs and DVDs. We are saved only through the grace of God. (Ephesians 2:8) It is His gift to us. (See Appendix)

Look Within – Stop My Own Sin

Therefore come out from them and be separate, says the Lord. Touch no unclean thing, and I will receive you, and you will be my sons and daughters, says the Lord Almighty. (2ⁿᵈ Corinthians 6:17-18)

Cutting Free

Elijah House Ministry speaks of a "cutting free" period where we release ourselves from the ungodly relationships. In order to become who God created us to be, we must cut free from the things that hold us back. [119] Just as I had to leave all homosexual relationships, I had to leave Mom until I learned how to relate as the "honest self" and until I had the Holy Spirit's leading. The "honest self" emerged as I got honest with myself and my own sins against the Father. And Jesus began to heal me from the inside out.

As I invited Jesus into each violation the Lord brought to my remembrance, this wall of self-protection came down, and the inferiority I felt with people disintegrated. I became God-conscious, not self-conscious. Not only did I need to learn new ways of relating to Mom to keep my healthy boundaries with her, but I also needed to experience God's love and get a revelation of my righteousness in Him. I began to speak God's Word and take Jesus' delegated authority and the spirit of fear began to come down. I worked to develop my heart of faith with surrender, repentance, and forgiveness. I then began to heal. This took years and is still a part of my deliverance today. Codependence had to be annihilated from my life and replaced with total dependence upon the Lord Jesus Christ, Whose presence in and with me would help me to set healthy boundaries with people.

However, I had to leave Mom first and the physical location per the leading of the Holy Spirit, several counselors, and my Pastor. Always receive godly counsel when making these decisions of separation and/or severance. I had to put Jesus back on the throne of my heart to be an effective warrior. I would only experience effective prayers of authority when I truly was under the divine authority of Jesus Christ, my Lord and Savior. I had to take Mom off the throne of my heart and place Jesus back upon it. I had to leave home and heal.

What kept me from speaking out was an attitude that I had developed over the years. It was peace at all costs. I did not like confrontation. There is arrogance in this attitude, which had to go. Why, you say? Because I thought I was the better person in not confronting and just loving. This is not only dishonesty; it is also self- righteousness and pride. It is very codependent and it is the enabler's role. When in a safe situation, it pays to speak the truth with love. Take a witness if you need. Be led of the Holy Spirit.

It is only when we are truly honest with discretion that we become free and also help to free others. I had to confront by writing a letter, because the demonic spirit between Mom and I caused enough turmoil to my soul just in normal conversations. I was not mature enough in Christ to deal with the wisdom of God in this situation. Seek wise godly Spirit filled Christian counsel and prayer, my friend, if you are experiencing anything that might be demonic.

Part of my healing was being honest enough with Mom to tell her that I just needed time away until I got stronger. I knew that I had work to do with the Lord to strengthen myself first. So I honestly and discreetly shared with her. "This is not about you. This is about me. I have formed judgments toward you and others and I must repent and look within myself and get healed." I also told her, "This is not easy for me either." "I cannot be what you want me to be." I had to grow apart from the enmeshment with her and find my identity in Christ, and mature as a woman totally dependent upon God.

Heal the Wounded Little Girl First – Dr. Bradshaw's Assertions

Going through Elijah House Prayer Ministry training was pivotal to my healing. It was during this time that I was confronted with "the wounded little girl." Elijah House gave me solutions. I was ready for this. I had enough of the enemy's torments. I could not fight this thing anymore on my own. I had to get to the root of the negative emotions, the inner vows, and the fears. My vow never to be controlled by another person had to be faced and issues dealing with trust of God, myself, and other people had to be worked through. I knew that I needed another person in my life whom I could trust.

In 2005, eight years after arriving home to New Jersey, I was at the deepest level of healing, my very deliverance. I was told once by a pastor that forgiveness is like an onion. You peel off layer by layer of unforgiveness until you get to the core of the onion. This is the most difficult layer to unfold.

The sense of hurt and resentment may to a greater or lesser degree be unconscious, and so the need for forgiveness may become more apparent as the healing process brings to light the hurts of the past. [120]

I also had to identify the deceptive lies that kept me caught in the perfection spiral. That lie had to do with shame, self-blame and a false sense of responsibility that was destructive to the very core. That lie had to die within my heart. It was already taken to its death on the cross of Calvary. But I had to accept its death. I had to accept the liberty that Jesus Christ bought for me as the ransom for my shame and self-blame. I had to receive His love and His righteousness. I had to take my healing and renounce these lies. This lie was deep seated in my heart and only the revelation of the Holy Spirit and an act of my will would be able to free me. It had to be accepted by faith, not by feelings.

At the core of homosexuality and the subsequent perfectionist spiral was a spirit of rebellion and the spirit of fear, including the fear of man. The fear of man brings a snare. (Proverbs 29:25) I had to repent for disobeying God and not trusting Him. There was self-doubt mixed into this which only the Holy Spirit could help me to release. During my checking and rechecking rituals, He would tell me it was done. As I learned to stop, listen, and trust God for the check in my spirit, God gave me a strategy to resist the tormenting doubts to recheck. There is a stopping point in all addiction where the divine intervention of the Holy Spirit helps us. And the Lord brings us His anointing to resist the driving spirits.(James 4:7,8)

I had to honestly look within my heart. The Holy Spirit showed me my selfishness. I had allowed the enemy to place me in a bubble of life and I wanted out. I had to repent of all my bitter root judgments against others; I had to look within my own heart and heal. I had to repent of being angry at God for putting me through this; I had to repent of despairing thoughts of not wanting to live as there was some part of me that wanted to die; suicide is the ultimate selfish act! It is murder against one's own soul and it is sin against God. I remembered when I was a young Christian that I had a stark presence of the Lord with me and there was no dread or fear present. I asked the Lord to restore this revelation to me so I could step out of fear and dread. And He answered me. Because it is His will that we live the abundant life. I discovered my purpose in life and this kept me alive and well, serving God and giving to other people whether in jobs or in other circles.

I had to honestly look at my life and see that I must have made inner vows which were keeping me in this victim mentality. I had to repent of vows that I would never let anyone control me. This vow kept me from seeking committed relationships even with godly men. It also kept me isolated. I thank God that I had the intimacy with Jesus to keep me safe and secure in His love for me throughout my life. I always knew He was with me as my friend as well as my Lord and Savior, my God, and my divine authority.

Coming out of the secrecy of homosexuality and perfectionism with the help of Holy Spirit filled counselors, I turned the lights on in Satan's camp. This was pivotal to my healing as I actually felt the tormenting spirit's grip on me in the presence of another person. Perfectionism was formed since childhood. I determined with the help of the Holy Spirit to close the door on this fantasy, the delusions, and the addiction to the law and to open a new door on the reality of life. I would learn to receive His grace, walking by faith, trusting that God would make a way for me one day at a time. I did eventually leave the nursing profession to get free from this addiction and I found the rest of God. You do whatever you must do to live free in your love relationship with Jesus.

I was not sure I liked reality. I felt so behind everyone else. I actually became nauseated for a while as I was experiencing life in a way I had never before known it. Nausea is what our spirit felt in the womb as we sensed the human condition. It is what our spirit feels as we first experience life. Dr. Bradshaw says you have to re-experience the pain, then leave home to be completely restored from the obsessive compulsive disorder. **[121]** This is how it unfolded for me. I went through the pain at home until my health was affected. Then I left home via direction of the Holy Spirit. Leaving home was like leaving my best friend. With no one to depend on except the Holy Spirit, the "core pain" is felt. And it must be felt in order to face it and to get free of it.

That "core" pain was not only just re-experienced, but also dealt with by identifying root issues and ungodly behavior patterns, facing them with repentance and forgiveness in one to one counseling sessions, releasing judgments against myself and others. As I stayed closely connected to my church and its activities in fellowship with other believers, the Lord changed me from the inside out. I experienced much healing in private fellowship spent in relationship with Jesus, one day at a time, in His Word and in prayer, learning to listen to the leading of the Holy Spirit. I found the balance of taking Jesus' delegated authority against the devil's attacks from the spirit realm together with defiantly obeying the Lord to silence my fleshly desires, my idols, and all ungodly habit patterns and behaviors through acts of my will, decisions of faith, and speaking prayers and the Word of God. I surrendered to His will for my life, not my will. And I developed a heart of faith as I submitted each day to the Lord as my loving authority, a heart with greater submission, with sincere daily repentance, and with heartfelt forgiveness; leaving the traumas and rejections at the foot of the cross. (See chapter <u>From Defiance to Repentance to Reverance – Dr. Bradshaw's Research – Receiving from God</u>)

I especially came to a deeper sense of His presence with me during both private and corporate praise and worship of the Lord. Tears of grief shed layers of hurt from my wounded heart and the Holy Spirit purged and cleansed the dark residues of trauma, loss, pain, and rejection in ways that only He could. He brought me revelations that cemented some of the healing I received. As the facades came down, and the dark spirits fled in the face of purity, the Lord revealed my "honest self," my true identity in Jesus Christ. The Kingdom of God is within us. (Luke 17:21)

My intimate relationship with the Lord along with a keen discernment of Jesus on the inside of my being was developing to eventually become the most important force of my life. As He becomes more real to us, the things of the earth grow dim. His voice within us becomes clearer and the lures of the world become dimmer. **Jesus replied, "The kingdom of God does not come with your careful observation, nor will people say, 'Here it is,' or 'There it is,' because the kingdom of God is within you. (Luke 17:20-22)**

Submit to God – Resist the Devil and He Will Flee – Listen to What You Say

I had to start loving others and giving again. I will choose the life of the Spirit over the life in the flesh. I will choose to give rather than to take. I will choose to obey and to come out of isolation. By an act of faith, we step out of the isolation and dare to live again. And the Holy Spirit will empower us and lead us. Seeking His perfect will, we will have peace within. **And this is the victory, even our faith. (1st John 5:4)**

I rose up out of the compulsive thoughts by speaking the Word of God. I taught myself to listen to myself when I spoke to others. Life and death are in the power of the tongue. (Proverbs 18:21) I acted in faith believing God to bring change. Then the Holy Spirit baptized me with His power. He said to me, "Lives are at stake!" It was a miraculous transformation! I knew God was really with me and I believed He took this torment from me at the cross of Calvary.

When I asked God what this was all about, He answered me and said, "Satan wants your integrity and your life." I actually heard an audible voice from an angel after Pastor Kenneth W. Hagin of Rhema Bible Church of Tulsa, Oklahoma laid hands on me. The voice spoke these words, "Resist death and the gates of hell shall not prevail against you." (These words are taken from God's Word in Matthew 16:18)

Jesus spoke to Peter in the Gospel of Matthew. **Blessed are you, Simon son of Jonah, for this was not revealed to you by man, but by my Father in heaven. And I tell you that you are Peter, and on this rock I will build my church, and <u>the gates of Hades will not overcome it</u>. I will give**

you the keys of the kingdom of heaven; whatever you bind on earth will be bound in heaven, and whatever you loose on earth will be loosed in heaven." (Matthew 16:17,18,19)

My need to control was given over to a greater power, that of the Holy Spirit. It was a combination of the Holy Spirit's power and an act of my will to surrender to the Lordship and the authority of Jesus Christ with reverence, daily repentance for sins, with forgiveness and release of blame against myself and all who have sinned against me that brought me deliverance. As I daily sought the place of complete surrender in obedience to the Lord's commands, I was free from the control of Satan's lies and stepped out as I now heard the voice of the Holy Spirit ever so clearly.

Repent and let every one of you be baptized in the name of Jesus Christ for the remission of sins; and you shall receive the gift of the Holy Spirit. For the promise is to you and to your children, and to all who are afar off, as many as the Lord our God will call. ---And the key is repentance. It puts you on the road to great fire and you will reach the destination God intends. [122] Repentance is a true sorrow for grieving the Lord. It requires an awareness of sin at the heart level; an understanding of how sin hurts others and God; a willingness to accept full responsibility for our actions; and the determination to change. [123]

Just like homosexuality, the addiction to perfectionism is pure deception. Because I had developed this habit since childhood, it had to be a work of the Holy Spirit to bring me conviction of faith from a deeper place than my mind and a deeper place than my emotions. I had to then exercise my will by faith to then subdue the flesh, to obey God and to resist the thoughts, to rebuke them, and to change the channel by replacing them with the spoken Word of God! I had to receive wise counsel to silence this addiction. I expected change and the miracle came!

I will make an everlasting covenant with them; I will never stop doing good to them, and I will inspire them to fear me, so that they will never turn from me. (Jeremiah 32:40)

Resist the Lust of the Flesh, the Lust of the Eyes, and the Pride of Life

All addiction brings torment. Breaking any addiction begins with an identification of the lies of Satan that we believe about the sins we have committed against God, an acceptance of the deception we have fallen for, and the problem that we are having leaving it. We must come out of the denial that we have no sin and that we do not need assistance. We must face the lie that we can handle this ourselves. This is Satan's trap.

We need to repent of the sin and submit to the Lord Jesus Christ. We have to come out of denial and admit that the addiction is holding us captive from life itself. It is giving authority and control of our lives to Satan himself. Jesus knows our hearts. He will honor every act of obedience toward His Lordship. He will bless our every attempt to come to Him, to submit, to repent, to forgive, and to obey Him.

With honesty and repentance, and with submission to His Lordship, Jesus turned my spiritual paralysis into a momentum and revival started in my life. I started to express sorrow to Him for displeasing Him. I had to humble myself to ask other Christians to help me.

This work is done in our quiet conversations with the Lord Jesus Christ. The work is also done with Spirit filled counselors with whom we are able to trust and to be accountable. We must reach out to the body of Christ to both receive prayer and to speak prayers of not only repentance but also of forgiveness that penetrates deep within our hearts. Prayer begins to identify the roots of all habit patterns.

Prayer invites the divine presence of Jesus to come into our humanity and it breaks the lies and the torment of the enemy! This is the place that you actually hear the Lord speaking to you, in your time with Him. He will reveal things to you that you would not otherwise have known. He wants you free. So it is very important to seek that quiet time alone with Jesus on a daily basis.

As I resisted the pride of life, I learned through example from humble men and women in the body of Christ how to walk in humility with Jesus as my Lord. I also realized that everything that I accomplish on this earth is a result of the gifts that the Lord has given me. He created everything and is in charge of everything in life and I am His servant.

As I resisted the lust of the flesh, walking in chastity and committing to celibacy, my body was dedicated as His temple, His place of residence. The Holy Spirit helped me to resist the impulses of my flesh. I had to choose to discipline myself to physical exercise to maintain my temple (my body) as dedicated to Him in holiness. As I made decisive steps to offer my body as a living sacrifice together with the discipline of physical exercise, the Lord blessed me with the gift of celibacy. And I had peace in my body. It is the unsettled issues of the heart that ignite the physical body to desire to sin. Once we face them head on and deal with them, we settle into the peace of God, not only in mind, and emotions, but in our bodies as well. **And if the Spirit of Him who raised Jesus from the dead is living in you, He who raised Christ from the dead will also give life to your mortal bodies through His Spirit, who lives in you. (Romans 8:11)**

As I resisted the lust of the eyes, I was fully healed and the harlot spirit left me. This spirit looks outside oneself and "wants" from others. We are so easily deceived by what we see. Our woundedness causes us to look outside ourselves because we have not settled into the rest of God. As I grew in my own identity in Christ, I was not so lured to attach myself to the worldly pull and its visual splendors. As I grew in Christ, I saw myself in Him and I saw people spiritually as Christ sees them. I wanted to let people see me naturally and spiritually, not masking myself with lots of makeup. As we heal from hurts, and submit to Jesus Christ, we became more aware of the presence of God within us and around us. The world's pull loses its lure as we determine to live for Jesus.**The eye never has enough of seeing, nor the ear its fill of hearing. What has been will be again, what has been done will be done again; (Ecclesiastes 1:8,9)**

Reawaken the Heart – We are Healed Socially

The mind and emotions reconnect and we have an active and clear thought life based on the Word of God. We work through issues with repentance and forgiveness. Inner healing awakens the brain; thoughts and memories are reactivated as we step out of the fog of negativity and out of the lethargy of apathy. The lure of physical and visual beauty loses its power to distract us from our focus on the Lord, and we desire to walk in His love, giving to others who are in need. It is a joy to converse with others and still maintain our honest identity.

When inner confidence returns, which I received as a result of my connection with the Jesus and a decision to receive the righteousness of God, we are then able to initiate and take control, saying "no" to the worldly distractions. The more we turn from the world's temptations to sin and walk led by the Holy Spirit, the more we heal and become our "honest selves." Eventually any immoral visual lures, as pornography, any sexual sin of thought or of deed, any ungodly imaginations, delusions, and any impure motives will become repulsive to us as we resist the flesh and enter into the walk of the Spirit. We also can fully appreciate and praise God for the beauty of what we do see. And chose to look at that which would only please the Lord.

Carnal comforts were replaced by listening to Christian radio and reading the Word and other Christian literature. I became a history buff as well. Walking with the Holy Spirit brought me a peace in my mind; where there was time spent thinking clearly and just being thankful to be alive and free, listening to the loving voice of the Holy Spirit or singing songs or hymns of worship in my mind. Good memories resurface with resolutions of hurtful emotions.

One small group could mean a complete change from isolation to accountability and friends in your life! I could have volunteered as a prayer partner. I could have been in conversation with a friend. I could have been doing something for somebody else who needed support. I could have set up a chat line on the internet to minister to folks in my position. There are countless opportunities on Face book, YouTube, MySpace, and twitter to stay connected with the world and with your purpose. Friend, as you give, it will always come back to you. Set up a website and share the gospel with folks! Share your relationship with Jesus on the internet. We are in the last days and we need to get His word out to as many people as possible before Jesus returns. **And pray in the Spirit on all occasions with all kinds of prayers and requests. With this in mind, be alert and always keep on praying for all the saints. (Ephesians 6:18)**

All idols are a result of turning from the "honest self" and the reality of God with us. The enemy tempted me in every way possible to stay under his deceptive control. It seemed that as I resisted one temptation, he put another one in my path. When you resist all for Jesus and completely surrender, then you know what it is to truly live as a vessel of honor. And what an honor it is to live and suffer for the one who died for us! You don't have to become a nun, a minister, or a priest to live a holy life. Holiness it is a lifelong process.

But we have this treasure in jars of clay to show that this all-surpassing power is from God and not from us. We are hard pressed on every side, but not crushed; perplexed, but not in despair; persecuted, but not abandoned; struck down, but not destroyed. We always carry around in our body the death of Jesus, so that the life of Jesus may also be revealed in our body. (2nd Corinthians 4:7-10)

Seek to Connect in Heart to Heart Relationships

I was so lonely for a relationship and He gave me a desire for a man. Yet I had to wait even though I had this desire for the "best" to arrive. I had to listen to the Holy Spirit's moving before I moved. I could not be moved by physical attraction alone. If I began a relationship with a man, it would have to start with a friendship in a heart to heart connection.

I was very careful that I did not move based upon my senses, especially by what I saw. I don't care how handsome someone looks or how much chemistry there is. I want someone who is completely sold out to Jesus for a partner. That is based upon a heart to heart connection and not merely a physical attraction. The Holy Spirit is guiding me in this area. Right now, I live content in Jesus. When and if I marry, I will also live content in Jesus with a desire to share the love of Jesus with my husband in a heart to heart connection.

As I release my habit structures to the Lord, my desire for a mate increases. As I give up the fantasy relationships which have served to isolate me from availability to normal relationships, I desire real friendships. As I learn to relax in His grace, I am yearning to blend in more with others and to share. As I repent and leave the addictions to perfection and homosexuality, I feel free to enjoy life again as I did as a child. **When tempted, no one should say, "God is tempting me." For God cannot be tempted by evil, nor does He tempt anyone; but each one is tempted when, by his own evil desire, he is dragged away and enticed. Then, after desire has conceived, it gives birth to sin; and sin, when it is full-grown, gives birth to death. (James 1:13-15)**

As we ask Him to guide us through the storm, we focus on the calmer of the storm and not the storm itself. And it is never our victory. The victory belongs to Jesus! It is all about Him.

There Can Be No Blame – Take Responsibility for My Own Transgressions

God is sovereign (has complete control, power, and authority) over every person and everything in this world. Therefore, the moment we consciously or unconsciously blame someone else for our problems, we block our own healing. I was blaming the devil for the attacks I experienced, but I also had to take responsibility for my own sins against the Father. There were deep wounds with ungodly reactions, which include sins and idols in my life. These had to be faced, repented of, and settled. The memories of some of them came late in the process. God knows when we are ready for each memory. He knows best!

In homosexuality, I had to face the childhood traumas, bringing Jesus into each place of violation, accepting His Lordship, and replacing codependence with complete dependence upon a loving and personal relationship with Jesus Christ. In so doing, I began the work of forgiving myself and others with a decision to release all judgments and blame, and to receive the loving presence of the Lord into my life in a personal way.

In perfectionism, I had to face my own humanity and accept the gift of God's perfect and unconditional love, acceptance, forgiveness, and His grace with no need to prove myself. Jesus Christ, Who died and rose again, sits at the right hand of God, forever making intercession for us. (Romans 8:34 ref.) We have an Advocate who believes in us. There is nothing to prove.

What showed that God loved me even though I was caught in these lies is that Jesus sent me the Holy Spirit to help me out of the sins. I was baptized with His power. I believe that God knew that I was buried in quicksand and His intentions were to get me out. He also knew I could not get out without His help. When I asked for His help, He was there. He always meets us at the point of our deepest need.

The humility and courage to ask are so essential to the Holy Spirit's working in our lives. Unless we open our mouths, God cannot work. He is a gentleman. He will not act until we reach out to Him and ask. **Ask and it will be given to you; seek and you will find; knock and the door will be opened to you. For everyone who asks receives; he who knocks, the door will be opened. (Matthew 7:7, 8)**

Honesty takes us to a place where we are comfortable in our own skin. We lose the fear of man because there is no need to compare ourselves to others anymore. I am not afraid of my mother or her reactions anymore. I actually see more of her strengths in my own behavior. As I stopped looking outward for the answers and looked to Jesus, cleaning up my own act, I became bolder to speak the truth in love. My own sins had kept me in a web of timidity and in a "role" which prevented me from being fully me, fully honest, and fully free. When I got honest with myself and then others, my life began to change. **And we know that in all things God works for the good of those who love Him, who have been called according to His purpose. (Romans 8:28)**

I Don't Want Anyone to Know I Have a Problem

I had to open up to someone. I was in hiding even in church. I made acquaintances but not many friends. This is pride to the core. I was so adept at discerning others' sins. The largest deterrent to my healing was seated in my own spiritual pride. I had to trust someone. It was not until things got really stretched that I started to "blend in" with others. I had to or I would have despaired! **Pride goes before destruction, a haughty spirit before a fall. (Proverbs 16:18)**

Criticism toward Others Changed to Self-Criticism

Sanctification is a process which takes a turning inward, an honest look at oneself for the purpose of purity in the Lord. The goal is to be used for His kingdom purposes and to know His perfect will for your life. It commands an honesty with oneself, with God, and with other people.

It was as if God provided me with a mirror to see my own heart. His purpose was to heal my heart, to reconnect my mind with my emotions, and to transform my spiritual eyesight. The Holy Spirit would show me how critical I was of other people while in actual conversations with them. He showed me my heart. I was shocked and had to change. As I asked God to help me change, He did, one day at a time.

As I dealt with my judgmental heart, I was not so quick to criticize others or to speak without thinking. I started to see myself as equal to and not inferior to others. (Job 12:3) I learned to respect myself first. And this brought me a respect for others. I saw myself in them and realized my need for other people in my life. I had to learn to respect others, no matter what their religious beliefs. With the respect came a control of my mouth. With the self-control came a more gentle spirit. Arrogance left as I humbled myself before the Lord. I became more careful with my words, unless the Holy Spirit was guiding me to small talk for the purpose of connecting with another person.

For this reason, make every effort to add to your faith goodness; and to goodness, knowledge; and to knowledge, self-control; and to self-control, perseverance; and to perseverance, godliness; and to godliness, brotherly kindness; and to brotherly kindness, love. (2ⁿᵈ Peter 1:5-7)

As a result of this change, something wonderful happened. I saw others in the light of their challenges and compassion started to spring from within me. I began to bond with others from the heart, now feeling for them while in conversation. My heart was opening. Praise God! **In repentance and rest is your salvation; in quietness and trust is your strength. (Isaiah 30:15)**

Reflections – Forgive Yourself

God brought me home for a reason. I promised myself, "I promise to forgive myself and lock this door of self-condemnation." I knew Jesus had forgiven me, but I had not fully forgiven myself. As a result, I could not receive the fullness of His power to work in my life. I knew I could not minister full comfort to others if I was not fully comforted and fully free. **Praise be to the God and Father of our Lord Jesus Christ, the Father of compassion and the God of all comfort, who comforts us in all our troubles, so** that we can comfort those in any trouble with the comfort we ourselves have received from God. (2nd Corinthians 1: 3, 4)

I recall Pastor Bob Yandian and his wife, Loretta, praying for me from the halls of Grace Fellowship in Tulsa. When I told him that I was finally going home to my family, I'll never forget their statement of prayer. As they held my hands, Pastor Bob prayed, "Stand back and watch the Holy Spirit work."[124] As I looked within myself, there was victory in Jesus because my prayers to open the eyes of my heart were being answered. The Holy Spirit had literally taken me by the hand and was walking with me through the process of inner healing. Only through this divine and intimate relationship are we truly escorted through this process. The Holy Spirit was ushering me into a higher and deeper level in Him. He wanted me to see, to feel, and to love myself. Years of living in the shame had kept me in an "invisible" existence. I neither saw myself nor felt myself when in the company of others.

The stony heart which is wounded will stay in isolation until the inner vows are faced and repented. The wounded heart shuts out the voice of God and others. The heart of stone must be loved to life by God and through people. [125]"I will give you a new heart and put a new spirit in you; I will remove from you your heart of stone and give you a heart of flesh." (Ezekiel 36:26)

As I took responsibility for my own sins, I was deeply humbled. As the inner mourning process reached its climax, I became more desperate for human contact. I could not live in this bubble anymore. I had to break out of the selfish cocoon and start giving to others. I had to say goodbye to the little girl who was still attached to "Mama" and live as an adult woman who was capable of loving and of living an abundant life. **Negative responses to early hurt have persisted unresolved, and in connection with this there will be a particular need for the healing of memories. Since the defensive detachment is essentially an unresolved 'mourning' process, such mourning must be worked through. [126]**

Go Deeper in God

After ten years of living close to family, it was then a season to go even deeper in the things of God and my relationship with Jesus Christ. I had to get stronger in my relationship to Jesus. The only way I could help my family was to step back in a place of trust in God's sovereignty over their lives. I literally had to "surrender all," even contact. Now I stood in a place of trust in the Lord and His unconditional love for them. The Lord wanted my undivided attention. I desired what was best for them and had to obey God, no matter what others' thought or what I felt. (I encourage you to seek wise counsel in making such critical decisions regarding separation or severance from family with at least two or three godly counselors and also with the confirmation from the Holy Spirit.)

I felt similar in 1981 when I left the homosexual lifestyle. Friend, we can have ungodly relationships in our family as well as in our homosexual contacts. The codependent relationship I had with female lovers was a result of codependent patterns formed earlier in my family bonding, especially with my mother. **Then the Word of the Lord came to Elijah: Leave here, turn eastward and hide in the Kerith Ravine, east of the Jordan. You will drink from the brook, and I have ordered the ravens to feed you there. (1st Kings 17:3, 4)**

I could not help anyone until I was fully healed of codependence. God hates idols. There is idolatry in codependent relationships. Until I totally yielded to the loving control and authority of the Holy Spirit, with no idols, I would not be strong enough or effective in ministry or in any relationship.

A Covenant Relationship – Silence
Torment and Unbalanced Grief

A covenant is a promise [127] that signifies a mutual understanding between two or more parties, each binding himself (herself) to fulfill specific obligations; it also refers to a solemn agreement to do or not to do a certain thing. [128] Accepting Jesus Christ as my Lord and Savior was a promise to live for Him alone from that moment of commitment on. It is the power of the Holy Spirit working within me and for me that seals that promise.

A seal is something which confirms that promise. [129] In the Gospels we find that Jesus Christ Himself, the New Covenant sacrifice, spoke many covenant words concerning the coming of the Holy Spirit. The Holy Spirit Himself is the seal of the New Covenant. [130] When I asked Jesus into my heart, He took up residence within me and the Holy Spirit, the third person of the Blessed Trinity, gave me the power to say "no" in faith and to resist the lying voices of any tormenting spirits. Benny Hinn explains it very simply: **"You see, you and I have no power to say no to Satan; there's no power in us to refuse him. The power only comes when the Holy Spirit is upon us. Giants of faith have fallen because they couldn't say no. They relied on their own power." [131]**

Our Father God provided us with a New Covenant as a promise of hope. That covenant offers us a "relationship" with God through Jesus Christ. [132] **"This is the covenant I will make with the house of Israel after that time," declares the Lord. "I will put my law in their minds and write it on their hearts. I will be their God, and they will be my people. No longer will a man teach his neighbor or a man his brother, saying, 'Know the Lord,' because they will all know me, from the least of them to the greatest," declares the Lord. "For I will forgive their wickedness and will remember their sins no more." (Jeremiah 31:33–34)**

If anyone acknowledges that Jesus is the Son of God, God lives in him (her), and he (she) in God. And so we know and rely on the love God has for us. (1st John 4:15,16)

With every covenant there are three parts. There are the promises of the covenant, the blood of the covenant, and the seal of the covenant. In the New Covenant, we are provided the promises through Our Father's Word. We are provided the blood of the covenant through the sacrificial blood of Jesus Christ, which represents the Son's work for us. And the seal is provided through the Holy Spirit's work in us. The Holy Spirit is the executer appointed to confirm the will and testament of the Father and the Son. [133]

Sanctification - Set Apart in Complete Honesty

We are given many great and precious promises as divine provisions of the New Covenant. The most important promise of the New Covenant is salvation of the soul. "Salvation" means "safety, security, preservation, deliverance, and wholeness." [134]

Praise be to God and Father of our Lord Jesus Christ, who has blessed us in the heavenly realms with every spiritual blessing in Christ. For He chose us in Him before the creation of the world to be holy and blameless in His sight. In love He predestined us to be adopted as His sons (daughters) through Jesus Christ, in accordance with His pleasure and will. (Ephesians 1:3-5)

Salvation's Promises

Salvation promises the following benefits:

Forgiveness and remission of the penalty of sin.

Justification or a declaration of right standing before God through Christ.

Regeneration by which we are born into the family of God and can call God "Father."

Assurance whereby we have the witness of the Holy Spirit that we are secure in obedience to the Word of God.

Sanctification whereby we are set apart unto the Lord for His holy service and use.

Adoption whereby we are placed as a son or daughter into the family of God.

Glorification by which we will be rendered glorious, honorable, and magnified as a completed work of redemption as perfected saints.

The New Covenant brings the believer into the fullness of the glory of God. **[135]**

As I stand firm in this covenant relationship with Jesus Christ, the promises are given as God's benefits. They are our divine inheritance. We can experience a little bit of heaven here on earth. However, standing firm requires that I do not look back on the mistakes of the past. I must continue to go forward in this new Christian lifestyle, living in the now and hoping for the future.

As Jesus prayed to His Father for His friends, the disciples, in the seventeenth chapter of John, He said, **I am coming to you now, but I say these things while I am still in the world, so that they may have the full measure of my joy within them. I have given them Your word and the world has hated them, for they are not of the world any more than I am of the world. My prayer is not that You take them out of the world but that You protect them from the evil one. They are not of the world, even as I am not of it. Sanctify them by the truth; Your word is truth. (John 17:17)**

Jesus asked His Father to sanctify His friends by the truth of His Word. He set an example for us. We also are sanctified (made holy) by the truth of the Word of God. And we also sanctify our friends and family by our prayers of intercession for them to our Father in the name of Jesus Christ. (John 16:23)

Webster's defines the word sanctify as "to set apart or to be free from sin; to purify." **[136]** Pastor Thomas Keinath of Calvary Temple says, "There is an honesty to dying to everything that is not of God." **[137]** We are sanctified in this place. It is complete honesty with ourselves and God that locks the door to any pretenses and allows the "honest self" to emerge fully free and set apart for the Lord to work for us, in us, and through us. The Holy Spirit is our teacher. As we look to Him, He will reveal to us what needs repentance, forgiveness, obedience, and change.

Teach Me Lord to Trust

Trust in the Lord with all your heart and lean not on your own understanding; in all your ways acknowledge Him, and He will make your paths straight. (Proverbs 3:5) These words are easier said than done. When you have lived for so many years relying on yourself to survive, trust does not come easily. But the Bible tells us that God gives us all a "measure of faith." (Romans 12:3) Faith is trust. This is a gift from God.

I am amazed at people who claim to be atheists. The proof of an almighty and all-powerful God is not just in the awesome world that He has created, but also in the magnificence of human life itself. Not only did He create us with a spirit, but He also created us with a body and a soul. The heart or soul also includes emotions that can feel love and have compassion for others, an intellect that can think and reason, and a will that can make healthy choices.

This could only be the product of a personal and a loving God. Love cannot be born out of anything, as Darwin would speculate in his hypotheses. God is love and He only could have created human beings with the awesome capacity to love. (1ˢᵗ John 4:7) **Do not think of yourselves more highly than you ought, but rather think of yourself with sober judgment, in accordance with the measure of faith God has given you. (Romans 12:3)**

It takes courage to trust. Just like any newly acquired skill, it takes practice to build up one's faith. Trial after trial, we learn to trust. I have watched God give me peace when I take the courage to trust. And I experience confusion and anxiety when I do not trust Him. There is a disease called introspection which fights against living with a childlike trust. The sure cure for introspection is reading the Word of God. God will speak to you through the Word. **He called a little child and had him stand among them. And he said: I tell you the truth, unless you change and become like little children, you will**

never enter the kingdom of heaven. Therefore, whoever humbles himself like this child is the greatest in the kingdom of heaven. (Matthew 18:3)

Prayer to Jesus – Declare Your Inheritance with a Heart of Faith

Prepare Your Heart - "Jesus, I humble myself to You. I believe You died for me and rose victoriously on the third day. (1ˢᵗ Peter 1:3) I repent of all sin and ask You to come into my heart and to be the Lord, Savior, and loving authority of my life. Fill me with Your Holy Spirit. I commit to forgive and release all judgment against myself and all who have sinned against me. I receive Your forgiveness and Your grace (loving kindness, unmerited favor, and power). Thank You, Lord Jesus, for Your sacrifice for me."

Enter into Your Father's Presence - "Father God, I enter into Your presence with thanksgiving and with my petitions in the name of Jesus Christ, my Lord, my Savior, and my loving authority." (John 16:23) (Psalm 100:4)

Receive Your New Bloodline Covenant Relationship with Jesus Christ in Jesus' Name

"Jesus, I surrender to You. You are my Lord, my Savior, and my authority. I now stand in covenant relationship with You, O Lord. (Romans 10:9,10)(Hebrews 8:10)(Rom. 10:13)(1ˢᵗ Cor. 11:25) I apply the blood of Jesus to my life and also to my body, my soul, and my spirit.(Heb. 9:14)(Heb. 10:19-22)(Rom.3:25) I have been redeemed, forgiven, and cleansed by Your blood. (1ˢᵗ Peter 1:18,19) (Hebrews 10:19-22) I declare myself saved in Jesus' name. (Romans 10:13) I belong to You, Jesus. (1st Cor. 6:19) I am a part of Your divine bloodline, Lord Jesus. (Romans 11:17) Praise God! I am no longer controlled by any tendencies, iniquities, or bondages from my ancestral bloodline. (1ˢᵗ Corinthians 11:25)(1ˢᵗ John 4:12-15)(Exodus 20:5,6)(Galatians 3:13) I declare, in Jesus' name, that I am cleansed and covered with the blood of Jesus Christ in the secret place of healing, of love, and of protection. (1ˢᵗ Peter 1:18,19)(Hebrews 9:14) (Psalm 91:1)(Isaiah 43:1-4)(Luke 4:18) I am submitted and drawing nearer to You, O God, each day. (James 4:7,8) I receive my inheritance in You, Lord Jesus. (Colossians 1:12)(2ⁿᵈ Peter 1:4) Thank You, Lord Jesus." (1ˢᵗ Thes. 5:18-20)(All scriptures personalized)

"My spirit is invigorated (made alive in Christ) in this divine covenant relationship.(1ˢᵗ Cor.15:22) I have become a new creature because I am now committed in my relationship with You, Lord Jesus.(2ⁿᵈ Cor. 5:17) You live within me.(John 15:5)(John 14:17,20) You are my hope of glory. (Colossians 1:27) You are the lover of my soul.(Isaiah 43:3,4) I am a new creation; the old has gone, the new has come! (2ⁿᵈ Cor.5:17) The Holy Spirit hovers upon me and He lives within me to empower me to do what I cannot do in my own strength. (John 14:17,20) (John 15:1-5)(John 16:13)(Acts 2:38)(Acts 1:8) You, Lord Jesus, Who live in me, are greater than the one who is in the world. (1ˢᵗ John 4:4) You have redeemed me from the curse of the law. You have become a curse for me so that I could receive the promise of the Holy Spirit by faith.(Galatians 3:13,14) I declare that I now receive the promises of eternal life, divine health and healing of my body, mind, and spirit, divine protection, divine provision, and divine prosperity, in Jesus' name, Amen." (John 3:16)(Isaiah 53:3-5) (Luke 4:18) (Psalm 91)(Phil 4:19) (3ʳᵈ John 2)(2ⁿᵈ Peter 1:4)(All scripture personalized)

...being strengthened with all power according to His glorious might so that you may have great endurance and patience, and joyfully giving thanks to the Father, who has qualified you to share in the inheritance of the saints in the kingdom of light. (Colosssians 1:11,12)

Renounce False Responsibility and Unbalanced Grief

My two friends who committed suicide I do miss. I miss my brother who also took his life. However, I am not responsible for their decisions to take their lives. I had to rebuke unbalanced grief and false guilt about their passing. And release my godly grief to the Lord. I miss them and believe they are with Jesus now. They stand in the heavenlies praying for me with the cloud of witnesses. (Hebrews 12:1) I will see them again.

Any unbalanced grief or guilt that takes me from my calling and purpose must be taken control over because it is rooted in a false sense of responsibility and lies about eternal life. I am not responsible for any other persons' decisions, only my own. (John 10:10) This is the truth. The enemy will have a party on you if you do not resist him in this area.

Anything I experienced as trauma, pain, hurt, rejection, abuse, or demonic intrusion as a child through to adulthood was paid for by my Lord Jesus Christ's sacrifice on the cross two thousand years ago. "The punishment (His punishment) that brought us peace was upon Him." (Isaiah 53:5) By faith, I am completely healed of all past abuses and injuries upon my soul because of the sacrifice of Jesus Christ who died to bring wholeness to me; body, mind, and spirit. "Surely He took up our infirmities and carried our sorrows, yet we considered Him stricken by God, smitten by Him, and afflicted.... The punishment that brought us peace was upon Him, and by His wounds we are healed." (Isaiah 53:4,5b) I respect my own life and thank God for it. Because of Jesus Christ, I am alive and well. And I will live my life to the fullest.

We must move away from all unbalanced grief which is worldly sorrow to get to God's work. **Godly sorrow brings repentance that leads to salvation and leaves no regret, but worldly sorrow brings death. (2nd Corinthians 7:10)** We must be wise and discern even our own emotions. My tears of submission, repentance, and forgiveness to the Lord continually cleanse me and bring me closer to Him! My tears that are shed as I cry out to the Lord have restored me to peace, to mental and emotional balance, and to His awesome presence. I celebrate my liberty in Jesus Christ! I celebrate my control over unbalanced worldly grief, self pity, and any emotions that hinder my faith and my joy in the Lord! Anything I subconsciously or psychologically missed as a child has been restored to me at the cross of Calvary through the blood bought sacrifice of Jesus Christ. And I receive it by faith. I cry out to the Lord for His presence within me to help me to accept all the traumas, losses, tragedies, and rejections as "settled." I now embrace my call as His servant to bring others to the Lord.

As my faith grows, I have learned to distinguish between the worldly grief and the godly grief. The anointing of the Lord has empowered me to take control over these emotions by acts of my faith and of my will. The anointing of the Lord has empowered me to release the godly grief to Him in exchange for His peace. The anointing of the Lord has also empowered me to rise up and to petition my Father and to take Jesus' delegated authority in the name of Jesus against the ungodly grief, saying with a heart of faith (submission, repentance, and forgiveness), "You will not rule or reign in my life, in Jesus' name." I do this in exchange for the faith of God which rules and reigns deeper and higher than any emotion.

The Holy Spirit guided me through the valley of Baca (weeping) through His still small voice. **Blessed are those whose strength is in You, who have set their hearts on pilgrimage. As they pass through the Valley of Baca, they make it a place of springs; the autumn rains also cover it with pools. They go from strength to strength, till each appears before God in Zion. (Psalm 84:5-7)** Remember Jesus wept for Lazarus, who had been dead for four days. "Jesus wept." (John 11:35) This was a godly grief which He knew He must first release to His Father. The Holy Spirit brought him a divine peace so that Jesus could then shift into His faith and exercise His gift of healing. Jesus was then enabled to heal Lazarus in the very same day, with a "loud voice!" Remember, it was in the same day that He wept that He also "spoke" with a loud voice, the voice of His human spirit empowered by the Holy Spirit, "Lazarus, come out!" (John 11:43) And Lazarus was raised from the grave!

In this example, Jesus released his deep emotions of grief to His Father so that He could then transition over to speak with a heart of faith, (submission, repentance, forgiveness), from his human spirit to raise Lazarus to life. Jesus knew He had an assignment from God for Lazarus' life. He knew He had to release the godly grief to be able to prioritize faith above even the godly emotions. Then He could also continue in faith to fulfill the assignment He was called to fulfill in the earth from His Father, sacrificing of His life on the cross.

When you have an assignment from God, you must prioritize! We all have a divine purpose in Christ Jesus, to share Jesus Christ the living God with the people that He places in our paths, no matter what occupation we are called to. (Matthew 28:18)(Mark 16:15) When we release and express godly grief in our own lives to the Lord, we are able to rise above the emotions, and resist them and their power over us in faith and in the name of Jesus. We are then empowered by the Holy Spirit to go forward in our call and purpose.

Jesus commissions all his disciples, both when He walked the earth and today.**Then Jesus came to them and said, "All authority in heaven and on earth has been given to me. Therefore go and** make disciples of all nations, baptizing them in the name of the Father and of the Son and of the Holy Spirit, and teaching them to obey everything I have commanded you. And surely I am with you always, to the very end of the age." (Matthew 28:18-20)

Jesus lives within us and grants us the fruits of the Holy Spirit to help us to be more like Him. One of these is self-control. When we surrender to the Lord, we are granted these fruits. So if you suffer from grief that is out of balance, which I had for many years, the Holy Spirit will help you with the fruit of self-control. If it is anger you have trouble with, the Holy Spirit will also help you. Depression is anger turned inward. **But the fruit of the Spirit is love, joy, peace, patience, kindness, goodness, faithfulness, gentleness and self-control. Against such things there is no law. Those who belong to Christ Jesus have crucified the sinful nature with its passions and desires. Since we live by the Spirit, let us keep in step with the Spirit. Let us not become conceited, provoking and envying each other. (Galatians 5:22-25)**

Both the natural and the divine work together. When we use what God has provided us with, a measure of faith and a will that is capable of making healthy decisions, God steps in and blesses us with His part, as in the fruit of self-control. We do our part. God does His part. When we take care of God's business, He intervenes and takes care of ours. It is a two way relationship.

Balance the Emotions and Enter Into the Peace of God

The Words of Jesus Christ, **"The Spirit of the Lord is on me, because He has anointed me to preach good news to the poor. He has sent me to proclaim freedom for the prisoners and recovery of sight for the blind, to release the oppressed, to proclaim the year of the Lord's favor." (Luke 4:18)**

Throughout the healing process, there is a grieving period but the Lord does restore us to a state of maturity in Him where the emotions find balance and are restored to normalcy. "Blessed are those who mourn, for they will be comforted." (Matthew 5:4) You do not have to and should not continually re-live the pain. Once you express and face the root pain, repent and forgive of your part in it, releasing all blame against yourself and others, it is over. The memories are still present, but the pain attached to them is not. Grieve and then leave the pain at the foot of the cross. Go in a different direction. Walk around it. Do whatever it takes to refocus. There is a deeper place of joy in our spirits in thanksgiving to the Lord for what He has done to free us from the world and its deceptions. .

I still have episodes of weeping before the Lord while interceding for others or in the midst of repentance to the Lord. These are spiritual tears. The Holy Spirit blesses me with His presence after tears of submission to Him. This is pleasing to the Lord because this is a godly sorrow from my human spirit. And I have the peace of God afterwards.

However, when I weep over negative circumstances, this is worldly sorrow and seeks to steal my faith and my strength. I refuse to let Satan take control of my emotions. With my will and by faith, I stop myself and take control of the tears. I petition my Father and take Jesus' delegated authority rebuking these emotions as I speak in the name of Jesus. I speak to them with my heart of faith (submission, repentance, and forgiveness). I sometimes use the modality of journaling to write down what the Holy Spirit is saying to me about the person or about the situation. Sometimes, He will give me revelation knowledge about the person or the situation. When the emotions are very strong, I will pray in the Holy Spirit for the person and/or the situation until the burden lifts. And move on as I transfer into the faith mode. **But you, dear friends, build yourselves up in your most holy faith and pray in the Holy Spirit. Keep yourselves in God's love as you wait for the mercy of our Lord Jesus Christ to bring you to eternal life. (Jude 20)**

Unbalanced Grieving Turned Around

My weakness was in the emotional realm of grieving losses, feeling the heart's pains for myself and others, and losing friends and family along the way. We will all be together in heaven. Sometimes I would cry and not even know why I was crying. This was an unbalanced grief that I carried for many years. I later identified it as a spirit of grief that was oppressing me. I did not know I had delegated authority in Christ over this until I went to Victory Bible Institute in Tulsa, Oklahoma. The road does narrow as you walk closer with Jesus. "But small is the gate and narrow the road that leads to life and only a few find it."(Matthew 7:14) **The blessing of the Lord brings wealth, and He adds no trouble (sorrow) to it. (Proverbs 10:22)**

Pray to Silence the Unbalanced Spirit of Grief

Prepare Your Heart - "Jesus, I humble myself to You. I believe You died for me and rose victoriously on the third day. (1st Peter 1:3) I repent of all sin and ask You to come into my heart and to be the Lord, Savior, and loving authority of my life. Fill me with Your Holy Spirit. I commit to forgive and release all judgment against myself and all who have sinned against me. I receive Your forgiveness. Thank You, Lord Jesus, for Your sacrifice for me."

Enter into Your Father's Presence - "Father God, I enter into Your presence with thanksgiving and with my petitions in the name of Jesus Christ, my Lord, my Savior, and my loving authority." (John 16:23) (Psalm 100:4)

Take Jesus' Delegated Authority over the Spirit of Grief, Rebuking It, and Speaking the Word of God over It, in Jesus' Name

"Spirit of grief, I rebuke you, in the name of Jesus. (Luke 10:19)(Mark 16:17)You have no authority in my life.(Matthew 21:27)(Col. 2:10,15) Lord Jesus, You are the Lord and loving authority of my life and of my spirit, my soul, and my body.(Rom. 10:13)(Rom. 10:9,10) Spirit of grief, the blood of Jesus is against you.(Heb. 9:14)(Heb. 10:19-22)(1st Peter 1:18,19)(Rom. 3:25) Go where Jesus sends you to be held captive by the angels of God.(Mark 5:8-13) I am grateful to You, Lord, for what You continue to do and have done in my life.(1st Thes. 5:18-20) I receive Your grace.(Ephesians 2:8,9) I declare that the very presence and power of the Holy Spirit in my spirit breaks the yoke of this bondage in Jesus' name. (Joshua 1:5) (John 15:1-5)(John 14:17,20)(Ezekiel 30:18)(Matthew 11:29,30) As I submit to You, Lord, You continue to empower me by Your Holy Spirit to take control over my emotions. (Acts 2:38)(Acts 1:8) I declare that streams of living water shall flow from within me through the Holy Spirit, in Jesus' name, the name that is above every other name. (John 7:37)(Phil. 2:9)(Ephesians 6:20) I commit to daily study of the Word of God and prayer with praise and worship of You, Lord, to keep my vessel filled. (Luke 11:25-26)(Romans 12:2)(Proverbs 4:20)(James 5:16)(Psalm 33:1-3)(John 4:24) I declare that the anointing of God will break the yoke of the spirit of grief off of me in Jesus' name. Amen." (Ezekiel 30:18)(Matthew 11:29,30)(All scriptures personalized)(See Appendix)

Speak the Word of God to the Unbalanced Grief

"For God did not give me a spirit of timidity, but a spirit of power, of love, and of self-discipline (sound mind). (2nd Timothy 1:7) I will not grieve, for the joy of the Lord is my strength. (Nehemiah 8:10) I rejoice in the grace of God as I rest in His precious promises. (Ephesians 2:8) (2nd Peter 1:4) I rejoice in my salvation, in my divine healing, in my divine protection, and my divine provision and prosperity, which I receive from the Lord my God. (Rom. 10:13)(Isaiah 53:3-5)(Luke 4:18,19)(Psalm 91:1,11)(Phil. 4:19)(3rd John 2) I rejoice in the peace of God that rules in my heart. (Isaiah26:3) For I am called to peace. (Colossians 3:15) (Habakkuk 3:18) I rejoice in the goodness of God that has rescued me out of all evil. (Colossians 1:13) (John 10:10) For I am now a citizen of the kingdom of God's dear Son."(Luke 17:21)(Colossians 1:13)(All scriptures personalized)

Victory Over Unbalanced Grief

Eventually, unbalanced grief lost its control over me. I have chosen to stop myself and pray myself through the unbalanced weeping to bring balance and hope to my sorrow. And the anointing (holy presence) of the Holy Spirit has now destroyed the bondage of the spirit of grief off of me. I offensively press in to take Jesus' delegated authority against it as I petition my Father, speaking with my heart of faith, with submission, repentance, and forgiveness, and in the name of Jesus Christ. I then meditate upon the Word of God and obediently leave sins and idols, severing all ungodly and codependent soul ties and remnants of those ties, and, defiantly pressing into living the sanctified life. And, with a decided act of my will, and by faith, I choose to also rise up and speak with my human spirit to my emotions and gain control over that which tried to destroy me. The human spirit, with the divine help of the Holy Spirit, rises above the fleshly emotions through conscious acts of the will and of faith. The "living waters" of the Holy Spirit now replaces the ungodly and the unbalanced emotions. I praise God for this healing!

Jesus stood and said in a loud voice, "If anyone is thirsty, let him come to me and drink. Whoever believes in me, as the Scripture has said, streams of living water will flow from within him." By this He meant the Spirit, whom those who believed in Him were later to receive. Up to that time the Spirit had not been given, since Jesus had not yet been glorified. (John 7:37-40)

Hope emerges as we realize that we have control over our ungodly emotions with the Holy Spirit ever assisting us. And so we live in deep gratitude for that which the Lord Jesus Christ has prepared for us to receive through His sacrifices for us at Calvary. Living for Christ, we will never be the same. We will always remember what He has provided for us. We are translated out of the darkness and the evil and brought into His marvelous light and into life itself. (Colossians 1:13) The joy of the Lord now becomes our strength. (Neh. 8:10) **To them God has chosen to make known among the Gentiles the glorious riches of this mystery, which is Christ in you, the hope of glory. (Colossians 1:27)**

Unbalanced grief that turns to depression, I believe, is also a result of a person living more in the flesh than in the spirit. When you live connected to the body of Christ and "in Christ," the Holy Spirit empowers you, shields you, and comforts you against the fleshly (worldly) grief. If we continue to sin, living in the flesh with idols and without accountability to others, however, we give the demonic spirits legal access to invade our souls and our bodies. Do not isolate yourself! I learned this lesson many times! The words of Jesus to the disciples, **If you love me, you will obey what I command. And I will ask the Father, and He will give you another Counselor to be with you forever – the Spirit of truth. The world cannot accept Him, because it neither sees Him nor knows Him. But you know Him for He lives in you and will be in you; (John 14:15-17)**

There are other people at the other side of our obedience. **"This day is sacred to the Lord your God. Do not mourn or weep." For all the people have been weeping as they listened to the words of the Law. Nehemiah said, "Go and enjoy choice food and sweet drinks, and send some to those who have nothing prepared. This day is sacred to the Lord. Do not grieve, for the joy of the Lord is your strength." (Nehemiah 8:9,10)**

My Uncle Walter always said, "I never had time to grieve the losses in my life." And, friend, we will see them all again – all those who have gone home to Jesus! So why waste time grieving for those who are in the very face of Jesus Christ? They are praying for us in heaven right now anyway. They are included in the cloud of great witnesses and are dancing before the Lord in another realm altogether. (Hebrews 12:1,2) We also are citizens of heaven as they. (Philippians 3:20)(Ephesians 2:6) We will be joined with them after we finish our race here on the earth. Jesus carried all our sorrows upon Himself at the cross two thousand years ago. (Isaiah 53:4) So why slow down your race here by any needless sorrow? Live your life to the fullest while you have it. **Surely He took up our infirmities and carried our sorrows. (Isaiah 53:4)**

Friend, you can never out give God. When you take care of His business, He will take care of yours. I sought out positive people in the body of Christ and positive activities to redirect me from dwelling on the negatives in my life. My training as a registered nurse was my "saving grace" in life. I was constantly helping others whether in or out of my career. I always was confronted with those less fortunate than I. When I could not nurse, I found other ways to reach out to others. I volunteered my time. I became an evangelist for God even on the streets, helping those less fortunate than I. I told God that every day I would bless Him to thank Him for taking me out of the darkness and the evil and bringing me into His marvelous light and life. (Psalm 145:2)(Colossians 1:13 ref.) **For he has rescued us from the dominion of darkness and**

brought us into the kingdom of the Son He loves, in whom we have redemption, the forgiveness of sins. (Colossians 1:13, 14)

In the Sermon on the Mount, Jesus spoke to the crowd: **Blessed are the poor in spirit, for theirs is the kingdom of heaven. Blessed are those who mourn, for they will be comforted. (Matthew 5:3, 4)**

Prayer to Silence Torment

Prepare Your Heart – "Jesus I humble myself to You. I believe You died for me and rose victoriously on the third day. (1ˢᵗ Peter 1:3) I repent of all sin and ask You to come into my heart and to be the Lord, Savior, and loving authority of my life. Fill me with Your Holy Spirit. I commit to forgive and release all judgment against myself and all who have sinned against me. I receive Your forgiveness. Thank You, Lord Jesus, for Your sacrifice for me."

Enter into the Father's Presence – "Father God, I come boldly into Your presence with thanksgiving in my heart in the name of Jesus Christ, my Lord and my loving authority. I now enter into my Father's presence with my petitions in the name of Jesus Christ." (John 16:23) (Psalm 100:4)

Take Jesus' Delegated Authority over All Torment in Your Life in the Name of Jesus Christ

"Through Your shed blood, Lord Jesus, (1ˢᵗ Peter 1:18,19)(1ˢᵗ Peter 2:24), and the crown of thorns on Your head, (Mark 15:17)((Matthew 27:29)(John 19:2), You conquered the curse of all mental and emotional torment for me. (Luke 4:18,19)(Isaiah 61:1)(Hebrews 10:19)(Galatians 3:13) I believe that You were buried and that You resurrected from the dead. (Luke 23:53)(Luke 24:46)(Matthew 28:6,7) You ascended to the right hand of Your Father and are interceding for me right now, Lord Jesus. (Romans 8:34)(Matthew 26:64)(Luke 24:50-53) You also conquered spiritual death, sin, sickness, and all torment for me. (1ˢᵗ Cor. 15:54,55)(Isaiah 53:3-5)(Col. 2:10,15) Lord Jesus, I believe that You suffered for me so that I could live the abundant life. (John 10:10)(Luke 4:18)(Isaiah 61:1) Thank You, Lord Jesus, for becoming sin for me, for taking my place that I might become the righteousness of God, (living in right standing with You). (Romans 1:16,17) (Romans 10:9,10) (Isaiah 53:4,5) (2ⁿᵈ Corinthians 5:21) I pray, in Jesus' name, Amen." (Phil. 2:9) (All scriptures personalized)

"Now, with my heart of faith, I speak to all tormenting spirits.(Mark 11:23-25)(Matthew 4:4,7,10) I rebuke you and will not allow you to enter my spirit, my body, or my soul; my thoughts, my will, or my emotions, in the name of Jesus Christ, the name that is above every other name. (Luke 10:19) (Phil.2:9) The blood of Jesus is against you, Satan. (Heb. 9:14)(Heb. 10:19-22)(Rom. 3:25) Go where Jesus sends you to be held captive by the angels of God. (Mark 5:8-13) I declare and loose (free) myself from all torment in Jesus' name. (Matthew 16:19)(Matthew 18:18)(Ephesians 6:20) Thank You for total forgiveness and cancellation of the debt and penalty for my sins.(1ˢᵗ John 1:9) You, O Lord, have forgiven and forgotten my sins. (Hebrews 10:16,17) You require no further offering to be made for my sins. (Ephesians 2:8,9) I am fully free and confident to enter into Your presence through the blood of Jesus Christ. (Hebrews 10:19) (Heb. 10:19-22)(Psalm 100:4) I have been purchased with the precious blood of Jesus Christ. (1ˢᵗ Peter 1:18,19)(Hebrews 10:19-22) I will not be moved by the enemy.(Acts 2:25)(1ˢᵗ Cor. 15:58)(Psalm 16:8) You, O Lord Jesus Christ, are my shield, my glory, and the lifter of my head. (Psalm 3:3) You are always before me with Your righteous right hand. (Acts 2:25) I choose to rise above and resist all torment, including worldly grief, worry, self-doubt, lust, false guilt, self-condemnation, anger, strife, fear, self-pity, and all perversions. (James 4:7,8)(2ⁿᵈ Cor. 10:4,5) I enter into Your rest, Lord Jesus. (Matthew 11:28) (Hebrews 4:3, 9-11)) (Romans 8:1,2) I release all my cares and concerns to You, Lord Jesus."(Psalms 55:22)(1ˢᵗ Peter 5:7)(All scriptures personalized)(See Appendix)

"My conscience is clear. (Heb. 9:14) I am covered by the blood of Jesus Christ. (Hebrews 10:19-22) No weapon of any enemy formed against me shall be able to prosper. (Isaiah 54:17) I commit to daily study of the Word of God and prayer with praise and worship to keep my vessel filled with God." (Luke 11:24-26)(Romans 12:2)(Proverbs 4:20)(James 5:16)(Psalm 33:1-3(John 4:24)(All scriptures personalized)(See Appendix)

Mom and Me – Ungodly Behavior Patterns Identified

I Am Sorry Mom

The coming home process began with an apology. God commands us to forgive. As a born again Christian, with the knowledge of the Word of God, I now had the responsibility to humble myself before my family. I remember saying "I am sorry" to Mom upon arrival. I also remember telling her, "I come here in peace. I came here to get my mother and my family back."

The Lord told me I had to take full responsibility for hurting my family and it did not matter how much I was hurt. I am only responsible for my own heart, and making amends to them was part of both my sanctification process and my deliverance. My responsibility to them is to love them as God loves them. **Let no debt remain outstanding, except the continuing debt to love one another, for he who loves his fellow man has fulfilled the law. (Romans 13:8)**

I went through a similar process with my sister, who had been hurt by my activity in the lifestyle and expressed anger toward me for some time. Sometimes we must wait for our loved ones to forgive us. I kept giving her gifts hoping that she would just "be my sister again." But I had to stop trying to buy her love back and wait on God to give her the conviction to forgive me, in God's time. The Word of God says that we are to do all that we are able to do and then "stand." **Therefore put on the full armor of God, so that when the day of evil comes, you may be able to stand your ground, and after you have done everything, to stand. (Ephesians 6:13)**

We cannot buy back someone's love. Reconciliation is a "God thing." We do our part and then wait for Him to work in the other person's heart. In your case, it may be writing a letter, sending a note, or a phone call that will be needed to start the process. Or it may be a season to pray for God's wisdom about the situation of a broken relationship. In any case, we must believe that the Lord will help us to resolve the hurts within our hearts whether or not we are reconciled to the persons. He says He will restore all that the enemy has stolen from us. (Joel 2:25)

Speak Life to Your Loved Ones

God did bless me with three and one-half years of very special <u>and</u> enjoyable time with Mom. We laughed and did so many wonderful things together. Mom is the life of any party and knows how to make everyone laugh. Mom and her friends became my social life. We had dinners together, went to the movies together, and went shopping together. We literally became friends. **No eye has seen, no ear has heard, no mind has conceived what God has prepared for those who love Him. (1st Corinthians 2:9)**

God ordained re-contact and good times with my three brothers, my sister, and the rest of the family. They were precious years and I thank God for them. I finally felt love from my mother that I so desperately needed in my "little girl part." Yes, God was restoring to me what the enemy had stolen through the dark years of practicing the lifestyle. I believe it was this love that I experienced during those years that gave me the courage to later leave and grow up, cutting free of the codependency upon Mom.

It wasn't easy to have a really deep conversation with Mom. A great part of my healing involved speaking life into my mother. The Holy Spirit gave me many opportunities to minister love to her. I remember having dinner with her at our favorite restaurant. In a conversation regarding my past homosexual lifestyle, I said to her, "I had to forgive myself." I looked her squarely in the eyes and I know I ministered to her in that statement as well as myself. Friend, we all have to forgive ourselves for our own mistakes. She always told me, "You have to forgive yourself."

One summer in the late 90's, I remember walking the boardwalk with Mom in Point Pleasant, New Jersey. We used to go there for summer vacations when I was a child. I said to her, "Mom, you are the greatest mother in the world!" On the fourth of July, I decorated her kitchen with colorful sunflower curtains to lift her spirits. This was the anniversary of my father's "home going." He had gone home to the Lord five years earlier. We sat at the kitchen table mostly in silence that day. We watched the Fourth of July celebrations together on television. These were precious times spent together!

Lord Give Me Wisdom

I knew Mom's pain was great after the "home going" of my father and I felt such a tremendous compassion for her. I wanted to be there for her. When living with her in her house, I loved to sing and play the piano for her. I knew it would warm her heart as it did when I was a child. It gave me joy to bring her comfort. It was such a special time wanting to help her through her pain, encouraging her with the music.

Later, I would have to release my care-taking role with her. I began taking on her burdens in an unbalanced way. It affected my mental and emotional health. I believe that this was a result of the codependency and also of an evil spirit that was between us. Many children become their parents' caretakers. This can be detrimental if the boundaries are not correctly set. If the child is not married, it becomes even more difficult to set healthy boundaries.

Later on in my healing process, I was able to share more deeply with Mom. I communicated to her that she "gave me everything." I was trying to convey to her that our relationship was enmeshed. I believe she "got the message" as her answer was, "I wanted to give you what I never had."

Her mom had passed when she was seven years old. Then she followed with this, "Had I let you make more decisions as a child, perhaps you would have made better decisions as an adult." These honest words of my mother brought me a deep healing!

For Such a Time as This – Golden Years of Reconciliation

These three and one-half years were probably the most challenging years of my life. Fresh out of Bible School, I was armed with God's Word as I entered the battleground of facing my past. I was in a born again personal and intimate covenant relationship with my Lord and Savior Jesus Christ. I had received His love, forgiveness, and approval. I knew that I stood in right standing with Him. I was now adopted into the family of God and assured of my covenant inheritance. The Holy Spirit had baptized me with His power and I was now relating to Mom as a free child of the living God.

This did not make me better than Mom. Yet it supernaturally changed the relationship to her at this time. It changed my position. I now saw her with the eyes of Jesus. I was enabled by the Holy Spirit's power within me to minister just what the Lord wanted me to say and do. She shared openly with me about her life and her losses. I listened and felt for her. We laughed. We cried. It was a precious season of my life!

Having the Word of God in me, I knew that I was dealing with the root of my problems. As I learned complete reliance upon the Holy Spirit, I became a prayer warrior for Mom and the family. Demonic influences were ever present to tempt and to destroy this relationship, and I was strong in the Lord against them. I worked daily to keep in covenant relationship with Jesus, staying close to Jesus and His Word with praise, worship, and prayer as well.

There was such a deep love within me for Mom during these years. This love and compassion kept me determined not to give in to the enemy's tricks to spoil the miracle of reconciliation.Coming home after seven years of preparation in Tulsa, Oklahoma, I was walking in a powerful anointing. The presence of God was strong upon me. Because of this, I was able to live with Mom for several months. After that short time, however, I needed to live in my own residence in order to keep rooted in the anointing of Christ's love and power within and upon me.

It is very difficult to keep one's boundaries while living on the home front. We are coming against early childhood patterns of relating. And there are familiar spirits lurking who know our every weakness. No matter how grounded we are in Christ, we must be alert and use wisdom on the home front, especially if our loved ones are not walking in a personal relationship with Jesus Christ.

While living in Dad and Mom's house, I went through some very difficult but healing times. I believe deep hurts of the past surfaced. I went through many grieving periods where I actively forgave as every painful memory surfaced. This purging was truly from the Holy Spirit. I know this because there were blessings of peace from the Holy Spirit after the times of grieving to the Lord. I believe living there brought out some subconscious hurts that I had buried years ago. I believe my heart was reopened to the normal childlike state which I had closed years prior.

Besides our true identity in Christ Jesus, there is also a historical identity we have with our family that the Lord will restore to some of us as we face the childhood pain – whether the people are still living or they are at home with Jesus. As the forgiveness process continues, some of the cherished early memories will resurface. Things you liked about the person you forgave will resurface. You also may identify with them. You may find there are strengths in you that resurface as well. The Lord will restore! (Joel 2:25)

Be Alert to the Plans of the Enemy

It was my very compassion for Mom which opened a door for Satan to enter. Why, you say? In my very compassion and love for her, I became deceived. My identity was fully centered in Christ upon arrival and I worked to keep it so. I came in filled with the Holy Spirit. But, as time progressed and the relationship progressed, the identity I had in Jesus Christ became compromised.

Parental Inversion

I became Mom's burden bearer. I would "feel her pain," and take it home with me after a perfectly wonderful time with her. Without realizing it, I was taking on "parental inversion." Parental inversion is not an easy sin to hate. What is it? It is the identity taken on by a child when a parent is unable or unwilling to fulfill his/her parental role. The parentally inverted child carries the weight of care and responsibility, which should rest on the father or mother. This wounding will drive him/her through childhood into adulthood, where it will reap destruction in the individual and in his/her relationships with other people. **[138]**

Friend, I must stress that the patterns of relating of both parties were never intentionally formed to hurt either party. Many of these patterns form without our conscious realization of them.

Now I am ready to visit you for the third time, and I will not be a burden to you, because what I want is not your possessions but you. After all, children should not have to save up for their parents, but parents for their children. (2ⁿᵈ Corinthians 12:14)

Parental inversion includes identities taken on by children in homes where one or both parents are absent or ineffective as a result of death, divorce, sin, or immaturity. The child tries to take responsibility, to fill the gap, unconsciously usurping the parental role: sometimes even consciously displacing a failing parent. **[139]**

One of the fruits of parental inversion is tremendous fear. The child believes, "If I stop doing what I'm doing, my family's lives (my life, the world) . . . will fall apart. It will be my fault." This is the primary motivating factor behind the need to control. Parental inverters have difficulty trusting God and see God as needing help. However, they see their role as "noble." Parental inverters have a sense of pride. They are "noble martyrs." **[140]**

I had to look at my own heart. While feeling "needed" by Mom and taking the role of "Mom's helper," I unconsciously assumed an improper position of authority and purpose. I was actually stealing from Mom her God-given role as a mother. After years of being away from my brothers and my sister, I started to pick up the "mother role" that I had assumed as a child, which now manifested in the "evangelist's" role. Without realizing it, I was also playing the "noble martyr" in this role. I would share the Lord with them, but I needed to let go and let the Holy Spirit convict them. We plant the seed of God's Word and the Holy Spirit brings forth the harvest. (Gal. 6:7) **Do not be deceived: God cannot be mocked. A man reaps (receives) what he sows (gives). (Galatians 6:7)** As a noble martyr, I was playing a role of caretaker, but I needed healing myself. You cannot give what you do not have.

I felt a false sense of responsibility for them and this brought me concern that belonged at the foot of the cross. After all, I had helped Mom raise my brothers and my sister when I was a child. My love and compassion for them is very deep. They are all adults now and responsible for their own lives. I had to relinquish this false responsibility and place Jesus back on the throne of my life and let God be God in theirs as well. **Cast your cares on the Lord and He will sustain you; (Psalm 55:22)**

I did, however, have the opportunity to share Jesus with all of them and I thank God for the opportunity. I believe that my balance of this role of evangelist was incorrect. It is difficult with family to find this balance when you want with all your heart for them to be saved. Only the Holy Spirit can convict and change another person. Our job is to share the gospel. It is then the work of the Holy Spirit to convict. My motive was pure but my position was incorrect. I needed to share the Lord and then let the Holy Spirit take over the job of convicting their hearts. .

Subconsciously, I was jealous of Mom's role as the mother. Having no children of my own, my heart became wicked. Did I consciously realize this? Of course not! Friend, I was so concerned for my sister's welfare that I actually kept myself from potential mates, with the desire to be available to her if she needed me later in life. I had to repent of this and give her over to the care of God. Again, I was taking on a false sense of responsibility. In taking on this role, I did not even look at my own needs or issues. It, like all other sins, kept me from my need for God because I again was helping God to do His job. The helper role led me right into an idol, my own family and a prideful heart. I needed to go forward in my life and pray for my family, but not assume responsibility for their lives and/or their decisions. (Exodus 20:5,6)

Now I understand why the Lord pulled me away from the "enabler's role." I had to let go and "go on" with my own life first. My role is and must remain as a servant of the Lord. My purpose is to spread His Word to others. I had to get myself back with my focus on Jesus and my own deliverance. Sometimes He takes us out to bring us in.

Every time we separated, I prayed and believed that God would make a way for me to see Mom and family again. The hardest part of the separations was embracing the time to work through my own heart lessons. Many of my homosexual relationships involved partners who were either drug addicts or alcoholics. This I see now was an outflow of the "noble martyr role" I assumed as a child. Perfectionism was also an outgrowth of the "noble martyr" role. In both examples, I was "taking care" of someone or something. I felt that my help was essential to the success of either the partners in the relationships or of the clients in the nursing profession.

A condition created when a parent relies inappropriately on a child of the opposite or same sex is called "substitute mate." The parent is seeking emotional support, gives the child the role of "confident," and, in the worst of cases, sleeps with the child in an incestuous relationship. This is a more serious form of parental inversion. The symptoms of this are the same as those for parental inversion. [141]

Healing from these ungodly relationships requires recognition of the condition. There must be confession for judgments against parents, for judging God as weak, and for the sin of usurpation. To usurp is to seize and hold in possession by force or without right. [142] There must also be forgiveness for what parents did or did not do in parenting. This is a daily discipline until fully accomplished in the heart. This requires time away from the childhood patterns and the familiar setting of the home as we "go on" in our lives.

Healing also requires a prayer to bring to death on the cross the structure of parental inversion and its accompanying practices. Then there is teaching involved in learning to walk a "new way." Teaching about "biblical" parenting and marital relationships is important. The person has a lack of understanding from childhood. The person must give up trying to control parents, spouse, and coworkers. The believer must learn to let parents, spouse, and co-workers be responsible for their own issues. As the parents are forgiven, changes in behavior will follow, taking away the driving force behind behaviors with other primary people. [143]

In balancing relationships, I had to mentally detach and consciously discipline myself against the driving forces until I had completed the heart work. In prayer, then, I consciously repented of my sins, my judgments, and my ungodly roles in these relationships. I released my family members to the care of God. I forgave Mom and repented for judging her, for judging God as weak, and for the usurping, (taking without a legal right), her role. By faith, I forgave myself for my part in this dilemma. I humbly asked the Lord to help me to accept the circumstances as they were. However, I continued to pray for change to come for my family for their salvation, divine protection, divine healing, and divine provision; for God to open their spiritual eyes and hearts to the truth of the gospel. (Luke 24:31,45) (See Appendix) I asked God to change and to balance my mercy gift, to remove the false guilt of the parental inverter, the false pride of the noble martyr, and the need to play God. I prayed for my trust in God to be increased. **Trust in the Lord with all your heart and lean not on your own understanding; in all your ways acknowledge him, and he will make your paths straight. (Proverbs 3:5,6)**

When I pray for Mom and family, I am released from the worries associated with my ungodly roles as the noble martyr, as the parental inverter, and from my false sense of responsibility. I believe that God is sovereign and has control, dominion, and power in every person's life situation. And, as I daily learn to trust God, He blesses me with His rest. And the driving lying spiritual force has to flee because it cannot live in the rest of God.

If you have the mercy gift, you may be prone to these relational bondages. It is my love for people without healthy boundaries that placed me in these roles. True love demands respect and it commands healthy boundaries. Attempting to form healthy boundaries in relationships where enmeshment has formed since early childhood is very difficult. It may require family counseling sessions.

No matter how I feel about the authority figures in my family, I must still respect their position. Even though I am in my adult years, the honor I must express to my mother and father is a command from the Lord. We must ask the Holy Spirit for the strategy to keep that honor and respect, no matter what the circumstances are. **"Honor your father and mother – which is the first commandment with a promise – that it may go well with you and that you may enjoy long life on the earth." (Ephesians 6:2)**

Leave and Heal

I could not judge Mom for this as the Lord Jesus Christ is the judge of all men and women. I did go to my mother and ask her about the tarot cards I found in the kitchen. She said she did not use them, that they were a door prize from a party she went to. She also did not believe in the devil, so she did not know her enemy. Also, I had friends in the gay lifestyle that played with tarot cards. I renounced, repented, and turned from all my New Age/occult activity with a Spirit filled counselor. I removed all related materials from my person and from my dwelling. **When we are judged by the Lord, we are being disciplined so that we will not be condemned with the world. (1ˢᵗ Corinthians 11:31,32)**

I spoke and rebuked the demonic spirits in a fleshly anger, not a holy anger. I also had unrepented sin. Friend, I was too close to the situation emotionally to pray correctly and in faith. I also did not have legal authority to pray to cast out any demons there. Thus both I and my family members were recipients of enemy harassment and retaliation as a result of praying in my flesh, because of my unrepented sins, which kept me out of submission to Jesus' authority, and also because of my illegal status. We must pray in faith. We must have a repentant heart to be under the Lord's authority to then take it successfully. And we must have legal authority to pray to cast out demons with Jesus' delegated authority. (Luke 11:24-26)(See Appendix)

I had no legal authority to cast out any spirits in my mother's house. The people there were not under my legal authority. And they were not asking for warfare prayers. They were not born again or filled with the Word of God. Therefore, praying warfare prayers illegally would have given the enemy access to our souls. (Luke 11:24-26) Any prayers to cast out spirits against the will of the people who lived in the house would bring reprucussions of seven more spirits in to reinvade their vessels and mine as well. (Luke 11:24-26)(See Appendix)

When an evil spirit comes out of a man/woman, it goes through arid places seeking rest and does not find it. Then it says, 'I will return to the house I left.' When it arrives, it finds the house swept clean and put in order. Then it goes and takes seven other spirits more wicked than itself, and they go in and live there. And the final condition of that man is worse than the first. (Luke 11:24-26) This is why we commit to the Word of God, prayer, praise, and worship to keep our vessels filled with God and to keep the enemy out. (See Appendix)

Remember, Jesus could do no miracles in His hometown. We must recognize our limitations. **Jesus said to them, "Only in His hometown, among His relatives and in His own house is a prophet without honor." He could not do any miracles there, except lay His hands on a few sick people and heal them. And He was amazed at their lack of faith. (Mark 6:4-6)**

I could have bound, gagged, and muted the demonic spirits, but not cast them out.(Matthew 18:18) We must respect the enemy but not fear him. These are the words of Jesus, **'I tell you the truth, whatever you bind on earth will be bound in heaven, and whatever you loose on earth will loosed in heaven.' (Matthew 18:18)**(See Appendix)

There may have been some occult activity in my mother's house, but I cannot be sure and I am not Mom's judge. I did, however, confront her with love. I verbally asked her to get rid of the tarot cards and also wrote her a letter of confrontation, being sure to tell her that I myself was also deceived in the same area of the New Age/occult, and that Jesus loves us. However, He hates sin and any idols that take us from His first place in our lives. I stressed His love for her and His wanting for her to reach out to welcome Jesus into her heart and to make Him Lord and Savior of her life in an intimate and personal covenant relationship. **If a brother (sister, mother, and father) sins against you, go and show him (her), his (her) fault, just between the two of you. If he (she) listens to you, you have won your brother (sister, mother, and father) over. But if he (she) will not listen, take one or two others along, so that every matter may be established by the testimony of two or three witnesses. (Matthew 18:15,16)**

As the Holy Spirit leads, our responsibility is to lovingly confront others, without judgment. The Lord is the judge. I know by experience there were demon spirits in the house. Territorial spirits is a whole other subject. They may have been present before we even moved into the house. I don't know. I may have been hallucinating. I do not think so. I believe that I was perceiving demonic voices from the spirit realm. It was all very real to me. I just left with love for my mother, in obedience to the Lord's voice, and with wise counsel from Spirit filled counselors as well as my Pastor's advice. I encourage strong Spirit filled counsel if you are considering separations and/or severance of family ties. **Do not judge, and you will not be judged. Do not condemn, and you will not be condemned. Forgive, and you will be forgiven. Give and it will be given to you. (Luke 6:37)**

Our Struggle is against Spiritual Principalities, Not against People

Had I not placed Mom's words higher than God's Word, had I not played the role of caretaker in my noble martyr role, where I was playing God, had I been further along in my own healing, without the need to please, without the idol of perfectionism, and had I had a witness, I would been able to be more effective. I would have kept my confidence in God and I would have petitioned my Father and taken my delegated authority in Christ with a heart properly positioned in faith, in submission to my Lord, and Savior, with repentence and forgiveness. I would have prayed correctly gagging and muting demon spirits, not illegally casting them out from the people who were not asking for prayer. (See Appendix)

I believe that since I was living with right intentions, however, God honored the seeds I planted into many lives. We never know the full amount of our harvest. The Holy Spirit never left me in this assignment. He helped me as I brought many people who were relatives and/or friends of the family to the Lord before the Lord took them home. I know I did the best I could do at the time. However, I had to seek God and turn within my own heart to seek my own healing. I had to resubmit my life and my heart back to Jesus.

My responsibility was to ask the Holy Spirit what my next step was. I relied on the Word of God and listened for the Holy Spirit's direction. I stood on Ephesians 6:12, "For our struggle is not against flesh and blood, but against the rulers, against the authorities, against the powers of this dark world and against the spiritual forces of evil in the heavenly realms." This scripture served as a battle ax against Satan's lure to try to deceive and bring me to a bitter heart against my mother. No matter what the circumstances, my friend, you must not judge or blame anyone else or the curse will not be broken over your life or anyone else's lives. It is when we come to Jesus in surrender, receive Him as Lord and authority, repent of our sins, forgive and release all judgment against ourselves and others, and obey the Lord, leaving all sins and idols, that the curse is broken over our own lives. It was broken two thousand years ago, but it is our responsibility to reach out and take that deliverance in order to receive the true freedom we have in Christ Jesus.

We come away with thanksgiving for His sacrifice for us. We come away standing with Him as Lord and best friend both with us and for us. We come away as new creatures in Christ Jesus, with a life of service to Him to share with others what the Lord has done in our lives. (2nd Cor. 5:17) Then we can become effective prayer intercessors for others with our hearts of faith.We can then stand in the gap for them for their salvation first, for their healing, and for their divine protection and provision as we boldly declare every demon spirit to be bound, muted, and gagged from operating in their lives, (Matthew 18:18) (Luke 11:24-26) in Jesus' name.(See Appendix)

It is the Lord Jesus Christ who has already broken the curse when He shed His blood for us. Jesus took the curse away from us two thousand years ago. (Isaiah 53:3-5) (Galatians 3:13) (Hebrews 10:19-22) But we live in a fallen world. And our part in receiving our freedom is declaring what God has already done for us by the precious blood of Jesus Christ. We believe that this mountain that is in our way will be removed as we speak to it and believe without doubting that God will act on our behalf. And obedience to the Lord's commands keeps us in the blessing. (Deuteronomy 28) We strive to live a holy life to humbly and graciously receive the blessings of God.

We make a mistake when we, through the flesh, try to straighten out someone who is causing us problems because the problem is not that person but the spirit that is driving that person. When we can't handle a situation ourselves, we can also glory in the fact that we can't correct the situation and trust God's anointing to come upon us at the appropriate time. When God's anointing comes, then we are well able, because His grace is sufficient. In Ephesians 6:10, Paul said, "Be strong in the Lord and in the power of His might." Not strong in yourself, not strong in your own fleshly impulses, but strong in the Lord, and in the power of His might, which is His anointing. Paul – through his weakness – became strong in the Lord by depending on the anointing of the Holy Spirit within him. **[144]**

I remained in the respectful position to Mom and the family, even though I had to leave and heal myself. Standing in prayer for Mom and my family served to keep my heart in the offensive side of the love walk and in that honor for them with unconditional love and forgiveness, with no blame! I could not heal in the home environment. I also could not heal if I were still connected to any lesbian relationships. I left in both arenas and resisted any temptations to judge any person.(See Appendix)

The Lord confirmed the decision by His still small voice in April of 2007, in which He spoke to me, "Leave the land," and I did obey. It was at this time that I launched back to Tulsa, Oklahoma, for restoration and healing of my heart, and transformation of my mind back to the Word of God. Obedience is better than sacrifice. It was the most difficult yet the most important decision of my life, next to accepting Jesus Christ as my Lord, my Savior, and my authority. **But Samuel replied: "Does the Lord delight in burnt offerings and sacrifices as much as in obeying the voice of the Lord? To obey is better than sacrifice, and to heed is better than the fat of rams. For rebellion is like the sin of divination, and arrogance like the evil of idolatry. Because you have rejected the word of the Lord, He has rejected you as king." (1st Samuel 15:22,23)**

My prayer was for the Lord to provide an opportunity for Mom and me to reconnect. When I became stronger in my walk with the Lord, then I believed that season would come. And I would know by the leading of the Holy Spirit. That opportunity did come four years later in 2010, and I was grateful for it. I was in a stronger place in the Lord and was able to minister to her. The Lord also confirmed to me that this truly was spiritual warfare, and not anyone's fault! **Do not judge, and you will not be judged. Do not condemn, and you will not be condemned. Forgive, and you will be forgiven. Give and it will be given to you. A good measure, pressed down, shaken together and running over, will be poured into your lap. For with the measure you use, it will be measured to you. (Luke 6:37, 38)**

Satan is a liar but he does have a certain amount of power. He will do all he can to take us from our faith and love for Jesus Christ. He wants our position also, which is sitting at the right hand of the Father with Jesus. **But because of His great love for us, God who is rich in mercy, made us alive with Christ, even when we were dead in transgressions – it is by grace you have been saved. And God raised us up with Christ and seated us with Him in the heavenly realms in Christ Jesus, in order that in the coming ages He might show the incomparable riches of His grace, expressed in His kindness to us in Christ Jesus. (Ephesians 2:4-7)**

Fasting and Speaking the Word in Prayer Changes the Circumstances

Always consult with your physician before fasting if you have any medical or health related conditions or issues, are pregnant or lactating, or are taking any medications. I knew that my home situation was a spiritual battle and required prayer. The vision of Daniel the prophet is an excellent example to us that heavenly battles are changed by our prayers. There are spiritual wars in the heavenlies that are forged between demonic and angelic beings.

As Daniel fasted and prayed for twenty-one days, he was visited by an angel who touched him and gave him strength. The angel reveals to Daniel that the answer to his prayers was detained because he was resisted by demonic forces in the heavenlies. But God sent Michael the Archangel to this angel to help him. **"Do not be afraid, Daniel. Since the first day that you set your mind to gain understanding and to humble yourself before your God, your words were heard, and I have come in response to them. But the prince of the Persian kingdom resisted me twenty-one days. Then Michael, one of the chief princes, came to help me, because I was detained there with the king of Persia. Now I have come to explain to you what will happen to your people in the future, for the vision concerns a time yet to come. (Daniel 10: 12-14)**

Do not be discouraged or deceived, friend. There is nothing that God cannot do. There is no Antichrist spirit, no generational spirit, no ancestral spirit, no territorial spirit, no familiar spirit, or any other demonic spirit that can win in their attempts against you. Nothing has the ability to separate us from the love of God. (Romans 8:39) Greater is He within us than He that is in the world. (1st John 4:4) You may not see the manifestation yet, but continue to pray in the midst of your circumstances and not only will your faith grow in Jesus Christ, but also your prayers of faith will touch the heart of God and turn the situation around both for you and for those for whom you pray. Lives and souls are at stake. This is spiritual warfare and prayer is our ammunition against Satan's attacks upon us and our loved ones. Jesus placed his hand on John in the book of revelation; **"Do not be afraid. I am the First and the Last. I am the Living One; I was dead, and behold I am alive forever and ever! And I hold the keys of death and Hades."** **(Revelation 1:17,18)**(See Appendix)

Silence against Making Slanderous Accusations Blesses the Heart of God

In the book of Job and Daniel, there are examples of keeping silent. The silence was kept, in Job's case, from making complaints or accusations against God for his losses. And God blessed him at the end of his life. Daniel refrained from making any accusations or complaints against King Darius, who sentenced him to the lion's den. And, because of his silence and his trust in God to deliver him through, he was released from the lion's den and he gained favor with the King.

These are the words of King Darius to the peoples, nations, and men of every language throughout the land of the Medes and the Persians: **May you prosper greatly! I issue a decree that in every part of my kingdom people must fear and reverence the God of Daniel. For He is the living God and He endures forever; His kingdom will not be destroyed, His dominion will never end. He rescues and He saves; He performs signs and wonders in the heavens and on the earth. He has rescued Daniel from the power of the lions." (Daniel 6:26,27)**

However, the Word of God tells us to pray without ceasing. We are never to refrain from prayer! The spoken Word of God carries power against the enemy. Remember that Jesus, after He was baptized by John the Baptist, was filled with the Holy Spirit. Led by the Holy Spirit, He spoke to the devil when He was tempted in the desert. He spoke the Word of God against his slanderous accusations saying, "It is written," three times. (Luke 4)(Matthew 4)(Scriptures referenced) He believed that what He said would bring Him results. **Be alert and always keep on praying for all the saints. (Ephesians 6:18)**(See Appendix)

Prayer Moves the Hand of God

After Solomon had finished the temple, the Lord actually appeared to him at night and said:

"If my people, who are called by my name, will humble themselves and pray and seek my face and turn from their wicked ways, then will I hear from heaven and will forgive their sin and will heal their land." (2ⁿᵈ Chronicles 7:14)

Judge Not!

I knew by faith that Christ in me had greater power over the enemy that was lurking in the environment. I could not blame Mom, Dad, or even myself. I refused to place blame on anyone as this would give Satan just what he wanted for me, a bitter heart. God did not ordain me as anyone's judge, only my own. Whenever we judge others, our judgment returns back upon us. When we judge ourselves, the Lord will be pleased as He will not have to correct or chastise us.

Does God sometimes chasten His people through sickness? Decidedly yes! When we disobey God, sickness may be permitted, through the Father's loving discipline. But God has told us just how it may be avoided and averted. "If we would judge ourselves, we should not be judged. But when we are judged, we are chastened of the Lord, that we should not be condemned with the world" (1ˢᵗ Cor. 11:31–32). These chastenings come to save us from final judgment. When we see the cause of the chastening, and turn from it, God promises it shall be withdrawn. As soon as "we judge ourselves" or learn our lesson, the absolute promise is "we shall not be judged." By self-judgment we may avoid chastening. Divine healing is not unconditionally promised to all Christians, regardless of their conduct. It is for those who believe and obey. "All the paths of the Lord are mercy and truth unto such as keep His covenant and His testimonies." (Psalm 25:10) [145] The words of Jesus in Revelation: **Those whom I love I rebuke and discipline. So be earnest, and repent. Here I am! I stand at the door and knock. If anyone hears my voice and opens the door, I will come in and eat with him, and he with me. (Revelation 3:19, 20)**

Instead of judging Mom, I wrote her a letter. I spoke to her in love and used the Word of God to educate her in an area I believe she was deceived. People suffer from lack of knowledge. (Hosea 4:6) We do need to speak the truth of the Word of God in love. (Hebrews 4:12). Then it is up to them to accept or reject it as the Holy Spirit convicts their hearts. **Make every effort to live in peace with all men and to be holy; without holiness no one will see the Lord. See to it that no one misses the grace of God and that no bitter root grows up to cause trouble and defile many. (Hebrews 12:14,15)**

Whatever your situation is, I just encourage you to look within your heart and let Jesus heal you first before asking God to use you on the home front. I believe this is the most difficult place to minister. If He sends you home, He will provide for you and protect you. If and when the season is over, obey Him. Whenever God guides, He provides. **"I tell you the truth," He continued, "No prophet is accepted in his hometown." (Luke 4:24)**

Godly discernment, however, should only serve to bring us to our knees in prayer for our loved ones. For we all are sinners. I noticed that as I became more submitted to Jesus, other people became softer to me. As I changed, it seemed that others around me changed. It really is not a cut and dry situation. There are many mixed emotions in this relationship between mother and daughter. All I know is, as I continue as my mother's daughter, that I must honor her in all that I do and say. And I trust that God will do what needs to be done, no matter how impossible I may think it is. (See Appendix)

I know that Jesus still performs miracles even today. My job is to obey the leading of the Holy Spirit and to look within my own heart and to change that which needs changing within me. Only as we change do the people around us change. Our mindset changes as we draw closer to truth. The things that distracted us before are no longer distractions but they become springboards from which we can share the love of God.

Now to Him who is able to do immeasurably more than all we ask or imagine, according

to His power that is at work within us, to Him be glory in the church and in Christ Jesus throughout all generations, forever and ever! Amen. (Ephesians 3:20)

It's No One's Fault!

See that no one is sexually immoral, or is godless like Esau, who for a single meal sold his inheritance rights as the oldest son. Afterward, as you know, he wanted to inherit this blessing, he was rejected. He could bring about no change of mind, though he sought the blessing with tears. (Hebrews 12:16,17)

Edom sold the birthright, so he obviously didn't think that the blessing was too important. Later he wanted to murder Jacob for what he had done. "It's Jacob's fault! It's Mama's fault!" He was so wrapped up in his self-pity that he never realized that godly repentance would remove his fault and change the situation! **[146]**

The instant you repent of your sins, the curse is broken. But as long as you cop out, as long as you dump the blame on everybody else and what you think they've done to you, then the curse will not be broken in your life. [147]

Judge Myself Only

I have learned the greatest lesson in all of this. For every deception I diagnosed on someone else, there is also another deception in which I am blinded. My homosexuality and perfectionism are just as much a deception as any sin I could judge in Mom or in anyone else. The Bible is true when it says, **Do not judge and you will not be judged. Do not condemn, and you will not be condemned. Forgive, and you will be forgiven. (Luke 6:37)**

The Lord spoke to the prophet Isaiah, **"If you do away with the yoke of oppression, with the pointing finger and malicious talk, and if you spend yourselves in behalf of the hungry and satisfy the needs of the oppressed, then your light will rise in the darkness, and your night will become like the noonday." (Isaiah 58:9,10)**

Sabbath Rest of God

There remains, then, a Sabbath-rest for the people of God; for anyone who enters God's rest also rests from his own work, just as God did from His. Let us, therefore, make every effort to enter that rest, so that no one will fail by following their example of disobedience. (Hebrews 4:9-11) Do you see why it is so important to leave the codependent relationships where your role as "savior," "helper," "enabler," or "partner" masks the "honest self" in the lesbian and the gay relationships? In my case, I had an ungodly soultie to my mother. It was codependent and there was an evil spirit between us due to the bloodline curse. We become blinded by what we think is love, when the gay relationship really is a hiding place for the broken heart. One person cannot heal another person's broken heart. Only Jesus can heal our hearts. My mother was my emotional fix. My gay girlfriends were the same. These relationships were codependent and temporary fixes as well as idols and sins against God. The real healing of the heart can only come through intimacy with Jesus. When we come to a stopping point with the sins and idols, Jesus is there. Only Jesus and His love can truly fill the empty places in our hearts.

The real healing can only be worked through in facing and identifying the root pains and issues, repenting of our sins and our ungodly reactions to the sins committed against us, and forgiving ourselves and all who have sinned against us with the help of the Lord and Spirit-filled counselor(s). When we do our part in the healing process and submit our lives, hearts, and wills to Jesus in an intimate relationship with Him, He heals our wounds. He takes up residence within us and replaces the empty places in our hearts with His love, acceptance, and forgiveness.

With humility and submission to the Lordship of Jesus Christ follows an ability to receive His love. When we truly submit to the Lordship and authority of Jesus Christ, repent, forgive, obey, and change, we emerge into the "honest self." His presence, power, and His Word changes us and the masks are removed. We become honest and transparent before Him and other people. We then receive the full blessing of God's grace, power, and loving-kindness in our lives. His voice becomes clear to us. We receive from the Lord and our confidence returns. There is nothing to hide from Him or prove to Him when we are honest with Him. It is an awesome transformation!

God blessed me in Tulsa, Oklahoma with a whole new lifestyle of Christianity. This brought me a joy and a peace I had never experienced. When I decided to leave homosexuality, I left by faith alone because the emotions would have kept me there. When I decided to leave perfectionism, I left full-time managerial nursing positions.

After the home going of my earthly father in 1992, I was blessed with a private duty job taking care of a little baby girl in Tulsa. The joys of caring for this child comforted me in ways I cannot explain. God always blessed me with spiritual children in the nursing profession, in music teaching, in babysitting positions, and in the ministry. **Sing, O barren woman, you who never bore a child; burst into song, shout for joy, you who were never in labor; because many are the children of the desolate woman than of her who has a husband, says the Lord. (Isaiah 54:1)**

The Holy Spirit knew what He was saying when He kept telling me to leave my full time nursing job. And Joanne, my counselor at L.I.F.E. Ministries in New York City, knew what she was saying when she said, "Do what you do well and do your best in it." [148] I believed the Lord would eventually lead me into full time ministry. **Not that I have already attained all this, or have already been made perfect, but I press on to take hold of that for which Christ Jesus took hold of me. (Philippians 3:12)**

Pastor Demola always helped me when I really needed a word from God. He expressed to the congregation one week, "When we sin, we call it a mistake. When someone else sins, it is blasphemy!" [149] Oh, the conviction I felt in those words! Who was I to judge Mom? I had my own sins against God. God does not measure sin. Who was I? I was wrong. I would only become that which I judged. When the judgments were brought to the cross, I found that I was a lot like my mother in much strength of personality and of integrity.

Coming to this truth within myself started me on the road to victory over the sins of homosexuality and then of perfectionism. In exposing the devil's lie by humbly confessing to another Christian, I was granted a compassion now for Mom. This was the beginning of a new way of loving and relating to her. Even though I did sever the tie with Mom, the Lord opened a short window of time to reopen communication and close it again. In two short phone calls, my heart opened and the Lord allowed closure with her and her with me as well. I shared the Word of God and my love for her via the mail until the Lord directed me to stop. The burden has been lifted and I believe the Lord answered my prayers and blessed me with the reconnection because of my obedience to make Him first in my life and to commit to pray for my family. (See Appendix)

When you take care of God's business, He takes care of yours!

Discernment is Not Judgment – Living by Faith

Because we have so much unresolved hurt within our own souls, our wounded "little girl" or "little boy" can become our worst enemy! The sadness that comes with the wounding can deceive and thus distract us from faith for the healing of our own wounds. It can cause insecurity in us that will drive us into a judgmental and controlling attitude against ourselves and others. We must ask the Holy Spirit to assist us to rise above that sadness, the judgments, and the need for control. Yielding to the Lordship and authority of Jesus brings the sadness into the proper perspective. Releasing the sadness breaks through the invisible concrete wall we have built. Humility before Him replaces the sadness with His joy. And His anointing and His presence will eventually break this yoke of bondage. We press into taking our part in forgiving ourselves and others and learning to yield our burdens over to the Lord. We believe God to take care of all that concerns us. Praising Him will break through the sadness. And the "living waters" (John 7:37) of the anointing of God will bring us the "joy of the Lord." (Nehemiah 8:10)

Humble yourselves before the Lord, and He will lift you up. (James 4:10)

These are the words of Jesus, **"Come to me, all you who are weary and burdened, and I will give you rest. Take my yoke upon you and learn from me, for I am gentle and humble in heart, and you will find rest for your souls. For my yoke is easy and my burden is light." (Matthew 11:28-30)**

Jesus died and resurrected for us. Faith in His sacrifice for us overrules any sadness we feel. When we take our eyes off of ourselves and onto His sacrifice for us, His loving presence with us, and His love for us, we become overpowered by His presence and faith replaces the negative emotions. When we live by faith and not by how we feel, the anointing or the presence of God covers us and the emotions are balanced by a deeper and a stronger force – our faith. He was "a man of sorrows and familiar with suffering." (Isaiah 53:3) **By faith, we will rise up from the pain when we experience His presence in our lives in gratitude to Him. He took our place on a cross at Calvary. We will turn it around by walking in love and giving to other hurting people.**

The enemy wants us to live by the wounded feelings, and not by faith. Yet it is our faith in Jesus Christ who loves us that will bring healing to these wounds. It is at these times when despair and discouragement come that we must rise up with a heart of faith with submission, repentance, and forgiveness in our hearts. And cry out to the Lord and say, "I believe that you are with me now, Jesus!" or just say, "Father!" And then, stop and listen to His voice, "I love you. I am with you. Do not be discouraged." Prayer meetings at my church have been a godsend, taking my bleeding emotional wounds to the very throneroom of God, interceding for my abusers.(See Appendix)

There comes a critical point in the healing process where the wounded child has to be courageous enough to say, **"I am wrong to judge any person no matter how hurt this child inside of me was or still is." The only way the homosexual struggler will resolve the defensive detachment problem in homosexuality is to look on the hated mother or father figure with love and compassion. The homosexual struggler must look within his/her own heart and deal directly with the wounds of childhood. And it is imperative to see and accept that the enemy is Satan and his influence upon the mother and/or father figure, upon the abusers, upon the generational bloodline, and upon the struggler as well. This is where hate and apathy is correctly redirected. Satan is the enemy, not "flesh and blood." And the enemy has been defeated through the blood of Jesus Christ. We must reach out with faith, take the resolution for the homosexual struggle, and receive the healing of Jesus Christ.**

It is the "hurting child" who lives by the felt emotions of the pain, the depression, the apathy, the anger, the inferiority, the bitterness, and the hate. It is the "victorious man or woman of Christ" who chooses to rise above the emotions and chooses godly compassion without compromise. He or she stands in intercession praying for the very people who have caused the harm. **For our struggle is not against flesh and blood, but against the rulers, against the authorities, against the powers of this dark world and against the spiritual forces of evil in heavenly realms. (Ephesians 6:12)(See Appendix)**

I learned that the only way to look on the mother or the father figure with compassion is to look within myself and repent of my own sins. I saw myself as a sinner also, so how could I judge anyone? In doing that, I then was able to see what loving parents I really had. Then and only then could I face my own emotions with honesty, work through them, and not be ruled by them anymore. I also saw many of my strengths and weaknesses as similar to theirs.

I became a prayer warrior for them.Intercessory prayer warriors pray for the nations. Mrs. Freda Lindsay spoke for the Generals of Intercession meeting in 1986. She is a powerhouse for God. Her husband, Gordon Lindsay, who is now with the Lord, was a great man of prayer who has influenced people all over the world. She quoted him at this meeting: **"Every man ought to pray at least one violent prayer every day." "And I think" she added, "that he had the world's record for praying the most violent prayers!" She cited the guideline of Matthew 11:12: "And from the days of John the Baptist until now the kingdom of heaven suffers violence, and the violent take it by force."** [150](See Appendix)

Subdue the Obsessive Compulsive Thoughts – God
Rewards Obedience with a New Momentum

New ways of thinking and behaving would replace the addictive and compulsive cycles and behaviors. Honesty and humility before God would allow me to receive the grace of God and this would carry me through every trial. I would replace the thoughts with the Word of God and realize what beliefs I held that were lies. I would stand in awe of God.

Once you face the deep hurt, forgive the person or persons who caused your inner pain and traumas, accept that it is over, and replace it with God's Word and His love, His divine presence and power takes over. As the burdens lift, the Lord blesses you with a new momentum. You will release the obsessions as you continue to enter into His grace, receiving it by faith.

"Faith is the belief we have that reaches out to receive His grace, His loving-kindness, His undeserved favor, His gift to us." **[151]** There is nothing we can do to earn it. We must humble ourselves and receive it. There is no other way! (Ephesians 2:8)

The secret things belong to the Lord our God, but the things revealed belong to us and to our children forever ... (Deuteronomy 29:2) I tried to get rid of the defiance of the perfectionist cycles intellectually by finishing project after project, but the rest only came with the repentance and forgiveness, and truly submitting my heart and making Jesus Lord. I spoke the Word of God over myself for each weakness to bring me the Lord's answer. Healing started when I no longer wanted to displease the Lord with this. I did not want any further chastisements. It came when I refused to worry and decided to trust God. My refusal to worry was the beginning of my resistance to the enemy's lies.

I had to give up my need for control and that came with time spent with other people and in relationships. He helped me through each project. But the reason I was striving so much with the sin of perfectionism was because I was living in false guilt for others' pain, for my mistakes, and punishing myself for my sins which were already forgiven by Jesus. I was trying to prove myself worthy to men and women, and to myself. No one is worthy no, not one! (Romans 3:10) We have nothing to prove to anyone! I had to receive His forgiveness. I had to forgive myself. When I did, He healed my wounded heart, and my heart reopened to live, to love, and to laugh again!

Love is our greatest weapon. (1ˢᵗ Cor. 13) The love of God working through me together with the rest of God that was brought to me due to my obedience to leave sin and idols all locked the door on Satan's illicit entrances to my body, my soul, and my spirit. (Romans 5:5) With my obedience to say "no" to sin, I entered into the secret place where the devil was now under my feet. (Psalm 91:1) He might try to tempt and harass, but I am alert to him and so deep in my faith and intimacy with Jesus, that he no longer has a portal of entry. I refuse to bring displeasure to my Father. With obedience, Jesus becomes my "shield" and His blood protects me as I change from living by what I feel to living by my faith in my Lord Jesus Christ. (Romans 10:17) (Hebrews 11:1)

As we starve the fears and feed our faith, we will be changed. As we choose to live led by the Holy Spirit, not by the flesh, the soul will come into agreement with the spirit, and the bodily pleasures will lose their control over us. There is a quiet rest when we walk in the Holy Spirit, when all is at peace with God. This is the entrance into the abundant life. (John 10:10) **Enter through the narrow gate. For wide is the gate and broad is the road that leads to destruction, and many enter through it. But small is the gate and narrow the road that leads to life and only a few find it. (Matthew 7:13–14)**

Jesus Loves You!

The Holy Spirit was always with me even through the sin part. I knew He still loved me and would help me to stop. I knew He was there and He continues to be with me through each step of life. Even though I had to continually repent of sin, I had to continually call upon the Lord and be renewed in His presence. I had to remind myself that He understood what I was going through as a result of early childhood traumas and the generational curse and sins on the bloodline. I knew that He was there with me through every childhood trauma. His presence kept me aware of His unconditional love for me even though I was not yet completely set free from this bondage. Remember, Jesus loves the sinner and hates the sin. He honors a heart that seeks after Him

Sanctification Brings Inner Healing – Fear, Panic, Anxiety

Forgive Them Father for They Know Not What They Do – Hatred to Compassion

With His words of faith, God created the universe. With His words of faith, Jesus healed the sick. So also, our words of faith carry power to speak life or death over our own lives and over the lives of others.

I was deeply moved by the story of Debbie Morris. She was kidnapped and raped, and her boyfriend was maimed for life by two criminals. Her decision to forgive changed her life and the lives of many others. She states in her book, Forgiving the Dead Man Walking, regarding her assailant, **I knew I had to forgive him – not for his sake, but for mine. Until I did, there was no escaping the hold his evil had on my life. [152]**

She says this in response to the reading of Lewis Smedes' booklet titled Forgive and Forget,

"If we say monsters are beyond forgiving, we give them a power they should never have. Monsters that are too evil to be forgiven get a stranglehold on their victims; they can sentence their victims to a lifetime of unhealed pain. If they are unforgivable monsters, they are given power to keep their evil alive in the hearts of those who suffered most." [153]

That evil, when kept alive in our hearts, will strike the body and bring on a physical malady. I knew I had to let go of the hurt and deep pain of my childhood, even if it was subconscious material. You say, "How can I let go of hurts I am not conscious of?" Jesus' will is for perfect health and healing. When I prayed prayers of forgiveness, I included anything that I had forgotten and anything that was hidden in the subconscious realm of my heart. And I believed that God honored my intentions to totally forgive. I prayed with my heart of faith with submission to my Lord, repentance for my sins, and with forgiveness and a release of all judgment, "Lord Jesus, I forgive and I release all judgment, even to the deepest crevices of my heart. Lord, help those who need You the most." **Dear friend, I pray that you may enjoy good health, and that all may go well with you, even as your soul is getting along well. (3rd John 2)**

Pray the Word of God – Take Control over Anxiety and Panic Attacks

I will tell you that I still experience very deep feelings, but these are not in the form of panic. However, I am still tempted with anxiety attacks. When this happens, I take control by breathing deeply and turning my attention away from the temptation. I quickly do something else. Get out of the cave! The devil likes to attack us when we are alone. Seek support! My first priority is to go to a church service and worship the Lord. I will play a worship tape and sing along with it. Worship brings you immediately into the presence of the Lord and the atmosphere will change.

Jesus declares in the gospel of John, chapter 4, **Yet a time is coming and has now come when the true worshipers will worship the Father in spirit and truth, for they are the kind of worshipers the Father seeks. God is spirit, and His worshipers must worship in spirit and in truth." (John 4:23,24)**

Prayer against Fear, Panic, and Anxiety

Prepare Your Heart of Faith – "Jesus, I believe You died on the cross for me and You resurrected on the third day. I ask You to come into my heart and to be the Lord and Savior of my life. I submit to Your Lordship and Your authority. (James 4:7)(John 3:3)(Romans 10:9,10) (Luke 10:19)(Romans 10:13) (John 3:16) I now repent and turn from all my sins and ask You to fill me with Your Holy Spirit. (Acts 2:38) I forgive and release all judgment against myself and all who have sinned against me." (Matthew 6:12) (Luke 6:37)

Enter into the Father's Presence – "Father God, I enter into Your presence with thanksgiving and praise in my heart with my prayers and petitions. I come boldly to Your throne of grace because of Your blood sacrifice that remits (forgives and forgets) all my sins, in Jesus' name."(Hebrews 10:19-22) (John 16:23) (Psalm 100:4)

Take Jesus' Delegated Authority against All Fear, Panic, and Anxiety in Jesus' Name

"I submit to You, Jesus, and I resist the devil, in Jesus' name. (James 4:7,8) Lord, Your Word says that You did not give me the spirit of timidity, but of love and of power, and of self-discipline (sound mind). (2nd Tim. 1:7) I thank You, Lord, that You sent forth Your Word and You healed me and rescued me from the grave and from all destruction. (Psalm 107:20) (Psalm 103:4) I believe that Your Word is living and active. It is sharper than any double-edged sword. It penetrates even to the dividing of soul and spirit, joints and marrow, judging the thoughts and attitudes of my heart. When I read the Word, You, O Lord, speak to me. (Hebrews 4:12) I thank You, Jesus, for giving me Your delegated authority to speak to this spirit of anxiety. (Luke 10:19) (Genesis 1:28) (Mark 16:17) I now rebuke the spirit of anxiety in Jesus' name. (Mark 11:23-25)(Luke 10:19) (Matthew 18:18) You have no authority in my life. (Col. 2:10,15)(Matthew 21:27) You must get out now, in the name of Jesus Christ. (Luke 10:19)(Mark 16:17) I am a child of the living God and I will not be moved by you.(Acts 2:25)(1st Cor. 15:58)(James 4:7)(Matthew 18:18)(Psalm 62:6)(Proverbs 12:3) Go wherever Jesus sends you to be held captive by the angels of God."(Mark 5:8-13)(See Appendix)

"The angel of the Lord encamps around me now and I am safe because I stand in awe and reverence before the Lord, and He has delivered me from all fear. (Psalm 34:7) You, Father God, have delivered (freed) me from the dominion of darkness and You, O Father God, have brought me into the Kingdom of Your dear Son Whom You love, in Whom I have redemption, the forgiveness of all my sins. (Colossians 1:13) You, O Lord Jesus, shall keep me in perfect peace, for my mind is stayed upon You and because I trust in You. (Isaiah 26:3) I now receive the peace of the Lord Jesus Christ to rule and reign in my heart, since I am Your child and I am called to Your peace. (Colossians 3:15,16) I will sing psalms, hymns, and spiritual songs with gratitude in my heart to You, O Lord, for Your sacrifice for me. I will sing to the Lord with my heart. (Ephesians 5:19) I will commit to daily study of the Word of God with prayer and praise and worship to keep my vessel filled with God." (Luke 11:24-26)(Romans 12:2)(Proverbs 4:20)(James 5:16) (Psalm 33:1-3)(John 4:24)(All scriptures personalized)(See Appendix)

These are the words of Jesus, **"I tell you the truth, whatever you bind on earth will be bound in heaven, and whatever you loose on earth will be loosed in heaven." (Matthew 18:18) And the peace of God, which transcends all understanding, will guard your hearts and your minds in Christ Jesus. (Philippians 4:7)**

Practical Hints against Anxiety

There are so many practical ways to thwart fear or anxiety. Take a good swim or walk the dog. Cooking can be a great activity to redirect the energy of anxiety. Read and speak the Word while doing this as well. I have taken countless drives through nature while singing to the Lord.

If I am so overwhelmed that I cannot sit and read or even pray, I say with my heart of faith in submission, repentance, and forgiveness, "Jesus" and this is very helpful. Just the mention of His name will change the spiritual environment. By speaking the name of the Jesus, you are calling out to Him, placing your faith in Him to come into the situation.

One strategy I love when anxiety comes is to worship Him. I just redirect my heart toward Him and my fears turn to faith. I am a worshiper and I love to praise Him. I have received countless healings from the Lord while in His presence during worship. Calling or emailing a friend can be a great help in times of any anxiety attack. If there is no one around, I go to the library or a restaurant to be around the life of other people. It is comforting just to be around people. Taking classes in various schools has been rewarding. It has kept me active and alert. **We are hard pressed on every side, but not crushed; perplexed, but not in despair; persecuted, but not abandoned; struck down, but not destroyed. We always carry around in our body the death of Jesus, so that the life of Jesus may also be revealed in our body. (1st Cor. 4:8-10)**

The Word of God Changes Us

Another great directive is to read the Word of God. Immediately, His Word has a settling effect upon my soul. After reading a chapter of the Old Testament, a chapter of the New Testament, and one from Psalms or Proverbs, I start talking to the Lord in prayer or start praying in the Holy Spirit prayer language and in my understanding. The Lord will speak to me through His Word. Meditating upon the Word of God is so encouraging to my spirit and it relieves my mind.

As the Word becomes a part of your heart and not just a recitation activity, it will help you out of any situation. It starts with meditation, memorization and then recitation in faith. It initially travels to your spirit. From there it enters the mind, which includes the thoughts and intellect, the emotions, and the will. It will first transform your mind in the thinking realm and eventually travel to your emotions as Jesus heals your wounds as you yield to Him. (Luke 4:18,19) (Isaiah 61:1-3) This is a process and it is a wonderful transformation of the mind. It is life changing!

As you agree with and believe the Word of God, and as you enter into an obedient lifestyle, the Word will become a part of your everyday life. It will change you from the inside out. Not only will your mind be transformed and renewed, but your emotions will also be healed, and you will be strengthened and transformed. Your thoughts and emotions will reconnect. Your thought processes will be organized and pleasant memories will return. And the more you yield to the Lord's authority and Lordship, with an obedient lifestyle, your will becomes lined up with His will. And He will help you to make good decisions with good judgment that is in line with His will for your life. **Call to me and I will answer you and tell you great and unsearchable things you do not know. (Jeremiah 33:3)**

Homosexuality is Not a "Thorn in the Flesh"

The apostle Paul was persecuted for his work for the Lord. Wherever he went, there was an enemy to stop his work for the Lord. But he valiantly kept submitted to the Lord and resisted the enemy. (James 4:7,8) You may believe your temptations toward homosexuality is your "thorn." I believe it is a challenge due to childhood influences and spiritual influences. You may disagree and believe it is a thorn in your flesh. This may be so until the Word of God convicts you that this is a choice to sin and not a "thorn in your flesh." (Romans 1:21-27) This may be so until you become so filled with the Holy Spirit and so deeply surrendered to Jesus Christ and His Word that you are personally and deeply convicted that homosexuality is sin. This may be so until you become honest with a Spirit-filled counselor, who will help you to face the deep hurts, freeing you from your mental and emotional vulnerabilities and the lies of this deception. This may be so until you are convicted by others within the body of Christ who are suffering with the same issues as you and are being changed through their relationship with Jesus Christ. This may be so until you seek accountability partners, Christian counselors, and mentors who care about you and who will assist you to work through the pain to get to the truth of your true identity in Jesus Christ. This may be so until you mature in Christ Jesus and experience your "honest self," with your true identity as identified with Jesus Christ, and heterosexuality becomes as natural as apple pie. This may be so until the soft, still voice of the Holy Spirit becomes stronger and more real to you than any temptation coming from this world. **No temptation has seized you except what is common to men. And God is faithful; he will not let you be tempted beyond what you can bear. But when you are tempted, He will provide a way out so that you can stand up under it. (1ˢᵗ Corinthians 10:13)**

As you ask the Lord for confirmation, you will know in your knower (human spirit) that homosexuality is sin and it is not a "thorn" in your flesh. Coming out of denial and calling it what it is; sin and addiction, you will face it, and emerge free from its hold upon your life. Then, with a decided surrender to Jesus Christ as Lord, Savior, and authority, with repentance for sin, and with forgiveness and release of all blame against yourself and others, you will begin to emerge free from the lies and the control of the driving spirits. Your conscience will be cleared as you make Jesus Christ the Lord of your life. You will be free from all condemnation as you receive His love, acceptance, and forgiveness with your obedience to repent and leave the sins and idols. You will be changed as you close and lock this door. **To the Jews who had believed**

Him, Jesus said, "If you hold to my teaching, you are really my disciples. Then you will know the truth, and the truth will set you free." (John 8:31,32)

In the Word, Paul asks the Lord to take away this "thorn in his flesh" three times and the answer the Lord gave him was, **"My grace is sufficient for you, for my power is make perfect in weakness. Therefore I will boast all the more gladly about my weaknesses, so that Christ's power may rest on me. That is why, for Christ's sake, I delight in weaknesses, in insults, in hardships, in persecutions, in difficulties. For when I am weak, then I am strong. (2nd Corinthians 12: 8-10)** The Scriptures show that Paul's "thorn" did not hinder him from laboring more abundantly than all others. Paul's thorn did not hinder him from finishing his course for God. **[154] I have fought the good fight. I have finished the race, I have kept the faith. Now there is in store for me the crown of righteousness, which the Lord, the righteous judge, will award to me on that day – and not only to me, but also to all who have longed for His appearing. (2nd Timothy 4:7,8)**

We Have to Come to Jesus

Repentance and a sense of desperation brought me to my knees. When I repented to Jesus, I felt His presence with me and I knew this was a real communication with Him. We started to have conversations, me and the Lord. I knew this was real. It was deep. I felt my heart change as I looked at my sins as "filthy rags" in the presence of a holy God who loved me in spite of myself. I lived in a place of dishonesty even with myself, not even wanting to look at my sin. I had to face my own shame, fears, and self doubt to be set free from it. Only through His felt love and presence, and through the love and acceptance in the body of Christ, my friend, did I face it. And in my persistence to get to the rest of God, I obeyed the Lord and, locking the door to sin, including worry, the devil could no longer steal from me.

The Holy Spirit showed me my dishonesty with people. At the same time, I knew that I was still deeply loved and accepted by Jesus, and this kept me going further in my Christian walk. We serve an awesome God. I knew He was there and that He loved me through the whole painful process. Pastor David Demola says, **"When we come face to face with our selves, then the Holy Spirit infills us."** [155] Anxiety, fear, and panic cannot live in the light of the Holy Spirit's presence.

Therefore there is no condemnation for those who are in Christ Jesus, because through Christ Jesus, the law of the Spirit of life set me free from the law of sin and death. (Romans 8:1-2)

Revelation Knowledge

I had three memorable experiences in which Jesus supernaturally healed me of my deepest wounds. One took place in my mother's house. I remember it was late at night. I was awakened by the Lord. I must have awoken with some family memories. I was crying and ran up to the third floor of the house. I sat down on the step and I remember speaking out the words, "Jesus, I forgive them all."

I know I went through many Christian counseling sessions in which I went through prayer after prayer of forgiveness. But, my friend, there was so much power in this prayer because it was said in the very place where I experienced many hurts. I observed and felt the pain of my family as a child, whether spoken or unspoken.

I had witnessed many arguments in that house. I know my spirit and soul were grieved by all the strife I had witnessed there. I know I felt rejected by being "left out" of many conversations. In a lot of ways, I did not feel included as much as the other children. I will never forget that prayer. It was as if the Lord supernaturally sutured wounds which penetrated deep in the recesses of my heart as I spoke these words of forgiveness. It is amazing what God does as a result of our obedience. It seems that He rewards us with the same measure that the obedience warrants.

Another deep healing I experienced was in the sanctuary of Faith Fellowship World Outreach Center under the anointing of Pastor David T. Demola in Sayreville, New Jersey. He was preaching the Word of God. As he spoke, the presence of God was "thick" in the sanctuary. I was led by the Holy Spirit to the memories of Mom being angry at me and losing control. I think her loud voice bothered me more than the wooden spoon when she corrected my brother and me in the midst of our sibling rivalries.

In this revelation from the Holy Spirit, I was challenged to identify with Mom's frustrations as a mother. When I accepted a position as a second grade teacher at Cornerstone Christian Academy, I also lost control and threw some books on the floor as a result of my frustrations with the children. I lost my position as a result of losing control. This experience helped me to understand what it is to lose one's control around children. Here was another opportunity to look compassionately instead of critically on my mother's behavior; with the wisdom of God instead of my hurt feelings. **Wisdom is supreme; therefore get wisdom, though it cost all you have, get understanding. (Proverbs 4:7)**

During Pastor Demola's preaching, I was empowered by the Holy Spirit. While in a submitted position of reverence to the Lord and with my heart softened in repentance for my own sins, my heart was moved to forgive Mom as an act of my faith and obedience. I remember speaking in a whisper to the Lord with my heart of faith with submission, repentance, and forgiveness, "Lord Jesus, I forgive Mom for every word and every deed that was ever committed against me. I repent of all the judgments I have made against her. I forgive her and I release her to Your care. I pray for her salvation. I call the angels to her for protection. I bind and gag the enemy from operating against her in Jesus' name." I did it in faith, not in feelings at all, and in obedience because I knew that I had to forgive "all" or my deliverance would never have been complete. Unforgiveness is one of the major roadblocks to receiving wholeness and healing from the Lord. And whatever I judged would come back to me until I stopped judging, forgave, and released the people I had made judgments against. (See Appendix)

Another revelation took place while I was lying face down in my bed. I remember talking to Jesus and asking Him to heal me to the deepest point of the wounding and remove every fragment of hatred from my heart. I asked the Lord with my heart surrendered in faith, with repentance and forgiveness, "Lord Jesus, take the hate." The Lord gave me a vision of seeing my mother as me, a woman experiencing much inner pain. I was filled with sorrow for the years of apathy and subconscious hatred toward her. Compassion then gripped my heart. I realized this was not hatred toward her at all but hatred of the hold that Satan had upon my family bloodline which influenced us all. I recall sharing with Mom on the phone one time, "Only Jesus could have taken <u>my</u> pain, Mom." I know those words ministered to her and I said them to help her to see Jesus as <u>her</u> healer also.

In the Bible, Daniel spoke of having visions while in a deep sleep. He was visited by one who looked like a man. **While he was speaking to me, I was in a deep sleep, with my face to the ground. Then he touched me and raised me to my feet. (Daniel 8:18)**

Eternal Perspective – Face the Fear of Death

After the September eleventh attack of 2001, I came face to face with my own fear of death. I made the decision to recommit my life to Jesus Christ as my Lord and Savior. I believe the Word of God that promises me eternal life through that commitment. To this day, I recommit my life to Him daily with repentance and faith. I know and believe that when I die I will go to heaven and I will be face to face with Jesus Christ Himself. **For the Lord Himself will come down from heaven, with a loud command, with the voice of the archangel and with the trumpet call of God, and the dead in Christ will rise first. After that, we who are still alive and are left will be caught up together with them in the clouds to meet the Lord in the air. And so we will be with the Lord forever. Therefore encourage each other with these words. (1st Thessalonians 4:16-18)**

The salvation of my loved ones became more important to me than anything else, even my own needs or wants for their acceptance. The Lord gave me an eternal perspective.**Therefore we do not lose heart. Though outwardly we are wasting away, yet inwardly we are being renewed day by day. For our light and momentary troubles are achieving for us an eternal glory that far outweighs them all. So we fix our eyes not on what is seen, but on what is unseen. For what is seen is temporary, but what is unseen is eternal. (2nd Corinthians 4: 16-18)**

I wrote a letter to all my family members. I told them that I had repented of my sins and had made Jesus Christ the Lord and Savior of my life. I shared that I trusted and believed in Jesus Christ for my eternal life and that I believed in His "finished" work for me at Calvary. I told them that I loved them and would like to see them all in heaven. (See footnote #156 for the prayer of salvation). I shared the sinner's prayer necessary to making Jesus Christ the Lord and Savior of their lives. I asked them if they would seriously consider making a commitment to trust and believe in Jesus Christ for their salvation. **Everyone who calls upon the name of the Lord shall be saved. (Romans 10:13)**

This letter gave me a great sense of peace. I had shared the gospel with them. This is the Great Commission, the call of every Christian. This is the heartbeat of God that we share Jesus Christ with the world. (Matthew 28:18-20) (Mark 16:15-18) I sent the letters out and then stood in prayer believing God for their acceptance of Jesus Christ as their Lord and Savior. Sharing the good news of Jesus Christ and the way to eternal life with those whom we love is the greatest gift we can give them, even greater than praying for someone's healing. For the greatest benefit of accepting Jesus Christ as Lord and Savior of one's life is the promise of eternal life.

However, I would have to work at a new attitude of humility. I had been "stubborn" all my life. My desire to educate Mom to the things of God did not make her any less of a believer. She is a believer in the Lord Jesus Christ, God's Son who died, was buried and resurrected for us all. However, the Word of God says, "You must be born again." This requires repentance and a committed personal covenant relationship with Jesus Christ. Soon after the terrorist attack of the Twin Towers in New York City, we held hands at her kitchen table and she said the words of the "sinner's prayer" with me.

"Heavenly Father, in Jesus' name, I repent of my sins and open my heart to let Jesus come inside of me. Jesus, you are my Lord and Savior. I believe that You died for my sins and that You were raised from the dead. Fill me with Your Holy Spirit. Thank You Father for saving me; in Jesus' name. Amen." [156] That if you confess with your mouth, "Jesus is Lord," and believe in your heart that God raised him from the dead, you will be saved. For it is with your heart that you believe and are justified, and it is with your mouth that you confess and are saved. (Romans 10:9,10)

Compassion Without Compromise

Webster defines "compassion" as the sympathetic consciousness for others' distress with the desire to alleviate it. [157] Only a godly perspective will get you to a place of real compassion for your loved ones. It is amazing to me how hatred turned to love which then matured into a deep compassion for my mother. This was a compassion which said, "I understand your pain. Let me be there for you." In my case, being there for Mom does not always mean being physically present. This commitment of love means that I commit to pray for her even when I cannot be there for her physically. Compassion never compromises who I am in Christ. It is of a much higher order to pity, which only says, "I feel sorry for you." **For all have sinned and fallen short of the glory of God... (Romans 3:23)**

I am so grateful that after years of conscious apathy and subconscious hatred toward this woman, I have been restored to a godly respect, love, and a compassion for her. I believe that true compassion is a divine work of the Holy Spirit through a submitted vessel. Compassion was the very tool that Jesus Christ used to heal others; **When Jesus landed and saw a large crowd, He had compassion on them and healed the sick. (Matthew 14:14)**

In my earlier years, I had a subconscious repulsion toward my mother. I never wanted to be like her. When I read My Mother, Myself, I learned that the hatred/apathy I felt was blocking me from my true personality. The hatred actually blocked the development of some of my strengths because I renounced everything about her. Refusing to reconcile was like saying, "You hurt me by not loving me. So I'm going to hurt you by not letting you love me."

It was my misperception that she did not love me. And this was brought about because of the enemy's control in the relationship and because of my lack of knowledge of the Word of God and my immaturity as a Christian. We were both deceived by the spiritual oppression from the enemy that was controlling us. We both were blinded by our own fears, traditions, and behavior patterns. Friend, someone has to start the ball rolling. Someone has to initiate the love to eradicate the hate.

The Cycle of Abuse Can Be Broken

Deep inner hurts and hatred/apathy, (whether conscious or subconscious), bring torment and our negative responses to them very often are ungodly reactions which cause us to sin. It is the viscous cycle of abuse. Sin, until repented of, separates us from our intimacy with Jesus. It reopens the wounds and vulnerable places of our heart and soul, thus allowing for further temptations, attacks, and oppression from Satan himself to distract and to steal our faith, our joy, our peace, and the very healing Jesus already purchased for us at Calvary two thousand years ago. **To break the cycle of abuse, we must stop reacting to Satan by sinning and submit to Jesus' Lordship and His authority. We must come to Him in our broken state for the healing to start and continue healing until we mature in Christ.**

Healing from the hatred and the deep hurt is a painful process which requires looking at our own hearts, taking responsibility for our part of the abuse, submitting to Jesus with repentance for our sins and our ungodly reactions to the sins committed against us, and forgiveness for ourselves and others with a heart that believes that God is a good God and that Jesus already took the torment and punishment for us at Calvary. Healing takes us to a place where we pray for other people, and want for them what the Lord has done for us. It releases all judgment against any other person. (See Appendix)

It takes a submitted and an honest heart to receive the healing from Jesus for all the brokenness, all the grief, all the tragedy, and all the pain. Jesus wants us whole and, with His divine hand upon our lives, we will be made whole. As you surrender, you will open your heart to receive your healing, and you will be quick to obey and to walk in repentance and forgiveness and get sin out of your life. With obedience, you will lock the door to allow Satan's entrance to your soul/heart and you will receive a fuller anointing. This is the very presence of God. And you will receive the gift of His grace, which is His loving-kindness toward you and His empowerment within and around you as a shield. (Ephesians 2:8) (Psalm 3:3)

But I tell you who hear me; Love your enemies, do good to those who hate you, bless those who curse you, pray for those who mistreat you. If someone strikes you on one cheek, turn to him the other also. (Luke 6:27) I love my mother and always will. And nothing Satan has, does, or will do to change my mind about this will have any effect upon me. I am so grateful that the Lord ordained and permitted the time we did share together. And that I obeyed Him when He called me to reunite with her. I believe that God will accomplish the full manifestation of my healing in this area of my life. My faith in His power to heal is greater than anything the enemy can do to try to deter it. **I have set (saw) the Lord always before me. Because He is at my right hand, I will not be shaken. (Psalm 16:8) (Acts 2:25)**

Let Go and Let God – Set Proper Boundaries

To release loved ones does not mean you stop loving them. On the contrary, love for others actually grows deeper as we release them to God's care. A mature love shares the Word of God, then releases our loved ones to the care of God and prays for them to make godly decisions. Only the Holy Spirit can convict a person to change. (See Appendix)

It is through the power of God working in and through us that His divine compassion helps to set other people free. People see life and hope when we reflect the living God. When we by faith, place the cross of Jesus between us and others, we set a healthy boundary which places us as separate from others, not enmeshed with them. As we rest in God in us, we allow Him to touch others through us.

It is not about us striving to change anyone. It is about resting and trusting in the love and presence of God living within us to bring His divine presence to others. And change comes to all people through the inner conviction of the Holy Spirit. **The Spirit of the Lord is on me, because the Lord has anointed me to preach good news to the poor. He has sent me to bind up the brokenhearted, to proclaim freedom for the captives, and release from darkness for the prisoners, to proclaim** the year of the Lord's favor and the day of vengeance of our God, to comfort all who mourn, and provide for those who grieve in Zion - to bestow on them a crown of beauty instead of ashes, the oil of gladness instead of mourning, and a garment of praise instead of a spirit of despair. They will be called oaks of righteousness, a planting of the Lord for the display of His splendor. (Isaiah 61:1-3)

I had to grow up and release that "wounded little girl" in me that needed Mom's love and approval and turn to Jesus and experience His divine love and total acceptance for me. I had to repent and turn from the "noble martyr" role, cut the umbilical cord, and become the woman Jesus had intended before I was even in my mother's womb. Then and only then the dynamic of that relationship with Mom would begin to change as I saw myself as a mature woman. I would never change her. I will always be her " little girl." But, as I changed, I would experience transformation in that relationship.

Personality Formed as Unique in Christ
Before I formed you in the womb I knew you. (Jeremiah 1:5)

Oswald Chambers speaks about personality only in terms of a merging of two. Personality is the characteristic of the spiritual man as individuality is the characteristic of the natural man. Our Lord can never be defined in terms of individuality and independence, but only in terms of personality, "I and My Father are one." Personality merges, and you only reach your real identity when you are merged with another person. When love, or the Spirit of God, strikes a man, he is transformed, he no longer insists upon his separate individuality. If you give up your right to yourself to God, the real true nature of your personality answers to God straight away. Jesus Christ emancipates the personality, and the individuality is transfigured; the transfiguring element is love, personal devotion to Jesus. Love is the outpouring of one personality in fellowship with another personality. [158]

Jesus had to become my mother, my father, my husband, and my best friend. As I decreased in my need for Mom and Dad (Dad is now with Jesus), and I took responsibility for all my sins and all my idols, the presence of God became like a fire. I turned to prayer actually out of desperation at first. And God did bless! He so much wants us to talk to Him. When we reach out to touch God, He then lovingly responds and touches us. **After Job had prayed for his friends, the Lord made him prosperous again and gave him twice as much as he had before. All his brothers and sisters and everyone who had known him before came and ate with him and consoled him . . . (Job 42:10-11)**

I Belong to Jesus

As I prayed for Mom and spent time with her again, I saw myself in her; her strengths, her weaknesses, and her pain. The very person who never wanted to be like this woman has now grown with a lot of strengths that I never thought I had which are her very strengths. I am so much like her.

I had to let go of the childish need for Mom, the noble martyr role, that dependency for her, the parental inversion, and the false sense of responsibility for her, but not my love for her. A lot of my fears and anxiety were grounded in my false sense of responsibility. In feeling overly responsible for others, I would not free myself to live the abundant life. (John 10:10)

And come to Jesus as a His child. God knows my heart's motives are to put Him first and He honors that obedience. I know that the best way I can help Mom now is to release her to the care of God and to step back and allow myself to grow apart from her. My true personality naturally is still developing as I let go of the "neediness" and transfer that desperation to my relationship with Jesus. The Lord is showing me even to this day how much I am like Mom. It's a good thing.

Jesus said, "I tell you the truth, unless you change and become like little children, you will never enter the kingdom of heaven. Therefore, whoever humbles himself like this child is the greatest in the kingdom of heaven." (Matthew 18:3,4)

Give Them Jesus

Depending on people for love is not only a sin before God, but it steals from that person the very relationship they need to develop in <u>their</u> intimacy with the Lord Jesus Christ. Jesus must be first and no other. The greatest gift we can give another is to give them Jesus. We must be desperately dependent upon God's love so that His love flows out of us to give to others.

Compassion is experienced when we draw our strength from Jesus. The Holy Spirit then works through us to reach out and touch others with the compassion of Jesus Christ. True love shows compassion for others. True love has pure motives. **Love is patient. Love is kind. It does not envy. It does not boast, it is not proud. It is not rude, it is not self-seeking. It is not easily angered; it keeps no record of wrongs. Love does not delight in evil but rejoices with the truth. It always protects, always trusts, always hopes, and always perseveres. (1st Corinthians 13:4,7)**

Nothing Left to Lose

The songwriter said, "Freedom's just another word for nothing left to lose." He forgot to mention that when one loses his life, he gains Christ and that is all we need. Like the Beatles so aptly sang, "All we need is love." **God is love. Whoever lives in love lives in God, and God in Him. In this way, love is made complete among us so that we will have confidence on the Day of Judgment because in this world we are like Him. There is no fear in love. But perfect love drives out fear, because fear has to do with punishment. The one who fears is not made perfect in love. (1st John 4:16b–18)**

Freedom only comes with a complete surrender. My friend, whatever it takes, let go of your secrets and your idols. You can never walk in the full power of the Holy Spirit if there are idols in your life. Take an honest look at your life. Any person, place, or thing that takes you away from Jesus Christ as being in first place is an idol. When Jesus is truly Lord, "the honest self" emerges.

The homosexual spirit is a driving and a lying spirit and it will do anything to keep you from the revelation of your "honest self." If your faith is weak and you are having a hard time releasing idols to God, ask Jesus to help you. Be honest with Him. He hears you and is there with you. I always felt His presence but when I actually spoke out loud to Him, I then knew His presence.

Seek an accountability partner. Sometimes it takes another person to tear us away from our rubble. **Call to me and I will answer you and tell you great and unsearchable things you do not know. (Jeremiah 33:3)**

Rubber Meets the Road

In January 2001, Mom was taken sick and rushed to the hospital. How incredibly the Lord works! I was placed in a position of nursing her and of helping her through pain and possible heart problems. I was moved with a deep compassion for her and a love for her after being away from her for some time. I know the Holy Spirit had ordained this time for further reconciliation and cherished moments of sharing together. We laughed and we cried. It was precious time!

Authority of the Believer Against Defilements
– We are Healed Socially

Jesus spoke these words as He appointed seventy two followers:

I have given you authority to trample on snakes and scorpions and to overcome all the power of the enemy; nothing will harm you. (Luke 10:19)

Then Jesus said to them, "All authority in heaven and on earth has been given to me." Therefore, go and make disciples of all nations, baptizing them in the name of the Father and of the Son, and of the Holy Spirit, and teaching them to obey everything I have commanded you. And surely I am with you always, to the very end of the age." (Matthew 28:18)

He said to them, "Go into all the world and preach the good news to all creation. Whoever believes and is baptized will be saved, but whoever does not believe will be condemned. And these signs will accompany those who believe: In my name they will drive out demons; they will speak in new tongues; they will pick up snakes with their hands; and when they drink deadly poison, it will not hurt them at all; they will place their hands on sick people, and they will get well." (Mark 16:15–18)

Jesus Gives Us Authority

In order to operate successfully in the divine authority of Jesus Christ, we must be properly positioned with our heart of faith under Jesus' authority in order to properly pray in faith. Being under His authority, we must be submitted to the Lordship and the authority of Jesus Christ. We must be in an attitude of daily repentance and forgiveness. We must be very careful in this arena. We must also have legal authority to pray to cast out demonic spirits oppressing or possessing others in our delegated authority in Christ. We do not have legal authority to cast out any demons against another person's will. And we do not have legal access to pray such prayers for someone we do not have legal authority over; unless they give us that authority and ask for such prayers. We can, however, bind, mute, and gag demon spirits from operating in their lives.(Matthew 18:18) Unsaved must be saved first before praying to cast out any demons.This is so they will work to keep their vessels filled with God and keep the enemy out. (Luke 11:24-26)(Romans 12:2) (See Appendix)

If you are still healing from wounds, use wisdom before taking authority and casting out any demonic spirits oppressing other people. You also invite enemy relatiation if you have doors open. Remember, the main ingredient is praying in faith in God and a repentant heart before the Lord, not a perfectly sinless person. Both we as intercessors and those for whom we have legal authority to pray to cast out demons must commit to keep our vessels filled with the Word of God, prayer, and praise and worship to keep the enemy out. (Luke 11:24-26)(See Appendix)

A Christian brother or sister who is strong in their walk of faith will be very helpful to pray these prayers of authority with us. Remember, Jesus sent them out in "twos". Once the vulnerable doors of our hearts are closed and locked, and sins of addiction are out of our life, we become stronger in our submission to Christ, our position of faith, and in our resistance against the attacks of the enemy. The trials do not stop, but our fight of faith is stronger against them. (See Appendix)

Submit yourselves, then, to God. Resist the devil, and he will flee from you. (James 4:7)

We are told by the Word of God that our real enemy originates in spiritual principalities in the heavenly realms. (Ephesians 6:12) However, Satan is the god of the carnal world and we must be equipped and ready for battle to fight properly in the earth. Spirits and principalities influence and work through people as well as through the heavenly realms. We do not fight in our own strength, but in our faith and in the power of Holy Spirit, Who meets us and Who also empowers us at the point of our surrender, of our faith, of our honesty, and of our repentance and obedience. (Acts 2:38)(Acts 1:8)(1st Cor. 12:3)(John 8:32)

Place your spiritual armor on before praying such prayers as well.(Ephesians 6:13-18)

Heed the Directions from the Holy Spirit

Only go where the Holy Spirit tells you to go! And only go when He tells you to go. There are seasons in everything! If He says not to go, do not go and just pray for the folks. If you do not know, do not go. Wait on the Lord until you get definite direction. If you have a clear and confirmed word from the Lord, obey Him. Always seek the Holy Spirit in all decisions. He speaks through persons as well as to you in His still small voice. He can speak to you in dreams, in visions, in revelations, and in visitations. But let the Word of God be your final confirmation. And, in important decisions, I always seek at least three confirmations from the Lord, through the Word, and through strong Christian leaders or friends. I do not make the decision until it is then confirmed in my spirit by the Holy Spirit. **The Lord replied, "My presence will go with you, and I will give you rest." Then Moses said to him "If your presence does not go with us, do not send us up from here." (Exodus 33:13, 14)**

You will see that in the numerous battles in biblical accounts, there are many different directives given to the Israelites as divine strategy necessary to win against their enemies. Some battles are won head on, some in outside territory, and some merely through prayer and praise. All battles, however, are won in direct obedience to the directions from the Lord.

We are Empowered by the Holy Spirit to Take Jesus' Authority

But you will receive power when the Holy Spirit comes on you; and you will be my witnesses in Jerusalem, and in all Judea and Samaria, and to the ends of the earth." (Acts 1:8)

These are the words of Jesus to His disciples;**"If you love me, you will obey what I command. And I will ask the Father, and He will give you another Counselor to be with you forever – the Spirit of truth. The world cannot accept him, because it neither sees Him nor knows Him. But you know Him, for he lives with you and will be in you. I will not leave you as orphans. I will come to you. " (John 14:15-18)**

Jesus' power is made perfect through our weaknesses (2nd Corinthians 12:9) when we come to Him in our broken state. When the lies come, we have been privileged to speak to any mountain with our hearts submitted in our proper position of faith to successfully take His delegated authority. Our hearts prepare in faith with submission to the authority and the Lordship of Jesus Christ. Our hearts humbly repent and turn from our sins, being truly sorry for having displeased the Lord, and seeking change. And we also stand and speak forgiveness and release of all judgment against both ourselves and all who have knowingly or unknowingly sinned against us. Then, with our hearts of faith, we enter into the Father's presence with our petitions in the name of Jesus. And we also take Jesus' delegated authority and rebuke the enemy and declare the Word of God in the name of Jesus Christ, which is the name that is above every other created name. (Philippians 2:9)

We place ourselves in the "secret place" (Psalm 91:1) by our faith that has believed in the death, burial, and the resurrection of Jesus Christ. (Romans 10:9,10) And in this place of faith in Jesus Christ, we are covered with the precious blood of Jesus Christ. This is a divine boundary line. It assures believers of divine protection against the enemy's entrance to our bodies, spirits, and souls. (1st John 1:7) When we speak with a heart of faith, we believe that whatever mountain we speak to will be removed, and that we will have what we say. (Mark 11:23-25) And we are empowered by the Holy Spirit to do what we cannot do in our own flesh, by the very Spirit of the living God. (Acts 2:38) (Acts 1:8)

With our repentance, we are seeking to leave our obsessive compulsive behavior patterns. God honors our hearts to want change in our lives. The Lord showed me that I had authority over the devil in my life by taking Jesus' delegated authority over my own spiritual battles; over spirits of fear, lust, depression, anxiety, shame, over my own flesh, over negative thoughts, emotions, and memories, fantasies, over all evil spirits, and any assignments of the devil. **He called His twelve disciples to Him and gave them authority to drive out evil spirits and to heal every disease and sickness. (Matthew 10:1) I will give you** the keys of the kingdom of heaven; whatever you bind on earth will be bound in heaven, and whatever you loose on earth will be loosed in heaven. (Matthew 16:19)

Our Lord was never beaten by any demon! He was never scratched, bitten, or clawed by one either! As you read on, you will discover that spiritual warfare cannot be waged in the flesh. If you attempt to battle from the realm of your flesh, you will be certain to fail. On the other hand, if you battle behind the Lord who abides in the supernatural realm, the result is always victory. There is nothing to fear when you fight the enemy in the power and authority of the Lord. **[159]**

Immorality and Idols Cause Defilement (Violations)

The words of Jesus are as follows,**"I tell you the truth, if you have faith as small as a mustard seed, you can say to this mountain, 'Move from here to there' and it will move. Nothing will be impossible for you." (Matthew 17:20,21)** Homosexual sin kept me in bondage to another person and their needs and also in bondage to the lies of Satan, denying to myself that I was even in sin. In homosexuality, I also gave the control of my life away to another person in the idol of codependence. This took Jesus off the throne of my heart and placed a person there in an idyllic relationship.

My perfectionism sin kept me in control. I had to give my control over to Jesus, trusting in Him for my every concern. Even if I spoke the Word of God, my heart was not fully in it. Why? Because the addiction kept my heart distracted and that is where faith operates. As I healed from the wounds, as I left the sins and idols, as I surrendered to the Lord, refusing to worry, my heart reopened. I became honest with God and the Word of God became alive in me. Prayer became a simple conversation with God.

We must speak with a heart of faith. We must believe what we say when we speak. Remember it was because of faith in the hearts of so many people in the Bible that the healings came to them. Without faith, our words are ineffective against the devil's lies. The devil is relentless. He will always try to badger us with something. (John 10:10)

All immorality and idols cause defilement, which will violate and trample upon a person. (Matthew 15:17-20)(Ezekiel 22:4)(Ezekiel 20:18)(Ezekiel 20:7)(Joshua 23:12-14)

Jesus asked the crowd, **"Don't you see that whatever enters the mouth goes into the stomach and then out of the body? But the things that come out of the mouth come from the heart, and these make a man 'unclean.' For out of the heart come evil thoughts, murder, adultery, sexual immorality, theft, false testimony, slander. These are what make a man (woman) 'unclean;' but eating with unwashed hands does not make him 'unclean.'"(Matthew 15:17-20)**

The words of the Lord to the prophet Ezekiel regarding Jerusalem's sins and idols that defile are, **'This is what the sovereign Lord says: O city that brings on herself doom by shedding blood in her midst and defiles herself by making idols, you have become guilty because of the blood you have shed and have become defiled by the idols you have made.' (Ezekiel 22:4)**

These words of the Lord also came to Ezekiel regarding defilement, **I said to their children in the desert, "Do not follow the statutes of your fathers or keep their laws or defile yourselves with their idols. I am the Lord your God; follow my decrees and be careful to keep my laws. " (Ezekiel 20:18)** The Lord spoke to Ezekiel regarding the Israelites, **And I said to them, "Each of you, get rid of the vile images you have set your eyes on, and do not defile yourselves with the idols of Egypt. I am the Lord your God." (Ezekiel 20:7)**

Joshua exhorted the Israelites regarding nations who worshipped false gods. He warns them against defilement. **"But if you turn away and ally yourselves with the survivors of these nations that remain among you and if you intermarry with them and associate with them, then you may be sure that the Lord your God will no longer drive out these nations before you. Instead, they will become snares and traps for you, whips on your backs and thorns in your eyes...."(Joshua 23:12-14)**

Since I was praying with fleshly anger and not in faith, I was open prey for enemy retaliation. And due to my own unrepented sins and idols, I had an open door for enemy relatiation. Due to my lack of legal authority to cast out demons from those who were unsaved and who did not ask for my prayers, we were all bait for Satan to attack in retaliation. I suffered with depression, anxiety, and demonic manifestations as the enemy attached his demons to me as I continued to fight illegally with unrepented sin, and in my flesh, using with my intellect and my emotions. Praying for unsaved family members, I should have interceded by binding, gagging, and muting the enemy from operating in their lives, but not by casting out demons. I had no legal authority unless I was asked to pray such prayers by the family members (mother, sister, brother, cousins...). I could intercede and still do asking the Lord to open up their spiritual eyes to the truth of the gospel and to send laborers to them to share the gospel with them. And I commit to keep my vessel filled with the Word of God with prayer, praise, and worship. (Luke 24:31.45)(Matthew 9:37.38)(Matthew 18:18) (Luke 11:24-26)(Psalm 33:1-3)(James 5:16)(John 4:24) (See Appendix)

The devil has a certain amount of power and is a being of a higher order than we. It is best to engage in spiritual warfare with another person who is anointed of God, especially on the home-front. **The focal point of our prayers should be God, not the devil. If the evil one is to be bound, it will take divine strength to do the job. Railing at the enemy is reckless and immature. It is also dangerous. We must never forget that we are dealing with a higher dimensional being whose capabilities greatly exceed our own. Spiritual swagger and clichés mean nothing to him. [160]** (See Appendix)

Praying to cast out demons, even if performed legally, will give the evil spirits access to the one prayed for as well as the intercessor, if we and they are not committed to keeping our vessels filled with the Word of God and prayer with praise and worship. The temple (house) must be filled with God and His Word, prayer, praise, and worship to keep the demons out.(Luke 11:24-26)(See Appendix)

When an evil spirit comes out of a man/woman, it goes through arid places seeking rest and does not find it. Then it says, 'I will return to the house I left.' When it arrives, it finds the house swept clean and put in order. Then it goes and takes seven other spirits more wicked than itself, and they go in and live there. And the final condition of that man (woman) is worse than the first. (Luke 11:24-26)

The Word exhorts us to "Encourage and rebuke with all authority." (Titus 2:15) The use of the word "encourage" in the very same sentence with "rebuke" exemplifies an attitude of firmness with compassion and respect in all such confrontations. The word "rebuke" connotes "to reprimand or to criticize sharply." **[161]** Our attitude is one of compassion and respect as we reprimand. The battle is not against the person(s), but it is against the demonic spirits in heavenly places. Trust that it is the Lord Who is working on our behalf as we speak out in faith. The Word tells us, "Be angry but sin not" (Psalm 4:4) It is not a reckless and uncontrollable anger that speaks. It is a controlled, firm, and a holy anger that speaks, an anger that is controlled by a deeper force called faith.

Break the Power of the Inner Vow/ Marriage Requires Proper Authority

An inner vow is a determination or promise made by the mind and heart early in life, and then forgotten. Inner vows program the computer of our mind and heart to resist change. Inner vows are often connected to bitter-root judgments and/or expectancies. They can be made during the formative years and have more power due to their unconscious and hidden nature. **[162]** I had to repent and confess of my lack of trust even in God, which was my sinful reaction to the vow. The vow I made was that I would never let anyone control me with the expectancy that if I let someone into my life that I would lose my identity. This was a blatant lie from Satan.

I had to repent and break the vow to never be controlled by a person, especially a man. Breaking the vow then changed the expectancy. Breaking the vow brought possibility to at least be open to the idea of dating and of a possible future marital situation. I would begin with friendships with godly and respectful gentlemen who loved the Lord. I would attend church group activities, as singles groups, prayer and church meetings, and recovery and support groups. In friendships, I experienced the success of establishing healthy boundaries. And, thank God, the work of forgiving and releasing both Dad and Mom tore down the walls of my heart and brought me a hope to trust myself in a relationship. I prayed for the Lord's perfect will.

In a good marriage, there should never be domination or control that defiles. Premarital counseling groups and godly counsel is advised. A godly marriage will bring security and peace in the interdependence of one partner upon the other as they both look to Jesus as their authority and their guide. The husband takes on the God-given role of leader in the home and the wife is submitted to his leadership because of her trust in him. She does not lose her identity in the relationship. Her identity is still found in Christ Jesus. A good husband will enhance her identity as a godly woman through his love for her. Jesus must be first in the heart of both the husband and the wife. So that even in a heterosexual marriage codependence does not develop.

When we judge another person and vow never to do what they did, the vow often works in reverse. **[163]** The vow of, "I'll never be controlled by anyone" turns into my need to be in total control myself, over my own world, and over other people. The possibility of sharing equally and in a healthy partnership with someone else is next to impossible until I cancel that vow and bring it to the cross of Jesus Christ. Change will be initiated with repentance for the vow and by first accepting Jesus as the divine authority of my life. Refusal to give up a vow that is an ungodly thought pattern is an idol. This is sin.

We become what we judge. Out of my ungodly vows and judgments, then, I developed the habit of perfectionism, which is actually played out in the control over the environment. When I realized I was living in a bubble of a prison, I had to start reaching out to others to get free of this lifeless existence. Life really starts when you come to the end of yourself. I broke through the isolation through reaching out in prayer groups, Bible studies, church activities, plutonic relationships and, of course, at various employments.

"Do not judge and you will not be judged. Do not condemn, and you will not be condemned. Forgive, and you will be forgiven. Give and it will be given to you. A good measure, pressed down, shaken together and running over, will be poured into your lap. For with the measure you use, it will be measured to you." (Luke 6:37,38)

Take Initiative in Your Own Life – Freedom from Trauma Memories – We are Healed Socially

Living the homosexual lifestyle for so long, I learned independence and a control of my own life. Even after becoming a Christian, I maintained an independent lifestyle, taking care of myself and my own needs. As I became closer to the Holy Spirit and actively involved within the body of Christ with volunteer ministerial activities, I began to relinquish some of that need to control my own life. I enjoyed my Christian friends and loved the safety I felt within the body of Christ. I established healthy relationships. I knew I had to first trust God and surrender to His divine control. I also had to connect in healthy friendships first before I could ever imagine trusting a man in my life.

My vow to not let anyone in was made in my early years. I remember thinking that my Dad could read my mind when I was a child. It was a scary feeling. I always felt vulnerable with him. This deception really affected me as a child, and into my young adult years, but the Lord restored me in my later years. There was a mental, or a "familiar spirit," which affected my father through the generational sins and which was passed down through many generations. Dad had no idea how this was affecting me as a child. I have no recollection of any sexual abuse, but, as stated earlier, something was not right. The details of the memories do not matter. The key is that I have faced the remnants of this deception and I am free from its defilement (violation). I have forgiven and released my judgments against Dad.

When I was a young adult, I actually asked Dad if he could read my mind. He said, "I am your father. Sometimes I know how you feel or what you may be thinking by the look on your face, but of course I cannot read your mind." And I believe that He was being honest. This was a spiritual attack from the world of Satan and his "familiar spirits." I also was very dependent upon my father as his child. Yes, to me, it felt very real. And it was frightening as I felt like I was being invaded. My spiritual and mental boundaries were violated, like a spiritual/mental rape if you will. I had no knowledge of familiar spirits, which are demonic spirits who are familiar with your soul and know how to harass you.

As a teenager, I had not yet learned the control I had of my own spirit, soul, and body with my will. Why? My sense of inferiority, my need to please people, and my need for their approval took precedence to my own self confidence. I had not grasped the art of setting healthy boundaries, especially with family members. I was ignorant to the Word of God, to the fact that the Lord was not only living within me, (Colossians 1:27) but that He was my shield, (Psalm 3:3) and that His presence within me was greater than any alien spirit.(1ˢᵗ John 4:4) Also, I had the ability to take control of that which I allowed into my spirit, my soul, and my body with an act of my will and with the use of my spoken words of faith! I had the ability to petition my Father in the name of Jesus with my heart of faith (with submission, repentance, and forgiveness). I also had the ability to then take Jesus' delegated authority to declare that the familiar spirits flee and declare the Word of God over myself, in the name of Jesus, also with my heart of faith. **To them God has chosen to make known among the Gentiles the glorious riches of this mystery, which is Christ in you, the hope of glory. (Colossians 1:27)**

We must always make room for the possibility that our imagination can also deceive us with these feelings of violation, especially if we have been violated in the past. These are "trauma memories" which can present. These are the same feelings we felt during past traumas that will present in a present day interaction where a person may ignite a memory and there may be no violation at all. The awesome rebound to these feelings of violation is that when we know by faith the presence of Jesus within and with us, our own identity and confidence in both Him and ourselves strengthens us against any memory. The memories are there but the pain attached to them is gone. It places us in the reality of the "now" in dealing with other people. If we are faced with a similar personality to a past abuser, we act in compassion instead of inferiority. Yet we must be aware of the vulnerable areas that Satan will attempt to deceive us with in order to have victory over them. We are more than conquerors in Christ Jesus Who loves us. (Romans 8:37)

Thus, what we feel and/or imagine does not take precedence to our present experiences in communication with others. We take control of these feelings through faith and by staying grounded in Christ Jesus. We take an active part in our own healing in the social arena through rising up in compassion and taking initiative in our conversations, by casting down every imagination to the obedience of Christ, and, also, in our prayers to the Father in the name of Jesus. I can speak God's Word under my breath in my heart when in any challenging situation in order to stay focused on the Lord. I can place the blood of Jesus between myself and anyone who is challenging me with a difficult memory. Remember, Satan knows our weaknesses.

I do not have to receive negative words or anything I may perceive as negative from any persons' spirits. We do not let others identify or control us. We have control of our own spirits, bodies, thoughts, emotions, past memories, and present imaginations by the proper use of our will. We are led by the promptings of the Holy Spirit. We are already identified in Christ. We are also no longer distracted by the memories of the past traumas because we have resolved them through repentance and forgiveness with a release of all judgment and/or blame against the persons who caused us the harm. And we have released ourselves of all guilt we took upon ourselves as a result of the traumas.

The weapons we fight with are not the weapons of the world. On the contrary, they have divine power to demolish strongholds. We demolish arguments and every pretension that sets itself up against the knowledge of God, and we take captive every thought to make it obedient to Christ. And we will be ready to punish every act of disobedience, once your obedience is complete. (2ⁿᵈ Cor. 10:4-6)

I had a fear of my own mother because the spirit that was oppressing her was coming against me. She had a controlling affect upon me because I was codependent and enmeshed in the relationship. Later in life, I had to learn to become assertive with controlling personalities and maintain my own personality in the process. As I forgave and released her, I was blessed with some of Mom's strengths and the Lord showed me how to use them against present day predators. And I became strong in the Lord with my own identity in Christ because of my obedience to forgive her. **Better a patient man (woman) than a warrior, a man (woman) who controls his (her) temper (spirit) than one who takes a city. (Proverbs 16:32)**

Therefore, we do not just mold to others' opinions because we have already formed our own. We are not moved by other people's negative words because we know that God is for us. (Romans 8:31) We are not changed by others' spirits because we are firmly grounded in Christ Jesus Who lives within us. (Proverbs

16:32) We are not identified by others' opinions and/or prophesies, because we always seek the Holy Spirit in confirming everything within us that comes to us from the outside. (John 16:13) **If God is for us, who can be against us? He who did not spare His own Son, but gave Him up for us all – how will He not also, along with Him, graciously give us all things? (Romans 8:31,32)**

Jesus heals all our traumas and wounding as we invite Him into each area of violation and allow Him to repair and to restore us. He heals us as we identify the wounding and the vulnerabilities to Him. The Holy Spirit, our divine Counselor, gives us strategies to strengthen that which is weak, whether it is a weakened will, a weakened emotional challenge, or a mental challenge. Today I understand the workings of this deception of mind control as demonic and just as another spiritual deception from Satan's kingdom. No one can control your thoughts unless you allow it! The Lord comes in to heal whatever is broken as the Holy Spirit quickens us to the enemy's deceptions and to our vulnerabilities. (Luke 4:18)(Isaiah 61:1) (Isaiah 53:3-5)(Scripture references) When we acknowledge and accept our vulnerable areas, we will then be wise to Satan's deceptions.

However, there are times when I am attacked spiritually and do not even know it. Satan knows our weak areas. He is a relentless foe. Stay alert in Christ at all times. The enemy is always on the prowl. I still am learning how to set healthy boundaries. I do not leave my home before spiritually dressing and, in that process, putting on the armor of God, spending time in the Word, and praying with my heart of faith (submission, repentance, and forgiveness), to my Father in the name of Jesus Christ.

With shame extinguished, walking free in my own identity in Christ, I emerged with spiritual eyes, seeing all people as one, all as distinctly different in abilities and talents, but all the same in humanness. It is as if we are all set together in a pot of stew. We do not change in our own distinct personalities and giftings, as the potato is still the potato as it sets next to the carrot or the beef. We retain our own individuality as we firmly stand strong in our identity of Christ in us, our hope, and our very identity, free to be whom He created us to be. (Col. 1:27)

I have forgiven Dad. In releasing all judgment, I am healing from the wounds and finding myself attracted to a man who reminds me of my father. He was placed in my life to remind me how much I loved my father who is now in heaven. When we forgive and release judgment, the Lord will restore the good memories and the precious bonding we had with the people we need reconciliation with. It is a natural law that whatever we give will come back to us. (Luke 6:38) Jesus said, **"Give and it will be given to you. A good measure, pressed down, shaken together and running over, will be poured into your lap. For with the measure you use, it will be measured to you." (Luke 6:38)**

The enemy is Satan, not flesh and blood, as much as our emotions will try to deceive us! I refuse to let the enemy control my life anymore, no matter what he throws at me. Life is too short to allow him to steal any more precious time from me. I will still rest in the deep peace of God and I will walk in love and compassion for even those that Satan tries to use against me. I am no better or inferior to any person. (Job 12:3) The hurt, with true forgiveness, will be transformed to compassion. I will say, however, that I am extremely particular about whom I choose to date. I stay closely connected with a church body and Christian singles groups to keep connected to men sold out to Jesus Christ in all my associations, whether business or social. I encourage group dating first before one to one dating. Keep temptation far from you.

Prayer for the Lord's Perfect Will

Prepare Your Heart of Faith – "Jesus, I believe You died on the cross for me and You resurrected on the third day. I ask You to come into my heart and to be the Lord and Savior of my life. I submit to Your Lordship and to Your authority.(James 4:7)(John 3:3)(Romans 10:9,10) (Col. 2:10,15)(Romans 10:13) (John 3:16) I now repent and turn from all my sins and ask You to fill me with Your Holy Spirit. (Acts 2:38) I forgive and release all judgment against myself and all who have sinned against me." (Matthew 6:12) (Luke 6:28,37)

Enter into the Father's Presence – "Father God, I enter into Your presence with thanksgiving and praise in my heart with my petitions. I come boldly to Your throne of grace because of Your blood sacrifice that remits (forgives and forgets) all my sins, in Jesus' name, Amen."(Hebrews 10:19-22) (John 16:23) (Psalm 100:4)

A New Beginning - Ask the Lord for His Perfect Will for Your Best Soul Mate

"Jesus, I speak to all of Satan's deceptions and lies in regards to pursuing a healthy relationship with a man; the need for control, unforgiveness, lack of trust, apathy, or any fears or judgments, whether conscious or unconscious.(Mark 11:23-25) I cancel all ungodly inner vows that I have made to disallow a significant other into my life and heart in Jesus' name. (Matthew 18:18) I now open my heart to the possibility for change.(Acts 16:14)(Psalm 51:10) Satan, I put you on notice in Jesus' name. (Luke 10:19) Go where Jesus sends you to be held captive by the angels of God. (Mark 5:8-13) I cast down every lie regarding my identity as a godly woman in Jesus' name.(Luke 10:19) I declare that I have forgiven and have released all judgments against my earthly father and against every abuser with the help of the Holy Spirit and in the name of my Lord Jesus Christ.(Luke 6:28,37)(Acts 2:38)(Phil. 2:9) I now repent of my part in all abusive experiences. (1st John 1:9) I also release myself of all guilt and/or shame that I may have falsely assigned to myself in Jesus' name. (Rom. 1:8)(Rom. 1:16) And, as a result, I retain the love I have for my father and for all men deep within my heart.(Lev. 19:18)(1st Cor.13) Today, I declare myself as Your child and as a godly woman, in Jesus' name.(Gen. 1:27,28) I stand in awe of You; whole and healed of all traumatic experiences.(Psalm 4:4)(Luke 4:18)(Isaiah 53:3-5) I believe and declare that I have been made brand new in Your sight, in Jesus' name, Amen." (Isaiah 43:1-4)(2nd Cor. 5:17)(See Appendix)

"I firmly am convinced that it is you, Satan, Who works to oppress, to control, to defile, and to destroy human beings. (John 10:10)(1st Peter 5:8)(Ephesian 6:12) And you, Satan, are under my feet because of the precious blood of Jesus Christ.(Matthew 22:24)(James 4:7,8) I declare that I am a woman of God and I am free and forgiven from all past ungodly soul ties, idols, and sins, in Jesus' name.(1st John 1:9)(Ephesians 6:20)) I declare that my body, my soul, and my spirit are washed clean by the sacrificial blood of Jesus Christ in the name of Jesus Christ.(Heb. 10:19-22)(Ephesians 6:20) I am in right standing with You, Lord Jesus. (Rom. 1:17) I commit to daily study of the Word of God and prayer with praise and worship to keep my vessel filled with God."(Luke 11:24-26)(Rom. 12:2)(James 5:16)(Psalm 33:1-3)(John 4:24)(See Appendix)

"I declare that I will come out of this dungeon of isolation in Jesus' name.(Ephesians 6:20) I do sincerely repent, O Lord Jesus, for my rebellion and living with this need for control.(1st Sam. 15:23)(1st John 1:9) You know the wounds I have endured and You, O God, have healed me. (Isaiah 53:5) Thank You, Lord Jesus. (1st Thes. 5:18-20) I cherish the peace I have with You in the intimacy we share, O God.(Col.3:15) (Isaiah 26:3)(John 15:5)(John 14:17,20) I enter into Your loving authority and I am honored to be under the loving control of the Holy Spirit. (Col. 2:10,15)(Acts 2:38)(Phil. 2,9) Your Word says that if I delight myself in You, O God, that You will give me the desires of my heart.(Psalm 37:4) I believe that You made men and women in Your image for fellowship and for sharing." (Gen., 1:26,27)(Psalm 133:1)(Ephesians 5:22-33)(All scriptures personalized)

"I desire a godly helpmate, Lord Jesus. (Psalm 37:4)(Matthew 7:7) I believe that if it is Your perfect will for me to be married, that You will lead me to the best person.(John 16:13)(Phil. 4:19) I ask You to speak to me about this in my soul and my spirit in the right season of my life. (Matthew 7:7)(John 10:5) I will follow Your lead because I seek Your perfect will in this matter. (1st Thes. 5:18-20) May Your will become mine, O Lord. I will make myself available in appropriate social situations. I believe that You will make a way for me. (Heb. 11:1)(Rom. 10:17) I believe that You, Lord Jesus, will supply whatever I need. (Phil. 4:19) I will rise up and reach out in faith to give of myself in relationships with godly men in friendships first in group situations. I believe and declare that You, Lord Jesus, will make a way through ever fear and every deception of the devil, in Jesus' name. (1st John 4:18)(Luke 10:19) I declare that I am now open to become active in heterosexual activities within my church, serving You, O God, as the first love of my life, in Jesus' name.(Ex. 20:3)(Ephesians 6:20) I commit to the setting of healthy boundaries. Whether I marry or not, Lord Jesus, I will remain faithful to my relationship with You, and will continue to cherish You, O God, and stay committed to a life of purity in Your sight.(Matthew 5:8)(Psalms 51:10) I ask You, Lord Jesus, to make Your will clear to me in this matter.(Matthew 7:7) I ask You to make this perfectly clear in my spirit first so that I will know what Your perfect will is first, without any doubt in my mind. Prepare me, O Lord, for this. (Luke 7:27) I ask for a godly man who loves You and who serves You even more than he may commit and declare to love and serve me.(Matthew 7:7) I will commit to place You first in my life in my singleness and, also, in marriage.(Ex.20:3)(Ephesians 5:22-33) Thank You, Lord Jesus. I pray and believe, in Jesus' name. Amen." (1ˢᵗ Thes. 5:16-18)(All scriptures personalized)

Delight yourself in the Lord and He will give you the desires of your heart. (Psalm 37:4)

Seek the Lord's Perfect Will

It is going to take a work of the Holy Spirit to convict me for the decision to marry. And I believe that when the right season comes, and the right man comes, I will be inspired and empowered by the Holy Spirit to say "yes" and to dare to explore the possibility by faith. I believe it will be a time when Jesus is fully my Lord, my Savior, and full authority in my life. I believe that the Holy Spirit will direct me to choose the soul mate who will be the best one. The Holy Spirit will help me to make the decision as He has with every other important decision. Premarital counseling is extremely helpful with decision-making for any couple desiring to become married. I have prayed and asked the Lord for the "God Man" whom I will not be able to refuse because I will be so convinced in my spirit that he is the right one.

I knew I had to at least come to a point of surrendering my need for control over my own life and over my environment before I would ever become serious about sharing my life with another human being. If the Holy Spirit led me to marriage, I would have to yield to His will. I know I would always favor the independent life which I have lived for so many years. It will be a change to marry, but, if it is God's will, it will be for the best for both myself and for the other person. The Bible does not say that you must marry to have the favor of the Lord, and Paul did more for the Lord because he was not responsible for the needs of a wife or children.

But there are numerous benefits to the married life that the single person will not have. There is lifelong companionship and friendship, intimacy, added protection from the enemy, the ability to pray in agreement with each other and to grow together; assisting, giving, and sharing life with each other are just some of the benefits. Marriage allows sharing love, heart to heart, with another person in a deep friendship first and foremost. And it legally allows for and purposefully provides for the bearing and sharing of children together. I encourage you to seek the Lord for His perfect will for you in this area.

For this reason a man will leave his father and mother and be united to his wife, and the two will become one flesh. This is a profound mystery – but I am talking about Christ and the church. However, each one of you also must love his wife as he loves himself, and the wife must respect her husband. (Ephesians 5:30-33)

Surrender Any Sense of Responsibility for Others' Failures

In Rev. Vinny Longo's book, <u>Victory in Jesus</u>, he explains how he stood at the crossroads of his ministry to help free people from the grips of the enemy's hold upon their lives. He candidly shares his frustrations and his decision for Christ after five years of ministry. He was overwhelmed in his heart at the loss of three people to AIDS, one to cancer, and one man to suicide;

"I soon realized that I was taking all of this personally. I thought I had failed these people. There was even a part of me (or a demonic force) that was trying to deceive me into thinking that I had caused these peoples' failures." "All of this wouldn't be happening" I reasoned, "if I was in the place God wanted me to be in. The discouragement was leading me into a prayerless depression. My personal hurt had turned to anger, and, as always happens, undealt with anger turns into depression."

"I began to feel quite alone, except for Nancy's (his wife) encouraging presence, as I examined my alternatives and wondered what was next for me. I was confused. Unbeknownst to me, it was the most crucial hour of decision I had ever faced."

"It was then that I heard God's voice once more: 'Vinny, instead of seeking answers, seek me. I have the answers. If you will seek me, you will find the truth. Seek me, and your direction will come.'"

"How could I have forgotten this so easily? I had to get back on my knees and seek the Teacher of Truth." **[164]**

The Word of God gives us another example of the sovereignty of God in all situations: The Spirit of the Lord spoke to King Jehoshaphat before facing the enemy at Moab and Ammon at Mount Seir. **He said, "Listen, King Jehoshaphat and all who live in Judah and Jerusalem! This is what the Lord says to you. Do not be afraid or discouraged because of this vast army. For the battle is not yours, but God's."** (2nd Chronicles 20:15)

God Will Get Our Attention- Leave "Lands" For His Namesake

Peter said to Jesus, "We have left everything to follow you!" "I tell you the truth," Jesus replied, "no one who has left home or brothers or sisters or mother or father or children or fields for me and the gospel will fail to receive a hundred times as much in this present age, (homes, brothers, sisters, mothers, children and fields – and with them, persecutions) and in the age to come, eternal life. But many who are first will be last, and the last first."(Mark 10:28-31)

I spoke with my heart of faith (with submission, repentance, and forgiveness), to the temptations to stay in the codependent homosexual relationship, "Not my will, Father, but thine be done in Jesus' name." (Luke 22:42) I mailed the letter of farewell to my last lover. I was determined that I would do the right thing for both myself and for my partner(s). "Lord Jesus, I commit to pray for_ (name the person(s)_, in Your precious name. I will obey You, O Lord, no matter how I feel. I will obey You by faith, Lord Jesus. I thank You for Your love, acceptance, and forgiveness of my sins against you. In Jesus' name, Amen." (See Appendix)

With the concerns for clients in the nursing field, I would speak to the Lord with my heart of faith (submission, repentance, and forgiveness), "Jesus, I believe that you know every detail about this (these) client(s) I am concerned about." These were legitimate medical concerns and I expressed them to the authorities in my written reports. I turned in the reports to the nursing authorities, saying with my heart of faith, (submission, repentance, forgiveness), "I cast all my cares about these clients upon You, Lord Jesus." There is always someone available to help you when you are stuck. I did my best to notify the authorities of the details that needed attention. Sometimes I would work with the authorities to solve the problems or, if I had left the case(s), I would turn in the reports to them and release my concerns to the authorities and to God.

If you do not know what to do, just stay close to the Word of God and prayer, stay committed to serving Jesus, and listen for the voice of the Holy Spirit. He will direct you into truth and He will honor your obedience to follow Him. (John 16:13) My doubts and fears attached to perfectionism I am still working through. But I keep close to Jesus and His Word, praying daily, with songs of worship in my heart and mind, and doing all I know to stay actively involved in the Christian lifestyle. Freedom from self doubt comes with prayer, following through with the strategies of the Holy Spirit, and casting our cares upon the Lord in faith. **Submit yourselves, then to God. Resist the devil, and he will flee from you. Come near to God and He will come near to you. (James 4:7,8)** It was not by my power that I left the homosexual lifestyle and the worries of perfectionism because they were so deeply a part of my habit structures. It is the spirit of fear that kept me in these habits. And faith continues to bring me out!

There were many major decisions to leave sin and temptations to sin. It was a combination of obedience to leave the ungodly soul ties to all gay contacts and lovers, leaving ungodly family soul ties and codependent relationships, and leaving the nursing field that fueled the sin of perfectionism that brought me the rest and the deliverance of God. The Holy Spirit knew I would be willing to first repent and then change, even if it meant going on social security. And, as He provided, I plunged into full time ministry.

I made a lot of money in the field of nursing, but my peace with God was more important. And I learned to be content with living simply with what I needed and not with what I wanted. It was sin and separation from God to stay connected to these habits. Just as in homosexuality, I had to stay away from the bars, the people, and do a three hundred and sixty degree turn toward Jesus and my relationship with Him. **No one can serve two masters. Either he will hate the one and love the other, or he will be devoted to the one and despise the other. You cannot serve both God and Money. (Matthew 6:24)**

Angels Watching Over Us

Whenever you are in God's will, there will always be demonic spirits that try to steal your joy and peace with God. They can try to cause harm and they can hover, but they can never come inside with Jesus in your heart. The Word of God tells us that for every demonic spirit, there are literally thousands of angels there protecting us. Satan and his fallen angels will still come to oppress. To the degree of our surrender, by our spoken words of faith, and by the power of the Holy Spirit, we will resist by an act of our faith and by an act of our will; not in our own flesh. (James 4:7) **The chariots of God are tens of thousands and thousands of thousands. (Psalm 68:17) For He will give His angels charge concerning you to guard you in all your ways; they will lift you up in their hands, so that you will not strike your foot against a stone. (Psalm 91:11-12)**

Honesty and Humility Destroys Pride

With each battle, I came to a deeper surrender in Christ, determined to continue on in my faith with a deeper anointing. Repentance is a daily activity. This is what the walk of sanctification is all about. We never "arrive" at perfection. We are still human beings. We must remember that it is God's forgiveness that saves us from all condemnation. We serve a loving God. As we press daily into Jesus, we enter into a closer relationship with Him. He teaches us through His Holy Spirit how to become more like Him. **For our light and momentary troubles are achieving for us an eternal glory that far outweighs them all. So we fix our eyes not on what is seen, but on what is unseen. For what is seen is temporary, but what is unseen is eternal. (2nd Cor. 4:17) "Watch and pray so that you will not fall into temptation. The spirit is willing, but the body is weak."(Mark 14:38)**

"Remember, communication is always a two-way street," says Pastor Demola. [165] I continue to get stronger in faith through each battle. Faith is a spiritual characteristic, not an emotional feeling. We speak by faith and stay steady in our love walk. **For surely, O Lord, you bless the righteous; you surround them with Your favor as with a shield. (Psalm 5:12) God opposes the proud but gives grace to the humble. Submit yourselves, then to God. Resist the devil, and he will flee from you. Come near to God and He will come near to you. Wash your hands, you sinners, and purify your hearts, you double minded. Grieve, mourn, and wail. Change your laughter to mourning and your joy to gloom. Humble yourselves before the Lord, and He will lift you up. (James 4:6-10)**

Daily repentance from dead works brings me to complete dependence upon Jesus. This union with Jesus Christ trades my fear for faith and trades my shame for self-respect, self-confidence, and the righteousness of God (right standing with Him). Because for each precious moment of humbling my wretched flesh to God, I receive a greater anointing of power from the Holy Spirit. Now as I walk with Him, I am convinced that it is only because of Him and His blood sacrifice for me that I walk with the presence of the Holy Spirit both within and upon me.

In Benny Hinn's book, <u>The Anointing</u>, he speaks about the promise of the power of the Holy Spirit: **And the key is repentance. It puts you on the road to great fire and you will reach the destination God intends. [166]** Peter said in Acts: **Repent, and let every one of you be baptized in the name of Jesus Christ for the remission of sins; and you shall receive the gift of the Holy Spirit. For the promise is to you and to your children, and to all who are afar off, as many as the Lord our God will call. (Acts 2:38)**

I now walk with a greater confidence in Jesus Christ dwelling on the inside of me and empowering me with the Holy Spirit's anointing, which is the power and presence of God. The struggle to fight this battle alone ended because I now am totally dependent upon my Creator, Father God, Jesus Christ, my Lord and my Savior, and the Holy Spirit, my Comforter and Counselor, Who guides me into all truth, one day at a time.(John 16:13)(John 14:16)

Becoming God Conscious

The Lord has showed me His heart for people. Many are suffering and need to know Jesus. They need to accept Jesus as the Lord of their hearts and of their lives. In other words, until they accept Jesus Christ as Lord and Savior, they will not inherit the promise of eternal life or His precious benefits and promises. We are called to share Jesus with those who need Him. This is the Great Commission which Jesus gave to His disciples. We are His present day disciples. (Matthew 28:19,20)

Benny Hinn speaks further about this transformation: **Fear is the first result of self-consciousness, and boldness is the first result of God consciousness. When we become God-conscious, we are no longer forced to trust in ourselves and our own strength, but God's presence resides within, bringing power and authority to our lives. We no longer must fight our battles in our own strength, but we can boldly call upon God Almighty through the authority of the Holy Spirit. [167]**

I thank God for the ministry of Victory in Jesus, under the anointing of Reverend Vinny Longo and his anointed wife, Nancy. I learned so much about spiritual warfare and have been blessed with their support during the most difficult times of this battle. Vinny says in his book, Violent Faith, Unless your faith is where it should be, you won't know how to "pull the trigger" that unleashes God's power and hits the intended mark. **[168]** A faith that is activated through the authority of the name of Jesus is God's faith. It is a violent faith that takes dominion over every situation and condition. The name of Jesus is the badge of authority that the devil and his legions recognize immediately. **[169]**

Faith is the Victory – Stay Involved in Life

All sin is rooted in pride because we seek for our own desires rather than the will of God. The sin of homosexuality and the sin of perfectionism are rooted in the same lie. It is the lie of "I want." Letting go of "I want" brings about the birth of the matured adult. The question now arises, "What do you want me to do, Lord?" As Jesus spoke to His Father at the garden of Gethsemane asking for the cross to be taken away, He spoke the words, "Not my will but thine be done."

I needed to die to self so that I could then accept God's supernatural strength and power in my life. In dying to self, the need to strive dies and that demon spirit that drives us has to go. As I shut the door on strife one day at a time, I began the faith walk. Little by little, I learned to trust God for my miracle of walking in the complete rest of God. God can only work through a committed and submitted vessel.

I think the hardest part of this process was being honest with myself. I was so deceived by the devil that I deceived even myself. If you told me I was selfish or prideful, I would not have believed it. If you told me I was not mature enough, I would have been insulted and surprised. Because I had suffered so long in self-pity, I must have thought I was a martyr. In actuality, I was very selfish, living in my own little bubble. When I became comfortable in the "bubble," I knew I had to change. I knew that this was a dangerous place. I was nurturing the hurt little child, licking her wounds, and wasting so much time. I had to change. I had to humble myself not only to God but to other people and connect to them. **Resistance to repentance because of old patterns of justified rebellion against those who have abused authority and abused us must be seen for what it is - sin - and turned from. [170]**

Give to Others

Did I realize that I still had pride and a bitter heart? Of course not! I saw it when I moved next door to a friend from my church. I saw my selfishness head on when I would rather spend the day off doing what I wanted to do. I actually had to force myself to give. And that giving began to break me free from the selfishness.

We see ourselves in relationship to others. That is why marriage is a God - given gift to His people. People grow in relationships and sharing with one another, not in isolation. As I grew first in my intimacy with Jesus, listening to the Holy Spirit, and speaking prayers to my Father, then my self-image developed. This divine relationship prepares us for marriage.

We heal through relationships and our own inner healing is primary. Relating with others, we are humbled by them, inspired by them, and they help us to see what we cannot see ourselves. They help us to face the pain. Other people are like mirrors. Through them we are able to perceive and see the good, the bad, and the ugly. **The path to freedom is from pain to truth.** [171]

And, once the truth has set you free, then you will walk in the anointing of the Holy Spirit and His power will be the only power that will be able to keep you free. **So if the Son sets you free, you will be free indeed! (John 8:36)**

Death Cannot Hold Me – Breaking Ungodly Soul Ties

We Are Promised Eternal Life in Christ Jesus
"Where O death, is your victory? Where, O death is your sting?" The sting of death is sin, and the power of sin is the law. But thanks be to God! He gives us the victory through our Lord Jesus Christ. (1st Corinthians 11:55)

The root of all addiction is the fear of death. We all must face death, which is our final enemy on this earth. We can only face death with faith. And Satan, the enemy of our soul, uses fear to block us from experiencing the very presence of God.

Fear disrupts communion with God. [172] The Spirit of fear strikes at the human mind! The mind is Satan's front line of attack. It is the "bull's eye" for attacks. And he knows if he conquers the mind, a person has no chance to lead a normal life. [173]

Satan job description centers on the propagation of fear. Fear is a destructive force which Satan uses to attempt to crush the soul first and then the spirit. This spirit of fear attempts to steal the very life force from every human being.

Once fear begins to take control of our human mind, it acts as a heavy fog. It is an awareness of this fog that motivates the believer to speak in faith even amidst the fog until it lifts its ugly hands off of us. No matter how thick the fog, we are always able to speak out and rise above its deceptive hold. We enforce the Lord Jesus Christ's dominion over the demonic spirits, over our negative thoughts and memories, over our negative emotions, and over our flesh with an act of our faith and our wills and by the power of the Holy Spirit, in the name of Jesus Christ. Our mouths are His instruments to enforce His dominion here in the earth. We, as born again believers, live in covenant relationship with Jesus Christ. In this covenant, we are privileged to take our delegated authority in Christ Jesus and to rise up and dare to speak against negative pulls. That is why our words spoken with a heart of faith (submission, repentance, and forgiveness), are essential to enforce God's will here in the earth.**The tongue has the power of life and death, and those who love it will eat its fruit. (Proverbs 18:21)**

People cannot have faith when they are filled with fear. Countries where Satan is most rampant have the greatest instances of fear. Heathen live in constant fear. Nearly all of their religious activities are designed to appease the wrath of pagan deities. [174] As born again Christian believers, we do not need to appease any gods. There is only one God. And our God has already won the victory over death for us by His Son Jesus' death and resurrection. Jesus' act of obedience to go to the cross finished our war against death and its threatening demons. We inherit eternal life in our born again covenant relationship with Jesus Christ. Because of Jesus' great love and sacrifice for us, we live with the security and with the promise of eternal life. No fear can stand in the way of that promise.(2nd Peter 1:4)

This ruler of darkness - this leader with authority over other wicked spirits - is the strongman. The strongman employs a clear-cut strategy in order to recover all that he has lost. Having been disarmed by the Lord at the person's new birth, or having been caught or cast out, he's unable to reoccupy the individual's <u>spirit</u> which is now permanently reconciled to God. The unclean spirit contents himself, however, with what's left - the person's <u>body and soul</u>. Since he is an evil, driven personality, he doesn't give up. He still seeks to rule the individual, so that he can destroy his or her temple (body) and wreak havoc on his or her mind (soul), doing whatever further damage the individual <u>allows</u> him to do on his eternal way out! The strongman is obsessive and compulsive about reaching this goal. [175]

Love is our greatest weapon against the strongman. **Dear friends, let us love one another, for love comes from God. Everyone who loves has been born of God and knows God. Whoever does not love does not know God, because God is love. This is how God showed His love**

among us: He sent His one and only Son into the world that we might live through Him. (1ˢᵗ John 4:7-9)

Surrender Your Right to Avenge – You Have a Purpose and a Call to Complete

I had no ammunition to fight the spirit of fear until I stepped into the surrendered life with Jesus Christ as Lord. I would remain ensnared by a lifestyle of addiction until I was fully submitted to the Lordship of Jesus Christ. To surrender means "to yield to the power, control, or possession of another under compulsion or demand." **[176]** When you surrender to the Lord, you give up your need to control any person, place, or thing. You put your trust in a loving God from a decision of your will, and by an act of your faith, not out of any compulsion. You surrender out of your need for His divine help and out of obedience to do His will.

The best strategy to surrender to Jesus is to come to Him as a child and say you are sorry for displeasing Him. This is repentance and God will meet the repentant heart. He will give you His divine strength to resist the enemy as you submit to Him. True surrender is not just giving up, but it is also a decided offensive action of a life of prayer on the part of the believer. It is a decision to walk with Jesus submitted under His Lordship and authority, in daily repentance for sin, with forgiveness without judgment, and with obedience and love for yourself and others. True surrender remains focused on the call that you have on your life. You cannot truly surrender to God until you have released your rights to be avenged of the injustices committed against you.

Relearning a new lifestyle, I was reprogramming myself to live without a need to control or to be in control and to simply live in a walking and talking relationship with the Lord. This was going to take time, a process, and many decided acts of my will to change my established patterns of living a life of a survivor to then enter into the abundant life. It would take faith to believe that no matter how long it took, I would learn that surrendering to a loving God would be the only way that I would ever live the abundant life of living in and for Jesus Christ.

Walk in Love

Remember, every time you make progress, Satan is angry. Always stay alert to the workings of the enemy to steal what you have already received from the Lord. I have forgiven my mother and my father so many times. And I have forgiven myself. The enemy will still try to deceive you with lies and negative thoughts about people you have already released. Just say "no."

You forgive with an act of your will and by faith. Eventually the enemy's distractions of the fleshly temptations, of the negative thoughts and emotions, of the painful memories, and of the hindering spirits lose their power to control you as you continue to walk in that love and forgiveness. Walking in love will become a way of life. You walk in love by faith, not by feelings! Remember, love is a fruit of the Holy Spirit. It is the greatest gift. And it is a decision of your will to walk in the love of God. (1ˢᵗ Cor. 13:13) (Galatians 5:6)

When I left the gay lifestyle, the devil would try to lure me back by placing different women in my path to tempt me back and to deceive me to the lie that I was not free. The devil still comes to humiliate and bring shame to me through the gestures and comments of others and through the silence of others because he knows my weak areas. I refuse to allow them to despise me.(Titus 2:15)

Revelation Knowledge to Counteract the Lies of Betrayal

Mom and Dad truly loved and cared for me, but there were demonic spirits that were oppressing them that were inherited through a bloodline curse. It brought oppression to them and it affected me and other family members as well. This was all a part of the generational curse. People suffer for the lack of knowledge that receiving Jesus Christ as Lord in an intimate and a personal relationship with Him would break the power of this curse. Jesus Christ became a curse for us. Accepting Jesus Christ as our Lord welcomes us into a new and divine bloodline, that of Jesus Christ with all its benefits, including the promise of the Holy Spirit. (Galatians 3:13)(Rom. 11:17)(Gal. 3:27-29)(2ⁿᵈ Peter 1:4)(Acts 1:8)(Acts 2:38)

I had to accept the tragedy of the consequences of their lack of knowledge, being grateful for the knowledge I was given, and then fight properly in prayer as their intercessor to break the power of the enemy over their souls and over mine as well. I had to acknowledge that I hurt them as well with my behavior. (See Appendix)

Receive Revelation Knowledge from God's Word

Friend, the knowledge of God's Word brought me freedom from the lie of Satan that Mom or Dad did not love me. It brought me freedom from the lie that I was not wanted. It brought me freedom from the deep hurt and deception that I was betrayed by Mom.

Anything negative that I experienced from my parents or siblings originated from Satan and his hold upon their spirits, souls (mind, will, emotions), bodies, and their lives. When you believe this, revelation knowledge enters your heart, and you are truly free from the deep hurt. Once you acknowledge and believe your enemy is truly Satan (Ephesians 6:12), not Mom or Dad, not any man or woman, or any abuser, to the depths of your heart, you are released. And you have, as a born again Spirit-filled believer, the power of the Holy Spirit within you to help you to forgive from your heart. You can forgive as an act of your faith and with a decision of your will, not as an act of your emotions! (Galatians 5:6) You do not have to be controlled by any driving spirit of grief, fear, anger, self-condemnation or any lying spirit that you were not wanted or loved! You are free from the deep hurt and deception that instigated the homosexual addiction, seeking perfect love and acceptance from the mother or the father figure that only Jesus Christ can truly give. Once you tackle this lie, you are free! We are all imperfect beings. We can only receive divine and perfect love, acceptance, and forgiveness from the Lord Jesus Christ because He is God.

Then Peter came to Jesus and asked, "Lord, how many times shall I forgive my brother when he sins against me? Up to seven times?" Jesus answered, "I tell you, not seven times, but seventy-seven times." (Matthew 18:21,22) When we forgive, we are placing Satan on notice because we know that he is behind the abuse. When we release the hurt and pray for the abuser, we are releasing any judgment and rising up in compassion for the abuser, who needs to be healed in the heart by Jesus. We identify with the abuser if you will. No one person is inferior or superior to another. We are all God's children. (See Appendix)

You Will Never Feel Like Doing This – Forgive and Receive the Love of God

When you by faith forgive and release the need for that perfect love you did not receive from your parents, and acknowledge, accept, and come to gratitude in your heart for the sacrifices they did make for you, accepting all the love, provision, and caring that you did receive from your parents, you are sitting on truth. Then you will open your heart to receive the divine perfect love from Your Lord and Savior Jesus Christ. Accepting this truth is what you need for the completed healing of your heart and for your true identity, which is found only in a relationship with Jesus Christ. He will shower you with His love as you continue to walk in fellowship with Him. (John 7:37)

Jesus stood and said in a loud voice, "If anyone is thirsty, let him come to me and drink. Whoever believes in me, as the Scripture has said, streams of living water will flow from within him." By this He meant the Spirit, whom those who believed in Him were later to receive. (John 7:37) That unconditional love you receive from Jesus Christ will become a wellspring of life to you that will replace the childlike need to be accepted by men and women; it will replace the performance mentality to do for others in order to be accepted by them. Because your completeness will now be found in your intimate relationship with Jesus Christ. You will be able to forgive yourself and all who have sinned against you in that place of unconditional love, acceptance, and forgiveness that you have received from the Lord Jesus Christ. Why? Because you will be walking in the power and the strength of the Lord with Jesus Christ dwelling on the inside of your heart and the Holy Spirit abiding closely upon and within you to empower you to do what you could not do in the natural. And you will live and give to others now walking in faith, not in the natural senses. Father God will be pleased. And all the broken and fragmented pieces of your heart will be restored.

In these words of Job, he accepted God's plan for his life and his spiritual eyes were opened. He began his walk of faith through his sufferings as he spoke to the Lord. **"My ears had heard of You but now my eyes have seen You." (Job 42:4)**

What are Ungodly Soul Ties?

A soul-tie is the joining or bonding between two or more persons through the doorway of the soul as described in the earlier chapter entitled, <u>Go Home to Be At Home</u>. There are godly and ungodly soul ties. Marriage is the most sacred covenant because it is ratified by God Himself. This is a godly and a holy soul tie. The relationship between husband and wife should be parallel to the relationship between Christ and the Church. **Husbands, love your wives, just as Christ loved the church and gave Himself up for her to make her holy, cleansing her by the washing with water through the Word, and to present her to Himself as a radiant church, without stain or wrinkle or any other blemish, but holy and blameless. In the same way, husbands ought to love their wives as their own bodies. He who loves his wife loves himself. After all, no one ever hated his own body. For this reason a man will leave his father and mother and be united to his wife, and the two will become one flesh. This is a profound mystery – but I am talking about Christ and the church. However, each one of you also must love his wife as he loves himself, and the wife must respect her husband. (Ephesians 5:25-32)**

An ungodly soul tie is a spiritually illegal joining of souls. It involves any vow, promise, an oath, or covenant made with another person outside of the marriage covenant which breaches the holy boundaries ordained by God. One does not have to be sexually intimate with someone for ungodly soul-ties to occur. Pornography can create a soul-tie with the object of lust. For example, a man who never met a Hollywood star can have a soul-tie with the image. Through masturbation, the person is idolized, (male or female), and is fantasized about by the person. There is a giving up a part of one's self to the object of lust. [177] This also is sexual sin. That part that is given up belongs to Jesus. **God takes a harsh view toward sexual sin: [178] But the cowardly, the unbelieving, the vile, the murderers, the sexually immoral, those who practice magic arts, the idolaters and all liars, – their place will be in the fiery lake of burning sulfur. This is the second death. (Rev. 21:8)** These are the words of Jesus. **"For out of the heart come evil thoughts, murder, adultery, sexual immorality, theft, false testimony, slander. These are what make a man (woman) 'unclean'; but eating with unwashed hands does not make him 'unclean.'" (Matthew 15:19,20)**

God Wants Us Completely Free To Love Him and He Us

God is a jealous God, concerned for our welfare. He wants our complete allegiance to Him so that we are strong in the Lord and His Word to guard against evil spirits, spiritual influences, and defilements (violations) that can enter into the doorway of our souls. He loves us and wants us free from all such bondage so that we may enjoy life and enjoy His love for us in our intimacy with Him. (Matthew 15:17-20)

As we develop our intimacy with Jesus, our identity and ways of thinking are changed. As we become clearly aware of His presence with us in our private time with Him, carnal fantasies are transformed to godly imaginations of the Lord being there with us and loving us. And He blesses us with a divine peace in His presence. For so long I had a fantasy of being overtaken by someone until the Lord transformed my thinking. The victim mentality and the carnal fantasy was annihilated and changed to a godly imagination of the actual presence of the Lord there with me and tenderly loving me. **I am the Lord your God, who brought you out of Egypt, out of the land of slavery. You shall have no other gods before me. (Exodus 20:2,3)**

Homosexual relationships are adulterous relationships in which, whether consciously or unconsciously, promises are exchanged with each other. Each partner becomes an idol to the other. Any person or thing can become an idol. **We may become soulishly attached to things. Thus idolatry occurs in various forms: to animals, to people, babies, and inordinate affection: anything can become an idol. [179]**

In homosexuality, the worship of God is illicitly shifted to the worship of a man (men) or a woman (women) through the deceptive lies of Satan who captures the minds and hearts of God's precious children. His lie to me was, "How can love be a sin?" Other lies included, "I must have been born this way." "I must have done something wrong to deserve this trial." "I don't know. I just always had these feelings." Satan attacks us from the feeling and thought realm with confusion, reasoning, self-condemnation, belittling the child of God to believe that she/he either is a bad person or that he/she is not wrong to follow the feelings. Lies! Friend, no one is born homosexual and all of God's creations are precious! We are all sinners saved by the grace of God. (Romans 3:23) God is a loving God, not a punishing God. We are all born in the image and the likeness of God, as male and female. (Genesis 1:27)

For although they knew God, they neither glorified Him as God nor gave thanks to Him, but their thinking became futile and their foolish hearts were darkened. Although they claimed to be wise, they became fools and exchanged the glory of the immortal God for images made to look like mortal man and birds and animals and reptiles.

Therefore God gave them over in the sinful desires of their hearts to sexual impurity for the degrading of their bodies with one another. They exchanged the truth of God for a lie, and worshiped and served created things rather than the Creator - who is forever praised. Amen.

Because of this, God gave them over to shameful lusts. Even their women exchanged natural relations for unnatural ones. In the same way the men also abandoned natural relations with women and were inflamed with lust for one another. Men committed indecent acts with other men, and received in themselves the due penalty for their perversion. (Romans 1:21-27)

An Open Door for Demonic Invasion

Having one or many ungodly soul ties through fornication or sex which is not divinely joined through the holy marriage covenant opens the way for demonic invasion into a person's life. Matthew states that one cannot serve both God and mammon. **[180]** All present and past ungodly soul ties, even if no longer relating to a partner or partners of the past, must be physically broken and spiritually severed in prayer through the authority of Jesus Christ. This is best done in the prayer of agreement with Spirit filled counselors who can help you to stay accountable to your commitment to the Lord Jesus Christ. (added by author to footnote). Along with prayer, several steps must be consciously and decidedly taken for the believer to be set free from the powers of the unclean spirits which have invaded and oppressed the person. With prayer and obedience, one will be set free in the heart (physical and emotional memories and attachments), in the mind (obsessive thoughts, longings, and fantasies toward the person(s) or the images(s)), in the body (carnal temptations), and in the spirit (oppressive harassing spirits of lust). (See four steps to breaking ungodly soul ties in the following several pages.)

Homosexuality, lesbianism, and other forms of perversion cause ungodly links of guilt, shame, and sin. Extremely strong soul-ties are often formed between such "lovers." [181] A common problem is that of evil soul-ties which exist between ex-lovers who have not married each other. By definition these individuals have entered into a sexual union by which they have been made one flesh, outside the covenants of God. They have entered into an ungodly union and consummated that evil union sexually, becoming thereby one flesh, creating an evil soul-tie. The problem of being "love-sick" or "heart sick" is a reality. Even Shakespeare wrote of such cases.

Some experience obsession, passion-lust-love ties with the objects of their affection which can become extremely tormenting. It is not uncommon to encounter those who testify that their minds are tortured, and that they are unable to get the words, or images, of the other partner out of their thoughts. Psychology speaks of this condition as a mind link; we see it as a soul-tie.

This phenomenon usually manifests when the relationship is threatened, when one of the lovers is attempting to break off contact with the other. This is not the compulsion simply to see one another, often experienced by those in love when a relationship is breaking up or doing badly, but rather a compulsion bordering upon an obsession to be with that person, even though mentally the person wills to be free from the other party.

There is a union that occurs when two individuals are sexually united as their bodies merge, so also, apparently, do their souls merge. The result is a union, albeit temporary. However, the fruit of that union can be relatively permanent. For instance, if human conception occurs, a child will be the result: a visible, tangible, lifetime, memorial expression of the union that occurred. There is also an invisible memorial, an expression of that union in the form of a sexual soul-tie, which will likewise last a lifetime, or until it is recognized, its hold broken, and its residue expelled. **[182]**

The born again believer is empowered by the Holy Spirit to break all ungodly soul ties. **Since, then, you have been raised with Christ, set your hearts on things above, where Christ is seated at the right hand of God. Set your minds on things above, not on earthly things. For you died, and your life is now hidden with Christ in God. When Christ, Who is your life, appears, then you also will appear with Him in glory. Put to death, therefore, whatever belongs to your earthly nature: sexual immorality, impurity, lust, evil desires and greed, which is idolatry. Because of these the wrath of God is coming. (Colossians 3:1-6)**

In this scripture, serving money is only one example of an idol that breaches the divine surrender of a soul to God. Any person, place, or thing, including the internet, social networking, a philosophy or a mindset, can become an idol in our lives. Even godly soul-ties can become perverted and idolized. **Remember that the less you are controlled by another, the more you will be able to yield yourself to God's control. [183]**

Breaking Ungodly Soul Ties

Virtually all battles with Satan are fought in the battlefield located in the mind. This is especially true with regard to deliverance in general, and breaking of soul-ties in particular. The candidate for freedom must come to recognize that a soul-tie problem exists, make the decision that he/she wants to be free, and determine to take steps in that direction.

These steps will include some or all of the following: repentance and confession, with renouncing; verbally breaking soul-ties and severing the tie; casting out evil spirits; and then calling back the fragmented portions of the soul that it might be restored and healed.

The degree of difficulty encountered in breaking a soul-tie will usually be affected by the duration and strength of that relationship. Soul-ties rooted in relationships presumed to be love, involving sexual contact, and those rooted in fear, or in the occult are usually the strongest and most difficult to break. However, even simple over-dependence upon a mother can be very strong if allowed to exist for a long time.

Jesus avoided all control from every source except God the Father, and He resisted all temptation to sin. Holiness requires the need to sacrifice temporary pleasure for the greater goal of personal and spiritual freedom.

Adam broke faith with God by disobedience. He failed to keep the Garden because of his lack of knowledge of Satan's intentions. **[184]**

General Prayer to Break Ungodly Soul Ties

Prepare Your Heart - " Jesus, I believe in Your death, burial, and resurrection. I surrender and commit my heart to You, Jesus, as my Lord, and my loving authority. I heartily repent of all sin. I forgive and release all judgment against myself and all who have sinned against me. Fill me with Your Holy Spirit. I receive the full payment, the forgiveness of my sins. In Jesus' name, Amen."

Enter into the Father's Presence - "Father God, I come to You with thanksgiving and with my petitions, in the name of Jesus Christ, my Lord and my Savior." (John 16:23) (Psalm 100:4)

Sever the Ungodly Relationships and Break All Ungodly Soul Ties

"Now I break all ungodly soul ties and sever the relationships to any person(s) whom I have either had sexual relationships with (whether married or unmarried) in fornication or whom I have had emotional adultery with, transgressing proper emotional boundaries. I also repent of and cast down any imaginations I have had regarding any other person(s) and/or image(s) sexually. (Exodus 20:3,4) (Romans 1:27,28) (2nd Corinthians 10:5) (Ephesians 5:3,7)(Rev. 18:4) Thank you, Jesus, for forgiving all my sins and healing all my diseases. (Psalm 103:3)(1st John 1:9) I commit to not judge or blame any other person, only myself. (Matthew 7:1) (Hebrews 10:30) (Luke 6:37,28) I ask for Your help in this, O Lord God. (Matthew 7:7) I believe that I do not fight against flesh and blood or any person, but against rulers, authorities, and powers of this dark world and against spiritual forces of evil in heavenly places. (Ephesians 6:12) I will not be defeated by my enemies or the devil because greater are You, O Lord Jesus, Who is in me than he who is in the world."(Proverbs 29:25)(1st John 4:4) Your blood covers me. (1st Peter 1:18,19)(1st Peter 2:24) I pray this and believe for these requests, in Jesus' name."(All scriptures personalized)

"My greatest concern for all persons I have had ungodly relationships with is for their salvation. I ask that you send laborers to them to bring them into a divine covenant relationship with You. (Matthew 9:37,38) I pray that you open their hearts to know the hope of their calling. (Ephesians 1:18) I pray that they will be convicted by Your gospel to come to repentance. (Romans 2:4)(2nd Cor. 4:3,4) (Romans 10:9,10) (John 3:16) (Isaiah 53:5) I bind and gag all satanic spirits and forces from operating in their lives, in Jesus' name. (Matthew 18:18) Amen." (All scriptures personalized)(See Appendix)

Step One: Renounce the Sin, Confession, and Repentance
Prayer to Pardon the Sin of Fornication

Prepare Your Heart - "Lord Jesus, I believe You died and rose again for me. I surrender to You. I repent of all sin. I ask You, Lord Jesus, to enter into my heart and to be my Lord and my Savior. I receive Your forgiveness. Thank You, Lord Jesus, for loving and forgiving me. I now forgive and release myself and all who have sinned against me. Today I surrender to You and call You my Lord. Fill me with Your Holy Spirit. In Jesus' name, Amen."

Enter into Your Father's Presence - "Father God, I enter into Your presence with thanksgiving and with my petitions in the name of Jesus Christ, my Lord, my Savior, and my loving authority." (John 16:23) (Psalm 100:4)(Scriptures personalized)

Repent of the Sin of Fornication in the Name of Jesus – Declare Your Cleansing in Jesus' Name

"Father God, in the Name of Jesus Christ, Your Son, I come to Your throne of grace, surrendering and recommitting my heart to the Lordship and to the authority of Jesus Christ. I repent for the sin of fornication which I have committed in violation of your laws. **[185]** I am sorry for having offended You, Lord Jesus. I ask you to forgive me. I forgive and release myself and all who have sinned against me. As you pardon me, dear Lord, I pray and believe that You also cleanse me and make me clean by Your precious blood. (Heb. 10:19-22)(Heb. 9:14) I now apply Your blood to my entire being; body, mind, and spirit, in Jesus' name.(Heb. 9:14) I declare that I am as white as snow because of Your shed blood in Jesus' name. (1st Peter 2:24)(1st Peter 1:18,19) I declare that I am divinely loved, fully accepted, and totally forgiven, in the name of Jesus Christ, my Lord and my Savior, Amen." (Isaiah 43:1-4)(1st John 1:9)(All scriptures personalized)

He Himself bore our sins in His body on the tree, so that we might die to sins and live for righteousness; by His wounds you have been healed. For you were like sheep going astray, but now you have returned to the Shepherd and Overseer of your souls. (1st Peter 2:24,25)

Take Jesus' Delegated Authority against the Consequences of Your Sins in the Name of Jesus Christ Your Lord, Your Savior, and Your Loving Authority

"Now, in your precious name, Lord Jesus, I cancel every curse that I have set in motion in the spirit realm as a result of my disobedience against You, in Jesus' name. (Deuteronomy 28:15-68)(Luke 10:19) (Gal. 3:13) Demons of those curses, go, in Jesus' name.(Luke 10:19) Go wherever Jesus sends you to be held captive by the angels of God. (Mark 5:8-13) I renounce, repent, and turn from of all ungodly soul ties, sins, idols, all beliefs and activities connected to the New Age mindset, and all occult practices.(2nd Cor.

6:17) I will now remove all remnants, books, games, crystals, articles, papers, pictures, cards, letters, statues, furniture, and remembrances of this belief system from my living quarters.(Rev. 18:4) I sever and leave all ungodly soul ties.(1st Cor. 6:19,20)(Ex. 20:3)(1st Cor. 6:17) I will obey You, Lord Jesus. (Phil. 2:8)(2nd Cor. 10;5) Your Word says that if I walk in obedience to Your commands, that I will inherit blessings and not cursings. (Deuteronomy 28:1-14) An undeserved curse cannot come to me. (Proverbs 26:2) I stand in the power and truth of the Word of God right now.(John 8:32)(Psalm 19:9) I declare every devisive plan that the enemy has designated for my life is now cancelled, in Jesus' name. (Luke 10:19)(Mark 16:15-18) I am redeemed from the hand of the enemy in Jesus' name. (Galatians 3:13) The promise of the Holy Spirit has shed divine light and power within me in this matter. (Galatians 3:13)(John 1:4)(John 16:13)(Acts 1:8) I cast every care upon You, Lord Jesus, because You care for me. (1st Peter 5:7) (Psalm 55:22) In the precious name of Jesus Christ, the name that is above every other name, (Phil. 2:9) I belong to You, Lord Jesus. (1st Cor. 6:19,20) I worship and adore You. (John 4:24) I place You higher than any other person, place, or thing in my life. (Ex. 20:3) (Phil. 2:9) Thank you, Lord Jesus, for the help of the Holy Spirit's conviction in this matter.(Acts 2:38)(Acts 1:8)(1st Thes. 5:16-18) For anything I have difficulty leaving, I will seek an accountability partner to help me.(Psalm 133:1)(James 5:16) I commit to daily study of the Word of God and prayer with praise and worship to keep my vessel filled with You, O Lord. In Jesus' name, Amen."(Luke 11:24-26)(Rom. 12:2)(James 5:16)((Pro. 4:20)(Psalm 133:1-3)(John 4:24)(All scriptures personalized)(See Appendix)

As I stand in obedience, the Word of God tells me that, **Like a fluttering sparrow or a darting swallow, an undeserved curse does not come to rest. (Proverbs 26:2)**

Step Two: Sever All Improper Soul Ties

Prepare Your Heart of Faith - "Lord Jesus, I believe You died and rose again for me. I repent of all sin. I ask You, Jesus, to enter into my heart and to be the Lord and Savior of my life. I receive Your forgiveness. Thank you, Lord, for loving me and forgiving me. I forgive and release myself from my sins and I forgive and release all judgment against all who have sinned against me. Today I surrender to You and call You my Lord. Thank You for saving me. Fill me with Your Holy Spirit."

Enter into Your Father's Presence - "Father God, I enter into Your presence with thanksgiving and with my petitions in the name of Jesus Christ, my Lord, my Savior, and my loving authority." (John 16:23) (Psalm 100:4)(Scriptures personalized)

Take Jesus' Delegated Authority and Break All Ungodly Soul Ties, in the Name of Jesus Christ, Your Savior and Lord - Pray to break the soul-ties to all persons, name them one by one, that you have had ungodly ties to in the past and/or in the present day. (1st Cor. 6:17)(Rev. 18:4) Pray this prayer aloud;

"Father God, in the Name of Your Son, Jesus Christ, I make a decision of my will to obey Your command and to separate myself from all ungodly soul-ties with (names each person you have ever been immorally involved with)_____, _____,_____. I am no longer in contact with these people, and I will rid myself of any remnants, any gifts, any letters, or pictures of them to completely sever the ties, allowing Satan no further entrance to my body, my spirit, or my soul. If I am still involved with anyone in an ungodly soultie, I will write him/her and serve the person(s) notice that the relationship is over. There will be no contact with them whatsoever through any avenue of communication; meetings, phone calls, and/or mail, or internet. I will dispose of all objects of remembrance. I commit to pray for these person(s) whenever the thoughts, desires, and/or memories of them come to me." (See Appendix)

"I forgive them for wrongdoing me and I ask You to forgive them as well. I give up my right to be angry with them. I ask You to forgive me for any sin I have held onto in my heart which has contributed to this ungodly soul tie. I commit to pray for their salvation, and their complete deliverance and healing and will renounce all obsessive and compulsive thoughts, desires, and/or fantasies to be a part of their lives again. I place them at your altar now and place my trust in You, Jesus, to take care of them. I ask You, Lord Jesus, to send laborers to them to share with them the truth about Your Son Jesus so that they will repent of their sins and accept You as their Lord and Savior to inherit eternal life, in Jesus' name, Amen."(Rom. 2:4)(Luke

24:31,45)(Matthew 9:37,38) **[186]** " I bind, mute, and gag the demons from them in Jesus' name. (Matthew 18:18) I ask that You, O Lord, to lead them to repentance for their sins. (Rom. 2:4) I pray they will commit to a relationship with You." (Rom. 10:9,10)(John 3:3)(All scriptures personalized)(See Appendix)

"I command any demonic spirits that have come to me through these soul ties to depart now in Jesus' name. (Luke 10:19)(Matthew 18:18) Depart and go where Jesus tells you to go to be held by the angels of God. (Mark 5:8-13) I consecrate my body, my soul, and my spirit to You, Jesus.(Rom. 12:1) I declare I am cleansed and made as white as snow in Jesus' name.(Heb. 10:19-22) I apply the blood of Jesus to my entire being; body, mind, and spirit. (Hebrews 9:14)(1st Peter 1:18,19)(Isaiah 53:3-5) I declare an end to all ungodly soul ties and an end to Satan's entry to my spirit, my soul, and my body in Jesus' name. (Luke 10:19) I will commit to daily study of the Word of God and prayer with praise and worship to keep my vessel filled with God, (Luke 11:24-26)(Romans 12:2)(Proverbs 4:20)(James 5:16)(Psalm 33:1-3)(John 4:24) in Jesus' name, Amen."(All scriptures personalized)(See Appendix)

Step Three: Casting Out Evil Spirits
We must cast out all possible spirits of lust, perversions, addiction, occult control, anger, resentment, hate, guilt, or fear. [187] These demonic spirits are all under the direct command of the leader of all demonic spirits, the "unclean spirit." We, as born again Christians, can cast out these spirits from our own body, soul, and spirit.We must, however, have legal authority to cast out demons oppressing or possessing other people.(See Appendix)

God has invested you with unbelievable power and authority to cast out every evil spirit and to break every demonic bondage. **[188]** This is true as long as you are staying true to the proper boundaries of authority. You have delegated authority in Jesus Christ as a born again believer to rebuke the spirits oppressing you. You have delegated authority in Jesus Christ to cast out and rebuke the spirits oppressing or possessing your children, as parents, until they are of age to take their own delegated authority in Jesus Christ as born again believers. You have delegated authority in Jesus Christ to pray for any born again believer who asks you for prayer to cast out demons. You can also lead them in the prayers to cast out the demons themselves in the prayer of agreement.(Matthew 18:19,20) If an unsaved person asks for deliverance prayer, ask them if they would first commit to become a born again Christian, to repent of sin, and to enter into a personal relationship with Jesus Christ. When they are born again, they also now have delegated authority in Christ Jesus to rebuke and cast out the demons with their own mouths. You, as a born again prayer partner, can also lead them into the prayers and pray in agreement with them if they ask you to. (Matthew 18:18,19,20)(See Appendix)

These are the words of Jesus, **"I tell you the truth, whatever you bind on earth will be bound in heaven, and whatever you lose on earth will be loosed in heaven. Again, I tell you that if two of you on earth agree about anything you ask for, it will be done for you by my Father in heaven. For where two or three come together in my name, there am I with them." (Matthew 18:18-20)**

We seal the prayers by sending the demons wherever Jesus sends them and/or to the depths of the earth to be held captive by the angels of God. (Mark 5:8-13)Then also ask them to commit to daily study of the Word of God and prayer with praise and worship to keep their vessels filled with God and thus to keep the enemy from reentrance. (Luke 11:24-26)(Romans 10:9,10)(Romans 12:2)(Proverbs 4:20)(Psalm 33:1-3)(John 4:24)(James 5:16)(See Appendix)

As a born again believer, the privilege of this authority is yours because of your commitment and relationship with Jesus Christ. Jesus has delegated His authority to you. (Luke 10:19) (Mark 16:15-18) It actually is the power of the Holy Spirit working through your faith filled words as you speak in proper position of heart; with submission to the Lordship and the authority of Jesus Christ in your heart, with repentance for sin, and with forgiveness toward yourself and all who have sinned against you, releasing all judgment. **Whoever believes and is baptized will be saved, but whoever does not believe will be condemned. And these signs will accompany those who believe: In my name they will drive out demons; they will speak in new tongues; they will pick up snakes with their hands; and**

when they drink deadly poison, it will not hurt them at all; they will place their hands on sick people, and they will get well. (Mark 16:16-18)

Prepare You Heart of Faith - "Jesus, I believe You died, You were buried, and rose from the dead for me two thousand years ago. I now surrender to You and recommit my heart and my will to Your authority and to Your Lordship. I am sorry for having offended You. I renounce and turn from all sin, in Your precious name, Lord Jesus. I receive Your forgiveness. I forgive and release all judgment against myself and against all who have sinned against me. I ask You now to come into my heart and to be the Lord of my life. Fill me with Your Holy Spirit. In Jesus' name I pray and believe. Amen."

Enter into the Father's Presence - "Father God, I come into Your presence with my petitions in the name of Jesus Christ, my Savior, Lord, and my authority." (John 16:23) (Psalm 100:4) (Scriptures are personalized)

Take Jesus' Delegated Authority and Rebuke the Evil Spirits from Yourself

Speak the Word of God in the Name of Jesus

"Father God, I now rebuke and cast out every foul, unclean, demonic spirit that has set up a habitation in my body and soul because of every illegal joining. I take authority over the spirit(s) tormenting me. I forever demolish them and break their power in my soul and in my life. I command every demonic spirit that has entered my life as a result of this (these) ungodly soul tie(s) to depart right now. I render the leader of all demon spirits, the unclean spirit, powerless. And I declare myself to be a vessel of the Holy Spirit: holy, pure, undefiled, and sanctified before the Lord my God. I claim the safety and protection of the blood of Jesus Christ over my life, and the lives of all of my descendants, all children, and all persons that my life has touched and will touch. Thank You, Lord Jesus, that Your blood washes the very residue, stain, and odor of this sin away from my life, and my children's lives forever, in Jesus' name. Amen. [189] I believe and declare that I am free from all sexual demons in the precious name of Jesus Christ.(Luke 10:19)(Phil.2:9) Demons, go in the name of Jesus. (Luke 10:19) Go where Jesus sends you to be held captive by the angels of God. (Mark 5:8-13) I apply the blood of Jesus to my entire being; body, mind, and spirit. (1st Peter 1:18,19) (1st Peter 2:24) I declare in Jesus' name that I am free from all demonic spirits and cleansed as white as snow. (Heb. 10:19-22)(1st John 1:9) I commit to daily study of the Word of God and prayer, praise, and worship to keep my vessel filled with God. In Jesus' name, Amen." (Luke 11:24-26)(Romans 12:2)(Proverbs 4:20) (James 5:16)(Psalm 33:1-3)(John 4:24)(See Appendix)

It is God's will that you should be sanctified: that you should avoid sexual immorality; that each of you should learn to control his/her own body in a way that is holy and honorable, not in passionate lust like the heathen, who do not know God: and that in this matter no one should wrong his brother (sister) or take advantage of him (her). The Lord will punish men/ women for all such sins, as we have already warned you. (1st Thessalonians 4: 3-6)

Do you not know that your body is a temple of the Holy Spirit, who is in you, for whom you received from God? You are not your own; you were bought at a price. Therefore honor God with your body. (1st Corinthians 6: 19-20)

Step Four: Call Back the Fragmented Parts of the Soul

Prepare Your Heart of Faith - "Lord Jesus, I believe You died, You were buried, and I believe that You, O Lord, resurrected from the dead for me at Calvary two thousand years ago. I surrender to You as my loving authority and as my Lord. I recommit my spirit, my (soul); my thoughts, my emotions, and my will; and my body, to You, O Lord. I repent of all sin. I am sorry for having offended You. I receive Your forgiveness. I forgive and release myself and all who have sinned against me. I ask You now, Lord Jesus, to come into my heart and to be the Lord of my life. Fill me with Your Holy Spirit. In the matchless name of Jesus Christ. I thank You, Lord, for saving me. Amen."

Enter into the Father's Presence - "Father God, I come into Your presence with my petitions and with praise in my heart for the finished work of Jesus Christ, in the name of Jesus Christ, my Lord and my Savior. The sacrifice of Your Son Jesus Christ brought me the completed healing of my soul, and I am forever grateful to You, O Lord Jesus." (John 16:23) (Psalm 100:4)(Scriptures personalized)

Take Jesus Delegated Authority Over Your Soul in the Name of Jesus

"I now command every portion of my soul that has been fragmented, torn, or broken, to come back into its proper place; to be healed; every piece of my heart to be returned; my soul to be restored, and every bondage of related soul ties to be completely broken. Lord Jesus, I now ask You to heal my heart and to guard it by Your power and Your love, and to keep my heart and mind through Christ Jesus. Now that I have closed, sealed, and locked the door of my heart with the blood of Jesus Christ, I now open my heart to reconnect with my mind, and to experience the freedom of living as a completely whole and healed vessel for God's use. I commit to study the Word of God and to pray on a daily basis so I can now work to replace the void with an intimate and a godly tie to my Savior and Lord Jesus Christ. In Jesus' name. Amen." [190] (See Appendix)

"As I commune with You, Lord Jesus, I discern Your very body, Your divine presence within my heart. I discern Your loving presence within me.(1st Cor. 11:23) I am now covered by Your divine and precious blood in Jesus' name.(1st Peter 1:18,19) I declare that I am as white as snow in Jesus' name. (Heb. 4:19.) I now declare and I humbly receive complete healing for my body, my (soul); mind, will, and emotions, and my spirit, in Jesus' name. Thank You, Lord Jesus, for Your have accepted me."

Restoration Comes After Obedience to Breaking Ungodly Ties

Today I can think about the past relationships because I have taken the steps to break the soul ties. Pastor David Demola so wisely discerned in his statement, "The memories are there, but the pain relating to them is not there."[191] When the past memories surface, I take the opportunity to thank the Lord for delivering me away from homosexuality and for giving me a new heart of love, an affinity with other women which is natural and not perverted. The need to depend upon them to meet my needs has been transferred over to my intimacy with Jesus Christ. I see myself as equal to them, not needing them or having to fix them. Jesus is my Lord and He has revealed to me my confident, unashamed, and honest identity in Him as His beloved. And I praise God for this transformational way of seeing with the eyes of faith and not just with my physical eyesight. I receive this healing by an act of my faith. I thank God that His Word has changed me from the inside out and has made me to be the woman I was always created to be.

Today, I am closer to Jesus, my conscience is clear. I am not perfect, but I am perfectly forgiven. Today I can process the memories because I have the Holy Spirit to guide me through facing, expressing, and releasing the pain to get to the truth. **But you are a chosen people, a royal priesthood, a holy nation, a people belonging to God, that you may declare the praises of Him Who called you out of darkness into His wonderful light. (1ˢᵗ Peter 2:9)**

I believe that the Lord has charge over what memories He brings to me. I thank Him for a certain amount of spiritual amnesia, because there is a lot I have forgotten. I choose not to run from the memories that do arise, because I can now face them with gratitude. God has grown me up and out of the snares of homosexuality. If He brings an x-lover to mind, as when He brings any other person to my mind, I pray for them. If, during my prayers for them, the enemy comes to tempt me back into the compulsion to be with them or to see them again, I quickly cast the thought down and replace it with prayers for their salvation, protection, and healing. (2nd Cor. 10, 4,5)(See Appendix)

Satan is a liar. Many thoughts we think are not our own. They are really thoughts which come from demons. [192] Satan and his demons will try to tempt you into the lie that you still lust for someone, but he cannot keep you in that lie if you cast the thought down. (2ⁿᵈ Cor. 10:4,5) Replace the thought with the Word of God. You cannot lust after someone you are praying for God to heal and to touch with His love and His healing power. When you are walking in the Spirit of the living God, lust has no place in your life. You are standing in the rest of God with Jesus as Lord, Savior, and loving authority.(See Appendix)

Run To the Lap of Your 'Daddy God'

I choose not to run anymore. I can face all things in the light of Jesus Christ in me and the power of His Word, His wisdom, and His love working within my heart. It is only in facing, expressing, and releasing the painful emotions that they lose their control over us. This is when the freedom comes. When the painful memories and emotions surface in the light of the presence of the Holy Spirit, a divine perspective is visualized and the bondage is broken.

Releasing the tears brings us to a new level of surrender in Christ. We see and understand more clearly our weaknesses as well as the other person(s) challenges and weaknesses. We come to a place of openness to settle issues and change behaviors. Forgiveness and release of judgment brings freedom from the pain. Repentance brings us to an openness to change. This is work that can be done between you and the Holy Spirit, with a counselor, and sometimes with the person(s) involved present. However, the other person or persons do not necessarily need to be present. This real work is done through the Holy Spirit as He works within your heart.

In the counsel I received from Dee, who is trained as an Elijah House prayer minister, I was ushered into the presence of 'Daddy God,' at the very scene of being in the arms of the first woman lover. Dee said the words, "You know that Father God was there when you were involved in this lesbian relationship." As the counselor continued to lead me, she then said, "What do you think your 'Daddy God' is saying to you?" I did not experience God speaking at that moment. I just saw myself in the bedroom with the Lord God looking at both of us from a distance in the room. The counselor said, "Go and sit on your 'Daddy God's' lap. As I did this, she then asked, "Do you hear Him saying anything now?" At that moment my Father God put His arms around me and He embraced me. At that moment I knew He loved me. It was the act of the sin He hated, not me. When the counselor asked me to picture myself in His arms, I saw my mother's face, not mine. I believe the Lord was showing me that I needed to see my own face and establish my own identity in Christ and that I needed to emerge out of the enmeshment and the codependence with Mom.

In another session, I took all my paperwork to Jesus to the foot of the cross. You know what He said? "You're a good girl, Bonnie." He, not Mom, gave me the affirmation I needed. When I knew that I had both His divine forgiveness and affirmation, I then had peace.

Godly Decisions

I was willing and God would meet me at the place of my willingness to change. I had to make a decision of my own will to turn away from the temptations, to say "no" to sin, and give the enemy no further entrance or control in my life. We cannot just blame the devil. Just as Adam and Eve had a free will to say "no" to sin, so also we are given free choice. We are inspired by the love of God to stop our sinning because we no longer want to separate from our intimacy with Jesus. We want to stay firmly established in our righteousness (right standing) with Him.

The Holy Spirit answers and gives us strategies when we ask Him. The Holy Spirit will empower us to take responsibility and to decide to stop sinning. This is a key decision which will subdue the control of the enemy's entrance into our spirits, our souls, and our bodies. Seek the Lord in prayer and listen for the Holy Spirit's leadings. Ask Him what the missing ingredient is that keeps you locked into the box. What is needed? More prayer, more fellowship, more exercise?

Using one's free will is the key to locking the door. I used free will to decide to choose Jesus Christ as my Lord and Savior. I used free will to leave the homosexual lifestyle. I used free will to completely surrender to the will of God and to forfeit my own desires, seeking that my will become the same as God's will for my life. And I used free will in my prayer closet to ask the Holy Spirit to come in and to cleanse me of any remaining wounds in my heart, even to the subconscious level. As I obeyed and daily repented and turned from sin, He brought me to a higher and a deeper level in Him.

What happened is that the Lord allowed the oppression of Satan in my life until I was humbled enough to make godly decisions. It was at each breaking point that I received a healing. When I decided to "obey the voice" within my spirit which went deeper than my feelings and even my thoughts, then the demonic and tormenting spirits left me. With each breakthrough, there is a decisive determination to continue walking with the Lord. Yes, we already have been healed by the cross of Jesus Christ two thousand years ago, but we are also working toward the full manifestation of the transformation of our souls as we make godly decisions. (Romans 12:2) (Phil. 2:12,13) **Therefore, my dear friends, as you have always obeyed – not only in my presence, but now much more in my absence – continue to work out your salvation with fear and trembling, for it is God Who works in you to will and to act according to His good purpoase. (Phil. 2:12,13)**

Each healing I experienced was life changing. I was actually comfortable in my own skin and I had, for the first time probably since I was a little girl, peace in my mind. I felt like I was floating, walking through the walk of life without that "horrible presence driving me." Obeying God is a form of taking authority. It is putting one's foot down and saying "no" to the devil. It can be saying "no" to an act of sin. It can be saying "no" to an unforgiving attitude. It can be saying "no" to judging someone else. Whatever the "no" is, we take a step of action by our will to resist the devil's ploys to keep us locked into his darkness. Whenever I am tempted to judge another person, I stop and prepare my heart of faith submitting to the Lord, repenting for my own sins, and, with forgiveness, saying, "Forgive me, Lord Jesus, for judging. I forgive this person, Lord. Bless this person today O Lord."

I knew that keeping my focus on Jesus would be my greatest strength against anything the enemy tried to distract me with. We cannot be neutral in this battle. This keeps us in remembrance of the fact that we are all human beings created by the same Lord. In all cases, the presence and the power of the Lord and His Word in your life is greater than anything the enemy brings to you.

God is in Us to Obey Him

Oswald Chambers has a beautiful way of expressing the battle which rages between the flesh and the spirit; **The thing in you which makes you say "I shan't" is something less profound than your will; it is perversity, or obstinacy, and they are never in agreement with God. The profound** thing in man is his will, not sin. Will is the essential element in God's creation of human beings – sin is a perverse nature which entered into people. In someone who has been born again, the source of the will is Almighty God. "...for it is God who works in you both to will and to do for His good pleasure." With focused attention and great care, you have to "work out" what God "works in" you – not work to accomplish or earn "your own salvation," but work it out so you will exhibit the evidence of a life based with determined, unshakable faith on the complete and perfect redemption of the Lord. As you do this, you do not bring an opposing will up against God's will – God's will is your will. Your natural choices will be in accordance with God's will, and living this life will be as natural as breathing. Stubbornness is an unintelligent barrier, refusing enlightenment and blocking its flow. The only thing to do with this barrier of stubbornness is to blow it up with "dynamite," and the "dynamite" is obedience to the Holy Spirit. Do I believe that Almighty God is the Source of my will? God not only expects me to do His will, but His is in me to do it. [193]

Do not despise the Lord's discipline and do not resent His rebuke, because the Lord disciplines those He loves, as a father the son he delights in. (Proverbs 3:11,12)

Because the heart issues needed to be worked through and because I was controlled by a demonic spirit, I did suffer. It was a stronghold which kept me from completed peace with God. "Stronghold" by definition is "a place of security or survival." **[194]** This habit became a comfort zone of hiding for me after years and years of habitual acting out of the pattern. It had to go. I had to step out and get help from within the body of Christ from a Spirit filled counselor who would provide accountability and lead me out of the bondage. The intimacy we have with Jesus Christ is our divine stronghold!

A friend once said, "Go around it." Whatever the sin is that tempts us, we must learn to ignore it, go around it,confront the root of it, and do whatever we need to do to get free of its hold. As I learned the Word of God, continued to talk to my Savior, and shared with friends in the body of Christ, I developed a new lifestyle of giving of myself to help others. I was no longer isolated and my selfish needs diminished. As I received help in the body of Christ through counseling and support groups, I became stronger to say "No" to every temptation which I knew was not God's will for my life. **Although He was a son, He learned obedience from what He suffered and, once made perfect, He became the source of eternal salvation for all who obey Him and was designated by God to be high priest in the order of Melchizedek. (Hebrews 5:8,9)**

Many are Suffering in the Valley of Decision- New Age Deceptions
Multitudes, multitudes, in the valley of decision! For the day of the Lord is near in the valley of decision. The sun and moon will be darkened, and the stars no longer shine. The Lord will roar from Zion and thunder from Jerusalem; the earth and the sky will tremble. But the Lord will be a refuge for His people, a stronghold for the people of Israel. (Joel 3:14-16)

We are living in the "New Age." Anything you so desire is condoned. The philosophy is, "If it feels good, do it!" This style of life is in direct opposition to faith, which operates on believing in the power of the Holy Spirit to work through a surrendered vessel.

I had developed an ungodly pattern and my conscience was seared to the point that I was blinded to the separation it was causing me from the Lord and from life itself. The habit structure locked me into a state of apathy about the sin I was committing. As also in homosexuality, I hopped from lover to lover, without feeling remorse. Webster defines "seared" as "to make withered or dry" **[195]**

Can I blame it on a spirit that was oppressing me? No. I had to accept responsibility for my own choices. I would never have become free if I kept blaming people, curses, demons, genetics, God, or even Satan! I would never get free until I called the sin the sin, stepped out of the complacency I had developed, and made a clear decision to stop. I had to look at how I was hurting God and others.

There are so many people suffering who do not even know they can live free with a relationship with Jesus Christ. Their lives and souls are at stake. Eternal life is at stake! Would I stay in this rut or reach out to others, giving purpose to both my own life and others' lives. This is the mission we are called to.

Discipline the Mind- Shake off All Distractions

My sin of homosexuality kept me ensnared in self-condemnation and from my very identity as a godly woman, and a woman with a God-given purpose. My sin of perfectionism kept me in the snares of worry which leads to panic. Both stole the peace and the joy I could have had in my life. These were addictions with the same force of control as the drink of alcohol is to the alcoholic or the pornographic picture is to the person controlled by the unclean spirit of lust.

I have to take responsibility for my thoughts. Just as Paul shook off the snake that had attached itself to his hand on the island of Malta, we also must learn to "shake off our temptations to sin." **When the islanders saw the snake hanging from his hand, they said to each other, "This man must be a murderer; for though he escaped from the sea, justice has not allowed him to live." But Paul shook off the snake into the fire and suffered no ill effects. (Acts 28:4,5)**

Finally, brothers, whatever is true, whatever is noble, whatever is right, whatever is pure, whatever is lovely, whatever is admirable - if anything is excellent or praiseworthy - think about such things. (Philippians 4:8)

Faith is the Victory

Mixing Faith with the Word

Faith is our victory. We never walk in the fullest capacity of faith that we are capable of carrying. But, as we step out in the measure of faith that we do have, our faith then grows. When I speak the Word of God, I need to be mixing faith with it and believing in my heart that my faith-filled words will rise above my own flesh, the negative thoughts and emotions, and any evil spirits. I believe that I will be changed. (Hebrews 4:12) These are the words of Jesus, **I tell you the truth, if you have faith as small as a mustard seed, you can say to this mountain, 'Move from here to there and it will move.' Nothing will be impossible for you. (Matthew 17:20,21)**

And, friend, it is awesome, how the Lord has changed circumstance after circumstance and has provided victory after victory. Prayer is amazing because God always shows up. The more I prayed and obeyed God, there was less room left for Satan to deter me. My submission to the Lord and my faith in God to work it through is the greatest deterrent to the enemy. The enemy will eventually flee in each particular battle as we continually submit to God and resist the devil. (James 4:7,8) Obedience to God is the natural result of a heart that is subbmitted in faith to the living God. We confidently expect results as we become serious about His will in our lives. Pastor David Demola said once that, "If you don't mix faith with the Word, you're not gonna get it!" [196] **For we also have had the gospel preached to us, just as they did; but the message they heard was of no value to them, because those who heard did not combine it with faith. (Hebrews 4:2)**

Jesus replied, "I tell you the truth, if you have faith and do not doubt, not only can you do what was done to the fig tree, but also you can say to this mountain, 'Go, throw yourself into the sea,' and it will be done. If you believe, you will receive whatever you ask for in prayer." (Matthew 21: 21, 22)

But when he asks, he must believe and not doubt, because he who doubts is like a wave of the sea, blown and tossed by the wind. (James 1:6)

Looking at the New Testament healings, there are several examples of people being healed through their faith alone. Look at the following examples of Jesus speaking:

"Daughter, your faith has healed you. Go in peace and be freed from your suffering." (Mark 5:34)

Jesus said to the woman, "Your faith has saved you. Go in peace." (Luke 7:50)

"Go," said Jesus, "your faith has healed you." (Mark 10:52)

Jesus said to him, "Receive your sight, your faith has healed you." (Luke 18:42)

Then he said to him, "Rise and go; your faith has made you well." (Luke 17:19)

"If you have faith as small as a mustard seed, you can say to this mulberry tree, 'Be uprooted and planted in the sea,' and it will obey you." (Luke 17:6)

I now strive for excellence, not perfection. Jesus has brought me far in the battle. I believe that it will manifest in complete deliverance as I put Jesus first in my life. I know I will be tempted in weak areas, but I do not sin if I do not give into the temptation. I will continue to fight the good fight of faith with the Word of God. (1st Tim. 6:12)

Then the Lord replied: After Jesus healed the woman who was bleeding for twelve years, He was approached by the synagogue ruler about his daughter. Some men were saying that his daughter was dead. Jesus ignored their death threats and said, **"Don't be afraid: just believe." (Mark 5:36)**

Face the Rebellion- Accept the Authority of Christ- Judge Not

I went through a period of four days of deep despair and mental torment, with thoughts racing in my mind in which I was unable to stop in my own strength. I slept through most of this period of time. I was weakened by it, and I was also humbled. I saw how I had reacted to a trial with a critical eye toward others. I needed to look within my own heart and repent of my own sins.

But God is faithful. He brought me out of the trial. I started to read a book about spiritual authority. In my reading I saw that I had no right to judge anyone, no matter how wrong they might appear to be. In Watchman Nee's book, Spiritual Authority, the author speaks with wisdom about the essence of our submission before the authority of God in our lives when he sites this example in Moses' life:

There can be no rebellion on the part of the Israelites more serious than that which is recorded in Numbers, Chapter 16. The leader of the rebellion was Korah, son of Levi, joined by two hundred and fifty leaders of the congregation. They assembled themselves together and with strong words attacked Moses and Aaron (verse 3).

Moses' first reaction was that "he fell upon his face" (verse 4). This is verily the attitude every servant of God should have. The people were excited and so many were speaking, but Moses alone was prostrating himself upon the ground. Here again we are confronted by one who knows authority. Being truly gentle, he was empty of personal feeling. He neither defended himself nor got stirred up. The first thing he did was to fall on his face. Then he told them: "Jehovah will show who are His, and who is holy, and will cause him to come near unto Him: even him whom He shall choose will He cause to come near unto Him": (verse 5). It was not necessary to strive. Moses did not dare say anything for himself, because he knew the Lord would show who was His. It would be better to let God do the distinguishing. Moses had faith and he dared to trust everything to God.

God came out to judge. He would consume not only Korah who was the chief instigator but also the congregation who followed Korah. But Moses fell on his face and pleaded for the congregation (verse 22). God answered his prayer and spared the congregation but ordered them to depart from the tents of the wicked. Then He judged Korah, Dathan, and Abiram.

So far as his own feeling went he (Moses) had no intention of judging anyone who rebelled against him. He proved himself to be the true servant of God when he insisted that these people had not sinned against him but that they had sinned against God. Let us learn how to touch a man's spirit. We find in Moses there was not the slightest thought of judging. He acted in obedience to God because he was God's servant. He had no personal feeling except that he felt they had sinned against God. He further explained that the Lord would prove this to them by creating something new. [197]

This was an act of deep faith in God on Moses' part. Why was I taking others' sins personally? Their rejection of me would find them out. It was an attack upon God Himself. And God would be their judge. When I humbled myself to the Lord, my focus changed to the Lord and away from the opinions of others.

When I reacted to others with judgment, I was in sin. Again, I found myself in the throws of spiritual pride. I thought I was better because I knew God's Word and had a relationship with Jesus. I found myself doing just what I was judging others for. I actually am held more accountable since I have the knowledge of God's Word and will. We are all sinners!

This is the result of an inner vow. When we vow never to act like someone else, we will find ourselves in the very sin which we are judging! We must give our bitterness to the Lord and forgive those who have rejected us. Otherwise we not only are filled with contempt toward them but we also will become contemptible. Do not take Satan's bait.

Do not be deceived: God cannot be mocked. A man reaps what he sows. The one who sows to please his sinful nature, from that nature will reap destruction; the one who sows to please the Spirit, from the Spirit will reap eternal life. Let us not grow weary in doing good, for at the proper time we will reap a harvest if we do not give up. (Galatians 6:7-9) There is so much contempt built up into the subconscious layers of our hearts. This is why it is essential that we prostrate ourselves before the Lord and repent of all negative attitudes and judgments asking the Lord to cleanse our hearts. We will be cleansed as we pray for others. **Those who sow in tears will reap with songs of joy. He who goes out weeping, carrying seed to sow, will return with songs of joy, carrying sheaves with him. (Psalm 126:5-6)**(See Appendix)

Speak Into Existence Your Miracle

I called out to the Lord and I knew that He would answer me. Joe Dallas spoke at a conference in New York City and I wrote down his statement. "It is in times of crisis that we find the truth."**[198]** When we respond to crisis through repentance to any ungodly lifestyle or sin in our lives, truth will be found. I spoke the words, "I am leaving this land of bondage and I am entering into the Promised Land."

When God created the earth and everything in it, He spoke into existence those things which were not as if they were. **And He said, "Let there be light, and there was light." (Genesis 1:3)** I believed my miracle healing would come and many healings came to me throughout the years. As I obeyed the Lord's voice, I experienced more breakthroughs and impartations from anointed men and women in the body of Christ. I can also attest to numerous healings throughout the years of walls of brokenness and deep pain removed from my heart through the cleansing of the Holy Spirit.

Respect Your Authorities

Since you call on a Father who judges each man's work impartially, live your lives as strangers here in reverent fear. (1st Peter 1:17) In repentance and rest is your salvation; in quietness and trust is your strength . . . (Isaiah 30:15)

God is faithful and He will give us strategy for every situation. He never gives up on us. The Holy Spirit has been my guide and continues to guide me every step of the way. I have stepped away from nursing and highly stressful situations which would tempt me to the perfectionism. I had to leave all lesbian relationships. To be in right relationship with Jesus is the most important thing in my life.

The Lord always provides a way out of any temptation! We just have to let our pride go to heed to the answers. I have found supervisors whom I could trust and they have helped me to overcome my concerns about the clients. I have to be honest with my authorities! This has been my greatest strategy for freedom from perfectionism. It may be humbling to admit weakness, but I must share the truth with them that this has been a difficult area for me and ask their help to let go of the details that concern me. I turn in my reports and let go. And learn to trust both God and the authorities over the clients as well.

Teamwork is precious! My admission of my problem to them takes away any judgment they may be interpreting from me. It places the light on amidst any darkness Satan will attempt to throw into the situation. Satan has no power or say in the midst of truth.

There were seasons in the healing process when I was not strong enough for certain job responsibilities. And there have been seasons in which I was strengthened to take on greater responsibility. I just remain honest with myself, my supervisors, and trust in the leading of the Holy Spirit. **Do nothing out of selfish ambition or vain conceit, but in humility consider others better than yourselves. Each of you should look not only to your own interests, but also to the interests of others. (Philippians 2:3,4)**

Fall Down - Pick Yourself Up

You cannot be intimate with someone you do not trust. [199] The devil uses people to plant seeds of self-doubt which can only be thwarted with bullets of faith. Whenever I feel rejected by another person, I have lost trust in God. I weaken as I allow my emotions to take control over my spirit first, and then my soul. In order to recover from the disappointment, however, I distance myself from the person and seek the Lord. I believe that my tears are of real sorrow because I have been hurt and also because I have failed myself. Why? I must take responsibility for the seeds I sow as a result of my own self-rejection. Self-rejection invites others' rejection. Remember, the Lord has commanded us to love our neighbors "as ourselves."

I may seek counsel with another person who will be able to give me godly wisdom and perspective about dealing with the issue. Sometimes a word said in a due season will completely change the course of a conversation. Had I not been in a victimized state, I would have responded to this person differently. I must remember that I have every right to say to a person who is speaking to me, "I do not receive that, but I still respect you."

As I enter into worship with my Creator, the grief I feel over the rejection from others is brought to the dust. As I imagine Jesus Christ on the cross saying, "I love you, Bonnie," a true perspective is gained. I need to take man or woman off the throne at these times and recommit to Jesus as my Lord. It doesn't matter who has hurt me.

As I deepen in my bonding with Jesus, the thoughts and opinions of other people diminish and I am able to rise above my own hurts. Because the "things of earth grow strangely dim in the light of His glory and grace." And I have grown to both love and respect myself. When I am connected with Jesus, I can react as Moses and fall on my face and pray for those who have rejected or abused me. With less of me and more of God, my viewpoint is changed from the flesh to the divine perspective as I see others' rejection as a sin against God and not against me. **The Lord is my strength and my song; He has become my salvation. (Psalm 118:14)**(See Appendix)

Speak and Believe God Will Make a Way

Homosexuality or perfection is never the salve for rejection. Jesus is the only way. In receiving His love and complete forgiveness for our sins, we enter a covenant of love with Him in which no man or woman can intercept. God will always make a way out of every storm. Our part is to believe God to bring us out. Pastor David Demola says, "Never make the storm the issue or you will fail."**[200]** In believing God, I surrender the solution of the problem to God and, just like a child, believe that He has the answer and will somehow show me the way.

We Don't Reach Heaven Until We Die

I had to reach the end of myself with all addiction. I had to stop and believe God would make a way out of the insanity of it all. Faith is deeper than all the rationalizations and introspections of the mind. Out of sheer desperation, I learned to trust. And He astounded me as He showed me how close He really was to me after I took the steps to resist the urges.

Once we think we have made it, we will be chastened by the Lord. For example, after the terrorist attack in New York City, I was at a Messianic Church in Garfield, New Jersey. Pastor Jonathan Cahn had an altar call for anyone who wanted to recommit his or her life to Jesus. I really wanted to "make sure" of my salvation at this time, yet pride held me back. I left the service feeling saddened that I did not take the opportunity and angry at myself for my pride.

The Holy Spirit showed me that I was spiritually proud and that I needed to correct this for further strength in Him. My family members would say, "You are so spiritual" These compliments built my pride. Had I been honest with them, I would have rebuked the false statements and given God the glory. Instead, I accepted false compliments and became more proud!

Homosexuality reeks with pride which says, "I do not need God." However, almost thirty years after leaving the lifestyle and living a Christian lifestyle, I still find myself in the tentacles of pride in areas that I am not even aware. Keeping accountable to a church helps me so much! I have lived so many years on my own and learned how to live without any commitment to a spouse. I learned self reliance which was strength in some ways, but a deterrent in many other ways. I have to kill this pride in all areas of my life. Marriage more than doubles your protection against pride in your life! In marriage, there is accountability and there is sharing.

The definition of pride is "self." Pride assumes superiority or arrogance. **[201]**

To counterattack it, we must praise and thank God who is our maker. This I learned through the trials. Out of sheer desperation, I learned the power of praise and thanksgiving.

The following week at another service, there was a call for recommitment. This was at my home church where I had worked with church leaders in the children's ministry. I felt embarrassed but I went forward for the call and obeyed God. I heard the voice of God say, "This day I will see you in paradise." Pastor Demola once said, "There is nothing you can do to embarrass God." **[202]** My going forward for this call showed to God and to myself that I was placing the Lord first before any one person. There were many people there who may have judged me as "not spiritually mature." But God honored my obedience. Settle it. Are you here to please God or man? In the end, who will you answer to?

Would you be willing to kneel down and praise God in the middle of Grand Central Station or a Starbuck's coffee shop? **The fear of the Lord is the beginning of wisdom. (Proverbs 111:10)**

The Manifestation Will Come

The manifestation of your answers to prayer will come. If your prayers are in line with what the Word of God says, petitioning the Father in the name of Jesus, (John 16:23), and you are praying God's will with a heart of faith, with surrender, repentance, and forgiveness, you can expect the answers to come. Keep your heart humble and honest before God and believe in the supernatural workings of God. Do not be moved by what you feel, see, sense, hear, or think. God's ways are not our ways. He will show Himself real to you and your faith will grow.

Jesus, My Husband

Now the Sabbath rest of the Lord can be entered, ending the power of the tormenting spirits because the believer surrenders to the Lord, has been humbled, and has taken decided steps of obedience. I will repent of sin and say "no" to the temptations. I will forgive and release myself and all who have sinned against me. True surrender, humility, repentance, forgiveness, and obedience is honored by God. With obedience, the believer is then blessed with His awesome and sometimes His felt presence. And she/he is graced with an experience of Jesus' divine love, total acceptance, and complete forgiveness.

With a clear conscience, His still small voice is keenly discerned. As Jesus spoke to the criminal who humbled himself to Him, He says to every repentant believer, "Today you will be with me in paradise." (Luke 23:43) With each step in this direction, the soul is transformed and the believer is changed by Almighty God, one step at a time. True identity in Christ Jesus is uncovered one day at a time.

The believer now connects in a divine union with Jesus Christ in a surrendered position of faith. The Holy Spirit seals this union . And Father God is pleased. With repentance of all idols and sins, leaving them, and turning toward Jesus, I am committed and connected to Jesus Christ now living on the inside of me. I belong to Jesus. The power of the Holy Spirit is provided to empower me to both obey my heavenly Father and to petition Him as I take Jesus' delegated authority over my flesh, over all ungodly mindsets and/or emotions, and over all evil spirits oppressing me, in the name of Jesus.

Therefore I am now going to allure her: I will lead her into the desert and speak tenderly to her. There I will give her back her vineyards, And will make the valley of Abhor a door of hope. There she will sing as in the days of her youth, as in the day she came up out of Egypt. In that day, declares the Lord, "You will call me 'My husband,' I will betroth you to me forever." (Hosea 2:14 -16; 19)

Receive Your Freedom in Christ Jesus by Faith – Honor the Lord's Sacrifice

Reach Out

Anything in the flesh has to go if we truly are to be used by God. Self-pity must go. Self- pity is anger turned inward. Self-pity develops an attitude of inferiority and failure within the heart. This attitude will block us from receiving the love, acceptance, and forgiveness we desperately need to mature in Christ Jesus. Jesus sacrificed His life for all of us. **So we therefore have no excuses regarding any personal inadequacies to prevent us from receiving His presence in our lives. [203]**

Religion that God our Father accepts as pure and faultless is this; to look after orphans and widows in their distress and to keep oneself from being polluted by the world. (James 1:27)

Bless Those Who Persecute You

Self-hatred takes away the ability of the believer to fully receive the righteousness of God. Righteousness gives us a fresh new start because we stand forgiven and in right standing with the Lord.

As I forgave others, I knew I was still not right. Something was missing because I did not have peace. Mom always told me, **"You have to forgive yourself."** No matter how many difficulties we face in the primary relationships, our parents know us the best! **Against You, You only, have I sinned and done what is evil in Your sight. (Psalm 51:4)**

Once God has forgiven us, it is over. If you do not forgive yourself and keep hanging unto the shame of it, Satan will use people to remind you of the shame. Friend, it is a sin to sit in the complacency of self-hate. Why? Because its apathy will keep you from caring for others. It will wipe out your joy within the body of Christ and for life itself. And the enemy will have a party on you until you give it up!

Just as I had to learn to forgive others, I had to face my own self- hate squarely in the face. I had to stop running from myself. I had to face it squarely. The beauty of God's plan is that once I forgave myself, I made a conscious decision to accept myself, mistakes and successes. I accepted myself as human.

It is interesting what occurs as we change. As I walk in the favor of God, I invite the favor of man. Because I now accept myself, mistakes and all, I have kicked out that spirit of rejection. Walking in divine favor and accepting of my own humanness, I have nothing to hide and I enjoy and invite communication with others. However, I still use discernment with what I share and with whom I share.

My defensiveness is changing as I walk as a free and accepted woman of God. I don't have to act like I'm ok. I am ok! Remember, we are "precious in His sight". (Isaiah 43:4) Even if I don't have children or live the same lifestyle as the married wife and mother, I am married to Jesus and I have spiritual children. I do not have to compare myself to others. I have accepted who I was called to be on this earth. In all honesty, mother's day is still difficult for me, but I still accept who I have been called to be in this life.

I know what it is to be in need, and I know what it is to have plenty. I have learned the secret of being content in any and every situation, whether well fed or hungry, whether living in plenty or in want. I can do everything through Him who gives me strength. (Philippians 4:12,13)

Turn It Around - Decide to Live and Love Again

Locking this door means that there is a decided turning away from any and all past offences against myself and others. Friend, I knew I had to conquer self-hatred. There is a wrath that I held against my own soul which had to go. I had to repent and accept Jesus' total forgiveness for my acts of flesh and lust against Jesus my Lord and King. I had to receive His sacrifice for me. And you must receive it as well, for yourself and for all whom your life will touch for Jesus. **In wrath, remember mercy. (Habakkuk 3:2)**

I think of the story of the prostitute who is cited in the book of Luke. She came to Jesus who was dining at the house of the Pharisee.**When a woman who had lived a sinful life in that town learned that Jesus was eating at the Pharisee's house, she brought an alabaster jar of perfume, and as she stood behind Him at His feet weeping, she began to wet His feet with her tears. Then she wiped them with her hair, kissed them and poured perfume on them. (Luke 7:37-38)** The Pharisees judged her and Jesus rebuked them with His words, **"Do you see this woman? I came into your house. You did not give me any water for my feet, but she wet my feet with her tears and wiped them with her hair. You did not give me a kiss, but this woman, from the time I entered, has not stopped kissing my feet. You did not put oil on my head, but she poured perfume on my feet. Therefore, I tell you, her many sins have been forgiven - for she loved much. But he who has been forgiven little loves little." (Luke 7:44-47)**

Friend, I had to take a long and honest look at myself. I did not deserve to be forgiven, but the grace of God is a gift which provides "undeserved favor" to the child of God. What did this prostitute do? She knew she was in sin. Her weeping at the feet of Jesus shows us that. She may have heard Jesus preach the gospel of repentance. In faith, she went to Him and humbled herself to Him even amidst the religious leaders of the day. And she showed Jesus her love for Him as she humbly anointed His feet with oil. In reaction to her act of love and repentance, she was forgiven. **Then Jesus said to her, "Your sins are forgiven." "Your faith has saved you; go in peace." (Luke 7:48,50)**

Here we have a perfect example of the benefits we reap as we look within ourselves, repent of our own sins, and refuse to judge others for theirs. This woman had a choice. She could have walked into that house, and, as the Pharisees criticized her, she could have been distracted from her act of repentance for her own sins. She could have retaliated verbally or walked out and lost her miracle of cleansing. Instead, she chose to stay focused on her own heart of repentance before Jesus.

The Bible says she had lived a "sinful life." I believe that this woman was dealing with many oppressive spirits attempting to keep her in torment. And she certainly was not of good reputation with the people of the town. There is proof of this in the verbal abuse against her from the religious leaders. However, she chose to stay focused on her own heart, in her submitted position of repentance before Jesus, and not on the evil within the hearts or in the words of others around her. She was wise not to be led astray with any more criticism from others. **Blessed are you when people insult you, persecute you and falsely say all kinds of evil against you because of me. Rejoice and be glad, because great is your reward in heaven, for in the same way they persecuted the prophets who were before you. (Matthew 5:11)**

I could have walked out of several church meetings had I not been focused upon the Lord and allowed the enemy to plant thoughts in my mind as to my "unworthiness." Friend, we are all unworthy of the grace of God and His forgiveness, acceptance, and love. We are made right with Him through our faith in His sacrifice for us, receiving His promises of love, acceptance, and forgiveness, and of our healing. **This righteousness from God comes through faith in Jesus Christ to all who believe. There is no difference for all have sinned and fall short of the glory of God, and are justified freely by His grace through the redemption that came by Christ Jesus. God presented Him as a sacrifice of atonement through faith in His blood. (Romans 3:23-25)**

Yes, we all fall short of His glory. But, we must fight for ourselves and our healing because the devil wants to steal it from us. You must seek accountability in a church membership. Ask the Holy Spirit to lead you to the church that He wants you to be in. There is no perfect church and there is only one perfect God. Stay planted where the Lord places you. Do not leave the accountability of the body of Christ. Do not isolate because of others' rejection!

You will find strength in staying amidst the very people who are coming against you. When you stop running, you will experience the breakthrough. You will know God's love when you no longer are moved by the sins and distractions of your fellow peers. There is no substitute for the growth you will experience under the corporate anointing of the body of Christ, under an anointed pastor, and among other leaders in a church membership. **Fight the good fight of the faith. Take hold of the eternal life to which** you were called when you made your good confession in the presence of many witnesses. (1ˢᵗ Timothy 6:12)

Receive Forgiveness from God

The woman with the alabaster jar was at the breaking point of her life. It was either "do or die." She needed a revelation and needed to "see" and "experience" forgiveness from Jesus so that she could absolve herself from her own self-hatred. I believe that she not only was forgiven by Jesus, but she also received that forgiveness. As a result of her faith in the authority of Jesus Christ as the Son of God and as a result of her humility before Jesus, she received His completed forgiveness. When she fully received the forgiveness from Jesus, she was then able to forgive herself. It was a revelation from God Himself, an experience that could not be taken away from her.

When I received my healing, I was in my apartment in Tulsa, Oklahoma, lying on the floor. Like the woman with the alabaster jar, I received forgiveness from Jesus as I listened to the sermon of the late Pastor Billy Joe Daugherty. I knew by faith that the Lord was with me and I said, "I receive my forgiveness for this. Thank you, Jesus!"

The words I spoke in complete surrender to Jesus Christ my Lord and Savior, with a humble and broken heart before Him, with a true repentance for displeasing Him, brought me to a place of receiving His complete mercy. This act of receiving His love, acceptance, and forgiveness put the enemy of self-condemnation in its place. I would no longer be a slave to this tormenting voice. I would live to declare what the Lord had done for me. This was a divine moment which no man or woman could ever take from my life. I was free from shame. You are also free from shame. Receive the mercy from the Lord!

Intercessory Prayer Has Great Benefits

After Job prayed for his friends, the Lord made him prosperous again and gave him twice as much as he had before. (Job 42:10) As intercessors, we place a supernatural covering over the person(s) we pray for and bring change to each situation by our prayers. It is God's promise to us to answer our prayers. Many desperate situations have been changed because people have decided to pray. Maturity learns to fight battles in the prayer closet. When we pray, God does the impossible in ways we could never have dreamed. (See Appendix)

In Genesis, we see an example of intercession when a mighty man of God, Noah, fell into drunkenness; **Noah, a man of the soil, proceeded to plant a vineyard. When he drank some of its wine, he became drunk and lay uncovered inside his tent. Ham, the father of Canaan, saw his father's nakedness, and told his two brothers outside. But Shem and Japheth took a garment and laid it across their shoulders; then they walked in backward and covered their father's nakedness. Their faces were turned the other way so that they would not see their father's nakedness. (Genesis 9:20-23)**

This attitude of these two sons should be our attitude in intercession - to use it as a garment to cover the nakedness of another. As our hearts are cleansed, we will be better able to discern the motive behind the prayers we pray. [204] Just like Noah's sons, we should press into such a deep love for our enemies that we are willing to "cover" their nakedness.

Jesus helped me the most because I could only truly release myself from my self-hate because of what He did for me. He died for my shame and gave me His unconditional love as a replacement. What a gift! I owe Jesus and many people of faith in the body of Christ for my life and for the peace I live in today. Even though I am still tempted in areas, I still have His peace deep within my heart to fight the good fight of faith against the temptations.

Self-hatred is sin because God commands us to love our neighbors as we love ourselves. It has always been easier for me to give than to receive. But God showed me His love for me through the love that I showed toward others, especially my enemies! In caring for others, I began to care about myself.

Create in me a pure heart, O God, and renew a steadfast spirit within me. Do not cast me

from Your presence or take Your Holy Spirit from me. Restore to me the joy of Your salvation and grant me a willing spirit, to sustain me. (Psalm 51:10-12)

Watch Your Words

My love for Jesus has become greater to me than life itself and certainly greater than my own self-contempt or even my jealousy or apathy/hatred toward others. I live because of Him and He has pulled me out of the quicksand of my bitter and stony heart: thus, my despair. I feel life today. **I tell you, get up, take your mat and go home. (Mark 2:11)** Pastor Demola says, "They may not like me, but they'll be at peace with me."**[205]**

Before you speak, ask the Holy Spirit if He wants you to speak. If yes, always stop and think. If you cannot speak with your spirit with a heart of faith (submission, repentance, and forgiveness), and with self-control over your emotions, do not speak at all. "If you show them love, they will get aggravated." per Rev. Vinny Longo. **[206]** You can only control what you think about yourself. You have no control over what other people think of you.

Rev. Vinny Longo of Victory in Jesus says, "We control the supernatural with our words." **[207]** It may be that being silent before the enemy will bring God the glory more than any words you may speak in a particular situation. The Holy Spirit will lead you. Always be safe! Travel in two's or teams of more than two. There is safety in numbers.

Jesus put the enemy to flight by His words. Words and prayers spoken with a heart of faith with submission, repentance, and forgiveness still have the power of God behind them. And two or more praying in agreement can put ten thousand to flight. (Psalm 91) Let the Holy Spirit guide you as you go. Pastor Demola says, "We need to learn how to disagree agreeably."**[208] A gentle answer turns away wrath, but a harsh word stirs up anger. (Proverbs 15:1)**

Accept Completed Freedom in Christ Jesus – Worship the Lord

Jesus declared, "Yet a time is coming and has now come when the true worshipers will worship the Father in spirit and truth, for they are the kind of worshipers the Father seeks. God is spirit, and His worshipers must worship in spirit and in truth." (John 4:23,24)

This a quote from Senior Pastor Sharon Daugherty of Victory Christian Center in Tulsa, Oklahoma from the Miracle Healing service of 10-24-10. She stated regarding worship, "Why do we worship? There is something about worship – that we allow the Holy Spirit to move within us. We know that our healing and our wholeness is in Him. There is something about worship that we draw on the power of God." [209]

Praise the Lord. Praise God in His sanctuary; praise Him in His mighty heavens. Praise Him for His acts of power; praise Him for His surpassing greatness. Praise Him with the sounding of the trumpet, praise Him with the harp and lyre, praise Him with tambourine and dancing, praise Him with the strings and flute, praise Him with the clash of cymbals, praise Him with resounding cymbals. Let everything that has breath praise the Lord. Praise the Lord. (Psalm 150:1-6)

Pastor Rema Spencer of Calvary Temple, Wayne, New Jersey spoke eloquently at one
of our Sunday services, In the face of death, I will say: "All is well." **[210]**

There is Freedom for Our Family through Our Prayers of Faith for Them

The root of all our iniquities, (tendencies toward sin), can be found in satanic bondage which manifests itself in generational sins which we inherit. As Marilyn Hickey states:

By now I'm sure you're beginning to understand that we all have inherited certain family iniquities. I'm sure you're beginning to realize that you and your future generations are free to walk in the blessings you've already inherited from Jesus through His death, burial, and resurrection. **[211]**

Prayer Asking for the Mercy of God for Yourself and Your Blood Relatives

Prepare Your Heart in Proper Position of Faith – "Jesus, I believe You died, were buried, and resurrected for me at Calvary. Today I surrender to Your Lordship and Your authority. I am sorry for my sins. I ask You to come into my heart and be the Lord and Savior of my soul. I receive forgiveness and cleansing for my sins. Fill me with Your Holy Spirit. I forgive and release all judgment against both myself and all who have sinned against me, in Jesus' name, Amen."

Enter into the Presence of the Lord – "Father God, I enter into Your presence with thanksgiving and praise with my petitions, in the name of Jesus Christ, my Lord and my loving authority."

Prayer Asking for the Mercy of God for Yourself and Your Blood Relatives– Cast the Devil Out of the Family Tree, in Jesus' Name

"Father, I confess that I have iniquities. I thank You today that when I confess my sins, that You are faithful and just to forgive me. I repent of my sins and my iniquities. I not only repent of my sins and iniquities, but I ask You to have mercy on my parents and grandparents for their sins as well. I also forgive them; I am not holding it against them. In Jesus' name, Amen." **[212]**(See Appendix)

You shall not make for yourself an idol in the form of anything in heaven above or on the earth beneath or in the waters below. Your shall not bow down to them or worship them; for I, the Lord your God, am a jealous God, punishing the children for the sin of the fathers to the third and fourth generation of those who hate me, but showing love to a thousand generations, of those who love me and keep my commandments. (Exodus 20:4-6)

Receive Your Freedom in Christ Jesus by Faith
Honor the Lord's Sacrifice

We receive God's grace (unmerited favor, loving kindness, and the power of God) through a decision of will, an action taken in faith. It is a free gift from God. It is a deep respect for the Lord's sacrifice for us that motivates and inspires us to receive this gift of His grace. If we do not receive this gift, we make the Lord's sacrifice of no effect. There is nothing we can do by our works that can bring us His grace. Jesus already earned it for us at the cross. So we can have no personal feelings or no opinions for or against grace. This is a gift that can only be received through an act of our faith in the finished work of Jesus Christ. **I do not set aside the grace of God, for if righteousness could be gained through the law, Christ died for nothing! (Galatians 2:21)**

Prayer to Honor the Lord and His Sacrifice for Us

Prepare Your Heart in Proper Position of Faith –"Jesus, I believe You died, were buried, and resurrected for me at Calvary. Today I surrender to Your Lordship and to Your loving authority. I am sorry for my sins. I ask You to come into my heart and be the Lord and Savior of my soul. I receive forgiveness and cleansing for my sins. Fill me with Your Holy Spirit. I forgive and release all judgment against both myself and all who have sinned against me, in Jesus' name, Amen."

Enter into the Presence of the Lord – "Father God, I enter into Your presence with thanksgiving and praise with my petitions in the name of Jesus Christ, my Lord and my loving authority."

Come to Jesus with Your Needs

"Lord Jesus, I am sorry for my sins. There are still areas in which I need to completely surrender and to change my mind about. I repent of the area of _____. I have been locked into a pattern of thinking and of acting out for many years. I know it is keeping me from living a free life. Lord, help me to change. I now ask You to give me the courage to completely let go and walk away. I believe that there are many other people at the other side of my obedience whose lives will be lengthened and whose souls will be saved by my decision to change."

"I truly do honor and thank You for the sacrifice of Your life for me at Calvary. I know that I will more effectively work to crucify my flesh as I draw my strength from You in a deeper surrender. Thank you for loving me in spite of myself, my sins, and my own deceitful heart." (Jer. 17:9)(Scripture personalized)

"I admit that I have reached a place where I need counsel. I will seek Christian counseling to help me process areas in my heart that are not yet resolved. I need another person to be a sounding board. I need an accountability partner to help me to face any compromise in my life, so that it can be seen for what it is and broken, once and for all. I need to come out of isolation. I choose to come out of this neutral place of apathy and to enter into the abundant and active life of purpose in giving to others. I also need at least one other person with whom to stop, to share, and to enjoy life."

"Today, I commit my life, my spirit, my body, my thoughts, my emotions, and my will to Your loving authority, Lord Jesus, in the precious name of Jesus Christ. Help me, Father, to come to the unselfish place of "no want," in Jesus' name, Amen."(Psalm 23:1)(Scripture personalized)

★★★★★

Final Comments of the late Pastor Billy Joe Daugherty and Senior Pastor
Sharon Daugherty of Victory Christian Center in Tulsa, Oklahoma
Prayer and Comment of the late Pastor Billy Joe Daugherty:
"I discern the Lord's body and receive all that He has provided for me, including healing for my physical body. (1ˢᵗ Corinthians 11:23-30) To discern the Lord's body is to examine yourself to make sure there is nothing blocking your faith, that there is no blockage to receiving the healing Jesus Christ bought at Calvary, understanding what Jesus did at Calvary."[213]

Sr. Pastor Sharon Daugherty of Victory Christian Center
in Tulsa, Oklahoma said these words at a
Miracle Healing Service on 10/24/10,
"He sent His Word to heal us and to deliver us from all our destructions. From Psalm 107:20: When we take this Word of God into our spirit it brings healing and deliverance. His Word is spirit. It's the speaking of His Word that produces spiritually into our beings what we need. It's alive! It's not like reading another book. It's powerful! It's alive! It's sharp like a sword. It pierces into us. It divides in our lives what is soul and spirit. It also pierces into us what the enemy has tried to bring against us. Why did Jesus say to the enemy, 'It is written. It is written. It is written!'? Three times. Because the Word of God is spiritually powerful against what the enemy has tried to bring against us."[214]

Conclusion

Our awe of God brings us to a position of surrender and honesty before Him. He is our Creator and once we bow to Him as Lord and loving authority of our lives, we accept our position as His servants created to worship Him here in the earth. We are committed in a born again relationship with Jesus Christ to bring as many people to the truth of His will, an intimate relationship with us to live an abundant life free from all of Satan's lies.

Because of the fall of man, we will always have challenges. But the greater one, Jesus, Who lives within us, gives us His power; which is our divine ammunition against all evil. The Word of God frees us as we speak prayers into existence for our completed redemption and divine inheritance. This includes eternal life for ourselves and for our loved ones, freedom from Satan's lies, complete health of body, mind, and spirit, divine prosperity, divine protection, and divine healing. It takes faith to believe this and to reach out and to receive it. (See Appendix)

In my case, I was called away from family for the full healing to manifest. Everyone is different. I simply told my testimony as it unfolded to me. I told it so you could glean from my life and take what is relevant for you. But, I in no way am your counselor. I encourage you to seek the Holy Spirit and wise Christian counselors for your journey to wholeness.

We will never reach perfection, but we work out daily our salvation in a sanctification process that brings us closer to the Lord. And He uses us in helping to bless others with a bit of His power working in and through us here in the earth.**Then Jesus came to them and said, "All authority in heaven and on earth has been given to me. Therefore go and make disciples of all nations, baptizing them in the name of the Father and of the Son and of the Holy Spirit, and teaching them to obey everything I have commanded you. And surely I am with you always, to the very end of the age." (Mathew 28:18-20)**

My greatest deterrent to my healing was my dishonesty with myself and with God. I had impure motives and sins that I kept in secret, believing the lie that I could get free without anyone else's help. When I opened my heart and disclosed my weakness to others, the enemy did not have such a hold on me. He still came to tempt, but my resistance against him was strong because I had the anchor of the Lord to fight back in His strength, and not in my own flesh. Honesty with God and man brought me out of the darkness.

In stressful times, I am still tempted to perfectionism, but I am able to take control of its hold on me with the help of the Lord who always gives me either a check in my spirit or a strategy against it. I do admire the beauty of the woman, but it is not out of want or desire of any kind. For I can truly and honestly say that I have entered into the peace and rest of God. Desires for companionship now originates from my healed heart which has now been made whole from the past woundings. And I am no longer envious of another woman's position, because I have developed an inner contentment of who I am in Christ, a godly woman made beautiful by my Creator God. My confidence is centered in Christ Who abides in me. I will always be challenged by others' opinions because the devil is still the God of this world, but I have the greater one, Jesus Christ, living within me and I have His approval, His love, and His forgiveness. I am forever grateful to the Lord for His peace and His rest amidst every deception. It is a deeper voice and its truth keeps me in His rest.

Prayer of Acceptance

There is a personal decision we all make at the crossroads of our healing. Will we sit back and thank God for the healing? Or will we accept the tragedy as over and dare to cross over to the next season? Will we go out and help others, to comfort them with the same comfort with which we have been comforted? If so, we continue in our own healing in the very midst of our giving to others. Inner healing is a lifelong process of sanctification.(2nd Cor. 1:3,4)

Prepare Your Heart of Faith - "Jesus, I believe that You died and resurrected for me. I surrender to You as my Lord and my authority. I am sorry for my sins against You and for the consequences of my disobedience. I turn from sin and surrender to You. I ask You to come into my heart and to be the Lord and Savior of my life. I forgive and release all judgment against myself and all who have sinned against me, in Jesus' name. Amen."

Enter into the Father's Presence - "Father God, I come into Your presence with thanksgiving and praise in my heart with my petitions and in the name of Jesus Christ, my Lord and my Savior." (John 16:23) (Psalm 100:4)(Scriptures personalized)

Take Jesus' Authority over All Tragedy and Declare Your Heart Healed and Whole to be Used of God to Minister to Others in Jesus' Name

"Thank you, Lord Jesus, for forgiving me of my sins. (1st John 1:9) By faith in Your finished work at the cross of Calvary,(Heb.11:1), I now receive complete forgiveness and I receive Your mercy and Your grace. (1st John 1:9) Thank You for loving me.(Isaiah 43:4) You are my strength and my song, Lord Jesus. I discern Your very presence in the very depths of my innermost being.(1st Cor. 11;23) I declare my body and my soul; my thoughts, my emotions, my will, and my spirit healed, in Your precious name, Lord Jesus. (Isaiah 53:3-5)(Phil. 2:9) Thank You, Lord Jesus. I know and believe that Your love covers me." (Jer. 29:11)(Isaiah 43:3,4)(Joshua 1:5)(All scriptures personalized)

"Father God, I now apply the blood of Jesus Christ to my life, my body, my soul/heart, and my spirit, (Matthew 26:28) (1st Cor. 11:25) in the precious name of Jesus Christ, the name that is above all other names. (Phil.2:9) I thank You, Lord Jesus, for giving Your life to me on this earth.(Luke 23:53)(Rom. 8:34) Thank You for giving me an abundant life to live. (John 10:10) Through Your sacrifice on Calvary, You rescued me from the dominion of darkness and brought me into the Kingdom of Your dear Son, the Son Whom You love. (Colossians 1:13) I declare in the name of Jesus Christ that I am in right relationship with You because of my faith in Your shed blood on Calvary. (Romans 1:16,17) With sincere thanksgiving, I believe and receive Your total forgiveness and cleansing for my sins. (1st John 1:9)(Heb. 10:19-22) I now close and lock the door on all fear, all shame, all guilt, all self-doubt, and inferiority in Jesus' name. (Romans 8:1) (Romans 1:16) (Rom. 1:17) I now commit through a decision of my faith and by an act of my will, to leave all that is not of You; idols, sins, all ungodly relationships and soul ties, co-dependencies, New Age/occult involvement, and materials. (2nd Cor. 6:17)(Rev. 18:4) You, Lord Jesus, despised these for me on the cross. (Exodus 20:3)(1st Thes. 5:22)(Romans 1:16) (Hebrews 12:2) I commit to daily study of the Word of God and prayer with praise and worship to keep my vessel filled with God." (Luke 11:24-26)(Rom. 12:2)(Pro. 4:20)((James 5:16)(Psalm 33:1-3)(John 4:24) (All scriptures personalized)(See Appendix)

"I am safe, covered by Your precious blood because I live in covenant relationship with You in the secret place of the Most High God. (Psalm 91:1) With the help of the Holy Spirit, I will overcome evil with good. (Rom. 12:21) Your precious blood sets a standard against all enemies in my life.(Isaiah 59:19) Thank You, Lord Jesus, for the provision that Your sacrifice has made for me.(Ephesians 2:8,9) I will reach out to comfort others with the same comfort with which You have comforted me."(2nd Cor.1:4)(Isaiah 43:4) (Psalm 118:14) (1st Cor. 11:23-30)(All scriptures personalized)

Appendix – Essential Points to Healing Prayers

Jesus Sends Out the Disciples by Twos

Then Jesus went around teaching from village to village. Calling the Twelve to Him, He sent them out <u>two by two</u> and gave them authority over evil spirits. These were His instructions: "Take nothing for the journey except a staff – no bread, no bag, no money in your belts. Wear sandals but not an extra tunic. Whenever you enter a house, stay there until you leave that town. And if any place will not welcome you or listen to you, shake the dust off your feet when you leave, as a testimony against them." They went out and preached that people should repent. They drove out many demons and anointed many sick people with oil and healed them. (Mark 6:6-13)

Whenever praying for and/or laying hands on anyone who is requesting you to cast out any demon spirits, follow the above teaching, and travel with a prayer partner. The disciples traveled <u>"two by two"</u> in obedience to the Lord Jesus Christ's instructions.

We Have Authority in Christ Jesus to Pray Over Ourselves as Born Again Believers

A born again believer cannot be possessed in his/her spirit because Jesus Christ has taken residence in his/her spirit. The reason it's impossible for a Christian to have an evil spirit in his spirit is that a Christian's spirit has been recreated by the Holy Spirit (2nd Cor. 5:17). Therefore, a Christian's spirit becomes the dwelling place of the Holy Spirit (John 14:23; 1st Cor. 6:17) and cannot also be the dwelling place of an evil spirit (2 Cor. 6:14-16; James 3:11,12).[215] However, these demonic spirits can oppress, harass, and even possess both believers and nonbelievers.

Those who say that a Christian can "have" a demon don't define their terms properly; they don't divide man correctly. They don't recognize that man is a spirit; he has a soul; and he lives in a body. And they don't make it clear that a demon can be affecting a person's soul or body, but not be in his spirit.[216]

If people mean a believer can be oppressed or obsessed in body or soul by a demon, that's one thing. Yes, a Christian can be oppressed or obsessed in body or soul by a demon. But it's quite another thing to say that a Christian can be possessed spirit, soul, and body by a demon.[217]

You can be saved and not know your authority in Christ to cast out demons. (Luke 10:19) To be saved is to be "born again." **In reply Jesus declared, "I tell you the truth, no one can see the kingdom of God unless he is born again." (John 3:3)** This requires repentance from sin and a verbal statement of belief in the death, burial, and the resurrection of Jesus Christ, the Son of God; with a welcoming of the Lord Jesus Christ into one's heart as Lord and Savior in a personal covenant relationship. (Romans 10:9,10)(John 3:3)(John 3:16)(Acts 2:21)(John 15:5)(1st Cor. 11:23) It is essential that we as born again Christians resist the devil and take Jesus' delegated authority rebuking and/or casting out all negative thoughts, emotions, and spirits in Jesus' name.

I'm going to go into quite a bit of detail in relating an account of a Spirit filled minister who became obsessed in her thinking with worry and fear, until she finally allowed the devil to possess her thinking, and she went totally insane. In other words, first she was oppressed by the devil's thoughts. But as she yielded to Satan's thoughts of worry and fear, she became obsessed with those thoughts, until finally she opened a door to the enemy and allowed her mind to become possessed with an evil spirit. [218]

This is the prayer to become born again, **"Heavenly Father, in Jesus' name, I repent of my sins and open my heart to let Jesus come inside of me. Jesus, You are my Lord and Savior. I believe** that You died for my sins and that You were raised from the dead. Fill me with Your Holy Spirit. Thank You, Father, for saving me; in Jesus' name. Amen." [219]

These are the words of Jesus, **"I am the vine; you are the branches. If a man remains in me and I in him, he will bear much fruit. (John 15:5)**

We, as born again believers, have been given the privilege and the responsibility by Jesus to take our delegated authority in Christ against these spirits oppressing our <u>own</u> bodies, souls, and spirits, in the name of Jesus Christ. Jesus speaks to the seventy-two disciples, **"I have given you authority to trample on snakes and scorpions and to overcome all the power of the enemy; nothing will harm you. (Luke 10:19)**(See prayers in the body of this manuscript.)

Blood Relatives and Friends

With our blood relatives and friends, whether saved or unsaved, we do not have legal authority over them to cast out demons unless they ask for prayer. We do not have legal authority to cast out demons against their will. We can, however, in intercession, bind and gag the evil spirits from operating in their lives in the name of Jesus. We can also ask God's mercy and protection upon them. We can ask for God to open their spiritual eyes and hearts to repent and renounce their sins and to come into a personal covenant relationship with Jesus Christ, to become "born again". (2nd Cor. 4:3,4)(2ndPeter 3:9)(John 3:3)(Romans 10:9,10)(Acts 2:21)(John 15:5)(Rom. 2:4)(Eph. 1:18)(Luke 24:31,45) (Matthew 18:18)

If an unsaved person asks you to cast out a demon, we first ask them to come to the Lord, leading them into the prayer of salvation with repentance for sin and faith in the Lord Jesus Christ, welcoming Jesus into their hearts. (See above prayer: footnote #215) After the prayer of salvation, they are then born again and able to pray prayers to cast out demons for themselves. Or, as newly born again Christians, they may ask you to lead them in such prayers in agreement with them. These are the words of Jesus, **"Again, I tell you that if two of you on earth agree about anything you ask for, it will be done for you by my Father in heaven. For where two or three come together in my name, there am I with them."(Matthew 18:19,20)**

If a saved person asks you to lead them in the prayer of recommitment, and repent and welcome Jesus to come inside their heart, then they may cast out any demon with their own delegated authority in Christ Jesus. They may also ask you to come into the prayer of agreement with them to cast out any oppressing spirits. (Matthew 18:19,20)(Scripture shown above) A born again believer cannot be possessed, but he/she can be oppressed by demons.

> **He (God) is patient with you, not wanting anyone to perish,**
> **but everyone to come to repentance. (2nd Peter 3:9)**
> **God's kindness leads you toward repentance. (Romans 2:4)**

Prayers of Intercession for Blood Relatives and/or Friends

Intercessory Prayer for our unsaved or saved blood relatives and friends are prayers said in the absence of the persons prayed for, believing God for the answers to these prayers. There is no distance in prayer. **The prayer of a righteous man (woman) is powerful and effective. (James 5:16)**

Intercessory Prayers for Unsaved Relatives and/or Friends

As born again believers, we intercede for our unsaved relatives and/or friends. We enter into the gates of our Lord with thanksgiving and praise, and petition our Father in the name of Jesus. (Psalm 100:4)(John 16:23) We pray with a heart of faith with submission, repentance, and forgiveness: "Right now I bind the god of this world (Satan) who has blinded the eyes of _____(name the person) to the truth of the gospel. I loose the light of the gospel to shine on him/her and open his/her eyes. (2nd Cor., 4:3,4) [220] I pray that the eyes of _____'s (name the person) understanding will be opened to know the hope of his/her calling. (Ephesians 1:18)[221] Lord, open ____'s (name the person) eyes to know You. Open his/her understanding that he/she can understand the Scriptures. (Luke 24:31,45)[222] I pray for laborers for the Lord of the harvest to be sent forth into ____'s (name the person) path." (Matthew 9:37,38)**[223]**I pray this all in Jesus' name, the name above all other names. (Phil. 2:9)

We can also bind, mute, and gag demon spirits that are oppressing and/or possessing these persons to render them powerless in Jesus' name. We do not, however, have legal authority to cast them out against their will or seven more spirits will go in and live there. **(Matthew 18:18)(Luke 11:24-26)**

These are the words of Jesus: **"I tell you the truth, whatever you bind on earth will be bound in heaven, and whatever you loose on earth will be loosed in heaven."(Matthew 18:18)**

When an evil spirit comes out of a man/woman, it goes through arid places seeking rest and does not find it. Then it says, 'I will return to the house I left.' When it arrives, it finds the house swept clean and put in order. Then it goes and takes seven other spirits more wicked than itself, and they go in and live there. And the final condition of that man (woman) is worse than the first. (Luke 11:24-26)

Therefore, we enter into the throneroom and petition the Father in the name of Jesus. (John 16:23)(Psalm 100:4) We pray with a heart of faith with submission, repentance, and forgiveness: "I bind, mute, and gag all demons from operating in ____'s (name the person) life; spirit, soul, and body, in Jesus' name. (Matthew 18:18)I pray, Lord Jesus, that you open ____'s (name the person) heart to repentance (Rom. 2:4) and to a personal relationship with You." (John 3:3)(2nd Cor 4:3,4)(2nd Peter 3:9)(Romans 10:9,10)

Prayers for Saved Relatives and/or Friends

As born again believers, we enter into the gates of our Lord with thanksgiving and praise, and petition our Father in the name of Jesus. (Psalm 100:4)(John 16:23) We pray with a heart of faith with submission, repentance, and forgiveness: "I ask you, Lord, to open the mind of ____(name the person) to the knowledge of his/her delegated authority in Jesus Christ. (Luke 24:45) Send laborers to ____(name the person) to teach him/her his/her authority in Christ to pray both for himself/herself and also in agreement with other believers.(Matthew 9:37,38)(Matthew18:18-20) I bind, mute, and gag all demons from operating in his/her life: spirit, soul, and body." (Matthew 18:18) I cover ____(name the person) with the blood of Jesus. I pray this all in the name of Jesus Christ."(1st Peter 1:18,19)(Hebrews 9:14)

For Our Children

A born again parent <u>does</u> have legal authority to pray for the spirit, soul, and body of his/her own children. We pray in Jesus' delegated authority for our children to rebuke and/or cast out demon spirits that are possessing and/or oppressing them. When they are of age and of maturity, they may decide to surrender and welcome Jesus into their hearts by faith and with repentance. They then receive the privilege and the responsibility from the Lord of taking Jesus' delegated authority to pray and take authority over demonic spirits that are oppressing them.

Prayers for Our Children

As born again believers, we may enter boldly into the gates of our Lord with thanksgiving and praise, and petition our Father in the name of Jesus. (Psalm 100:4)(John 16:23) We pray with a heart of faith with submission, repentance, and forgiveness: "I declare ____ (name the child) is free from the generational curse on his/her ancestral bloodline.(Galatians 3:13) In Jesus' name, I cast out and rebuke any demon spirits from operating in his/her life; spirit, soul, and body, whether in oppression or in possession.(Luke 10:19)(Mark 16:17) Go, in Jesus' name. (Luke 10:19) Go wherever Jesus sends you to be held captive by the angels of God. (Mark 5:8-13) I declare ____(name the child) is the redeemed of the Lord, free from all evil, in Jesus' name. (Galatians 3:13) (Matthew 6:13) I ask that when ____ (name the child) comes to an age of understanding and maturity, that ____(name the child) will, by an act of faith, will, and submission to You, Lord Jesus, repent of sin and enter into a personal and intimate covenant relationship with You.(John 3:3)(John 15:4) (Romans 10:9,10)(John 3:16)(John 14:6) I cover ____(name of child) with the blood of Jesus.(1st Peter 1:18,19)(Hebrews 9:14)(1st Peter 2:24) I declare that the angel of the Lord encamps around him/her in Jesus' name.(Psalm 34:7) I declare him/her saved, protected, healed, provided for, prosperous, and free from any bondages, in Jesus' name.(Galatians 3:13)(Isaiah 53:3-5)(Luke 4:18-19)(1st Peter 2:24)(Phil. 4:19)(Rom. 10:13)(Psalm 91:11) I commit to daily study of the Word of God, prayer, praise, and worship to keep my vessel filled with God and to keep the enemy out. (Luke 11:24-26) I pray and declare this in Jesus name, Amen."

Seal the Prayers

After these prayers to rebuke and/or cast out demons, we seal the prayers by sending the demons wherever Jesus sends them and/or to the depths of the earth to be held captive by the angels of God. Read the example of Mark 5. Jesus, after taking authority over the demons possessing the man at the Gerasenes, sent the demons into the pigs that were feeding in the nearby hillside. (Mark 5:8-13) After praying these prayers, both the person(s) who has received the prayer and the ones who have prayed need to commit to daily study and meditation of God's Word with daily repentance and prayer, speaking the Word of God with ongoing praise and worship, thus filling his/her vessel with God and preventing any further demonic invasions. (Luke 11:24-26)

Conclusion

As born again believers, we <u>do</u> have delegated authority from Jesus to rebuke and/or cast out demons from operating against ourselves and against another born again believer who asks for prayer, thus giving us legal authority to pray such prayers. We also have delegated authority in Christ as well as legal authority to pray to rebuke and/or cast out demons that are oppressing and/or possessing our children (as parents). If an unsaved person asks you to cast out a demon, they are giving you legal authority to then take Jesus' delegated authority to rebuke and/or cast out any spirits oppressing and/or possessing them. They must first come to the Lord and welcome Jesus into their heart with repentance and faith. After the prayer of salvation, they are born again Christians and are able to take Jesus' delegated authority against all demon spirits oppressing and/or possessing them. If they ask a born again believer(s) for such prayers of agreement, their hearts and spirits will also be ready to receive any prayers to cast out and/or rebuke any spirits in the name of Jesus Christ.(Matthew 18:18-20)

The words of Jesus: "I tell you the truth, whatever you bind on earth will be bound in heaven, and whatever you loose on earth will be loosed in heaven. Again, I tell you that if two of you on earth agree about anything you ask for, it will be done for you by my Father in heaven. For where two or three come together in my name, there am I with them." (Matthew 18:18-20)

Endnotes

1   Pastor Billy Joe Daugherty, "Breaking the Chains of Bondage," (Tulsa: Thomas Nelson Publishers, Inc.), p.7.

2   Ibid., p. 23.

3   Pastor Billy Joe Daugherty, "Jesus Heals the Broken Hearted," (video online @ www.youtube.com/user/VictoryTulsa) by Impact Productions, Tulsa, Ok., produced on 3/4, 5/09.

4   Charles Capps, "The Messenger of Satan," (Tulsa: Harrison House, Inc.), p. 12.

5   Charles Capps, "Authority in Three Realms," (Tulsa: Harrison House, Inc.), p.123.

6   Ibid., p. 112.

7   George Otis, Jr., "Informed Intercession," (Ventura: Renew Books, 1999), p.223.

8   Capps, "Authority in Three Realms," p.14,15.

9   Capps, "The Messenger of Satan," p. 24.

10   Kenneth E. Hagin, "Steps to Answered Prayer," (Tulsa: Faith Library Publications, 1998), p. 20.

11   Capps, "Authority in Three Realms," p. 15.

12   Ibid., p. 5.

13   Ibid., p. 27,28.

14   Ibid., p. 28.

15   Elijah House, "Elijah House School for Prayer Ministry," (Post Falls: Elijah House, 2004), p. 31- 33, and p. 123.

16   David T. Demola, "Dominion and Authority to Rule and Reign," (Tulsa Christian Publishing Services Inc., 1987), p. 17.

17   Ibid., p. 17.

18   Marilyn Hickey, "Breaking Generational Curses," (Denver: Harrison House, 2000), p. 32.

19   Stephanie Boosahda, "Somewhere It's Snowing" from cassette tape The Early Years.

20   Kate McVeigh, "Conquering Intimidation," (Tulsa: Kenneth Hagin Ministries, 2000), p. 80.

21   Pastor David T. Demola, p.17.

22   Hickey, p.21.

23   Ibid., p.194.

24   Ibid., p. 217.

25   Ibid., p. 217.

26   Rev. Dr. Leo Natalie, "When Spirit and Soul Agree," (Plainfield: Bridge Publishing Co., 1994), p. 37.

27   Ibid., p. 37, 38.

28   Ibid., p. 83.

29   Merriam Webster, "Webster's Ninth New Collegiate Dictionary," (Springfield: Merriam Webster Inc., Publishers, 1981), p. 362.

30   Dr. Bill Consiglio, Hope Ministries Conference, New York City, December, 2001, Church for All Nations, N. Y. C., (Quotation).

31   Rev. Dr. Natalie, p. 27.

32   John Bradshaw, "Healing the Shame That Binds You,"(Deerfield Beach: Health Communications, Inc., 1988), p. 82, 83.

33   Ibid., p. 14.

34   Ibid., p. 15.

35   Ibid., p. 14.

36   Pastor Billy Joe Daugherty, "Jesus Heals the Broken Hearted" (video online @ www.youtube.com/user/VictoryTulsa2009 by Impact Productions, Tulsa Ok., produced on3/4, 5/09.

37   Ibid.

38   Ibid.

39   Ibid.

40   Pastor Billy Joe Daugherty, "This New Life," (Tulsa: Thomas Nelson, Inc., Publisher, l982), (inside cover).

41   Pastor Demola, Faith Fellowship World Outreach Center, (Quotation).

42   Joanne Highley, "The Best Words of L.I.F.E.,"(New York: L.I.F.E. Inc. Publishers, 2003), p. 128.

43   Billye Brim, "The Blood and the Glory," (Tulsa: Harrison House, Inc., l987), p. 40.

44   Webster, p. 623.

45   Ibid., p. 453.

46   Bradshaw, p. 136.

47   Ibid., p. 136.

48   Elijah House, p. 33, 34.

49   Ibid., p. 197.

50   Benny Hinn, "The Anointing," (Nashville: Thomas Nelson Publishers, l987), p. 1.

51   Rev. Dr. Natalie, p. 82, 83.

52   Webster, p. 607.

53   Ibid., p. 55.

54   Ibid., p. 815.

55   Ibid., p. 271.

56   Ibid., p. 268.

57   Ibid., p. 1173.

58   Pastor Dr. Thomas Keinath, (Quotation).

59   Ron and Joanne Highley, "The Best of Words of L.I.F.E.," p. 228.

60   Bonnie Doebley, (Quotation).

61   Highley, "The Journal," L.I.F.E. Newsletter, 1990.

62   Robert Schaeffer, "The Best Words of L.I.F.E.," p. 259.

63   Ibid., p. 259.

64   Webster, p. 265.

65   Dr. Bill Consiglio, Hope Ministries Conference, (Quotation).

66   Morton Hunt, "The Story of Psychology," (New York: Banton Doubleday Dell Publishing Group, Inc., l993), p. 392.

67   Ron and Joanne Highley, "The Best Words of L.I.F.E.," p. 228.

68   Webster, p. 223.

69   Pastor Billy Joe Daugherty, (Quotation).

70   Pastor David T. Demola, (Quotation).

71   Ron Highley, "Understanding Homosexuality," (pamphlet) (New York: L.I.F.E., Inc.).

72   Bill and Sue Banks, "Breaking Unhealthy Soul-Ties," (Kirkwood: Impact Christian Books, Inc., 2004), p. 99.

73   Ibid., p. 15.

74   Ibid., p. 8.

75   Ibid., p. 5, 6.

76   Ibid., p. 6.

77   Ibid., p. 6.

78   Ibid., p. 6.

79   Webster, p, 980.

80   Billy Joe Daugherty, "Breaking the Chains of Bondage," (Tulsa: Thomas Nelson Publishers, Inc., 1988), p.101-103.

81 William Sudduth, "So Free! An In-Depth Guide to Deliverance and Inner Healing," (Grand Rapids: Chosen Books, 2007), p.45.
82 Webster, p. 918.
83 Vinny Longo, "Victory in Jesus," (New Brunswick: Bridge-Logos Publishers, 1996), p.72.
84 Rev. Dr. Leo Natale, (Ideas taken from a conversation with Dr. Natalie in January, 2003).
85 Pastor Bob Yandian, (Quotation).
86 Leanne Payne, "The Healing of the Homosexual," (Westchester: Crossway Books), p.37.
87 Webster, p.597.
88 Elizabeth Moberly, "Homosexuality a New Christian Ethic," (Greenwood: The Attic Press, Inc., 1988), p.24.
89 Moberly, p.4.
90 Webster's, p.118.
91 Ibid., p.623.
92 Moberly, p. 44.
93 Ibid., p. 46.
94 Webster, p.1253.
95 Moberly, p.42, 47.
96 Webster, p. 486.
97 John and Paula Sandford, "Healing the Wounded Spirit," (Tulsa: Victory House, Inc., 1985), p. 209.
98 Moberly, p.49.
99 Elijah House, p.187.
100 Elijah House, p.189.
101 Hickey, p.266.
102 Capps, "Authority in Three Worlds," p. 34, 35.
103 Hickey, p.265.
104 Hickey, p.266.
105 Capps, "Authority in Three Worlds," p. 127.
106 Capps, Ibid., p. 145.
107 Capps, Ibid., p. 144,145.
108 Capps, "The Messenger of Satan," p. 36.
109 Capps, Ibid., p. 23.
110 Sumrall, p.99.
111 Sumrall, p.87.
112 Hickey, p. 266.
113 Ibid., p. 267.
114 Sanford, p. 209.
115 Ibid., p. 209,210.
116 Ibid., p. 210.
117 Brim, p.12
118 Oswald Chambers, "My Utmost for His Highest," (Nashville: Thomas Nelson Publishers, 1993), July 16th.
119 Elijah House, p.197.
120 Moberly, p.46, 47.
121 Badshaw, p.136.
122 Benny Hinn, "The Anointing," (Nashville: Thomas Nelson Publishers, 1992), p.129.
123 Elijah House, p.69.
124 Pastor Bob Yandian, (Quotation).
125 Elijah House, p.126,127.
126 Moberly, p.45.

127 Webster, p.300.

128 Kevin Conner and Ken Malmin, "The Covenants," (Blackburn Acadia Press Pty L.T.D., 1976), p. 1.

129 Webster, p.1058.

130 Conner, p.89.

131 Hinn, p.77.

132 Conner, p.70.

133 Ibid., p.4.

134 Ibid., p.73.

135 Ibid., 73, 74.

136 Webster, p.1040.

137 Pastor Dr. Thomas Keinath, (Quotation).

138 Elijah House, p.113.

139 Ibid., p.114.

140 Ibid., p.117.

141 Ibid., p.118.

142 Webster, p.1300.

143 Elijah House, p. 119.

144 Capps, "The Messenger of Satan," p. 32.

145 F.F. Bosworth, "Christ the Healer," (Grand Rapids, Revell Books, 2000), p.68.

146 Hickey, p.217.

147 Ibid., p.217.

148 Joanne Highley, (Quotation).

149 Pastor David T. Demola, (Quotation).

150 Cindy Jacobs, "Possessing the Gates of the Enemy" (GrandRapids:ChosenBooks, 2000), p.73.

151 Pastor Mark Brazee, (Quotation).

152 Norris, "Forgiving the Dead Man Walking," (Grand Rapids: Zondervan Publishing House, 1988), p.248.

153 Norris, p.248.

154 Bosworth, p. 204.

155 Pastor David T. Demola, (Quotation).

156 Pastor Billy Joe Daugherty, "This New Life."(Tulsa: Thomas Nelson, Inc., Publishers, 1982), inside cover.

157 Webster, p.268.

158 Oswald Chambers, "My Utmost for His Highest," (Uhrichsville: Barbour Publishing Inc., 1963), December 12.

159 Rev.Vinny Longo, "Victory in Jesus" (North Brunswick: Bridge-Logos Publishers, 1996), p.66.

160 George Otis, Jr., p.223.

161 Webster, p.982.

162 Elijah House, p.130.

163 Elijah House, p.129.

164 Rev. Vinny Longo, p.67.

165 Pastor David T. Demola, (Quotation).

166 Rev. Hinn, p.129.

167 Ibid., p.121.

168 Rev.Vinny Longo, "Violent Faith," (Gainsville: Bridge-Logos Publishers, 2000), p.20.

169 Ibid., p.21.

170 Joanne Highley, "The Journal," L.I.F.E. Newsletter, 1990.

171 Ibid., "The Journal."

172   Lester Sumrall, "Commanding Spirits That Rule the Hearts of Men," (South Bend: LeSea Publishing Company, Inc., 1994), p. 99.

173   Ibid., p.96.

174   Ibid., p.94.

175   Rev. Vinny Longo, p. 73.

176   Webster, p.1188.

177   Bill and Sue Banks, "Breaking Unhealthy Soul-Ties," (Kirkwood: Impact Christian Books, Inc., 2004), p. 62.

178   Ibid., p. 62.

179   Ibid., p. 80.

180   Ibid., p. 22.

181   Ibid., p. 66,67.

182   Ibid., p. 63, 64.

183   Ibid., p. 102.

184   Ibid., p. 97.

185   Ibid. p. 98.

186   Ibid., p. 106.

187   Ibid., p. 106.

188   Ibid., p. 107.

189   Ibid., p. 110.

190   Ibid., p.110.

191   Pastor David T. Demola (Quotation).

192   Dr. Adriana Mueller (Quotation).

193   Chambers, June 6.

194   Webster, p.1059.

195   Webster, p.933.

196   Pastor David T. Demola, (Quotation).

197   Watchman Nee, "Spiritual Authority", p. 133-135.

198   Joe Dallas, (Quotation).

199   Dee Verhagen, (Quotation).

200   Pastor David T.Demola, (Quotation).

201   Webster, p.933.

202   PastorDavid T. Demola, (Quotation).

203   Rev. Marlene Burdock, (Quotation).

204   Cindy Jacobs, p. 47.

205   Pastor David T. Demola, (Quotation).

206   Reverend Vinny Longo, (Quotation).

207   Reverend Vinny Longo, (Quotation).

208   Pastor David T.Demola, (Quotation).

209   Pastor Sharon Daugherty (Quotation).

210   Pastor Rema Spencer, (Quotation).

211   Hickey, p.74.

212   Ibid.,p.74.

213   Pastor Billy Joe Daugherty, "You Can Be Healed," (Shippensburg: Destiny Image Publishers, Inc., 2006), pgs.80, 81.

214   Pastor Sharon Daugherty (Quotation).

215   Kenneth E. Hagin, "The Triumphant Church," (Tulsa, Faith Library Publications, 1993), p. 95

216   Ibid., p. 95

217   Ibid., p. 95

218 Ibid., p. 80
219 Pastor Billy Joe Daugherty, "This New Life," (Tulsa: Thomas Nelson, Inc., Publisher, 1982), (inside cover).
220 Pastor Billy Joe and Sharon Daugherty, "Word Confessions for Championship Living," (Tulsa, Oklahoma, 2009), p. 30.
221 Ibid., p. 30.
222 Ibid., p. 30.
223 Ibid., p. 30.

Bibliography

- Banks, Bill and Sue. <u>Breaking Unhealthy Soul-Ties</u>. Kirkwood, Missouri: Impact Christian Books, Inc., 2004.
- Bosworth, F.F. <u>Christ the Healer</u>. Grand Rapids, Michigan: Revell Books, 2000.
- Bradshaw, John. <u>Healing the Shame That Binds You.</u> Deerfield Beach, Florida: Health Communication, Inc., 1988.
- Brim, Billye. <u>The Blood and the Glory</u>. Tulsa, Oklahoma: Harrison House, 1995.
- Capps, Charles. <u>Authority in Three Worlds</u>. Tulsa, Oklahoma: Harrison House, 1992.
- Capps, Charles. <u>The Messenger of Satan</u>. Tulsa, Oklahoma: Harrison House, 1993.
- Chambers, Oswald. <u>My Utmost for His Highest.</u> Uhrichsville, Ohio: Barbour Publishing Inc., 1963.
- Chambers, Oswald. <u>My Utmost for His Highest</u>. Nashville, Tennessee: Thomas Nelson Publishers, 1993.
- Cominsky, Andrew. <u>Pursuing Sexual Wholeness - How Jesus Heals the Homosexual</u>. Lake Mary, Florida: Creation House, 1989.
- Conner, Kevin and Malmin, Ken. <u>The Covenants</u>. Blackburn, Victoria: Acacia Press Pty. LTD., 1976.
- Daugherty, Billy Joe. <u>Breaking the Chains of Bondage</u>. Tulsa, Oklahoma: Thomas Nelson Inc., Publishers, 1982.
- Daugherty, Billy Joe. <u>This New Life</u>. Tulsa, Oklahoma: Thomas Nelson, Inc., Publishers, 1982.
- Daugherty, Billy Joe. <u>You Can Be Healed</u>. Shippensburg, Pennsylvania: Destiny Image Publishers, Inc., 2006.
- Daugherty, Billy Joe and Sharon. <u>Word Confessions for Championship Living</u>. Tulsa, Oklahoma: 2009.
- Demola, David T. <u>Dominion and Authority to Rule and Reign.</u> Tulsa, Oklahoma: Christian Publishing Services, Inc., 1987.
- Elijah House. <u>Elijah House School for Prayer Ministry - Basic 1</u>. Post Falls, Idaho: Elijah House, 2004.
- Goodrick, Edward W. and Kohlenberger, John R. III. <u>The NIV Complete Concordance, the Complete English Concordance to the New International Version</u>. Grand Rapids, Michigan: Zondervan Publishing House, 1981.
- Hagin, Kenneth E. <u>Steps to Answered Prayer</u>. Tulsa, Oklahoma: Faith Library Publications, 1998.
- Hagin, Kenneth E. <u>The Triumphant Church</u>. Tulsa, Oklahoma: Faith Library Publications, 1993.
- Hickey, Marilyn. <u>Breaking Generational Curses</u>. Tulsa, Oklahoma: Harrison House, Inc., 2000.
- Hinn, Benny. <u>The Anointing</u>. Nashville, Tennessee: Thomas Nelson, Inc., 1997.
- Jacobs, Cindy. <u>Possessing the Gates of the Enemy</u>. Grand Rapids, Michigan: Chosen Books, 2000.
- Members of L.I.F.E. Ministry. <u>The Best of Words of L.I.F.E.</u> New York, New York: L.I.F.E., Inc., Publishers, 2003.
- Longo, Vinny. <u>Violent Faith</u>. Gainsville, Florida: Bridge-Logos Publishers, 2000.
- McVeigh, Kate. <u>Conquering Intimidation</u>, Tulsa, Oklahoma: Harrison House, Inc., 2000.
- Moberly, Elizabeth. <u>Homosexuality - a New Christian Ethic</u>. Greenwood, S.C.: The Attic Press, Inc., 1988.
- MacInTosh, Ron. <u>Keep the Flame Burning</u>. Tulsa, Oklahoma: Harrison House, Inc., 1994.
- Meyer, Joyce. <u>Beauty for Ashes</u>. Tulsa, Oklahoma: Harrison House, 1994.
- Morris, Debbie. <u>Forgiving the Dead Man Walking</u>. Grand Rapids, Michigan: Zondervan Publishing House, 1998.
- Natalie, Leo. <u>When Soul and Spirit Agree</u>. South Plainfield, New Jersey: Bridge Publishing, 1994.
- Nee, Watchman. <u>Spiritual Authority</u>. Richmond, Virginia: Christian Fellowship Publishers, Inc., 1972.
- Payne, Leanne. <u>The Healing of the Homosexual</u>. Westchester, Illinois: Crossway Books, 1985.
- Sandford, John and Paula. <u>Healing the Wounded Spirit</u>. Tulsa, Oklahoma: Victory House, Inc., 1985.

- Sudduth, William. <u>So Free! An In-Depth Guide to Deliverance and Inner Healing</u>. Grand Rapids, Michigan: Chosen Books, 2007.
- Sumrall, Lester. <u>Commanding Spirits That Rule the Hearts of Men</u>. South Bend, Indiana: LeSEA Publishing Co., Inc., 1994.
- Strong, James. <u>The Comprehensive Concordance of the Bible</u>. Iowa Falls, Iowa: World Bible Publishers, Inc.
- Strong, James, LL.D., S.T.D. <u>The New Strong's Exhaustive Concordance of the Bible</u>. Nashville, Tennessee: Thomas Nelson Publishers, 1995, 1996.
- <u>The Amplified Bible</u>. Grand Rapids, Michigan.: Zondervan Publishing House, 1965.
- The Holy Bible. <u>The NIV Study Bible</u>. Grand Rapids, Michigan: Zondervan, 1985.
- Webster, Marian. <u>Ninth New Collegiate Dictionary</u>. Springfield, Mass.: Merriam Webster, Inc., Publishers, 1981.
- Words of Life Newsletters. L.I.F.E. Ministry. New York, New York, 2002.

★★★★★★★★★★★★★★★★★

Websites, "Free Read" Info, and Ordering Information
To purchase book or EBook:
Go to http:// <u>www.westbowpress.com/</u> Go to bookstore link

http://www.barnesandnoble.com / (Look for: See inside book)

http://www.amazon.com/

http://www.google.com/

Personal Email Address: bonnieegglehand@yahoo.com

Ministry Website Address for Alive Ministry
and for
"<u>Free Read</u>" of entire book – go to: www.speakyourhealing101.com